James Summers

A Handbook of the Chinese Language

Parts I and II: Grammar and Chrestomathy

James Summers

A Handbook of the Chinese Language
Parts I and II: Grammar and Chrestomathy

ISBN/EAN: 9783743393653

Manufactured in Europe, USA, Canada, Australia, Japa

Cover: Foto ©Thomas Meinert / pixelio.de

Manufactured and distributed by brebook publishing software (www.brebook.com)

James Summers

A Handbook of the Chinese Language

A HANDBOOK

OF THE

CHINESE LANGUAGE.

"Die Sprachlehre lehrt nicht eigentlich, wie man *sprechen soll*, sondern nur, wie man *spricht*..... Die Sprachlehre ist nur eine Physiologie der Sprache; sie kann nur in so fern lehren, wie man sprechen *soll*, als sie in uns die innern Bildungsgesetze der Sprache zum Bewusstsein bringt, und uns dadurch in Stand setzt, zu beurtheilen, ob die Sprechweise im Einzelnen diesen Gesetzen gemäss sei, oder nicht."—BECKER's *Organism der Sprache*, page 9.

A

HANDBOOK

OF THE

CHINESE LANGUAGE.

PARTS I AND II,

GRAMMAR AND CHRESTOMATHY,

PREPARED WITH A VIEW

TO INITIATE THE STUDENT OF CHINESE IN THE RUDIMENTS

OF THIS LANGUAGE, AND TO SUPPLY MATERIALS

FOR HIS EARLY STUDIES.

BY

JAMES SUMMERS,

MAGDALEN HALL, OXFORD,

PROFESSOR OF THE CHINESE LANGUAGE AND LITERATURE, KING'S COLLEGE, LONDON,
LATE AN ASSISTANT IN THE LIBRARY OF THE BRITISH MUSEUM.

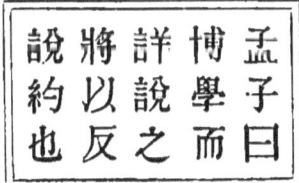

OXFORD:
AT THE UNIVERSITY PRESS.
MDCCCLXIII.

"Study things profoundly, and investigate the precise meaning of what you learn, and then you will acquire the means of forming a comprehensive system of principles."—*Free translation of the extract from the works of* MANG-TSZ, *which is printed on the title-page.*

ADVERTISEMENT.

It has been deemed advisable to publish, in their present form, Parts I and II of the *Handbook of the Chinese Language*, in order to meet the demand which now exists for the work. They are complete in themselves, but when Parts III and IV—the Exercises and Dictionary—are finished, (which, it is hoped, may be done in a few months,) the whole will form a perfect apparatus for the student of Chinese to commence with in this country.

PREFACE.

THE intention of the author in preparing this work for the press was to make a text-book for students of the Chinese language who attend his lectures at King's College, London, and to assist others who might commence the study of the language in this country, as well as to aid those who enter for the first time upon this study in China itself.

In order to show the need of some such book, it will be necessary fairly to pass in review the various works which are within reach of, or which may be supposed to exist for the student,—to point out candidly what appear to be their defects, and also to note their real value as aids to the study of Chinese.

The investigation of Chinese in this country, and even in Europe generally, is but of recent date. The vague expressions collected from the works of the Jesuits on the subject, though correct for the most part in themselves, needed a Jesuit to explain them and to guard the wayward fancy from misinterpreting them. The best rules and the deepest truths are often misunderstood because there is no teacher at hand to purge the *idola* from the mind and clear it of its earlier prejudices. The colouring of every thing that concerns the Chinese has been heightened by the romantic accounts of this nation given by the early historians of the East, and the imagination has supplied much that was not found in the reality.

The first work of a systematic character on the Chinese language was written by a Dominican, Père Varo, and printed from wooden blocks in Canton in 1703 [*].

Theoph. Sigefr. Bayer wrote a work in Latin, which was published in St. Petersburg in 1730 [†]. He was however not in a position to render much service to the subject which he attempted to explain. The work is made up

---

[*] The title ran thus:—"Arte de la lengua mandarina, compuesto por el M. R⁰. P⁴. Francisco Varo, de la sagrada orden de N. P. S. Domingo, acrecentado y reducido a mejor forma, por N⁰. H⁰. Fr. Pedro de la Piñuela, p.ᵒʳ y commissario prov. de la Mission serafica de China; Añadio se un Confesionario muy util y provechoso para alivio de los nuevos ministros. Impreso en Canton, año de 1703." It consisted of 64 double leaves, 8⁰., printed in the Chinese manner. The work is very rare, but a copy is to be found among the Sloane MSS. of the British Museum.

[†] Museum Sinicum, in quo Sinicæ linguæ et litteraturæ ratio explicatur. Petropol. 1730. 2 vols. in 8⁰.

of various matter collected from the works of the Jesuits, which are commented on in a very vague and unsatisfactory manner. *M. Abel-Rémusat* writing, in the preface to his *Grammaire*, on this book says: " The greater part of this Grammar is taken up with details on the writing, the dictionaries, and the poetry; about fifty pages present nothing but the most ordinary notions on the mechanism of the language, and almost without any examples. The original characters are printed upon copper plates, to which the reader is referred. They are moreover so badly executed, that only those experienced in the subject can recognise them."

The next writer of note on Chinese was Fourmont *, who was quite incompetent for the task which he undertook; but in those times he was able to palm upon his countrymen many incorrect and absurd views of his own, while the little good and true information, which his books contain, was the production of other minds. The student may spare himself the trouble of examining them, as they are only calculated to mislead him. Several other works, unworthy of consideration, were published in various parts of Europe; but no book on the subject of Chinese was produced which can be recommended as worth perusal before the learned and able treatise of Dr. Marshman. His knowledge of the Sanskrit and the classical languages of antiquity, coupled with a practical acquaintance with Chinese, through his private studies with native teachers, enabled him to arrive at correct views on the genius and composition of the Chinese language. The *Clavis Sinica* † of Dr. Marshman is still worthy of a careful perusal by the earnest student, although, as a whole, it falls short of the requirements of the present day.

Dr. Morrison's Chinese Grammar issued the next year (1815) from the same press at Serampore. This work contains some valuable matter, but from the haste with which it appears to have been prepared for publication, and from the fact of its having been published at so early a period after Dr. Morrison's entrance upon the study, the student must not expect to derive much positively practical advantage from its perusal.

The first work that appeared in some measure to correspond to the wants of the student was the very clear and scientific grammar of M. Abel-Rémusat ‡, the first Professor of the Language and Literature of China in the Royal

---

* Meditationes Sinicæ, 1737, in fol., and Linguæ Sinarum Mandarinicæ hieroglyphicæ Grammatica duplex, 1742, in fol.

† The Clavis Sinica was published at Serampore in India in 1814. Dr. Marshman had had the opportunity of reading with several native Chinese scholars while in India, he availed himself of the aid of M. Rodrigues, a Jesuit from Peking, and he was assisted by Mr. Thomas Manning, who had also resided in China.

‡ Élémens de la grammaire chinoise, ou principes généraux du Kou-wen ou style antique, et du Kouan-hoa, c'est-à-dire, de la langue commune généralement usitée dans l'Empire chinois. Par M. Abel-Rémusat, de l'Académie royale des Inscriptions et Belles-Lettres, Professeur de Langue et de Littérature chinoises et tartares au Collége royal de France. Paris, 1822, in 8º. A new edition was recently printed in Paris, edited by M. Léon de Rosny, with a supplement.

PREFACE. vii

College of France. The author had read the valuable examples given in the MS. of Prémare's *Notitia Linguæ Sinicæ*, and had carefully consulted the original works referred to by that writer. M. Rémusat analysed these examples, and produced a work drawn out upon scientific principles, which keep in view the genius and peculiarities of the Chinese language.

The work of Prémare, mentioned above, remained for many years in manuscript in the Imperial Library of Paris. The author resided in China from 1698 until his death, about the year 1735. His plan was to teach by examples, and instead of giving rules, he gave the material from which rules might be formed. He recommended imitation and the practice of committing passages to memory. It will be seen therefore that although his work is an immense storehouse, it leaves the learner very much to himself in arriving at conclusions respecting the nature and genius of the language. It is not to be expected that every young man, who takes up such a work as this of Prémare's, can form a judgment of much grammatical significance from the examples before him. It is the duty of the grammarian to form the rules and to prove his propositions by examples. The value therefore of the work of Prémare is limited to affording a number of examples from which the advanced student may acquire a good deal of information on the style of the novels, and of a few other books from which they were drawn. The versions given of some of the examples are incorrect, but as a general rule they are sufficiently true to the original to be of service in acquiring the idiom of the language *.

In the year in which Dr. Morrison's Grammar was printed at Serampore, the first portion of his Dictionary was published at Macao, having been printed at the sole expense of the East India Company. This great work in six quarto volumes, the last of which was not published until 1821, contains so much that is interesting and profitable to the student of Chinese that it is indispensably necessary to all who wish to collect information that may be depended upon. But with all praise of Dr. Morrison's ability and indefatigable labour, we cannot conceal the fact that his Dictionary is very imperfect, and often fails to render that assistance to the student which he requires. The enormous labour, almost without any help, which it involved, renders it a matter of surprise that so much was done and so well; and it behoves the author of the present small work to speak with diffidence on the subject of its demerits. Another work was written about the same time by Dr. Morrison, entitled: *Dialogues and detached sentences in the Chinese language, with a free and verbal translation in English.* This was a great help at the time it was published; but since China has been more largely opened to Europeans, and the facilities for learning the language are become greater, some parts of this work are found to savour of the Canton provincial phraseology. It is however

---

* *Notitia Linguæ Sinicæ*, auctore P. Premare, Malaccæ cura academiæ Anglo-Sinensis. M.DCCC.XXXI. It was printed in 4º., at the expense of a British nobleman. A version of the Latin was made by the Rev. J. G. Bridgman, and was printed in 8º. at Canton in 1847. Copies of this work are now very scarce.

likely to prove very useful to those who can obtain it, but it is now difficult to be procured, as copies of it are scarce.

A useful little book appeared in 1823, compiled by Sir John F. Davis, Bart., F. R. S., &c., entitled *Hien wun shoo.—Chinese moral maxims, with a free and verbal translation, affording examples of the grammatical structure of the language*. These maxims are likely to be useful to those students who will commit them to memory; and, as the literal rendering of each word is given, as well as the free translation, it will be found useful to beginners.

The next writer who made an immense addition to the aids for learning Chinese was Père J. A. Gonçalves, a missionary at Macao. His *Arte China*, which was published in 1829, is the most complete work on the Chinese language which we possess. He spent great labour on an analysis of the characters, the result of which was what he called an "*Alphabeto China;*" but from its being explained in the Portuguese language, comparatively few study it. Every student of Chinese ought, however, to possess this work, on account of the valuable store of good phrases which it contains. After the alphabet he has ranged a collection of phrases and sentences, both in the colloquial idiom (*kwān-hwá*), and in the style of the books (*kü-wǎn*), graduated in difficulty to suit the beginner; then follows a *grammar*, in which he occasionally tortures the Chinese to adapt it to some peculiarity in the grammar of his own language. There is also a very good collection of sentences in the form of *dialogues*. The allusions made to facts in history, the great names, the epistolary style, extracts from prose and poetry, and the principles of elegant composition (*wǎn-chāng*), all enter into this fund for the Chinese student. Unfortunately very meagre explanations are given; while the sounds of the characters, except in the *alphabeto*, are omitted, and the translations appear in some cases to be not the most happy. For study with a native instructor the book is invaluable; but without such assistance it must fail to aid the beginner. Père Gonçalves also prepared several other great works, dictionaries, in Portuguese and Latin, all of which are worthy of consideration.

Two works by Mr. Robert Thom, H. B. Majesty's Consul at Ningpo, also deserve mention here, as calculated to assist the student in his initiatory studies; *Æsop's Fables* in Chinese, with interlinear translation in the Canton and Mandarin dialects; and the *Chinese Speaker, or extracts from works written in the Mandarin dialect as spoken at Peking*. The author however had not much opportunity of hearing the Peking dialect spoken, and being under the necessity of following the work from which he translated, which was a book used to teach the Mandarin dialect in the provinces, he fell into some errors of pronunciation; and what is to be regretted still more, he entirely disregarded the "tones," and neglected to insert any mark by which to guide the student in learning them.

The works of Dr. Medhurst call for some notice at this point. We can only speak of them in a general manner, as it would occupy too large a space to criticise them with any degree of minuteness. The most useful and important work of Dr. Medhurst's on the Chinese language is his Chinese-English

Dictionary, published in Batavia in 1843, 2 vols. 8º. The whole was lithographed, and therefore is so far inferior to Dr. Morrison's Dictionary, but in other respects it is far superior and more complete than Dr. Morrison's first part, to which it corresponds in arrangement. Dr. Medhurst next edited "Notices of Chinese Grammar" by Philosinensis (Dr. Gützlaff). This work was prepared in haste, and consequently neither the author nor the editor did justice to his abilities and acquirements. Dr. Medhurst afterwards published a book of Dialogues, which are good, and an English-Chinese Dictionary, as well as a Dictionary of Chinese in the Hok-kiën dialect. All his works are useful. He was a Chinese scholar of very extensive reading and indefatigable in labour.

M. Callery's Dictionary, entitled, *Systema Phoneticum Scripturæ Sinicæ*, published in 1842, was on a new plan, which is worthy of the student's attention (cf. Arts. 50 and 51 of this Grammar); but the meanings given of each character are few, and the absence of words which are formed with the characters diminishes the usefulness of the book. We have found however that the meanings are very correct, and we should recommend the student to procure a copy, if possible. Mr. Williams, the editor of the Chinese Repository, now connected with the United States Mission to China, has produced several very practical works for the beginner, from among which the *Vocabulary* (English-Chinese) in the Mandarin dialect, and his recently published *Dictionary* in the Canton dialect, may be recommended. His *Easy Lessons in Chinese* are universally spoken of with praise; they are however in the Canton dialect; but much that is common to the Mandarin dialect is also to be found in the book.

The sinologues of France and Germany claim some notice at this period. Professor Julien of Paris, whose learning in Chinese is unquestioned, his accurate knowledge of the language having been proved by his excellent translation of Mencius in 1824, stands first among them. But unfortunately he has not published any grammar or dictionary of the language, tasks for which he must be eminently qualified. His writings consist chiefly of translations and critiques, and we consider his views of such weight that we recommend the student of Chinese to procure any of his works which he can meet with, especially his critical translation of the works of Mencius into Latin. Professor Bazin also deserves well of all students of Chinese for his various papers on Chinese literature, and for his *Grammaire Mandarine*, which is a good work on the subject, and may be read with profit, notwithstanding some blemishes, owing probably to the author's not having studied the language in China.

Among the Germans, Dr. Stephen Endlicher of Vienna has written a very perspicuous work on Chinese Grammar, as far as the language of the books is concerned.

Dr. Julius Klaproth was engaged upon Chinese many years, and his criticisms are generally marked by shrewd discernment and accurate distinction, but he did not write either a grammar or a dictionary, although he added a

Supplement of great value to the Dictionary of De Guignes. This latter, which we omitted to mention above, may well be noticed here. It was published by order of the Emperor Napoleon I. in huge folio. The basis of it was the Manuscript Dictionary of Père Bazil de Glemone. The editor added very little to the original MS. excepting probably the French renderings, which are given as well as the Latin. The meanings are singularly correct; they had been made from the native Chinese Dictionary of *K'ang-hi*. The deficiency however among the words which occur as compounds under each character, and the unwieldy size of the book, render it, even with the Supplement of Klaproth, inferior to the Dictionaries of Morrison, Medhurst, and Williams.

In 1857 a *Chinesische Sprachlehre* by Dr. Schott was published in Berlin. This work is in our opinion superior to all others in its simple system of grammatical analysis for the Chinese language, and although it does not extend to the spoken language—the Mandarin dialect—at all, what is said therein respecting the book-style or learned language of China, and the analysis of the same, is well worthy of the most careful study. Dr. Schott's Sketch of the Literature of China is another great acquisition to the aids in the study of Chinese. We recommend both of these to the student's attention.

In the same year in which Dr. Schott's Grammar appeared in Germany, the Rev. Joseph Edkins, B. A., of Shanghai, published a Grammar of the Mandarin Dialect. He had previously given to the public a Grammar of the Dialect of Shanghai, in which much accurate knowledge of the language was displayed; and in his next work on the Mandarin he eclipsed all his predecessors in exhibiting not the mere language of the novels, which had sufficed for Prémare, Gützlaff, and others, but the language which he had obtained *vivâ voce* from the natives, and by a comparison with many native scholars. We cannot agree with him in every thing he says respecting the tones or with his mode of spelling Chinese syllables in every instance, but we are bound to give unqualified praise to a work which shows so much laborious research, and which has made such an advance in the mode of treating the subject. Every student should possess himself of a copy as soon as he arrives in China.

Another work which it behoves us to mention is by the present Chinese Secretary, Thomas Francis Wade, Esq., C. B. It is entitled, *The Hsin-tsing-lü, or Book of Experiments, being the first of a series of Contributions to the Study of Chinese*. It was published at Hongkong in 1859. It is devoted to the dialect of Peking, the species of Mandarin which is affected by the court and the officials of the empire; but not employed throughout the provinces as Mandarin, excepting by the high officials who come direct from the northern capital. This work of Mr. Wade's is very limited in its scope, for the 362 sentences given in the first part are confined to the single subject of "heaven" and the phenomena of the skies. The second part contains a passage from the Paraphrase of the Sacred Edict; and the third, some good sentences explanatory of the tones of the Peking dialect. The notes which the work contains are calculated to prove useful, and there is no question about its being a *bonâ-fide* work on Pekinese. It is to be regretted that greater care was not bestowed on revision, and that the subject of the first part was not made more extensive in its range, so as to have answered more immediately to the wants of the student-interpreters, for whose benefit the work was composed. With the enormous labour which has devolved upon Mr. Wade as Chief Interpreter and Secretary, coupled with his own close habits of study, we may well wonder that he found time to bring any work of this kind to a completion; and we hail the "Contributions" as being likely to serve a very good purpose, and as the earnest of much more as soon as leisure affords the opportunity for its preparation.

The last work which we must notice is by Dr. James Legge, of the London Missionary Society. This bids fair to supersede all its predecessors in the field of Chinese classics. The work is entitled, *The Chinese Classics: with a translation, critical and exegetical notes, prolegomena, and copious indexes:* roy. 8vo. *Hongkong,* 1861. The whole work will consist of seven volumes, one of which has recently appeared; and the remaining six volumes are expected to be ready for publication during the course of the next five years. The enormous labour which must be expended upon a critical translation and explanation of the classical books of the Chinese, executed in the style which this first volume indicates, could hardly have been undertaken by a scholar more likely to succeed in the task than Dr. Legge. The Prolegomena contains digested information, on the lives and opinions of Confucius and his disciples, never before presented to European readers. Dr. Legge has drawn largely upon native sources, and the facts which he has collected, and his own remarks upon them, cannot fail to be interesting and instructive to students of Chinese in common with many others. The native text is in bold clear type, and is accompanied by a translation and critical notes on each page. The indexes will be found most valuable to the student; they form at once a concordance and dictionary to the volume; and the book as a whole will render a great service to Chinese scholars generally. We earnestly hope that Dr. Legge's health may not suffer from his close application in the climate of Hongkong.

After reading this list of the principal works on the subject of Chinese, the reader may ask what need there was of another. Our answer to this is, that no one of these books meets the wants of the beginner; they do undoubtedly *en masse* give almost all that is needed, certainly more than the author of the present work could on his sole responsibility lay before the student, but each individually cannot answer all the common questions which suggest themselves to the mind of the student on entering upon the study of Chinese. Among the questions which we may suppose to arise are, "As the Chinese have no letters, how shall I write down the sounds of their words? How do they represent words in writing? How do they pronounce? How do they distinguish one syllable from another of the same sound? What is their mode of writing? How are their words constructed? Where shall I obtain copies for writing? — text to read, — explanation to this text?" The reply might be: "You must purchase the works of Morrison or Schott or Williams for one thing, you must buy those of Edkins and Wade for another, you must send to China for text, and buy a Dictionary which will cost you from four to ten guineas for explanations, and then you will find you want a native teacher or a European proficient in the language to help you."

In the work which the author now ventures to present to the public, he thinks a sufficient answer to the above questions will be found, as well as all the aids which a *beginner* needs in this most difficult study. He has availed himself of all the help which he felt he needed from the above authors, and he freely acknowledges the great assistance which the works of Drs. Morrison and Williams have afforded him for lexicography, and the works of Prémare, Gonçalves, Gützlaff, Schott, Edkins, and Wade, for grammar and examples to grammatical rules.

For translations of some of the passages in the Chrestomathy he is under obligation for help derived from the works of Dr. Medhurst, Sir John Davis, Bart., F. R. S., Père Gonçalves, and Professor Bazin.

Having noticed the various works on the subject of Chinese grammar and lexicography, and having pointed out the need which exists for a book adapted to the wants of the beginner, it remains for the author of the present work to explain the plan of it, and to show wherein it is likely to fulfil the purpose for which it was prepared. In a work which professes to initiate the student in the rudiments of a language, three things are generally looked for; 1. Some account of the letters employed to represent its sounds, with the character and quality of those sounds; 2. An explanation of its forms of words, and, if possible, a complete classification of these words as parts of speech; 3. An exposition of its arrangement of words in sentences, showing how words and clauses are dependent upon each other, either on account of their relative positions, or the peculiar inflexions of the words themselves.

These considerations naturally lead to the formation of three divisions in the grammar of the Chinese tongue. And in order to adapt it to this arrangement, we have to consider, in the first place, the best mode of representing its sounds and syllables. But as the Chinese language possesses no alphabet, we are compelled to employ that with which we are best acquainted, viz. the Roman. And then we have to consider what value each Roman letter shall possess in a system for spelling Chinese words. Shall the uncertain value of English letters be taken? or shall we assume for each letter, which we employ, a value which shall remain constant and uniform, as is the case in some of the languages on the continent of Europe? We have preferred the latter course, and have followed in the footsteps of Sir William Jones, Dr. Lepsius, and many other Orientalists. As we have to invent an alphabet to represent Chinese sounds, we deem it best to avoid the eccentricities of the English mode of spelling, and we have chosen the regular orthography of the German and the Italian in preference. It may be observed that the system of orthography adopted presents scarcely any deviation from that now acknowledged to be the best suited for writing down the sounds of strange tongues,

PREFACE.

being most in accordance with the fundamental laws of speech. A glance at the tables given on pages 3 and 5 will suffice to show the extreme simplicity of Chinese syllables, as regards their formation, and the ease with which the mere syllable may be read. The value of each letter has been explained very fully by examples in English, French, and German, so that no mistake need arise on that score.

A more difficult subject, however, presented itself in the elucidation of the Chinese "*tones.*" The explanation which the author has given of them will, he thinks, assist the student. They were the subject of his careful study while in China, and he has more than once proved his views respecting them to be correct. That there are slight variations in these Chinese tones there is no denying. But the mode of illustrating them by the accentuation or emphasis given to English words under certain circumstances will enable the foreign student to acquire the first elementary power to enunciate them; and with such an attainment, although rude and in a measure unpolished, he will have made progress in the right direction. His object should be to pronounce the tones with the full force and modulation at first, and to rely on future practice with the natives for making the unevenness and crudeness of his pronunciation to disappear. It must be remembered that a large majority of those who study to speak foreign languages *never* speak them exactly as the natives do; that refinement in the pronunciation which a native would admire is rarely attained by a foreigner, and even when it *is* mastered, it is only after a considerable degree of practice.

In the next place, the formation of words, or, as it is frequently called, "Word-building," claims our attention. If there exists in Chinese any process for the formation of words, by which a classification of them may take place, it must be for the interest of the student to know what it is. And this process, which does exist, we have endeavoured to indicate, and we leave it to the student himself to develope the principles which have been laid down on the formation of nouns and verbs. This part of Chinese grammar is vast in extent, and many years of discriminating study will be required to exhaust it. We are now but upon the threshold of the subject. Some earnest workers in this mine of the East will enter into it very much further, and will, we hope, complete the work.

And thirdly, the sentence in Chinese has been analysed with a view to a comparison of its parts, and to show the effect which certain forms of the sentence have upon the meaning and grammatical value of the words in it.

But without native text the student would find the abstract rules of grammar excessively dry and uninteresting. This want has been supplied, in some measure, by about forty pages of extracts from Chinese authors, explained at length, with translations and notes. To these we have added a third part, consisting of exercises, by which the student may acquire a practical acquaintance with Chinese prose composition, and an ability to speak the language with correctness. The fourth part of the Handbook consists of a dictionary of all the characters in general use, and it is hoped that this portion may prove

PREFACE.

very useful to the beginner, and that the whole may answer the purpose for which it was intended.

One of the great difficulties which beset a beginner in a language like the Chinese is the enormous number of words and phrases which present themselves, without his being able to distinguish those best suited for the early stages of his course from the less common expressions which are used in books only. And no simple tales and stories exist in Chinese, as in European languages, to supply him with a stock of useful words. The examples taken from books are seldom the expressions employed in common parlance; and unless the student is in a position to avail himself of native help and proper advice, he may labour for a long time without much profit. The object, therefore, in this work has been to bring together chiefly such expressions as are of frequent occurrence in every day life. Some terms which will be met with in the Dictionary will readily be distinguished by the significations given, as belonging to the higher classes of literature. It would be useless and absurd in a writer of an English grammar for foreigners to collect words from Chaucer and Spenser, or even from Shakespeare, in order to teach them the English language of the nineteenth century. To avoid such a mistake with respect to Chinese, we have selected the most common words, and have endeavoured to clear the path of the beginner, and to give a more simple exposition of the Chinese language than has hitherto appeared.

In the absence of a teacher, a few hints on the use of this work and on the method of study which it will be advisable to adopt will perhaps be acceptable to the beginner. His first object should be to master the system of orthography which is given in this work, and exercise himself in it, by reading aloud the list of syllables on page 5, or a page of the native text in Roman letter. Then the instructions relating to intonation should be thoroughly understood and applied practically by reading again a page of the Chrestomathy. He should then commit to memory the words given to exemplify the tones (pp. 9—11, without the characters); and commence learning to read and write the elementary characters (pp. 19—28). And in learning Chinese characters, the student should on no account attempt too many at once. The first fifty radicals may be speedily acquired, but afterwards he will find that ten characters a day, thoroughly learnt, will test his powers; and at this rate, if it can be sustained, he will know three thousand characters at the end of a year; and if these include two thousand of those in common use, he will have made most satisfactory progress. In his choice of characters the Grammar will supply him first, and then the Chrestomathy. It is, moreover, desirable that couples and triples of characters, which form phrases, should be sought for and committed to memory, so as to store the mind with good expressions, either for positive use, or that they may be readily recognised when uttered by native Chinese. But while pursuing this mere plodding study by memory, he must not neglect to read passages in the Chrestomathy (Part II), and make sentences upon the model of those given in the Exercises (Part III). And in the Chrestomathy some passages will be found better adapted than others

PREFACE. xv

for this purpose: we should recommend him to begin by learning to read the syllables which stand for the characters in pages 8—12 of the native text (*Haŭ-k'iŭ chuén*); and pages 27—30 (*Mandarin Phrases*). The syllables will be found in the Chrestomathy. The Mandarin Phrases should be committed to memory as soon as they are understood, and daily practice in copying the characters with the Chinese pencil should be persevered in.

Four hours a day ought to be the *minimum* of time given to the study during the first year; but this is only general advice, the time allotted to the subject and the method of study must depend on the ability and power of application in each individual;—

Sumite materiam vestris, qui discitis, æquam
Viribus, et versate diu, quid ferre recusent,
Quid valeant humeri.

Some apology is necessary for the occasional defectiveness of the Chinese type used in this work; although as a whole, and when the characters are in a perfect state, they are in very good proportion, and in some cases beautiful, a few are deficient in regularity of form. But thirty-four pages of the Chrestomathy, which were printed in Hongkong with the new type, will supply to the diligent student any deficiency which may be noticed in the Grammar.

In conclusion, the author, in common with all the friends of Anglo-Chinese literature, has to thank the Delegates of the Oxford University Press for their liberality in undertaking so expensive a work upon the ground of its utility alone; and the author has only to regret the errors which may have crept in to mar the work, and render it a less worthy object of such distinguished patronage. Unlike many works of this kind, it has had but one fostering hand; and the author has none to thank for friendly counsel or assistance. It will therefore, he trusts, be accepted with a generous criticism as the first work on the subject ever published in this country, and as having been prepared under very many disadvantages.

J. SUMMERS.

KING'S COLLEGE, LONDON, Jan. 1863.

INTRODUCTION.

THE language which we call Chinese is to the languages of eastern Asia what Sanskrit is to the Indian and to the Indo-Germanic stock of languages, or what Arabic is to some of the other eastern tongues; that is to say, Chinese is the parent, in some sense or degree, of Japanese, Corean, Cochin-Chinese, and Annamese, as well as of all the numerous dialects of China Proper. It is a sort of universal medium of communication throughout the vast territories of the emperor of China, which include Manchuria, Mongolia, Tibet, and other countries, which are together equal in extent to the whole of Europe. The use of Chinese in some of these countries is indeed confined to official communications, but by about 300,000,000 of the Chinese race it is spoken, and among these it forms the only colloquial medium of intercourse. In Japan, Annam, and some other regions, the written characters of China, and frequently the original words, have been so much changed by the *literati*, that they cannot be readily distinguished from the native characters and words [*].
In Japan, for example, the Chinese word *tꞌiēn*, 'heaven,' is changed to *ten;* the nasal *ng*, at the end of some Chinese words, being always omitted, the syllable *liang* would become *liau* or *lau*. Sometimes the Chinese character will represent a mere syllable, at other times it is allowed to represent an idea, and to go under a Japanese name of perhaps two or three syllables, e. g. the Chinese character *kia* or *ka* 加, changed to カ, is the common letter for the syllable *ka*, and scarcely ever carries with it the signification which the Chinese character bears (i. e. 'to add'); but the character *chꞌáng* 長, 'long,' is allowed to stand for the same idea in Japanese, its name however being changed to *naga*. In Annamese the Chinese characters are more frequently taken for syllables alone, and they have undergone a variety of changes to adapt them for use in that language.

But notwithstanding these peculiar changes and modes of usage with respect to the Chinese language among the neighbouring nations, it stands

---

[*] Numerous examples of similar changes both in the characters and the words employed in European languages might be given. Let the following suffice. The Slavonic *sha* Ш (*sh* English) from the Hebrew *shin* שׁ; the letter D altered from the *daleth* ד and *delta* Δ. The F from the *digamma* ϝ, &c. &c. Swedish *somnar*, 'to sleep,' from the Lat. *somnire*, i. e. a Teutonic termination is appended to a Latin root. The verbs *stare, stand, stehen,* from στάω.

c

pre-eminent as a classical language to them, and it occupies the same position as Latin and Greek do among Europeans. The philosophers, historians, and poets of China are read and studied diligently by the Japanese; their works are annotated and explained by writers of that country, and every child of respectable parentage begins the study of Chinese as soon as he goes to school, and carries it on simultaneously with the study of his native tongue. The works of Confucius and Mencius have exerted a mighty influence over the minds of all these eastern tribes. Confucius was to China and her tributaries what Aristotle has been to Europe. Would that his doctrines had been more energising and more fructifying! But we may attribute the comparative failure of Confucianism not to its author, but to the recipients of his instruction. Probably Confucius would have been an Aristotle had he lived in the west, and Aristotle a Confucius in the east. The πολιτική and ἠθική of the one find their counterpart in the other, and while the Greek republics with their social and moral science have passed away, the Chinese empire still remains, a monument of political coherency and wisdom, in some respects at least, with the quality of marvellous endurance and steadfastness.

The antiquity of the Chinese language and written character invests them with peculiar interest, for in them may be discovered facts connected with the social and political history of a nation which flourished two thousand years before our era. It is remarkable too, that Chinese has suffered little change through this great period of time, compared with the mutations which have taken place in other languages. While the pronunciation of its written symbols has varied, and ever will vary in consequence of its want of an alphabetic system to represent the syllables which are uttered, the written characters have been altered scarcely at all during a period of two thousand years. Commencing with the rude pictures of objects within the sphere of life in those early times, as the Chinese mind developed, and the forms of government and society became fixed, the symbols to express authority and the various relationships of life were invented to correspond to the wants of public and private intercourse *.

---

* Writing, which may be defined to be a representation of language and an exhibition of it to the eye, is divided into two kinds:—1. *Notion-writing*, which is independent of any given language, and conveys its meaning to the understanding *immediately* through the eye;—2. *Sound-writing*, which exhibits the sounds of a particular language, the understanding of which depends upon a knowledge of that language.

Notion-writing, again, is divided into two kinds, viz. *Picture-writing* and *Figure-writing*. The former, which is the most natural and probably the most ancient, consists in this, that the figure which is pictured to the eye represents the thing delineated, and by this figure are also symbolized the other notions, which admit of no immediate representation, such as the tropical and symbolical meanings of the object. The mere representation of the visible thing is called *Curiological writing* (from κύριος, *proprius*), and to this belong most of the hieroglyphics (v. *Champollion*, Gram. Egyptienne. Paris, 1836. Fol. I. p. 3). Such a kind of writing the Chinese had originally (v. *Kopp*, Bilder und Schriften II. 66. *Abel-Rémusat*, Gram. Chin. §§. 2. 4, 5), as had also the Mexicans. The same kind of writing however has another element,—the *symbolic* meaning, which rests upon a comparison of the real and possible representations with the intellectual and the abstract; and the thousandfold

INTRODUCTION.

These symbols are partly hieroglyphic and partly ideographic, that is, representations of objects or marks of notions. The hieroglyphs from which the forty thousand characters have been derived were originally signs of concrete notions; symbols for abstract terms and general notions were subsequently formed, as the Chinese mind developed and literature increased. The combinations, which can be effected by means of the four or five hundred elementary forms, give the Chinese language, as far as its written character is concerned, a power of expression unknown in other languages. And the simple and logical character of its formation renders it a far more efficient medium for the communication of ideas, and as an instrument of thought, than the languages of Europe.

The Chinese has a double advantage; it presents to the eye of the initiated the pictures of things, the general term derived from them, or the common notion deduced from a combination of elementary figures. It addresses to the ear, by the simple form of its constructions, the most complex notions and the most general expressions, without disturbing the necessary unity, which should always exist in the sentence; while it conveys in a few words, compactly arranged, the full idea with emphasis and logical precision. There is the language of the books and the language of conversation. These differ from each other, for, in writing, a few monosyllabic characters are made to express much, while, in speaking, many syllables are required; but they are the same in their principles of construction,—the same simplicity and logical order run through both.

---

combinations which are possible in this kind of writing approach the ridiculous. According to Diodor. (III. 4), the *hawk* among the Egyptians signified 'swiftness;' the *crocodile*, 'evil;' *flies*, 'impudence;' the *eye*, 'a watchman;' an *outstretched hand*, 'liberality;' a *closed hand*, 'greediness and avarice;' but most of the other tropical meanings of hieroglyphics rest upon more remote comparisons: e. g. the *bee* for 'the king;' *sparrow-hawk* for 'sublimity;' *eye of the sparrow-hawk* for 'vision' and 'contemplation;' the *vulture*, on account of its maternal love, for 'mother.' Indeed in many of those which are called ænigmatical hieroglyphs, the reason for the combination is sometimes doubtful and sometimes wholly unknown; as when the *ostrich feather* stands for 'justice,' because all the feathers of the wing of the ostrich are of equal size; or the *palm branch* for 'the year,' because the palm tree brings forth every year regularly twelve branches. Among the Chinese, *two men, one following the other*, stands for the verb 'to follow;' the *sun and moon* for 'light;' a *man on a mountain* for a 'hermit;' a *woman, a hand,* and a *broom*, for a 'matron.'

The other kind of *Notion-writing,—Figure-writing,*—expresses the notion by means of figures taken arbitrarily, which have no similarity to the thing intended. A rude example of this kind were the gay-coloured threads (*quipos*) of the Peruvians, who understood how to knot them and to twist them in so many ways (v. *Götting. Hist. Magaz.* III. p. 422. Lehrgeb. der Diplom. II.305). The Chinese have a very complete system of this kind; they have from 20 to 30 thousand characters, which may be reduced to 214 radicals (called *keys*). To the same category belong also the technical marks used by medical men, and perhaps also the astronomical signs for the planets and the signs of the zodiac; while *such figures often seen to be only arbitrary marks, they really have proceeded from hieroglyphics,* in which the figures have been so very much contracted and mutilated that they have lost all resemblance to the original object intended to be represented (v. Ersch and Grüber's *Encyclopædie*, art. *Paleographie* by Gesenius, of which the above is a translation).

INTRODUCTION.

An eminent writer on logic observes, that "the chief impediments to the correct performance of the process of reasoning lie in the defects of expression *," but we think that such defects will not be found in Chinese, while no difficulty will be experienced in forming a complete apparatus for this or for any other science as soon as the native mind becomes alive to the importance of more vigorous and systematic thinking. The subtle distinctions and exact meanings, which may be referred to a vast number of Chinese words, prove the analytic character of the language, as does also the complexity of the syntax and the arrangement of words and sentences,—a remedy, as it were, for the want of inflexions. If inflexions have arisen by the agglutination of separate and distinct words,—by pronouns, prepositions, &c., being placed after and joined to the words to which they refer; if they were produced, not merely by a scientific process, but by a vulgar and careless pronunciation of the words, and so were agglutinated, the reason why Chinese has never undergone this process, and obtained inflexions, appears to be, because the original terms, which were employed as the names of objects and relations of things, were so definite and distinct from each other, and the characters, which at a very early period represented them, so unique and separate, that union of two of the latter being impossible, two of the former could not well be agglutinated. Be this as it may, the Chinese, without any sort of inflexion in its words, affords a remarkable specimen of the power of syntactical arrangement to express the multitudinous variations of human thought. Instead of being composed, as is frequently supposed, of a vast number of arbitrary and complicated symbols, the characters of the Chinese language are compounded of very simple elements, which carry along with them into their derivatives something of their own meaning, while each generally preserves its figure unchanged. These elementary characters supply the place of an alphabet,—but it is an alphabet of ideas, not of sounds. With it may be produced thousands of different radical words, and with these words hundreds of thousands of compounded words have been and may be formed. It is not even necessary to become acquainted with more than four or five thousand of these radical words and characters to enable the literary man to understand, with etymological accuracy, the meaning of myriads of expressions which are, or may be, formed by them. The task to the foreign student is trifling, when he considers that these four thousand characters are systematically derived from two hundred and fourteen simple figures, and that when these are mastered, all other difficulties vanish entirely, or diminish to such a degree that the rest of his labour is easy and pleasant. The process however of derivation and composition is not without some arbitrary and, at first sight, absurd deviations from rules, but such exceptions are found in every language, and we do not see that the Chinese exhibits many more of them than our own tongue.

Dr. Morrison's view of Chinese etymology to be derived from the hieroglyphic

---

* See "Outline of the Laws of Thought" by Dr. Thomson, Provost of Queen's College, Oxford. 12°. London, 1849, p. 42.

INTRODUCTION. xxi

forms of characters is worth noting *: "The ancients formed characters from things; these gradually came to be used metaphorically to denote the operations of the mind, and to serve as auxiliaries in speech. As the number of such characters increased, it was necessary to modify them again in order to distinguish them. Thus *chī* 之 was originally *chī-t'saŭ* 芝 茝. (i. e. 'the *chi* grass,' now a particle of relation, demonstration, &c.), *hū* 乎. was 吁 欻 *hū-k'i* (i. e. 'the breath issuing forth in exclamation,' now a particle of interrogation), and *yên* 焉 was *yuén* 鳶. (i. e. 'a kite or fish-hawk,' now used as a final particle of assertion, interrogation, &c.). When the etymology of a word or the various metaphorical changes of a hieroglyphic can be traced, it is amusing; but the present usage alone can fix what the meaning of a word is at the present time.

"Assuming the truth of the above critic's remark, it may be inferred, that many characters are so mutilated or increased that to trace the gradual changes up to their original form is hopeless." While these remarks indicate the scope which Chinese affords for the sound discrimination of the ingenious mind, the student who follows such an authority as Dr. Morrison will not be discouraged on finding his efforts frequently unavailing to fathom the sense of a Chinese character, and to trace its origin and history.

The extent of Chinese literature and its praises cannot be expressed more fully than in the enthusiastic description of Prof. Abel-Rémusat, a translation of which we will subjoin: "There are few Europeans," he says, "who would not smile at hearing one speak of the geometry of the Chinese, of their astronomy, or of their natural history; although it is true that the progress, which these sciences have made amongst us during the last two centuries, causes us to dispense with having recourse to the knowledge of those distant nations, ought we therefore to be ignorant of their present state, and especially of what their former state was amongst a nation which has never ceased to cultivate and honour them? The proportion of the right-angled triangle was known in China B. C. 2200; and the works of *Yu* the Great, to restrain two streams equal in impetuosity and almost in breadth to the great rivers of America; to direct the waters of 100 rivers, and to guide their flowing over a space of ground of more than 100,000 square leagues, are more than sufficient proof of this. If the astronomical and physical theories of these people are defective, their catalogue of eclipses, of occultations, of comets, and of aërolites are not the less interesting; and if people maintain that the Chinese make mistakes in their calculations, at least we must confess that they have, like us, observant eyes.

"Besides this, rural and domestic economy is sufficiently perfected amongst them for them to teach us many useful things; of this, at least, we are assured by those who have made a study of this science. As to their descriptions of

---

* Cf. *Chinese Dictionary*, Part I. vol. I. p. 34, where Dr. Morrison translated the above passage from a native author.

natural beings, since nothing can supply their place whilst Europeans have not free access to their country, they are not to be despised from a people so exact and circumstantial: and I hope to prove by several extracts from their books on botany and zoology that the writers in this department are as much above the Latin naturalists, or those of the Middle Ages, as they are inferior to Linnæus, Jussieu, or Des Fontaines. But if we pass to polite literature, philosophy, and history, some Chinese, in these subjects, may even set us an example.

"An immense fund of literature, the fruit of 4000 years of assiduous efforts and labours; eloquence and poetry enriched by the beauties of the picturesque language, which preserve to the imagination all its colours, metaphors, allegory, and allusion, all combining to form the most smiling, energetic, or imposing pictures; on the other side, the most vast and authentic annals which ever came from the hands of men, unfolding to our view actions almost unknown, not only of the Chinese, but of the Japanese, Coreans, Tartars, Tibetans, and of the inhabitants on the peninsula beyond the Ganges; unfolding the mysterious dogmas of Buddha, or those of the sect of the Tauists, or consecrating, in short, the eternal principles and the philosophic politics of the school of Confucius:—these are the objects which Chinese books present to the student, who, without leaving Europe, may wish to travel in imagination to these distant countries. More than 5000 volumes have been collected, at great expense, in the Royal Library; their titles have scarcely been read by Fourmont; a few historical works have been opened by De Guignes and by Des Hauterayes; all the rest still await readers and translators*."

These are the words of one who in his day stood high among the Orientalists of Europe, and whose opinions will always be regarded with respect by the student of Chinese. M. Rémusat had actual experience on the subject, and had read much of the literature on which he dilated. His evidence is worthy of our full credit, and, while so much has been written and said which is adverse to China and the Chinese, his testimony calls for our honest acceptance, for he views China through the writings of its great minds, and not, as too many do, by the exhibitions of some of its vulgar rulers or the acts of some low unruly mob. Even from those who should understand the subject well, we too often hear statements which, although they have some appearance of truth, are yet unfair, because they are based on insufficient grounds, but they tell nevertheless to the prejudice of this people and their language. For instance, it has been stated that "this language does not afford much scope for oratorical display," a view which we consider very erroneous, for Chinese is just that kind of language which leaves the speaker free from the technicalities of grammar and of artificial forms of expression, and allows him to rise in sublimity by the power of allusion and the various figures of the rhetor's art, and through the various styles of composition to affect his hearers; or to descend into the vulgar colloquial, and raise a smile at his antagonist's expense, or ridicule the cavils of a supposed objector.

---

* V. Mélanges Asiatiques par Abel-Rémusat, vol. II. p. 14.

INTRODUCTION. xxiii

It cannot be asserted that the speeches of the Chinese ministers of state exhibit much oratorical power, but there can be no reason why the Chinese should not display as much power in this way as did Demosthenes himself, if they once fell into the circumstances which would call it forth, and were gifted with the same argumentative powers as he was. The fault is in the mind of China, and not in the language. When the Chinese mind is elevated, the language will be found to be not only sufficient for the requirements of this development, but also a valuable agent in the work of its advancement.

But it will be necessary to notice the dialects of which Chinese is composed. The mother-tongue, which is every where expressed by the antique characters, finds a different utterance in every province of the empire. So various are the dialectal changes that the inhabitants of adjacent provinces cannot understand each other. If a native of Canton meet with a native of Shanghai he can communicate with him only by some language common to them both, or by the learned characters, which are used in books. The dialects (for there are several) between Canton and Shanghai differ very much from each other. They have, it is true, a common basis and groundwork; but the pronunciation of syllables in them, especially of diphthongal sounds, varies considerably, though these changes are in accordance with the general laws of such variations in other tongues. Their idioms, moreover, are peculiar, and these therefore present a further obstacle to the communication of ideas. The comparative tables of dialects will explain our meaning in some degree.

It must not be supposed that these dialects are so different as to present to a native a formidable task in the acquisition of several of them. Native merchants and traders frequently have a smattering of three or four; but we think that foreigners are in a position to acquire a more exact knowledge of them than natives themselves. As they are all derived from the same written language, so when this is acquired, or at least when the mandarin or court dialect is learnt, the others may be mastered with comparative ease, after a few months' practice. The foreigner in representing by Roman letters the precise sounds of the language, has an advantage over the native, who cannot do so, unless he learn the system of European orthography. The European soon perceives that certain letters of his Roman alphabet undergo regular changes in the different dialects, and this affords him an immense assistance. For example, he may observe that the primary vowel sounds, *a, i, u* (*ah, ee, oo*), generally remain in the language of each province,—thus *pa* in Shanghai remains *pa* in Canton; *ki* in Nanking remains *ki* in Peking, with a little stronger aspiration; *ku* in Ningpo is *ku* every where else: but, on the contrary, *kai* in Mandarin becomes *koi* in Canton and *ke* in Shanghai; *yau* in Mandarin becomes *yiu* in Canton and *yǫ* (*yaw*) in Shanghai. Thus he finds that only the diphthongs (that is, those sounds formed by the combination of two primary vowels) are affected by dialectal changes. The same fact in articulate sounds is shown in our own words *clause, pause,* &c., where the diphthong *au*, which is formed of the two primary vowels *a* and *u*, and is generally represented by the secondary vowel *o*, has been changed in course of time to the sound of *o* in *order*. These regular changes suggest the importance of having but one system of orthography for writing Chinese in Roman letter, so that various dialects may be acquired with greater facility. With how much greater ease, than under the present systems, would French, German, and the other European tongues be learnt, if only one system of writing existed, and but one uniform value were given to the letters employed!

It is no longer necessary to advise the public of the importance of a knowledge of Chinese to those who are connected with China; now that the whole empire is, by the late treaty, declared open to travellers with passports, the language is indispensable to those who would penetrate into the interior. The advantages to the merchant, the missionary, the traveller, and the scientific explorer, of an acquaintance with the Chinese language, cannot well be overrated. And when the vast territories under Chinese rule, and their relations to Great Britain are considered, the perfect medium of communication, which this language would afford, renders the attainment of it an object of primary importance. With this object in view, the cultivation of it should be commenced before leaving this country, that no time may be lost in entering upon a work which will require so much time and arduous effort to accomplish. Very much may be done by the young student before he leaves England, especially in the acquisition of the style of the books, and also in some degree the language of conversation. The written characters of the Chinese may be acquired any where by means of books alone, and, as the pronunciation of these written symbols is exceedingly simple, considerable progress may be made, with a little assistance, in learning such simple sentences as have the stamp of being native, but he should avoid those which are made up to suit foreign expressions. Where native teachers, good grammars, and perfect dictionaries of Chinese are wanting, this language can only be studied to perfection in its native land. Some knowledge however may and ought to be acquired under a European tutor, who can generally explain far better than a native Chinese the difficulties which will beset a beginner. The plan which we would suggest for cementing our new relations with China, and removing the numerous misconceptions which exist on both sides, is the establishment of a College in this country for the education of young Chinese in English, and for affording to young Englishmen the means of acquiring the rudiments of Chinese; and also the foundation of a College in Peking, or in some other city of China, for the preparation of such Chinese youths in the rudiments of English, and for the instruction of English youths in the Chinese language. Each College should have two departments, and these should be directed by English and Chinese tutors. The Chinese youths would cultivate the languages and sciences of Europe to the best advantage in England, while the English youths in China would learn perfectly, as natives do, the Chinese language, and would make themselves acquainted with the products and the resources of China, and gain a knowledge too of the home and foreign policy of the Chinese. Such an arrangement would be productive of most beneficial results. The plan of an Anglo-Chinese College was carried out at Malacca about thirty-

INTRODUCTION.

five years ago, and much good was done thereby, but from its position out of China and from a deficiency in means, less was accomplished than might have been under more favourable circumstances. For an institution of this kind to succeed, it should receive the countenance and support of the governments of both countries; but the education should not be gratuitous, as it would be desirable to obtain the better class of boys for instruction; and the relatives of such youths would be in a position to defray the expenses of their education, and thus lessen the amount of expenditure on the part of the promoters of the plan. But while the civil war in China is raging, and the government of that country is so insecure, no extensive plans of amelioration can be carried out. As commerce and Christianity advance, civilization and peace will follow in the steps of the missionary and the merchant. In the meantime it is not from the partial knowledge of European languages in the case of a few natives that much good may be anticipated, but the full and frequent dissemination of religious and political truth, by means of translations into Chinese, will affect the national mind, which is now very fully alive to the influence of Europe on the well-being of the "Middle kingdom."

Many such translations have already been made within the last few years. Improved versions of the Holy Scriptures, and of standard religious publications, have been issued in China. Valuable treatises on astronomy, algebra, arithmetic, and geometry, natural philosophy and political economy have been turned into Chinese recently*. Many more are however needed, especially on the subjects of European history, the science of mind and the laws of thought.

---

* Such are *Herschel's Astronomy* and *De Morgan's Algebra*, and works on *Arithmetic* and other subjects translated by A. Wylie, Esq.; works on Geography, the History of England, by the Rev. William Muirhead; several works on Anatomy, Physiology, and Medicine by Dr. Benjamin Hobson; treatises on Electricity, the Laws of Storms, and other subjects by Dr. Macgowan; and various educational works by the Rev. W. Lobscheid.

CONTENTS.

PART I. CHINESE GRAMMAR.

CHAP. I. ETYMOLOGY.

Sect. I. *Articulate sounds and their symbols.*

PAGE

§. 1. Elementary sounds and their orthography 1
§. 2. Syllables and their intonation 4
§. 3. Words and their composition generally 12
§. 4. The characters, and how to write them 14
§. 5. Arrangement of characters in books, punctuation, &c. 34
§. 6. On writing the characters 36

Sect. II. *The forms of expression.*

§. 1. Preliminary remarks 40
§. 2. On nouns and their formation 41
§. 3. On adjectives and their formation 55
§. 4. The numerals 60
§. 5. The pronouns 63
§. 6. The verb 69
§. 7. The substantive verbs 77
§. 8. Mood and tense 79
§. 9. The adverbs 84
§. 10. The prepositions 91
§. 11. The conjunctions 93
§. 12. The interjections and other particles 95

CHAP. II. SYNTAX.

Sect. I. *On simple constructions.*

§. 1. Preliminary remarks 97
§. 2. General rules relating to the position of words 97
§. 3. The construction of simple terms 99

CONTENTS.

§. 4. The principles involved in the grouping of words 102
§. 5. The uncommon use of certain words in phraseology 103
§. 6. The modifications and relations of the parts of speech 105
§. 7. The syntax of the particles 142
    I. Attributive particles 142
    II. Connective particles 147
    III. Affirmative particles 152
    IV. Negative particles 158
    V. Adversative particles 162
    VI. Causative particles 165
    VII. Conditional particles 167
    VIII. Illative particles 169
    IX. Interrogative particles 169
    X. Dubitative particles 173
    XI. Intensitive particles 174
    XII. Exclamatory particles 175
    XIII. Euphonic particles 176

Sect. II. *On sentences.*

§. 1. Preliminary remarks 180
§. 2. The forms of the simple sentence 183
§. 3. The noun sentence 184
§. 4. The adjective sentence 184
§. 5. The adverbial sentence 185
§. 6. On complex sentences 187
§. 7. On compound sentences 188
§. 8. On figures of speech 188
§. 9. On varieties of style 189

APPENDICES.

I. Examples of antithesis, repetition, &c., and select phraseology 191
II. A list of the Chinese family names (*Pĕ-kiā síng*) 201
III. A list of the dynasties, and the emperors, with dates 205
IV. A list of the characters in the *niên-haú*, with a table of the *niên-haú* ... 212
V. A comparison of some of the Chinese dialects 225
VI. Tables of weights, monies, measures, and times 230

PART II. CHINESE CHRESTOMATHY.

A short introduction to Chinese literature.

Preliminary notices on the character, extent, and wants of Chinese literature. —Division of Chinese literature into (1) classical, (2) historical, (3) professional, (4) miscellaneous.—Another classification into ancient and modern literature.—The *Wù-kīng* or "Five classics."—The *Yĭ-kīng*, the *Shŭ-kīng*, the *Shī-kīng*, the *Lĭ-kì*, and the *Ch'ăn-tsiú.*—The *Sź-shū* or "Four books." —The *Tá-hiŏ* of *Tsăng-tsź.*—The *Chūng-yŭng* of *K'ūng-tsź.*—The *Lŭn-yû* of *K'ūng-tsź.*—The *Măng-tsź* (first and second).—The commentator *Chū-fū-tsź.*—The *Cheū-lĭ.*—*Hiaú-kīng.*—*Ts'ŭ-tsź.*—*Shān-haĭ-kīng.*—*Sź-mà-tsiên.* —*Taú-tĕ-kīng.*—The *Shĭ-tsź.*—(1) *Laù-tsź.*—(2) *Chwáng-tsź.*—(3) *Siūn-tsź.*—(4) *Lĭ-tsź.*—(5) *Kwăn-tsź.*—(6) *Hān-fĭ-tsź.*—(7) *Hwaí-nán-tsź.*— (8) *Yáng-tsź.*—(9) *Wăn-chūng-tsź.*—(10) *Hŏ-kw'ăn-tsź* .... Pages 3–8.

List of Chinese works arranged in classes: (1) Ethics, politics, and mental science. (2) Mathematics and astronomy. (3) Language and the meanings of words. (4) Jurisprudence. (5) Medicine and materia medica. (6) History and statistics. (7) Biographical notices. (8) Geography, topography, &c. (9) Mythology. (10) Poetry. (11) Painting, engraving, &c. (12) The drama. (13) Works of fiction. (14) Agriculture and weaving. (15) Encyclopædias and compilations .... Pages 9–18.

The various styles of composition,—the *Kŭ-wăn*, the *Wăn-cháng.*—Metrical composition in Chinese.—The different kinds of poetry ...... Pages 19, 20.

List of the passages in the native character .... Page 21.

Extracts from native authors, in Roman letter, with English translations:—

The *Shŭ-kīng* (text, pp. 1, 2) .... Pages 22–27.
Epitaph of *Kĭ-tsź* (text, p. 2) .... Pages 26–29.
Sź-shū (text, pp. 3, 4, 5), *Lŭn-yû*, *Shàng-măng*, *Hiá-măng*... Pages 28–35.
Shíng-yù (text, pp. 6, 7) .... Pages 36–41.
Haú-k'iû chuén (text, pp. 8–12) .... Pages 40–51.
Shwüĭ-hù chuén (text, pp. 13–16) .... Pages 50–57.
Sān-kwŏ chí (text, pp. 17–20) .... Pages 58–66.
Æsop's Fables, translated (text, pp. 21, 22) .... Pages 66–70.
Lin's letter to Queen Victoria, translated (text, pp. 23, 24) ... Pages 70–76.

CONTENTS.

Supplementary treaty, translated (text, p. 25) .... Pages 76–78.
A notice and a petition, translated (text, p. 26) .... Pages 78–80.
Mandarin dialogues, translated (text, pp. 27–30) .... Pages 80–86.
Extract from the *Chíng-yīn-tsüï-yaü*, translated (text, p. 31)... Pages 86–88.
Epistolary style, translations (text, p. 32) .... Pages 88–90.
Poetical extracts, translated (text, p. 33) .... Pages 90–94.
Proverbs, translated (text, p. 34) .... Pages 94–96.
Extracts from the *Chíng-yīn-tsüï-yaü*, translated (text, litho. pp. 9, 10)
Pages 96–98.
Extract from the *Sān-kwŏ chí*, translated (text, litho. pp. 11–13) Pages 98–103.
Æsop's Fables, translated (text, litho. p. 14) .... Pages 104, 105.

PART I.
CHINESE GRAMMAR.

Chap. I. ETYMOLOGY.

Sect. I. Articulate sounds and their symbols.

§. 1. *Elementary sounds and their orthography.*

1. The Chinese language does not possess, like the European languages, a series of letters with which to express elementary sounds; nor are figures employed to represent syllables merely, as in the syllabaries of the Japanese and Manchu languages. It is therefore necessary in the outset to lay before the student a clear system of orthography, in order that he may acquire as speedily as possible a correct pronunciation of the Chinese characters; and we propose making use of the Roman alphabet for this purpose.

2. The articulate sounds of the human voice are produced by the united action of the breath and the organs of speech, the lips, the tongue, and the larynx. As these organs are the same every where, the articulations of every language must partake of many sounds in common; and though they may be modified by the shape of the organs and other circumstances, they are fundamentally the same. It follows, therefore, that in learning a foreign tongue a consideration of the elementary sounds of the human voice, and the exhibition of them in that tongue, will facilitate the progress by placing the subject from the first upon a reasonable basis.

3. There are three primary vowel sounds, *a, i, u,* and from these the other vowels and the diphthongs spring*. This fact has been proved by the absence of the *ĕ* and *ŏ* in the Sanskrit, and by the vowels of the Hebrew in its ancient form being only א *aleph,* י *yod,* and ו *vav.* These primary or fundamental vowels, with the vowel-sounds derived from them, are thus exhibited:

α) By the union of *a* and *i* the diphthong *ai* is produced, as *ai* in *aisle;* then by gradually closing and contracting the organs we form the German *ä,* the flattened *ŭ* in *shamo,* and the open French *é* in *forêt, même;* to these may be added *ạ* with a dot beneath to represent the obscure sound like *ir, er,* and *o,* in *Sir, her, son,* respectively.

β) By the union of *a* and *u* the diphthong *au* is formed, as *ou* in *plough* or *au* in *Baum* (German); then by contraction we have *ō* long in *no, nos* (French); to which may be added *ọ* with a dot beneath to represent the

---
* It should be understood from the first that the pronunciation of these vowels is the German or Italian; *ah, ee, oo* in English.

sound of *o* in *order* or *au* in *clause*. In the ancient Arabic, *ai* and *au* were used instead of *e* and *o*. So in the Greek and Latin, Καῖσαρ became *Cæsar*, θαῦμα in the Ionic dialect was θῶμα, a case exactly similar to that which takes place in Chinese, and which will be found noticed under the Comparative Table of Dialects. The modern pronunciation of the French words *lait*, *mais*, *aussi*, illustrates the same facts, as does also the vulgar German *öch* for *auch*.

γ) By uniting *i* and *u* we produce *ew* in *yew*, *hew*, *new*, &c.; and in like manner any variety of simple vowel sound or diphthongal compound may be formed with the three vowels *a*, *i*, *u* *.

4. We shall employ the letters of the Roman alphabet to express Chinese sounds; and the student should make himself thoroughly acquainted with the system of orthography given below. An absolutely true pronunciation can only be attained by long and regular practice, by imitating a teacher, and by a residence among the Chinese; yet, by careful attention to the advice here given, considerable advance may be made with the aid of books alone.

T. T. Meadows, Esq., one of H. B. Majesty's Consuls in China, proposed a new orthography several years ago, and made some very just remarks on the *obscure vowel sounds*, with especial reference to their delicate modifications in the Pekin dialect. (See *Desultory Notes on China*. London: Allen, 1847.)

The variations however in the pronunciation of native scholars speaking the same dialect are many, whilst all are sufficiently correct. Just as distinctions may be drawn between the pronunciation of individual scholars in this country and considerable difference be found to exist in their pronunciation of single words; but to alter the spelling of English words because the letter *a* is sounded somewhat broader or made a little longer by one than by another, would lead to endless changes. To illustrate this point—the German *ä* is not the same as the English *a* in *shame* or *ay* in *play*, nor is the German *eu* accurately expressed by *oy* in *joy*, *toy;* yet these examples may stand in a Grammar for Englishmen, because each answers so nearly to the foreign sound as to be a sufficient guide to the pronunciation, though the French *ê* in *même* and the *eui* in *feuille* correspond more nearly to the German *ä* and *eu*.

5. The quantity of each of the vowels in the following table is *long* in all positions which allow of it; that is to say, in some rare positions they will be short; as, for instance, when affected by the *jĭ-shīng* (902, 2291) or 'entering tone,' which is always designated by the ordinary mark ⌣ for a short vowel.

The pronunciation of the short vowels is exemplified by the words enclosed in brackets.

The short *ŏ*, which should correctly be written with the dot beneath, will be without the dot, as the corresponding short of *ō* long rarely, if ever, occurs.

The equivalent of each vowel is also given according to Dr. Morrison's system of spelling, as the student will have to refer to his Dictionary.

---

* For further information on this subject the student may refer to Karl F. Becker's *Organism der Sprache;* Jacob Grimm's *Geschichte der Deutschen Sprache;* and Wilhelm von Humboldt's work, *Ueber die Kawi Sprache*, vol. I. *Einleitung*.

ORTHOGRAPHY BY ROMAN LETTERS. 3

The system of orthography adopted.

I. The vowels, simple and combined.

Form.	Morr.	The value of each illustrated by examples.
i ĭ	e eĭh	i in *police;* i in *wir* (Germ.); i in *aussi* (Fr.); (*bĭt.*)
e ĕ	ay ĭh	a in *lame;* ä in *fähig* (Germ.); ê in *même* (Fr.); (*bĕt.*)
a ă	a ăh	a in *father;* a in *darf* (Germ.); a in *pas* (Fr.); (*băt.*)
ą ą̆	ă uh	a in *organ;* e in *haben* (Germ.); ue in *que* (Fr.); (*bŭt.*)
o ŏ	o ŏ	o in *no;* o in *oder* (Germ.); ô in *côté* (Fr.); (*nŏt.*)
ǫ	aw	(Canton D. and Shanghai D.) o in *order;* aw in *law.*
ö	–	(Shanghai D.) ö in *Löwe* (Germ.); nearly œu in *sœur* (Fr.)
u ŭ	oo ŭh	u in *rule;* u in *du* (Germ.); ou in *vous* (Fr.); (*bŭll.*)
ü ü̆	eu uĕ	u in *lune* (Fr.); ü in *Mühe* (Germ.); (eu in *peut-être.*)
ie iĕ	eay ĕĕ	ie in *pied* (Fr.); yea (Eng.); (yĕ in *yesterday.*)
ia iă	ea ĕă	ia in *lia, plia* (Fr.); ja (Germ.); (yă in *yankee.*)
io iŏ		io in *million* (Fr.); (Shanghai D.); (yă in *yacht.*)
iu iŭ	ew eŭh	ew in *hew, yew;* (jŭ in *juchhe!* (Germ.))
ei	ei	ei in *sein* (Germ.); ie in *pie* (Eng.)
eu	ow	e + u, peculiar. French MSS. would have *éou.*
ai	ae	ai in *aisle;* so *iai*=*eae* in Morr.
au	aou	ow in *cow;* au in *Frau* (Germ.); so *iau*=*eaou* in Morr.
oi	oy	(Canton D.) oi in *voice.*
ui	uy	(Canton D.) u+i; ui in *ruin.*
üi	uy	eui in *feuille* (Fr.); eu in *Beute* (Germ.)

II. The consonants, single and combined.

Form.	Morr.	The value of each illustrated by examples.
b	–	as in English, not in Mand. D. (in Shang. D. and Hok. D.)
ch	ch	ch in *hatch;* chw in *hatchway;* chh in *catch him.*
d	–	(Shang. D. Ningpo D. &c.) as in English; dj=Eng. j.
f	f	f in *fit.* The *tone* in some dialects changes it to v.
g	g	g in *good* always, never g in *gin.*
h	h	h in *heart;* before i and ü it is a strong aspiration, nearly sh.
j	j	j in *jeune* (Fr.); z in *azure* (Eng.); ju or jw.
k	k	k in *king;* kw as qu in *queen.*
l	l	l in *line;* lw as in *bulwark.*
m	m	m in *mine;* mw as in *homeward.*
n	n	n in *nine;* nw as in *inward;* ng in *anger.*
p	p	p in *pine.*
r	r	r in *run;* rather more rolling than the English r.
s	s	s in *see;* sw as in *swain.*
sh	sh	sh in *shine;* shw as in *a rash wish.*
t	t	t in *tiny;* tw us in *twist;* ts as in *wits;* tsw as in *Cotswold.*
v	–	v in *vine* (Shang. and Ning. D.)
w	w	w in *way,* or v in *vine.*
y	y	y in *you.*
z	z	z in *squeeze,* sz=s+z, i. e. the hissing sound of s, then the buzzing sound of z, and in tsz=ts+z.

6. Exercise for reading.

Ts'ing ts'au k'ì laî, kiáu haî-tsz̀-mǫ̀n, saú-saú tí, kiaū-kiaū hwā, gaú shwùi sù lién, paù wàn haù ch'á k'ï-k'ï; mŭ-yiù sź tí shî-heú, k'ān-k'ān shŭ siè-siè tsź; sān-liàng-kó sz-wǫ̀n páng-yiù, tsŏ kó shī, hiá kó weî-ki, kiái-kiái mǫ̀n-ǫ̀r. tsiù k'ô-ì kwó-tǐ jī-tsź liaù.

§. 2. *Syllables and their intonation.*

7. After having thus considered elementary sounds and the symbols suited to express them, we naturally proceed to view them as they are united to form syllables. The characters of the Chinese do not represent elementary sounds or articulations, but each character stands for an entire syllable. The syllable then in Chinese is simply the *name* given to a symbol; that is, each character is expressed by a syllable, the sound of which cannot be discovered from the composition or formation of the character. In fact, the same characters have different names in the different provinces in which they are read, just as the Arabic numerals are called by different names in the various states of Europe and Asia.

8. Every syllable in the Court dialect ends with a vowel or nasal, but commonly with a vowel. The dialectic peculiarities may be seen in the Comparative Table.

9. The Chinese divide the syllable into two parts, the initial and the final; and they define the pronunciation of characters by a process called *fán-tsĕ* 反切 'to cut off in opposite directions;' thus the initial of the syllable *ke* may be taken and the final of the syllable *mung*, and they together constitute the syllable *kung*. In K'anghi's Dictionary the pronunciation of characters is always explained in this way; e. g. the sound of the character 正 is explained thus: *chi shing tsĕ, chi* and *shing* being cut in the above way into *ch-ing*, which is the pronunciation of the character *ching*.

10. The number of different Chinese syllables is between four and five hundred. In the Mandarin or Court dialect—the *Kwān-hwá* 官話 —there are four hundred and ten syllables, besides those with aspirates, as *thien* or *t'ien*. They are here arranged in alphabetic order, and the student will do well to read them as an exercise in orthoëpy.

Table of the syllables in the *Kwān-hwá*.

1 *a*	13 *chĕ*	25 *chŭi*	37 *fu*	49 *gŏ*	61 *hiá*	73 *hiun*
2 *an*	14 *chen*	26 *chung*	38 *fŭ*	50 *hai*	62 *hiai*	74 *hiung*
3 *ǫr*	15 *cheu*	27 *chwa*	39 *fung*	51 *han*	63 *hiang*	75 *ho*
4 *au*	16 *chi*	28 *chwai*	40 *gai*	52 *hǫn*	64 *hiau*	76 *hŏ*
5 *cha*	17 *chí*	29 *chwang*	41 *gan*	53 *hang*	65 *hiĕ*	77 *hu*
6 *chá*	18 *chin*	30 *fá*	42 *gǫn*	54 *hǫng*	66 *hien*	78 *hŭ*
7 *chai*	19 *ching*	31 *fan*	43 *gang*	55 *hau*	67 *hin*	79 *hŭ*
8 *chan*	20 *chŏ*	32 *fǫn*	44 *gǫng*	56 *hĕ*	68 *hing*	80 *hung*
9 *chǫn*	21 *chu*	33 *fang*	45 *gau*	57 *heu*	69 *hiŏ*	81 *hwa*
10 *chang*	22 *chŭ*	34 *feu*	46 *geu*	58 *hi*	70 *hiu*	82 *hwo*
11 *chau*	23 *chŭ*	35 *fi*	47 *gĭ*	59 *hï*	71 *hiŭ*	83 *hwai*
12 *che*	24 *chuen*	36 *fŏ*	48 *go*	60 *hia*	72 *hiuen*	84 *hwan*

SYLLABLES OF THE COURT DIALECT.

85 hwan	132 kiun	179 lŭ	226 niŏ	273 shă	319 swan	365 tsu
86 hwang	133 kiung	180 lüi	227 niu	274 shai	320 sz	366 tsŭ
87 hwqng	134 ko	181 lung	228 no	275 shan	321 ta	367 tsü
88 hwŏ	135 kŏ	182 lwan	229 nŏ	276 shqn	322 tă	368 tsŭ̈
89 hwŭ	136 ku	183 ma	230 nu	277 shang	323 tai	369 tsüi
90 hwüi	137 kü	184 mă	231 nŭ	278 shau	324 tan	370 tsung
91 i	138 k-ü	185 mai	232 nü	279 she	325 tqn	371 tswan
92 jqn	139 kŭ	186 man	233 nüi	280 shĕ	326 tang	372 tsz
93 jang	140 kung	187 mqn	234 nung	281 shen	327 tqng	373 tu
94 jau	141 kwa	188 mang	235 nwan	282 sheu	328 tau	374 tŭ
95 je	142 kwă	189 mqng	236 o	283 shi	329 tĕ	375 tüi
96 jĕ	143 kwai	190 mau	237 ŏ	284 shĭ	330 teu	376 tung
97 jen	144 kwan	191 me	238 pa	285 shin	331 ti	377 twan
98 jeu	145 kwqn	192 mĕ	239 pă	286 shing	332 tĭ	378 ung
99 jĭ	146 kwang	193 mei	240 pai	287 shŏ	333 tiau	379 wa
100 jin	147 kwqng	194 meu	241 pan	288 shu	334 tie	380 wă
101 jing	148 kwei	195 mi	242 pqn	289 shŭ	335 tiĕ	381 wai
102 jŏ	149 kwo	196 mĭ	243 pang	290 shwa	336 tien	382 wan
103 ju	150 kwŏ	197 miau	244 pqng	291 shwă	337 ting	383 wqn
104 jŭ	151 kwă	198 mie	245 pau	292 shwai	338 tiu	384 wang
105 juen	152 la	199 mien	246 pĕ	293 shwang	339 to	385 wei
106 jüi	153 lă	200 min	247 pei	294 shwŏ	340 tŏ	386 wi
107 jung	154 lai	201 ming	248 peu	295 shwüi	341 tsă	387 wo
108 kai	155 lan	202 miu	249 pi	296 si	342 tsai	388 wŏ
109 kan	156 lqn	203 mo	250 pĭ	297 sĭ	343 tsan	389 wu
110 kqn	157 lang	204 mŏ	251 piau	298 siang	344 tsqn	390 wŭ
111 kang	158 lqng	205 mu	252 piĕ	299 siau	345 tsang	391 ya
112 kqng	159 lau	206 mŭ	253 pien	300 sie	346 tsqng	392 yă
113 kau	160 lĕ	207 mung	254 pin	301 siĕ	347 tsau	393 yai
114 ke	161 leu	208 mwan	255 ping	302 sien	348 tsĕ	394 yqn
115 keu	162 li	209 na	256 piu	303 sin	349 tseu	395 yang
116 ki	163 lĭ	210 nă	257 po	304 sing	350 tsi	396 yau
117 kĭ	164 liang	211 nai	258 pŏ	305 siŏ	351 tsĭ	397 ye
118 kia	165 liau	212 nan	259 pu	306 siu	352 tsiang	398 yĕ
119 kiă	166 liĕ	213 nqn	260 pŭ	307 siŭ	353 tsiau	399 yen
120 kiai	167 lien	214 nang	261 pung	308 siuen	354 tsie	400 yi
121 kiang	168 lin	215 nqng	262 pwan	309 siun	355 tsiĕ	401 yin
122 kiau	169 ling	216 nau	263 să	310 so	356 tsien	402 ying
123 kie	170 liŏ	217 neu	264 sai	311 sŏ	357 tsin	403 yiu
124 kiĕ	171 liu	218 ni	265 san	312 su	358 tsing	404 yŏ
125 kien	172 liŭ	219 nĭ	266 sqn	313 sŭ	359 tsiŏ	405 yu
126 kin	173 liuen	220 niang	267 sang	314 sü	360 tsiu	406 yŭ
127 king	174 lo	221 niau	268 sqng	315 sŭ̈	361 tsiuen	407 yŭ̈
128 kiŏ	175 lŏ	222 niĕ	269 sau	316 süin	362 tsiun	408 yuen
129 kiu	176 lu	223 nien	270 sĕ	317 sung	363 tso	409 yün
130 kiŭ	177 lŭ	224 nin	271 seu	318 süi	364 tsŏ	410 yung
131 kiuen	178 lüi	225 ning	272 sha			

11. The syllable *ąr* (No. 3. of the preceding list) is variously spelt by Morrison and others *urh, eul, 'll, irr, ri*. It represents a peculiar sound, probably of modern origin, as it is not found in the Imperial Dictionary of *K'anghi* 康熙. The characters it expresses are called *i* in the Canton and some other dialects, and it rhymes with *i* in the *Shi-king* 詩經 or Classic Odes.

12. The articulate sounds in every language must have preceded the written character. There is no positive proof that the syllabic sounds in present use in China are of very great antiquity, though this may be inferred from one or two facts. *a.* The two hundred and fourteen elementary characters called *Radicals*, contain one hundred and fifty of the above-mentioned four hundred syllables; and this is a large proportion unless we suppose that they had those sounds attached to them in a very early stage of the language, when, as yet, but few other characters had been invented.

b. The *Primitives*, one thousand seven hundred in number, another set of elementary characters, which, with the Radicals, make up the body of material out of which the thirty or forty thousand characters have been constructed, contain nearly every syllable found in the language.

c. Ancient poetry also goes to prove the antiquity of the present oral system, by the rhymes in the *Shi-king*. Some of these odes are very ancient. One of them, on the marriage of *Wăn-wăng* 文王, a celebrated emperor, father of the *Cheū* 周 family, and which was without doubt written at that period, leads us back three thousand years, or about two hundred years before the reputed date of Homer [*].

13. Every syllable in Chinese is uttered with a certain intonation or modulation of the voice, which is commonly called its 'tone' by Europeans; by natives the tone is called *Shing-yin* 聲音, i. e. *tone-sound* (v. 2291).

14. The tones are of essential service in adding distinctness to the expression; in many cases a phrase would be quite unintelligible without its proper tones, and often convey an entirely different idea from the one intended.

15. The difficulty of learning these tones has been much exaggerated, and the published opinions of some who had a right to be heard on subjects connected with the Chinese language, have tended to confirm misconceptions. We shall here endeavour to state clearly their nature, and give directions for their acquirement.

16. In the first place, the tones are not mere *accents* or the elevated utterance of syllables in words, nor *accent*, as when we speak of the French accent, Scotch accent, a point in which every language differs, nor the wayward and uncertain intonation of words and phrases as we hear frequently in animated dialogue and oratory; but they are certain fixed intonations, peculiar to each character when uttered, and they change only when euphony would be disturbed by their accustomed sound being retained.

17. The Chinese *Shing-yin* are from *four* to *eight* of these latter intonations proper to the language of the orator, and they add as much force and vigour to the Chinese tongue as they do to our own. Only one of them is peculiar and uncommon, and this is a sort of whine or drawl; but in union with others in the same word it assimilates in some degree to the general or predominating tone, and so loses its unpleasant sound.

---

[*] V. Marshman's Clavis Sinica, pp. 83, 84, etc.

18. The number of the tones appears to have been four in the first instance, but in the various dialects of China they rise to seven and eight. They are as follows:

— 1. The *p'ing-shīng* 平 (2291) 'even, level tone.'

\ 2. The *shàng-shīng* 上 (2291) 'rising tone.'

/ 3. The *k'ŭ-shīng* 去 (2291) 'departing tone.'

\/ 4. The *jĭ-shīng* 入 (2291) 'entering tone.'

By uttering these four at a low pitch of the voice and then at a higher, eight different intonations are produced; those pitched high being denominated *shàng* 上 'upper,' and those pitched low being called *hiā* 下 'lower.'

19. The Mandarin dialect, or *Kwan-hwá*, acknowledges five of these tones, the whole of the upper series and the first of the lower. In common parlance they are called, 1. *P'ing*, 2. *shàng*, 3. *k'ŭ*, 4. *jĭ*, and 5. *hiá-p'ing*.

20. The *Shàng-p'ing-shīng* is the 'upper even tone,' and may be illustrated by the sound of calling to a person at some distance, thus: '*John, fetch* my *horse*,' the syllables in Italics expressing the tone.

21. The *Shàng-shàng-shīng* or 'upper rising tone' agrees nearly with our tone of the final syllable in an interrogation with surprise, 'Will he say that *now?*' 'Can he come, *eh?*' The voice is first depressed and then suddenly raised.

22. The *Shàng-k'ŭ-shīng* or 'upper descending tone' is well illustrated by a phrase of exclamation with scorn or reproach.

23. The *Shàng-jĭ-shīng* or 'upper entering tone' is equivalent to the short abrupt utterance in such a phrase as 'tit for tat,' without pronouncing the final letters. In the Peking dialect this tone is changed into the *k'ŭ-shīng*.

24. The *Hiá-p'ing-shīng* or 'lower even tone' is similar to the corresponding upper one, but is pitched *lower*, as in the tone of a direct reply to a question, '*Yes*,' '*No*,' 'Who fetched it?' '*John.*'

25. The *Hiá-shàng-shīng* or 'lower rising tone' is very much like the Scotch accent, the voice is depressed and quickly raised again. This tone and the remaining three are not recognised in the Mandarin dialect, and will therefore not be explained here. The student is referred for further information on the subject of the tones to the works of Dyer, Medhurst, Bridgman, and Edkins, all of whom have taken great pains to elucidate them.

26. The diacritical marks used by the early Jesuits to distinguish the tones we shall employ in this work. They are as follows: ‾ \ ′ ˘ ^ 1. *P'ing*, 2. *shàng*, 3. *k'ŭ*, 4. *jĭ*, 5. *hiá-p'ing;* placed above the vowel of the syllable to be intonated thus, *tā, tà, tá, tă, tâ*.

27. The following passages are intended to illustrate the character of tones. The numbers attached to the words, and the diacritical marks also, refer to the tones employed in the pronunciation of them.

I. "Thēre I sāw Rhadamânthus (5), one of the judges of the dead, seated at his tribûnal (5). He interrogated each separately. 'Mādām' (1), says he, to the first of them, 'you have been upon thè earth above fifty yèars; whāt have you been dōing there all this while?' 'Doìng!' (2), says she, 'really I don't know whāt I've been doing!'" *Guardian*, No. 158.

II. LEAR.   But goes this with thy heàrt? (2)
CORDELIA.   Ay, good my lord.
LEAR.   So yoùng, and so untènder?
COR.   So yoûng, my lord, and trûe (5).
LEAR.   Let it bê sô.—Thy trûth then be thy dôwer;
For, by the sacred rádiance of the sún;
The mysteries of Hécate, and the níght;
By all the operátions of the órbs (3),
From whom we do exíst and céase to bê;
Hêre I discláim all my patêrnal câre,
Propínquity and próperty of blóod,
And as a strânger to my heârt and mê
Hold thēe, from thîs, for êver.
KENT.   Gōod my liēge—
LEAR.   Peâce, Kênt!
Cōme not betwixt the drâgon and his wrâth:
I lov'd her most, and thought to set my rest
On her kind nûrsery.—Hénce, and avoid my sight.
          SHAKESPEARE, *King Lear*, Act I. Sc. 2.

28. The Chinese sometimes distinguish the tone of a syllable by a mark placed at the corner of the character, but not generally. As each character is inscribed in a square, the four corners serve as positions for tone-marks in the order shown here:

29. The tone of a character is sometimes changed to show that it has an uncommon meaning or that its relation to the sentence is altered; thus *nouns* become *verbs*, and *adjectives* become *nouns*, but not by any constant rule: *chù* 主 'a lord' becomes *chú* 'to rule;' *ŏ* or *gŏ* 惡 'bad' becomes *wú* or *hú* 'to hate;' *shǎng* 上 'upper' becomes *shǎng* 'to go up, ascend;' *chúng* 重 'heavy' becomes *chúng* 'to repeat.' In such cases a small circle called *kiuên* (1282) is placed at one corner of the character to intimate the change.

30. The Chinese aspirate many of their syllables very strongly, and the absence of the aspiration nearly always renders the phrase unintelligible. For example, *kai* 解 'ought,' but *k'ai* 開 'to open.' We shall express the aspiration by the Greek *spiritus asper* ('). When the letter *h* is used it will be understood to be a very strong aspiration; thus *hai* 海 'the sea' is pronounced as if written with the German guttural *ch, chai*.

31. The Chinese are accustomed to arrange the characters in Dictionaries according to the *final sounds* of the syllables which they represent; thus, *sien, lien, mien, kien,* &c., come together as they rhyme with each other, and then they follow according to the *tones, p'ing, shàng, k'ú, jì*. In the Canton dialect there is a Dictionary of this kind, in which the syllables are arranged in thirty-three classes according to their terminations. The first of the series is *sien;* and the syllables which rhyme with this are taken through the four tones of both upper and lower series. The practice of reading these syllables after a native instructor, in the order of the tones, will be advantageous to the student: thus, *siēn, sièn, siēn, siĕ;* and then, as a second exercise, he should select dissyllabic and trisyllabic combinations whose sequences as regards tone are similar.

32. The following table will show what we mean by sequence in tone, and the accompanying exercises will serve to accustom the student to practical intonation.

	P'ing	*Shàng*	*K'ú*	*Jì*	*Hiá-p'ing*
P'ing	1 --	2 -- \	3 -- /	4 -- ᵕ	5 -- ʌ
Shàng	6 \ --	7 \ \	8 \ /	9 \ ᵕ	10 \ ʌ
K'ú	11 / --	12 / \	13 / /	14 / ᵕ	15 / ʌ
Jì	16 ᵕ --	17 ᵕ \	18 ᵕ /	19 ᵕ ᵕ	20 ᵕ ʌ
Hiá-p'ing	21 ʌ --	22 ʌ \	23 ʌ /	24 ʌ ᵕ	25 ʌ ʌ

From this it appears that twenty-five combinations of tones may be formed, though some occur more frequently than others. We shall now give several combinations intoned according to the numbers in the table:

1. *kīn-t'iēn* 'to-day;'[a b] *kūng-fū* 'work;'[c d] *siāng-kūng* 'Mr., Sir.'[e f]
2. *tō-shaù* 'how many ?'[g h] *t'iēn-chù* 'God *;'[b i] *gān-tièn* 'favour.'[j k]
3. *sāng-í* 'trade, business;'[l m] *chī-taù* 'to know;'[n o] *ī-kiú* 'as before.'[p q]
4. *ī-fŭ* 'clothes;'[r s] *sheŭ-shĭ* 'to collect together;'[t u] *sāng-jĭ* 'birthday.'[l v]

* The word used by the Romanists.

[a] 今 [b] 天 [c] 工 [d] 夫 [e] 相 [f] 公 [g] 多
[h] 少 [i] 主 [j] 恩 [k] 典 [l] 生 [m] 意 [n] 知 [o] 道
[p] 已 [q] 久 [r] 衣 [s] 服 [t] 收 [u] 拾 [v] 日

5. *shū-fáng* 'a library;'^{a b} *sz̄-wǎn* 'polished, refined;'^{c d} *kǎn-tsʻúng* 'to follow.'^{e f}
6. *tǎ-saú* 'to sweep;'^{g h} *tǎ-tʻīng* 'to listen;'^{g i} *tiēn-hiāng* 'to kindle incense.'^{j k}
7. *laú-tsz̀* 'the old one, father;'^{l m} *yin-tsiù* 'to drink wine;'^{n o} *tʻù-chǎn* 'land produce.'^{p q}
8. *hŏ-kí* 'an assistant;'^{r s} *tsaù-fǎn* 'morning rice, breakfast;'^{t u} *tǎng-heū* 'to wait for.'^{v w}
9. *wei-kiŭ* 'hardship;'^{x y} *tǎ-fŭ* 'to send;'^{z a'} *yěn-mŭ* 'the eyes.'^{a' b'}
10. *taú-chʻá* 'to pour out tea;'^{c' d'} *wǎng-niēn* 'last year;'^{e' f'} *tiěn-tʻeú* 'to nod.'^{j g'}
11. *waí-piēn* 'outside;'^{h' i'} *chúng-hwā* 'to plant flowers;'^{j' k'} *paú-chī* 'to inform.'^{l' m'}
12. *chě-lī* 'here;'^{n' o'} *sí-siǎng* 'to think of carefully;'^{p' q'} *shǎng-mǎ* 'to mount a horse.'^{r' s'}
13. *fí-yúng* 'expenses;'^{t' u'} *yǔ-pí* 'to prepare beforehand;'^{v' w'} *kaú-sú* 'to inform.'^{x' y'}
14. *lúng-shā* 'to kill;'^{z' a''} *heū-shǐ* 'liberal;'^{b'' c''} *kʻí-lì* 'strength.'^{d'' e''}
15. *pí-mǎn* 'shut the door;'^{f'' g''} *hiá-kʻí* 'to play at chess;'^{h'' i''} *sz̄-tsing* 'affair.'^{j'' k''}
16. *tǔ-shū* 'to study;'^{l'' a} *fǎ-chī* 'to be mad;'^{z m''} *chǔ-sāng* 'domestic animals.'^{n'' o''}
17. *tsŏ-chù* 'to act as master;'^{p'' q''} *kí-kwŏ* 'to bear fruit;'^{r'' s''} *jǐ-tsz̀* 'a day.'^{t'' m}
18. *tǎ-yíng* 'to answer;'^{u'' v''} *shwŏ-hwá* 'talk;'^{w'' x''} *tsě-pí* 'to blame.'^{y'' w'}

---

^a書 ^b房 ^c斯 ^d文 ^e跟 ^f從 ^g打
^h掃 ⁱ聽 ^j點 ^k香 ^l老 ^m子 ⁿ飲 ^o酒
^p土 ^q產 ^r移 ^s計 ^t早 ^u飯 ^v等 ^w侯
^x委 ^y曲 ^z發 ^{a'}眼 ^{b'}目 ^{c'}倒 ^{d'}茶 ^{e'}往
^{f'}年 ^{g'}頭 ^{h'}外 ^{i'}邊 ^{j'}種 ^{k'}花 ^{l'}報 ^{m'}知
^{n'}這 ^{o'}裏 ^{p'}細 ^{q'}想 ^{r'}上 ^{s'}馬 ^{t'}費 ^{u'}用
^{v'}預 ^{w'}備 ^{x'}告 ^{y'}訴 ^{z'}弄 ^{a''}殺 ^{b''}厚 ^{c''}實
^{d''}氣 ^{e''}力 ^{f''}閉 ^{g''}門 ^{h''}下 ^{i''}棋 ^{j''}事 ^{k''}情
^{l''}讀 ^{m''}痴 ^{n''}蓄 ^{o''}生 ^{p''}作 ^{q''}主 ^{r''}結 ^{s''}果
^{t''}日 ^{u''}答 ^{v''}應 ^{w''}說 ^{x''}話 ^{y''}責

19. tsŏ-ji 'yesterday;'[a][b] tsĭ-k'ĕ 'forthwith;'[c][d] yŭ-fŭ 'so much the more.'[e][f]
20. ch'ŭ-lai 'going in and out;'[g][h] hiŏ-fáng 'a schoolroom;'[i][j] yĭ-t'ăng 'together.'[k][l]
21. năng-kăn 'power;'[m][n] jŭ-kīn 'now;'[o][p] niên-kāng 'age'[q][r] (of a person).
22. wăn-lĭ 'elegance of composition;'[s][t] jŭ-tsz̆ 'thus;'[o][u] yaŭ-sheŭ 'to wave the hand.'[v][w]
23. mĭng-tsz̆ 'name and title;'[x][y] yŭng-maŭ 'countenance;'[z][a'] k'ĭ-kwaĭ 'marvellous.'[b'][c']
24. năn-shwŏ 'difficult to say;'[d'][e'] fáng-ŭ 'a house;'[i'][f'] mĭng-jĭ 'to-morrow.'[g'][b]
25. hwŭĭ-lai 'to return;'[h'][i'] ch'á-hŭ 'tea-pot;'[j'][k'] nŭ-ts'aĭ 'a slave.'[l'][m']

33. The following may serve as an exercise for reading the different tones with the same syllable aspirated as well as unaspirated:

Chāng [n'] 'chapter;' ch'áng [o'] 'long;' chăng [p'] 'palm of the hand;' cháng [q'] 'a curtain;' cháng [r'] 'constant;' ch'áng [s'] 'to reward;' chī t' 'to know;' chĭ [u'] 'to point out;' ch'ĭ [v'] 'to begin;' chĭ [w'] 'to come;' chĭ [x'] 'slow;' chūng [y'] 'middle;' ch'ŭng [z'] 'insect;' chúng [a''] 'to plant;' fān [b''] 'to divide;' făn [c''] 'flour;' făn [d''] 'all;' făn [e''] 'to reverse;' fī [f''] 'not;' fi [g''] 'to spend;' fĭ [h''] 'fat;' hŏ [i''] 'fire;' hŏ [j''] 'what?' hiūng [k''] 'an elder brother;' hiúng [l''] 'a bear;' hwā [m''] 'a flower;' hwá [n''] 'to change;' hwâ [o''] 'flowery;' kī [p''] 'a foundation;' kĭ [q''] 'self;' kĭ [r''] 'to remember, record;' k'ĭ [s''] 'he, that;' k'ĭ [t''] 'to insult;' k'ĭ [u''] 'to begin.'

[a] 昨	[b] 日	[c] 即	[d] 刻	[e] 越	[f] 發	[g] 出
[h] 來	[i] 學	[j] 房	[k] 一	[l] 同	[m] 能	[n] 幹	[o] 如
[p] 今	[q] 年	[r] 康	[s] 文	[t] 理	[u] 此	[v] 搖	[w] 手
[x] 名	[y] 字	[z] 容	[a'] 貌	[b'] 奇	[c'] 怪	[d'] 難	[e'] 說
[f'] 屋	[g'] 明	[h'] 回	[i'] 來	[j'] 茶	[k'] 壺	[l'] 奴	[m'] 才
[n'] 章	[o'] 長	[p'] 掌	[q'] 帳	[r'] 常	[s'] 償	[t'] 知	[u'] 指
[v'] 始	[w'] 至	[x'] 遲	[y'] 中	[z'] 虫	[a''] 種	[b''] 分	[c''] 粉
[d''] 凡	[e''] 反	[f''] 非	[g''] 費	[h''] 肥	[i''] 火	[j''] 何	[k''] 兄
[l''] 熊	[m''] 花	[n''] 化	[o''] 華	[p''] 基	[q''] 己	[r''] 記	[s''] 其
[t''] 欺	[u''] 起						

These will afford practice for the student in the regular sequences of *p'ing, shàng, k'ŭ*, and some others:

ts'iĕn-lĭ-king 千里鏡 'thousand-mile-mirror—a telescope.'

chaŭ-sheù kiaŭ jĭn 招手叫人 'beckon with hand—call man.'

gān-tiĕn tsŭi tá 恩典最大 his 'favour very great.'

t'ān-tsiŭ kwó tō 貪酒過多 'desire wine passover much—he is too fond of wine.'

It remains for the student to collect phrases with the same consecutive tones, and to practise reading them aloud. Such short sentences may be found already marked with the proper tones in the body of this work.

§. 3. *Words and their composition generally.*

34. Up to this point we have considered only the *sounds* and *syllables* of the Chinese, independent of any meaning that might be attached to them. We next turn to *words* as the expression of ideas. By a word is here meant one or more syllables, which, on being pronounced, convey but one signification; e.g. *jĭn* 人 'man,' *t'iĕ-tsiāng* 鐵匠 'a blacksmith.'

35. A word in Chinese *may* consist of *one* syllable, but from the want of grammatical inflexions, and from the limited number of syllables in use, a monosyllable is rarely intelligible when alone; it generally requires some adjunct to limit or strengthen its meaning. To illustrate this; *ti* 地 signifies 'earth;' *ti* 帝 'ruler;' *ti* 弟 'younger brother:' the syllables and tones of all these being alike, there is nothing to distinguish them when uttered, and it is only by some syllable or syllables being attached to them, that any notion is to be acquired from them. Thus in the phrase *t'iĕn-ti* 天 | 'heaven and earth,' the meaning of the syllable *ti* becomes known by its juxta-position with the syllable *t'iĕn*. In *ti-fāng* | 方 'a place,' the syllable *ti* 'earth' is limited by *fāng* 'a square,' making the compound to signify 'locality, region' merely. Again, *ti* 'ruler,' as a general term, is limited in the spoken language to 'emperor' by prefixing *hwáng* 皇 'emperor,' and is made to signify 'God' by prefixing *shang* 上 'upper.' Then again, *ti* 'younger brother' is made intelligible at once to a Chinese by the addition of *hiūng* 兄 'elder brother;' *hiūng-ti* meaning 'brethren.'

36. When two or more syllables come together in the above way to form one word or phrase, though each syllable may have a distinct meaning of its own, the compound becomes in many cases a perfect word with a new meaning, varying according to the nature of the relation existing between the syllables of which it is composed. These syllables either represent (*a*) *syno-*

nyms, as *yèn-mŭ* 眼目 'the eye,' *chūng-sīn* 中心 'middle-heart—the centre', *mŭ-wi* 末尾 'end-tail—the end,' where each is as much a dissyllable as *workhouse, washstand*, &c., in English; or they form (β) a *phrase*, as in *t'iēn-tī* 'heaven and earth,' *k'ŭng máng* 孔孟 'Confucius and Mencius,' which amounts to enumeration of objects; or (γ) words of *opposite* meaning are united to form the general or abstract term implied by each, e. g. *hiŭng-tī* 'elder brother, younger brother—brethren *,' *tō-shaŭ* 多少 'many, few—quantity, or how many?' or (δ) one of the syllables stands as *an attribute* of the other, e. g. *shíng-jín* 聖人 'holy-man—a sage, a philosopher,' *tá-hwáng* 大黃 'great-yellow—rhubarb,' *k'ŭ-niên* 去年 'gone year—last year;' or (ε) the two are in *apposition*, e. g. *shí-tsź* 石字 'shí, the character—the character *shí*' (stone), *jín-kiā* 人家 'man-family—a person,' *k'ĭ-jín* 客人 'guest-man—a guest.' Similar unities may be formed by joining verbs which are synonymous or antithetical in meaning; and innumerable phrases of two and three syllables are constituted, by conventional usage, perfect words, their elements being inseparable. This subject will be found further explained in the section on the formation of nouns and verbs. The following English words and phrases will lead the student to anticipate what he may find in Chinese compounds: (a) *wire-worker, silver-smith, tin-man, plum-tree, craw-fish, load-stone, the three kingdoms* (for the whole country), *church-warden, feather-bed, sea-port, fox-hound;* (b) *to injure a man, to kill a man, to obey an order.*

37. From the above, however, it must not be inferred that Chinese words, thus formed, always remain in their original form when brought into construction in the sentence. The rhythm often causes the exclusion of one syllable from a word when the sense is unaffected by its absence. Thus *mŭ*ᵃ*-tsīn*ᵇ is 'mother-relation—mother;' *ǎr*ᶜ*-tsź*ᵈ is 'son-child—son;' 'to die' is *sź*ᵉ, and *sź*ᵉ*-liaŭ*ᶠ means 'die-finish—died:' but in the expression 'The mother and son died together,' *tsīn* and *ǎr* and *liaŭ* would be omitted for the reasons just given, and the expression would be *mŭ*ᵃ *tsź*ᵈ *liǎng*ᵍ*-kó*ʰ *yī*-*t'ŭng*ⁱ *sź*ᵉ, or *liaŭ*ᶠ might be also attached.

38. The same principle of rhythm, which leads to the elision of one of two syllables in a word, under certain circumstances, also leads to the addition of a meaningless particle when the sound of the whole would be improved thereby. This fact is shown most clearly in the local dialects, each of which has euphonic particles peculiar to it.

---

* Cf. the phrase 'The long and the short—all.'

ᵃ母 ᵇ親 ᶜ兒 ᵈ子 ᵉ死 ᶠ了 ᵍ兩
ʰ個 ⁱ一 ʲ同

39. Although Chinese words are not built up from roots by the addition of terminations, nor modified by changes of the vowels in them, there are certain syllables which take the place of terminations, and these give nominal and verbal forms to the words they thus affect. We have called such syllables *formatives*. Among them are, *ąr*[a] 'child,' *tsź*[b] 'son,' *t'eŭ*[c] 'head:' thus, *t'sió*[d]*-ąr*[a] 'sparrow-child—a sparrow, or any small bird;' *siāng*[c]*-tsź*[b] 'box-son—a chest;' *jĭ*[f]*-t'eŭ*[c] 'sun-head—the sun.' The subject will be found further explained in the next chapter.

§. 4. *The characters, and how to write them.*

40. We now come to the consideration of the symbols employed to express the sounds and syllables of this language. They are not merely arbitrary figures, but ideographic characters; they express notions rather than sounds. They are very ancient, and are unique in every point of view.

41. The inventor or originator of the characters is said to have been *Fŭ-hi*, or, with his proper title, *Tai-hau Fŭ-hi* 太昊伏羲 'the most illustrious *Fŭ-hi*.' He was born in *Shen-si* 陝西 Prov., circ. B. C. 2200, and was the first of five ancient emperors (v. Table of Dynasties and Emperors, Appendix A.), and successor of the three mythical sovereigns. He built his capital, *K'ai-fung-fu* 開封府 in *Hu-nan* 河南 Prov., on the *Hwang-ho* 黃河 or 'yellow river *.' Fŭ-hi taught his rude subjects the arts of domestic life; and he invented the eight diagrams, *pă-kwá* 八卦, or combinations of whole and broken straight lines, as a substitute for the knotted cords used for recording events by one of his predecessors, *Süi-jin* † 燧人. Fŭ-hi also subsequently invented the *Lŭ-shū* 六書, or six classes of characters given below (44).

42. Another account is, that *Hwang-ti* 黃帝, the 3rd Emperor from Fŭ-hi, ordered *Ts'ang-hiĕ* 蒼頡, a man of extensive genius, and president of the Board of Historians, to work at the composition of the characters, and to follow the six rules of *Fŭ-hi*. One day, while walking by the river-side, he perceived some traces of birds' claws on the sand, and sat down to ponder on the Emperor's command. Some of the marks he copied on slips of bamboo with a pencil dipped in varnish. On his return home he multiplied the forms, always keeping in view the foot-prints of the birds, and thus produced five hundred and forty characters, which were called *niaŭ-tsź-wąn* 鳥字文 or 'bird-mark characters.'

---

* A colony of Jews settled in this city in later times.

† *Süi-jin* is said, by the Chinese, to have first discovered the use of fire.

[a] 兒   [b] 子   [c] 頭   [d] 雀   [e] 箱   [f] 日

43. But the father of letters in China was *Paù-shí* 保氏 'a scholar in the reign of *Ching-wáng* 正王 of the *Cheù* 周 dynasty, circ. B. C. 1100. In his work it is stated that the greater part of the characters were originally hieroglyphic; but that for the sake of appearance and convenience they were gradually changed. See Morrison's Dictionary, vol. I. *Introduction;* Marshman's Clavis Sinica, pp. 15, 16; and *Kang-kien* 綱鑑, or the translation of this work by Père Mailla—*Histoire Générale de la Chine,* tom. I. pp. 19, 20.

44. The *Lü-shū,* mentioned above (41), deserve some notice. The names of them, with explanations, are here given in a tabular form.

No.	Name.	Meaning of name.	Technical name.	No. in each.
1	像形 *Siáng-hing*	Similar-figure	Hieroglyphic	608
2	指事 *Chì-sz̀*	Indicating-thing	Significative	107
3	會意 *Hwùi-í*	Combining-ideas	Ideographic	740
4	轉註 *Chuèn-chù*	Inverting-signification	Antithetic	372
5	假借 *Kià-tsiè*	False-borrowed	Metaphorical	598
6	聲形 *Shīng-hing*	Sound-form	Phonetic	21,810

45. The following are illustrations of the above-mentioned six classes of characters. The modern forms are given as well as the ancient, that the student may be learning a few characters in every day use, while he sees the change which has taken place in the ancient hieroglyphic.

CLASS I. HIEROGLYPHIC.

Ancient.
Meaning. 'sun' 'moon' 'mountain' 'eye' 'child' 'horse' 'fish' 'tree' 'teeth'
Modern.   日   月   山   目   子   馬   魚   木   齒
Sound.   jĭ   yŭ   shān   mŭ   tsz̀   mà   yû   mŭ   chi

丁 *ting* represents 'a nail;' 弓 *kūng* 'a bow;' 井 *tsing* 'a well;' 巛 and 川 *ch'ūen* 'a stream;' 口 *k'eù* 'a mouth;'))) *hŏ* 'fire;' and 予 *shuuĭ* 'water.'

46. The second class includes those which indicate the meaning by their very form or composition.

ILLUSTRATIONS OF THE SYMBOLS.

CLASS II. SIGNIFICATIVE.

Ancient.	☉	夕	●	▼	△	中
Meaning.	'dawn'	'evening'	'above'	'below'	'unite'	'middle'
Modern.	日¹	夕²	上	下	入³	中
Sound.	tăn	sĭ	shăng	hiá	tsĭ	chŭng

屮 *chĕ* represents a plant springing from the ground, 'to come out,'—the common character for this is *ch'ŭ* 出 'to go out;' 本 *pŭn* 'a root—beginning;' 曰 *yŭ*, something in the mouth, 'to say.'

47. The next class includes those which are formed by the union of two figures belonging to class I; and which together give rise to an idea, sometimes of an abstraction, sometimes the name of a real thing.

CLASS III. IDEOGRAPHIC.

Ancient.	☽))	閑	林	見	坐	从
Meaning.	'brightness'	'obstruction'	'forest'	'to see'	'to sit'	'to follow'
Modern.	明⁴	閑⁵	林	見⁶	坐⁷	從⁸
Sound.	míng	hiên	lin	kiên	tsŏ	tsŭng

拜 *pai* (two hands) 'to salute'—the Chinese clasp their hands together in salutations—also 'to visit;' 恤 *siŭ* (heart and blood) 'pity;' 夜 *yĕ* (roof, man, dark) 'night.'

48. The following are specimens of the fourth class; they show by the inversion of the figures the antithetic significations which are attached to them. These inversions are, however, not so apparent in the modern characters as in the ancient hieroglyphic; and whenever the original elements of a compound are sought for, the ancient forms must be consulted *.

---

1. The sun above the horizon.
2. The moon beginning to appear.
3. The common character is 合 *hŏ* 'to unite.'
4. The sun and moon together, suggesting the idea of *brightness*.
5. A tree in a doorway,—*obstruction*.
6. A man with a large eye,—*seeing*.
7. Two men on the ground,—*sitting*.
8. Two men following,—*following*.

* An idea of the number of ancient forms for the same character may be obtained by reference to M. Callery's "Systema Phoneticum." Introduction, pp. 31—34. He there gives from twenty to forty different forms in the ancient character.

CLASS IV. ANTITHETIC.

Ancient.					
Meaning.	'right-hand'	'left-hand'	'to cut off'	'to continue'	'body'	'body turned'
Modern.	右¹	左¹	斷²	繼³	身	月
Sound.	yiù	tsŏ	twán	kî	shīn	yin

49. The fifth class is more numerous than the preceding, as well as more important. All particles and proper names are included under this class. The usages with respect to these and the figurative meanings of words will be explained in the syntax and in the dictionary.

CLASS V. METAPHORICAL.

Ancient.						
Meaning.	'mind'	'character'	'to imprison'	'peace'	'the world'	'ancient'
Modern.	心⁴	字⁵	囚⁶	安⁷	世⁸	古⁹
Sound.	sīn	tsz̀	ts'iù	gān	shĭ	kù

So 堂 *t'áng* 'a hall' is used for 'mother;' 室 *shĭ* 'a house,' for 'wife;' 昇 *shīng* 'the sun ascending,' for 'tranquillity;' 興 *hīng* 'to raise,' for 'to flourish.'

CLASS VI. PHONETIC.

50. The sixth class, under which the great mass of characters are found, has been called *Phonetic;* because, in the characters classed under it, one part gives its own sound to the whole figure, and thus acts as a symbol of sound merely. This part does sometimes convey also its symbolic meaning as well as its sound. The number of really useful phonetic characters amounts to about one thousand and forty. These, when united to the two hundred

---

1. The 口 and 工 were not represented in the ancient form, but the figures for *hand* were reversed.
2. The modern character for this idea is *twán*, with *an axe* by the side of *the silk threads divided.*
3. The modern character *kî* has *silk* added to strengthen the meaning.
4. *Sin* is the common word for *heart* in nearly all the senses in which this word is used in English;—*mind, disposition.*
5. This is a child under a roof, it means properly, *to produce,* but commonly, *a character.*
6. A man in an enclosure,—in prison, *to imprison.*
7. A woman under a roof,—sitting quiet at home, *peace, tranquillity.*
8. Three figures for ten,—thirty years, a generation, this generation, *the world.*
9. Ten and mouth,—through ten generations, *ancient.*

and fourteen elementary figures (the Radicals), produce from fifteen to twenty thousand derivatives (cf. 12 and 53).

記², 起³, 忌⁴, 紀⁵, are all called *kì*, after 己 ¹ the common part.

訪⁷, 放⁸, 坊⁹, 房¹⁰, are all called *fāng*, after 方 ⁶ the common part.

囹¹², 苦¹³, 枯¹⁴, 姑¹⁵, are all called *kù*, after 古 ¹¹ the common part.

51. The Chinese division of the characters into classes has now been given and illustrated. The figures in the margin of the table (44) show the number of characters under each class. It will be seen that the ordinary process of forming new symbols is the sixth;—by adding to a character a figure, to convey a sound merely, a new symbol is formed, which has a name corresponding to its phonetic element. Thus the figure 丁 *ting* being added to the character 金 *kīn* 'metal,' a new symbol, 釘 *tīng* 'a nail' is produced; so, also, being added to 頁 *hiĕ* 'a head' the symbol 頂 *tīng* 'a peak,' or 'top of any thing,' is formed. By this ingenious plan any number of new characters might be created; one part of which would designate the generic notion of the new name, and the other would indicate the *sound* by which to call it. As an illustration of this:—A newly discovered insect or fish might be called *ling* by certain rude tribes who had never expressed the sound in writing, some character having this sound *ling* would be taken by a Chinese scholar and united to the generic word *chúng* 'insect,' or *yù* 'fish,' as the case might be, and the new character, thus formed, would ever after be used as the proper name for that particular insect or fish *.

52. The hieroglyphic element in the Chinese characters is not of frequent occurrence, that is to say, we find but a very limited number of characters whose meaning can be gathered from their formation out of simple significant rudiments; and though the hieroglyphic element may have prevailed in many characters under their primitive forms, it is now seldom to be traced through the changes which the characters have undergone. An enquiry into this branch of the Chinese would be very interesting, and would perhaps throw some light upon the acceptations of words at the present day, but as it is not of a directly practical nature it would be out of place here. The following is an example; the character 家 *kiā* 'a family' is composed of *miĕn* 'a roof' placed above, and 豕 *shi* 'a pig' beneath; and these con-

---

1 *kì* 'self,' 2 with *words = to remember*, 3 with *walk = to rise up*, 4 with *heart = to fear*, 5 with *silk = to record*; 6 *fāng* 'a square,' 7 with *words = to enquire*, 8 with *a blow = to set free*, 9 with *earth = a dwelling*, or *a street*, 10 with *dwelling = a room*; 11 *kù* 'ancient' (cf. 49, note 9), 12 in *an enclosure = firm, constant*, 13 with *grass = bitter herbs*, meton. for *trouble, hardship*, 14 with *wood = a rotten tree, withered*, 15 with *woman = a matron, a lady*.

* The phonetic system of arrangement for lexicographical purposes has been adopted by M. Callery in his work entitled "Systema Phoneticum Scripturæ Sinicæ." 8vo. Macao, 1841.

stituent parts would lead to the erroneous impression that pigs under a roof was the original notion to be conveyed; but a Chinese authority, noticed by Dr. Schott, makes the figure below to consist of the character *jĭn* 人 'man' placed in three different positions, and this would at once suggest the idea of *a family* †.

53. The elementary figures or characters are technically termed *radicals* and *primitives*. The *radicals*, which were formerly about five hundred in number, are now reduced to two hundred and fourteen; the *primitives* amount to about one thousand seven hundred in common use. These, with the radicals and the characters compounded with both classes, include nearly all the characters existing in Chinese.

54. The radicals have been sometimes denominated *keys;* but the term *radicals* is very suitable when we consider their meaning and use. They include the names of simple objects, natural and artificial, and serve as generic heads for classes of characters; and, in the absence of an alphabet, they are employed as an index to the whole language, just as an alphabet is used in European tongues.

55. The Chinese term for the radicals is *tsź-pŭ* 字部 'character-class or classifier.' They are arranged according to the number of strokes required to form them. We have given them below under this arrangement, and recommend the student to use his best efforts to acquire them so as to write them correctly.

TABLE OF THE RADICALS.

Note.—Of the two numbers given after each radical, the former represents the number of characters extant under that radical, and the latter the number of those in common use. The words in brackets show the position of the radical in its derivatives. (*Com.*) means that the radical is in use as a common word. The asterisk marks those radicals which are frequently found in compounds.

Formed with one *stroke.*

1. 一 *yĭ* * 'one, the same' (various). 44. 16.

2. | *kwān* 'perpendicular' (through). 22. 2.
   This radical is used as a sign of the repetition of a character.

3. 丶 *chŭ* 'a point,' also called *tiĕn* 點主 when used as a stop or dot. 11. 2.

4. 丿 *pĭ* 'a curve, a sweep to the left' (various). 24. 8.

5. 乙 *yĭ* 'a crooked line, one;' a horary character. 42. 8.

6. 亅 *kŭ* 'a hooked stroke' (various). 20. 3.

---

† See Dr. Schott's "Chinesische Sprachlehre." 4to. Berlin, 1857, p. 22.

THE ELEMENTARY CHARACTERS.

Formed with two *strokes.*

7. 二 *ár* 'two' (com.) (encloses, above, below). 31. 9.

8. 亠 *teŭ*, no signification is given of this radical. (above). 39. 10.

9. 人 *jin* * 'a man' (com.) (above). Its contr. form 亻 on the left always. 800. 141.

10. 儿 *jin* 'a man walking' (obs.) (below). 52. 14.

11. 入 *jĭ* 'to enter' (com.) (above). 29. 5.

12. 八 *pá* 'eight' (com.) (below). 45. 12.

13. 冂 *kiŭng* 'a desert, an empty space' (obs.) (encloses). 51. 5.

14. 冖 *mĭ* 'to cover' (obs.) (above). 31. 2.

15. 冫 *pĭng* * 'an icicle' (obs.) (left). 51. 16.

16. 几 *kĭ* 'a table, a bench' (encloses, right, below). 40. 4.

17. 凵 *kăn* 'a receptacle' (obs.) (encloses). 24. 3.

18. 刀 *taŭ* * 'a knife; a sword' (com.) (below, or right in this form 刂). 378. 33. The hook should be written first.

19. 力 *lĭ* * 'strength' (com.) (below or right). 163. 19. The hook should be written first.

20. 勹 *paŭ* 'to wrap up, to envelop' (obs.) (encloses). 66. 4. The dash should be written first.

21. 匕 *pĭ* 'a spoon' (right). 20. 2.

22. 匚 *fāng* 'a chest' (obs.) (encloses). 65. 4.

23. 匸 *hĭ* 'to hide' (obs.) (encloses). 18. 3.

24. 十 *shĭ* 'ten' (com.) (various—below). 56. 11.

25. 卜 *pŭ* 'to divine' (above, right). 46. 4.

26. 卩 *tsĭ* 'a seal' (obs.) (right, or below in this form 㔾). 39. 7.

27. 厂 *hăn* 'a shelter' (obs.) (hangs over). 128. 8. This is often interchanged with radical 53.

28. 厶 *meŭ* 'crooked, perverse' (obs.) (above). 41. 2.

29. 又 *yiŭ* 'the hand; again' (com.) (right, below). 92. 12.

THE ELEMENTARY CHARACTERS.

Formed with three *strokes.*

30. 口 *k'eŭ* * 'a mouth' (com.) (left, below). 1047. 128.
31. 囗 *hwŭī* * 'an enclosure' (obs.) (encloses). 119. 16.
32. 土 *t'ŭ* * 'earth, soil' (com.) (left, under). 579. 56. Sometimes radicals 170 and 150 are used instead of this.
33. 士 *sź* 'a scholar; a statesman' (com.) (above, right). 25. 4.
34. 夂 *chī* 'to follow' (obs.) (above). 12. 1.
35. 夊 *shuī* 'to walk slowly' (obs.) (below). 24. 2.
36. 夕 *sī* 'evening; darkness' (com.) (various). 36. 6.
37. 大 *tá* * 'great' (com.) (above or below). 133. 23.
38. 女 *nŭ* * 'a woman' (com.) (left or below). 690. 61.
39. 子 *tsź* * 'a son' (com.) (below, left). 87. 17.
40. 宀 *miēn* * 'a roof' (obs.) (above). 249. 52.
41. 寸 *tsąn* 'the tenth of a *chĭ* 尺 or Chinese foot' (com.) (right or below). 41. 11.
42. 小 *siaŭ* 'small' (com.) (above, combined). 32. 4.
43. 尢 尤 尢 尣 *wáng* or *yiŭ* 'crooked-leg' (obs.); *yiu* 'still more' (com.) (left). 67. 2.
44. 尸 *shī* * 'a corpse' (above). 149. 20.
45. 屮 *ch'ĕ* 'a sprout' (obs.) (above). 39. 1.
46. 山 *shān* 'a mountain' (com.) (left, above). 637. 17.
47. 巛 or 川 *ch'uēn* 'a stream' (com.) (combined). 27. 4.
48. 工 *kūng* 'work' (com.) (various). 18. 5.
49. 己 *kĭ* 'self' (com.) (below). 21. 5. Distinguish this from 已 *ī* and 巳 *sź*.[1]
50. 巾 *kīn* * 'a napkin' (com.) (left, below). 295. 19.
51. 干 *kān* 'a shield' (com.) (combined). 18. 6.
52. 幺 *yaŭ* 'young' (left, doubled). 21. 4. E. G. 幾 *kĭ* 'several.'
53. 广 *yen* * 'a covering' (obs.) (covers). 287. 29.

---

1 *ī* signifies 'already;' *sź* is a horary character, '9-11 o'clock A. M.'

THE ELEMENTARY CHARACTERS.

54. 辶 *ying* 'a long journey' (obs.) (left). 10. 5. Used for radical 162.
55. 廾 *kŭng* 'folded hands' (below). 51. 2.
56. 弋 *yĭ* 'a dart' (right). 16. 2.
57. 弓 *kŭng* * 'a bow' (com.) (left, below). 166. 15.
58. 彐 *kì*, 彑 or 彑, 'a pig's head' (obs.) (above). 26. 2.
59. 彡 *shan* 'long hair' (right). 53. 7.
60. 彳 *chĭ* * 'to walk' (obs.) (left). 227. 26.

Formed with four *strokes.*

61. 心 *sīn* *, contr. 忄, 'the heart' (com.). (The contr. form on the left; the full form, below or elsewhere). 1077. 142.
62. 戈 *kō* * 'a spear' (com.) (right). 111. 15.
63. 戶 *hŭ* 'a one-leaved door; a family' (com.) (above). 45. 5.
64. 手 *sheŭ**, contr. 扌, 'the hand' (com.). (The contr. form on the left; the full form, below). 1092. 46.
65. 支 *chĭ* 'a branch' (com.) (right). 27. 2.
66. 攴 *pŭ* *, contr. 攵, 'to touch' (right). 296. 21.
67. 文 *wăn*, contr. 攵, 'to paint letters' (com.). Contr. form seldom used. (below). 23. 2.
68. 斗 *teŭ* 'a dry measure, the North Star' (com.) (right). 33. 5.
69. 斤 *kīn* 'an ax; a Chinese pound' (com.) (right). 56. 8.
70. 方 *făng* 'a square, a place' (com.) (left). 83. 9.
71. 无 *wŭ*, in comp. 旡, 'wanting, not.' 13. 2.
72. 日 *jĭ* * 'the sun; a day' (com.) (left, and elsewhere). 455. 51.
73. 曰 *yŭ* * 'to speak' (com.) (below, and elsewhere). 38. 13.
74. 月 *yŭ** 'the moon; a month' (com.) (left). 70. 11.
75. 木 *mŭ* * 'wood' (com.) (left, below). 1358. 17.
76. 欠 *k'iĕn* * 'to owe, to want' (right). 236. 18.
77. 止 *chĭ* 'to stop at a point' (com.) (various). 91. 9.

THE ELEMENTARY CHARACTERS. 23

78. 歹 *taì** 'a rotten bone; bad, putrid' (com.) (left). 232. 12.
79. 殳 *shu* 'to kill' (right). 84. 8.
80. 毋 *wû* 'not, without' (com.) (below). 17. 5.
81. 比 *pì* 'to compare' (com.) (various). 22. 1.
82. 毛 *maù* 'hair (not human), fur, feathers' (com.) (left.) 212. 4.
83. 氏 *shì* 'a family' (com.). 15. 3. 民 *mîn* 'the people' is under *shì*.
84. 气 *k'î* 'vapour' (obs.) (right, above). 18. 1. The character in use is 氣.
85. 水 *shwuì**, contr. 氵, 'water' (com.) (contr., on the left; full form, below). 1586. 148.
86. 火 *hò**, contr. 灬, 'fire' (com.) (contr., below; full form, left). 639. 43.
87. 爪 *chaù*, contr. 爫, 'claws' (com.) (above). 37. 7. See radical 97.
88. 父 *fù* 'a father' (com.) (above). 11. 2.
89. 爻 *hiaù* 'to imitate' (left). 17. 3.
90. 爿 *chwâng* 'a couch' (obs.) (left). 50. 2.
91. 片 *pién* 'a splinter' (left). 78. 4.
92. 牙 *yâ* 'molar teeth' (com.) (left). 9. 2. Cf. radical 211.
93. 牛 *niû**, contr. 牜, 'an ox' (com.) (contr., on the left; full form, below). 232. 12.
94. 犬 *k'iuèn*, contr. 犭, 'a dog' (com.) (contr., on the left). 445. 28. Interchanged with radical 153.

Formed with five strokes.

95. 玄 *hiûen* 'colour of the sky; dark' (com.) (combined). 7. 2. E. G. 率.
96. 玉 *yù** 'a jewel' (com.) (left). 473. 25.
97. 瓜 *kwâ* 'fruit of the melon kind' (com.) (right or left). 56. 2.
98. 瓦 *wà* 'tiles, bricks' (com.) (right, below). 173. 2. Interchanged with radicals 32, 108, and 112.
99. 甘 *kân* 'sweet' (com.). 23. 2.
100. 生 *sâng* 'to be born, to live' (com.). 23. 2.

101. 用 yŭng 'to use' (com.) (combined). 11. 2. E. G. 甫 fŭ 'great.'
102. 田 t'iĕn* 'a field' (com.) (left, below). 193. 26.
103. 疋 p'ĭ 'a piece of cloth; a foot' (com.) (below). 16. 5.
104. 疒 nĭ* 'disease' (left). 527. 25. The common character is 病 ping.
105. 癶 pŭ 'to stride' (above). 16. 3.
106. 白 pĕ 'white; clear' (com.) (left, above). 109. 8.
107. 皮 p'ĭ 'skin; bark' (com.) (right, left, below). 95. 1.
108. 皿 ming* 'dishes' (com.) (below). 129. 16.
109. 目 mŭ* 'the eye' (com.) (left, or contr. form 罒 above). 646. 29.
110. 矛 meŭ 'a barbed spear' (left). 66. 3.
111. 矢 shĭ 'an arrow' (left). 65. 8.
112. 石 shĭ* 'a stone, a rock' (com.) (left, below). 489. 23.
113. 示 shĭ*, contr. 礻, 'an omen from heaven' (com.) (left, below). 214. 25. The contr. form is similar to the contr. form of 145.
114. 禸 jeŭ 'the print of an animal's foot; a trace' (below). 13. 2.
115. 禾 hô* 'grain' (com.) (left). 433. 31.
116. 穴 hiŭ 'a cave, a hole' (com.) (above). 300. 18.
117. 立 lĭ 'to stand, to establish' (com.) (left). 102. 7.

Formed with six *strokes.*

118. 竹 chŭ*, contr. 竹, 'bamboo' (com.) (above). 954. 45
119. 米 mĭ* 'rice (uncooked)' (com.) (left). 321. 16.
120. 糸 mĭ*, also written 系 and 糹, 'silk, (threads)' (com.) (left, below). 821. 71. This radical has also been called sz; prob. for sz 緕.
121. 缶 feŭ 'an earthenware vase' (left). 78. 2.
122. 网 wăng, contr. 罒, 罓, and 冈, 'a net' (above). 164. 15. E. G. 罕 hăn 'rare.'
123. 羊 yăng 'a sheep' (com.) (left, above). 157. 9.
124. 羽 yŭ 'wings' (com.) (various:—above, below, right). 210. 9.

125. 老 laŭ 'old' (com.) (above); contr. into 耂 in 考¹ and 者². 23.5.
126. 而 ǎr 'whiskers; and, yet' (com.). 23. 3.
127. 耒 lǎi 'a plough handle' (left). 85. 3.
128. 耳 ǎr* 'the ear' (com.) (left, below). 172. 16.
129. 聿 yŭ 'a pencil' (left and below). 20. 2.
130. 肉 jŭ*, contr. ⺼, 'flesh' (com.) (left, below). The contr. form is printed like yŭ 'the moon.' 675. 56.
131. 臣 chǐn 'a subject; a statesman' (com.) (left). 17. 4.
132. 自 tsź 'self; from' (com.) (various). Sometimes used for 白 pĕ 'white.' 35. 2.
133. 至 chí 'to come to' (com.) (below, and elsewhere). 25. 3.
134. 臼 k'iù 'a mortar' (various). 72. 7.
135. 舌 shĭ 'the tongue' (com.) (left). 35. 6.
136. 舛 ch'uĕn 'to turn the back on; to oppose' (obs.). 11. 3.
137. 舟 cheŭ 'a boat' (com.) (left). 198. 3.
138. 艮 kǎn 'disobedient; limits' (right). 6. 2.
139. 色 sĭ 'colour; appearance' (com.) (right). 22. 2.
140. 艸 tsaŭ*, contr. ⺿, 'grass; plants' (com.) (above, in the contr. form). 1902. 95.
141. 虍 hŭ 'a tiger' (obs.) (above). 115. 9.
142. 虫 chŭng* 'an insect; a reptile' (com.) (left, below). 1067. 22.
143. 血 hiŭ 'blood' (com.) (left). 61. 3.
144. 行 hǐng 'to walk; to do' (com.) (encloses). 54. 8.
145. 衣 ī*, contr. 衤, 'clothing; covering' (com.) (contr. form on the left; full form below; sometimes half above and half below). 611. 36.
146. 襾 yǎ, also written 西³, 'to cover over' (obs.) (above). 30. 3.

---

1 k'aŭ 'aged,' com. 'to examine.'   2 chĕ 'this, he who, &c.'   3 sī 'the west.'

Formed with seven *strokes.*

147. 見 *kién* * 'to see' (com.) (right, below). 162. 14.
148. 角 *kiŏ* 'a horn; a corner' (com.) (left, below). 159. 5.
149. 言 *yên* * 'words; to speak' (com.) (left, below). 861. 105.
150. 谷 *kŭ* 'a valley' (left). 55. 2.
151. 豆 *teŭ* 'a wooden sacrificial vessel; beans' (below, left). 69. 5.
152. 豕 *shĭ* 'a pig' (left or below). 50. 3.
153. 豸 *chĭ* 'reptiles' (left). 141. 5.
154. 貝 *pêi* * 'a pearl shell' (com.) (left, below). 278. 46.
155. 赤 *chĭ* 'flesh colour' (com.) (left). 32. 2.
156. 走 *tseŭ* * 'to walk, to run' (com.) (left). 236. 11.
157. 足 *tsŭ* *, contr. ⻊, 'the foot, enough' (com.) (left, below). 581. 30.
158. 身 *shīn* 'the body; trunk' (com.) (left). 98. 4.
159. 車 *kŭ* * 'a carriage' (com.) (left). 362. 22. Sometimes called *chē*.
160. 辛 *sīn* 'bitter,' H. C. (com.) (doubled, right). 37. 7.
161. 辰 *shīn* 'time; an hour,' H. C. (com.) (various). 16. 3. Cf. radical 168.
162. 辵 *chŏ* *, contr. 辶, 'motion' (obs.) (left). 382. 59.
163. 邑 *yĭ* *, contr. 阝, 'a city' (com.) (right c. contr. form). 351. 27. Cf. radical 170.
164. 酉 *yiŭ* * 'new wine,' H. C. (com.) (left). 291. 20.
165. 釆 *pién* 'to distinguish' (left). 14 2.
166. 里 *lĭ* 'a Chinese mile; a village' (com.) (below). 14. 5.

Formed with eight *strokes.*

167. 金 *kīn* * 'gold; metal' (com.) (left). 803. 46.
168. 長 *ch'áng*, contr. 镸, 'long, old' (com.). 56. 2.
169. 門 *mǎn* * 'a door' (com.) (encloses). 249. 27.
170. 阜 *feŭ* *, contr. 阝, 'an artificial mound of earth' (left c. contr. form). 347. 38. Cf. radical 163.

171. 隶 *tai* 'to reach to' (right). 13. 1.
172. 隹 *chuī* * 'short-tailed birds' (right). 234. 17.
173. 雨 *yü* * 'rain' (com.) (contr. form 𠂇 above). 298. 18.
174. 青 *tsing* 'azure, sky-blue' (com.) (left). 18. 3.
175. 非 *fī* 'not so, false' (com.). 26. 3.

Formed with nine *strokes.*

176. 面 *mién* 'the face' (com.) (left). 67. 1.
177. 革 *kě* 'untanned hide, without hair' (left). 307. 5.
178. 韋 *weí* 'tanned hide' (left). 101. 2.
179. 韭 *kiù* 'leeks' (various). 21. 1.
180. 音 *yīn* 'sound, tone' (com.). 43. 3.
181. 頁 *yě* * 'the head' (com.) (right). 373. 30.
182. 風 *fūng* 'wind' (com.) (left). 183. 3.
183. 飛 *fī* 'to fly' (com.). 13. 1.
184. 食 *shí* *, contr. 𩙿, 'to eat' (com.) (contr. form on the left). 395. 38.
185. 首 *sheù* 'the head; the chief' (com.). 20. 1.
186. 香 *hiāng* 'fragrance' (com.). 38. 1.

Formed with ten *strokes.*

187. 馬 *mà* * 'a horse' (com.) (left, below). 473. 28.
188. 骨 *kǔ* * 'a bone' (com.) (left). 186. 4. Interchanged with radicals 130 and 181.
189. 高 *kaū* 'high' (com.). 35. 1.
190. 髟 *piaū* 'long hair' (above). 245. 7.
191. 鬥 *teù* 'to fight' (obs.) (encloses). 24. 1.
192. 鬯 *chǎng* 'fragrant plants' (below). 9. 1.
193. 鬲 *lì* 'a tripod with crooked feet' (left, below). 74. 7.
194. 鬼 *kweì* 'a departed spirit, a ghost' (com.) (left). 142. 4.

Formed with eleven *strokes.*

195. 魚 *yû* 'a fish' (com.) (left). 572. 10. Interchanged with radicals 110 and 205.
196. 鳥 *niaŭ* 'a bird' (com.) (right). 761.21. Interchanged with radical 180.
197. 鹵 *lŭ* 'salt' (left). 45. 1.
198. 鹿 *lŭ* 'a stag' (com.) (above). 106. 9. Interchanged with radical 120.
199. 麥 *mĕ* 'wheat' (com.) (left). 132. 1.
200. 麻 *má* 'hemp' (com.) (above). 35. 3.

Formed with twelve *strokes.*

201. 黃 *hwâng* 'yellow, colour of earth' (com.) (left). 43. 1.
202. 黍 *shŭ* 'millet' (com.) (left). 47. 2.
203. 黑 *hĕ* 'black' (com.) (left, below). 173. 4.
204. 黹 *chǐ* 'to sew, to embroider' (left). 9. none in common use.

Formed with thirteen *strokes.*

205. 黽 *mùng* 'a frog' (com.) (below). 41. 2. Interchanged with radicals 140, 195, and 212.
206. 鼎 *tĭng* 'a tripod' (com.). 15. 1.
207. 鼓 *kŭ* 'a drum' (com.) (above). 47. 1.
208. 鼠 *shŭ* 'a rat' (com.) (left). 103. 2. Interchanged with radical 111.

Formed with fourteen *strokes.*

209. 鼻 *pí* 'the nose' (com.) (left). 50. 1.
210. 齊 *ts'î* 'to adjust, to adorn' (com.) (above). 19. 3.

Formed with fifteen *strokes.*

211. 齒 *chǐ* 'front teeth' (com.) (left). 163. 3.

Formed with sixteen *strokes.*

212. 龍 *lûng* 'a dragon' (com.). 25. 2.
213. 龜 *kwêi* 'a tortoise' (com.). 25. 1. Interchanged with radical 205.

Formed with seventeen *strokes.*

214. 龠 *yŏ* 'a flute with three holes' (left). 20. 1.

56. The meanings attached to the above elementary characters have been thus classified; we give them here because they may be useful both to the general reader, to show the kind of words denoted by the elementary figures, and to the student to test his knowledge of the radicals themselves.

Parts of bodies.—Body, corpse, head, hair, down, whiskers, face, eye, ear, nose, mouth, teeth, tusk, tongue, hand, heart, foot, hide, leather, skin, wings, feathers, blood, flesh, talons, horn, bones.

Zoological.—Man, woman, child; horse, sheep, tiger, dog, ox, hog, hog's head, deer; tortoise, dragon, reptile, mouse, toad; bird, fowls; fish; insect.

Botanical.—Herb, grain, rice, wheat, millet, hemp, leeks, melon, pulse, bamboo, sacrificial herbs; wood, branch, sprout, petal.

Mineral.—Metal, stone, gems, salt, earth.

Meteorological.—Rain, wind, fire, water, icicle, vapour, sound; sun, moon, evening, time.

Utensils.—A chest, a measure, a mortar, spoon, knife, bench, couch, clothes, crockery, tiles, dishes, napkin, net, plough, vase, tripod, boat, carriage, pencil; bow, halberd, arrow, dart, axe, musical reed, drum, seal.

Qualities.—Colour, black, white, yellow, azure, carnation, sombre-colour; high, long, sweet, square, large, small, slender, old, fragrant, acrid, perverse, base, opposed.

Actions.—To enter, to follow, to walk slowly, to arrive at, to stride, to walk, to reach to, to touch, to stop, to fly, to overspread, to envelope, to encircle, to establish, to overshadow, to adjust, to distinguish, to divine, to see, to eat, to speak, to kill, to fight, to oppose, to stop, to embroider, to owe, to compare, to imitate, to bring forth, to use, to promulge.

Parts of the world and dwellings; figures; miscellaneous.—A desert, cave, field, den, mound, hill, valley, rivulet, cliff, retreat. A city, roof, gate, door, portico. One, two, eight, ten, eleven. An inch, a mile. Without, not, false. A scholar, a statesman, letters; art, wealth, motion; self, myself, father; a point; wine; silk; joined hands; a long journey; print of a bear's foot; a surname, a piece of cloth.

57. Some radical appears in every symbol, and the Chinese classify the characters under that radical, which is easily distinguishable from the rest of the figure. In some cases, however, the selection appears to have been arbitrary, for occasionally we find characters classified under a radical which is so intermingled with the remaining part of the figure that it is only by practical experience that it can be recognised. The student will find a list, taken from K'ang-hi's Dictionary, of all the characters whose radical is difficult to discover, in Dr. Morrison's Dictionary, part II. vol. II.

58. When the radical is found, we proceed to count the number of strokes in the remaining part, often called the *primitive*. The primitive is composed of strokes, from one to twenty and upwards; these strokes are made in one consecutive order, which depends upon the figure itself, and this order can only be learnt by practice. (The rules in Art. 76. may be consulted.) As

examples:—the character 下 hiá 'below' is under rad. 一 yĭ, with two strokes in its *complement*; 世 shí 'an age' is also under rad. — yĭ, with four strokes; 乃 naĭ 'it may be, it is, but,' is under rad. 丿 pĭ, with one stroke; 事 sź is under 亅 kiŭ, with seven; 五 wŭ 'five,' under 二 ąr 'two,' with two; 井 tsìng 'a well,' under the same rad., with two; 況 hwàng 'more,' under the same rad., with five strokes; 亞 á or yá 'second,' under the same rad., with six strokes; 以 ĭ 'to use' is under the rad. 人 jîn 'a man,' with two strokes. If, while learning the radicals, the student will write them with the rules in Art. 76. before him, he will have little difficulty in counting the number of strokes in them, or in any character compounded with them. As the number of the radical is rarely known, even by advanced students of Chinese, the following table of the *Tsź-pú* is arranged alphabetically to assist the beginner in referring to his Chinese-English Dictionary.

An alphabetic arrangement of the Radicals.

二 ąr 7	彳 chĭ 60	飛 fí 183	黃 hwáng 201	几 kĭ 16
而 ąr 126	赤 chĭ 155	父 fú 88	囗 hwüĭ 31	己 kĭ 49
耳 ąr 128	臣 chîn 131	風 fûng 182	衣 ĭ 145	彐 ki 58
長 ch'âng 168	彡 chŏ 162	厂 hăn 27	肉 jeŭ 114	气 k'í 84
鬯 chàng 192	丶 chù 3	黑 hĕ 203	入 jĭ 11	欠 k'iĕn 76
爪 chaŭ 87	竹 chŭ 118	匸 hĭ 23	日 jĭ 72	見 kiĕn 147
車 chĕ 159	巛 ch'uĕn 47	香 hiāng 186	人 jîn 9	巾 kîn 50
屮 ch'ĕ 45	夕 ch'uĕn 136	爻 hiáu 89	儿 jîn 10	斤 kîn 69
舟 cheŭ 137	隹 chuì 172	行 hîng 144	肉 jŭ 130	金 kîn 167
攴 chĭ 34	虫 chŭng 142	穴 hiŭ* 116	干 kān 51	角 kiŏ 148
支 chĭ 65	爿 chwâng 90	血 hiŭ 143	甘 kān 99	臼 k'iù 134
止 chĭ 77	匸 fāng 22	亥 hiŭen† 95	凵 kăn 17	非 kiù 179
至 chĭ 133	方 fāng 70	火 hŏ 86	艮 kĭn 138	犬 k'iuĕn 94
豸 chĭ 153	缶 feŭ 121	禾 hŏ 115	高 kaŭ 189	冂 kiŭng 13
鬲 chĭ 204	阜 feŭ 170	戶 hú 63	革 kĕ 177	戈 kŏ 62
齒 chĭ 211	非 fí 175	虍 hŭ 141	口 k'eŭ 30	車 kŭ 159

* Also called yŭ.   † Also called yuĕn.

ALPHABETIC ARRANGEMENT OF THE RADICALS.

亅	kŭ 6	宀	mĭ 14	生	sāng 100	糸	sz 120	毋	wŭ 80
鼓	kŭ 207	亠	miēn 40	山	shān 46	大	tá 37	牙	yă 92
谷	kŭ 150	面	miēn 176	彡	shan 59	歹	taì 78	而	yă 146
骨	kŭ 188	皿	mĭng 108	手	sheŭ 64	叒	taì 171	羊	yáng 123
工	kūng 48	木	mŭ 75	首	sheŭ 185	刀	taū 18	幺	yaū 52
廾	kūng 55	目	mŭ 109	尸	shī 44	士	teŭ 8	頁	yĕ 181
弓	kūng 57	黽	mŭng* 205	氏	shì 83	斗	teŭ 68	广	yen 53
瓜	kwă 97	广	nĭ 104	氺	shì 113	豆	teŭ 151	言	yên 149
丨	kwăn 2	鳥	niaŭ 196	豕	shì 152	門	teŭ 191	一	yĭ 1
鬼	kweĭ 194	牛	niŭ 93	十	shí 24	田	tiên 102	乙	yĭ 5
龜	kwêi 213	女	nŭ 38	石	shí 112	鼎	tĭng 206	弋	yĭ 56
老	laŭ 125	八	pă 12	舌	shí 135	寸	tsăn 41	邑	yĭ 163
里	lĭ 166	勹	paŭ 20	食	shì 184	艸	tsaŭ 140	音	yīn 180
力	lì 19	白	pĕ 106	矢	shì 111	走	tseŭ 156	辶	ying 54
鬲	lì 193	貝	péi 154	身	shīn 158	齊	ts'í 210	叉	yiŭ 29
立	lì 117	匕	pĭ 21	辰	shîn 161	卩	tsĭ 26	尢	yiŭ 43
鹵	lŭ 197	比	pĭ 81	殳	shu 79	青	tsīng 174	兀	yiŭ 43
鹿	lŭ 198	皮	p'ĭ 107	黍	shŭ 202	足	tsŭ 157	酉	yiŭ 164
耒	lùi 127	鼻	pí 209	鼠	shŭ 208	子	tsź 39	龠	yŏ 214
龍	lúng 212	丿	p'ĭ 4	水	shuĭ 35	自	tsź 132	羽	yù 124
馬	mà 187	飛	p'ĭ 103	水	shwuĭ 85	土	t'ŭ 32	雨	yŭ 173
麻	mà 200	彡	piaŭ 190	夕	sĭ 36	歹	wà 98	魚	yŭ 195
門	măn 169	片	piên 91	色	sĭ 139	文	wăn 67	曰	yŭ 73
毛	maŭ 82	釆	piên 165	小	siaŭ 42	尢	wáng 43	月	yŭ 74
麥	mĕ 199	冫	pīng 15	心	sīn 61	王	wáng 96	聿	yŭ 129
厶	meŭ 28	卜	pŭ 25	辛	sīn 160	网	wăng 122	玉	yŭ 96
矛	meŭ 110	支	pŭ 66	厶	sz 28	韋	weí 178	用	yúng 101
米	mĭ 119	癶	pŭ 105	士	sź 33	无	wú 71		

32   ANCIENT AND OTHER FORMS OF CHARACTER.

59. Various forms of character have been used at different periods, and some of them are still employed for certain purposes. The sheet facing this page will show six of these forms. Beginning on the right hand and reading downwards we have in the first column—shū [a] yiù [b] lŭ [c] t'ĭ [d]; yŭ [e], chuén [f]; yŭ [e], lĭ [g]; yŭ [e], kiaĭ [h]; yŭ [e], hĭng [i]; yŭ [e], tsaù [j]; yŭ [e], sŭng [k]; i. e. 'There are six forms of writing, viz. the *seal* character, the so-called *official*, the *pattern*, the *cursive*, the *grass* (or abbreviated cursive), and the *Sung* dynasty character.'

60. 1) Of the *Chuén-shū* [f a] (col. 1.) there are several varieties, from the stiff straight lines used on seals and stiff spike-like strokes cut on brazen vessels, to the rounded angles as seen here and upon porcelain, cakes of ink, &c.

2) The *Lĭ-shū* [g a] (col. 2.) was invented by officials under the *Tsin* dynasty; it is often employed for inscriptions, titles and prefaces to books, and was formerly used for official papers.

3) The *Kiaĭ-shū* [h a] (col. 3.) is the model for good writing; works are sometimes printed in this form, but not commonly.

4) The *Hĭng-shū* [i a] (col. 4.) or *running* hand is frequently used in prefaces, and for business purposes. Many varieties of it may be seen in Morrison's Dictionary, part II. vol. II.

5) The *Tsaù-shū* [j a] (col. 5.) or *grass* character is an abbreviated form of the *Hĭng-shū*. These abbreviations are so various, according to the whim of the writer, that sometimes they can scarcely be read even by educated natives. This form is employed in prefaces, manuscripts, and shop-ledgers, &c.

6) The *Sŭng-shū* [k a] (col. 6.) or as it is also called the *Sŭng-pàn* [k l] was first used, under the *Sung* dynasty, for printing from wooden blocks; an art which was invented about that time (A. D. 900). This form has continued in use for letter-press ever since.

61. In addition to these six forms, the Chinese indulge their taste and fancy in ornamental writing. They have, for example, the *wheat-ear*, the *dragon-head*, the *tadpole*, the *bamboo-sprout*, and other forms of character. The Emperor *K'ién-lǔng's* [m n] Poem on *Shĭng-kĭng*, [o p] the city of Moukden, the metropolis of Manchuria, has been printed, both in Chinese and Mandchu, with every variety of fanciful character. A very beautiful copy of this work may be seen in the Library of the British Museum.

62. Many characters have undergone a series of changes at different periods, and some are frequently used for others. The various descriptions

---

[a] 書 [b] 有 [c] 六 [d] 體 [e] 曰 [f] 篆 [g] 隸
[h] 楷 [i] 行 [j] 草 [k] 宋 [l] 板 *pàn* means 'a board, plank or block.' The common word for a boat of small dimensions is *Sān-pàn* 'three planks.'

書有六體曰篆曰隸曰楷曰行曰草曰宋
書有六體曰篆曰隸曰楷曰行曰草曰宋
書有六體曰篆曰隸曰楷曰行曰草曰宋
書有六體曰篆曰隸曰楷曰行曰草曰宋
書有六體曰篆曰隸曰楷曰行曰草曰宋
書有六體曰篆曰隸曰楷曰行曰草曰宋
書有六體曰篆曰隸曰楷曰行曰草曰宋

書其六體曰籇曰蘛曰隸曰蔡曰䋣曰虫
書其六體曰籇曰蘛曰隸曰蔡曰䋣曰虫
書其六體曰籇曰蘛曰隸曰蔡曰䋣曰虫
書其六體曰籇曰蘛曰隸曰蔡曰䋣曰虫
書其六體曰籇曰蘛曰隸曰蔡曰䋣曰虫
書其六體曰籇曰蘛曰隸曰蔡曰䋣曰虫
書辰究鼎曰籇曰蘛曰永曰虫曰南

VULGAR AND ABBREVIATED FORMS. 33

have been classified under the following designations: 1. The *Ching-tsz̀*,[a,b] or 'correct character,' without variations; 2. *T'ǔng-tsz̀*,[c,b] those having 'corresponding forms,' duplicates and triplicates; 3. *T'ǔng-tsz̀*,[d,b] those conveying a corresponding signification though differing in form; 4. *Pùn-tsz̀*[e,b] and *Kù-tsz̀*,[f,b] the 'original' and 'ancient forms;' and 5. *Sù-tsz̀*,[g,b] 'vulgar forms' of characters. Abbreviated forms are called *Sǎng-tsz̀*,[h,b] and spurious ones *Weí-tsz̀*;[i,b] e. g. 恩 for sz̀ 思 'to think.'

63. The standard works in Chinese literature are generally printed with the full form (*Ching-tsz̀*) of the characters, but some works contain a few abbreviations (*Kù-tsz̀* or *Sù-tsz̀*); and books in the lower style of composition—such as novels, ballads, &c.—contain numerous contracted forms. The list here given should be learnt by the student, as the forms in it are likely to occur frequently. Many more will be found in the Dictionaries of *K'ǎng-hī* (in Chinese), of Drs. Morrison and Medhurst (in English), and in that of *Père* Gonçalves (in Portuguese).

List of abbreviated forms in common use.

(N. B. They are arranged according to the number of strokes in the abbreviations.)

1	万	萬	13	与	與	25	边	邊	37	还	還	49	觘	能
2	厼	錢	14	头	頭	26	孛	學	38	鸟	焉	50	写	2379*
3	亡	亾	15	厺	26³³*	27	似	從	39	具	與	51	与	與
4	几	凡	16	尔	爾	28	斦	所	40	变	變	52	点	點
5	刂	刂	17	处	處	29	过	過	41	画	畫	53	肏	賢
6	么	麼	18	佢	信	30	两	兩	42	叚	叚	54	尭	覺
7	久	久	19	仝	同	31	声	聲	43	毡	氊	55	敉	數
8	斤	勛	20	圣	聖	32	听	聽	44	观	觀	56	鸡	鷄
9	号	夯	21	对	對	33	乱	亂	45	类	類	57	旧	舊
10	从	從	22	号	號	34	国	國	46	爱	愛	58	台	臺
11	双	雙	23	礼	禮	35	囬	回	47	畨	留	59	亲	親
12	气	氣	24	灯	燈	36	实	實	48	难	難			

[a] 正 [b] 字 [c] 同 [d] 通 [e] 本 [f] 古 [g] 俗
[h] 省 [i] 僞   * These numbers refer to the sheet of characters.

F

64. Besides the use of these abbreviations and vulgar forms of characters in the lower class of compositions, when expressing purely local idioms, colloquial or provincial phrases, characters well known, but of an entirely different meaning from that which is to be conveyed, are sometimes employed; and the reader is supposed to understand that the character used, is so used merely on account of its sound, that is both syllable and tone. At other times characters are made by the addition of the radical 亻 *jîn* 'man,'—as in the phrase 傢伙 *kiā-hỏ* 'utensils, implements, furniture,' or the radical 口 *k'eù* 'mouth,'—to some common character. All the local dialects, the Canton, the Amoy, the Fŭcheu, and the Shanghai especially, contain such characters, which are often not to be found in the Dictionaries.

65. It will be desirable here to point out some characters which, though similar in form, or with a very slight variation, differ in sound and meaning. 己 *kì* 'self;' 已 *ì* 'to stop, finished, now, already;' 巳 *sź* '9 o'clock to 11 A. M.:' *kì* and *ì* are often written and printed interchangeably for each other. 予 *yû* 'to give' and 子 *tsź* 'son' are confounded by beginners, the former requires four strokes, the latter only three. 干 *kān* 'a shield,' 于 *yû* 'in, at, with respect to,' and 千 *ts'iēn* 'a thousand,' are similar. Compare also 未 *wî* 'not yet' and 末 *mŭ* 'the end;' 了 *liaù* 'finished' and 丫 *yā* or *chā* 'forked;' *tá* 大 'great,' *t'aî* 太 'very great, very,' and 犬 *k'iuén* 'a dog;' 天 *t'iēn* 'heaven' and 夫 *fû* 'a man, a person.'

66. The Dictionary edited by the Emperor *K'āng-hī* contains about forty-four thousand characters; but of these, six thousand five hundred are obsolete forms, four thousand two hundred are without name or meaning, and, of the remainder, about twenty thousand are very rarely met with, being either duplicate forms, names of unimportant places and persons, or found only in rare and ancient works. From ten to twelve thousand is understood to be the number employed in Chinese literature, but a much smaller number suffices for ordinary purposes. The manual native Dictionary,—the *Fān-yŭn* 分韻 'divided rhymes,'—in use in the province of Canton contains seven thousand three hundred and twenty-seven characters. Even this number includes many characters not in common use. Four, five, and six thousand have been mentioned as an approximation to the number of characters in general use. The manual Dictionary appended to this work contains nearly three thousand five hundred, and these will be found sufficient for all ordinary purposes.

§. 5. *Arrangement of characters in books, punctuation, &c.*

67. The characters are arranged in native works in columns, and are read from the top of the page downwards, always beginning on the right hand side and proceeding column by column towards the left. This arrangement

renders it necessary to begin at, what appears to us to be, the end of the volume, as is the case in the Hebrew, Arabic, and some other languages. Two pages only are printed at a time, and these upon the same side of the paper. The leaf is folded with its blank sides placed together, and on the folded edge, which remains uncut, the general title, the running title, the chapter, section, page, and often the designation of the edition, are printed parallel to the other columns. When the characters are arranged in horizontal lines they are read from right to left.

68. The sizes of books vary from folio and quarto, which are uncommon, to imperial octavo for the classics and history; duodecimo, designated 'sleeve' editions, alluding to their portability, are taken for novels; and various smaller sizes are in use for popular poetry, ballads, and works on arithmetic: but, although these sizes predominate in, they cannot be said to be confined to, the above classes of literature. Various qualities of paper are used; works being sometimes printed on white paper; large paper copies are also found. Poems and other works are occasionally printed in white letters on a black ground. Vermillion coloured characters are a mark of Imperial design or patronage. The yellow title-page with the dragon depicted on the margin indicates the Imperial editions.

69. The divisions of a work are commonly *pǎn* 本 or *kiuèn** 卷 'volumes,' *hwùi** 回 'chapters,' the latter especially in novels; *twán* 段 'section,' *chāng* 章 'chapter,' *tsiĕ* 節 'section,' used for 'verse,' are also found. In extensive works the characters used in the cycle and for the time of day are employed for divisions of the *kiuèn*. The first four characters of the *Yi-king* 易經 are sometimes used for works in four parts (v. *Numerals*). Works in three volumes or parts are distinguished by the characters 上 *shàng* 'upper,' 中 *chūng* 'middle,' 下 *hiá* 'lower.'

70. To the text of the classics, ancient history and poetry, there is generally attached some note, comment, annotation, or paraphrase. These are always distinguished by the size of the character, and often by the characters 註 *chū* 'comment' or 解 *kiaì* 'explanation.' The comments are mixed up with the text, or they are placed above it, after it, or at the foot of the page. Interlinear translations of the old classics are also common; the phrase 旁合 *pāng-hŏ* is then used in the title-page, and 訓講 *hiún-kiàng* is the expression applied to general explanations of the text.

71. It is not usual to punctuate the sentence in any way. The paragraph is marked by a large circle, or the first character of it is placed at the top of the column. When the period is shown, it is by a small circle, in the place of our full-stop; a dot, called *chù* or *tièn* 點, takes the place of our comma

---

* *Kiuèn* and *hwùi* both signify 'something rolled up,'—'a scroll.'

or semicolon. The sentence or clause is called *kü* 句 ; a smaller division is stopped by a point, called *teü* * 讀, equivalent to our comma. Small circles are placed on the right of the characters when the passage is deemed important or worthy of notice, and black dots are used when the passage is less important; the characters so pointed take the place of *italics* in English. The names of books quoted are enclosed by a line. Names of places, when marked at all, have two parallel lines on the right; names of nations are sometimes surrounded by a line; names of persons have one line only on the right. The names of emperors and others deemed worthy of honour are always made to begin a new line, and to project above the tops of the other columns, to the extent of one, two, or three characters.

§. 6. *On writing the characters.*

72. The Chinese write the characters with great care, and make it their study to give them an elegant form. The importance to the student of writing them correctly is self-evident; the practice of writing them will give accuracy, and will help the memory; while, as an eminent writer on the subject has said, " no man can properly be considered to learn the language who does not devote a portion of his time to this important branch of the subject †."

73. The materials for writing were in early times of the rudest kind; but the *varnish*, the *style*, and the *bamboo slips* have given place to the *wǎn-fǎng-sź-paǔ* 文房四寶 'the four precious implements of the study,' viz. *pencil, ink, paper,* and *ink-stone*. The *pencil*, 筆 *pĭ*, is made of the hair of the sable, the fox, the deer, the cat, the wolf, or the rabbit; a small bundle of it, properly adjusted, is secured in a piece of bamboo, about the length and thickness of an ordinary lead pencil. The hair of which the best pencils are made is that of the *hwǎng-shǔ-lǎng* 黃鼠狼, a kind of squirrel: it is sent from the Northern provinces to *Hú-cheǔ* 湖州 in *Chĕ-kiang* Prov., where the pencils are manufactured. A noted shop for this article bears the name of *sǎn-pĭn-tsaì* 三品齊. The pencil generally has some inscription, the name of maker, &c. The *ink*, 墨 *mĕ*, which is a compound of fine soot and some glutinous liquid, is cast in oblong cakes, with inscriptions, stanzas of poetry, and the maker's name impressed thereon. The use of ink became general about the seventh century. About A. D. 400. ink was made from soot obtained by burning millet or fir. In the *T'ang* dynasty, A. D. 650, ink was an article of annual tribute from Corea; this

---

* Commonly pronounced *tŭ* 'to read.'

† See *Eugraphia Sinensis*, Art. XIX. in Transactions of the Royal Asiatic Society, vol. I. part II. p. 306, by Sir John F. Davis, F. R. S., &c. &c. The lithographed copies, which are the same as those on the sheet given in this work, are well worthy of the student's attention.

was made from the pine soot. In the *Sung* dynasty, A. D. 1085, *Ch'ang-yu* 張 遇 made ink from soot produced by burning oil, he scented it with musk, and called it 'dragon-composition *.' The best ink comes from *Hwuï-cheü*,[a b] in the Prov. of *Gan-hwui*, the native place of *Chu-fu-tsz*, the philosopher; hence the impress on the ink—*Chū-tsź-kiā-hiún* 朱子家訓 'the family teachings of *Chū-tsź*;' an extract from which appears upon the reverse side of the cake. Chinese *paper*, 紙 *chí*, is made of bamboo fibre; it is soft, absorbent, and smooth, commonly of a yellowish tint, and well suited to the Chinese pencil and ink. There are various qualities of it; a large proportion of the best for writing purposes is manufactured in *K'ü-cheü*,[c b] in the Prov. of *Chě-kiang*. Paper was first made in China in the first century of our era. *Ink-stones*, 硯 *yên*, are small oblong slabs of stone, or hard brick; they should be hard and smooth, and should not absorb water quickly. Various forms of ink-stone are in use; some of these stones are very ancient, and are elaborately carved in fantastic shapes, with ornamental cells for water. The price varies from a hundred Chinese cash (fourpence) to several hundred dollars; these latter are valuable as relics of the past, and are seldom found in the shops.

74. The two characters 永 *yǔng* 'eternal' and 衣 *ī* 'clothing' contain every stroke used in forming characters. The character *yǔng* is thus formed:—

The common designations and forms of these strokes are here given. They should be copied frequently, and their names should be learnt by the student, as his Chinese tutor will frequently employ them in explaining the formation of characters.

[a] 徽   [b] 州   [c] 衢   * See Morrison's Dictionary, vol. I. p. 546.

RULES FOR WRITING CORRECTLY.

The strokes used in forming Chinese characters.

點 *tiĕn* 　　畫 *hwă*　　　直 *chí*　　　鈎 *keŭ*
a point,　　a horizontal line,　a perpendicular line,　a hook,

刁 *tiaŭ*　　乀 *p'ĭĕ*　　捺 *pă*　　曲 *kŭ*
a spike,　　a sweep,　　a dash,　　an angle.

75. It is of the first importance that the student should regard the *order of making* the strokes when forming a character, as correctness in this will facilitate his reading the *cursive* hand. A few rules will be given below; and by comparing the various examples of cursive forms, given in Dr. Morrison's Dictionary (vol. II. part II.), he will see which stroke to make first.

76. The following rules may be observed:—1. Begin either at the top or on the left-hand side. 2. When a perpendicular or dash cuts a horizontal line or one leg of an angle, the latter are to be written first, (cf. radicals 19, 24, 29, 32, 33, 41, 43, &c.) 3. An angle at the top on the right side is made with one stroke, and unless *pĭ* (rad. 4.) or *kwăn* (rad. 2.) is affixed to the left of it, the angle is made first. In radicals 18, 19, 26, 29, 39, 44, 49, 105, 124, 129, 178, 183, it is made first. In radicals 13, 20, 34, 35, 36, 76, 122, 130, the angle is made second. 4. An angle at the bottom on the left is also made with one stroke, if it be alone, or be joined to a perpendicular on the right, leaving the top or right side open, (cf. radicals 17, 22, 23, 28, 38, 45, 46, 49, 90, 206.) The characters in which 丑 (five strokes) occurs are exceptions to this rule; the angle on the left is made first; then the angle on the right; the points, next; and the horizontal, last. 5. The angles ㇆ and ㇄ in 門 *măn* 'a door' are made first on each side respectively. 6. Horizontal lines precede perpendiculars, when these cross each other; but should the perpendicular terminate with the base line, then the base line is final. 7. In such characters as the radicals 42, 85, 77, 141, 197, 204, 211, the perpendiculars above, or in the middle of the symbol, are made first. 8. In such characters as *k'eŭ* 口 'mouth' (rad. 30.) the perpendicular on the left is to be written first; and the interior of such characters as 國 *kwŏ* 'a kingdom,' 園 *yuĕn* 'a garden,' is filled up before the base line is written.

77. The style of writing usually taught in schools is the *Kiaĭ-shŭ* (cf. 60. 3.), the copies for which are after the writing of *Shaŭ-yīng* 邵瑛, a noted caligraphist. The characters on the fly-leaf facing this page are *Shaŭ-yīng's* copies. It will be observed that they are arranged by fours, beginning with the first column on the right-hand side. To these the author has appended observations, some of which we shall now give as briefly as possible.

風鳳飛氣先見元毛庭居尹底友及反皮參修須形
沿洪流海是足走氽者耆老考馨聲繁繫繼繡纏纚
車申中巾卓犖單畢易乃毋力正主本王身目耳貝
白工日四會合金命琴吝各谷土止山公了寸卜才
上下千小羸齋龜黽晶磊轟森爨鬱麼
丁芋寧亭遠邊逯逮莫矣契作仰冲行叵巨柠佳
官空宥宰鷓赫鬭驚卬印叩邨邠郊鄭鄰啫隬阪
登癹癸祭蔡察登氺泉眾聚家象豪豕仁儀俯休
從徐徧後乳亂色包

目自因固川升邢邢伊佟傐修亦赤然無三册冊㐰
願顧體御謝樹術鑒響需留章意素累吸呼峰峻
知鉏細嚚嚚器器齒爾奭齾此七也乜云去且旦
尺史又武成或幾恩息必志勉旭魁拋天父外文
鵝鳩輝頻鳥馬焉為師明旣野朝故辰後爕談茶黍
林森槑棗爻哥柔冠晃筮宅雲普皆齊衆表萬禹
騰讓靖敬獻歆劉弼辨衍仰蕃筆衝擲鸞驚驚譽

78. Observe:—1. The upper part covers the lower *. 2. The lower supports the upper. 3. The left exceeds the right in size and elevation. 4. The right exceeds the left. 5. The horizontal through the middle is extended. 6. The perpendicular is perfectly straight. 7. The hook should not be too crooked or too short. 8. The hook should not be too straight or too long. 9. The horizontal, short; the sweep, long. 10. The horizontal, long; the sweep, short. 11. The horizontal, short; the perpendicular, long; the sweep and dash extended. 12. The horizontal, long; the perpendicular, short; the sweep and dash diminished. 13. The horizontal, long; the perpendicular, short. 14. The reverse of rule 13. 15. The horizontal above, short; at the base, long. 16. The perpendicular on the left shorter than on the right. 17. The sweep on the left is shorter than the perpendicular on the right. 18. The perpendicular on the left is shorter than the sweep on the right. 19. The points of the dots converge towards the centre of the character. 20. Several horizontal lines should not be made of equal length. 21. When both sides contain nearly the same number of strokes they are written of equal size. 25. If the left portion be small, it should be level with the top of the right. 26. If the right be small, it should be level with the bottom of the left †.

79. The preceding information on the *sounds* and *characters*, with their proper pronunciation and formation, should be accurately learnt by the student before he proceeds with the next section on the forms of words, as far as they can be distinguished. Dialectic peculiarities would be out of place here, though it may be observed with regard to the pronunciation of words in the Peking dialect, that various modifications are necessary. In the northern parts of China aspirated syllables are pronounced very strongly, and letters which partake of the nature of aspiration have increased aspiration, which changes their orthography in a slight degree: e. g. *kia, kiang, k'ü* and *kiun* change into *chia, chiang, chü* and *chiun; tsiang,* &c., in the same way. The rule may be given thus:—All syllables having for their initial *k* or *ts* followed by *i* or *ü* change *k* and *ts* into *ch;* and it may also be observed that after *ch* or *sh* the *i*, if final, is not sounded at all. This latter rule may be said to be common also in southern Mandarin. It ought also to be observed, that the *u* after *ch* and *sh* is pronounced more like the *u* in French, that is *ü;* so that the syllables *kü* and *chu* in this work ought to be pronounced as if written *chü* in both cases. After all that can be said upon the subject of orthography, correctness in speaking lies more in the tones than in the utterance of the syllables. Various other modifications take place in the Peking dialect; but attention to the above rules and explanations will enable the persevering student to pronounce with sufficient correctness to be intelligible, though he may fail in acquiring the exact accent of the capital.

---

* Each of these rules refers to four characters in the sheet.
† The remainder of these rules, some only of which are important, will be found in Dr. Bridgman's Chinese Chrestomathy, in the Canton dialect.

40   CHINESE NOTIONS OF GRAMMAR.

SECT. II. FORMS OF EXPRESSION.

§. 1. *Preliminary remarks.*

80. The Chinese do not analyse the sentence, or classify their words and expressions in any way at all approaching to the exact method pursued in European tongues; their language is therefore wanting in those grammatical terms, which are necessary for this purpose. They do indeed distinguish between nouns and verbs: the noun they call *sz̽-tsz̽* 死字 'dead word;' and the verb, *hwŏ-tsz̽* 活字 'living word.' Again, they divide words into two classes; 實字 *shĭ-tsz̽* 'real words,' and 虛字 *hŭ-tsz̽* 'empty words;' the former class includes nouns and verbs, the latter particles, in which they include all except nouns and verbs. A native author has however recently treated the subject with considerable care; and has made other distinctions, not heretofore noted by the Chinese*.

81. As a compensation for the want of grammatical rules on ordinary construction, Chinese scholars study *wǎn-fǎ* 文法 'the laws of style,' and strive to bring their compositions into accordance with *wǎn-lĭ* 文理 'the rules of style.' We shall do well also to follow their example; and, after commencing with an exact knowledge of the *shīng-yīn*, 'the tones and syllables,' and the characters and words, we may proceed to the syntax of the language, in which lies the whole of its grammatical significance and force.

82. It is however necessary to acquire words before we can, as a native would, examine the structure of the sentence; and, therefore, though all Chinese words cannot be classified under European denominations, yet many may be placed in grammatical categories and be distinguished by the respective terms for the parts of speech. This method will be more convenient for our purpose of analysis; but it will be necessary to forewarn the foreign student of the fact that Chinese words have really no classification or inflexion, and that the distinctions of *case, number, person, tense, mood*, &c., are unknown to natives of China.

83. The meaning of a character or word and its position in the sentence will generally determine to what category it belongs. Auxiliary syllables and particles do however frequently distinguish the parts of speech. The sentence may often be broken up into groups of syllables, and each group will then form one expression. It will be the object of this portion of the grammar to show upon what principles these groups are formed, to enable the student to realise the various classes of expressions which will come under his observation.

84. The syllables, which are appended to strengthen the original notion conveyed by the prime syllable, are such as denote the *agent*, an *object;*—the

---

* See *Grammar of the Shanghai Dialect by J. Edkins, B. A., Lond.* 12mo. *Shanghai,* 1853.

VARIOUS FORMS OF NOUNS IN CHINESE. 41

completion or the *expansion* of the idea conveyed by the word to which they are joined;—or they are purely *formative* in character, and produce nouns or verbs, adverbs or adjectives, as conventional usage has determined.

§. 2. *On nouns.*

85. Chinese words which may be placed in this class may be considered, either with reference to general usage or to their derivation, as,

1. Nouns *primitive;* i. e. such as are monosyllables bearing their primitive signification, and being most commonly used in their monosyllabic or crude form.

2. Nouns *derivative;* i. e. such as are formed by the addition of some formative syllable, and in this connection, as dissyllables or trisyllables, are always used as nouns.

3. Nouns *composite;* i. e. such as are formed by the union of two syllables bearing one of the following relations to each other:—

α) The *appositional* relation, when synonymes or words conveying accessory notions are joined together.

β) The *genitival* relation, when the former of the two may be construed as if in the genitive case.

γ) The *dativaI* relation, when the former may be construed as if in the dative case with the words *to* or *for*.

δ) The *antithetical* relation, when words of an opposite signification are united to form a general or abstract term.

86. No fixed rules can be laid down with respect to any of the above distinctions; and it must be borne in mind that in the colloquial generally, and in some dialects more particularly, combinations of two, three, and four syllables, to form nouns, are very common, while the same notions would in the books frequently be conveyed by one syllable only.

87. *Primitive* nouns, or those which are monosyllabic, and are generally understood to be nouns, are such as the following :—

人 *jĭn* 'man,'   飯 *fán* 'rice,'   茶 *ch'á* 'tea,'

風 *fŭng* 'wind,'   血 *hŭ* 'blood,'   馬 *mă* 'horse.'

This class is not a large one, and the monosyllable is not intelligible to a Chinese when pronounced by itself, it must have some syllable or syllables with it: e. g. 'a man' must be called *yĭ-kó* (one) *jĭn; fán,* ' rice,' must enter into some phrase, as *k'ĭ-(chĭ)-fán* ' to eat rice,'—' to dine,' or *tsaŭ-fán* ' early rice,'—' breakfast,' or *wán-fán* ' late rice,'—' dinner ;' *ch'á* ' tea,'—' the infusion,' must be distinguished from the leaf, by such phrases as *yĭn-ch'á* 'to drink tea,' or *ch'á-yĭ* ' tea-leaf.' Nouns which designate objects that may be numbered take with them a word in apposition with the number prefixed ; e. g. *mă*, ' horse,' takes *yĭ-p'ĭ* (1988), ' one,' before it, *yĭ-p'ĭ-mă* ' a horse,' *sān-p'ĭ-mă* ' three horses.'

G

FORMATION OF NOUNS.

88. *Derivative* nouns, or such words as have acquired the form of substantives by the addition of a *formative* syllable, are much more numerous than primitive nouns, or monosyllables. These always remain nouns, while some primitive nouns may be used as verbs. This class of words belongs chiefly to the colloquial and the lower style of composition.

89. *Formative* syllables, or those used as such, being similar to terminations in European languages, may be classified thus:—

a) Those which generally indicate an agent: e. g. *jin* 人 'man;' *nü* 女 'woman;' *sheü* 手 'hand;' *fū* 夫 'man, person;' *tsz̈* 子 'child.'

β) Those which refer to a class, and form appellatives relating to *position* or *gender:* e. g. *tí* 帝 'a ruler;' *nü* 女 'a woman.'

γ) Those which imply a round shape: e. g. *t'eú* 頭 'head.'

δ) Those which relate to objects of various forms and combinations: e. g. *kwei* 塊 'a lump;' *tsz̈* 子 'child.'

90. Many characters are used as formative syllables, like the words *man, boy,* in *herdsman, handicraftsman, footman, stable-boy, post-boy, errand-boy.* The characters of this class, which generally indicate an agent, are *sheü* 手 'hand,' *jin* 人 'man,' *tsiáng* 匠 'workman,' or *kŭng* 工 'artisan,' 夫 *fū* 'fellow,' 戶 *hú* 'householder,' *tsz̈* 子 'son,' *ǎr* 兒 'child.' This latter—*ǎr*—is used especially in the north of China:— 頭 *t'eú* 'head,' 生 *sāng* 'born,—produced,—a performer.'

91. Of those formatives which generally indicate a person or agent, the following examples illustrate the use of *sheü* 'hand:'

shwuǐ-sheü 水, 'water-hand,'—'a sailor.'

yiú-sheü 遊, from *yiú* 'to wander,'—'a vagrant.'

p'aú-sheü 炮, from *p'aú* 'a cannon,'—'a gunner.'

k'iaú-sheü 巧, from *k'iaú* 'skilful,'—'an adept.'

Examples of the use of *jin* 'man.'

fú-jin 婦 'a woman, a matron.' | *kŭng-jin* 工 'a workman.'
k'ĕ-jin 客 'a guest.' | *ch'aī-jin* 差 'a messenger.'
fū-jin 夫 'a lady.' | *paú-jin* 報 'a reporter' (of news &c.).

92. Nouns formed with *tsiáng* 'workman,' *kŭng* 'artisan—labourer,' and *fū* 'a man—a fellow,' are such as these:

FORMATION OF NOUNS.

mŭ-tsiáng 木, from *mŭ* 'wood,'—'a carpenter.'
yín-tsiáng 銀, from *yín* 'silver,'—'a silversmith.'
t'iĕ-tsiáng 鐵, from *t'iĕ* 'iron,'—'a blacksmith.'
h'wá-kŭng 畫, from *h'wá* 'to sketch,'—'a painter.'
t'ù-kŭng 土, from *t'ù* 'earth,'—'a husbandman, a gardener.'
mà-fŭ 馬, from *mà* 'a horse,'—'a groom.'
t'iaŭ-fŭ 挑, from *t'iaŭ* 'to carry on the shoulders,'—'a porter.'
kiaŭ-fŭ 轎, from *kiaŭ* 'a sedan-chair,'—'a chair-bearer.'
kiŏ-fŭ 脚, from *kiŏ* 'a foot,'—'a courier or messenger' (1246).
nŭng-fŭ 農, from *nŭng* 'to cultivate the ground,'—'a husbandman.'

93. *Tsz̀* 'child' and *r̀* 'infant' are very common formatives for designations of persons and agents, though they frequently help to form names of things, and often form diminutives.

Examples of the use of *tsz̀* 'child.'

niáng-tsz̀ 女 'a mother' (1823).
cháng-tsz̀ 長 'the eldest son.'
t'iĕn-tsz̀ 天 'the son of heaven,' i. e. 'the emperor.'
sān-tsz̀ 孫 'a grandchild.'
láng-tsz̀ 浪 'a fop,—a rake' (1498, 'wave').
chŭ-tsz̀ 廚 'a cook.'

kwūn-tsz̀ 木 'a cudgel' (1434).
kwó-tsz̀ 'a fruit' (1468).
yín-tsz̀ 銀 'money.'
shīn-tsz̀ 身 'the human body.'
siáng-tsz̀ 箱 'a box.'
chŭ-tsz̀ 主 'the master.'

Examples of the use of *r̀* 'infant.'

haí-r̀ 孩 'a child.'
nŭ-r̀ 女 'a girl.'
jín-r̀ 人 'a man.'

míng-r̀ 名 'a name' (of any thing).
hwá-r̀ 話 'a word.'
hwŭ-r̀ 物 'a thing' (esp. antique &c.).

94. *T'eú* 'head' and *kiā* (*chiā*) 家 'family' also designate persons and agents, but *t'eú* often means *things* of a round shape, or all in a piece, and *places;* and *kiā* frequently denotes a whole *class,—faculty, sect,* &c.

FORMATION OF NOUNS.

Examples of the use of *t'eú* 'head.'

yā-t'eú 丫 'a servant-girl *.'
tüi-t'eú 對 'an enemy *.'
laù-t'eú 老 'a gaoler.'
fán-t'eú 飯 'a cook.'

shí-t'eú 舌 'the tongue.'
jï-t'eú 日 'the sun.'
kŭ-t'eú 骨 'a bone.'
pié-t'eú 鼻 'a nose,' met. 'a servant.'

Examples of the use of *kiā* 'family.'

jin-kiā 人 'people.'
laù-jin-kiā 老人 'an old man,—gentleman.'
pàn-kiā 本 'a clansman.'
tūng-kiā 東 'a master.'
tién-kiā 店 'a shopkeeper.'

i-kiā 醫 'the medical faculty.'
taú-kiā 道 'the Tauists.'
ch'uên-kiā 船 'ship-owners.'
fú-kiā 富 'the rich.'
kwei-kiā 貴 'the noble.'

95. Some other words, as *hú* 戶 'a house-door,'—for 'householder,' *ti* 帝 'a ruler,'—'a prince,' *nù* 女 'a woman,' and *sāng* 生 'born,' form nouns in a similar way to the preceding, though some of these may perhaps be considered to be in apposition to their prime syllables: e. g.—

k'ai-hú 丐 'beggars.'
liáng-hú 糧 'a tax-collector.'
pin-hú 貧 'the poor.'
siēn-sāng 先 'a teacher.'
ch'ŭ-sāng 畜 'domestic animals.'
heú-sāng 後 'a young man.'
hiŏ-sāng 學 'a student.'

i-sāng 'a medical man' (848, as above, line 7).
hwáng-ti 皇 'an emperor.'
shàng-ti 上 'God.'
yŭ-ti 禹 'God,' acc. to Budd.ᵗ religion.
chi-nù 姪 'a niece.'
tūng-nù 童 'a virgin.'
chú-nù 處 'a young lady not yet introduced to society.'

Here also we may notice those nouns formed with *sẕ* 師 'a teacher,' *chù* 主 'a lord,' and *sheù* 首 'a head, a chief:' e. g.—

ch'á-sẕ 茶 'a tea-inspector.'
tién-chù 店 'a shopkeeper.'

ch'uên-sheù 船 'a captain' (of a ship).
hwúi-sheù 會 'the principal' (of a society).

---

* The more common words are *yǔng-jin* 傭人 'servant, male or female,' and *ch'eú-jin* 仇人 'enemy.'

FORMATION OF NOUNS. 45

96. The designations of agents are very commonly formed by the periphrasis of an active verb and its object with the addition of the genitive particle *tī* 的, which throws the whole into the form of a participial expression similar to the Greek form ὁ πράττων, ὁ πράγματα πράττων, &c.

tă-yü-tī 打 魚, lit. 'strike-fish (sub. *person*), one who takes fish,'=a fisherman.

nă-yü-tī, fr. *nă* 拿 'to take,' has the same meaning.

tsŏ-săng-ĭ-tī 做 生 意 'make trade (*person*),'=a tradesman.

k'ăn-chaĭ-tī 砍 柴 'cut fuel (*person*),'=a woodcutter.

tsŭng-mĭng-tī 總 明 'clear-bright (*person*),'=an intelligent person.

năng-kăn-tī 能 幹 'able to transact affairs,'=an able man.

păn-sź-tī 辦 事 'manage business (*person*),'=a manager.

Nouns formed in this way are very numerous, but they are not often used in the presence of the individual whose calling or character they signify.

tŭ-shū-tī 讀 書 'one who reads books, a scholar, a learned man.'

kiaú-shū-tī 教 書 'one who teaches book-lore, a teacher.'

97. In addition to the above names of persons, others will be found under the articles treating of *composite* nouns. We will now consider those derivative nouns which designate *objects* and *localities*. Besides the use of *tsź* and *ặr* 'child,' and *t'eŭ* 'head,' for general objects, we have *t'eŭ* 'head,' *k'eŭ* 'mouth,' and *mặn* 'door,' as formatives for designations of places.

Examples.

taū-tsź 刀 'a knife.'		*mĭng-ặr* 名 'a name.'
yĭn-tsź 銀 'silver,—money.'		*huá-ặr* 話 'a word.'
kĭn-tsź 金 'gold.'		*shĭ-t'eŭ* 舌 'the tongue.'
tŭĕ-tsź 帖 'an invitation card.'		*ku-t'eŭ* 骨 'a bone.'
shên-tsź 扇 'a fan.'		*mŭ-t'eŭ* 木 'a piece of wood.'
jĭ-tsź 日 'a day.'		*chĭ-t'eŭ* 指 'a finger.'
tīng-tsź 釘 'a nail.'		*shăn-t'eŭ* 山 'a mountain-top.'
tiĕn-ặr 點 'a little.'		*ch'uên-t'eŭ* 舟 'a roadstead' (324, 'ship').
mặn-ặr 門 'a door.'		*mă-t'eŭ* 馬 'a jetty,—a landing-place.'

ch'wāng-k'eŭ 窗 'a window.'   *yá-mǎn* 衙 'magistrate's office.'

shān-k'eŭ 山 'a mountain-pass.'   *laŭ-mǎn* 牢 'a gaol.'

lŭ-k'eŭ 路 'a thoroughfare.'   *wŭ-mǎn* 午 'the ante-rooms.'

98. *Composite* nouns are such as are formed by the union of two or three syllables, each preserving its individual signification when in composition. They have been divided into four classes according to the relations which these syllables bear to each other. We now proceed to consider the first of these classes, namely, that in which the *appositional relation* predominates.

Observe.—We understand by the term *apposition*, words, identical or cognate in meaning, placed together and explanatory of each other; e. g. *Victoria Queen of England, Cicero orator, Urbs Roma*, &c.

99. One division of this class consists of words formed by the union of two syllables identical in signification or synonymous, one syllable standing as the exponent of the other. And, in the first place, those which are identical are simply *repetitions* of the same word: thus—

t'ai-t'ai 太 'aged lady,' used in addressing or speaking of a mandarin's lady.

nai-nai 奶 'married lady of rank,' with similar usage.

kō-kō 哥 'elder brother,—Sir,' in speaking to one of inferior rank.

100. In the next place, *synonymes* are united to form common nouns: thus—

fáng-ŭ 房屋 'a house.'   *sīn-cháng* 心腸 'the heart, the feelings.'

yên-tsîng 眼睛 'the eye.'   *yîng-ŭr* 嬰兒 'an infant.'

ĭ-fŭ 衣服 'clothing.'   *lĭ-li* 律例 'statute-law.'

101. Two verbs are sometimes united to form nouns: e. g.—

hîng-wei 行為 'actions,' both verbs meaning *to do* (synonymes).

fĭ-yŭng 費用 'expenses,' lit. *to expend—to use* (cognate).

shwŏ-hwá 說話 'conversation,' lit. *to talk—to say* (synonymes).

fàn-lwán 反亂 'revolution,' lit. *to reverse—to rebel* (synonymes).

Nouns expressing the abstract notion of verbs are generally formed in this way, just as the infinitive is used in German and Greek; *das Leben, das Haben,* τὸ τυχεῖν, &c.

102. Two adjectives are united to form nouns: e. g.—

chīn-paŭ 寶 '*precious-precious*—a jewel' (216).

jĭn-ts'ź 仁慈 'benevolent-kind—kindness.'

yiŭ-mún 憂悶 'sad-sorrowful—sorrow.'

103. Two nouns of a series are used to form the name of the class which the series expresses: e.g.—

kŭng-heŭ 公侯 'a nobleman,' lit. *duke—marquis;* the series being *kŭng-heŭ-pĕ-tsz̀-nán* 'the five degrees of nobility.'

kiă-tsz̀ 甲子 'the cycle;' these two characters being the signs of the 1st year of the cycle. Cf. Alphabet. A. B. C.

104. Many nouns are formed by placing generic terms, the equivalents for *tree, stone, flower, fish,* &c., after the special object: e.g.—

lĭ-yŭ 鯉魚 'the carp.'   *kweí-hwā* 桂花 'the flower of the cassia.'

sŭng-shŭ 松樹 'the fir-tree.'   *yĭng-shĭ* 英石 'limestone.'

105. Under the appositional relation we must also consider the very large class of nouns formed by the use of what have been called *numeratives* or *classifiers*. These correspond to our words *gust* of wind, *flock* of sheep, *cup* of wine. The words *gust, flock, cup*, are not in the genitive or possessive case, but in apposition to the words *wind, sheep, wine* *. The Chinese, in conversation, extend the use of such words to every object; they say, for example, 'one handle fan' for *a fan*, 'one length road' for *a road*. They are here called *appositives*, a term more appropriate than numeratives or classifiers. We shall now give a list of these appositives, and point out those which claim our first attention, and the classes of words to which they are prefixed in order to form nouns.

106. *List of appositives, with the nouns and classes of nouns to which they are united in composition.*

1. *kó* 個, 箇 or 个, is the most common app.; it is used with almost all objects: thus, *yĭ kó jĭn* 'a man.'

2. *chĭ* 隻 'an individual thing, single;' with names of *animals, ships*, and *things that move*.

3. *kiĕn* 件 'a division;' with *things, affairs, clothes*.

4. *k'weí* 塊 'a clod, a lump;' with *dollar, land, stone*, and things of an irregular shape.

5. *t'iaŭ* 條 'a twig, a division;' with long things, *roads, fish, snakes*, &c., *laws*, &c.

6. *tsó* 座 'a seat;' with *house, hill, clock*, of things *fixed* in a place.

7. *pạn* 本 'root, origin;' with *book*. This is a *borrowed* character.

---

* Compare Lat. *Urbs Roma*, Ger. *ein Glas Wein*.

8. *pà* 把 'a handle;' with *knife, chair*, things that may be held.

9. *kān* 根 'a root;' with *tree, pole, club*, &c.

10. *chāng* 張 'a sheet;' with *paper, table, bow*, &c., things spread out.

11. *chī* 枝 'a branch;' with *pencil, branch*, &c.

12. *p'ĭ* 匹 'a piece or a pair;' with *horse, ass*, &c.

13. *tuì* 對 'a pair;' with *shoes*, or any thing in pairs.

14. *shwāng* 雙 'a couple;' used as the above (13).

15. *kiēn* 間 'an interval, a space;' with *house*, and buildings generally.

16. *fūng* 封 'to seal;' with *letters*, &c.

107. The above are the appositives in most general use. A list of those characters which are less frequently used in this way is now given. The student may by reference to Mr. Edkins' *Grammar of the Mandarin Dialect* find a more particular notice of each.

1. *chạn* 陳 'a gust of wind.'
2. *ch'ing* or *shing* 乘 'a carriage.'
3. *chŭ* 軸 'an axle.'
4. *chu* 處 'a place.'
5. *fŭ* 幅 'a fold, a piece.'
6. *kān* 杆 'a pole.'
7. *kiá* 架 'a frame, a stand.'
8. *k'eŭ* 口 'a mouth.'
9. *kiuén* 卷 'a roll.'
10. *k'ŏ* 顆 'a grain.'
11. *kō* 科 'rank, examination.'
12. *kwàn* 管 'a pipe.'
13. *lĭng* 領 'a collar.'
14. *mạn* 門 'a door.'
15. *meî* 枚 'a stem.'
16. *mien* 面 'the face.'
17. *ping* 柄 'a handle.'
18. *p'ú* 鋪 'to spread out.'
19. *pú* 步 'a pace.'
20. *sŏ* 所 'a place.'
21. *t'eŭ* 頭 'a head.'
22. *tĭng* 頂 'a top.'
23. *tŏ* 朵 'a bunch.'
24. *tŭ* 堵 'a low walk.'
25. *ts'ān* 'a meal' (2786).
26. *ts'áng* 層 'a layer, a story.'
27. *tsĭ* 節 'a joint.'
28. *twán* 端 'a piece of cloth, &c.'
29. *tsūn* 尊 'honourable.'
30. *wạn* 文 'the tenth of a copper cash.'
31. *wei* 'a tail' (3121).
32. *wei* 位 'a person.'

FORMATION OF NOUNS. 49

Besides the above, many words are used as *appositives*, especially such words as express *quantity* of any kind, a *collection* or a *class* of objects *.

108. The second class of composite nouns includes all those whose first part may be said to stand in the *genitive* case, and which expresses the *origin* or *cause* of the second part, or that person or thing to which the second part *belongs* or has *reference*. Under this class also will come such compounds as have an attributive attached to them, whether an adjective or a verb in its participial form.

109. Examples of nouns of two syllables, the former of which is in the genitive case:—

t'ŭ-chăn 土產 lit. 'soil's produce,'=produce.

t'iēn-kí 天氣 lit. 'heaven's breath,'=the weather.

shǎng-hǎng 商行 'a merchant's house and premises.'

măn-k'eŭ 門口 lit. 'door's mouth,'=door.

tiēn-chŭ 店主 lit. 'shop's lord,'=innkeeper or shopkeeper.

niŭ-jŭ 牛肉 lit. 'cow's flesh,'=beef.

110. Examples of nouns of two syllables, the former of which is an adjective or a participle:—

tá-mĕ 大麥 lit. 'great-corn,'=wheat. tá-hwǎng 大黃 '(yellow) rhubarb.'

tsŏ-jĭ 昨日 'yesterday.' tsŏ-yé 夜 'last night.'

wăn-yŏ 文約 'a written agreement.'

chŭng-sīn 中心 lit. 'middle-heart,'=centre.

kì-síng 記性 lit. 'recording-faculty,'=memory.

kiaì-fă 解法 lit. 'explaining-method,'=explanation.

hí-yěn 戲言 lit. 'sporting-words,'=a joke.

míng-t'iēn 明天 lit. 'bright-heaven, or when the heaven becomes bright,'= to-morrow.

hiēn-shwŏ 閒說 'idle-talk.' siaŭ-sž 小斯 'a waiter or valet.'

chaŭ-p'aí 招牌 lit. 'calling-board,'=a sign-board.

fī-k'iaŭ 飛橋 lit. 'flying-bridge,'=drawbridge.

111. Sometimes designations of place and time, which are commonly used as prepositions or adverbs, enter into the composition of nouns: e. g.—

---

* See *Grammar of the Mandarin Dialect* by Rev. J. Edkins, pp. 129, 130.

H

siēn-fūng 先 鋒 lit. 'forward-point, van,'=the van of an army.

kīn-jĭ 今 日 lit. 'now-day,'=to-day. Cf. uses of νῦν and πάλαι.

tsaù-fán 早 飯 lit. 'early-rice,'=breakfast. Cf. Ger. *Früh-stück*.

wán-fán 晚 | lit. 'late-rice,'=the evening-meal. Cf. Ger. *Abend-brod*.

112. The third class of nouns is much smaller than the preceding, but it includes many idiomatic expressions. The first syllable of the two stands to the other in what we shall call the *dativa*l relation to its associate. The examples will show what is meant by this expression:—

hiŏ-fâng 學 房 lit. 'learning-room,' i. e. a room for that purpose,=a school-room.

tsiù-liâng 酒 糧 lit. 'wine-measure,'—'the capacity for drinking.'

ch'á-hú 茶 壺 'a tea-pot, a pot for tea.'

pīng-lĭ 兵 律 lit. 'soldiers'-law,'—'discipline.'

yín-k'ú 銀 庫 lit. 'silver-store,'—'treasury.'

113. In addition to the names of agents mentioned already, the expression *sz̄-fú* 師 傅 'a teacher,' and the verb *tsŏ* 作 'to make,' are used to form nouns: e. g.—

ní-kū-sz̄-fú 尼 姑 lit. 'pure-lady,'=nun.

t'ĭ-t'eú-sz̄-fú 剃 頭 lit. 'shave-head,'=a barber.

shĭ-tsŏ 石 lit. 'stone-make,'=a stone-mason.

shwui-tsŏ 水 lit. 'water-make,'=a confectioner or baker.

114. A verb and its object are sometimes used as a noun with and sometimes without the particle 的: e. g.—

k'ĭ-t'eú 起 頭 lit. 'begin-head,'—'beginning.'

hwui-sìn 回 信 lit. 'return-letter,'—'a reply,' to a letter.

115. The verb sometimes stands in the second place with a noun before it, without any apparent construction existing between them: e. g.—

shĭ-mó 石 磨 lit. 'stone-grind,'=a grindstone. *mó-shĭ* too is used.

shú-lung 樹 礲 lit. 'tree-grind,'=a wooden mill for grinding grain.

FORMATION OF NOUNS.

116. Many of the appositives are placed *after* words, and they then help to form general terms: e. g.—

mǎ-pǐ 馬匹 'horses.' *pú-pǐ* 布匹 'piece-goods.'
ch'uên-chě 船隻 'ships.' *shǐ-kw'ei* 石塊 'stones.'

117. Nouns formed by uniting words *antithetical* in meaning are very common, and they generally signify the abstract notion implied by these extremes: e. g.—

k'ing-chúng 輕重 lit. 'light-heavy,'=weight.
tŏ-shaù 多少 lit. 'many-few,'=quantity, which is the common phrase for 'how many?' or 'how much?'
ch'áng-twǎn 長短 lit. 'long-short,'=length.
kaŭ-tī 高低 lit. 'high-low,'=height.

118. The union of syllables of an opposite signification gives rise to a *general term:* e. g.—

hiūng-tī 兄弟 lit. 'elder brother and younger,'=brethren.
chí-meì 姊妹 lit. 'elder sister and younger,'=sisters.

119. The student should notice the class of *abstract* nouns which are formed by the addition of such words as *k'ì* 氣 'breath,' *fūng* 風 'wind,' *sīn* 心 'heart,' *sìng* 性 'nature,—disposition,—faculty:'—

ì-k'ì 義 'integrity.' *wǎn-fūng* 文 'literary taste.'
nù-k'ì 怒 'anger.' *siaù-sīn* 小 'attention.'
k'ě-k'ì 客 'etiquette.' *chūng-sīn* 中 'the centre.'
t'ì-k'ì 地 'climate.' *liàng-sīn* 良 'conscience.'
mǎn-k'ì 悶 'sadness.' *kŭ-sīn* 懼 'fear.'
weī-fūng 威 'dignity.' *kì-sìng* 記 'memory.'
mín-fūng 民 'nationality.' *sīn-sìng* 心 'disposition.'

120. Other *abstract* nouns are formed upon the same principle as those noticed in the foregoing articles; viz., (1) by uniting synonymes, (2) by placing one noun in the genitive case before another, (3) by joining two verbs or (4) an adjective and its noun:—

(1) *jîn-ngai* 仁愛 'benevolence, philanthropy.'
 gān-tièn 恩典 'favour, grace.' Ger. *Gunst.*
 chūng-kiēn 中間 'the midst.'
(2) *chù-ì* 主意 'the will,' lit. 'the idea of the master.'
 mîng-shīng 名聲 'reputation,' lit. 'sound of the name.'
 taū-lî 道理 'doctrine,' lit. 'the rule of reason.'
(3) *maì-maí* 買賣 'trade,' lit. 'to buy, to sell.'
 siaù-hwà 笑話 'joking,' lit. 'to laugh, to talk.'
 wán-tà 問答 'dialogue,' lit. 'to ask, to answer.'
 fán-pì 分別 'difference,' lit. 'to divide, to distinguish.'
 kūng-laù 功勞 'merit,' lit. 'to merit, to labour.'
(4) *siaù-sīn* 小心 'attention,' lit. 'small heart.'
 pán-fán 本分 'duty,' lit. 'own part.'
 kaū-mîng 高名 'celebrity,' lit. 'high name.'

121. Proper names may be mentioned appropriately here. Chinese names proper are always significant. Foreign names are put into Chinese form by simply representing the syllables of which they are composed by Chinese characters. There are about five hundred characters used as the names of families. (See Appendix.) In addition to this *sing* 姓, 'surname,' each individual has several designations, the principal one, which follows the *sing* immediately, is the *ming* 名 or common 'name,' and sometimes a *tsè* 字 or 'title.' In addressing a person the *sing* is used with some polite expression suffixed, such as *siēn-sāng* 'elder-born,' *siāng-kūng* 'Mr.' A few of the most common geographical and other proper names will be found in the Appendix.

122. *Diminutives* are formed by means of certain words, signifying *little, small*, prefixed; *siaù-yâng* 'small sheep,'=a *lamb*, *siaù-mà* 'small-horse,'=a *colt*; or by the word *tsè* 'child,' *ár* 'infant,' suffixed, *haî-ár* 'a little boy.'

123. The distinctions of gender and number are made in a similar way by prefixes or suffixes:—

nân 男 'male' and *nù* 女 'female' are prefixed to *jin*, 'man,' to express the gender; so also are *kūng* 公 'male' and *mù* 母 'mother,' to names of animals, to distinguish the gender.

fù 父 'father' and *mù* 'mother,' *tsz̀* 'son' and *nǔ* 'daughter,' are employed with the names of relations; as, *uncle, aunt, nephew, niece*. They are however suffixed.

Examples.

nán-jín 男 'a man.'		*kūng-chū* 猪 'a boar *.'	
nǔ-jín 女 'a woman.'		*mǔ-keù* 狗 'a bitch.'	
pĕ-fù 伯 'uncle.'		*chí-nǔ* 姪 'a niece.'	
pĕ-mǔ	'aunt.'		*sān-nǔ* 孫 'a granddaughter.'	

The Chinese ascribe certain genders to various objects of nature, according as they belong to the male and female principles, the *yáng* 陽 and the *yīn* 陰, the dual powers of the universe. The 'sun,' *jí*, is masculine, the 'moon,' *yǔ*, is feminine. But this does not affect the form of the words or their construction. Frequently the gender is shown by a distinct appellation; as, *tsz̀* 'son,' *nǔ* 'daughter.'

124. A proper name may be used as a common noun either by itself or with the addition of *táng* 等 'sort, class;' instead of saying "He was a perfect Confucius," the Chinese would say "He is of the Confucius sort." But this form of expression is scarcely ever used; the notion would be conveyed in some other way, especially in the colloquial style.

125. When the plural is expressed in Chinese it is done in several ways, each having reference to the extent of the notion of plurality. The simplest form of the plural is the reduplication of the syllable, a method common to Japanese as well as to Chinese †. It expresses *all* in a general sense, in some expressions indefinite, but in others limited by locality or the nature of the subject; e. g. *jín-jín* 人 signifies either 'every body' (but not without exception) or 'all men,' if the nature of the case or sense of the passage require it; just as we say, *most men*. The same may be said of *jí-jí* 日 'daily,' which is an adverb.

126. The following are the syllables commonly prefixed to express plurality: those common to the conversational form are marked thus—(*c.*); the others are only used in the books:—

眾 *chúng* (*c.*) 'all;' either 'every,' or merely 'all' the party in a certain place, generally of persons, followers, attendants.

諸 *chū* (*c.*) 'all,' in a more general sense applied to smaller classes.

庶 *shù* 'all,' chiefly in the books.

---

* Cf. σῦς κάπρος of Homer.
† In Japanese *fíto* is 'man,' *fíto-bíto* 'men.'

多 tō (c.) 'many, or much, or often,' of men or things. 許 hŭ-tŏ or 好 haŭ-tŏ are stronger colloquial forms.

凡 făn (c.) 'all,' of number or quantity; also tá-făn. 兆 chau 'all, generally' (seldom).

悉 sĭ 'all, completely,' often as an adverb.

並 píng is used both before and after the noun, but only in books.

127. These below are placed after the noun, and are emphatic, and commonly imply universality as well as mere plurality:—

皆 kiaĭ (c.) 'all,' in company,—*in universum*, it comprehends the whole class.

都 t'ū (c.) 'all, entirely, altogether.' This is also used as an adverb, to intensify; and then gives the sense of, *at all, quite*.

俱 k'ū 'all,' chiefly in books and the higher colloquial.

咸 hiĕn 'all,' also uncommon in speaking.

舉 kŭ 'all,' lit. 'to raise up,' confined to the books.

均 kūn 'all, equally.' 僉 tsiĕn 'all,' in books especially.

等 tăng (c.) 'a class, sort.' This is common in books too.

輩 peĭ (c.), as in *chăng-peĭ* 長 'elders, superiors.'

全 ts'uĕn (c.) 'complete,' also used in the books.

們 măn (c.), the common mandarin particle for 'all;' it may be looked upon as a *formative* particle.

128. The most common method is to employ some number or expression which sufficiently defines the plurality of the noun to which it is attached; just as the vulgar expression 'three foot' for 'three feet,' and in German *drei hundert mann*, &c. The numeral determines the plurality; and frequently in Chinese a special number prefixed serves to form a general or universal notion: e. g.—

sź-haĭ 四海 'the four seas,' i. e. the world.

pă-kwān 百官 'the hundred mandarins,' i. e. the officials.

lŭ-făng 六房 'the six rooms, departments,' i. e. the six boards of government.

wăn-min 萬民 'the ten thousand people,' i. e. all the people. kĭ 幾 and sŭ 數, 'several,' and some other syllables determine the plural. Cf. the use of μύριος in Greek.

FORMATION OF ADJECTIVES.   55

129. Those relations of words to each other, which are shown in the classical languages of Greece and Rome by the *cases* of nouns and by the *persons* and *tenses* of verbs, are exhibited in Chinese by the arrangement and sequence of the words themselves. The consideration therefore of the cases of nouns must be referred to the syntax of the language.

130. The only case which can be distinguished by the form of the expression is the *genitive*. The particles which show this are *tĭ* 的 and 之 *chī;* the former in speaking, the latter in the books. They have the nature of demonstratives, and stand for the *s* with an *apostrophe*—*'s* or *s'*.

§. 3. *On adjectives.*

131. Adjectives in Chinese may be divided, as the nouns have been, into three classes. Some syllables are used exclusively as adjectives, and are but seldom employed in the other grammatical relations; they may therefore be looked upon as *primitive:* e.g. *haù*, 'good,' is most commonly used as an adjective, although sometimes, with a change of tone—*haú*, it means 'to love.' Others seem to require the genitive particle to *form* them into attributives, and may be considered as *derivatives.* Others again are formed by the union of two or more syllables, and may be called *compounds.* Examples of this classification are to be found in the following articles.

132. The common formative particles, which strengthen the attributive force of the adjective, are *tĭ* 的 in the mandarin and *chī* 之 in the books. When these must be used depends in a great measure upon the rhythm of the expression: e.g. we may say *fú-kweí-jín* 富 貴 人 or *fú-kweí-tĭ-jín* 'a rich man,' but *lí-haí-jín* 利 害 would not pass, because it might signify 'to injure a man,' *haí* being a verb 'to hurt,' but *lí-haí-tĭ-jín* is 'a hurtful man,'—'a fierce, bad person.' The *tĭ* is required generally when a verb enters into the composition of the adjective, therefore especially after verbal adjectives and participles.

133. Adjectives of cognate signification come together and strengthen each other: e.g.—

t'sièn-pŏ 淺 薄 'shallow—thin,'=poor, weak.

k'iaù-miaú 巧 妙 'clever—marvellous,'=ingenious.

kièn-kú 堅 固 'firm—strong,'=firm.

134. A substantive sometimes stands before an adjective, as one noun stands before another in the genitive case, and thus intensifies the adjective: e.g.—

pīng-liâng 冰 凉 'ice's cold,'=icy-cold.

sŭ-pá 雪 白 'snow's white,'=snowy-white.

135. A noun and an adjective combined sometimes form an epithet, which is used as an adjective: e. g.—

tá-tăn-tĭ 大 胆 lit. 'great-liver,'=brave.

kŭng-taŭ-tĭ 公 道 lit. 'just-doctrine,'=just.

Such compound adjectives always require 的 *tĭ*. 的 之

136. An adjective or a noun is prefixed to an adjective with an adverbial force, and it is sometimes doubled to intensify the meaning: e. g.—

tsīng-sĭ-tĭ 精 細 'fine-small,'=fine.

tsīng-tsīng-sĭ-tĭ 'very elegant.'

wặn-yà-tĭ 文 雅 'letters-elegant,'=of literary elegance.

wặn-yà-yà-tĭ 'of a very fine style of composition.'

137. The addition of *k'ŏ* 可 'can,' or *haŭ* 好 'good, much,' to a verb forms adjectives which terminate in *-able* in English; they must always be followed by *tĭ*: e. g.—

k'ŏ-liên-tĭ 憐 lit. 'can-pity,'=pitiable, miserable.

k'ŏ-yŭng-tĭ 用 lit. 'can-use,'=that may be used.

haŭ-yŭng-tĭ, lit. 'good-use,'=useful.

haŭ-siaŭ-tĭ 笑 lit. 'good-laugh,'=laughable.

138. The quality of a verb may be attributed to a noun by a participle formed by suffixing *tĭ* to the verb itself: e. g.—

hwān-hĭ-tĭ 歡 喜 lit. 'to be pleased with,'—'pleasant.'

hwŏ-tŭng-tĭ 活 動 lit. 'to live and move,'—'lively, active.'

139. The quality or possession of the quality of a noun may be attributed to another noun by prefixing *yiŭ* 有 'to have,' and suffixing *tĭ* to the noun whose quality is concerned: e. g.—

yiŭ-tŭng-tsiên-tĭ 銅 錢 lit. 'has-money,'=monied, rich.

yiŭ-lĭ-k'ĭ-tĭ 力 氣 lit. 'has-strength,'=strong.

yiŭ-liàng-sīn-tĭ 良 心 'conscientious.'

yiŭ-haŭ-ĭ-sź-tĭ 意 思 'with a good meaning or intention.'

140. Many adjectives are formed from nouns, especially when they are descriptive of the shape or material of which any thing is made: e. g.—

FORMATION OF ADJECTIVES. 57

sź-fāng-tĭ 四方 lit. 'four-square,'=square.

chĭ-tĭ 紙 'of paper.'   *kīn-tĭ* 金 'of gold,'=golden.

These latter sometimes take the verb *tsŏ* 做 or *tsŏ* 作, 'to make,' between the noun and the particle *tĭ*:

mŭ-tsŏ-tĭ 木作 'made of wood,—wooden.'

Such are however to be regarded as the participles from compound verbs, corresponding to the German compound verb *handhaben*.

141. Some adjectives with an intransitive or passive signification are formed by prefixing *jîn*, 'man,' to the verb: e. g.—

jîn-hąn-tĭ 恨 lit. 'men-hate,'=hated.

jîn-ngai-tĭ 愛 lit. 'men-love,'=esteemed.

Such adjectives as *wolfish, hateful*, &c., are sometimes expressed by conventional terms, sometimes by circumlocutions: e. g.—

yiŭ-chaī-láng-tĭ sîng-tsîng, lit. 'has-wolf's-disposition,'=wolfish; or,
siáng-chaī-láng-tĭ, lit. 'like-wolf,'=wolfish.
jîn-kʻŏ-hąn-tĭ, lit. 'men-can-hate,'=hateful.

142. Adjectives formed in European languages by means of a privative syllable are made by prefixing *pŭ* 不, 'not,' to the simple word, and adding *tĭ*, the genitive particle: e. g.—

pŭ-siāng-kān-tĭ 相干 'unimportant.'

pŭ-shwáng-kwʻai-tĭ 爽快 'unwell' or 'unwholesome.'

pŭ-hŏ-mŭ-tĭ 和睦 'inimical.'

143. In this way many adjectives are formed in Chinese as equivalents for adjectives not produced by means of a privative syllable, but of a more emphatic power: e. g. for *bad, ugly, hearty*, the Chinese would frequently say *pŭ-haŭ-tĭ*, 'not good,'—'bad,' instead of *ŏ* 惡. All such require *tĭ*, the genitive particle.

144. There is no form of the adjective which expresses the degree of intensity or comparison. Words which may be mentioned in this connection as affording a means of expressing the comparative and superlative are, *kạng* 更 'more,' *chĭ* 至 'to come to (the extreme point):' e. g.—

kạng-haŭ-tĭ, lit. 'more good,'—'better.'

kạng-yúng-ĭ-tĭ 容易 lit. 'more easy,'—'easier.'

I

chĭ-kaŭ-tĭ 高 lit. 'extremely high,'—'highest.'

chĭ-jĭn-ngaĭ-tĭ 仁愛 lit. 'extremely benevolent,'—'very benevolent.'

145. The verb *kiā* 加 'to add' is sometimes joined to *kăng:* e. g.—

kăng-kiā-k'ĭ-kw'aĭ-tĭ 奇快 'more wonderful.'

kăng-kiā-paŭ-peĭ-tĭ 寶丨 'more precious.'

146. Several words are used to express the superlative or the intensity of the attribute, such as *tĭng* 頂 'the top,' *kĭ* 極 'the extreme point,' *hăn* 狠 'to hate,' *ts'ŭ* 絕 'to cut off,' *haŭ* 好 'good,' *t'aĭ* 太 'great,—very,—too,' *shīn* 甚 'very,' *tsŭĭ* 最 'very.'

Examples.

tĭng-siaŭ-tĭ 小 'very small,'—'the smallest.'

tĭng-haŭ-tĭ 好 'the best.'

kĭ-tá-tĭ 大 'very great,'—'the greatest.'

hăn-tō-tĭ 多 'very many,'—'the most.'

ts'ŭ-miaŭ-tĭ 妙 'most wonderful.'

haŭ-tō-tĭ 多 'very many *.'

t'aĭ-ts'iĕn-tĭ 淺 'very shallow.'

shīn-k'ŭ-tĭ 苦 'very bitter.'

tsŭĭ-yaŭ-kĭn-tĭ 要緊 'very important.'

147. The relations expressed by the forms of comparison, and by what is commonly called the superlative, are *often* produced by syntactical arrangements; the consequence is that the simple adjective must often be construed into European tongues by the forms of comparative and superlative: e. g.—In choosing long articles a person might say, 'This is longer by a foot;' the Chinese would say, 'This is long by a foot,' i. e. *longer* than some others, or 'this is a good one' for 'this is a better one.' This is syntactical; the duration and the extent being expressed *after* the word to which they respectively refer.

148. There are certain words with which it may be well to make the student acquainted here, because they are employed to state the comparison of the adjective in circumlocutions: e. g.—*pĭ* 比 'to compare,' thus 'you compared with him are tall' for 'you are taller than him.'

---

* Cf. the English phrase, a *good many*.

yiù 又 'again, still,' *tsai* 再 'again, more.' Cf. the use of *encore* in French and *noch* in German:—*encore mieux, noch mehr.*

hwán 還 'still, again, beside;' pron. *hai* in coll.

yŭ 越 'to pass over,' and *yŭ-fă* 發, which is more colloquial, in such phrases as 'the more, the better.'

yŭ 愈 'to exceed, more,' used as *yŭ*.

149. Sometimes verbs are used to express the idea of adding to or lessening the force of the adjective: e. g.—

kiā 加 'to add,' e. g. *kiā-tō* 'add-many,'=greater.

kiēn 減 'to subtract,' e. g. *kiēn-siaŭ* 'reduce-small,'=smaller.

150. The particle *yŭ* 於 'in, at,' which is used chiefly in the book-style, is also employed in conversation in the sense of 'in comparison with,'—'than.' Likewise several other words and expressions which signify 'a little.' These are placed after the adjective, as adverbs, and induce the notion of comparison: e. g.—

ché-kó   shi   tá   yĭ-tièn-ǎr   'This is great a little,'
這 个 是 大 一 點 兒 for, 'This is a little greater.'

151. Another very common way of forming the superlative is by prefixing the ordinal number *tĭ-yĭ* 第 一 'first,' or the expression *shĭ-fán* 十 分 'ten parts,' to the adjective in its simple form. Both these expressions give the notion of *entirety, completeness*. The Chinese employ the decimal system, and therefore *ten parts* means the *whole*. The word *mán* 萬 'ten-thousand, all,' is also used as an intensifier.

152. When the verb *tĭ* 得 'to obtain' is employed after the adjective, and is itself followed by some word which signifies *limit, extremity, urgency, severity*, &c., as 狠 *hǎn*, 極 *kĭ*, 緊 *kin*, 利害 *li-hai*, the superlative is formed by the whole expression, which denotes a very high degree of the quality signified by the adjective: e. g.—

kw'ai-lŏ-tĭ-hǎn 快 樂 'very glad indeed.'

sīn-siēn-tĭ-kĭ 新 鮮 'very fresh indeed.'

k'ŭ-nán-tĭ-kin 苦 難 'very hard to bear.'

hiūng-tĭ-li-hai 凶 'very fierce indeed.'

153. The following expressions are often suffixed to show the degree of

the attributive: *pŭ-kwo* 不過 'not pass-over,' *pŭ-shíng* 不勝 'not over-come,' 不完 *pŭ-wán* 'not finish;' also 了不得 *liaŭ-pŭ-tĭ* 'finish not obtain,' i. e. extremely. The characters 殊 *shū* 'to kill,' *tsín* 盡 or 儘 'to complete,' *k'ĭ* 綮 'strict,' *k'ai* 凱 'excellent,' *ts'úng* 從 'to follow,' *shá* 殺 'to kill,' *sān* 森 'abundant,' are also used in this connexion.

154. Certain other words, which signify *great, upper, good*, are used for the same purpose: e. g.—

tá-fān-pĭ 大分別 'very different.'

shàng-ku-tĭ 上古的 'most ancient.'

liàng-kiù-tĭ 良久的 'of a very long time ago.'

§. 4. *The numerals.*

155. The cardinal numbers are,

一　二　三　四　五　六　七　八　九　十
yĭ,　ĕr,　sān,　sź,　wŭ,　lŭ,　ts'ĭ,　pá,　kiŭ,　shĭ.
one, two, three, four, five, six, seven, eight, nine, ten.

156. The remaining numbers are formed thus:

shĭ-yĭ, 11; *shĭ-ĕr*, 12; *shĭ-sān*, 13; *shĭ-sź*, 14:

ĕr-shĭ, 20; *ĕr-shĭ-yĭ*, 21; *ĕr-shĭ-ĕr*, 22:

kiŭ-shĭ-kiŭ, 99; *yĭ-pĕ* 百, 100:

yĭ-ts'iēn 千, 1000; *yĭ-wán* 萬, 10,000.

157. The ordinal numbers are formed by prefixing *tĭ* 第, 'order,' to the cardinal numbers; and up to the *tenth*, *ch'ū* 初, 'to begin,' may be prefixed instead of *tĭ*. In expressing the days of the month, the cardinal numbers may be used alone for the ordinals.

158. Fractional parts are expressed by the character *fān* 'to divide,—a part;' the *half* by *pán* 半, and the *quarter* by *kĕ* 刻.

Examples.

pán-jĭ 半日 'half a day.'

jĭ-pán 日半 'a day and a half.'

sān-fān-chĭ-yĭ 三分之一 'one of three parts,' = ⅓.

kiŭ-fān-chĭ-sź 九分之四 'four of nine parts,' = 4/9.

159. Many characters not properly numerals are used as numerals in

Chinese as in Hebrew and Greek. The characters in passages from noted authors are employed as numerals. Such are the first four characters of the *Yĭ-kīng;* viz. *yuên* 元, *hîng* 亨, *lì* 利, *chíng* 貞, which serve for the numbers *one, two, three, four,* for volumes of books &c. The characters *shàng* 上 'upper,' *chūng* 中 'middle,' and *hiá* 下 'lower,' are used for works in three parts or volumes. The three months of each season are designated by *mâng* 孟, *chūng* 仲, and *kí* 季.

160. The characters commonly used for the purposes of higher calculation and chronology &c. are two series, one consisting of *ten*, the other of *twelve* characters; viz.—

(α) 甲, 乙, 丙, 丁, 戊, 己, 庚, 辛, 壬, 癸, and
    kiă, yĭ, pĭng, tīng, wŭ, kĭ, kāng, sīn, jîn, kweî,

(β) 子, 丑, 寅, 卯, 辰, 巳, 午, 未, 申, 酉, 戌, 亥.
    tsź, ch'eŭ, yîn, maŭ, ch'ên, sź, wŭ, wî, shīn, yiŭ, sŭ, haī.

The principal use of these is for the production of the names of the sixty years of the Chinese cycle, which is called *Hwā-kiă-tsź* 花甲子. The number of the cycle must be determined by the 年號 *niên-haŭ* 'year's designation,' by the title of the reign, or by the name of the emperor, and then the two characters from the two series given above will show the number of the year in the cycle. A list of the *niên-haŭ* and of the emperors will be found in the Appendix. The date is frequently noted both by means of the emperor's title and the year of his reign, and by the characters of the cycle for that particular year: thus, *K'iĕn-lûng sź-shĭ-ạr-nien, süĭ-tsź tīng-yiŭ shĭ-ạr-yŭ shĭ-kiŭ-jĭ;* that is, 'The forty-second year of *K'ien-lung*, the year *ting-yu* (A. D. 1778), in the twelfth month, on the nineteenth day.'

161. The following diagram and dates of the first year of each cycle since the birth of Christ will be of use to the student.

A. D. 4. was the first year of the 45th cycle.

A. D. 64.	46th.	A. D. 664.	56th.	A. D. 1264.	66th.
124.	47th.	724.	57th.	1324.	67th.
184.	48th.	784.	58th.	1384.	68th.
244.	49th.	844.	59th.	1444.	69th.
304.	50th.	904.	60th.	1504.	70th.
364.	51st.	964.	61st.	1564.	71st.
424.	52nd.	1024.	62nd.	1624.	72nd.
484.	53rd.	1084.	63rd.	1684.	73rd.
544.	54th.	1144.	64th.	1744.	74th.
604.	55th.	1204.	65th.	1804.	75th.
				1864.	76th.

	甲	乙	丙	丁	戊	己	庚	辛	壬	癸
子	1		13		25		37		49	
丑		2		14		26		38		50
寅	51		3		15		27		39	
卯		52		4		16		28		40
辰	41		53		5		17		29	
巳		42		54		6		18		30
午	31		43		55		7		19	
未		32		44		56		8		20
申	21		33		45		57		9	
酉		22		34		46		58		10
戌	11		23		35		47		59	
亥		12		24		36		48		60

162. The *distributive* form of the numeral is expressed by a circumlocution; thus 'one a-piece' might be translated *kŏ-yĭ-kó yiŭ yĭ-kó*, lit. 'each one has one.' The phrases 'by ones, twos, threes,' are turned into *yĭ-kó, yĭ-kó; liàng-kó, liàng-kó; sān-kó, sān-kó*. Repetitions of the words or expressions have a distributive force; thus, *yĭ-tsʻáng, yĭ-tsʻáng* 層 'in layers' or 'by layers,' *tiʻaŭ-tiʻaŭ* 條 | 'each article.'

163. *Proportionals* which answer to the question 'How many times as much or as great?' are expressed by adding the word *peí* 倍 to the cardinal number, and placing both after the adjective; thus, *tō-shĭ-peí* 多十倍 'ten times as great:' and if a fractional part, by adding the word *fąn*;— *tō-wŭ-fąn* 多五分 'five-tenths greater.'

§. 5. The pronouns.

164. The *personal* pronouns commonly used in the Mandarin dialect are,

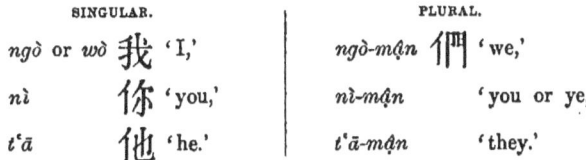

SINGULAR.			PLURAL.	
ngò or wò	我	'I,'	ngò-mǎn 們	'we,'
nǐ	你	'you,'	nǐ-mǎn	'you or ye,'
t'ā	他	'he.'	t'ā-mǎn	'they.'

In the dialects these syllables change or are replaced by others: e. g.—In Peking, tsǎ 咱 'I.' In Shan-tung, ngàn 俺 'I.' In Shanghai, nùng 儂 'you,' and nā 那 'ye or you,' and ī 伊 'he.' While the plural is formed by adding nǐ to the 1st person, making ngò-nǐ 'we;' and kǎ to the 3rd, making ī-kǎ 'they.' In Fŭ-kien, lán and gwa 'I,' lǐ 'you.' In Canton, k'ü 渠 or 佢 'he.'

165. There are besides many characters used as pronouns in the books, which are seldom found in the conversational style; e. g.—

wù 吾, yü 余, yü 予, for 1st person, 'I.'

jü 汝, ǎr 爾, jü 若, (also ǎr 而 and naǐ 乃 sometimes,) for 2nd person, 'you.'

k'ǐ 其 and kiü 厥 are used for the 3rd person, 'he.'

The plural is formed by tàng 等 'series;' ch'aǐ 儕 and tsʻaù 曹.

166. The Chinese have no *possessive* pronoun, but its place is supplied by the genitive case of the personal pronoun: e. g. ngò-tǐ 'my or mine,' nǐ-tǐ 'thy or thine,' t'ā-tǐ 'his,' ngò-mǎn-tǐ 'our or ours,' nǐ-mǎn-tǐ 'your or yours,' t'ā-mǎn-tǐ 'their or theirs.' No difference is made between the possessive pronoun when used as an attribute to a noun and when used as the predicate to a sentence: e. g.—

'This is our house,'=ché-lǐ shí ngò-mǎn-tǐ fāng-tsz̀;
'This house is ours,'=ché-kiēn fāng-tsz̀ shí ngò-mǎn-tǐ.

Sometimes the particle tǐ 的 is omitted when the euphony of the expression would be injured by its presence.

167. For the *reflexive* pronouns *self, own*, &c., tsź 自 'self,' kǐ 己 'self,' and their compounds tsź-kǐ and tsź-kiā 家 are used *after* the personal pronouns: e. g.—

ngò-tsź-kǐ 'I myself,' or tsź-kǐ alone;
nǐ-tsź-kǐ 'you yourself.'

When the subject of the proposition is well known, tsź-kǐ may stand for any person, but it usually is employed for the first person only. tsīn 親 'dear, related,' is used for 'self;' as well as *shĭn* 身 'body' and 射¹ *kŭng* 'body:' also the compounds *tsĭn-tsź, kŭng-tsĭn* *.

168. The most common pronoun is the *demonstrative*, and of this class the Chinese possesses a large number; some of these are peculiar to the books, others to the colloquial style. They may almost all be used as pronouns of the third person (see Art. 165). Such are, (a) *tsź* 此 'this, = hic,' and (β) *k'ĭ* 其 'that, = ille.' Under (a) may also come *tsź* 茲, *sź* 斯, *shĭ* 是, and *chè* 這, (coll.) Under (β) are also 彼 *pĭ*, 夫 *fŭ*, 者 *chè*, 厥 *kiŭ*, 那 *nā*, and 個 *kŏ*, (coll.) The Chinese have no demonstrative for the second person, like *iste* in Latin. The student should remember that the *appositives* (Arts. 106 and 107) will be required after these pronouns: e. g.—

chè-chĕ-mă 'this horse.' | *tsź-fūng-sĭn* 'this letter.'
k'ĭ-pā-tau 'that knife' or 'his knife.' | *nā-kŏ-jĭn* 'that man.'

169. Our English word *such*, for *that or this sort*, considered as a demonstrative pronoun, would be rendered into Chinese by any of the above pronouns followed by *yáng* 樣 'sort, fashion:' e. g.—

chè-yáng tí sĭn-tsíng 心情 'such a disposition.'

nā-yáng tí tsiāng-kiŭn 將軍 'such a general.'

170. The plural of these demonstrative pronouns, when not shown by the context, is expressed by the addition of *siē* 些, 'a few,' to them: e. g.—

chè-siē-kwō-tsź 'these (few) fruits.'

171. The want of *relative* pronouns in Chinese is supplied partly by the demonstratives and partly by the interrogatives, to which they are correlative: e. g. *nā-kŏ*, 'that,' is also 'which?' interrogative, and 'which,' the relative; *shuí* 誰 'who?' interrogative, is also 'who,' the correlative of it; *sŏ* 所 'that which,'—'what,' which seems to be a relative, is in its nature, first, indicative of place, and, secondly, an adjunct to a demonstrative expression, and is frequently a substitute for *chè* 者, i. e. the definite article. The method of expressing relative clauses must be referred to the syntax, where examples will be found.

172. The *interrogative* pronouns most common in Mandarin are the following: *shuí* 誰 'who?' *nā-kŏ* 那個 'which?' *shĭn-mô* 甚麼, pron. *shimmo*, 'what?' also written *shĭ-mô* 什麼. 'Who?' may also be expressed by *shimmô jĭn*, lit. 'what man?' *shuí-tí* 'whose?' or *shimmô-jĭn-tí?*

---

* So the old English adjective *sib*, for 'self,' meant 'related.' Cf. Key's Lat. Gr. p. 49.

THE PRONOUNS.   65

The book word *hŏ* 何 'what' is sometimes used in the colloquial style: e. g. *hŏ-jín* 'what man?' for *shuî-jín* 'who?' *Kî* 幾 'several' is used as an interrogative in such phrases as 幾時 *kí-shî* 'what time?' for *when?* Some other characters and phrases having reference to this subject will be found under the adverbs.

173. The interrogative pronouns used in the books may here be mentioned. Such are, *shú* 孰 'who?' *cheû* 疇 'who?' *hŏ* 曷, *k'ĭ* 豈, and *yên* 焉 sometimes take the place of *hŏ* 何 in the books. See the articles on the interrogative particles.

174. The *indefinite* pronouns are sometimes merely the interrogatives used as correlatives: *shuî* 'who?' used for *any body;* *shímmŏ* 'what?' used for *any;* *meú* 某 'a certain,' for *some.* *None* is expressed by 'not any,' therefore by *mŭ-shímmŏ* 沒, i. e. 'not what.' So also *kî* 幾 'several,' for *some*, is an indefinite pronoun, as well as an interrogative. *Ling* 另 and *pí* 別 express 'other' and 'another:' *kŏ* 各 'each,' *meî* 每 'every;' *tō* 多 'many, much;' *sïĕ* 些 'a few, a little,' and *sú* 數 'several.'

175. *Whoever, whatever, whichever,* and *wherever* are formed by prefixing *suî-pién* 隨便 lit. 'follow convenience,' *pŭ-lún* 不論 lit. 'not talk of,' or *pŭ-kwǎn* 不管 lit. 'not control,' or *pŭ-k'ū* 不拘 lit. 'not prevent,' to *shímmŏ-jín* 'who?' *shímmŏ tūng-sī* 東西 'what thing', or *shímmŏ sź-tsíng* 事情 'what affair;' or to 那裏 *nà-lî* 'where:' e. g.—

(1) *suî-pién shímmŏ* = 'whatever' or 'whichever.'
(2) *suî-pién shímmŏ-jín* = 'whoever.'
(3) *suî-pién shímmŏ-tūng-sī* = 'whichever thing.'
(4) *pŭ-kwǎn shímmŏ-sź-tsíng* = 'whichever affair.'
(5) *pŭ-k'ū nà-lî* = 'wherever' (properly an adverb).

176. When these expressions take a general sense and mean 'all,' one of the following words is employed: *fǎn* 凡, *tá-fǎn* 大凡, *chū* 諸, *chúng* 眾, *tá-kaí* 大概, and several others. The *whole* is very often expressed by the numeral 'one' with a word signifying to *complete,* to *cut off,* and the like: e. g. *yí-tsùng* 總, *yí-t'úng* 統, *yí-ts'ĭ* 切. The words meaning 'all' are too numerous to mention here; reference may be had to Articles 126, 127, and to the Dictionary for the rest.

177. *Both* is expressed by *liàng-kŏ* 兩個, 'two,' after the personal pronouns; and *neither* by *kŏ* 各 or 每 *meî,* 'each,' followed by a negative: e. g.—

ngŏ-mǎn liǎng-kó = 'both of us' or 'we two;'
kŏ-jin or *meī-jin mŭ* = 'neither of them.'

Only or *alone* is expressed by *tŭ-yĭ-ko* 獨 一 个 'one alone.'

178. Before leaving the present section, upon the pronouns, we must notice some of the nouns which the Chinese employ when in European tongues the pronouns would be used. These expressions arise out of the desire to excel in politeness and courtesy, and some of them are of very ancient origin; they correspond to our terms *Sire, Sir, your worship, your honour,* and other titles of respect. Their terms of humility are not used among us, except in the close of a letter, *your humble servant,* &c.

179. The substitutes for the personal pronoun *I* and *my* are,

 siaù-tí 小弟 lit. 'small younger brother,' for *I*.

 siaù-k'iuèn 小犬 lit. 'small dog,' for *my dog*.

yû 愚 lit. 'stupid,' for *I*, especially in letters. *chīn* 朕 'I, the emperor.' A merchant calls himself 'trader,'—*shāng* 商 or *pùn-shāng* 本; and this word *pùn* 'own' is frequently prefixed to the names of offices and professions, in edicts especially, in which the personal pronoun is never used; e. g. *pùn-hièn* 縣 'I, the district magistrate,' and *pùn-chīng* 丞 'I, the assistant magistrate.' In addressing the emperor various titles are used; a tributary prince says *kwá-jin* 寡人 or *kū-jin* 孤, *yû-yĭ-jin* 予 or *yu-siaù-tsž* 小子; a minister of state calls himself *chīn* 臣 'your subject;' if a Manchu, *nú* 奴 'your slave.' The people in writing to superiors call themselves *tsüĭ-jin* 罪人 'sinners,' and *ĭ* 蟻 'ants.'

180. The characters which most commonly enter into such phrases are *siaù* 小 'small;' *tsién* 賤 'mean, poor;' *hân* 寒 'cold, chilly;' *pí* 敝 'bad, vulgar;' *ts'aù* 草 'grass, coarse.' The characters *shé* 舍 'cottage' and *kiā* 家 'family' are often used for *my*.

Examples of the above.

 pí-sing 姓 'vulgar surname,' for *my name*.
 hân-shé 舍 'chilly cottage,' for *my house*.
 hân-mǎn 門 'cold door,' for *my home*.
 siaù-t'ŭ 徒 'little scholar,' for *I*.
 ts'aù-tsž 字 'coarse title,' for *my title*.
 kiā-fú 父 'family father,' for *my father*.

shé-tí 弟 'cottage younger brother,' for *my younger brother.*

ts'iēn-fū-jin 夫人 'mean lady,' for *my wife.*

181. Substitutes for the second personal pronoun are commonly the names or titles of honour of the individuals addressed; and the possessive pronouns corresponding to *thy, your,* &c., are such expressions as the following, made with the words *kweí* 貴 'noble,' *tsūn* 尊 'honourable,' *kaū* 高 'high,' *ling* 令 'good,' *laŭ* 老 'old,' *tá* 大 'great,' &c.

Examples with *kweí* 貴 'noble, generous, honourable.'

kweí-sing 姓 'your noble surname.'

kweí-kwŏ 國 'your noble country.'

kweí-kāng 庚 'your noble age.'

kweí-fŭ 府 'your noble palace,' for *your house.*

kweí-i'ĭ 體 'your noble body.'

182. Examples with *tsūn* 尊 'honourable,' *kaū* 高 'high,' *ling* 令 'good,' and *tá* 大 'great.'

tsūn-ming 名 'your honourable name.'

tsūn-kiá 駕 'your honourable carriage,' for *you, Sir.*

tsūn-pĭ 筆 'your pencil,' for *your handwriting* or *your composition.*

kaū-sheú 壽 'your high age.'

kaū-kién 見 'your high opinion.'

ling-lâng 郎 'your good son'* (*lâng*=pavilion).

ling-t'áng 堂 'your good mother' (*t'áng*=hall).

ling-ngaí 愛 'your good daughter' (*ngaí*=love). She is also called *tsiēn-kīn* 千金 (lit. '1000 gold pieces') 'your treasure.'

tá-haú 號 'your great title,'=your literary designation.

tá-ming 名 'your great name.'

The same words are applied to form other designations and forms of address, but chiefly in letters, in novels, and in the language of etiquette.

---

* Cf. *Monsieur votre fils* in French and *Liebe Mutter* in German.

183. Examples with *laù* 老 'old.'

laù-yê 爺 'old father,' for *Sire* or *Sir*.

laù-hiūng 兄 'old elder brother,' for *you*.

So also *tá-hiūng* 大 ('great'), *t'aī-hiūng* 台 ('eminent'), *jîn-hiūng* 仁 '(benevolent'), *hiēn-hiūng* 賢 ('wise'), in addressing superiors, for *you*.

tá-jîn, laù-tá-jîn, and *laù-tá-fū* 夫 are used in addressing people of rank and position in society. And instead of the personal pronouns, the name of the individual, or of his office or his title, is substituted in speaking or writing: e. g.—

shîn-fù 神父 'spiritual father,' for *I, you* or *he*.

tá-laù-yê 大老爺 'your Excellency' or 'your Highness.'

t'aí-sz̄ 太師 'great general,' to military mandarins, for *you*.

wán-suí-yê 萬歲爺 'Sire of 10,000 years,' *of* or *to* the emperor.

t'aí-hwáng-tí 太皇帝 'great emperor,' *of* or *to* the emperor.

pí-hiá 陛下 'your Majesty' (*pí* = steps to a throne).

tsù-hiá 足下 'you,' especially in letters and documents.

184. The characters *fán* 範 'a pattern, a rule,' *yên* 顏 'the countenance,' in conjunction with *t'aī* 台 'exalted' or 臺 *t'aī* 'a high tower or terrace,' are used in elegant writing for *you*: e. g.—

kwāng-fán 光 'bright pattern,' for *you*.

k'ù-fán 苦 'earnest rule,' for *you*.

ī-yên 儀 'polite figure,' or *t'aī-yên* 'exalted face.'

t'aī-fū 甫 'your honoured name,' when asking a person's name.

nī-fū 尼 'you,' used for Confucius.

t'aī-tîng 鼎 'lofty tripod,' when addressing high officers of state.

lĭ-weì 列位 'distinguished persons,' = Gentlemen!

185. A few other expressions of this kind are formed with *paù* 寶 'precious, valuable,' *sháng* 上 'upper,' and *hiá* 下 'lower:' e. g.—

paù-háng 行 'valuable line of buildings,' for *your shop*.

THE VERB. 69

paù-cheŭ 舟⋅ 'precious barge,' for *your boat*.

fù-sháng 府 'up in your palace,' for *your house*.

shé-hiá 舍 'down in my cottage,' for *my house*.

kŏ-hiá 閣 'under your pavilion,' for *you*.

Also *t'aĭ-sháng* or *t'aĭ-hiá* for *you*.

§. 6. *The verb.*

186. Some syllables in Chinese are the representatives of characters, which are commonly used as verbs; these are *simple* and *primitive:* many others however are formed into verbs by their connexion with certain auxiliaries and adjuncts; these may be designated *compound* or *derivative*.

187. Although monosyllables are sometimes found to express a verbal notion, they are almost always assisted by some word of cognate signification, or by some syllable which completes the crude notion expressed in the primitive. This is most general in the spoken language of China, and makes it a polysyllabic rather than a monosyllabic tongue, as it is commonly supposed to be. The stems in all languages are monosyllables in the same way.

188. *Moods* and *tenses*, as such, are quite unknown to the Chinese. No distinction is made between *active* and *passive* verbs; nor are the *persons* or *numbers* noticed at all by them. The context and the circumstances under which any thing is said are the chief guides to the exact sense of any passage. *Time* and *mode* are very clearly shown by the meaning of the whole sentence, or by the conditions under which it has been uttered.

189. The composition of verbs may be considered under nearly the same heads as the composition of nouns. We have compound verbs formed (α) by repetition, or by the union of synonymes or words bearing a cognate meaning; (β) by joining to the primitive an auxiliary verb, without which the former would convey only a general notion; (γ) by prefixing to one verb another, denoting *power, origin, fitness, desire, intention, obligation,* &c.; (δ) by placing certain verbs *before* or *after* others, to give the idea of intention or completion to the action; (ε) by uniting two verbs, similarly to those mentioned above (β), but which when united give rise to a notion different from the meanings conveyed by the parts separately, or one of them is equivalent to a preposition; and (ζ) by adding the proper object to the verb, like the cognate accusative in Greek, and thus forming a new verb, (cf. Art. 36.) These are general heads merely; it will be necessary to notice other formations below.

190. Verbs of the first class are very common, and are such as the following:*

(a) *k'ān-kién* 看 見 lit. 'look-see,' i. e. *see!* or *seeing*.

* The Chinese verb, when standing alone, must be construed into the imperative mood, or the infinitive mood as a substantive.

k'ān-k'ān 看看 lit. 'look-look,' i. e. *look!*
hwān-h'ĭ 歡喜 lit. 'rejoice-joy,' i. e. *being pleased with.*
k'ĭ-húng 欺哄 lit. 'cheat-deceive,' i. e. *cheat.*
hiŭn-kiaŭ 訓教 lit. 'instruct-teach,' i. e. *teach.*
yíng-kaĭ 應該 lit. 'should-ought,' i. e. *ought.*

191. One verb follows another as an auxiliary to limit or perfect the notion of the primitive: e. g.—

(β) lúng-shá 弄殺 lit. 'do-kill,' i. e. *kill.*
lúng-hwaĭ 弄壞 lit. 'do-injure,' i. e. *spoil.*
kweĭ-paĭ 跪拜 lit. 'kneel-worship,' i. e. *prostrate.*
tiĕ-sž 跌死 lit. 'fall-die,' i. e. *fall down dead.*
kĭ-chíng 結成 lit. 'unite-complete,' i. e. *knot and become,* or *clot.*

192. The following verbs, denoting *power, origin, fitness,* &c., require another verb as a complement:—

(γ) náng 能 'able, can' (*physically*). | k'ŏ 可 'can, may' (*morally*).
k'ĭ 起 'arise, begin.' | k'ú 去 'go;' cf. Hebrew idiom.
yŭ 欲 'long for, wish.' | yaŭ 要 'will, intend.'
yíng 應 'it is fit.' | kaĭ 該 'it is proper.'
ĭ 宜 'it is right.' | táng 當 'ought.'

193. Examples of the above with their complements are,

náng-fĭ 飛 'can fly.' | yíng-t'ĭng 聽 'should listen.'
náng-siĕ 寫 'can write.' | k'ŏ-k'ú 去 'may go.'
náng-tsŏ 做 'able to do.' | k'ŏ-tsŏ 做 'may do (it).'
k'ú-tsŏ | 'go to do.' | k'ĭ-tsŏ | 'begin to do.'
yaŭ-tŭ 讀 'will read,' fut. 'read!' or 'wish to read.' | yŭ-sž 死 'wish to die.'
 | kaĭ-táng 當 'ought to bear,' = *ought.*

194. The common auxiliary verbs which stand *before* or *after* the principal verb and determine the tense into which it must be construed are, (1) for the *perfect* tense, liaŭ 了 'to finish,' kwŏ 過 'to pass over,' yiŭ 有 'to have,'

or *wân* 完 'to finish,' placed *after* the other verb; and *ì* 已 'already,' *kí* 既 'finished,' and *tsǎng* 曾 'already done,' placed *before* it. (2) For the *future* tense, *yaú* 要 'will,' *yuén* 願 'desire,' *k'ǎng* 肯 'shall' or 'will,' *tsiāng* 將 'to approach,' or *pì* 必 'certainly, must,' placed *before* the verb.

195. Compounds of two of these are also formed in the colloquial style, and thereby the particular tense is more clearly defined: e. g.—

(δ) *sž-liaù* 死 'is or was dead.'   *k'ú-liaù* 去 'is or was gone.'

tŭ-kwó 讀 or *tŭ-kwó-liaù* 'has read or studied.'

siĕ-kwó 寫 or *siĕ-kwó-liaù* 'has written.'

k'ĭ-wân 吃 or *k'ĭ-wân-liaù* 'has eaten.'

yiŭ-shǎ 有殺 or *yiŭ-shǎ-liaù* 'has killed.'

ì-chí 至 or *ì-kīng* 經 *chí-liaù* 'has arrived.'

tsǎng-shĭ 食 or *tsǎng-kīng shĭ-liaù* 'has eaten.'

tsǎng 曾 is more commonly found with a negative prefixed: e. g.—

pŭ 不 'not,' or *wî* 未 'not yet.'   *wî-tsǎng-laî* 'not yet come.'

ch'ǎng 嘗 'to taste, to try,' is also prefixed occasionally to the verb to form the past tense; thus, *ch'ǎng-tsŏ* 作 'already done.'

196. Examples of the forms by which the *future* tense is expressed:

yaú-k'ú 要去 lit. 'wish-go,'=*will* or *shall go*.   *tsiāng* 將 may be prefixed.

tsiāng-tsŏ 將做 lit. 'approach-do,'=*shall do*, or *about to do*.

pì-híng 必行 lit. 'certainly-walk,'=*shall walk*, or *must walk*.

The distinction of tense is often shown in the context by some adverb of time: e. g. 'to-morrow I shall go' would be expressed in Chinese by 'to-morrow I go;' 'yesterday I came' would be expressed by 'yesterday I come.' These peculiarities do not belong to this part of the grammar, but will be found treated of in the syntax, under the section on tenses.

197. The next class of verbs is formed by the union of two verbs, the latter of which is supplementary to the former; and from the union of their separate notions a third verbal notion is formed. The adjuncts which serve for this purpose are very numerous. The most common are mentioned here:—

(ϵ) 得 *tĭ* 'to obtain.'   開 *k'aî* 'to open.'

出 *ch'ŭ* 'to go out' (cf. *aus-*).   上 *sháng* 'up' (cf. *ǎva-*).

去 k'ú 'to go away' (cf. ἐκ-, weg-).
散 sān 'to scatter' (cf. dis-, zer-).
見 kién 'to see.'
罷 pá 'to cease.'
着 chŏ 'to take effect.'
進 tsín 'to enter in' (cf. hinein).

住 chú 'to rest in, to fix.'
下 hiá 'down' (cf. κάτα-).
來 laí 'to come' (cf. εἰς-).
攏 lùng 'to collect' (cf. zusammen-).
k'ĭ 'to arise, to begin' (v. Art. 192).
定 tìng 'to fix.'

過 kwó 'to pass over or by,' 完 wán, 畢 pí, 盡 tsín, 'to finish,' and some others are used as the above, and occupy the place of inseparable prepositions in the compound verbs of some languages.

198. As examples of the uses of the above we may give the following:—

(e) kì-tĭ 記 lit. 'record-obtain,' 'to remember.'
t'īng-tĭ 聽 lit. 'listen-obtain,' 'to hear.'
ná-ch'ŭ 拿 lit. 'take-go out,' 'to bring out.'
t'aú-ch'ŭ 逃 lit. 'run-go out,' 'to escape.'
fạ̄n-k'aī 分 lit. 'divide-open,' 'to separate.'
tseŭ-k'aī 走 lit. 'walk-open,' 'to walk away.'
tseŭ-shảng | lit. 'walk-above,' 'to walk up.'
tiū-k'ú 丟 lit. 'throw-go away,' 'to throw away.'
fă-săn 發 lit. 'shoot out-scatter,' 'to expend (money &c.).'
wặn-kién 聞 lit. 'hear-see,' 'to hear of.'
yŭ-kién 遇 lit. 'meet-see,' 'to meet with.'
tsô-pá 做 lit. 'make-cease,' 'to finish making.'
shuí-chŏ 睡 lit. 'sleep obtain,' 'to go to sleep.'
paù-tsín 跑 lit. 'walk-enter,' 'to walk in.'
k'aú-chú 靠 lit. 'rely on-rest in,' 'to depend upon.'
ān-hiá 按 lit. 'lay-down,' 'to deposit.'
lā-lùng 拉 lit. 'drag-collect,' 'haul up.'
chán-k'ĭ 站 lit. 'stand-arise,' 'stand up.'

THE COMPOSITION OF VERBS. 73

shwŏ-tíng 說 lit. 'say-fix,' 'decide.'

yaŭ-kwó 搖 lit. 'row—pass over,' 'row past.'

yŭng-wán 用 lit. 'use-finish,' 'use up.'

t'án-pì 彈 lit. 'harp-finish,' 'finish playing.'

hing-tsin 行 lit. 'walk-complete,' 'go through entirely.'

laî 來 'come,' *k'ŭ* 去 'go,' or *liaŭ* 了 'finish,' are added to these compounds to express that the action of the verb has taken effect.

199. Other syllables of like meaning are sometimes used instead of the above; e. g. *taŭ* 到, 'to arrive at,' is used for *laî* 來, 'to come,' in some expressions: and many other words, which signify *to complete, end, die, kill, conquer* or *spoil*, help to strengthen the verb; such are, *ch'ing* 成, *yi* 訖, *shá* 煞 or *shá* 殺, *sz̆* 死, *shing* 勝, *yíng* 贏, *shū* 輸, and *pai* 敗.

200. Another class of verbs is formed by the addition of the cognate object, or that on which the action of the verb naturally falls. This object is not often added in English, but it is in Chinese, and it increases the perspicuity of the expression. The following are examples:—

tŭ-shū 讀書 lit. 'read-book,' for *read*, (for study.)

siè-tsz̆ 寫字 lit. 'write-character,' for *write*, (for practice.)

kĭ or *chĭ-fán* 吃飯 lit. 'eat-rice,' for *eat*, (any meal.)

shê-tsŭĭ 赦罪 lit. 'forgive-sin,' for *pardon*.

t'ing-ming 聽命 lit. 'listen to—order,' for *obey*, (cf. *obedio*, fr. *ob-audio*.)

k'iuèn-jín 勸人 lit. 'advise-man,' for *exhort*.

201. Adjectives sometimes enter into the composition of verbs to intensify or limit the meaning of the primitive: e. g.—

lin-kín 臨近 lit. 'come-near,'—'approach.'

cháng-tá 長大 lit. 'increase-great,'—'enlarge.'

paí-chíng 擺正 lit. 'place-correct,'—'arrange.'

wá-k'ŭng 挖空 lit. 'scoop-hollow,'—'excavate.'

202. There are a few idiomatic verbal compounds made by the union of a verb and an adjective or a noun: e. g.—

tí-tsŭĭ 得罪 lit. 'obtain-fault,'—'offend.'

chùng-i 中意 lit. 'hit the centre—idea,'—'please, suit.'

L

203. In addition to the above, the following idiomatic forms of expression may come under the head of compound verbs:

1. Those formed with *tă* 打 'to strike;' e. g.—

tă-swán 算 lit. 'strike-calculate,'—'plan, reckon.'

tă-kĭ 結 lit. 'strike-knot,'—'tie.'

tă-shuì 睡 lit. 'strike-sleep,'—'go to sleep.'

tă-t'ĭng 聽 lit. 'strike-listen,'—'listen.'

tă-saú 掃 lit. 'strike-sweep,'—'sweep.'

tă-shwuĭ 水 lit. 'strike-water,'—'draw water.'

2. Impersonals and phrases in which the subject follows: e. g.—

hiá-yü 下 雨 lit. 'falls-rain,'—'it rains,' (or *lŏ-yü* 落.)

hiá-sŭ | 雪 lit. 'falls-snow,'—'it snows.'

fān-fūng 翻 風 lit. 'change-wind,'—'the wind is changeable.'

204. Many nouns are used as verbs, though they do not differ from them in form; such being always monosyllables, the context only can determine the part of speech to which they belong: e. g.—

tiēn 點 'a point, a dot;' also means 'to punctuate, to blot out, to light, to nod.'

taú 道 'a road, reason;' also means 'to say,' (cf. λόγος=*ratio* and *oratio*.)

shwŏ-hwá 說 話 'conversation;' also means 'to talk.'

205. *Frequentatives*, or verbs which express the repetition or continuation of an action, are formed in Chinese by repeating the primitive syllable: e. g.—

mô-mô 磨 'to go on rubbing.'

t'iaú-t'iaú 跳 'to jump about.'

hŏ-hŏ 喝 'to keep on drinking.'

ch'ŭ-ch'ŭ k'ĭ 出 氣 'giving off steam constantly.'

t'án-t'án siaú-siaú 談 笑 'keep talking and laughing.'

The repetition of the verb does not always give it the frequentative force, but only intensifies the meaning of the simple primitive.

206. *Iteratives*, that is, verbs which express the reiteration of the action, as in English when the phrases *backwards and forwards*, *again and again*,

THE COMPOSITION OF VERBS. 75

up and down are used, are formed in the following manner with *lai* 來 'come,' *k'ü* 去 'go,' *sháng* 上 'above,' and *hiá* 下 'below:' e. g.—

tseŭ-laî-tseŭ-k'ü 走 'walk backwards and forwards.'

fi-sháng-fi-hiá 飛 'fly up and down.'

siàng-laî-siàng-k'ü 想 'think again and again.'

207. *Inceptives*, or verbs which indicate the beginning of an action, are formed by adding *k'ĭ-laî* 起來, 'begin-come,' to the primitive: e. g.—

hwá-shwŏ-k'ĭ-laî 話說 'begin to talk.'

k'ŭ-k'ĭ-laî 哭 'begin to cry.'

tŭ-k'ĭ-laî 讀 'begin to read.'

liŭ-ch'ŭ-k'ĭ-laî 流出 'begin to flow out.'

k'ĭ-laî has not always this force; sometimes it stands as the complement to another verb: e. g.—

lĭ-k'ĭ-laî 立 'stand up!' or 'stood up,' as the context may require.

208. *Desideratives*, or verbs which express the desire or wish to do anything, are formed by prefixing *yaŭ* 要 'to want,' *yŭ* 欲 'to wish,' *yuén* 願 'to desire,' followed by *tsó* 做 'to make,' or *weî* 爲 'to become,' to the primitive, if it be a noun, but without *tsó* or *weî* if it be a verb: e. g.—

yaŭ-k'ĭ 吃 'wish to eat.'

yŭ-tsó 坐 'wish to sit.'

yuén-hîng 行 'wish to do.' (B.)

yaŭ-tsó-wáng 王 'wish to be a king.'

yuén-weî-chŭ 主 'wish to be master.'

209. *Diminutives*, or verbs which indicate the diminution of the action expressed by the primitive, are formed by adding *yĭ-tiēn-ŭr* 一點兒 'a little,' or by the repetition of the verb with *yĭ* 一 'one' placed between: e. g.—

k'aî-yĭ-tiēn-ŭr 開 'open a little.'

shaŭ-yĭ-tiēn-ŭr 少 'lessen a little.'

tàng-yĭ-tàng 等 'wait a little,—delay.'

tseŭ-yĭ-tseŭ 走 'walk a little,—promenade.'

210. Verbs which express *being provided with* are formed by prefixing *yiŭ* 有 'to have' to some noun. These verbs are mostly employed as participles (cf. Art. 139): e. g.—

yiŭ-kŏ-tĭ 角的 'having horns.'

yiŭ-yên-tsing-tĭ 眼睛 'having eyes.'

211. *Causative* verbs are formed by prefixing *kiaŭ* 叫 'call,' *kiaŭ* 教 'teach,' *shĭ* 使 'cause,' *lĭng* 令 'command.' *kiaŭ* 交 is used for 教 incorrectly; and *jĕ* 惹 'provoke' is also used in the colloquial style: e. g.—

kiaŭ-laĭ 教來 'cause to come.'

The object of the verb always comes between the two parts of it.

kiaŭ-ngŏ-tsŏ-kwān 我做官 'cause me to be a magistrate.'

kiaŭ-ngŏ-pŭ-nâng-kiăng 不能講 'prevented my speaking.'

shĭ-t'ā-sheŭ-k'ŭ 他受苦 'caused him to be miserable.'

212. The *passive* form of the verb is produced by prefixing one of the following verbs to the active form, which may be then considered as a dependent noun; thus with

kiên 見 'to see,' *kiên-siaŭ* 笑 'to be laughed at.'

sheŭ 受 'to receive,' *sheŭ-k'ĭ* 欺 'to be insulted.'

k'ĭ or *ch'ĭ* 吃 'to bear,' *k'ĭ-kw'eĭ* 虧 'to be reduced.'

lĭng 領 'to receive,' *lĭng-kiaŭ* 教 'to be instructed.'

ts'aŭ 遭 'to meet with,' *ts'aŭ-k'în* 擒 'to be seized.'

weĭ 為 'to become,' *weĭ-jîn-sŏ-hǎn* 人所恨 'to be hated.'

213. Several auxiliary verbs are also used with some primitive verb and a noun to express the *passive*, by which form they must generally be translated: such auxiliary verbs are,

peĭ or *pĭ* 被 'to suffer, to reach to,' usually translated 'by.'

nâ 拿 'to take, to use;' also *yŭng* 用 'to use.'

yaĭ 挨 'to rest upon, depend on,' (seldom.)

tsiāng 將 'to take, to seize;' with *ĭ* 以 'to use.' (B.)

Also *yŭ* 於 or 于 'in, by,' and *mûng* 蒙 'favoured by' (in books).

THE SUBSTANTIVE VERBS.

214. The following are examples of the uses of these auxiliary verbs, showing how they help to form the passive:—

pí-hŭ-shí-liaŭ 被虎食了 'was eaten by a tiger.'
pí-t'ā-hwá-ngò 被他話我 'I was told by him.'
ná-shí-t'eŭ-tă-sź-tí 拿石頭打死的 'was killed by a stone.'
tsiāng-taŭ-tsź-shă-tí 將刀子殺的 'was killed with a knife.'
yŭng-piēn-tsź-tă-tí 用鞭子打 | 'was beaten with a whip.'
k'î-yü-jîn-chè 欺於人者 'one hated by men.' (B.) (Cf. Art. 212.)
mŭng-k'î-paŭ-hú 蒙其保護 'protected by him.' (B.)

215. Two other modifications of the verb, the *reflexive* and the *reciprocal*, which in Greek are effected by the middle voice, are produced in Chinese by the syllables *tsź* 自 'self' and *siāng* 相 'mutual' being placed before the verb: e. g.—

tsź-shă-tsź-kiā 自殺自家 'to kill one's self.'
siāng-lŭn 相論 'to discourse together.'
siāng-yŭ | 遇 'to meet with any one.'
siāng-haŭ | 好 'to be on good terms with.'

§. 7. *The substantive verbs.*

216. Of these there are several, which vary according to the nature of the case in which they are used, and the connexion of the subject with the predicate in a sentence. The *logical copula*, 'is,' is expressed by the verb *shí* 是. It denotes either that the predicate is, or, that it is generally supposed to be, an attribute of the subject by nature; it corresponds to the original use of φύω, πέφυκα in Greek, from which come *fui, fuerim* &c. in Latin, used as tenses of *esse* 'to be.' *Shí* in the *kŭ-wǎn* 故文 'ancient style,' i. e. the language of the classics, is used as a demonstrative.

With *shí*, *tsiŭ* 就 'then,' *yè* 也 'also,' and *tŭ* 都 'all,' are united; thus *tsiŭ-shí*, lit. 'there-is,' 'that is;' in Peking dialect sometimes *k'ò-tsiŭ* or *k'ò-chiŭ* (可): *yè-shí*, lit. 'also-is,' 'besides it is:' *tŭ-shí* (都), lit. 'all-is,' 'completely is,' 'is quite.' These are recognised phrases in the colloquial mandarin dialect.

217. The verb *wei* 爲 'to do, to exist, to become,' is also used as a substantive verb, but only when the notion of *becoming* something by some

conventional arrangement is implied, not as is the case with *shí* 是, when the relation between the subject and predicate is a natural consequence. In "Fire is hot" use *shí*. In "The Yellow River is the boundary" use *weí*. Also especially before designations in the predicate: "He is (*weí*) a slave." This distinction may be said to apply more particularly to the style of the books than to that of conversation. The adjuncts used with *weí* will also serve to indicate its meaning in some passages: e. g.—

náng-weí 能爲 'able to be' or 'to become.'

ĭ-weí 以爲 'consider to be, take to be.'

使喚之女爲婢 *shĭ-hwăn-chī-nû weí pī*
'Servant women are called *pī*,' i. e. slaves.

天子以四海爲家 *t'iĕn-tsź ĭ sź-h'aĭ weí kiā*
'The son of heaven considers (all within) the four seas to be (his) family.'

218. When the substantive verb implies *location*, the verb *tsaí* 在 'to exist or consist in' is used; and when the *possession* of some attribute, the verb *yiù* 有 'to have;' e. g. in "he is here" use *tsaí*, in "this is polite" use *yiù:* thus—

t'ā tsaí ché-lĭ 他在這裡 'he is here.'

ché-yáng yiù lĭ 這樣有禮 lit. 'this has politeness,' i. e. *this is polite.*

t'ā-tsaí-kiā 他在家 lit. 'he is in family,' i. e. *he is at home.*

tsź-yiù-lĭ 此有理 lit. 'this has reason,' i. e. *this is reasonable.*

219. The verb *tsaí* 在 refers to *place* or *position*, and means *to be in* or *to consist in;* the verb *yiù* 有 means 'to have *some quality*,' as an acquired possession, or as an accident, so 'to happen to be;' and consequently in the beginning of the sentence it always means 'there is' or 'there was,' like the use of *avoir* in French (cf. *il y a, il y avait*).

Examples.

tsaí sīn mĭn 在親民* 'consists in renovating the people.'

yiù jĭn shwŏ 有人說 'there are men (who) say,' *on dit.*

220. The word *naĭ* 乃 (rar. 迺), which was originally demonstrative, and

---

* This is from the *Tá-hiŏ* 大學 'The Great Science,' the first of the "Four books," a work belonging to the Chinese classics. It begins with the sentence, "The principle of the great science consists in renovating the people, in perfecting the original virtue (in self), and in resting only in the summit of excellence."

signified *'there'* as a designation of locality, and afterwards as a mark of time *'then,'* seems to take the place of the substantive verb occasionally, especially in the book-style. It is found with all the preceding substantive verbs, and may be said to partake of the meaning of each. It denotes also 'to wit, it may be.' In the following example 乃 and 是 are in parallel clauses of the same nature:

德乃天理，色是人慾 *ti nai t'iĕn-li, shi shi jin-jü*
'Virtue is heaven's order, vice is man's lust.' (v. Dict. 3311. for *jŭ*.)

The word *hi* 係 'belong to, is, am,' which is used in the books and in the Canton dialect, corresponds in force to *shi* 是 and *nai* 乃.

221. The words *tsŏ* 做 'to do,' *tsŏ* 作 'to make,' and *tāng* 當 'to bear, to meet with,' are also used in the senses of the substantive verb. The two former are used as *wei* 'to be called, to become;' the latter conveys the notion of a definite article, or of a demonstrative pronoun, like *ille* in Latin; e. g. *tāng-ch'ŭ* | 初 'that early time,' i. e. 'in the beginning:' *tāng-ch'ai-ti* | 差的 'that sent one,' i. e. 'he who is (or was) sent.' And when *tāng* is used in this way, it serves to point out the subject or predicate, and so renders the use of a positive copula unnecessary; (cf. the use of *shi* 是 in the *kŭ-wăn*, v. Art. 216.)

222. Very frequently the verb substantive is understood in consequence of the form of the sentence, or when an adverb or conjunction follows: e. g.—

sŭng ni tsi haŭ 送你即好 'to present it to you will be good.'

mai-mai pŭ t'ŭng 買賣不通 'commerce cannot be carried on.'

§. 8. *Mood and tense.*

223. A Chinese verb when uttered by itself expresses (1) the notion of the verb in the *imperative* mood; e. g. *tseŭ-k'ai* 走開 'walk away!' *lai* 來 'come!' or (2) the abstract notion of the verb as given in the infinitive mood; it then stands as a substantive: e. g. *tseŭ-k'ai* 'to walk away,—walking away,' *lai* 'to come,—coming,' are virtually nouns; so *t'aŭ-ch'ŭ* 逃出 'to run away,' i. e. 'the act of running away,' is either a noun or simply the imperative 'run away!' When however we construe *t'aŭ-ch'ŭ* 'running away,' something more is expected,—it is then only the subject to a sentence. It might for example be said, *t'aŭ-ch'ŭ pŭ-haŭ* 'running away (is) not good.' So that in truth a Chinese verb can only be construed properly into the imperative when it stands *alone*.

224. The *indicative* mood has no special sign. When the subject,—a noun or pronoun,—precedes a verb, that verb is generally in the indicative mood, but not always, for it may be a verb which is a mark of some other mood, or

80   MOOD AND TENSE.

it may be in the *imperative;* e. g. *nĭ laî*, lit. 'you come,' may be (1) *you come* (ind.), (2) *come!* (imp.), or (3) *when you come;* in the first and third cases being entirely dependent upon the context: thus 'you come here twice a-day' would be *nĭ laî chê-lĭ yĭ t'iĕn liâng-tsź;* and 'when you come, I shall go,' *nĭ laî wŏ tsiŭ k'ú.*

225. We have seen that the *subjunctive* mood is only distinguished from the indicative by the context; and the discussion of some peculiarities of this mood may be reserved for the syntax, by which alone they are to be distinguished. Certain particles however require that the verb following them should be in the subjunctive: such are, *jŏ* and *jŏ-shî* 若是 'if' (*si*); *hwŏ* and *hwŏ-chĕ* 或者 'perhaps' (*si forte*); *t'âng* 倘 'if' and *t'âng-jên* 儻然.

226. The *potential* mood is designated by the verbs *may, can, would, should, must* being prefixed, and by the addition of certain particles and auxiliary words to the primitive: e. g.—

k'ŏ-tŭ 可讀 'you may read' (permissive).

nâng-lá 能拉 'I can pull it' (potential, physically).

hwŭi-tsô 會做 'I can do it' (potential, intellectually).

yaú-k'ān 要看 'I would look' (optative).

yaú-k'ān 要看 'you should look' (hortative).

pĭ-kì 必記 'you must remember' (obligatory).

pĭ-sź 必死 'he must die' (necessarily.)

227. The following particles and auxiliary words affixed to the verb also show that some tense of the potential mood will be required:—

tĭ 得 'obtain' is suffixed, and followed by *laî* 'come,' *k'ĭ* 'arise,' or *chŏ* 'take effect,' or some other auxiliary to mark the direction or completion of the action (see adjuncts, Art. 197). Examples will be found in the syntax.

k'ŏ-ĭ 可以, lit. 'can-use,' is prefixed commonly to indicate the potential, either of permission or capability.

haŭ 好 'good' is used before verbs for the potential: e. g. *haŭ-k'ú* 'it is well to go,' i. e. *go!* (hortative), or 'it is well (for you) to go,' i. e. *you may go* (permissive). The word *pá* 'to cease,—it is enough,' is put after the verb in this latter sense: e. g. *k'ú-pá,* lit. 'go, and that is sufficient,' for *you may go*.

228. The *infinitive* mood, that is, the verb without an adjunct, which is construed into English with 'to,' is always appended to some word, which expresses *capacity, fitness, readiness, goodness, facility, difficulty,* and the like,

---

* Cf. Naaman's reply to Gehazi, "Be content, take two talents," 2 Kings v. 23.

MOOD AND TENSE. 81

and by this it is governed. It also follows such words as require the infinitive of *purpose* or *result*, just as in English. The position alone shows the infinitive mood: thus—

(1) *ngò nâng-tsó tsź* 我能做此 'I am able to do this.'

t'ā k'ò-ì tseù 他可以走 'he is able to walk.'

nì yíng-kaī k'ü 你應該哭 'you ought to cry.'

yü-pí hîng-wai 預備行外 'prepared to travel.'

haù-k'ān í-pīng 好看義兵 'it is good to look at the volunteers.'

yúng-ì siè-tsź 容易寫字 'it is easy to write characters.'

nā-yáng nân-tsó 那樣難做 'in that manner it is difficult to do.'

(2) *t'ā-laî kién-ngò* 他來見我 'he came (or is come) to see me.'

ngò-mạn laî k'ï-fân 我們來吃飯 'we are come to dine.'

229. The *participles* are generally shown by the genitive particle *tĭ* 的 or *chĭ* 之 being suffixed to the verb in one or other of its tenses; by a preposition being prefixed; or by the position of the verb after certain words denoting *like* or *dislike*: e. g.—

(α) *pién-tĭ* 辯 'discussing' (pres. part.).

hwüî-tĭ 回 'returning.' *paî-tĭ* 拜 'paying respects.'

pién-liaù-tĭ 辯了 'discussed' (past part.).

hwüî-liaù-tĭ 回了 'returned.' *pĭ-liaù* 避 'escaped, fled.'

(β) *tsaî-k'aù* 在考 'in examining' or 'in being examined' (gerund).

tsaî-múng | 夢 'in or whilst dreaming.'

(γ) *haù yaù* 好遙 'fond of rowing.' *haù-lún* 論 'fond of arguing.'

hạn-tü 狠讀 'hates reading.'

haù-yaù might be, 'good to row;' and with *tĭ*, 'well-rowed.'

hwān-hì pién-lún 歡喜辯論 'fond of arguing.'

230. The participles thus formed by the verb and some appended particle hold a very important place in Chinese construction, the syntax and the context however determine the precise meaning in each case: e. g. The above (α) *pién-tĭ*, in *ngò pién-tĭ*, makes, 'what I am discussing,' or *pién-tĭ* 'he who discusses.' The preposition *tsaî* 在, 'in,' must be prefixed, if the sense of

M

82   MOOD AND TENSE.

the present participle is to be given; thus, *tsai-piēn-tí* 'discussing,' or 'in the discussion of.' (See the constructions with *tí* 的 in the syntax.)

231. The *tenses* of the verb can be distinguished only by the various adverbs of time or by the context; and all that can be done here is to give the auxiliaries, which may be said to form the principal tenses, the *present*, the *past*, and the *future*. The numerous modifications of the time of an action are produced by the arrangement of the words and the form of the sentence, for which the student may refer to the syntax. It will be necessary even here to follow the synthetical rather than the analytical method, and to show the student how the exact meanings of the tenses found in European languages are conveyed in Chinese.

232. Pronouns and adverbs of time must be used in order to show the true state of the verb. If the verb *tú* 讀 'read' be taken, the forms of the *present* tense are,—

'I read (habitually or constantly)' *ngò cháng-shí tú* (常 時 'always').

'I am reading (now or periodically)' *ngò ín-tsaí tú* (現 在 'now').

'I do read (truly)' *ngò shí-tsaí tú* (實 在 'truly').

233.   The *past* tense with *liaù* 了, *kwó* 過, &c.

'I read (last year)' *k'ú-niên ngò tú-liaù* (去 年 'last year').

'I have read (at some former time)' *siēn-shí ngò tú-kwó-liaù* (先 時 'before time').

'I have read (what you wrote)' *ní siè-tí, ngò tú-liaù*.

The past tense is sometimes formed by the auxiliary verbs *yiù* 有 'have,' and *wán* 完, *í* 已, *kí* 既, *ts'áng* 曾, &c. (v. Art. 194): thus—

'I have written (the thing in hand)' *ngò yiù-siè-liaù* 寫.

'I have passed over (this river before)' *ngò tú-kwó-liaù* 渡.

'(We) have known (the contents &c.)' *chí-taú-liaù* 知 道 了*.

'He once said (so and so)' *yiù-shí t'ā kiàng-liaù* 有 時 他 講 了.

Without *liaù* it would be 'sometimes he says or speaks.'

234. The rule about the past tense appears to be, that when the perfect with 'have' is required, and refers to an action recently performed, it is sufficient to add *liaù*, *kwó-liaù*, *wán*, or *wán-liaù* to the simple verb; but when the past indefinite is meant, either the context must show it, or some word such as

---

* This is the phrase written by the emperor in vermilion on the documents which are presented to and perused by him.

MOOD AND TENSE. 83

siēn 先 'before,' *siēn-shî* | 時 'formerly,' *ts'ŭng-ts'iên* 從前 must be used as well as the above auxiliaries, and if the action refer to a definite time, and that time be mentioned, the auxiliaries may be dispensed with, if the rhythm permit: e. g.—

'I loved her most' (past indef.) *siēn ngaí t'ā tǐng-tŏ* 先愛他頂多.

'He wandered ever' (past indef.) *t'ā ts'ŭng-ts'iên yiŭ-hǐng* 遊行.

'We learnt too late' (past indef.) *ngò-mạn t'ai-chí hiŏ liaù* 太遲學.

'Last night I heard it' (past def.) *tsŏ-yè ngò t'ǐng-liaù tsz̀* 昨夜聽了此.

'To-day I forgot' (past def.) *kīn-t'iēn ngò wáng-kì-liaù* 今天望記了.

235. The *perfect* tense of impersonal verbs is formed by adding *liaù* 了: e. g.—

hiá-liaù-yŭ 下了雨 'it rained,' (occ. in replies.)

Probably the following expression may be referred to this form:

tseŭ liaù shwŭi liaù 走了水了 'it has been run with water,' i. e. *water has been fetched*: (v. Mr. Wade's *Hsin-tsing-luh*, Cat. of *t'iēn*.)

236. *Tsāng* or *ts'ǎng* 曾 (1) 'to add,' (2) 'already past,' prefixed to the principal verb, denotes the past tenses, often the *pluperfect*, but this depends upon the sense of the passage and the sequence of clauses:—

sĭ-niên t'ā ts'ǎng-yŭ .... *jǐn-shî* 昔年他曾與....認識
'In former years he had formed acquaintance with ....'

tsŭ-sháng ts'ǎng-tsŏ-kwŏ 祖上曾做過....*
'Among his ancestors there had been ....'

237. The expression of *future* time is effected by the words *yaú* 要, *tsiāng* 將, or *pĭ* 必 being prefixed to the verb:—

yaú gives the force of *will, shall, should*, or *must*, and is frequently used in compounds; e. g. with *k'ŭ* 去 'to go,'

'I shall go (to-morrow)' *ngò yaú k'ŭ.*
'You shall go' or 'you must go (to-morrow)' *nĭ yaú k'ŭ.*
'Go!' or 'Do you go (now)!' *nĭ yaú k'ŭ.*
'He must go (any time)' *t'ā yaú k'ŭ.*

---

* These examples are from the *Háng-leŭ-múng* 紅樓夢 'Dreams of the Red-chamber,' a modern work in the Peking dialect.

M 2

tsiāng is used with *yaú*, and gives the force of *about to;* e. g. with *laî* 來 'to come,'

    'I am about to come,' *ngò tsiāng laî.*
    'He is about to come,' *t'ā tsiāng-yaú laî.*

pĭ is also joined to *yaú*, and then the force of the compound is *must, certainly shall* or *must;* e. g. with *t'aú* 逃 'to run away,'

    'I must run,' *ngò pĭ t'aú.*
    'You must certainly run,' *nì pĭ-yaú t'aú.*

The addition of an adverb of future time always compensates for the absence of these special words: e. g.—

'To-morrow I shall go,' *míng-t'iēn ngò k'ú* (明天 *míng-t'iēn* 'to-morrow').

'In the afternoon you will go,' *hiá-wù nì k'ú* (下午 *hiá-wù* 'this afternoon').

'By and by he will come,' *mân-mân t'ā laî* (慢 | *mân-mân* 'by and by').

§. 9. *The adverbs.*

238. Monosyllables commonly used in an adverbial sense are *primitive* (α); those of two or more syllables formed by the addition of a distinctive or formative particle are *derivative* (β); and those formed by a locution, and which may be resolved into their separate parts, are *compound* (γ): e. g.—

(α) *Primitives* are not very common in the colloquial dialect, but are frequently met with in the books.

    ì 已 'already,' *kīn* 今 'now,' *heú* 後 'after,' *siēn* 先 'before.'

(β) *Derivatives* are such as the following, formed by adding *jû* 如 'as,' *ì* 以 'to use,' or *jên* 然 'yes,' to the primitive: thus—

hwŭ-jên 勿 |	'suddenly.'	*kwò-jên* 果 |	'certainly.'
twàn-jên 斷 |	'decidedly.'	*chă-jên* 輒 |	'immediately.'

(γ) *Compounds* are such as are made up of two primitives, or of two or more syllables which constitute a phrase: e. g.—

    ì-kīng 已經 lit. 'already-now,' = *now.*

    ch'ā-pŭ-tō 差不多 lit. 'error not much,' = *almost.*

    ts'ûng-tsiên 從前 lit. 'from-before,' = *formerly.*

    t'iēn-t'iēn 天天 lit. 'day-day,' = *daily.*

    tsiāng-laî 將來 lit. 'about to come,' = *afterwards* or *hereafter.*

mân-mân-tĭ 慢 | 的 lit. 'slow-slow,' = *slowly*.

tá-kiā 大家 lit. 'great-family,' = *altogether*.

yĭ-ts'z̆ 一次 lit. 'one-series,' = *once*.

239. It will be seen that nouns, adjectives, and verbs enter into the composition of adverbs, and that the same principle of formation is followed as was observed with respect to the other parts of speech. Synonymes are united or syllables are repeated to intensify the meaning; or the repetition implies the continuation of the prime notion; or the words are in construction, viz. as subject and verb, as adjective and substantive, or as attributive genitive and the word which it qualifies; or the compound is an idiomatic locution.

240. Before giving lists of the adverbs, it will be well to classify them with regard to their meanings and uses in Chinese.

1. Adverbs of *time;* in reply to the questions 'when?' and 'how long?'
2. Adverbs of *place;* replying to 'where?' 'whence?' and 'whither?'
3. Adverbs of *manner;* in answer to 'how?'
4. Adverbs of *intensity and frequency;* in answer to 'how often?' 'how much?'
5. Adverbs of *quantity;* in reply to 'how great?' or 'how much?'
6. Adverbs of *quality;* in reply to 'of what sort?'
7. Adverbs of *affirmation,* of *doubt,* and of *negation.*
8. The *interrogative* adverbs are the correlatives of the above.

241. The common adverbs of *time*, simple and compound, which answer to the question 'when?' are the following:—

1. The simple or primitive adverbs.

kīn 今 'now' (*nunc, νῦν*).   *hién* 現 'now' (*jam, ἤδη, à présent*).

fāng 方 'now, just now' (*nunc* or *tunc*).   *kāng* 剛 'recently, just now.'

pién 便 'then' (*tunc*).   *tsiú* 就 'then' (*tum*).

siēn 先 'before' (*antea*).   *heú* 後 'after' (*postea*).

ch'ū 初 'at first' (*ἀρχήν*).   *sĭ* 昔 'formerly' (*olim, pridem*).

kŭ 古 'of old' (*τὸ παλαίον*).   *hiáng* 向 'hitherto' (*adhuc*).

cháng 常 'always' (*semper*).   *wĭ* 未 'not yet' (*nondum*).

2. The compound adverbs of time.

kīn-t'iēn 天 'to-day.'   *hién-kīn* 現 ⎫

tsŏ-t'iēn 昨 'yesterday.'   *tāng-kīn* 當 ⎬ 'now' or 'at present.'

míng-t'iēn 明 'to-morrow.'   *jŭ-kīn* 如 ⎭

ts'iēn-t'iēn 前 'day before yesterday.'   *hién-tsai* 現在 ⎫ 'now' or 'at
fāng-ts'ai 方纔 'then, just now.'   *i-kīng* 已經 ⎭ present.'
pién-shi 是 'then.'   *tsiú-shi* 就是 'then.'   *tsĭ-k'i* 卽刻 'immediately.'
tsai-siēn 在先 'formerly.'   *si-shi* 時 'in ancient times.'
ch'ang-shi 時 'always,' or *shi-shi* | 'at most times.'   *wú-shi* 無 'never.'
yiù-shi 有 'sometimes.'   *tō-shi* 多 'often.'   *tsaù* 早 'early.'
wi-ts'ǎng 未曾 'not yet.'   *heú-lai* 來 'afterwards.'   *chi* 遲 'late.'
haù-kiù 好久 'a long time ago.'   *mŭ-hiá* 目下 'at present.'
sháng-kŭ 上古 'in high antiquity.'   *wán-sháng* 晚上 'in the evening.'
ts'iēn-sān-jĭ 前三日 'three days ago.'   *kwai-kwai* 快 'soon.'
kwó-sź-t'iēn 過四天 'four days hence.'
ts'ǎng-ts'iēn 從前 'formerly, from of old.'
tsùng-yiù 總有 lit. 'generally have,'= *always*.

Duration of time is shown by the position of the adverb *after* the verb.

242. The common adverbs of *place*, which answer to 'where?' are the following:—

ché-li 這裡 lit. 'this interior,' for *tsai ché-li* 'in this interior,'= *here*.

ná-li 那 | lit. 'that interior,' for *tsai ná-li* 'in that interior,'= *there*.

The syllables *ti* 他, *kw'ei* 塊, *t'eù* 頭, *ch'ú* 處, *fāng* 方, *mién* 面, and *piĕn* 邊, which all denote *place*, are used with the demonstrative (cf. Art. 168), often preceded by the preposition *tsai* 在 'in:' thus—

tsai-tsź-ti, lit. 'in this place,'= *here*.
tsai-ché-piĕn, lit. 'on this side,'= *here*.
tsai-ná-t'eù, lit. 'on that head (for *place*),'= *there*.
tsai-pĭ-ch'ú, lit. 'in that place,'= *there*.

yü-tsź 於此 and *tsai-tsź* 此 lit. 'in this,'= *here*.

tsai-pĭ 彼 lit. 'in that,' and *ná-sò-tsai* 那所 lit. 'that place,'= *there*.

243. It will be seen that almost all the adverbs are produced by the construction of words with one another. Many of the prepositions are used as adverbs in construction with verbs, as we say 'he is gone before,' *t'ā-ts'iên-k'ŭ*.

Examples of adverbs of place ('where?').

ché-li 'here' (*hic*).   *ná-li* 'there' (*ibi*).

nì-piēn-ché-lĭ, lit. 'your side here,' 'here by you' (*isthic*).
t'ā-piēn-ná-lĭ, lit. 'his side there,' 'there by him' (*illic*).
tsaí-yĭ-yáng-tí-fāng, lit. 'in the same place' (*ibidem*).
tsaí-liáng-piēn, lit. 'in two (for *the two*) places,' 'in both places' (*utrobique*).
ch'ú-ch'ú* or kŏ-ch'ú 'every where' or 'in each place' (*ubique*).
pŭ-hiaú-tĭ-tsaí-ná-lĭ, lit. 'not know in which place,' 'in some place' (*alicubi*).
suí-piēn-tsaí-ná-lĭ 'anywhere you please' (*ubivis* and *usquam*).
tsaí-pĭ-tĭ-tí-fāng, lit. 'in other's place,' 'elsewhere' (*alibi*).
pŭ-kū-shimmó-tí-fāng 'wherever' (*ubicunque*).
pŭ-tsaí-ná-lĭ 'no where' (*nusquam*).

244. The adverbs of place, which express *direction from* a place, are formed by prefixing *ts'ŭng* 從 'to follow' to the simple adverb of position: e. g.—

ts'ŭng-ché-lĭ 'hence' (*hinc*);
ts'ŭng-ná-lĭ 'thence' (*inde*);
ts'ŭng-nì-piēn-ché-lĭ 'from your place' (*isthinc*):

and so of all the others.

245. The adverbs of place, which express *to* or *towards* a place, are formed by prefixing *taú* 到 'to reach to' or *hiáng* 向 'towards' to the simple adverb of position: e. g.—

taú-ché-lĭ 'hither' (*huc*).
taú-ná-lĭ 'thither' (*eo*).
taú-nì-piēn-ná-lĭ 'to your place' (*isthuc*).
taú-kŏ-piēn-ná-lĭ 'to that place' (*illuc*).
hiáng-ché-lĭ 'towards this place.'

246. Adverbs of *manner* are generally derivatives formed by the addition of *jên* 然 to some adjective or verb. Such are, *hwŭ-jên* 'suddenly,' *twàn-jên* 'decidedly,' in Art. 238.

Other examples of adverbs of manner are,—

ché-yáng 這樣 'thus' (coll.).   jú-tsż 如此 'thus' (B.).

Like is expressed by the form

jú 如 ..... yĭ-yáng 一 | or yĭ-pwān 一 般.
pĭ-yáng 別 | lit. 'other fashion,' = *otherwise*, (or *liáng-yáng*.)

247. The repetition of the adverb or adjective forms an adverb of manner frequently: e. g.—

pîng-pîng-ān-ān 平 | 安 | 'peacefully, comfortably.'
hwān-hwān-hĭ-hĭ 歡 | 喜 | 'gaily.'   mán-mán-tĭ 慢 'slowly.'

---

* The notion conveyed by repetition is *most, a good deal*, and never seems to mean absolutely *all* or *every*.

248. Adverbs of *intensity* and *frequency* are such as the following; they are sometimes called adverbs of comparison:—

> kăng 更 'to change,' adv. 'more, again.'
>
> tsai 再 'again,' also yiú 又.
>
> tĭng 頂 'the top,' adv. 'very.'
>
> kĭ 極 'the extreme point,' adv. 'very.'
>
> hwán 還 'moreover.'   fŭ 復 'again.'

Some other syllables, used to form the comparative and superlative of adjectives, are adverbs (v. Arts. 146, 148). Words denoting 'to pass over, exceed,' and the like, are used adverbially; e. g. kwó 過, yŭ 越, &c.

> t'ai 太 and t'ĭ 忒 denote 'too.'
>
> tŏ 多 'many or much' is used adverbially.
>
> pŭ-kwó 不過 lit. 'not pass over,'=*only*.
>
> shĭ-fạn 十分 lit. 'ten parts,'=*very*.
>
> tá-fán 大凡 lit. 'great, general,'=*mostly, generally*.
>
> yĭ-siĕ 一些 lit. 'one few,'=*a little*.
>
> shaŭ 少 'few' and liŏ 畧 'an outline' are also used for *little*.
>
> p'ó 頗 'rather' is less frequent in conversation.
>
> sháng-hiá 上下 'almost.'   tá-yŏ 大約 'nearly, about.'

249. The adverbs which express *frequency*, and answer to the question 'how often?' are such as,—

> jĭ-jĭ 日 | or t'iĕn-t'iĕn 天 | 'daily.'
>
> niĕn-niĕn 年 | or sut-sut 歲 | 'yearly.'
>
> tŏ-shĭ 多時 'often.'   yiù-shĭ 有 | 'sometimes.'

250. Several adverbs of *quantity* have already been given, and others are formed by the following constructions: e. g.—

> chê-yáng-tŏ 多 lit. 'this manner much,'=*so much (tantum)*.
>
> t'ai-tŏ or t'ŏ-tŏ 太多 'too many,' or 'too much' (*nimium*).
>
> taú 到 'to arrive at,'=*so much as*, or *up to*.

Especially after pŭ 不 'not:' e. g.—

ché-kó yáng-ts'ién pŭ-taú sān pĕ kweī, 'these dollars do not reach to three hundred pieces.'

251. The adverbs of *quality* are generally formed by uniting an adverb of *manner* to an adjective; e. g.—

ché-yáng-haù-jîn 'so good a man.'
yĭ-yáng-haù-jîn 'an equally good man.'
pĕ-pwán 百般 'all kinds of,' lit. 'a hundred classes.'

252. The adverbs of *affirmation,* of *doubt,* and of *negation* are the following:—

Affirmative adverbs.

shí 是 'it is,'=*yes;* e. g. in 'Is there?'—'Yes.' *hí* 係 for 'yes,' is peculiar to the Canton dialect; e. g. *haí-lŏ* 'yes.'

jên 然 denotes *acquiescence;* it is especially used in the books.

yiù 有 'there is,' after appropriate questions; e. g. 'Have you?'—'Yes.'

kwŏ-jên 果 | 'certainly.'   *shí-tsaí* 實在 'truly.'
tsź-jên 自 | 'certainly.'   *chíng-jên* 誠* | 'surely.'

sin 信, *kú* 固, *ching* *, *kŏ* 果, *shīn* 甚 are all used in the books, but not in the colloquial style, except in compounds.

The affirmative is also expressed by *pŭ-ts'ŏ* 不錯 lit. 'not mistake,' or *wú-ts'ŏ* 無 'without mistake.' *ch'ā* 差 often stands for *ts'ŏ*.

253. Adverbs of *doubt* are such as the following:—

hwŏ-chĕ 或者 'perhaps.'   *chĕ-p'á* 只怕 'perhaps.'
shū-kí 庶幾 'perhaps' (B.), and *wí-pĭ* 未必 (B.).
k'ŭng-p'á 恐怕 'lest perhaps' (coll.).

254. The *negative* adverbs are these:—

mŭ 沒 'to be without,'=*no* or *not;* opp. to *yiù* 有 'to have,'=*yes, there is.*

pŭ 不, 'not,' is the most commonly used negative, and it has no other use.

fī 非 'not to be,—false,'=*it is not;* opp. to *shí* 是 'to be,'=*yes, it is.*

wú 無 'not to have,'=*without,*=*mŭ-yiù* 沒有, which is also common.
The negative of possession is expressed in Canton dialect by *mò* 冇.

mŏ 莫 'not, do not,' is a synonym of *pŭ* 不 'not.'

m 唔 (in the Canton dialect)=*mŏ* and *pŭ* of the books.

wú 无, *wàng* 亡, *wáng* 罔, *wí* 靡, *wù* 勿, *feī* 匪, *wí* 未, and *feù* 否 are used in the books, and some of them in local dialects, but seldom in the Mandarin, except in compounds.

255. The *interrogative* adverbs correlative to the above classes are:—

kǐ-shí 幾時 'at what time?'=*when?*
kǐ-cháng-yuén | 長遠 'how long? how far?'
kǐ-tō-t'iēn | 多天 'how many days?' ⎫
kǐ-tō-niēn | | 年 'how many years?' ⎬ =*how long?*
siēn-kǐ-niēn 先 | 年 'how many years ago?'
shímmò shí-heú 什麼時候 'at what time?'=*when?*
tsǎ-mó-yáng* 怎 | 樣 'how? in what way?'
tsai-nà-lǐ 在那裡 'where?'
ts'úng-ná-lǐ 從 | | 'whence?'
taú-ná-lǐ 到 | | 'whither?'
kǐ-ts'è 幾次 'how many times? how often?'
kǐ-peī | 倍 'how many fold?'
kǐ-tō | 多 'how much?'   *kǐ-tá* | 大 'how great?'
hó-yáng 何樣 'of what sort?'
siáng-shímmò 像 | | 'like what?'
shí-pǔ-shí 是不是 'is it so or not?'
yiù-mǔ-yiù 有沒有 'have you or not?'

256. *yēn* 焉, *hó* 何, *kú* 故, and several other words are used in the books as interrogative adverbs or particles. They are prefixed generally.

wei-hó 爲何 'why?' (coll.) or *wei-shimmó?*

ān or *gān* 安 is interrogative, chiefly in books; *ān-tsai* 在 = *where?*

k'ǐ 豈 at the beginning of a sentence is interrogative, (*quomodo*.)

The interrogative particles will be found further on (Art. 272), and the forms of the interrogative sentence in the syntax.

---

* *Tsǎ* is also pronounced *tsèn*, *tsěng* or *tsǎng*, and formerly it was called *tsǐm*: v. Edkins' *Grammar of the Mandarin Dialect*, p. 153.

§ 10. *The prepositions.*

257. The relations expressed by the prepositions are shown in Chinese partly by prepositions properly so called, and partly by the union of these in construction with postpositions. The former are generally verbs; the latter, commonly nouns.

The following are words used as prepositions:—

taú 到 'to reach to,'—*to* (*ad*), and *up to* (*usque ad*).

tsai 在 'to be in a place,'—*in* (locative) (*in*) or *on*.

ts'ǔng 從 'to follow,'—*from* (*de* or *per*) or *through*.

hiáng 向 'to go towards,'—*towards* (*versus*).

i 以 'to use, to take,'—*with* (instrumental) (*de* or *ex*) (B.).

ki 及 'to arrive at,'—*with* (*cum*).

liên 連 'to connect,'—*with, united with* (*cum*).

tai 代 'to act as a deputy,'—*instead of* (*pro*).

yü 與 'to give,'—*for* or *to* (*pro* or *ad*) (B.).

ki 給 'to give,'—*for* or *to* (*pro* or *ad*).

tá 打 'to strike,'—*from*, but only in colloquial, and especially in the Shanghai dialect, in which it is pronounced *tǎng*.

tāng 當 'to meet with,'—*in, at* (cf. Art. 221); it occupies the place of *tsai* 'in,' mentioned above.

wei 爲 'to do, to become,'—*for, on account of* (*propter*).

tui 對 'to be opposite to,'—*towards, opposite to,* and *for*.

t'ǔng 同 'the same, together with, in company with' (*cum*).

hô 和 'concord,'—*along with*.

tsź 自 'self,'—*from* (B.), used with *ts'ǔng* 'from.'

t'ï 替 'for, instead of;' also *to* or *for* (*ad*).

yīn 因 'because of' (*propter*).

yiû 由 'origin,'—*from, by* (*ex* and *per*).

yü 於 and *yü* 于 are equivalents of *tsai* 'in,' and several other prepositions, but they are used only in the books.

258. The words used to express the relations of place in construction with

the preposition *tsai* 在 are treated as nouns, and may be called *postpositions*. The most common are these:—

nüi 內 (pron. *nei* occ.) 'interior,' *tsai-fáng-tsz̀ nüi* 'within the house.'

wai 外 'exterior,' *tsai-fáng-tsz̀ wai* 'outside the house.'

li 裡 'interior,' is used similarly with *tsai* for *within*.

sháng 上 'above,' *tsai-shān-sháng* 'upon the mountain.'

hiá 下 'below,' *tsai-mà-hiá* 'under the horse.'

chūng 中 'middle,' *tsai-ü-chūng* 'in the middle of the house.'

ts'ién 前 'before' (*coram*), *tsai-mǎn-ts'ién* 'before the door.'

heú 後 'after,' *tsai-ngò-heú* 'behind me.'

259. The same words may stand after nouns without *tsai* being prefixed: e. g.—

ch'ing-nüi 城 內 'within the city.'

kwŏ-wai 國 外 'outside the kingdom,'=*abroad*.

shān-hiá 山 下 'at the foot of the mountain.'

mà-sháng 馬 上 'upon a horse,'=*on horseback*.

heú 後, 'after,' is also used as a *preposition*;—*heú-ngò* 'after me.'

260. Some explanatory locutions and phrases, such as the following, supply the place of prepositions: e. g.—

mŭ-yiù 沒 有 lit. 'not to have,'=*without* (*sine*).

pŭ-yúng 不 用 lit. 'not use,'=*without* (*sine*).

pŭ-tsai 不 在 lit. 'not present,'=*without* (postposition).

wai-t'eú 外 頭 lit. 'outside head,'=*beyond* (*extra* or *ultra*).

kwŏ-k'ü 過 去 lit. 'pass over go,'=*beyond* (*extra*).

Examples of the above in construction.

mŭ-yiù li-k'i 有 力 氣 'without strength.'

pŭ-yúng fǎn-hiāng 不 用 焚 香 'without incense.'

t'ā-mǎn pŭ-tsai 他 們 不 在 'without them' (they being absent).

miaú-mán waí-t'eú 廟門外頭 'outside the temple-gate.'

Meî-lĭng kwó-k'ú 梅嶺過去 'beyond the *Mei ling*' (Mt.).

§. 11. *The conjunctions.*

261. *Copulative* conjunctions are of rare occurrence in Chinese, but *disjunctive* and *adversative* conjunctions and those with the *hypothetical* and *illative* force are frequently found.

The ordinary copulative conjunctions are:—

k'í 及 'with;' *hŏ* 和 'with;' *pĭng* 並 or *pĭng* 幷 'together with;' 也 *yĕ*, the final particle of the books, is used in colloquial style for *and*, especially in the phrases *yĕ-yiŭ* 'also have' and *yĕ-shí* 'also is;' *hwán* 還 (occ. *haí* in coll.) 'still, moreover,' is used in the same sense. *yí* 亦 'also,' *yiŭ* 又 'again,' *ts'iĕ* 且 'moreover,' and 而且 *ár-ts'iĕ* are found in books; so also is *liên* 連 'to connect,'=*with, through.* *kiên* 兼 'together with,' is seldom used in coll. The copulative conjunction is frequently omitted.

262. The *disjunctives* are such as the following:—

hwŏ-chĕ 或者 ... *hwŏ-chĕ*, lit. 'perhap ... perhaps,'=*either ... or.*

yĭ 抑 ... *yĭ* are used in the same way for *either ... or.*

pŭ-shí 不是 ... *shí*, lit. 'not is ... is,'=*either ... or.*

pŭ-shí pŭ-kwŏ 不 | 不過 'not only' (*non solum*),=*fī-tŭ* 非獨 (B.).

tán-shí 但 | or *hwán-shí* 還 | 'but is' or 'also is' (*sed etiam*),=*tsiú-shí.*

yĭ-miên 一面 ... *yĭ-miên* 'on the one side ... on the other side' (*tum ... tum*).

yĭ-shí 一時 ... *yĭ-shí* 'now ... then' (*modo ... nunc*).

263. The *concessive* conjunctions are these:—

suĭ-jên 雖然 'although' (*etsi*).

jên-ár | 而 'although, yet' (not often in colloquial style).

264. The *adversatives* are principally,—

tán-shí 但是 'but' or *taŭ-tĭ* 倒底 'yet, but.'

pŭ-tán 不 | 'not only,' *ár-ts'iĕ* 而且 'but also.' (B.)

tān 單, *tán* 僅, *weí* or *wĭ* 惟 or 維, and *naĭ* 乃 are used in books, both singly and in composition with *ár* 而 and *jên* 然, for *but, only*, &c. *chĭ* 祇 and *tĭ* 第 are used for *but, only*, in edicts.

265. The *conditional* or *hypothetical* conjunctions in common use are,—

jŏ 若, *jŏ-shi* 若 | 使, and *jŏ-shi* 若 | 是 'if;' *hwŏ-chĕ* 或者 'if' (*si forte*); *chĕ-p'à* 只怕 'suppose, if;' *t'ăng* 倘 'if,' and *t'ăng-jên* | | ;

p'i-jū 譬如 'suppose, if,' or *pi-jū* 比如 (coll.) or *kiă-jū* 假如 (B.);

shĕ-jŏ 設若 'if;' *chǐng-jŏ* 誠 | 'if indeed' (*sin vero*);

shŭ-ki 庶幾 'if perhaps;' *keŭ* 苟 'if;' and many other words are used in the book-style.

266. The *causal* conjunctions are,—

yin 因 and *yin-wei* 因爲 'because' (coll.).

ki 既 and *ki-jên* 'since' (B.).

i 以 and *i-wei* 以爲 'on account of' (B.).

yuên 緣, *yuen* 原, *kŭ* 故 and *i-kŭ* 以故, and *kai* 蓋 are common to the literary style.

267. The *conclusive* or *illative* conjunctions are,—

sŏ-i 所以 and *kŭ-sŏ-i* 故所以 'therefore,' and *tsiŭ* 就 'then.' *kŭ-tsz̆* 故此 and *yin-tsz̆* 因此 are less common.

268. The *final* conjunctions are these:—

i 以 'in order that, so as to' (*ut*).

k'ùng-p'à 恐怕 'lest, so that not' (*ne*).

269. The *temporal* conjunctions are expressed by the adverbs and the form of the sentence: e. g.—

Before he came (*prius quam*), *t'ā wi-ts'ăng lai*, lit. 'he not yet come.'

After he was gone (*post quam*), I &c., *t'ā k'ŭ-liaŭ, ngò tsiŭ*, lit. 'he being gone, I then.'

As soon as he came, I &c., *t'ā lai, ngò tsiŭ*, lit. 'he comes, I then.'

So long as he reads, I &c., *t'ā-tŭ-tĭ-shi-heŭ, ngò* &c., lit. 'while he reads, I &c.'

As often as he eats, he sleeps, *t'ā-k'ï, tsiŭ chăng-shi shui*, lit. 'he eats, then always sleeps.'

Whilst I am here, *ngò chè-li*, i. e. 'I, being here.'

The position of words and clauses affects the nature of their connection very considerably. In the syntax this will be further elucidated.

§. 12. *The interjections and other particles.*

270. The *interjections*, which are the involuntary expressions of feeling, are rather numerous in Chinese. The following are among the most common:—

aī-yā 愛呀 'ah!' is an expression of joy or surprise (cf. *eja* in Latin).

tsâng-t'iēn! tsâng-t'iēn 蒼天 'heavens!'

k'ŏ-lièn 可憐 or *k'ŏ-sī* 可惜 'alas! mercy!'

k'ŭ-pá 去罷 'away! be off!'

kiū-jĭn 救人 'help! help!' lit. 'save man.'

wăn-haŭ 甚好 'very good! beautiful!'

kî-miaŭ 奇妙 'wonderful!'

271. Besides the ordinary interjections of surprise, admiration, &c., there are in the Chinese colloquial style a great number of expressions in imitation of the various sounds heard in nature (*onomatopœia*), as the *falling of water, jingling of crockery, bursts of laughter*, &c. &c. Such are,—

aī-aī 哀哀 'Oh! oh!' (to indicate pain.)

hī-hī 喜喜 'Hi! hi!' (to resemble laughter.)

fān-fān jáng-jáng 紛紛嚷嚷, to express the noise of business in a market-place.

272. The euphonic and interrogative particles remain to be mentioned. They vary in the different dialects. In the Mandarin the following are the most common:—

lī 哩, *mà* 嗎, *lā* 拉, *yā* 呀, and *lŏ* 咯 are final euphonic particles.

mò 麼 is a final interrogative particle. (Mandarin.) Contr. 么.

nī 呢 is a final interrogative particle. (Canton D.)

ọ 阿 and *aī* 愛. In replies for 'Oh,'—'very well,' &c.

273. The following particles should also find a place here as they are used in the ordinary colloquial style:—

yuên-laí 原來 lit. 'originally come,'=*lo! just then!* This is used at the beginning of clauses as an exclamation.

uh 兀 and *uh-tī* is a sign of the vocative case, especially in the Plays of the *Yuen* dynasty.

pā-pŭ-tĭ 巴不得 'would that!' (*utinam,*)=*I hope, I desire;* and with a change of tone it applies alternately to the speaker and the person addressed, e. g. 'would that I were &c.!' or 'would that you were &c.!'

nĭ-taŭ 你道 lit. 'you speak,'=*speak! tell me!* introduces a question.

nán-taŭ 難道 lit. 'difficult to say,' also introduces a question, generally followed by *whether*, that is, a dependent question.

p'ĭ 啵 or 咶, particles used at the beginning of a sentence, are expressive of contempt or irony.

naĭ-fán 耐煩 lit. 'bear trouble,' and *naĭ-hô* 奈何 lit. 'happen what,' may be regarded as particles. They occur in many phrases, sometimes as an exclamation; e. g.—

naĭ-hô! naĭ-hô 奈何！！ 'what shall we do!'

The remaining particles, more common to the books than to the colloquial idiom, will be found treated of at the end of the syntax.

274. We have now reached the end of the first division of the grammar, in which has been noticed, 1st, the sounds and syllables, the characters which represent the syllables, and the manner of writing the characters; 2ndly, the formation and grouping of the words and syllables, which enables the student to analyse the sentence with greater ease than he can when each character and each syllable is considered as a separate word. The fact that the Chinese generally put two and three syllables together to form a simple notion is enough to show that the term monosyllabic is not applicable to this language.

275. The first object of the student should be to group the words or syllables in the sentence so as to be able to say as nearly as possible to what category each group belongs; the more complete and certain classsification of the words cannot be made until their relations to each other in the sentence are viewed in accordance with the rules given in the syntax.

CHAP. II. SYNTAX.

SECT. I. ON SIMPLE CONSTRUCTIONS.

§. 1. *Preliminary remarks.*

276. By etymology we intended to describe the *forms* of Chinese words, with their true meaning and classification under those forms, in so far as they are distinguishable by the prefixes and suffixes attached to them; by syntax we mean to denote that *arrangement* of the words which expresses the relations existing between them, and the various forms of the sentence by which simple and complex ideas are exhibited.

277. The words of the Chinese language being without inflexion, the external form of the word cannot be introduced as an element to be considered in the construction of sentences. The case of the Chinese is similar to that of the English language in this particular, that the *position* of a word shows to a great extent its grammatical relation to the other words of the sentence. We have to consider then as we proceed to analyse the Chinese sentence; (1) the relative position of the words, (2) the relative position of clauses, and (3) the presence of certain particles, or words used as such.

278. It is assumed that the student is able to recognise in the sentence the particles and other words which help to form nouns, verbs, adverbs, &c. In order to do this he must have an accurate acquaintance with the earlier sections of this work, especially with Arts. 89, 90, 106, 107, 126, 127, and 130, for nouns; and Arts. 192, 194, 197, 211, 212, and 213, for verbs; also the Arts. on the adverbs and prepositions. The student will also do well to refer again to Arts. 35 and 36, on the composition of words, for the same general principles, there noticed, hold good with respect to the syntax of words and sentences.

§. 2. *General rules relating to the position of words.*

279. The expression of the time *when* of an action generally stands first in a sentence; e. g.—

kīn-niên kwŏ-tsz̤ tō 今年菓子多 'this year there is much fruit.'

kīn-t'iēn haŭ 今天好 'to-day it is fine.'

t'iēn-t'iēn wǎn-sháng | | 晚上 'every day at eventide.' [122.]*

hiĕn-tsai kŏ-chú-ạr &c. 現在各處兒 'now in every place &c.' [125.]

---

* The numbers in brackets refer to Mr. Wade's *Hsin-tsing-lŭ*, (Peking dialect.)

280. The designation of *place* follows the expression of time; e. g.—

tsŏ-t'iēn tsaì Pĕ-kīng &c. 昨天在比京 'yesterday in Peking &c.'

281. The subject of a sentence, when it is expressed, is placed before its verb, though not always immediately before it, for sometimes adverbial expressions come between it and the verb; e. g.—

jĭ wi ch'ŭ 日未出 'the sun not yet being out.' Chrest. p. 8. a. 13.

t'ā tsai Kwǎng-tūng pŭ haù 他在廣東不好 'he was not well in Canton.'

jĭ-yŭ tsaì-t'iēn cheū-hīng 日月在天週行 'the sun and moon revolve in the sky.' [90.]

282. The subject is often understood from the previous clause, and then it is generally a pronoun of the first person; e. g.—

kiŭ nĭ kĭ ngò tsŏ ché-kó 求你給我作這個 '*I* beg you to do this for me:' cf. Dialogues in Mandarin. Chrest. p. 27. a. 17.

283. The adjective precedes its noun always; when it *appears* to follow it, it should be looked upon rather as the predicate of a sentence, in which the noun that it qualifies is the subject, as in the example above, the literal rendering would be, 'this year the fruit is much :' e. g.—

haù-jîn 好人 'a good man.' | *ché-kó jîn haù* 'this man is good.'

284. Words and phrases, which qualify other words and phrases, regularly precede them; thus the attributive genitive is shown by its position before the noun: e. g.—

kwān-fŭ tĭ ché-tsz̀ 官府的車子 'the mandarin's sedan.'

ts'iū-t'iēn tĭ kĭng-ǎr 秋天丨景兒 'the aspect of autumn.'

t'iēn liáng tĭ shî-heù 丨亮丨時候 'the time of sunrise.'

285. In accordance with this rule the relative clause, being a qualifying expression, is thrown into the form of an attribute to the noun, which would otherwise be its antecedent: e. g.—

nĭ chŭ tĭ tĭ-fāng 你住的地方 'the place, in which you live,' lit. 'you dwell's place.'

kiaū lūi p'ĭ tĭ nà-kó-jîn 叫雷霹丨那個人 'that man, who was struck with lightning.'

lūi, lit. 'thunder,' *p'ĭ* 'to rend by lightning.' *kiaū* here = *pei*, v. Art. 213.

286. Adverbs generally precede the words they qualify, but they sometimes follow them; e. g.—

yĭ-sz̄ wú ts'ŏ 一絲無錯 'without the least mistake.'

chĕ-tĭ yĭ-kó 只得一个 'only one.'

shīn-t'ĭ* p'ó gān 身體頗安 'I am pretty well.'

liĕn-liĕn tă-kùng 連連打拱 'repeatedly bowing.'

287. The expression of length, height, or duration is placed after the phrase to which it belongs; e. g.—

kaū lŭ ch'ĭ 高六尺 'six cubits high.'

taū-lú sź-lĭ 道路四里 'the road is four miles *long*.'

hiá-yŭ sān-t'iēn 下雨三天 'it has rained three days.'

§. 3. *The construction of simple terms.*

288. When two nouns come together, the former of them is in the genitive case, or they are one of the following constructions; viz. (1) an enumeration of two objects, *and* being understood between them; (2) in apposition to each other; (3) the former is the subject, the latter, the predicate of a sentence; (5) the latter of them is an adverbial expression of time, place, or manner: e. g.—

chūn t'iēn 春天 lit. 'spring's sky,'—'the sky in spring;' cf. Art. 109.

kwān-fŭ shīng-ming 官府聲名 'the mandarin's reputation.'

(1) *yŭ, sŭ* 雨雪 'rain and snow.'

jĭ, yŭ, sīng-sŭ 日月星宿 'sun, moon, and stars.'

(2) *chŭ-tsaī* 主宰 'lord or master;' cf. Art. 100, &c.

(3) *fŭ haĭ, sheú shān* 福海壽山 '*his* happiness *be it* a sea, *his* age, a mountain.'

jin-shān, jin haĭ 人山人海 'men *as many as* mountains and seas.'

(4) *kiuĕn yê sheŭ kiā* 犬夜守家 'the dog by night keeps the house.' *yê*, 'night,' is here an adverb of time.

289. A noun before an adjective is either (1) the subject of a sentence of which the adjective is the predicate, or it is (2) construed as an adverb; e. g.—

(1) *sīn chá* 心窄 '*his* heart is narrow.'

---

* *shīn-t'ĭ* 'body,' cf. the use of *corpus* for the personal pronoun in Latin.

ch'ĭ-tsŭn pŭ-tui 尺寸不對 'the measurement is not the same.'

yŭ-liáng haŭ 月亮好 'the moonlight is beautiful.'

(2) *pīng liáng* 冰凉 'cold as ice;' v. the first example in Art. 297.

fūng kw'ai, pĭ chĭ 風快, 壁直 'sharp as a needle, straight as a wall.'

290. A noun after an adjective is qualified by that adjective, or it forms an adverbial expression in composition with the adjective; e. g.—

(1) *shíng-jîn* 聖人 'a holy man,—a sage.'

weĭ-fūng tĭ mién k'ūng 威風的面空 'a dignified countenance.'

(2) *míng-niên* 明年 lit. 'bright year,'=*next year*.

gán-tĭ-lĭ 暗地裏 lit. 'dark place within,'=*secretly*.

291. A noun before a verb is either (1) the subject of that verb, or (2) an adverbial expression of time, place, or manner, formed by the two words; e. g.—

(1) *K'ŭng-tsz̆ shwŏ-taŭ* 孔子說道 'Confucius said,'

p'ăng-yiŭ hwŭi-lai 朋友回來 'my friend is returned.'

(2) *hiaŭ-kíng fú-mŭ* 孝敬父母 'reverenced his parents with obedience;' pron. also *fú-meŭ*.

mă p'aŭ tĭ kw'ai 馬跑的快 'as quick as a galloping horse.'

292. A noun after a verb is either (1) the object of that verb, or (2) an adverbial expression of time, place, or manner, formed by the two words; e. g.—

(1) *lŏ-liaŭ shĭn-fă̱n* 落了身分 'lost his position.'

tă-fă liaŭ jĭn-chaī 打發了人差 'sent a messenger.'

(2) *făng-sīn shwŏ-pá!* 放心說罷 'freely speak!'

liên-yé t'ā k'ŭ 連夜他哭 'all night she cried.'

făng-sīn is literally, 'release heart;' cf. Chrest. p. 27. a. 13.

liên-yé is literally, 'connect night,'='all night,' sometimes, 'day and night;' cf. *San-kwŏ-chi*, Chrest. p. 17. a. 24, 25.

293. When two adjectives come together they follow the same rule in several particulars as that in Art. 288 with respect to two nouns; viz. (1) the first is an attributive to the second, and qualifies or intensifies it; or (2)

they express simply an enumeration of two qualities; or (3) they are in apposition, and form a compound adjective; or (4) they form an adverbial expression of time, place, manner, or degree: e. g.—

(1) *ch'âng-yuèn* 長遠 'long-distant,'=distant.

ts'ing-ts'ù 清楚 'clear-distinct,'=distinct.

(2) *fāng, yuên* 方圓 'square and round.'

kaū, tī 高低 'high and low.'

(3) *kān-saū* 乾燥 'dry.' Cf. Art. 136.

ts'ūng-ming 聰明 'intelligent.'

(4) *yīn-yīn yà-ngaí* 殷｜雅愛 'most affable and courteous.'

yīn means 'full, complete.'

tsî ts'ù siaŭ 濟楚笑 'respectfully and heartily laughing.'

294. An adjective before a verb either (1) qualifies it as an adverb; (2) it is used as an abstract noun, and is then the subject to the verb; or (3) they form an adverbial expression: e. g.—

(1) *t'ā kw'aí tseù-liaù* 他快走了 'he walked fast.'

tō yúng sīn sz̄ 多用心思 'he thinks much.'

(2) *ŏ pù tī gān* 惡不得安 'the wicked cannot obtain peace.'

shên yiù shên paù 善有善報 'virtue has a good reward.'

(3) *ts'iŏ-ǎr shaú-tī haù-t'īng* 雀兒哨得好聽 'the birds sing sweetly,' lit. 'good to hear.'

295. An adjective after a verb follows a similar rule; either (1) it is used adverbially, or (2) as an abstract noun, and is then the object of the verb; e. g.—

(1) *t'ā kiàng haù* 他講好 'he speaks well.'

shwŏ ming 說明 'to speak plainly.'

paì ching 擺正 'to arrange properly.'

(2) *tsz̄ pî yiù î* 此彼有異 'there is a difference between this and that.'

hiŏ haù wei shên 學好為善 'to learn goodness is a good thing.'

296. When two verbs come together they are in composition or in construction either (1) as a compound word, or (2) the second is the natural

complement of the first, or (3) they are used as an adverbial or attributive expression; e. g.—

Examples for (1) and (2) will be found in Arts. 190—198.

(2) *ngò pŭ-năng tseŭ* 我不能走 'I am not able to walk.'

tsż jìn k'ŏ-ĭ tŭ 此人可以讀 'this man can read it.'

tsiŭ yaŭ shí lĭ 就要施禮 'then he was about to go through the rites,' or 'to make the proper greetings.'

(3) *tsî ts'ŭ siaŭ hă hă* 齊楚笑哈 | 'respectfully-heartily laughing.'

liĕn-liĕn tă kŭng kùng 連 | 打恭拱 'repeatedly bowing reverently.'

§. 4. *The principles involved in the grouping of words.*

297. Besides the ordinary formation of the parts of speech by the union of two, and sometimes of three syllables, the Chinese are fond of grouping together syllables, which form a rhythmical expression, and which are attached to each other upon principles often different from the *primary* rules, but which accord with the *less common* rules of composition and construction: e. g.—

tsŭĭ-t'iĕn sīn-k'ŭ 嘴甜心苦 'on the lip sweet, in the heart bitter.'

tă-t'ŭng siaŭ-ĭ 大同小異 'in a great degree the same, in a small degree different,' = *nearly alike:* cf. Arts. 289 (2) and 293 (4).

298. The first important principle of grouping is the appropriate selection of words having an opposite meaning, or which are generally connected in dissyllabic phrases: e. g. *t'iĕn-tĭ* 天地 'heaven and earth;' *wăn-wŭ* 文武 'civil and military.' These are separated, and compounded with two other words to form a set phrase or group: e. g.—

t'ăn-t'iĕn shwŏ-tĭ 談天說地 'to talk about every thing, to gossip.'

tŭng taù sī waī 東倒西歪 'to fall in all directions,' lit. 'eastward and westward.' *Hau-k'iu-chuen,* p. 12. h. 16.

299. Another leading feature in the grouping of words is *repetition.* This is extremely common, and has the effect of intensifying the meaning of the single syllable, and gives the notion of *a good many*, often *all, every*, to the single noun. It is true, however, that it gives occasionally a meaning somewhat at variance with the original notion conveyed by the word: e. g.—

kăn-kăn kw'ăn liŭ 懇 | 欵留 'to detain as a guest with importunity.'

tĭ tsŭĭ-hiŭn-hiŭn 得醉醺 | 'intoxicated completely.'

haŭ-haŭ sŭng ngŏ 好 | 送我 'conduct me properly.' Chrest. p. 12. i. 23.

jı̆n-jı̆n tŭ shwŏ 人 | 都 說 'every body says.'
chĕ-chĕ sāng-pı́ng 隻 | 生 病 'each (animal) is sick:' (cf. Arts. 106. 2.)
shı̆-shı̆ k'ŏ-liĕn 實 | 可 憐 'truly to be pitied.'

300. These repetitions must be construed according to the sense of the passage, sometimes as nouns, sometimes as adverbs, and sometimes as expressions of plurality, and very often as the imitation of natural sounds: e. g.—

yiŭ wán-wán 遊 玩 | 'to roam for pleasure.'
mwán-t'iēn tŭ shı̆ sı̄ng-sı̄ng 滿 天 都 是 星 | 'the whole sky is starry.'
siaŭ hă-hă tı̆ 笑 哈 | 的 'laughing with a Ha! ha!'

301. Words expressing cognate notions or commonly associated ideas are placed together, and become phrases in groups of two, three, and four characters each. These are virtually nouns or verbs, general terms, or special designations of objects: e. g.—

k'ai-t'iēn p'ı̆-tı̆ 開 天 闢 地 lit. 'open heaven, split earth,'= *creation.* (1997.)
yên, hı̆ng, túng, tsı̆ng, 言 行 動 靜 'words, ways, and deeds,'= *conduct.*
wù-hú sź-haı̆ 五 湖 四 海 lit. 'the five lakes and the four seas,'= *the world.*
hiaŭ-chán wàn-chán 餚 饌 碗 盞 lit. 'the food and cups,'= *the feast.*
wáng-heŭ wáng-heŭ 望 候 望 | lit. 'to look and wait,'= *to visit friends.*

§. 5. *Uncommon use of certain words in phraseology.*

302. The employment of single words in Chinese is very various, and frequently is quite exceptional, and to be explained only by reference to conventional usage; e. g. in

hŏ-pà 火 把, 'a torch,' we have the noun *fire* and the verb *to hold* united to form a conventional term for *torch.*
k'eŭ-wı̆ 口 味 'taste,' from *mouth* and *to taste.*
k'eŭ-kŭng 口 供 'evidence,' from *mouth* and *to declare.*
fŭng-p'ı̆ 封 皮 'the government confiscation paper posted on the front-door,' from *fŭng* 'to seal,' and *p'ı̆* 'skin, bark.'
shı̄-sheŭ 尸 首 'a corpse,' from *corpse* and *head.*
pŭ jı̆n yên k'ŭ 不 忍 言 去 'cannot bring himself to speak of going,'

lit. 'not suffer to say to go,' where *k'ŭ* 'to go' stands as the object to the verb *yên* 'to speak, talk of.'

sheŭ-î 壽 衣 lit. 'long-life's garments,' or 'the apparel of old age,'=*shroud*.

303. Phrases are often affected by ellipsis, and would according to the ordinary rules of composition appear to be absurd, but, when the customs of the people of China are considered, these phrases become intelligible, and frequently display elegance and vigour of expression : e. g.—

paî-sheŭ 拜 壽 lit. 'to bow to, or worship age,—long life,'=*to pay compliments on a birthday.*

paî-niên 拜 年 lit. 'to worship year,'=*to pay compliments at the new year.*

304. So also many technical and legal terms are formed by an extraordinary use of words, for which the student should be prepared : e. g.—

hô-pǎn 貨 本 'goods for a beginning,'=*capital, funds.*

tŭng-sī 東 西 lit. 'east-west,'=*thing, any thing.*

yuên-kaŭ 原 告 lit. 'origin-accuse,'=*plaintiff.*

pî-kaŭ 被 | lit. 'one being accused,'=*defendant.*

305. The student of Chinese must also expect to meet with very many designations formed by the metaphorical use of words. Such are,—

siŭ-ts'aî 秀 才 lit. 'sprouting talent,'= B. A., the first degree in scholarship.

yŭn-ngŏ 雲 額 lit. 'cloud-forehead,'=*a headband.*

306. In like manner the names for many officers of government are formed by metonomy, using the name of the place, or of the employment : e. g.—

lǎng-chŭng 郎 中 lit. 'pavilion centre,'=*gentleman usher.*

t'ŭng-chī 同 知 lit. 'with-know,' but *chī* is here put for

chī-hiên 知 縣 lit. 'knows the *hien* (town)' or

chī-fŭ 知 府 lit. 'knows the *fu* (city),' therefore *t'ŭng-chī* means 'an assistant of the *chī-hiên* or *chī-fŭ*.' And these are equivalents for 'prefect' or 'mayor.'

307. Many expressions are purely foreign, and, although represented by Chinese characters, those characters are not to be taken in their ordinary sense, but simply as the equivalents for certain foreign sounds : e. g.—

yà-p'iên 鴉 片 'opium.'

pō-lî 玻 璃 'glass,' acc. to Mr. Edkins, from the Sanskrit *sphatika*.

The words referred to in this section are to be employed as compounds, excepting in such a case as *chī-hién*, when the *chī* may stand in another compound for *chī-hién*. This habit of eliding a syllable is common in Chinese *.

§. 6. *The modifications and relations of the parts of speech.*

308. The meanings of words are modified by their connexion with other words. A *noun* may be the expression for a general notion, or an abstract term; or it may be used to designate an individual only. In the expressions ' *man* is mortal,' ' what will *a man* give for his life?' ' *the man* came again,' the word *man* stands in different relations; in the first case it means *mankind;* in the second, *any man* or *every man;* and in the third, *some particular man.* In Europe, grammarians call the words prefixed to the noun, by which the definite and indefinite or general notions are indicated,—*articles*. These articles are in their nature demonstrative pronouns; and accordingly the Chinese use such pronouns when they desire to circumscribe the notion of the noun: e. g.—

jîn=man, mankind; *kó-jîn* 'that man,'=*the man;* *yĭ-kó-jîn* ' a man.'
mà-pĭ 'horses;' *ch'uên-chĕ* 'ships,' (cf. Art. 116.)
kó-chĕ-mà ' the horse;' *nà chĕ ch'uên* ' the ship.'
nǜ-jîn ' woman;' *kó-nǜ-jîn* ' the woman;' *yĭ-kó-nǜ-jîn* ' a woman.'

These are in the colloquial idiom; in the books various words (cf. Arts. 168 and 174) are employed to limit or to render indefinite the substantival notion. For the general term the simple monosyllable is often sufficient in classical composition.

309. It must however be borne in mind that these distinctions in the meaning and use of words are not confined to the noun. Chinese verbs are used in a general sense or with a special application according to the form of the sentence or to the circumstances of their position and the addition of certain particles or adjuncts. If the student will refer to Arts. 189 &c. on the verb, and will compare them with the examples here given, he will obtain a clearer idea of these remarks than by the following examples alone. In Art. 301. *yên-hìng-tûng-tsĭng,* ' words, ways, and deeds,' for the whole *conduct*, illustrates this remark. The words mean literally ' to speak, to act, to move, to rest.' *Tûng-tsĭng* especially is an expression for a general term, the scope of which is indicated by the two opposite terms of *moving* and *resting* implied by its component parts. In epistolary correspondence, and in the style of the classics, such forms of expression are common : e. g. in the preface to the *Shing-yü* or ' Sacred Edict' we have

  ĭ - chĭ - yü kāng-sāng tsŏ - sĭ chī kiēn
以 至 於 畊 桑 作 息 之 間
' Even to that which concerns the culture of the land and the mulberry and labour in general.'

---

* As the examples, which will be given in what follows, will be made up generally of words previously used in this work, the characters belonging to them will not be printed, excepting those not likely to be known by the ordinary student.

310. Verbs formed in the manner described in Art. 200, belong to those used in a general sense, or as abstract terms, and they may stand as the subjects of simple sentences, or as the *result* or *purpose* in a compound sentence: e. g. in the expressions *tŭ-shŭ shí yaú-kīn-tĭ* 'to read is important,' *nĭ k'ŏ-ĭ tŭ-shŭ mô?* 'Can you read?' the word *read* is used in a general sense independent of any special act of reading. Again, in *t'ā laí tŭ-shŭ*, 'he comes (or came) to read,' the word *tŭ-shŭ* expresses a purpose; and in *yúng sīn tsiŭ k'ŏ-ĭ tŭ shŭ*, 'take pains and then you will be able to read,' it expresses a result. When such expressions as *tŭ-shŭ* 'to read,' *siĕ-tsz̆* 'to write,' *kĭ-fán* 'to eat rice,' *k'aī ch'uên* 'to sail,' *haí-jīn* 'to injure,' *shĕ-tsuī* 'to forgive,' are used in construction in the sentence, except in cases such as the above, the nouns compounded with them are dropped or separated from the verbal element. Thus: *t'ā tŭ-liaù sān-pặn-(shŭ)* 'he has read three volumes.' But *tŭ* is also a special word for *studying* books: *nĭ tŭ-kwó Sz̆-shŭ mô?* 'Have you read the Four books?' that is, 'Have you studied them thoroughly?' To *read* simply is, *k'ān* 'to look at.' The uses of such words will be found exemplified in the exercises, which follow the grammar.

311. The union of opposite terms has already been referred to in Arts. 117, 118, and there it was shown that two nouns of opposite significa- tion form a *general* term; and that two adjectives in a similar way form an *abstract* noun. The same may be said of two verbs which represent two opposite notions; e. g. *to labour,—to rest*, gives the general or indefinite notion of *labouring,—working*.

312. The position marks the *nominative* case of the noun. Any word which stands before the verb may be the subject of that verb, unless it be inconsistent with the sense of the passage to construe it as such. In any other case it would be an adverbial expression, or as it were the accusative case placed absolutely, denoting the thing or part affected by the verb: e. g. (cf. Arts. 91, 92, 93, and 198, for the characters; and Hom. Od. a, 274, for acc. abs.)—

k'ĕ-jīn tseù-k'aī, pŭ chūng-i k'ī-ch'ā
'The guest walked away, he was not pleased to drink tea.'
hw'á-kūng wặn-kiēn ch'aī-jīn tĭ shwŏ-hwá, tsiŭ pŭ hwān-hĭ
'The painter heard the messenger's words, and (then) was displeased.'
ī-fŭ yĕ táng-wān-liaù 'clothes, even they were pawned.'

313. The *genitive* case is also shown in most cases by the position of the word before the noun to which it belongs, and very frequently by the pre- sence of the particle *tĭ* 的 between them, or *chī* 之 if it be in the literary style: e. g.—

t'iĕ-tsiáng tĭ nŭ-ặr 'the blacksmith's daughter.'
kiă-fŭ tĭ kwặn-tsz̆ 'the courier's cudgel.'
mà-fŭ tĭ siāng-tsz̆ 'the groom's box.'
mà-kiă or *mà chī kiă* 'the horse's foot.'
siēn-sāng chī hiūng 'the teacher's brother,' or 'the gentleman's brother.'

314. The *dative* case is shown by the use of certain verbs which signify *to give, to offer*. Such are *kĭ* 給 and *sŭng* 送 and *yŭ* 與, the two first being used in the colloquial idiom, the other in the book style*: e. g.—

kĭ nĭ fán k'ĭ 'give rice to you to eat.'
kĭ ngò tsŏ chê-kó 'do this for me.'
sŭng yŭ t'ā yĭ-kweí yáng-tsʻiên 'to present a dollar to him.'
kiáng yŭ jĭn-jĭn 'to speak to every body.'

315. Other words, which are commonly used as prepositions, supply the want of case in the noun. Article 257 contains almost all the words which are employed for this purpose. But as they are to be regarded as prepositions or postpositions, we must refer the student to the syntax of that part of speech.

316. The *accusative* case is shown merely by the position of the word after its verb, or between the parts of a separable verb: e. g.—

ngò kiaŭ-liaŭ kó jĭn laí 'I have called the man here.'
k'ĕ-shāng pŭ yaú maí ch'á 'the merchant does not wish to buy tea.'
siēn-sāng ch'ĭ fán liaŭ 'the teacher has eaten the rice,'—(*has dined*.)

317. The *vocative* case is distinguished by being cut off from the rest of the sentence, either by the addition of a particle of exclamation, by the repetition of the word or the appropriate pronoun, or by the sense of the passage and the context: e. g.—

Laŭ-yê-ya! k'ŏ-liên ngò, 'O Sir! pity me!'
siaŭ-ár! nĭ pŭ-yaú k'ŭ, 'Boy! weep not!'
Châng-ngó! Châng-ngó! nĭ, 'O Luna! Luna! you &c.' †

Cf. Mr. Wade's *Hsin-tsing-lŭ*, Category of *T'iên*, [5.]

318. The *ablative* and the *locative* and *instrumental* cases will be found fully exemplified under the Articles on the syntax of the prepositions. Two or three examples may here be given:—

From (a place) is expressed by *tsʻŭng*, 'to follow,' or *tsź;* e. g.—
t'ā shí tsʻŭng Sháng-haí laí tĭ 'he is from Shanghai.'

With (instrumental) is translated by *yúng*, 'to use,' or *ĭ;* e. g.—
ngò yúng niuŭ-tsʻiāng, tă t'ā, 'I struck him with a gun,' i. e. *I shot him.*

By or *through* (causal) is expressed by *yĭn-weí* or *weí-tsź* 'on account of;'—
t'ā tau-k'ŭ, yĭn-weí yiŭ p'â, 'he fled through fear,' lit. 'because he had fear.'

319. The modifications of the noun with regard to *gender* and *number* are seldom made. When this is done, special words are employed to mark the gender of the noun, and certain adjuncts are used to show the plurality. Some of these words will be found in Arts. 123—128. The following are examples of the use of such words:—

---

* *tĭ* 替 and *taí* 代 are used to translate *for*, (instead of.)
† Vide J. G. Bridgman's translation of Premare's *Notitia Linguæ Sinicæ*, p. 29.

yiŭ nân-jĭn, yiŭ nŭ-jĭn shắng-hiả sān-pă-kó, 'there were men and there were women, about three hundred.'

nĭ tĭ chĭ-nŭ laĭ mô? 'Is your niece come?'

kīn-t'iēn tă-liĕ, tă-shă yĭ-chĕ kūng-chū, 'to-day in hunting, (we) killed a boar.'

K'ŭng-tsż tẵng mŭ-yiŭ liăng-kó, or *mŭ-yiŭ liắng-kó K'ŭng-tsż,* 'there are not two of the Confucius sort.'

320. Examples of the use of the plural particles and adjuncts, given in Arts. 126 and 127, now follow:—

chúng-jĭn hwán wĭ-kĭ tă-yíng 'before the men had replied;' v. Chrest. *Haŭ-k'iŭ,* p. 11. b. 10.

chŭ-wei siēn-sāng! 'Gentlemen!'

shŭ-min (B.) = *pă-sĭng-mận* (coll.) 'the people.'

chŭ-siēn-sāng kiaĭ wŭ píng 'none of the teachers are ill.'

hŭ-tō jĭn pŭ k'ŏ-ĭ tă-hŏ-ts'iāng 'many men cannot shoot.'

chê-ti-hiŭng-mận 'your brothers' (often); v. *Hsin-tsing-lŭ, Shing-yŭ.* [19.]

nĭ-mận píng-min-mận 'you, soldiers and people.' [39.]

chúng-shin kŏ yiŭ sò kwăn tĭ sż-tsĭng 'each of the gods has his own affairs to manage.' [358.]

pă-sĭng-mận sò paĭ tĭ kŏ-chŭ-ạr, pŭ t'ŭng, 'the places where the people worship are various,' lit. 'each place not the same.'

pĭng-min-jĭn tẵng 'soldiers and people all.'

321. Further examples to illustrate the plural particles in Arts. 126, 127:—

jĭn-kiaĭ chĭ tsż 'all men know this.'

kiūn-chīn kiaĭ kŭ 'the prince and the minister both wept;' v. *San-kwŏ,* p. 18. d. 12.

k'ŭ-kŏ t'ŭng-k'ŭ 'all and each wept bitterly;' v. *San-kwŏ,* p. 18. k. 25.

jŭ-hiēn ts'ŭng chī 'the scholars all followed him.'

shŭ-hwán-ch'ăn-shwŏ 'all obstinate detractors;' v. *Shu-king,* p. 1. i. 23.

nŭng-fŭ kūng-tsiáng tằng 'husbandmen and artisans.'

shí yiŭ hwán-kwān Tsaŭ-tsĭ tằng 'at that time there were the eunuchs of Tsau-tsĭ's party;' v. *San-kwŏ,* Litho. p. 11. g. 13.

Tàng[a], *peĭ*[b], *lui*[c], *tsĭ*[d], *tsaŭ*[e], and *cheŭ*[f] are all used after nominal notions to express plurality,—*a class* or *party:* e. g.—

ŏ-peĭ 'the wicked;' *ts'iĕn peĭ* 'predecessors,' *heŭ-peĭ* 'successors.'

wáng[g]-*ĭ chī peĭ* 'those who forget right principle.'

t'ŭng-peĭ chī jĭn 'men of the same class,' i. e. *equals.*

kwān-tsaŭ, 'officers, mandarins,' (not commonly used.)

fī[h]-*lui* or *fĭ-t'ŭ*[i] 'vagabonds;' *wŭ-tsĭ,* 'we,' belongs to the literary style.

chŭ-fắn wŭ-kién 'the universe of things,'—*all things.*

yiŭ-sò-tsż-wŭ k'ŭ pŭ sheŭ 有所賜物俱不受 lit. 'the things that were given, all he did not receive,' i. e. *he received none of the things that were given.*

[a] 等 [b] 輩 [c] 類 [d] 儕 [e] 曹 [f] 儔 [g] 忘 [h] 匪 [i] 徒

MODIFICATION OF THE ATTRIBUTE. 109

Tŏ 多, 'many,' sometimes follows the noun to which it belongs: e. g.—
Chūng-kwŏ jin tō ch'ŭ wai-fâng 'many Chinese go abroad.'

322. A few of the ordinary phrases denoting plurality, or the whole group or collection of objects, may here be given. The Chinese in naming certain classes of things have attached a number to the generic term, according as they conceived the genus to be divided into more or fewer species; and these expressions have come to mean the whole class accordingly: e. g. they say—

*sān-kwāng*ᵃ 'the three lights,' i. e. *sun, moon, and stars.*
*sān-tsai*ᵇ 'the three powers,' i. e. *heaven, earth, and man.*
*sān-kiaú*ᶜ 'the three religions,' i. e. *jŭ*ᵈ, *shi*ᵉ, *taú*ᶠ, 'Confucius, Buddhist, and Tauist.'
*sź-kí*ᵍ 'the four seasons,' i. e. *chūn, hiâ, ts'iú, tūng,* 'spring, summer, autumn, and winter.'
wù-hîng 'the five elements,' i. e. *kīn, mŭ, shwuí, hŏ, t'ŏ,* 'metal, wood, water, fire, and earth.'
wù-lŭn 'the five relations of life,' i. e. between *kiūn* and *chin, fú* and *tsź, fū* and *fú, hiūng* and *tí, pâng* and *yiù,* '1. Prince and subject, 2. father and son, 3. husband and wife, 4. elder and younger brothers, and 5. friends.'
wù-k'ŭ 'the five kinds of grain;' *wù-tsiŏ* 'the five degrees of nobility.'
wù-wí 'the five tastes,' i. e. *sour, sweet, bitter, acrid, and salt.*
wù-châng 'the five virtues,'—*jin, í, li, chí, sin,* i. e. *benevolence, justice, propriety, prudence, and truth.*
lŭ-í 'the six arts,'—*li, yŏ, she, yü, shū, sú,* i. e. *etiquette, music, archery, driving a carriage, writing, and arithmetic.*
tsī-tsing 'the seven passions or emotions,'—*hí, nú, gai, lŏ, ngai, wú, yü,* i. e. *joy* (external), *anger, grief, delight* (internal), *love, hatred, desire.*
pā-kwā 'the eight diagrams,' the theme of the *Yí-king.*
kiù-t'iēn 'the nine heavens;' and *kiù-cheŭ* 'the nine islands,' for *the world.*
wán-tí 'all the virtues,' and *wán-shí* 'all ages.'

They also sometimes express multitude by using adverbially such terms as *swarms of insects, vast forests, oceans, seas, mountains,* &c.: v. Art. 288. (3.)

323. The modifications of *adjectives*, in respect of *degree*, are very various, and are effected by the addition of certain words and particles to the adjective. No alteration however can be made in the adjective to show the distinctions of gender, number, and person. It stands generally *before* its noun, either immediately, or it is connected with it by the particle *tí* 的 (c.) or *chī* 之 (B.) being placed between them. Some adjectives seem to require these particles, either to avoid ambiguity in the expression, or for the sake of the rhythm; e. g. *shén-jin* 'a virtuous man,' not *shén-chī-jin,* but *kūng-taú tí jin*

ᵃ 光 ᵇ 才 ᶜ 教 ᵈ 儒 ᵉ 釋 ᶠ 道 ᵍ 季

'a just man.' The rule given in Art. 132 should be observed, that when a verb enters into the composition of the adjective, the *tĭ* or *chī* is required.

324. Examples of the construction of adjectives *.
ché-lĭ, tsiĕn-shwuĭ, 'here it is shallow water.'
t'ā-tĭ kién-shĭ ª, *ts'iĕn,* 'his knowledge is superficial.'
lĭng-lĭ-tĭ jĭn or *ts'ŭng-mĭng-tĭ jĭn* 'a clever man.'
k'iaù-miaú-tĭ tsiáng-kūng 'a dexterous artisan.'
sŭ-pā-tĭ chī 'snow-white paper.'
pīng-liâng-tĭ shwuĭ 'icy-cold water.'
tá-tàn-tĭ haú-kī ᵇ 'a brave hero.'
kūng-taú-tĭ hwâng-tí 'a righteous emperor.'
wặn-yà tĭ siĕn-sāng 'a scholar of great attainments and polish.'
ché-kó-tsź tsīng-sí-tĭ siĕ 'these characters are written with elegance.'
k'ŏ-lién-tĭ jĭn-kiā 'a miserable individual.'
k'ŏ-yúng-tĭ fă-tsĕ̆ ᶜ 'a method which may be used.'
haù-yúng-tĭ niaù-ts'iāng ᵈ 'a useful fowling-piece.'
haù-siaú-tĭ sź-tsīng ᵉ 'a laughable affair.'
ché-lĭ hwān-hĭ-tĭ tí-fāng 'this is a pleasant place.'
ché-kó siaù-ạr hwŏ-túng-tĭ 'this boy is active.'
t'ā yiù yiù-t'ŭng-ts'iên tĭ pâng-yiù 'he has rich friends.'
tsź jĭn yiù lĭ-k'ĭ-tĭ 'this man is strong.'
mŭ-yiù liàng-sīn-tĭ 'a man without a conscience.'
shĭ yiù-haù-i-sź-tĭ '*he* is a well-intentioned person.'
ché-kó tūng-sī shĭ chĭ tĭ 'this thing is *made of* paper.'
pŭ shĭ, shĭ mŭ-tsŏ-tĭ, 'no, it is made of wood.'
shĭ jĭn-hặn-tĭ kwān-fú 'he is a hated mandarin.'
tsź sź shĭ jĭn-k'ŏ-hặn-tĭ 'this affair is hateful.'
pŭ-siāng-kān-tĭ 'it is of no consequence,'—'*n'importe.*'
kīn-t'iēn t'ā pŭ shwâng-kwaí-tĭ 'to-day he is unwell.'
Chūng-kwŏ, Ying-kwŏ, pŭ-hŏ-mŭ-tĭ, 'China and England are inimical *to each other.*'

325. The *comparison* of the adjective can best be shown by means of examples. For the auxiliary adjuncts the student may refer to Arts. 144, 145, and 148—150.
ché-kó haù-tĭ, nà-kó kāng-haù-tĭ, 'this is good, *but* that is better;' and *nà-kó kāng-kiā-haù* 'and that is better still.'
ngŏ tsŏ-t'iēn maí kāng-kiā-paú-peí-tĭ tūng-sī 'I bought a still more precious thing yesterday.'
nĭ pĭ t'ā kaū 'you are taller than he is.'
t'ā pŭ jŭ-nĭ kaū 'he is not so tall as you,' or
t'ā mŭ-yiù nĭ-kaū 'he has not your height.'

* For the words the student may refer to Arts. 133—142, p. 55.

ª 見識   ᵇ 豪傑   ᶜ 法則   ᵈ 鳥鎗   ᵉ 事情

nằ-kó haù nī 'this is better!' lit. 'this is good!' We must suppose some one making a selection, and taking up one article, which he conceives to be superior to the rest.

pŭ haù tĭ tŏ, haù tĭ shaù, lit. 'the not good are many, the good, few,' which is equivalent to 'there are more bad ones than good ones.'

326. The expression of the comparative degree is further effected by means of the words yiŭ 'again, more,' and tsaí 'again,' hwăn 'still, besides,' yŭ 'to pass over,' yŭ 'to exceed,' and some others of a similar meaning: cf. Art. 148.

Examples.

yŭ-tsaù-yŭ-haù 'the earlier the better;' yŭ is used in the same way, but not often in speaking.

hô k'aĭ-liaù k'eù-tsz̀, hiá-yŭ yiŭ tŏ, 'when the river had overflowed its banks, the rain fell still more.'

mŭ-yiù tsaí sĭ-tĭ 'there is no finer.'

pŭ náng pì ché-kó sĭ-tĭ 'you cannot get finer than this.'

yaù-ch'uên hwăn yaŭ kw'aí 'row faster.'

ngò k'ān t'ā pì pĭ-jin tŭ chúng 'I look upon him as certainly more honest than other men;' chúng = 'heavy,'—'well-principled.'

fŭ tá liáng tá 'the greater his fortune, the greater his bounty.'

ngĕ waí kiā siū 額 外 加 修 'give a higher salary,' lit. 'allowance beyond add recompense.' Hsin-tsing-lŭ, Part III. 22.

kāng k'í chùng-liaù 更 氣 腫 了 'the more inflamed it swells.' Hsin-tsing-lŭ, P. III. 29. The chùng-liaù in this place is like the impersonal in Latin.

Most of these sentences might be otherwise translated in respect of form, but no difference in meaning would arise therefrom.

327. The form for the limitation of the quality of the adjective is the following. Various words may be used for *rather*.

maì kweĭ yĭ siē 'bought it rather dear.'

tù-liáng tièn ặr 'a little more generous.'

nā yĭ-kó twàn yĭ ch'ĭ 'that one is shorter by a foot.'

328. The word in Chinese forms of comparison which seems to take the place of *than* in English is yŭ 於: e. g.—

tsiù haù yŭ shwuí 'wine is better than water,' or

tsiù pì shwuí kāng haù would express the same, although it is not so exact as the former, for in it the goodness of both is implied, which might not be true of some other articles under comparison.

shīn yŭ haì 'deeper than the sea' (B.).

jin feŭ yŭ sź 'men more than work *for them*' (B.); feŭ 'to float,'—'to exceed.'

於 yŭ has the sense of 'with respect to,' and so 'in comparison with;' v. Arts. on the particles, and the examples in the exercises.

329. In Arts. 146 and 151—154 the student will find the forms of the *superlative* degree, and it remains only to give here a few examples of their usage. The various degrees of the superlative are shown by the same words, which must be translated by *most, very, too,* according to the sense required by the context: e. g.—

t'ā tĭ hing-weí tĭng-pŭ-haù 'his actions are very bad.'

haù k'ĭ-kwʻaí yĕ (他) 'very wonderful' (B.).

haù pŭ k'ù yĕ 'very much afflicted;' this expression, in which *pŭ* 不, 'not,' intensifies, is equivalent to *shĭ-fān k'ù tĭ;* and *mŭ* 沒, 'to be without,' is sometimes substituted for *pŭ* in such phrases. The adjective with the negative before it must be looked upon as one word, and the negative particle then stands as a privative particle; e. g. *haù mŭ-liáng-sīn* is 'very wanting in conscience,' not 'well may he have no conscience,' as translated after Premare by Bridgman *. The other examples given by Premare prove this view to be correct,—for *wû* 無, 'without,' is used occasionally in the same sense: thus—

nĭ haù mŭ-taú-lĭ 'you are very unreasonable.'

haù wû-pā[a]*-pi*[b] 'entirely without method,' or 'very unmethodical.'

k'ĭ ts'ūng-ming shīn pŭ shĭng[c] 'his intelligence is quite unsurpassable.'

tĭ-mŭ t'aí ch'ŭ yûng-ì 'the theme turns out to be a very easy one.' The *ch'ŭ* here belongs to the *yûng-ì; tĭ-mŭ* is the subject, the remainder the predicate of the sentence.

330. It may be observed that the particles which form the superlative are very frequently suffixed instead of being prefixed,—and this is especially the case in the books, and in the higher colloquial style; e. g.—

meí shĭ shīn kĭ 'a very beautiful countenance.' (1700, 1071.)

k'ò-gaí shīn ì (矣) 'very amiable.'

331. Examples of the superlative with *t'aí* 太, *t'ĕ* 忒, and *kwó* 過 are the following:—

pŭ yaú t'aí k'iĕn[d] 'do not be too modest.'

chê kĭ t'aí hièn[e] 'this plan *is* too dangerous.'

hiá sheù t'ĕ hĭn-liaù 'it is struck too much,' this is the impersonal form,
  but it is equivalent to 'you struck me too hard.'

t'ĕ tsīng-sì liaù 'it is too delicate.'

nĭ yĕ t'ĕ tŏ sīn 'you are a person of too much heart.'

tsiù t'ĕ k'ĭ kĭ liaù 'the wine—it was drunk too quickly.' (1068, 1074.)

wăn-lĭ pŭ shīn t'ŭng-t'eŭ[f] 'in learning not very profound.'

sīng-ts'ing kwó ngaú 'he is too proud;' *sīng-ts'ing*='temper, mind.'

---

* Vide Bridgman's translation of Premare's *Notitia Linguæ Sinicæ*, p. 83.

[a] 把 [b] 鼻 [c] 孵 [d] 謙 [e] 險 [f] 通透

332. The following expressions illustrate the use of *kí* 極, *tsŭ* 絕, *tsüí* 最, and *hản* 狠 :—

chè-kó shí k'ò-siaù-kí-liaù 'this is most laughable.'
kí-tá yǐ-tsó-miaú 'a very large temple.'
kí-k'iaù-tǐ hwā-kūng 'a most clever painter.'
kí-mŭ-k'iaù [a] *-tǐ hwá* 'most unintelligible language.' *k'iaú* (1129).
tsŭ wú kī-hwuí [b], lit. 'entirely without opportunity.' Mr. Bridgman has rendered it 'exceedingly unfortunate.'
tsüí-kaŭ sheù-twān [c] 'very skilful.' *kaŭ* 'high.'
miaú pŭ-k'ò-yên 'wonderful, unspeakably.'
hản-shīn-tǐ tsìng 'a very deep well.'
tsŭ-miaú, tsŭ-miaú, 'very good! very good!'
shí kó tsŭ-miaú-tǐ fă-tsż 'it is a most admirable plan;' v. *Shing-yü*, p. 7. h. 24, &c.

333. The phrases *shí-fān* and *tí-yǐ, pŭ-shǐng, pŭ-kwò,* and *liaù-pŭ-tí* (v. Arts. 151 and 153) should be remembered as adjuncts to form the superlative notion: e. g.—

sāng-tǐ shí-fān ts'ing-siú [d] 'born very well-favoured.'
pŭ tá-shí-fān-haù 'not very very good.'
tí-yǐ miaú 'very wonderful;' cf. Americanism *first-rate*.
* *shí-ạr-fān jìn ts'aî* [e] 'very beautiful in countenance;' so
wù-fān haù means 'five parts good,'—'pretty good,' and
kí-fān haù 'several parts good,'—'in some degree good.'
pŭ-shíng hì-hwān, lit. 'not conquer joy,'—'extremely glad;' or
hì pŭ-tsź-shǐng, lit. 'joyful not conquer himself,' like ἔκστασις.
hì-hwān liaù-pŭ-tǐ 'most joyful,' lit. 'cannot end his joy.'
hwān-hì wú-sò-pŭ-kǐ [f], lit. 'joy—interminable.'
tsüí k'ù pŭ-kwó 'most miserable beyond compare.'
kūng-taú pŭ-kwó-tǐ 'surpassing just.'
kw'ai-sŭ [g] *mò* [h] *kwó yü tsż* 'insurpassably swift.' (B.)
cheŭ-ŏ shīn-pŭ-shǐng 'desperately wicked.'
ts'ản-niŏ wú yú yü tsż 殘虐無踰于此 'incomparably cruel.' (B.)

334. There are other phrases and words used for the purpose of intensifying the attribute, but these will be found under the section on the particles and in other parts of this work. The following however must come in here (cf. Arts. 152 and 153 for the characters used) :—

hiūng tǐ lí-haì 'most cruel;' (*tǐ* 'to obtain,' or *ti* the gen. pa.)
nǐ yè shă laù-shí liaù 'you are too honest;' (*ye* 'also,' the fin. pa.)
t'ān tsiù kwó-tō 'he is too fond of wine.'

---

* *shí-fān* meaning 'ten parts,' which is like saying the whole of any thing. *shí-ạr-fān* would mean 'twelve parts,' and be a stronger intensifier than *shí-fān*.

[a] 竅 [b] 機會 [c] 手叚 [d] 清秀 [e] 材
[f] 及 [g] 快速 [h] 莫

ch'aŭ-kiŭn 超羣 lit. 'to surpass the common herd.'

chŏ-li 卓立 lit. 'to establish as pre-eminent.'

chŏ-tsŭ | 絶 lit. 'to surpass exceedingly.'

chŏ-yŭ | 越 lit. 'surpassing excellent.'

chŭ-lŭi 出類 lit. 'to stand out from his class.'

sai-kwó 賽過 lit. 'to excel and overpass.'

sai-shing | 勝 lit. 'to excel and conquer.'

tsŭi-kwei 罪魁 lit. 'sin's chief,'—'chief of sinners.'

ŏ-kwei 惡 | lit. 'wicked head,'—'the most wicked.'

kai-shi 蓋世 lit. 'cover age,'—'the most eminent of his age.'

These expressions do not occur in common conversation, but are used with elegance in literary composition.

335. The measure of a thing, as regards *number*, is denoted by the numeral being placed before the noun, with the proper appositive between them, or by placing the numeral and the appositive after the noun, thus *sān-pĭ-mă* or *mă sān-pĭ* is 'three horses,' *sź-chĕ-ch'uên* or *ch'uên-sź-chĕ* 'four ships,' *yĭ-kiĕn kŭ-kwai tĭ sź-tsing* 'a strange affair;' and when it refers to *quantity* it is expressed by the numeral and some special word denoting the measure of quantity, and these are placed after the noun to which they apply (cf. 287): e. g.—

sān-sź-kó-jĭn yĭn-liaŭ sān-wŭ-pei-tsiŭ 'three or four men drank from three to five cups of wine.'

ngò yaŭ mai ĭ-chăng sān-t'aŭ 'I wish to buy three suits of clothes.'

tiŭ-pĭ[a] *sān-niên, yĭ-tān t'ŭng-li*[b], 'separated for three years, on a sudden we are united.' (Prov. and Epistolary.)

336. The following examples will show how numbers are constituted and modified:—

sān-sź-kó 'three or four;' *shĭ sź-wŭ kó* 'fourteen or fifteen;'
wŭ-lŭ-shĭ kó 'fifty or sixty;' *lŭ tsĭ ts'iĕn* 'six or seven thousand;'
tsĭ pă mán 'seventy or eighty thousand.'

337. It should be noted that a *point* of time is placed first generally, but not before the subject of the sentence, and especially if this be a pronoun; and that *duration* of time is placed after the expression to which it belongs: e. g.—

ngò tsŏ-t'iĕn tŭ-shŭ liaŭ 'I read yesterday.'

t'ā tŭ-shŭ sān-t'iĕn 'he has read for three days.'

---

[a] 丟別   [b] 旦同列

THE SYNTAX OF PROPER NAMES. 115

nì ts'ién-jì pŭ laì 'you did not come the day before yesterday.'
ts'ién-sān-t'iēn t'ā pŭ-shì ché-yáng 'three days ago he was not so.'
ts'ién-sān-t'iēn t'ā pŭ k'ï-fán 'three days ago he would not eat.'
t'ā pŭ k'ï-fán yiù sź-t'iēn 'he has not eaten any thing for four days.'
ts'ién-sān-t'iēn t'ā sź-liaù 'he died three days ago.'
t'ā sź-liaù sān-t'iēn 'he has been dead three days.'

338. The measures of *length* or *breadth*, *weight* or *quantity* of any kind are put after the verb:—

kó-tsĕ p'aù-ch'ŭ shì lī liaù 'the robber ran ten *li**.' (2826, 1919.)
ché yĭ-tiaŭ-hô k'wān-tĭ yĭ-lī-lŭ 'this river is one *li* wide.'
nì laì-tĭ-ch'ĭ yĭ-tiēn-chŭng 'you came late by *an* hour.'
ché-yĭ-tsó-t'ā kaŭ-tĭ shì cháng 'this pagoda is ten *cháng** high.' (2529.)

339. Many measures of *time*, *space*, *weight*, &c., are used as appositives, and then stand in the place of the appositive, between the numeral and the noun: e. g.—

lŭ tsĭ meù t'iēn 'a six or seven acre field.' (1710.)
yĭ tān mĭ 'a pecul of rice.' (2559.)
wŭ t'iēn shĭ-heŭ 'a period of five days.' (584.)
t'ā k'ï-liaù sān-wān-fán 'he has eaten three bowls of rice.' (饭碗.)
See Appendix for the tables of times, weights, and measures.

340. The syntax of proper names and their relative positions may here be noticed, and the student may refer to Art. 121 for the same subject.

The name of an individual consists of his *sĭng*, the name of his family (*gens*), which is commonly but one syllable, and is placed *first*; and then follows his *mĭng* (*cognomen*), which is generally dissyllabic: e. g. in

T'ang Hiŏ-hiun, *T'ang* is the name for the whole *gens*, and *Hiŏ-hiun*, the name (*cognomen*) for the individual of that *gens*.

Sometimes in books the word *shì* 氏, 'family,' is added after the *sĭng*, but only when the *mĭng* is omitted. In asking a person's name we should always enquire what his *sĭng* is, and then address him by that name with the appropriate addition of *siēn-sāng* or *siāng-kŭng*, &c.: e. g.—

Siēn-sāng, kaŭ sĭng á? 'Sir, your eminent name?'
siaù sĭng Li 'my insignificant name is Lee.'
Li siēn-sāng k'ò haù má? 'How do you do Mr. Lee?'

No distinction is made by the Chinese between the name of the clan (*gens*) and the name of the family (*familia*), but the name of the whole *gens* is attributed to each individual. It will be seen that the Chinese and the Roman order of announcing the names is similar; first the *nomen*, then the *cognomen*; first the *sĭng*, then the *mĭng*. In his writings the author uses his *mĭng* by way of humility, but in addressing any one worthy of respect the *sĭng* is invariably used. The *tsź* 子 or 'title' is taken by every youth of education

---

* A *li* = 1897½ feet English, or 27¾ *li* = 10 miles English; and a *cháng* = 10 *ch'ĕ*, or 141 inches English.

Q 2

on attaining his majority. In writing this follows the other two names. In addition to these there is a name given to honour the dead, this is called the *huuí* 諡 ('to respect'); and if it be in honour of a great man, or of an emperor, the expression is *miaú-haú* 廟號 'temple designation,' because the memorials of such persons are preserved in the temple of ancestors, like the images of the Roman ancestors in the *atrium* *.

341. All the *titles of honour and of office* precede the *sing*, which is used alone in such cases : e. g. *Kīn-ch'ai, Tá-chīn, Pīng-pú Shǎng-shū, Liàng-Hú Tsùng-tǔ, Līn*, i. e. lit. 'Imperial Commissioner, Minister of State, a President of the Board of War, and Governor of the Two-Hu ('lake') Provinces,—*Lin*:' (cf. the notes upon the Chinese text in page 23 of the Chrestomathy.) This rule does not however hold good with respect to the terms *siēn-sāng* 'teacher,' *siāng-kūng* 'Sir,' and such expressions of civility; these invariably follow the *sing*.

342. The names of places in China are all significant, although, as with European local names, the meaning is seldom thought of: e. g. *Kiāng-sī* 'the river's west,' *Hú-nân* 'the lake's south,' are names of provinces. But the names of foreign places and persons are given in a changed form, according as the Chinese are able to pronounce them †: e. g. *Ying-kă-li* for 'England;' *Fă-lan-si* for 'France;' *Ngo-lo-sz* for 'Russia;' *Lạn-tạn* for 'London.' 'Alexander' would be *A-lǎ-shan-ta-ạr* in Chinese; 'Elgin,' *E-ạr-kin*. But foreigners in China generally choose a Chinese family name (*sing*), which is like the first open syllable of their own surname, and they adopt this for their surname: e. g. 'Mr. Hobson' might use *Ho*; 'Mr. Cave,' *Ka* or *Kai*; 'Mr. Brown,' *Lau* or *Lo*.

343. The names of *cities* and *towns* are simply the names of the provinces or districts of which they are the chief places: e. g. *Shún-t'iēn-fù*, i. e. 'chief place of the department of *Shún-t'iēn* is Peking.' The word *Pě-kīng* means the 'northern capital,' just as *Nán-kīng* means the 'southern capital.' *Kwàng-cheū-fù*, i. e. 'chief place of the department of *Kwàng-cheū* is Canton,' a word which is a corruption of *Kwàng-tūng*, written by the Portuguese in former times *Can-ton*.

344. The names of *countries, islands, rivers, mountains*, are followed by the words *kwǒ*[a] 'kingdom;' *t'aù*[b] or *cheǔ*[c] or *sǔ*[d] 'island;' *kiāng*[e] or *hô*[f] 'river;' *shān*[g] or *ling*[h] 'mountain or peak:' e. g. *Jǐ-pạ̀n kwǒ* 'Japan;' *Yīng-kǎ-lǐ-kwǒ* or *Ying-kwǒ* or *Tá-ying-kwǒ* 'England,' put for 'Great

---

* M. Bazin says, in his *Grammaire Mandarine*, p. 2, that there are two thousand three hundred different family names given in the "Universal Biography." This is a large Chinese work called the *Shǐ-sing-p'ǔ*, i. e. 'Records of families,' a copy of which is preserved in the Royal Asiatic Society's Library.

† This is similar to the French pronunciation of foreign words: e. g. *Grenvish* for *Greenwich*.

[a] 國 [b] 島 [c] 洲 [d] 嶼 [e] 江 [f] 河 [g] 山 [h] 嶺

THE CONSTRUCTION OF PRONOUNS. 117

Britain;' *Kiau-i-cheü* commonly called 'Green Island' (near Hongkong); *Tàng-lûng-cheü*, i. e. 'Kellet's Island;' *Chŭ-sŭ* 'Bamboo Island;' *Hĕ-shān* 'Black mountain;' *Mei-ling* 'Plum-peak or ridge' (to the north of Canton).

345. The construction of *pronouns* now claims our attention. In their isolated state, without the addition of any grammatical particle, their position alone will show the case to which they belong: e. g. in *t'ā t'ŭng-nì yaú k'ŭ́*, 'he wants to go with you,' the pronoun *t'ā* must be in the nominative case, and the pronoun *nì* in the accusative after *t'ŭng:*

t'ā pŭ hwān-lì nì 'he does not like you:' *t'ā* is nom.; *nì*, acc.

346. The *personal pronoun* is frequently omitted in Chinese: when it is expressed its position shows the case in which it must be construed; if before the verb, it will almost always be in the nominative case; if after the verb, in the accusative. The words used for the pronoun of the first person vary according to the style of the composition in which they occur. Some of these distinctions will be seen by referring to Arts. 164, 165, and 179, where the characters will be found.

ngò yaú nì t'ŭng-ngò k'ŭ́ 'I want you to go with me.'
pŭ yaú t'ŭng-nì k'ŭ́ 'I will not go with you.'
nì tà ngò, pŭ-haù 'you strike me and do wrong,' or 'in striking me, you do wrong.'

In the books the student may expect to find the pronoun occasionally placed before the verb as the object of the verb, not the subject; e. g. in the Lun-yu of Confucius—

pŭ ngù chī 不 吾 知 lit. 'not me know,' 'when I am unrecognised.'
ngò shuí k'ì 我 誰 欺 lit. 'I whom insult,' 'whomsoever I insult.'

347. The nature of the expression enables the Chinese sometimes to dispense with the pronoun; e. g.—

kaū sìng á? '*Your* great name Sir?'
kiù wán taī-hiūng '*I* have long heard of *you* Sir.'
kĭ sź yĭ-hwüí '*I* have ardently desired a meeting *with you;*' v. *Haú-k'iŭ-chuên* (1), p. 8. h. 20 and 28.

348. The designation of the person is frequently used for the personal pronoun:—

Li siēn-sāng k'ò haù má? 'Are *you* well, Mr. Lee?' (v. Art. 340.)
chŭ-kūng tsiè sŭ pí chī 'My lord *you* should avoid him;' v. *Sān-kwŏ-chí* (4), p. 20. d. 13.
k'ǫn-k'iŭ tá-yê chê kó gạn-tiên '*I* beg of *your* excellency *to grant me* this favour;' v. Dialogues &c. (1), p. 27. b. 1.
waí-shāng fú t'aí - jîn taī tsiên, fú - ki chui - kú pǫn-shāng
外 商 赴 太 人 臺 前 伏 祈 垂 顧 本 商
'*I*, the foreign merchant, hasten to your excellency's tribunal, and humbly beg *you* to bestow a glance on *me*, a merchant.'

siaù-tì tsŏ-jĭ tsin-yĕ 'I (lit. 'younger brother') yesterday proceeded to wait upon *you*;' v. *Haû-k'iû-chuên* (1), p. 8. d. 13.

349. As the Chinese have no *possessive* pronoun in form, they use constantly the personal pronouns with the particle *tĭ* 的 attached to them, and this is equivalent to the genitive case, which answers the purpose for which the possessive pronoun is commonly used: e. g. *nĭ-tĭ fŭ-mŭ* 'your parents;' *t'ā-tĭ hiŭng-tĭ* 'his brother;' *ngò-tĭ fāng-ŭ* 'my house.'

350. In questions and commands or invitations the pronouns are frequently omitted: e. g.—

tsìng-tsŏ 'pray be seated;' *yaú shímmô?* 'what do *you* want?'
yaú chĭ fán '*I* want my dinner;' *pŭ pĭ tō-lĭ* 'do not be extreme in etiquette.'
yaú ngò tsŏ shímmô? 'what do *you* wish me to do?'

351. The reflexive pronoun *tsź-kĭ* regularly follows the personal pronouns, but it is often used alone when the other pronoun is understood: e. g.—

ngò tsź-kĭ pŭ-k'āng k'ŭ 'I for my part will not go.'
nĭ tsź-kĭ shwŏ-taú-liaù chê-kô 'you said that yourself.'
t'ā tsź-kĭ pŭ hwān-hí 'he himself is not pleased.'

But other words are used for the reflexive pronoun, such as *shīn* 'body,' &c.

352. The demonstrative pronouns follow the same rules as the personal pronouns, but the syntax of the *relative* pronoun, or rather of the demonstrative used for the relative, will require further elucidation: e. g.—

nà tă ngò tĭ 'the man who struck me.'
ngò sŏ shwŏ tĭ 'what I said.'
nĭ sŏ tŭ tĭ shŭ 'the book, which you are reading.'
yiù pŭ ts'úng chĕ, chăn-chī, 'if there are any who will not follow, cut them down;' v. *Sān-kwŏ-chí* (3), p. 19. b. 15.
shân-ngò chĕ, săng; yĭ ngò chĕ, sź, 'those who obey me, *shall* live; those who oppose me, *shall* die;' v. *Sān-kwŏ-chí* (3), p. 19. i. 11.
gai-fŭ-mŭ-chĕ 'those who love their parents;' v. the Arts. on the particles *chĕ* 者 and *sŏ* 所.

353. Sometimes there is no sign for the relative, but the context shows that the words must be construed with a relative pronoun in English: e. g.—

tsŏ-shăng yĭ-jĭn t'ui-găn 'one man, of those who were sitting, pushed the table;' v. *Sān-kwŏ-chí* (3), p. 19. g. 7.

354. The use of the *shuí*, 'who,' and *shímmô*, 'what,' for *any body* and *any thing* may here be exemplified: thus, a master speaking to his servant might say, *lai tĭ shĭ shuí?* 'who is that come?' the servant might reply, *mŭ yiù shuí lai* 'there is not any one come.' *Nĭ yaú shímmô, ngò tsiú tsŏ shímmô*, '*If* you want any thing, then I will do *it* (any thing);' v. Mandarin Phrases, p. 27. d. 6.

355. The characters in Art. 174 are further illustrated by the following examples:—

meù-jĭn kaú-sŭ-liaù ngò 'a certain man told me.' Chrest. p. 28. a. 20.
nĭ yiù kĭ-tō yĭn-tsiên? 'how much money have you?'
ngò mŭ yiù shímmô 'I have not any.'
ché-kĭ-t'iên hiá-yŭ-liaù 'it has rained for some days.'
līng jĭ tsai î 'another day again consult;' v. *Sān-kwŏ-chí* (4), p. 20. b. 18.
pŭ yaú hai pĭ-jĭn 'do not injure others.'
nĭ k'ŏ-ĭ pĭ-yáng tsó 'you may do it another way.'
pĭ-yáng mŭ yiù 'there is no other kind.'
sŭ-pĕ jĭn mà 'several hundred men and horses;' v. *Sān-kwŏ-chí* (2), p. 18. d. 4.
meī-jĭ k'ŏ tŭ 'you may read every day.'
mŭ-yiù yĭ-siē 'I have not even a little (or a few).'
kŏ-jĭn yiù yĭn-ts'iên tō 'each man has much money.'

356. The forms for *whoever*, &c., given in Art. 175, need further exemplification. A few examples of their uses may be given here, and an exercise upon them will be found in the third part of this work.

nĭ suí-piên shwŏ 'say whatever you like.'
pŭ-kwàn shímmô jĭn kiàng 'whoever speaks.'
pŭ-k'ŭ hô jĭn shwŏ tsź 'no matter who says this.'
pŭ-k'ŭ tō-shaù yĭn-ts'iên 'whatever quantity of money,' or 'no matter how much money.'
jĭn pŭ-k'ŭ taú nà-lĭ 'wherever a man goes,'
tŭ yaú kiàng lĭ-sing 'he ought to speak common sense.'

Some of the forms used in the books are occasionally employed in the higher colloquial style.

pŭ-lṳ́n hô shí 不 論 何 時 'whenever.'

meī yĭ niên 每: 一 念 'whenever I think.'

ngò meī-tsź taú t'ā nà-lĭ k'ü, kĭ ngò sŭng-lĭ 'every time I go to his place, he gives me presents.'

suí yŭ, chĕ ch'aū 隨 遇 輒 抄 'whenever I met with any, I at once copied *them*.'

Suí, lit. 'to follow,' conveys the signification of 'as often as, according to, in consequence of:' cf. *sequence* from *sequor*, Germ. *Folge, folgend* from *folgen*, *yŭ* 'to meet with.' The other words which mean *to follow, to use, to take, to meet with*, correspond with the usages of Greek words: cf. ἀκολούθως 'in accordance with,' ὁ τυχών = Lat. *quivis*, and the use of χρώμενος, ἔχων, φέρων, λαβών. See ĭ 以, *yúng* 用, *yiù* 有, *nā* 拿, *pà* 把. Cf. also *ts'ŭng* 從 and *sŭ* 率 'to accord with, to cause to follow, to lead,' in the phrase *tá-sŭ* 'generally, on an average.'

357. The expressions *tá-fán* and *fán* alone, *tá-kaí*, *yĭ-tsŭng* for the *whole*, often convey the sense of *whoever, whatever*, &c., especially when followed by *sŏ* (cf. Art. 176): e. g.—

tá-fán sŏ shwŏ tĭ 'whatever is said.'
fán yiù t'iĕn-hiá chī kwŏ 'every country of the world,' or, if in a dependent sentence, 'whatever country of the world.'
yĭ-tsŭng tĭ tsuĭ tŭ kweī yŭ kaŭ-gaú 'all sin is reducible to pride,' i. e. 'whatever sin, or every sin which is committed;' cf. πᾶς, for *any one*.

358. It has already been remarked that the designation of the person is put for the personal pronoun (v. Art. 348). The use of the title and the various substitutes for the pronouns may now be exemplified. The characters are given in Arts. 179—185.

Examples.

siaù-tĭ tsŏ-jĭ tsín yĕ 'I yesterday proceeded to wait upon *you*;' v. *Haú-k'iŭ-chuên* (1), p. 8. d. 13.
siaù-tĭ yĭ pŭ-jĭn yên-k'ŭ 'I cannot bring myself to speak of going;' v. *Haú-k'iŭ-chuên* (1), p. 9. a. 26.
chĕ shí míng-k'í siaù tĭ 'this is plainly to insult me;' v. *Haú-k'iŭ-chuên* (1), p. 10. o. 11.
yŭ-tĭ meŭ-meŭ-tsź tąn 'your humble servant so-and-so bows;' v. Epistolary style, p. 32. o. 19.
pąn tāng líng kiaú 'I ought to receive your commands;' v. *Haú-k'iŭ-chuên* (1), p. 8. k. 6.
chīn siĕn-chaŭ sź-tŭ.... '*I* (lit. 'your subject') *am* the Minister of Instruction of the late dynasty's....;' v. *Sān-kwŏ-chí* (1), p. 27. l. 18.

síng-shīn míng-shuí, lit. 'surname what, name who?'
sháng-síng kaŭ míng, lit. 'superior surname, exalted name?'
kaŭ-míng yá-haú, lit. 'exalted name, elegant designation?'
These expressions are all equivalent to, 'Will you favour me with your name?' *

wĭ sí[a] *kweī-pù*[b], lit. 'not yet acquainted with *your* honourable position.' This is used by classmen when unknown to each other. *Pù*, lit. 'a place for planting trees' (2084), is elegantly used for *place* or *position* in the list of prizemen, for which *fŭ*[c], 'eminent,' is used; e. g.—

t'aī-fŭ hŏ míng = '*Pray* what is your name Sir?'
The following is employed by ordinary scholars or passmen:
wĭ wąn tsąn-haú, lit. 'not yet heard of *your* honourable designation.'
And this by merchants and others for 'I have not the pleasure of knowing you:'
wĭ-chī tsŭ-hiá, lit. 'not yet know *you* Sir.'

---

* See Bridgman's translation of Premare's *Notitia Linguæ Sinicæ*, p. 143.

[a]   [b]   [c]

ts'iēn mŭng-jŭ lĭn pĭ-yĭ shĭ ' when on a former occasion you condescended to come to my poor place;' v. *Haŭ-k'iŭ-chuên* (1), p. 8. i. 2.

kweī-kwŏ suī tsaī chŭng-yâng ạr wán lĭ waī 'although your honourable kingdom is in the great ocean above two myriads of miles away;' v. Official papers, Lin's letter, p. 23. d. 11.

yiŭ kĭ weī lĭng-lâng 'there are how many of your sons?' v. Dialogues &c. (2), p. 28. j. 10.

359. Many other designations of persons are used for the personal pronouns. The signification and use of each will be indicated in the Dictionary. (Part IV.) Some are more commonly used than others; each province and place has its own peculiar words of this kind; and the language of etiquette, the rank of the persons speaking, and various other conditions determine the particular epithet to be employed. The following dialogue may exemplify this:

Q. *Lĭng-tsặn haŭ-mô?* 'Is your respected father well?'
A. *Kiā-fŭ haŭ*, lit. 'the *paterfamilias* is well;' v. Dialogues, Chrest. p. 30. l. 5.
Q. *Yiŭ kĭ-weī kweī-nŭ?* ' How many young ladies (for *daughters*) have you?'
A. *Yiŭ sān-kô kū-niâng* 'I have three girls' (for *daughters*); v. Dialogues, Chrest. p. 28. j. 15.

The following may be noticed here as they were omitted above:

hân-kīng 寒 刾, lit. 'cold-thorn,' is used for *my wife:* (cf. Chr. 9. j. 19.)

siaŭ-kiuèn 小 犬, lit. 'little dog,' for *my son.*

siaŭ-t'ŭ 小 徒, lit. 'small scholar,' for *I, your pupil.*

ts'aŭ-tsź 草 字, lit. 'grass title,' for *my name.*

jîn-hiūng 仁 兄, lit. 'benevolent elder brother,' for *you, Sir.*

laŭ-shīn 老 身, lit. 'old body,' for *I,* used by old women in the novels.

360. In treating of the modifications which the verb undergoes, we may begin by considering those simple verbs which stand between the subject and predicate of a sentence to express that the subject *is, has, becomes, makes, exists in* or *happens to be* something. They are commonly called *substantive* verbs, because they express the reality or the assumed reality of the predication. But this reality may exist under various conditions or modes of existence, for example: 'Victoria *is* (by nature) a woman, she *has* a crown, she *becomes* a queen, she *makes* a good queen, she *exists in* her palace, and she *is* (but not by nature) an accomplished lady.' Some languages express more definitely than others these distinctions. In Chinese they are each marked by a separate word, and the syntax of these may be here noticed in addition to the remarks given in Arts. 216—222.

R

361. The substantive verbs may be arranged thus:

1. *shí* 是 'to be, is, was,' that is a *being by nature*, or at least *apparently so being*. The verb *hí* 係, 'is,' is used in the Canton dialect for *shí*, and in the books in this sense, and in a manner similar to the use of *nai* 乃, which is also employed occasionally where we might expect to find *shí*.

2. *yiù* 有 'to have,' which implies the *possession* of some object or quality by the subject. Instead of saying, 'he is rich,' the Chinese would say, 'he has wealth.'

3. *wei* 爲 'to become,' which indicates that the subject was not naturally such as the predicate asserts, but that it *was made* or *became* such. 'He was king,' would be, 'he became king.'

4. *tsai* 在 'to exist in.' This refers especially to the *location* of the subject. Instead of saying, 'the master is at home,' the Chinese would say, 'the master is in the house.'

5. *tsŏ* 做 'to do' or *tsŏ* 作 'to make,' which both stand as the verb *to be* in the sense of *makes, acts as,* or *means*. When we say, 'that man is a good magistrate,' the Chinese idiom would require, 'that man makes (or acts as) a good magistrate.' The character *tāng* 當, 'to bear,' is used in a similar way: cf. *Hsin-tsing-lü* [I. 1 and 2]. *Kiaū* 'to call,' *swàn* 'to reckon,' *sāng* 'to be born,' all stand in the same category with this; see the examples below.

6. *nai* 乃 'to wit, it may be,' which often takes the place of *shí* (1), but it seems to differ in this, that it is most correctly used in sentences where the predicate is not so positive an assertion as in those in which *shí* is used. It occurs also for *yiù* (2) in the *kŭ-wǎn*, when that character would signify 'there is, there happens to be.'

It must be observed that all these verbs partake more or less of the nature of the demonstrative pronouns, especially *shí, tāng,* and *nai,* which are commonly used as such in the literary style of composition*. *Shí* and *nai, wei* and *tsŏ* (*tsŏ, tāng,* &c.) form pairs; *wei* and *nai* are more common in books than in the colloquial style.

362. These substantive verbs come invariably *between* the subject and

---

* This curious fact, that the demonstrative pronoun and the substantive verb are of cognate origin is clearly shown in Chinese, but it seems to exist in almost all languages. Cf. the pron. *is* and the verb *esse* in Latin ; and see Becker's *Organism der Sprache*, p. 223, where he says: " Wenn man die Lautverhältnisse des Aussagewortes und die ganze Art seines syntaktischen Verhaltens in den bekannten Sprachen näher betrachtet ; so kann man kaum mehr bezweifeln, dass das Aussagewort, wie das Pronom, ein *ursprüngliches* Formwort, und mit dem Pronom ursprünglich sehr nahe verwandt ist."

predicate in a sentence, and not at the end of the clause or at the beginning unless the subject or the predicate be omitted: e. g.—

chê-kó shí laù-jîn-kiā 'this is an old man.'
yiù yĭ cháng-kaū 'it is one foot high.'
tsź-jîn yiù tá-tàn 'this man is brave.'
tsź-tí yiù hŭ-tō yê-sheŭ 'there are many wild beasts about here.'
wei chúng sŏ sin 'he was believed of all,' lit. 'whom all believed.' (B.)
t'ā tsán[a] *ngò wei shên-jîn* 'he praised me, as being a virtuous man.' (B.)
sź tsai mŭ ts'iên 'the business is before your eyes.'
hiŏ kwān-hwá, yaú tsŏ kwān-fŭ, 'learn the mandarin dialect, in order to act as a mandarin.'
ngò tsŏ Chī-hién[b], *nĭ tāng-pīng,* 'I am the Chi-hien, and you are a soldier.'
t'ā nai hiá-chē 'he then was dismounting from the carriage,' i. e. 'it so happened that &c.'
wù nai wâng tí, Chīn-liŭ Wâng yè, 'I am the prince's brother, Chin-liu, the prince.' (17. l. 3.)
hwân pŭ chī-taú shímmô kiaū[c] *yiù-fŭ-kí tĭ jîn* 'I do not yet know what is a happy man.'
chê-kó pŭ swān[d] *chān-t'iēn* 'this is not spring weather.' (29. n. 7.)
sheù hí síng Lĭ 'the chief is surnamed Li.'

363. The negation and intensification of these verbs is effected by placing the negative and intensive particles before each respectively. But it will be necessary to show which particles accompany the different verbs by giving a few examples of the usage in each case.

The verb *shí* 是, 'to be,' takes *pŭ* 不, 'not,' before it to form the negative, and also the antithetical word *fī* 非, 'not to be,' occasionally in the same sense; e. g. *pŭ shí chê-yáng* 'it is not so.'

kó tsiāng-kiūn pŭ-shí tá-tàn tĭ 'that general is not brave.'

fī before *shí*, to negative it, is an idiom which belongs to the book-style. *fī-shí* 非是 or *shí-fī* is a phrase which means 'true and false.'

364. The modification of this verb, as far as regards the intensification of its meaning, is effected by means of such words as *yiú* 又 'again,' *yè* 也 'also,' *piên* 便 'then,' *tsiŭ* 就 'then,' *tsĭ* 郎 'then,' *chĕ* 只 'only,' and other particles of similar meaning: e. g.—

t'ā yiŭ shí pŭ haù 'he is still bad.'
tsĭ shí tsīn-hiŭng 'he is forsooth my own brother.'
yè-shí nĭ sŏ shwŏ tĭ 'it is just what you said.'
piên-shí Tī Chūng-yŭ 'I am indeed Tī Chung-yu:' cf. Chrest 11. c. 16.

---

[a] 讚　[b] 知縣　[c] 叫　[d] 算

tsiŭ-shí tà-jĭ Hwâng-kūng tĭ 'it is the very same who broke into the Imperial palace:' cf. Chrest. 10. d. 14.

jĭ-t'eŭ tsiŭ-shí t'aí-yâng 'jĭ-t'eŭ is the same as t'aí-yâng (the sun).' [I. 57.]

tán chĕ-shí tsīng-shin &c. 'but it is just this, that in early morning &c. :' cf. Chrest. 9. c. 11.

365. The verb *yiù* 有, 'to have,' takes the place of the substantive verb, when the notion of the attribution is *accidental* or *acquired*, or at least to be considered as such: e. g. *t'ā yiù píng* 'he is sick,' which is an abnormal state; the regular phrase is *t'ā sāng-píng-liaù* 他生病了, lit. 'he has produced disease.' *T'ā yiù ts'iên* 'he is rich,' lit. 'he has money,' which is an attribute acquired. Instead of saying, 'what is your plan,' the Chinese would say, 'you have what plan,' *nĭ yiù shimmó fā-tsz̆* [a]. This verb *yiù* is the common word for 'there is' at the beginning of a sentence: e. g. *yiù yĭ chĕ-*[b]*yâng-ch'uên taŭ-liaù* 'a foreign vessel is arrived,' or 'there is a foreign vessel arrived;' but before numerals it means *ago*, as the Fr. *il y a*.

Further examples to illustrate the use of *yiù*.

kŏ-chŭ kŏ-tĭ yiù chíng-kīng jìn 'every where there are upright men.'

ts'iên-jĭ yiù k'ĕ-jìn laí paí 'the day before yesterday there was a gentleman (lit. 'guest') who came to make a call.'

chê-kó yiù shimmó fān-pĭ [c] 'what difference is there in this?'

yiù shíng-jìn, yiù kweī-shín, 'there are saints, and there are spirits.' [I. 2.]

This verb is used also as an auxiliary to form the past tense with *have*: e. g.—

yiù tŭ-kwó-liaù 'I have read it.' *yiù sié-kwó-liaù* 'I have written it.'

366. There is a special negative for *yiù*, the opposite of it, *mŭ* 沒 'to be without,' just as *fĭ*, 'not to be,' is used as the negative of *shí* 'to be:' e. g.—

k'ān-pŭ-ch'ŭ-laí, mŭ-yiù kwāng-liâng [d], 'I cannot see, there is no light.'

chê-kó ch'á mŭ-yiù yên-sĭ [e] 'this tea has no colour,' or 'there is no colour in this tea.'

nĭ shwŏ tsŏ liaù, mŭ-yiù shimmó kwān-hi [f], 'if you make a mistake, it will not be of any consequence.'

laù-t'iēn-yê mŭ-yiù pŭ-paù-yiù [g] *tĭ* 'heaven will not be wanting in protecting *him*.' [I. 31.]

fĭ 非 also occurs as the negative of *yiù*: e. g.—

fĭ yiù sŏ k'iŭ yĕ 'there is nothing else to ask;' v. *Haŭ-k'iŭ-chuén,* Chrest. 8. o. 30.

---

[a] 法子　[b] 洋　[c] 分別　[d] 光亮
[e] 顏色　[f] 關係　[g] 保佑

It will be seen in the Arts. on the forms of interrogation that *mŭ-yiù* at the close of a sentence often means, 'or not?' And this compound verb *mŭ-yiù* 'there is not, not to have,' also helps to form the perfect tense: e. g.—

    kīn-jĭ mŭ-yiù făn shĭ 'there is no rice to eat to-day.'
    jĭ-t'eŭ mŭ-yiù ch'ŭ-shān 'the sun has not arisen.'

367. The modifications of the verb *yiù* 有, 'to have,' are effected by means of the following particles among others: *yè* 也, which means, 'also,' *hwán* 還 'moreover,' *tsaí* 再 'again,' *yiù* 又 'again,' *tū* 都 'all,' *chĕ* 只 'only,' *pĭ-tíng* 必定 'must, certainly.' And in the style of the classics words of similar meaning are used: e. g. *yĭ* 亦 for *yè* 也, *kiaī* 皆 for *tū* 都. Examples of these latter will be found under each particle respectively.

    t'ā pŭ sź, ngò tsiŭ-yiù ĭ-kaŭ, 'if he had not died, I should have been supported.'
    tsai-yiù t'ŭng-ts'iên 'I have more money;' cf. Fr. *j'ai encore de l'argent.*
    yè yiù fŭ-kweī tĭ mô? 'are there any more rich ones?'
    hwán-yiù shinmô kiàng-tĭ? 'what more have you to say?'
    liáng-mîn pĭ-tíng-yiù liáng-sīn 'good people always have a good conscience.'

These particles may also precede *mŭ-yiù*: e. g.—

    tsai-mŭ-yiù chê-mô waí[a]*-tĭ* 'there never was such a dwarf.'
    yè-mŭ-yiù chê-kó nâng-lĭ 'I have not indeed such strength.'

368. The verb *weî* 爲 'to do or make,' as a substantive verb, is used to signify that the subject *holds the office of*, or *becomes* what the predicate expresses: e. g.—

    Chǎng yè pŭ weî lĭ 'but Chang was not polite,' or 'did not perform the salutations;' v. *Haŭ-k'iŭ-chuén*, Chrest. 11. f. 6.
    k'î weî jîn yè tō-tsaí tō-nâng 'this is a man of great talent and ability.'
    shīn[b] *weî k'î-kwaí*[c] 'truly it is wonderful;' *shīn* is lit. 'deep.'
    weî jîn yĭ-shî[d] *pŭ-tsó sǎn-jîn*[e] *lĭ-kĭ tĭ sź* 'should a man all his life do no injury to others for his own advantage, &c.;' v. 366. for the apodosis.

This verb is most frequently used in the style of the books. It corresponds to *tāng* 當, *tsó* 做, &c., in the style of conversation.

369. The substantive verb *tsaí* 在, 'to be in,' comes next. There are a few idiomatic uses of it, but generally the notion of the locality of the subject in the sentence will indicate the case in which it must be used.

    pŭ chĭ tsaí yè pŭ tsaí 'I do not know whether he is there or not.'
    laù-yè tĭ maŭ-tsź tsaí chê-lĭ 'your cap, Sir, is here.'

[a] 矮   [b] 深   [c] 怪   [d] 世   [e] 損

nì tī fú-mù tū tsaí mô? 'are your parents alive?' v. Dialogues &c., Chrest. p. 28. i. 13.
jĭ, yŭ, sīng-sŭ tū tsaí nà-lĭ, 'the sun, moon, and stars are there' (in heaven); cf. *Hsin-tsing-lŭ*. [I. 10.]

370. The common negative which is used with *tsaí* is *pŭ* 不 'not:' e. g.— *t'ā pŭ tsaí* 'he is not in' (=*not at home*).
mù-tsīn pŭ tsaí shí 'my mother is not in the world,' for, *is deceased*.

371. The verbs *tsó* 做 'to make,' *tsŏ* 作 'to do or make,' *tăng* 當 'to bear the office or act the part of,' 叫 *kiaū* 'to call or be called,' 算 *swàn* 'to reckon, to count,' *săng* 生 'to be born,' are used as substantive verbs, the various accessory notions implied in them being understood. *Kiaū* is followed by *tsó* or *tsŏ* sometimes, and the two may be translated 'is said to be' or 'is called:' e. g.—

nì *kiaū-tsó shimmŏ ming*? 'what is your name?' cf. *Hsin-tsing-lŭ*. [75.]
hô-kù tsŏ tsè t'aū-yên? 'what reason is there for these formal expressions?' cf. *Haū-k'iù-chuén*, Chrest. p. 9. f. 24.
nà sān-kô tsiăng-kiūn tăng nù-ts'ai 'took three generals and made them slaves:' cf. also *săng-ping* 'to be sick,' and *săng-k'i* 'to be angry.'
These are negatived by the usual word *pŭ* 不 'not.'

372. The verb *nai* 乃 'to wit, is,' remains to be noticed. It is more common to the books than to the conversation; it sometimes corresponds with *shí*, and sometimes with *yiù*.
haú shên ár wú-ŏ nai jin chī chăng-ts'ing 'to love the good and hate the evil is man's common disposition.'

373. Two of these substantive verbs are often united to strengthen the expression: e. g.—
yi-haú [a] *kià-tsiĕ* [b] *shí mŭ-yiù tĭ* 'there is not a particle of fiction in it.' (Prém. Brid. p. 51.)

374. *Shí* 是 is often redundant, and *wei* 爲 is used at the beginning of a sentence sometimes, where it is hardly wanted, and where some expression for 'if' would seem to be needed. Thus when we say, 'if such a thing were to happen,' the Chinese might say, 'it being so and so:' and the modifying particles are used with the verb; e. g.—
hwân-shí laù-tá-jin shwŏ-tĕ t'ŭng-kw'ai 'of a truth, the old gentleman speaks very shrewdly.' Chrest. 9. m. 1.
shí t'ā pŭ shí haù jin 'he is not a good man.'

375. In simple sentences, in which the predicate is the natural attribute of the subject, the substantive verb is generally understood: e. g.—

[a] 一毫   [b] 假借

nà-kó yŭn-ts'ai[a] *kaŭ* 'those clouds are high.' [157.]
t'iēn yīn-liaŭ 'the sky is cloudy.' [147.]

376. When a description of the subject forms the matter of the predicate then *shí* seems invariably to be used: e. g.—
lŭ shí hĕ-hiá tĭ ch'aŭ-k'í, hwā-ch'ŭ-lai-tĭ shwuĭ, 'dew is the damp vapour of night changed into water.' [247.]

377. For the expression of tense and mood as regards these substantive verbs very few rules can be given. The ordinary auxiliary particles, which distinguish tense and mood, are not employed with these verbs, but the circumstances of *time* and *manner*, either expressed or understood, define the relations of tense and mood: e. g.—
wăng-niên ngò shí fú-kweĭ-tĭ 'last year I *was* rich,' or
wăng-niên ngò yiù ts'iên 'last year I *had* money.'
lai-niên ngò tsó fú-kweĭ-tĭ 'this year I *shall be* rich.'
tsŏ-t'iēn t'ā pŭ-tsai 'yesterday he *was* not at home.'
yiù-shí-heŭ ngò shí yiù tŭng-ts'iên-tĭ 'I *have been* rich,' lit. 'there was a time (when) I *was* a person who had money.'

378. The *pluperfect* and *future perfect* tenses will be dependent upon some circumstance: thus —
t'ā wí-tsāng lai chē-lĭ, ngò sāng-ping, 'before he came here, I *had* been sick.'
ts'iên-sān-niên ngò tsó sāng-i tsai Chūng-kwŏ 'three years ago, I *was doing* business in China.'
nĭ ming-t'iēn lai tĭ t'eŭ-lĭ, t'ā tsó wáng, 'before you shall have arrived tomorrow, he *will have been made* king.'

379. The tenses of the subjunctive mood are expressed by *k'ŏ-ĭ* 可以 and *k'ŏ*, and certain particles, such as *jŏ* 若 'if,' *hwŏ-chĕ* 或者 'perhaps' (cf. Arts. 263, &c.), followed by the substantive verbs just given: e. g.—
k'ŏ-ĭ tsó chē-yáng 'it *may be* so.'
Hwâng-tí sź-liaŭ, hwŏ-chĕ shí chē-yáng, 'when the Emperor died, it *might* perhaps *have been* so.'
nĭ yè-lĭ mân-waí shüĭ, k'ŏ-ĭ sāng-ping, 'if you sleep out of doors at night, you *may be* ill.'
pŭ yaŭ k'i chē-kó, K'ŭng-p'á nĭ swàn hŏ-sāng, 'do not eat this, lest you *should be* taken for a Buddhist priest.'

380. So much information has already been given upon the formation of the kinds of verbs, in Arts. 189—215, that it remains to notice here only the same in construction, and to point out the *form of the sentence*, which affects the tense or mood of the verb; and the remarks will have reference to the words and forms given on pp. 70—76.

The various modifications of the verbal notion are produced in four ways:
1. By a change of the tone or the syllable; 2. By the position of the word in

---

[a] 雲彩

the sentence; 3. By the juxta-position of some particle or auxiliary word, or 4. By the circumstances under which the expression occurs.

The changes of voice, mood, tense, and person in construing a Chinese verb frequently leave the word unchanged; the conditions under which it is uttered being a sufficient guide to the limitation of its meaning. Adverbial expressions of time, and indeed a whole clause in which a certain time is indicated, force the construing of the simple verb into particular moods and tenses; while the subject of the verb (often understood) shows the person which must be construed with the verb unchanged.

381. By a change in tone, the *voice* or kind of the verb may be altered,— an *active* verb may become *passive*, a *transitive* verb may become *neuter* or *causative*: e. g.—

為 *weí* 'to make, to do' (trans. v.), changes into *weí* 'to be made, to be considered as' (pass. v.).

占 *chén* 'to seize upon' (trans. v.) becomes *chĕn* 'to divine' (neut. v.).

行 *háng* 'to baste, to beat' (trans. v.), becomes *híng* 'to walk, to act' (neut. v.).

聽 *t'íng* 'to hear' (trans. v.) becomes *t'íng* 'to hearken, to obey' (intrans. v.).

382. The position of the verb in the sentence may determine its relation to the other parts of the same, according to the following general rules:

1. A verb standing alone or as the first word in a clause is commonly in the imperative mood; e. g. *laí ché-lí* 'come here!' *tsǐng-tsó* 'please to sit:' or it is intended to express the general notion of the verb, which is about to be spoken of, and is consequently the subject of the sentence; e. g.—

tǔ-shū shí shǐ-fān yaú-kīn-tí 'to study is a very important thing,'

t'íng-míng shí nì tí pān-fān 'to obey is your duty:'

or the verb belongs to an absolute clause,—the expression of some circumstance connected with the principal clause; e. g.—

taú tsź-jì 'having arrived at the next day,' = *when the next day had come*; cf. *Haú-k'iǔ-chuén*, Chrest. p. 8. a. 10.

2. A verb between two nouns belongs to the former as its subject, and to the latter as its object (cf. Arts. 291, 292, and 296); or the first noun being put for an adverbial expression of time or place, the verb stands with the subject understood in the present or past tense, according as the other conditions of the clause will allow; e. g.—

yé, pŭ yaú híng-lú, 'in the night do not travel;' the fuller colloquial form is *yé-lí* 'in the night.'

Pĕ-kīng, tseŭ pŭ haŭ, 'in Peking it is bad walking.'

jǐ-jǐ kǐ-fán liáng-tsź 'every day he eats twice.'

3. One verb following another directly or indirectly, without a particle being between, must be considered as expressing a *purpose* or a *result*: e. g.—

t'ā laî, k'ān, 'he is come to look.'
ngò hîng lú tŏ, săng-píng, 'I walked much and fell sick.'

In these rules we cannot take cognizance of the auxiliary verbs as such, because they are often attached to the simple verb, and become part of a compound with it.

383. The auxiliary verbs and particles which are used to modify the verbal notion have been given in Arts. 192, 194, 197, and 199. And here it may be remarked, that the verbal notion may be viewed under two aspects: 1st, as expressing the entire and general notion of the verb as an abstract idea, and independent of any positive act; 2ndly, as entering into relation with some real transaction. Two expressions therefore commonly occur, which correspond to this distinction; one, *general,* the other *particular*.

384. Verbs which express a general notion are such as those given in Arts. 200 and 203: e. g.—

(Gen.) *tŭ-shŭ̄, shí nĭ-tî pàn-fān,* 'to study is your duty.'
(Par.) *t'ā pŭ-k'ạng tŭ Sź-shŭ̄* 'he will not learn the *Sź-shŭ̄.*'
(Gen.) *kĭ-fán, shí jîn-jîn pĭ-tíng tsŏ tí,* 'to eat, is what all men must do.'
(Par.) *taú-tî ngò mŭ-yiù shimmô fán k'î* 'but I have no rice to eat.'
(Gen.) *nĭ k'ò-ĭ tă-swán mô?* 'can you calculate?'
(Par.) *tsiú swán chê-kĭ sú-mù* 'then reckon up these numbers.'
(Gen.) *kiaū siaù haî-ạr, tà-saú,* 'call the little boy to sweep.'
(Par.) *t'ā saú-liaù chê-kó tí-fāng* 'he has swept this place.'
(Gen.) *tă-fă yĭ-kô-jîn, tă-t'îng,* 'send a man to listen!'
(Par.) *ngò t'îng-kiên-liaù t'ā-tî hwá* 'I have heard what he said.'

Those compounds with *tà,* 'to strike,' do however frequently keep the *tà* when particular acts are mentioned: e. g.—

hiŏ-făng tà-saú-liaù 'the schoolroom is swept.'

But with such compounds as *tà-shwŭĭ,* 'to draw water,' *shwŭĭ,* 'water,' would be dropped in construction: e. g.—

ngò yaú nĭ kĭ-ngò tà-shwŭĭ 'I want you to draw water for me.'
shwŭĭ tà-liaù 'the water is drawn,' or *tà-liaù* 'it is drawn.'

385. It will be well to show, by a few examples, how each of the auxiliary words affects the principal verb when it is joined with it.

The character *liaù* 了, 'to finish,' is very commonly used after verbs, to indicate that the action of the verb is accomplished, and the expression may therefore be construed in one of the perfect tenses or by the perfect participle. The following examples will show its use:

chĕ-tĕ t'eù-liaù míng-tĭ 'he only *presented* his card.' (8. f. 23.)
lĭ-kĕ tsiú-yaú hîng-liaù 'at once I *should be* on my journey.' (8. k. 18.)
chĕ-kiên Shwŭĭ-yuên, hwŭ tseù-liaù, tsìn-laî, 'who should they see but Shui-yun, *having suddenly walked* up, enter.' (9. g. 4.)
k'ān-liaù yiú k'ān '*having looked,* he looks again.' (11. f. 13.)

130   THE CONSTRUCTION OF AUXILIARY VERBS.

yaú yī-chāng ṛ̀r chī, shī k'ī- siaù-tí -liaù, lit. 'wishing to take one cup and then stop, is *to have insulted* me.' (11. l. 13)

pŭ kai laî tsź-kú-liaù, lit. 'ought not to come, *to have taken notice* of me.' (8. n. 28.) Cf. 10. n. 4. also.

In oblique narration *liaù* must sometimes be construed into the pluperfect tense: e. g.—

'The attendants announced, that the second son of academician Li (*laî-liaù*) had arrived' (or 'to have arrived'). (10. h. 15.)

This character often means 'has become;' e. g. *húng-liaù* 'has become red;' *pĕ-liaù* 'has become white;' *míng-pĕ-liaù* 'has become clear,'=*has understood*. Thus an adjective is changed into a verb when followed by *liaù*.

When *liaù* is repeated, the first *liaù* must be taken as the verb 'to finish,' and the second as the auxiliary particle to express the perfect tense or the participle. It is however seldom found thus, though Prémare gives one or two examples of it.

sheū-wǎn-liaù ts'iēn 收完了錢 'having received the money.'

chǎng kwó-liaù 嘗過了 'having tasted.'

Liaù is very commonly used in the court dialect, and in the mandarin generally; also in the ordinary novels, but seldom in the *Sān-kwŏ-chí* and the better class of books.

Sometimes the object of the verb is placed between the verb and the auxiliary *liaù* 了 : e. g. *k'ī- siaù-tí -liaù* '*you* have insulted me.'

386. The addition of *kwó* 過, 'to pass over,' as an auxiliary verb, is very common; it regularly forms the perfect tense when used in this way: e. g.—

nì t'ŭng-tĕ t'ā shwŏ-kwó-tĭ 'you understood what he *said*.' (28. d. 24.)

kiĕn-kwó t'ā kĭ-tsź ? 'you *have seen* him, how many times?' (28. g. 10.)

Liaù is frequently superadded to *kwó* in the same sense of *completing* the action of the verb. *Kwó* sometimes enters into the composition of a word, and then it cannot be looked upon as an auxiliary verb, but the verb 了 seems to be used to form the perfect tenses in that case: e. g.—

nâ-kwó-laî 'bring over;' *nâ kwó-laî liaù* 'it is brought over.'

387. The verb *yiù* 有, 'to have,' also occurs as an auxiliary verb, like *have* in English, but this use of it is not common in Chinese. When used in this sense, it must stand *immediately before* the verb to which it belongs: e. g.—

yiù kī-fân 'I *have eaten* rice (i. e. dined).'

tsŭng mŭ-yiù-k'ān-kiĕn chĕ-yáng-tĭ yī-kŏ-tsź 'I never yet *have seen* such a character as this.' (30. i. 16.)

hwǎn mŭ-yiù-tà sān-hiá 'it *has* not yet *struck* three o'clock.' (29. k. 19.)

THE CONSTRUCTION OF AUXILIARY VERBS. 131

388. The verb *wán* 完, 'to finish,' is also set after the verb to form the perfect tenses with the other auxiliary verbs and particles: e. g.—

t'ā siĕ-wán chĕ-yi-sheù-shī 'he has written this ode.'

Sī-chăn pŭ tăng t'ā shwŏ-wán 'SI-chun did not wait until he *had done* speaking.'

ngò wí-tsāng tsó-wán chĕ-kô sź-tsíng 'I have not yet finished this business.'

Kĭ 訖 'to stop speaking,' *pĭ* 畢 'to finish,' and some other words have a similar force and usage in the books, where they will present no difficulty.

389. The particle *ĭ* 已, 'already,' is used as an adjunct to form the *perfect* and *pluperfect* tenses: e. g.—

ĭ-fŭ hiá-jĭn tsaí hiá-chŭ 'he had hidden a menial in the lower room.' (8. b. 25.)

nà Lī kŭng-tsz̀ ĭ-tseù taú sĭ-ts'iĕn 'this Mr. Li had walked up to the festive board.' (10. h. 29.) *sĭ-ts'iĕn* is 'before the mat,' by met. 'feast.'

hîng sūī tsăn ǎr sīn ĭ-sź 形 雖 存 而 心 已 死 'the body indeed may remain, but the soul is departed.'

This word is however more frequently used as a book-particle than in the colloquial idiom. It is used with adjectives like *liaù*, but *prefixed*, and then it signifies *had become:* e. g.—

t'iĕn-sĭ [a] *ĭ-wán t'ŭī-pīng* [b] 'when the day had become late he withdrew his soldiers.'

And in phrases it often loses its grammatical force, or, to say the least, the value of the word is hidden by the figure *ellipsis:* cf. 9. f. 12.

390. *Kĭ* 既 'finished, to exhaust,' is employed in a similar way, and is placed before the verb to form the *perfect* and the *pluperfect* tenses, or the *past participle* of the verb, according as the circumstances require each form of translation respectively: e. g.—

kĭ mŭng tsʻź-kú 'having *favoured* me with this regard.' (8. o. 4.)

kĭ Wáng Lì ǎr-hiūng k'ŭ-liĕn sān-shāng 'having taken with our two friends, Mr. Wang and Mr. Li, three cups in succession.' (11. k. 30.)

kĭ yaú-hîng, hô pŭ tsaù-k'ŭ? 'if *you wished* to go, why did you not go earlier?' (10. n. 21.)

kĭ sź t'ai-hiūng, pŭ ĭ pâng-yiù wei ts'îng, 'it *being* thus, Sir, that you make no account of friendship as a motive.' (9. b. 18.)

391. *Tsāng* 曾, 'already done,' stands before the principal verb as an auxiliary to form the *perfect* tenses and participles: e. g.—

tsù-shâng tsāng-tsó-kwó yĭ-kô-siaù-siaù Kīng-kwān 'one of their ancestors *had been* an insignificant official at the Capital.' (*Húng-leú-múng.*)

tsāng-kīng k'ĭ-ch'îng [c] 'he *has already set out* on his journey.'

[a] 天色   [b] 退兵   [c] 起程

392. It must be observed too, that particles such as *tsiú* 就, *piĕn* 便, *kiŏ* 却, *tsaù* 早, *yīn* 因, each of which means 'then,' commonly throws the succeeding verb into the *past* tense, the *past participle* or the *future* tense. They occur naturally in the apodosis of a sentence where the perfect or future tense is often required: e. g.—

jī-wí-ch'ŭ, tsiú k'ĭ-laí, 'before the sun came out, (*then*) he *arose.*' (8. a. 13.)
Kwó tsiú săng tsŏ 'Kwo *then having invited* his guests to sit.' (9. n. 15.)
tsaù fī paú-yŭ Kwó kŭng-tsz̀ '*then* he *hastened* to inform Mr. Kwo.' (8. c. 11.)
yīn liĕn-liĕn tà kŭng-kùng '*then* he continuously *bowed* profoundly.' (8. c. 4.)
yīn kiĕn shīn-ts'íng heŭ-maŭ '*when he saw* the deep feeling and generous manner displayed.' (19. e. 15.)
tsiú-yaú hîng-liaù 'I am *about* to proceed on my journey.' (8. k. 20.)
wàng-waí tsiú-tseù 'he went out, *being about* to depart.'

But in parallel clauses, or those joined with *and* understood, the verb which follows these particles must be construed like the verb in the corresponding clause preceding. And when the protasis is a hypothetical proposition, the verb in the apodosis will be in the *future* tense: e. g.—

393. Several verbs which are placed before the principal verb may be considered as belonging to the class of auxiliaries, since they serve to define the notion of time more clearly. For the *future* tenses and *future participles*, *yaú* 要, *tsiāng-yaú* 將 |, and *tsiú-yaú* 就 | are used. The following examples will show how they are employed:

ngò mîng-t'iēn yaú k'ú 'to-morrow I *shall* go.'
laí niĕn nĭ tsiāng-yaú laí 'next year you *will come.*'
k'ĭ-fán-liaù, tsiú-yaú k'ú, 'having eaten his rice, he was *about* to go.'

But after *nĭ*, 'you,' *yaú* would signify *should* or *must:* e. g.—
nĭ mîng-t'iēn yaú laí 'to-morrow you *must* come.'

394. Many words are used to modify the notion expressed by *yaú*, as well as other words employed to mark the future time, and to change the expression so as to mean *must, should, would,* &c.; as, for example, *pĭ* 必 'must, certainly;' and adverbs of intensity, with certain verbs of like signification: e.g.—

t'ā pĭ-yaú tŭ-shū 'he *must* study.'
hwáng-tí yĕ yaú sz̀ 'the emperor *must* also die.'
kiaù-fū shĭ-tsaí yaú-laí 'the chair-bearer *will* really come.'
nĭ kwò-jên yaú-k'ĭ-fán 'you certainly *will* dine.'
siēn-săng pŭ-k'ăng laí tŭ 'the teacher *will* not come to read,' (won't.)

395. The verbs given in Art. 197 will need some further exemplification, as they play an important part in the modification of the verbal notion. We will take each in order. 1st, *tĕ* 得, 'to obtain,' *follows* verbs whose signification requires some such supplementary notion to complete their sense: e. g.—

ngò tŭng-tĕ nĭ-tĭ shwŏ-hwá 'I *can* understand your language.'

nĭ k'ŭ-tĕ, k'ŏ-ĭ, 'you *may* go,' where *k'ŏ-ĭ* is redundant, but idiomatic.

The negative *pŭ* 不 comes between the verb *tĭ* and its associate, and denotes that the action of the principal verb does not or cannot take effect; and this is common with all these auxiliary verbs: e. g.—

chĕ-yĭ-t'iaŭ-lŭ kw'ān-pŭ-tĭ 'this road *cannot* be widened.'

kŏ yŭng-jĭn k'ŭ-pŭ-tĭ 'the servant *may not* go.'

Tĭ also forms, with certain verbs, an expression equivalent to *utinam* in Latin, in wishes, 'would that!' e. g. *hắn pŭ-tĭ* 恨 'annoyed at not getting,'= '*would that!*' but the more common phrase in conversation is *pā-pŭ-tĭ* or *pà-pŭ-tĭ*, which signify respectively, 'would that I' and 'would that you,' i. e. with one tone it refers to the subject who speaks, with the other, to the object spoken of, or to the person addressed. *Pŭ-tĭ* enters into a variety of phrases, as *liaŭ-pŭ-tĭ*, 'finish not obtain,' for an intensitive, = *very;* and sometimes for 'it will not suffice:' cf. Chrest. 30. e. 21.

396. The verbs *k'ŭ* 去 'to go,' *ch'ŭ* 出 'to go out,' *k'ai* 開 'to open,' and *sān* 散 'to scatter,' have a good deal in common. They express the *present* or the *perfect* tenses of the *indicative* mood;—the *imperative* mood; or the *potential* mood, with *can* as the sign in English: e. g.—

k'ān pŭ ch'ŭ-lai, mŭ-yiŭ kwāng-liāng, 'I *cannot see*, there is no light.'

t'ā ná-ch'ŭ yĭ-kweī yáng-ts'iên 'he took *out* a dollar.'

shwŭĭ ts'ŭng shān-lĭ liŭ-ch'ŭ lai 'water *flows out* from the mountains.'

t'aŭ-ch'ŭ, pŭ-yaú tàng chĕ-lĭ, '*Flee!* do not tarry here.'

ngò pĭ-k'ai yĭ kweī mŭ-t'eŭ 'I *split* a log of wood.' (Indic.)

nĭ pĭ-k'ai yĭ kweī mŭ-t'eŭ '*split* a log of wood!' (Imper.)

jŏ t'ā chĕn-mei nĭ, lĭ-k'ai t'ā yuên, 'if he flatters you, *keep* at a distance.'

nà-kiên mĭ-sź ᵃ *lŭ-ch'ŭ* ᵇ *lai-liaŭ* 'that secret *has* come out.'

ngò piĕn-yaú nĭ kĭ-liaŭ-k'ŭ 'I am determined you *shall* drink it:' (*now*, so pres.) (12. a. 2.)

397. The verb *pá* 罷, 'to cease,' corresponds in force to *liaŭ* 了, 'to finish,' as an auxiliary verb. But it very commonly has the effect of turning the sentence either into an *imperative* sentence, or it gives to it a *hortative* force. The following examples will show both these uses of *pá:*

Tĭ kūng-tsź ch'ā pá 'Mr. Tĭ *having* done tea.' (8. j. 20.)

shwŏ-pá, yiŭ wai tseŭ, '*having* spoken, he again made for the door.' (8. m. 19.)

siaŭ-tĭ kīng-tsiŭ tsŏ-pá 'I am already *seated*.' (10. i. 15.)

fáng-sīn shwŏ pá! 'speak freely!' (27. a. 12.)

tsā-mắn tū yĭ-kweī-ắr tseŭ-pá! '*let* us all walk together!' (30. b. 17.)

ngò-mắn sháng-chīng pá! '*let* us go up into the city!' (28. l. 19.)

Hō-kí, nĭ tai ngò kwŏ hô pá! 'Friend! *carry* us over the river!' (28. n. 10.)

Cf. also 28. l. 5. and 27. l. 28.

ᵃ 密事　ᵇ 露出

After a conditional clause, referring to the second person, or after an absolute clause, it will generally give the sense of *may*, or some tense in the *potential* mood, or be construed into the *imperative:* e. g.—

nì pŭ yaú tàng, k'ŏ-ì k'ŭ pá (or tsiú k'ŭ-pá), 'if you will not wait, then you *may* go.'

k'ì-fán heú, tsiú k'ŭ pá ! 'after dinner, then you *may* go !' (or 'then go.')

tàng-yì-tàng ngò chē-yáng tsŏ pá ! 'wait a little, I will do it so !' which would be also, 'let me do it so.' (27. k. 5.)

398. The verb chŭ 住 'to rest in, to stay,' partakes of the same nature and grammatical force as the preceding verb. It may be said to attach itself to the verb in almost every mood and tense, to show that the action of its associate, which always precedes it, has taken effect: e. g.—

Kwó lán-chŭ taú 'Kwo *opposed* him and said.' (8. 1. 8.)

Kwó yì-sheŭ chì-chŭ taú 'Kwo with one hand *stopped* him and said.' (8. m. 25.)

chì-tĕ chŭ-hiá 'he *stayed* there.' (9. c. 26.)

ì-tseŭ taú sì-ts'iên chì-chŭ taú 'he had walked in to the banquet and *stopped* them, saying.' (10. h. 29.)

piên lì-chŭ tă-yíng taú 'then he *arose* and answering, said.' (11. e. 8.) Cf. also (12. c. 1) and (12. f. 1).

In its own proper sense we have chŭ in (10. b. 15) yiù chŭ-sheŭ chī-ì 'he had the idea of desisting (from drinking).'

399. The verbs lai 來 'to come,' tsìn 進 'to enter,' and lûng 攏 'to collect,' may be classed together as auxiliaries, being allied in meaning and use, and being often united in the same phrase. All three convey the notion of *direction towards* the subject, just as k'ŭ 'to go,' ch'ŭ 'to go out,' and k'ai 'to open,' express the *direction from* the subject of the sentence. Lai precedes liaù when it helps to form the perfect tenses of neuter verbs, but when an object comes in between, liaù goes with the chief verb, and lai is suffixed after the object mentioned: thus—

nâ-liaù tì-tsz̀ laî 'he took his card.' (8. b. 10.)

ngò hwân mŭ-yiù k'ì laî 'I have not yet *arisen.*' (30. o. 18.)

Tsìn and lûng precede liaù in the sentence, and come immediately before it: e. g.—

tsìn-laî 'to come in' (cf. *hineinkommen*), or 'come in !'

lûng-laî 'to collect together' (cf. *zusammenhaufen*).

t'ā t'ì-k'ì pi laî 'he *takes* up his pencil.'

t'ā t'ì-k'ì pi laî-liaù 'he *took* up his pencil.'

hŏ-lûng nà-kó tūng-sī laî '*collect* those things.'

hŏ-lûng-liaù 'they *are collected.*'

The student must learn to distinguish between words which stand as grammatical adjuncts from the same when used as principal verbs: cf. ngŏ-fŭ ặr laî, ngŏ-fŭ ặr k'ŭ, 'to come fasting,' 'to go fasting.' (9. c. 16.)

THE CONSTRUCTION OF AUXILIARY VERBS. 135

Many of these auxiliary verbs form the various tenses, or stand for the prepositions found with the verb in some European languages. The Chinese may be said to correspond with the idiom of the English in this respect. We may say either, 'he *offered up* tea, or he *presented* tea.' In colloquial Chinese, '*offered up*' is the form of more correct phrase: cf. Chrestomathy.

yĭ-miên hiên-sháng ch'á laî 'while they offered up tea.' (8. h. 10.)

400. The verbs *sháng* 上 'to go up' and *k'ĭ* 起 'to arise' are similar in their grammatical use, for they both signify the *beginning* or *raising* of the action of the chief verb; but they do not seem to have any effect in forming the tenses of the verb, although they *assist* in producing the perfect tense sometimes: e. g.—

tsiù lĭ-k'ĭ shĭn lai 'then he *arose*.' (8. j. 25.)
yĭ-miên hiên-sháng ch'á laî 'while they *were offering* up tea.' (8. h. 10.)
pŭ tŏ-shî peí-sháng tsiù laî 'not long after they *prepared* and brought up wine.' (9. n. 8.)
yiú yiù Hwüi-tsz̆ tsŏ-lwán-k'ĭ-laî-liaù 'there were also the Turcomans who had rebelled.' Gonç. *Arte China.*
yīn ná-k'ĭ ná-peī-tsiù laî 'then he *took* that cup of wine.' (12. a. 9.)
kiaŭ tsó-yiú chīn-k'ĭ liàng-cháng 'he called the attendants to *pour* out two goblets.' (11. j. 24.)

K'ĭ is used sometimes to form the *inceptive* verb, even with a verb of an opposite signification, e. g. with *hiá* 下 'down, to descend,' while *k'ĭ* means 'to arise:' thus—

hiá-k'ĭ tá-yŭ 'it began to rain heavily.'

This is exceptional usage, for the auxiliary is commonly suited to the action of the verb to which it is joined; *hiá* 下 is generally used for a downward movement and *sháng* 上 for an upward movement: e. g.—

hiá kó-weî-kí 'to play the game of *siege* (a kind of chess).' Chrest. litho. p. 9. c. 4.
nĭ tù-sháng tŏ-shaù 'how much will you wager?' (lit. 'bet-up,'=Eng. *lay*.) (27. g. 9.)
pä . . . . . siáng-sháng yĭ siáng, lit. 'touching . . . . . enter upon thinking!' (6. m. 22.) = 'with regard to . . . . . take a thought!'

401. Many other verbs are used in senses similar to the preceding, and assist in forming the tenses or in conveying the notion of direction implied in the verbs to which they are attached. From the preceding articles the principle involved will be seen; but many additions to the examples may be given by the student as he proceeds in his reading. The following expressions must suffice to exemplify these remarks:

yēn-hiá 咽下 'to swallow down,'=coll. *t'ān-hiá* 吞下.
jĭ 入 'to enter' is used for *tsìn* 進 'to enter,' and both are occasionally

used together; e. g. *tsìn-jî* 'enter!' *tsìn-laî* 'come in!' *tsìn-k'ŭ́* 'go in!' and *sháng-tsìn-k'ŭ́*, lit. 'ascend-in-go,' for 'go in!' *kàn-sháng-k'ŭ́* 'to pursue after.'

Each of these adjuncts is affixed to some verbs, just as prepositions are to assist in forming compounds in European languages. The student of the Greek will at once perceive the analogy between Chinese and that language on this point, as he will too in many other Chinese forms of construction and usages of words. (Compare πρός with *laî;* ἀπο with *k'ŭ́;* ἐξ with *ch'ŭ;* ἐν with *tsìn*, &c.)

Thus—*ná-laî* 'bring!' *ná-k'ŭ́* 'take away!'

ts'ŭ́-kwó 取 'to bring over :' e. g.—

kiaŭ-jìn ts'ŭ́-kwó pĭ laî 'tell a man to bring a pencil over here ;' so *ts'ŭ́-ch'ŭ* 'to take out,' *ts'ŭ́-k'ŭ́* 'to take away.'

402. When verbs compounded with these auxiliary adjuncts are negatived, the negative particle is placed either between the principal and the auxiliary,—and they then generally signify *cannot* do what the verb expresses,—or before the two verbs as a compound, when they mean *does not, has not*, or *will not:* e. g.—

ᵃ *ná-pŭ-laî* 'cannot bring it.' *ná-pŭ-k'ŭ́* 'cannot take it away.'
siĕ pŭ sháng laî 'cannot go on writing.' *taŭ pŭ ch'ŭ laî* 'cannot speak.'
ᵇ *k'ĭ-pŭ-tĭ* 'cannot eat it.' ᶜ *t'aŭ-pŭ-ch'ŭ* 'cannot escape.'
pŭ ná-laî 'does not bring it, has not brought it,' or 'will not bring it,' according as the circumstances of the case require.

t'ā pŭ tsìn-laî 'he will not enter.' *nì pŭ tsìn-laî* 'you, do not enter!' (Imp.)
hŏ-pŭ-lŭng-laî 'cannot be brought together.'
nì tsìn-pŭ-laî 'you cannot enter.' *ngò tŭ-pŭ-tĭ* 'I cannot read it.'
ngò pŭ k'ĭ-tĭ 'I do not eat it,'=*I will not eat it*.
ᵈ *kiàng-pŭ-tíng* ᵉ 'cannot be settled by discussion.'
ngò t'īng-pŭ-kiĕn 'I cannot hear.' *ngò pŭ t'īng-kiĕn* 'I do not hear.'
ᶠ *maĭ-pŭ-laî* 'I cannot buy it.' ᵍ *maĭ-pŭ-k'ŭ́* 'I cannot sell it.'

403. After these remarks upon the value of the above-mentioned auxiliary verbs, the explanation of such phrases as the following will present no difficulty.

tseŭ̆-laî tseŭ̆-k'ŭ́ 'to walk backwards and forwards.'
shwŏ-laî shwŏ-k'ŭ́ 'to say again and again.'
siàng-laî siàng-k'ŭ́ 'to think of this and that,'=*to keep on thinking*, in which form all such expressions may be construed. They cannot however be affected by the auxiliaries for the *past* and *future* tenses as the simple verb can; they signify merely the general notion in the infinite mood.

404. The *imperative* mood in Chinese is marked by certain verbs, which signify to *invite* or *beg*, to *yield*, to *cause*, to *call*, to *exhort*, and the like, being prefixed to the principal verb; but very frequently the command is

ᵃ 拿   ᵇ 吃   ᶜ 逃   ᵈ 講   ᵉ 定   ᶠ 買   ᵍ 賣

conveyed simply by the verb alone ; e. g. *laî* 'come!' *k'ú* 'go!' *k'àn* 'see!' or with the subject only placed before it ; e. g:—

nì pŭ-yaú-k'ú 'do not go!' (Lat. *noli ire.*)

t'ā pŭ-yaú-k'ú would be 'he will not go' or 'he may not go.'

The verbs just referred to are, *tsĭng* 請 'to invite,' *k'iû* 求 'to beg,' *jáng* 讓 'to yield,' *shí* 使 'to cause' or *ling* 令 'to cause,' *kiaŭ* 叫 'to call,' *kiuén* 勸 'to exhort,' of which the following examples will show the use in this connection :

ts'ĭng nì tsĕ maú-tsz̀ 'take off your cap,' lit. 'invite you to remove the cap.'

hiū 休 is *prohibitive;* e. g. *hiū-shwŏ* 'do not say !'

405. In pursuing the method of European grammar, and seeking equivalents for the voices, moods, and tenses, we may wander from the proper sphere of the grammar of Chinese : in the analysis of this language we ought rather to confine ourselves to the physiology of it, and leave the consideration of the method of expressing moods and tenses until we come to the third part (the Exercises), which may be looked upon as the synthetical portion of the grammar.

It remains however to mention the verbs which act as auxiliaries in forming the *passive* voice. They have been already given, but a few more examples may be of service to the student. The verbs referred to are, *kién* 見 'to see,' *sheú* 受 'to receive,' *k'ĭ* 吃 'to eat,' *ling* 領 'to receive,' *ts'aŭ* 遭 'to meet with,' *peí* 被 'to suffer,' &c.: (cf. Arts. 212 and 213.)

pí Tí chĕ yĭ-tuī taú: 'by Tí he was pushed away, with these words :' (12. f. 29.)

li-weí! pŭ-yaú kién-siaú 列位不要見笑 'Gentlemen! Do not be inclined to smile,' a phrase made use of when a scholar reads his own essays before the learned: (v. Prém. under 見, p. 61.)

Kién 'to see, to seem, to be affected by,' forms the passive here just as in other cases, although we do not so express the sentence in English, for we may say, 'do not smile!' It is literally, 'do not be seen to smile!'

t'ā pŭ kién-hwān-hǐ 'he was not pleased.'

suī-jên ngò k'ĭ-tièn-kw'eī 雖然我吃點虧 'although I shall be a loser.'

pí tsĕ-jîn kiĕ-k'ú 被賊人劫去 'was carried off by robbers.'

406. The student may refer to Arts. 211—213 for several auxiliary or formative verbs and examples, and seek for further examples under the following section on the meaning and use of the particles.

Few precise rules can be given for construing verbs into certain moods and tenses, beyond those already noticed, because the mood and tense often depend upon the circumstances of the action, or upon the previous sentence.

Examples of both will be seen in the passages given in the Chrestomathy. We must now proceed to the consideration of the syntax of the verbs and nouns, which serve to supply the place of the prepositions.

407. The verbs which are used as substitutes in some sense for the prepositions are given in Art. 257, p. 91. Examples of their use is all that is needed here.

1. *taú* 到, 'to arrive at,' implies *motion towards* and *arrival at:* e. g.—
t'ā taú-ché-lī lai-liaù 'he has arrived here,'—'*at* this place.'
ngò yaú taú-Pĕ-kīng k'ŭ 'I wish to go *to* Peking.'
nī kĭ-shí taú-Kwáng-tūng lai? 'When did you come *to* Canton?'
t'ā-mṇ̌ shă taú t'iĕn ming 'they went on killing *until* break of day.'
yü̆ lŏ taú pwàn yĕ 'the rain fell *until* midnight.'

Phrases: *lai-taú* 來 'come, arrived.' *tsĭ-taú* 接 'received.'

taú-chú 處 'every where.' *taú-tí* 底 'but, still, after all.'

2. *tsai* 在, 'to be in a place,' implies *position, rest in a place:* e. g.—
tsai-Kwáng-tūng tsŏ sáng-í haù 'trade is good *in* Canton.'
tsai-kiā-lī pŭ-haù 'it is not pleasant *in* the house.'

Phrases: *tsai-kiā* 家 'at home.' *tsĭ-tsai* 自 'to be without absence of mind.'

tsai-hŭ 乎 'to consist in.' (B.)

3. *ts'ŭng* 從, 'to follow,' implies *motion from, through,* or *out of:* e. g.—
t'ā ts'ŭng Pĕ-kīng lai liaù 'he is come *from* Peking.'
t'ā tseù ts'ŭng ching-lī kwŏ-k'ŭ 'he walked all *through* the city.'
ts'ŭng hwáng-sháng taú hiá-min '*from* the emperor down to the lowest of the people.'
ts'ŭng fáng-tsĕ ch'ŭ 'he went *out of* the room:' (cf. 27. l. 1.)
ts'ŭng yuĕn ḍr-lai 'come *from* a distance.'
With a negative preceding, it implies *means from or by which:* cf. *tsĭ* (15) below.

4. *hiáng* 向, 'to go towards,' implies *motion towards,* but it is not so commonly used as *taú* (1).
hiáng-ngò lai 'come *towards* me!'
pŭ yaú taú-ngò lai 'do not come *to* me.'
kŏ-chĕ-niaù fī hiáng-t'iĕn k'ŭ 'that bird flies *towards* heaven.'

Phrases: *hiáng-nán* 南 'southward.' *hiáng-tsiĕn* 前 'forward.'

hiáng-sháng 上 'upward.'

Hiáng 向 and *yàng* 仰 are sometimes used for *yù* 於 'to, at:' e. g.—
hiáng páng-yiù shwŏ 'to speak *to* a friend.'
wei-tsĕ-shí yàng kŏ-kwŏ ch'uĕn-chĕ 'by this notification we address ourselves *to* the ships of all nations.'

Wáng 望 and *yàng* 仰, 'to look towards,' are also used like *hiáng*.

5. *ì* 以 'to use, to take,' implies the *means by which*, and it precedes the *instrument* by which any thing is done, or the *cause* or *motive* for an action.

Yúng 用, 'to use,' is more commonly employed in this sense in the colloquial style; and as *ì* is looked upon generally as a book particle, the student is referred to the section on particles for examples of its grammatical use.

ngò yúng-taú-tsz̀ shà-t'ā 'I killed him *with* a knife.'

yīn yúng-sheù chí-chŏ Tì, taú, 'then *with* his hand he pointed to Tì, and said.'

Ná 拿, 'to take,' is also used in the same sense as *yúng*, for *by* or *with*.

6. *kí* 及, 'to arrive at or reach to,' is used for *with, and, until,* and *with reference to;* but this word is more common in the books than in the colloquial style.

k'ì-chă mŏ kí jù 稽察莫及汝 'the examination has no reference to you.'

kí ạr yû 及二月 'until the second month.'

It also has the sense of *about* in some phrases: e. g. *lạ́n-kí* 論及 'to talk about;'—a book is 'about' (*lạ́n-kí*) a certain subject. In this sense it agrees with that of *pà* 把 'to take,' which often means *taking, touching, concerning.*

7. *liên* 連, 'to connect,' is used in the sense of *and, with* (like *cum* or σύν); and at the beginning of a clause it often means *in addition to.*

liên hô-kí maú sż̀ 連夥計冒死 'he braved death with his companions.'

The verbal signification of *liên* admits of its being construed by several words, such as *both, and,* &c., and it often appears to be redundant at the head of a sentence: e. g.—

liên ĭ-fŭ sheù-shĭ[a] *tŭ pŭ kiên-liaù* 'she found neither her clothes nor her head-dress.'

liên nĭ yè-mŭ ching-kīng 連你也沒正經 'you too are without right principle.'

Phrase: *liên-yè* 連夜 'day and night.'

8. *tai* 代, 'to act as a deputy,' is equivalent to the prep. *instead of*:

tai-tĭ t'ŭng-hiāng-jîn[b] *sheù-k'ŭ* 'he suffered trouble in the place of his townsmen.'

---

[a] 首飾　　　[b] 同鄉人

t'ā tai-jîn shŭ-tsüi-liaŭ 'he, instead of men, made atonement for sin.'

9. yŭ 與, 'to give,' involves the notion of the *dative* case with the prep. *to or for*. But more examples will be given of its use under the section on the particles.

tsaŭ fĭ paŭ-yŭ Kwó-kūng-tsz̀ 'then he hastened to give information to Kwo-kung-tsz.' (8. c. 11.)

容小弟去與仁兄作伐如何 yŭng siaŭ-tì k'ŭ yŭ jîn-hiŭng tsŏ-fă jŭ-hô? 'allow me to go for you, Sir, and negotiate the marriage, will you?'

10. kĭ 給, 'to give,' is more commonly used in the conversational style for *yŭ*, as the mark of the *dative* case.

kiŭ nĭ kĭ ngò tsŏ chê-kó 'I beg of you to do this *for* me:' (cf. 27. a. 25.)
súng chê-kó kĭ t'ā k'ŭ-liaŭ 'presented this *to* him.'
tsai [a] kĭ-ngò yĭ-pŭ-k'ān [b] 'give (to) me another copy to look at.'

11. wei 爲 'to do, to become,' is used for the prep. *on account of, for*, and it enters into several phrases in this sense: e. g.—

yīn-wei 'because,' wei-shimmô 'for what,' = *why*.
weî nĭ laŭ-Yu ngò kaŭ chê-kó 'on your account, Mr. Yu, I will change this.'
weî shimmô lai liaŭ? 'why are you come?'
î-hô wei kiaì 依河爲界 'taking the river *for* the boundary.'
wei t'iĕn-hiá siaŭ 'to be a laughing-stock *for* the world.'

12. tüì 對, 'to be opposite to,' makes the prep. *towards, opposite to (adversus)*, &c. :
nĭ tüì t'ā shwŏ 'speak *to* him!'
tüì t'iĕn shwŏ-shì 'he swore *by* heaven.'

Phrase: tüì-miên 面 'on the opposite side.'

13. t'ŭng 同, 'the same,' stands as the prep. *together with (cum)*:
ngò pŭ-yaŭ t'ŭng-nĭ k'ŭ 'I do not wish to go *with* you.'
shĭ t'ŭng nà-kó yĭ-yáng 'it is the same *as* (with) that.'

14. hô 和, 'concord,' is commonly employed as the prep. *with, in company with*, = *t'ŭng* (q. v. 13. above):
ngò yaŭ hô nĭ hîng-lŭ 'I wish to walk *with* you.'
liên-jîn hô mà 'both men *and* horses.'
hô hiŭng-tì yĭ-k'ĭ hiáng-lĭ-miên tseŭ 'with my brother I went in.'

15. tsz̀ 自, commonly 'self,' has the same force and usage as ts'ŭng (q. v. 3.

---

[a] 再 [b] 部

above) 'to follow,' and therefore signifies 'from.' This is more frequently the case in the book style than in the colloquial idiom; and will be exemplified under the particles.

16. *t'ì* 替 'for, instead of,' is a more frequent colloquial expression than *tai*, mentioned above (8). *T'ì* also corresponds with *yü* 'for, to,' as a mark of the dative (9).

ngŏ kiŏ t'ì nì siŭ 我却替你羞 'well, I am ashamed of you!' (*Hsin-ching-tu* III. 76.)

t'ì-jìn ch'ŭ-lì 人出力 'to exert one's self for people.'

yāng-jìn t'ì t'ā ŕr-tsz̀ tsŏ-fá 央人 | 他兒子作伐 'he solicited a person to negotiate a marriage for his son.'

17. *yīn* 因 'because of' and *yiŭ* 由 'origin' are both used for *on account of, by* or *through*, although the manner of using them varies: e. g.—

yīn taŭ-tsz̀, sz̀-liaŭ, 'he died by the sword.'

yīn nì pŭ-nì 因你悖逆 '*because* of your obstinacy.'

yīn weí p'á, pŭ k'ì-fán, 'he could not eat *through* fear.'

yiŭ tsz̀ mǎn tsìn 'enter *by* this door!'

yiŭ yuên jì ŭ '*by* the garden enter the house!'

yiŭ wŭ-kwān chīng-pán[a] 'transacted *by* the military officers.'

408. The forms of construction, which stand as equivalents for the *relations of time and place*, commonly expressed by prepositions in European tongues, need some elucidation: (cf. Art. 258.)

Any general term for a relation of place or time may be used in construction, as a noun, with the preposition *tsai* 在 'in' or *ts'ŭng* 從 'from,' (according as the notion of *rest in* or *motion* is implied,) placed before the noun to which such relation of place or time refers; the expression then becomes equivalent to a preposition with its case in Latin or English: e. g.—

ngŏ kŭ tsai-chîng-lì 'I reside *in* the city,' lit. 'in the city's interior.'

t'ā t'ŭng-chîng-lì k'ŭ 'he went *through* the city.'

nì tseŭ tsai-chîng-waì 'walk *outside* the city,' lit. 'in the city's exterior.'

409. It is of great importance for the student to be able to divest his mind of the idea of a Chinese word being a noun or a verb, and to be able to treat any word as a noun or a verb, according as the case may require. The value of this is especially observable in the construction of words to express the relations of time and space, where we use adverbs and prepositions. Instead of saying 'upon the table,' the Chinese would say 'iu the table's upper part,' *tsai chŏ-tsz̀ sháng*. Several examples of this form of expression have already been

[a] 武官承辦

given in Arts. 258—260, and to these the student may refer. When the phrase thus formed, as an adverbial expression, stands as the nominative case, or the subject of a sentence, *tsai* need not be used: e. g. *ch'ing-nūi yiŭ mĭ mai* 'in the city there is rice to sell,' lit. 'the city's interior has rice to sell.' But the method of expressing these relations will find its appropriate place in Part III, where the exercises will necessitate a number of rules for turning English into Chinese. One caution should be always remembered, that the *position* of the words alone can determine how the expression must be construed. A noun may become a verb, simply from its position, and a noun may so stand with another noun, as to form a preposition in signification, although it is not prefixed (*præpositum*). Thus *hiá-shān* 'descend a mountain,' but *hiá-fāng* 'lower room,' and *shán-hiá* 'at the foot of the mountain.' *Waî-kwŏ* 'foreign countries,' *kwŏ-waî* 'out of the country,'= *abroad*. *Shàng-mă* 'to mount a horse,' *mă-shăng* 'on horseback.'

410. The adverbs do not admit of any modification of a grammatical nature, excepting their intensification, either by being *repeated*, or by an intensifying particle being prefixed to them. (Cf. Arts. 238—256, p. 84.)

It will be necessary to notice, in the next place, the particles which affect words and sentences, and thus modify them, but in a manner so peculiar as to call for a separate section, and a distinct analysis of their uses as *attributive, connective, affirmative, negative, adversative, causative, conditional, illative, interrogative, dubitative, intensitive, exclamatory,* and *euphonic* particles.

§. 7. *The syntax of the particles.*

I. *Attributive particles,* 的 *tĭ,* 之 *chī,* 者 *ché,* and 所 *sŏ.*

411. The very first principle of Chinese construction is, that the qualifying words and clauses precede those which they qualify, and though there is frequently nothing to show the point at which the attribute ends and where the object of that attribute begins, several particles do exist, which, under certain circumstances, show this. They have been referred to above in Arts. 130, 132, and 313.

As the effect of these particles is to throw that which precedes them into the form of a qualifying or attributive expression, that is, either the genitive case of a noun, the adjective, or the relative clause, we shall call them *attributive* particles; and here it will be well to illustrate their use by several examples. They were all originally demonstratives, excepting *sŏ*, and the two first may be looked upon as equivalent to our *s* with an apostrophe, which appears to be only a contraction of *his, its,* or *hers* * ; the last—*sŏ*—contains the notion of ' place.'

---

* Since the above was written we have met with the following extract from a native author on the subject : ª *Fán yèn chī chè* 'Whenever *chī* is expressed,' ᵇ *wŭ yiŭ sŏ chi* 'there is a thing pointed out,' ᶜ *sz' yiŭ sŏ shŭ* 'there is an affair connected with it,'

ª 凡言之者 ᵇ 物有所指 ᶜ 事有所屬

的 *tī* is used only in mandarin and in the novels. After a noun it produces the genitive case, after a verb it makes the participle, and after a sentence it must be construed into the form of the relative clause: e. g.—

hwâng-tí-tī 'of the emperor,' *hwâng-tí tī mà* 'the emperor's horse.'
hwâng-sháng 'imperial,' *hwâng-sháng-tī* 'that which is imperial.'
chê-kó shī ngò tsŏ tī 'this is what I made.'
yiù tseù-tī, yiù fī-tī, 'there are those which walk and those which fly,' or 'some walk, others fly.'
nà-kó shī tsŏ jī laì tī jīn 'that is the man who came here yesterday.'
kąng-tàng-tī 'just waiting,' or 'who was just waiting.'

412. With respect to the particle *chī* 之, Dr. Morrison says, that in the ancient books it occurs in the sense of *yū* 於, *shī* 是, *tsż* 此, *ī* 遺, *chī* 至, and *piēn* 變. (See these words in the dictionary.) Its original meaning was the same as *chī* 至 'to proceed, to go to,' or as a demonstrative particle, 'that' or 'this.' The meanings of all these words run into each other. Compare the notion in *chī* 至 as a particle to form the superlative; it signifies 'to proceed to the extreme,' or 'that;' e. g. *chī-haù* 'that good thing or person,' *par excellence*, therefore 'the best.' Although the characters 之, 此, 是, 至 are different, the ideas first attached to them were probably the same, and perhaps the sound too, for *chi, tsz, shi, chi* are all cognate in sound. As the Chinese language became more analytic, the characters were invented and diversified, and words (by which syllables merely are intended), which had at first but one primitive meaning, came to receive special significations in certain connections, and, as a matter of course, distinct characters to represent them. Examples of the uses of *chī* *:

jīn chī k'ì sò tsin-gaì 人 之 其 所 親 愛 'men, as to those things which they love.' (Tá-hiŏ.) Here *chī*=*yū* 於 'with respect to.' Cf. *Classics*, vol. I. p. 233.

chī tsż yū hwoi 之 了 于 歸 'this girl is on the return *to her husband's house*.' (Shī-king.) Here *chī*=*shī* 是. Cf. *Classics*, vol. I. p. 236.

---

d *tī yiù sò wàng* 'there is a place which is visited;' e *liēn shŭ chī tsż yè*,—it is an expression of connection and relation. See Dr. Morrison's Dictionary, vol. I. p. 34. See also the extract given in the Introduction, p. xxi.

* The references are to vol. I. of Dr. Legge's recently published work: *The Chinese Classics, with a translation, critical and exegetical notes, &c.* Roy. 8vo. Hongkong, 1861. The author here wishes to acknowledge his indebtedness to this first volume, and to recommend it to the student of classical Chinese. The student may compare also the classic usage of *chī* f 'these,' com. = 'only,' and *tsī* g 'to go to,' com. = 'then.'

d 地 有 所 往   e 連 屬 之 辭 也   f 只   g 郎

Mậng-tsź chī Ping-lù 孟子之平陸 'Mencius went to Ping-lù.' (Chūng-yūng.) Here *chī=chí* 'to proceed to.'

wí chī yiù yĕ 未之有也 'there never was such a thing,' where *chī* is merely euphonic, though in such a position it sometimes appears to represent the object of the verb *yiù*.

413. *Chī* 之 frequently stands after a verb, as a pronoun, the antecedent for which is either expressed or understood; e. g. 學而時習之 *hiŏ ąr shí sź chī* 'to learn and constantly to practice it,' viz. 'what you learn,' (*Lun-yü, ad init.*) Here *chī* is *objective*, and occupies the same place as *tsź* 子, in the Shanghai dialect, after verbs. There *tsź* is looked upon as a euphonic particle, and *chī* in the books, when in this position, is probably nothing more, or merely like *it* in some English phrases (cf. "*Thu' es heute,*" in the Prologue to Goethe's *Faust*). The following is an example of two uses of *chī*; 1st, as a verb; 2nd, as a euphonic particle, as that just referred to: cf. *kiù-chī* 久 | 'a long time past.'

yiù shí ąr chī-yên-chī weí taú 由是而｜焉｜謂道 'from this place proceeding is called *taú*' ('road'). The *yên* is put in to separate the former *chī* from the latter more clearly, and to make the expression more rhythmical.

Chī, used as the object, has also the effect of making *tsź* 自, which precedes the verb, the subject, and prevents it from being the reflexive pronoun and object, which is commonly the case: e. g.—

ch'áng tsź shĕ chī 常自射｜ 'he always shot them,' but

yìn taú tsź kīng 引刀自剄 'with a sword he killed himself:' v. *Schott. Chin. Sphr.* p. 80.

414. *Chī* 之 is also *subjective,* and used as such in the *kù-wąn* for *chĕ* 者; e. g. *kù-chī* 古｜ 'the ancients;' and it has the same effect as *chĕ* (i. e. as a formative), and then it corresponds with *tsź* 子 in the colloquial idiom. In this way it occurs very frequently, and it must be considered either as a formative or as a rhythmical or euphonic particle.

415. *Chĕ* 者 is also an attributive particle, for it unites the whole sentence which precedes it, and makes the noun or verb to which it is affixed an attributive: thus, *shwŏ-chĕ* 說｜ 'he who speaks,—the speaker or speakers;' *kù-chĕ* 古｜ 'those of ancient times,—the ancients.' But although the attributive force may generally be referred to this particle, it will be needful to notice the other more common explanations of it.

Chè 者 is frequently to be regarded as a *demonstrative* pronoun, and stands after words, as the article ὁ, ἡ, τό, in Greek, stands before words, to individualize or make special, particular persons, things, or expressions; and most commonly where an explanation is about to be given of the object thus specified. This explanation which succeeds, determines not only the meaning of that which precedes, but also the grammatical value of the word itself; e. g. *jin-chè* 仁 | would be either 'benevolence' or 'the benevolent,' according to the definition which followed: thus,

jin-chè jin yè 仁者人也 'humanity is man,' (i. e. 'to fulfil all the demands involved in the human relations is to act as a man,') but

jin-chè lŏ shān 仁 | 樂 山 'the benevolent delight in the mountains.'

So also the addition of the particle *yè* 也 or *chī* 之, between the verb and *chè*, separates the verbal notion, and causes the whole to form an abstract noun: thus,

sāng-chè 生 | 'those which are born or which grow,—the living.'

sāng-yè chè 'that in which growth is or consists,—life.'

416. When in an explanatory sentence the subject is marked by *chè* being attached, and the explanation consists of several words, or includes a relative clause, another *chè* often precedes the final particle *yè* 也. It would be so in a sentence like this: "God is the all-wise and beneficent creator and preserver of all things."

jù - tsz̀ chè tsaī kī k'ī shīn chè - yè
如 此 | 災 及 其 身 | 也
' He who does so will bring evil upon himself.'

Prémare says that *Ngaū-yâng* 歐陽 used *chè-yê* | 耶 for *chè-yè*, and also *shí-yè* 是 也 for the same, in common with writers of the first class; and he gives one example which goes to prove that *chè* 者 and *shí* 是 alike mean *this* or *is*, as we choose to render the sentence *.

kù · chī jin yiù hìng chī chè, Wū-wâng shí yè,
故 | 人 有 行 | 者 武 王 是 也
' Among the ancients there were those who did it, Wu-wang was *one of them*.'

417. When *chè* is placed after a complete sentence the whole will form an abstract notion, or it will represent some particular action in an abstract point of view: e. g. after the sentence 'the soldier braves death,' *chè* would make the whole to signify 'the soldier's braving death,' which might form either the

---

* Cf. note on page 122.

subject or the predicate of a new sentence. 'Alexander went to India,' followed by *chě*, would become, 'Alexander's going to India.' Sometimes *chě* follows two clauses, as in this example:

t'iaū - chě lwàn - p'ó chě, hô ? Siūn-tsź.

茍折卵破者何

'The cracking of the reed, and the breaking of the egg, how *is it?*'
(The nest was well formed and strong, but the support was infirm: cf. The house built on the sand.)

Yaū-Shūn sing chě, T'ang Wŭ fán chī,

堯舜性者湯武反之

'The principles of Yau and Shun were perverted by T'ang and Wu.'

chī - chī - chě, pŭ jû haú - chī - chě,

知之者不如好之者

'Knowing it is not like loving it,' or 'those who love it are better than those who know it.'

418. *Chě* frequently serves only to mark the subject of the sentence, and to separate it from the predicate: e. g.—

kiūn - tsź taú chě, sān. Cf. Chrest. 3. e. 13—23.

君子道丨三

'The principles of the superior man are three.'

k'ŏ - chě, yŭ chī; k'í pŭ k'ŏ - chě, k'ü chī,

可丨與之其不可丨拒之

'With those who are worthy, treat; those who are unworthy, reject.'

419. *Chě* appears to stand like *chī* 之, for the object of the verb, and after the predicate, in the following examples (cf. Art. 413):

fū hô-weî chě? 夫何爲丨 'but how are you to do it?'

Chūng-nī pŭ - weî ì shìn chě

仲尼不爲已甚丨

'Chung-ni never went to excess.'

420. The use of *chě* 者 does not date so early as that of *chī* 之. It is rarely, if at all, to be found in the *Shū-king* and the most ancient classics, but it is very common in the *Sź-shū* and all later classical writings. It is sometimes difficult to give any definite signification to *chě*, but if the student will bear in mind that it unites the whole clause and makes it participial, as when *the* is prefixed to a clause in English, or ὁ, ἡ, τό in Greek, he cannot be very far from apprehending the notion which the passage conveys.

421. The remaining particle *sŏ* 所, which originally signified 'place,'

THE SYNTAX OF THE PARTICLES.

perhaps 'that place,' has been classified with attributive particles, because it often has the force of the relative pronoun, and the relative clause is undoubtedly an attributive clause. The common rendering of *sŏ* is 'that which, what;' *nĭ sŏ yiŭ* 你 所 有 '*what* you have.' This character, like *chĕ*, appears to have been seldom, if ever, used in the ancient books, though common enough in the later classics of Confucius and his disciples: e. g. in the *Sz̀-shū* (4. c. 23), *sŏ weî kŭ-kwŏ chĕ* 'the kingdoms *which* are called ancient,' or, as is said in English, '*what* is called an ancient kingdom is &c.' Again (4. l. 15), ..*fĭ jĭn sŏ năng yĕ* '.. is not *what* men are able to do,' and (4. d. 17) *sĭ-chĕ sŏ tsĭn, kīn-jĭ pŭ chī k'ĭ wáng yĕ*, 'the former ministers *whom* you advanced, to-day you are not cognizant of their loss.'

sŏ-weî hŏ sz̀? 所 爲 何 事. lit. 'that which he is doing is what business?'= *what is he doing?* (B.)

sŏ-kiên pŭ shū 所 見 不 殊 'our opinions (*the views which we take*) are not diverse.'

p'ĭ k'ĭ sŏ-pŭ-weî 毗 其 所 不 爲 'to slander is what he will not do.'

422. There are several phrases into which this particle enters; e. g. *sŏ-ĭ* 所 以, 'the means by which,' is commonly translated 'therefore:' 幾 所 *kī-sŏ* 'several which, a good many, some.' The following formula should be remembered, and the classical scholar may observe that it accords with he Greek expression for the same form with two negatives:

wû sŏ-pŭ-náng 無 所 不 能 lit. 'there is nothing which he could not do,'=*omnipotent*.

wû sŏ-pŭ-súng 無 | | 送 'there is nothing which they would not have given,' or 'which they would not give;' and this corresponds exactly with the Greek of Demosthenes, οὐκ-ἔσθ' ὅ-τι οὐκ ἐδίδοσαν: v. Dem. de Coronâ, Reiske 261.

II. *Connective particles*, 亦 *yĭ*, 而 *ărr*, 又 *yiú*, 幷 *píng*, &c.

423. Characters which may be called *connectives* in Chinese are rather numerous, but they cannot be designated as simply *copulative*, for they generally convey some accessory notion. The above however are the common equivalents for 'and, also;' and they imply an addition of something to the previous clause. We must consider each separately.

424. *Yĭ* 亦, 'also,' generally comes second in the clause, and then, like καί in Greek, it means 'even' or 'indeed:' e. g.—

pŭ yĭ yŭ hû? 不 亦 說 乎. 'is it not indeed pleasant?' (*shwŏ* is here used for 悅 *yŭ*.) Chrest. 3. d. 17.

pŭ yĭ lŏ hû? | 亦 樂 乎. 'is it not indeed enlivening?' Chrest. 3. d. 25.

jên, Chĭng wáng, Tsz̀ yĭ yiù pŭ lĭ yên,

然 鄭 亡 子 亦 有 不 利 焉

'Yea, if Ching were lost, Tsz indeed would not have any advantage.'

And in many expressions it is simply intensive : e. g.—

pĭ pŭ haŭ, tsz̀ yĭ pŭ haŭ,

彼 不 好, 此 亦 不 好

'That is not good, this too is not good.'

Phrases yĭ-k'ŏ 亦 可 and yĭ-haŭ 亦 好 are terms of assent, = *Well! Good!*

425. 而 *r̨* 'and, and yet, and then, but, and consequently,' is commonly used as a connective particle, but sometimes it has an illative force, and sometimes it is merely euphonic. It should be observed, however, that it never connects substantives : e. g.—

hŏ ĭ shĭ k'ĭ pŭ tsaî r̨ shè chĭ

何 以 識 其 | 才 | 舍 之

'Whereby shall I know his want of talent and reject him?' Chrest. 4. e. 1, also 3. e. 26. and Art. 439.

kīng sĭng r̨ hĭ chĭ 驚 醒 而 戯 之 'he awoke in a fright, and then played with him.' (Chrest. 21. g. 19.)

pŭ lŏ shên-taú, r̨ wáng k'ĭ kwŏ,

不 樂 善 道 而 亡 其 國

'He delighted not in virtuous principles, and so he lost his kingdom.'

It is joined with *tsiĕ* in the following example :

r̨-tsiĕ jĭ pīn 而 且 日 貧 'and moreover he daily grew poorer.'

And it is euphonic in the following *apodosis*:

..r̨-hwàng yū jĭn hŭ! 而 況 於 人 乎. '..much more as regards man!'

426. The difference between yiŭ 又 and yĭ 亦, each of which means 'also,' seems to be that the former has a more purely connective force, and often stands at the beginning of a clause, though it does sometimes take the second or third place with the signification 'again :' e. g.—

yiŭ weí weí pŭ k'ŏ 又 未 爲 不 可 'and it is not yet considered impossible.'

k'ŭng-p'à yiŭ shĭ chĭ-tūng-hwá-sī

恐 怕 又 是 指 東 話 西

'I fear that he will again say one thing and mean another,' lit. 'point to the east and talk about the west.'

yiŭ chĕ - shí siaù, píng pŭ shwŏ - ch'ŭ ch'áng-twăn,

又只是笑並不說出長短

'Again he only smiled, and uttered nothing for or against,' (lit. 'long or short.')

In the following example, which is purely idiomatic, *yiŭ* is repeated, and may be rendered 'then' or 'and then:'

má - liaù yiŭ tă, tă - liaù yiŭ má,

罵了打，打了罵

'Having scolded, then he beat; having beaten, then he scolded.'
This form of expression is admired by the Chinese. Cf. Chrest. litho. *Săn-kwŏ*, 11. c. 7, *făn-kiù pĭ hŏ, hŏ kiù pĭ făn.*

An intensifying form is *k'ăn-liaù yiŭ k'ăn* 看了看 'having looked he looked again:' v. *Haŭ-k'iŭ chuén*, 11. f. 13.

427. *Yiŭ* 又 is also used where *yiù* 有 or *shí* 是 might be looked for, as in the two following examples:

t'ŭ - chūng yiŭ kī; sīn - hiá yiŭ k'i,

肚中饑心下氣

'In his belly he had hunger; in his heart he had wrath.'

ts'z̆, yiŭ ts'z̆ - pŭ - tĕ; tsiŭ, yiŭ tsiŭ - pŭ - tĕ,

辭辭不得，就就得

'As for refusing, he could not refuse; as for accepting, he could not accept.'
Yiŭ must here be left untranslated, but it corresponds precisely with the colloquial usage of *shí* 'to be,' which means 'it was *this*' in such expressions.

kwān yiŭ kaū, kiā yiŭ fŭ,

官又高，家富

'His office was high, his family was wealthy.'

428. When *yiŭ* 又 is repeated thus in two parallel clauses, it may occasionally be construed by 'neither' and 'nor:' e. g.—

tsŏ yiŭ pŭ gān, lĭ yiŭ pŭ níng,

坐又不安，立寧

'He could neither sit nor stand with comfort.'

For several examples of the use of this particle the student may refer to the Chrestomathy: 9. i. 8; 9. k. 2; 10. j. 2; 10. h. 6; and elsewhere.

429. *Píng* 并 (also very commonly 並, and formerly 竝), which properly signifies 'two standing together,'—'together with, in union with,' is used as a simple copulative conjunction in the style immediately above the ordinary colloquial. In the *Săn-kwŏ chí*, for example, *píng* and *yiŭ* are used together: (see also the first example on this page, where *pŭ* follows *píng*.)

yiú píng jĭ yŭ Hàn 又 | 入 于 漢 'and together united in Han:'
v. *Sān-kwŏ chí*, Chrest. litho. 11. d. 9.
And on the same page at c. 21. *píng* is used alone in a similar sense.

Píng is used as an intensifying particle before a negative; it then signifies 'even, indeed, forsooth' (cf. the use of καί in Greek): *píng-pŭ-shí* 'no, forsooth!'

píng wú-wáng 並 無 望 'utterly hopeless.'

430. *Píng* sometimes means 'both,' as in these two examples:

tsiĕ-mĕi píng mei 姐 妹 並 美 'the (elder and younger) sisters were both alike beautiful.'

laù - yiú píng-kiaī nâ - hiá
老 幼 並 皆 拿 下
'The old and the young were both alike seized.'

Like many other words in the same category, *píng* enters into several phrases to signify the *whole;* e. g. *yĭ-píng* 'one and all.'

Phrase: *píng-kiēn* 並 兼 'together with.'

431. *Kiēn* 兼 is commonly used in official papers for 'and, together with:' e. g.—

Píng - pú, Shảng-shū; kiēn Tū-chă-yuên, yiú Tū - yŭ - shĭ,
兵 部 尚 書 | 都 察 院 右 都 御 史
'Of the Board of War, President; and of the Metropolitan College of Censors, an Imperial officer.'

The following belong to a higher style of composition:

kiēn ár yiù chĭ 兼 而 有 之 'altogether to have them.'

kiēn tsż ár ì | 此 二 義 'both these meanings.'

432. *K'í* 暨, 'together with,' is used like *kiēn* in the official style of composition for 'and,' and generally as a copulative conjunction: e. g.—

Hiēn-lìng k'í Hiĕ-taì 縣 令 | 協 臺 'the Worshipful the Mayor, and His Excellency the Commandant.'

433. *Tsiĕ* 且 'moreover, and,' is used as a conjunction, and also means sometimes 'now' or 'anon,' and 'still, then,' &c. It also enters into several adverbial phrases. But it is not frequently found in the colloquial style.

nĭ chè siē hwá tsiĕ màn shwŏ
你 這 些 話 | 慢 說
'If you say this, then speak deliberately.'

THE SYNTAX OF THE PARTICLES.   151

tsiĕ k'ŭ tsiĕ tseŭ 且 拒 且 走 'anon visiting and running.'

yû, tsiĕ laŭ, maí tiên 余 | 老 買 田 'I, being then an old man, bought a field.'

434. *Tsiĕ* also seems to be a common prefix to the imperative sentence: e. g.—

Siāng-kūng! tsiĕ pŭ yaú k'ŭ!
相 公 | | 要 哭
'Sirs! do not weep!'

tsiŭ, tsiĕ fāng-hiá 酒 | 放 下 'as for the wine, do desist.'

tsiĕ k'ān hiá-hwiĭ fān-kiaĭ
| 看 下 回 分 解
'Just look at the following chapter for explanation.'

435. *Tsiĕ* is frequently redundant at the beginning of a clause: e. g.—

tsiĕ k'ān t'ā tsăng-tĭ 且 看 他 怎 的 'behold, how he is.'

tsiĕ mŏ shwŏ t'ā! | 莫 說 他 'now, do not speak to him!'

tsiĕ chĕ-p'á | 只 怕 'I only fear indeed.'

Phrases: *hwáng-tsiĕ* 況 | 'so much the more:' *ăr-tsiĕ* 而 | 'but yet, and besides:' *chĕ-tsiĕ* 只 |, at the end of sentences, 'only' or 'alone' (B.): *tsiĕ-shwŏ* is the regular phrase at the beginning of a new chapter in novels for, 'the story goes on to say' (cf. Chrest. 17. a. 6); and 却 | *kiŏ-shwŏ*, 'to return to the story' (cf. Chrest. 17. m. 22): 姑 | *kū-tsiĕ*, 權 | *kiuên-tsiĕ*, both mean 'then, the case being so:' *keŭ-tsiĕ* 苟 | 'carelessly;' *tsiĕ-fŭ* | 夫 'now, further;' *tsaí-tsiĕ* 再. | 'again.'

436. *Kĭ* 及 and *liên* 連, which have been spoken of in Art. 407. 6, 7, as verbs acting the part of prepositions, also stand frequently as conjunctions. This might indeed be expected, inasmuch as *with* frequently stands for *and* in our own language: e. g.—

liên jin mă 連 人 馬 'men and horses.'

ngò liên nĭ 我 連 你 'I and you' or 'I with you.'

ngò kĭ jŭ | 及 汝 'I and you.' (B.)

kĭ fūng Chaŭ-siēn.. 及 封 朝 鮮 'and being appointed governor of Corea,'..

Other examples may be seen in page 139, Art. 407.

Kúng 共, 'together with,' is also used in the same sense and manner.

437. The particle *yè* 也, which will be more fully discussed in another place as a final particle of assertion, is used very frequently in the style of conversation for *and, also,* and stands at the beginning of the clause; or for *even, indeed,* as an intensifying particle, and then it stands immediately before the word which it affects: e. g.—

ngǒ yè t'úng nì k'ú 我也同你去 'I also will go with you.'

tsiú yǐ-kě yè-pǔ-náng liú! 就一刻也 | 能留 'then you could not even stay ten minutes!' Chrest. 10. o. 4. Comp. Art. 364.

438. The particle *fū* 夫 is used at the beginning of the sentence for *now*, as a particle of transition, like *then* (cf. ἤδη in Greek): e. g.—

fū Tsz̀ chī k'iú-chī yè.. 夫子之求 | 也 'now the Master's seeking,'..

fū jîn-chě, tś'z̀ yè | 仁者慈 | ' now benevolence is just kindness.'

fū hiaú-chě, t'iēn chī kīng, tī chī ì, mîn chī hìng yè,
夫孝 | 天之經地 | 義民 | 行也
'Now filial piety is (what accords with) the order of heaven, the sentiment of earth, and the conduct of the people.'

fū jîn yiú q̀r hiǒ chī,chwáng q̀r yǔ hìng chī,..
夫人又 | 學之壯 | 欲行 |
'Now when a man has learnt any thing in his youth and being grown wishes to practise it,'.. (Cf. Chrest. 4. h. 25.)

439. At the end of a sentence *fū* is merely expletive, or a mark of exclamation: e. g.—

mǒ ngǒ chī yè-fū! 莫我知也夫 'no one knows me!'

náng kaū k'í mù q̀r hiá k'í q̀r chě, fī t'iēn yè-fū!
能高其目 | 下其耳者非天也夫
'He who can exalt his eye and depress his ear is no other than heaven!'

III. *Affirmative particles,* 是 *shì,* 然 *jên,* 也 *yè,* 矣 *ì,* &c.

440. The common form of affirmation in Chinese is the repetition of the principal verb used in the question: e. g.—

Q. *nǐ lai mó?* 'are you coming?' A. *lai* 'I am coming.'

Q. *t'īng ngǒ tī shwǒ-hwá mó?* 'do you hear what I say?' A. *t'īng-kiēn-liaù* 'I have heard.'

The simple assertion or affirmation of any fact is generally expressed by *shì* 是 'it is so, it is the truth.'

441. But in the book style the particle of acquiescence or affirmation is *jên* 然, which may stand at the beginning of a sentence or alone. At the beginning of a sentence *jên* may mean 'it was thus:' e. g.—

jên Súng-jin yiŭ mìn 然宋人有閔 'it was thus that a man in the Sung dynasty was grieved.'

When *jên* follows an adjective or a verb it is a formative particle, and helps to make an adverb. (Cf. Art. 238. β.)

Phrases: *jên-heŭ* | 後 'afterwards,—then.' (Chrest. 4. f. 30.)

    kī-jên 既 | 'since it is thus.' (Chrest. 9. b. 18.)

    tsz̀-jên 自 | 'certainly.'

    suī-jên 雖 | 'although it is so.'

    wí-pí-jên 未必 | 'not necessarily so.'

    tsz̀-jên ǎr-jên 自 | 而 | 'of itself,'—'*suâ sponte*.'

442. *Yĕ* 也 is a very common particle of affirmation, and stands at the end of sentences with the sense of 'forsooth, it is true,' attached to it: e. g.—

ĭ - wei năng shíng k'ì jìn yĕ
以爲能勝其任也
'Because you would consider it sufficient for the purpose.' (Chrest. 4. h. 2.)

fĭ jìn sǒ năng yĕ 非人所能 | 'it is not indeed what man can do.' (Chrest. 4. l. 5.)

Meŭ lì wàn - ch'ŭ - chī, tsĭ ts'ī yĕ!
某力挽出之卽妻也
'M. with force dragged it out, and behold it was his wife!'

wáng-yáng pú - laŭ, wí wei chí yĕ,
亡羊補牢未爲遲也
'Though the sheep is lost, it is never too late to mend the fold.'

Yĕ seems to be used in sentences conveying an assertion, whether affirmative or negative, and it helps to affirm the truth of each respectively.

443. Sometimes *yĕ* merely creates a pause in the sense of the passage, or makes a division of the members of the sentence itself: e. g.—

    k'ì yên yĕ shén 其言也善 'his words are good.'

    hiaŭ - tí - yĕ - chĕ k'ì wei jìn chī pàn yŭ!
孝弟 | 者其爲仁之本與
'Filial piety and fraternal love,—these are the sources of benevolence!'

Phrases: *wĭ chī yiŭ yĕ* 未之有也 'there never was such a thing.'
   tsè chī weí yĕ 此之謂也 'this is the meaning.'

444. *Yĕ* is sometimes used after proper names, especially when the name consists of a monosyllable, and when it seems to require some expletive to support it. It also stands as an expletive at the end of an answer to a question: e. g.—

Yiŭ yĕ 由也, *K'iŭ yĕ* 求也, 'Yiu, K'iu (names of philosophers).'

k'ŏ-hŭ? pŭ-k'ŏ-yĕ! 可乎, 不可也, 'May he? He may not!'

yiŭ-hŭ? wĭ-yiŭ-yĕ! 有乎, 未有丨, 'Is there any? There is not!'

Yĕ is found as an adjunct with *chĕ* 者, *chĕ-yĕ* and *yĕ-chĕ* (cf. Arts. 415 and 416); also with *fŭ* 夫, *yĕ-fŭ* (cf. Art. 439); and with *tsaī* 哉, *yĕ-tsaī*; with *yŭ* 與, *yĕ-yŭ*; with *ĭ* 已, *yĕ-ĭ*; and with *yĕ* 耶, *yĕ-yĕ*.

445. *Yên* 焉 is found either at the beginning, in the middle, or at the end of sentences. At the beginning it is an interrogative particle; in the middle it marks a pause in the sentence; and at the end it has an affirmative or assertive force, and has sometimes the value of a mark of admiration.

Examples.

fŭ yên yiŭ sŏ ĭ? 夫焉有所倚 'now what was there to rest upon?'

shă kī yên yŭng niŭ taū? 殺雞焉用牛刀 'in killing a fowl why use an ox knife?'

pŭ nâng k'āng shīn, yên nâng k'āng tsūng?
不能亢身焉能亢宗
'Not being able to screen myself, how can I screen my kinsmen?'

kiŭn' tsè chī kwó jŭ jĭ - yŭ chī shĭ yên!
君子之過如日月之食丨
'The good man's errors are like the eclipses of the sun and moon!' (i. e. they are but partial obscurations.)

446. The particle *ĭ* 矣 is commonly *final*, either at the end of a clause or of a sentence.

siàng pĭ jên ĭ 想必然丨 'I think it must be so.'

jîn ĭ ąr-ĭ-ĭ 仁義而已丨 'humanity and justice, and nothing else.'

wŭ wĭ chī-chī ĭ 我未知之丨 'I do not yet know it.'

taú - chī   pŭ - híng   yĕ   wŭ   chī - chī   ĭ
道之不行也吾知之矣
'That principles are not followed I know it,' (i. e. the reason) =
'I know why right principles are not acted upon.'

447. The particle *ĭ* closes the predicate of an affirmative or of a negative sentence, but it most commonly ends an affirmative clause or sentence. *Yĕ* 也 seems to be preferred for closing a negative sentence, though it is often found at the end of an affirmation. The following two examples will illustrate this: (1) *K'ĭ weí-jín yĕ hiaú-tí ạr haú-fán-shàng-chĕ, siĕn-ĭ*, 'those who, with respect to men, show themselves dutiful, both as sons and as younger brothers, and yet like to resist their superiors, are few.' (2) *Pŭ haú-fán-shàng ạr haú tsŏ-lwán chĕ, wí-chī-yiù yĕ*, 'men who dislike resisting superiors, and yet like creating rebellion, are not to be found:' (v. Chrest. *Sz̆-shū, Lạ́n-yŭ̂*, 3. d. 13. et seq.) This particle *ĭ* stands in the following affirmative sentences with the force of the Greek particle πέρ, implying the reality of what is asserted:

wŭ pĭ weí chī hiŏ ĭ 吾必謂之學 | 'I must call him learned.'
(Chrest. 3. j. 24.)

fŭ sz̆ ạr-ĭ 弗思耳 | 'not merely to be aimed at.' (Chrest. 5. h. 13.)

..*ạr kwŏ weí ĭ* 而國危 | '..and the country will be in danger.'

yúng-chī   wŭ   tŭ   ạr   tsaí   lĭ   kweí   ĭ
用之無度而財立匱 |
'Use them without measure and your means will soon be exhausted.'

yĭ   yiù   jín - ĭ   ạr - ĭ - ĭ!
亦有仁義而已 |
'Surely there are benevolence and justice, and they are sufficient!'

wŭ   wĭ   chī   hô   yĕ - ĭ - ĭ
吾未之何也 | |
'I have nothing more that I can do.'

448. The combinations of the particle *ĭ* 矣 with other particles are many, and the signification and force of each particular combination must be sought for in the passages where they occur. They will generally assist in strengthening the assertion, or in intensifying the expression if it be an exclamation. Such are the following:

Combinations: *ĭ-hŭ!* | 乎..   *jên-ĭ* 然 |.
         ĭ-fū! | 夫.   *ĭ-ĭ* 已 |.
         ạr-ĭ 耳 |.   *hô-ĭ* 何 |.

449. The two last examples in Art. 447 will serve to illustrate the use of 到 已 as a particle of affirmation, or rather of assertion. It properly signifies 'already done' (cf. Art. 194); and, as a particle, it adds to the force of the statement to which it is appended: e. g.—

tsĭ yĭ ậr-ĭ 則 一 而 | 'just one and no more.'

wĭ chĭ yè-ĭ | 之 也 | 'do not go there at all.'

pŭ tsŭ kwān yè-ĭ 不 足 觀 | | 'not at all worthy of notice.'

450. But in the following example 到 conveys its own proper meaning simply: e. g.—

ĭ-hû! ĭ-hû! | 乎 | 乎 'Have done! have done!' or

ĭ-ậr! ĭ-ậr! | 而 | 而 'Enough! enough!' or 'No more! no more!'

Combinations: *ĭ-ĭ* | 矣. Also *yè-ĭ* 也 | .

ĭ-hû | 乎, and

ĭ-ĭ-hû | | 乎, or

ĭ-ĭ-fû | | 夫.

451. Particles are accumulated with 到 in the two sentences following:

wû wĭ chĭ hô yè - ĭ - ĭ
吾 未 之 何 也 | |
'I have not indeed any thing left that I may do.'

jĭ - yŭ chĭ yĕn ậr ĭ ĭ
日 月 至 | 而 | |
'They continue for a day or a month, and no more.'

ậr-ĭ produces the equivalent for the English expression 'nothing else to do but,' in some sentences: e. g.—

wei fāng-sīn ậr-ĭ 惟 放 心 而 已 'but only take courage' (lit. 'let go heart'), which might signify, 'you have nothing else to do but to banish sorrow from your heart,' &c.

Chū-hĭ yĭ-jin ậr-ĭ! 朱 熹 一 人 | | 'Chu-hi, a man, and that's all!' (See Schott's *Chin. Sprach.* p. 132.)

452. The double negative forms of expression *mŏ-fĭ* 莫 非, *mŏ-pŭ*, and *wû-fĭ* 無 | , each give the force of an affirmative particle, and therefore the examples to illustrate them may come fitly in this place. They usually bear the signification of 'surely.' Compare the following examples:

mŏ-fĭ tsiŭ-shĭ tà-jĭ yàng-hiĕn-t'âng tĭ Tĭ t'ĭng-sāng mó! 'Why, surely, it is the very Tĭ who forcibly entered the summer palace!' *Haŭ-k'iŭ chuén*, Chrest. 10. d. 12.

ngò mŏ - fĭ shwŏ-hwâng pŭ - ch'ing!
我 莫 非 說 謊 不 成
'I surely do not lie at all!'

mŏ - fĭ shĭ t'ā kiĕn-liaù kweĭ!
莫 非 是 他 見 了 鬼
'Surely he has seen a ghost!'

t'iĕn - hiá mŏ - pŭ chĭ k'ĭ kiaù yè! Mǎng-tsź.
天 下 莫 不 知 其 姣 也
'In the empire there was not one unconscious of his beauty!'

wŭ - fĭ hiaŭ - chĭ t'iĕn - hiá chĭ ĭ
無 非 孝 治 天 下 之 意
'Filial piety alone he considered to be the means of ruling the empire.' Chrest. *Shĭng-yû*, 6. b. 17.

453. The expression *nân-taú* 難道, lit. 'hard to say,' has a force similar to the preceding. *Nân-taú* is however common only to the lower style, while *mŏ-fĭ, mŏ-pŭ*, and *wŭ-fĭ* belong especially to the higher class of compositions. In the *Haŭ-k'iŭ chuén* and the *Shwŭĭ-hù chuén* we find *nân-taú* frequently, and it is generally followed by a negative. The negative in *nân-taú*, with this negative particle, combine to form a strong affirmative: e. g. *nân-taú pŭ-jŭ kŭ-jîn!* 'Surely they are as good as the ancients!' Chrest. 9. l. 8.— *nân-taú taĭ-hiūng hwân-pŭ-k'ǎng fŭ-tsûng!* 'Surely, Sir, you are not still unwilling to comply with my request!' Chrest. 9. e. 1.

nân-taú tsiú pá-liaù! 難 道 就 罷 了 'Surely this is not all though!'

454. *Pŭ-ch'ing* 不 成 is added as a particle at the close of sentences which begin with any of the above combinations—*mŏ-fĭ, mŏ-pŭ, wŭ-fĭ*, and *nân-taú*. If *pŭ-ch'ing* were added to the last example, it would mean, 'Surely this will not be the end of it!' (See an example with *pŭ-ch'ing* in Art. 452.)

nân-taú shĭ [a]*kià-tĭ pŭ-ch'ing!* 'Surely it cannot be all false!'
nân-taú shĭ ngò t'ing-tsó-liaù[b] *pŭ-ch'ing!* 'Surely I did not hear incorrectly!'
mŏ-pŭ kĭ-liaù[c] *ngò pŭ-ch'ing!* 'Surely he will not exactly eat me!'

Nĭ-shwŏ 你 說 and *nĭ-taú* 你 道 may be regarded as initial particles of the same kind, and may be construed in a similar way.

---

[a] 假   [b] 錯   [c] 吃

IV. *Negative particles,* 不 *pŭ,* 弗 *fŭ,* 勿 *wŭ,* 否 *feŭ,* &c.

455. Negative particles in Chinese are numerous and of distinct classes;— there are direct or absolute negatives, such as *pŭ* and *fŭ,* &c., 'not;' and there are prohibitive and conditional negatives, such as *wŭ, mŏ,* &c., 'do not;' and others, which *imply* a negation, such as *wŭ* and *mŭ,* &c., 'without.'

456. The particle *pŭ* 不 stands before the word which it negatives. It may be placed before a verb, an adjective, or a noun. Before a verb it is a direct negative, but occasionally prohibitive, and often means 'cannot;' before an adjective it has the same effect as *un-, in-,* in *unkind, insincere;* before a noun it denies the existence of the object, or the amount of duration, if it be a noun of time. It also enters into several adverbial phrases. The force of two such negatives should also be noticed.

Examples.

pŭ ĭ páng-yiù weí tsîng 'you do not take friendship as a motive.' Chrest. 9. b. 22.
siaù-tí yĭ pŭ jèn yên k'ŭ 'I cannot bring myself to speak of going.' Chrest. 9. a. 26.

pŭ k'ò pŭ hwŭi 不可不會 'you could not dispense with meeting him,' = *ought not to miss meeting him.* Chrest. 10. d. 6.

So also *pŭ-tĭ-pŭ* signifies 'cannot be avoided,' = *must:* e. g.—

pŭ-tĭ-pŭ k'ŭ 不得不去 'I cannot avoid going.'

pŭ-yûng-pŭ jŭ-tsz̀ | 容 | 如此 'it cannot be otherwise.'

This force of two negatives exists only when an auxiliary verb accompanies the principal verb. When two different verbs are each affected by *pŭ,* the expression means 'neither —,' 'nor —:' e. g.—

pŭ-kī pŭ-hán 不飢不寒 'neither famished nor starved.' *Mǎng-tsz̀.*

But *pŭ weí pŭ-tō ĭ* | 爲 | 多 | signifies 'cannot be considered few,' *pŭ-tŏ,* 'not many,' forming an adjective, in one word,—*few.*

457. The position of *pŭ* in many colloquial expressions, in which it negatives the verbal notion, is between the principal verb and its auxiliary or the word which conveys the notion of its action having taken effect: e. g. *t'îng-pŭ-kiên* 'I do not hear' (i. e. so as to understand); *miên-pŭ-liaù* (28. k. 27) 'cannot avoid,' lit. 'avoid not finish;' *pŭ-tŭi* (29. l. 24) is a complete sentence, 'it does not agree,' = *it is not right,*—said of a time-piece.

458. After some words it enters into adverbial phrases, and may be occasionally construed by 'without :' e. g.—

siāng fûng pŭ-yĭn .. 相逢不飲 'for good friends to meet without drinking ..' Chrest. 8. l. 12.

siaù-tí sŭi pŭ-ts'aí .. 小弟雖 | 才 'although I am without talent ..' Chrest. 4. e. 5.

Phrases: *pŭ-siaŭ* 不消 'needless.' (10. i. 11.)

pŭ-siaŭ | 肖 'degenerate.'

pŭ-chŭng | 忠 'insincere.' (3. g. 20; 6. j. 19.)

pŭ-shí | 時 'soon.'

pŭ-k'í | 期 'no great time' (before or after). (8. b. 20.)

pŭ-jí | 日 'not a day,' or 'not many days,'—*soon*.

pŭ-fǎ | 法 'lawless.'

pŭ-kiŏ 不覺 'unexpectedly.' (8. n. 1.)

pŭ-weí | 惟 'not only,' in opposition to *yĭ-tsiĕ* 抑且 'but also.'

pŭ-piĕn | 便 'inconvenient.' (8. g. 20.)

pŭ-kwŏ | 過 'only.'

pŭ-yaú | 要 'do not' (*noli*).

shaŭ-pŭ-tĭ 少 | 得 'soon.' (9. o. 18.)

459. *Fŭ* 弗 is a synonym of *pŭ* 不, and, like that particle, precedes the word which it affects, but its use is less general than that of the latter. It occurs, however, frequently in classical writings. The following are two examples from the *Chŭng-yŭng*:

fŭ weí chī ǐ! 弗爲之矣 'I will not do it!'

shí chī ǎr fŭ kiĕn; t'ing chī ǎr fŭ wǎn,
視之而弗見聽之而弗聞
'To look at them and see them not; to listen to them and hear them not.'

ǐ fŭ mwǎn k'í chǐ shí yíu
以弗滿其職是憂
'Because he had not fulfilled his duty he was grieved.'

460. *Wŭ* 勿 is a prohibitive negative, and stands generally at the head of the sentence. It is found less frequently in the colloquial style than in that of the books: e. g.—

wŭ weí yên chī pŭ tsaŭ yĕ!
勿謂言之不早也
'Do not say that I did not speak early *about it*!'

fī lǐ; wŭ-shí, wŭ-t'ing, wŭ-yên, wŭ-tŭng! Lǎn-yŭ.
非禮勿視勿聽 | 言 | 動
'If improper, do not look at, or listen to, or speak of, or do it!'

wŭ wǎng wŭ tsù chǎng yĕ! Chrest. 4. m. 18.
勿亡勿助長也
'Do not forget! do not help things to grow!'

wŭ shê kĭ yŭn jĭn | 舍 己 芸 人 'don't neglect yourself and weed out *other* men's *faults*.' Canton Proverb. Cf. also Chrest. 22. n. 23.

461. *Feŭ* 否, which is also read *p'ei* and *p'ĭ* with the significations 'wicked, bad,' and 'to obstruct' (cf. the meanings of *fĭ* 非), is a negative particle, equivalent to 'no!' 'it is not so,' and is sometimes used interrogatively as a final particle. It is undoubtedly allied to *fĭ* in the ancient language. The examples of its use and its occasional meanings prove this. Thus *shĭ-fĭ* 是 |, lit. 'is, not is,'='truth—falsehood,' or 'good—bad;' an expression which might also signify 'is it so or not?' But we find *shĭ-feŭ* 是 否 is also used in this latter sense, 'is it true or false?' Other examples of its use as a negative particle are the following:

sŏ   yên   wĭ   chĭ   shĭ   feŭ
所 言 未 知 是 否
'What I say, I know not whether it be true or not.'

kĕ,   tsĭ   chĭng chĭ,   yŭng chĭ; feŭ,   tsĭ   wei   chĭ.   Shū-kīng.
格 則 承 之 庸 之 | 則 威 之
'If they repent, recommend them and employ them; if not, overawe them.' Chrest. 1. k. 1.

462. The word *fĭ* 非 'it is not' (opp. to *shĭ* 是 'it is') is a strong negative particle, and often stands, just as *pŭ* 不, like inseparable prepositions in compound words, in which a negative is implied: e. g. *fĭ-lĭ-tĭ* 'unreasonable;' *fĭ-lĭ-tĭ* 'irrational;' *fĭ-chăng-tĭ* 'uncommon.'

fĭ t'ŭng yŭng-i | 同 容 易 'not alike easy.'

fĭ-fă mŏ tsŏ | 法 莫 作 'do not unlawful things.'

(Cf. Art. 442; the second example. Compare also Chrest. 6. j. 5. *et seq.*; and 9. l. 22.)

463. *Fĭ* goes with *pŭ* in the same sentence, and unites with *wŭ* and *mŏ* to form strong affirmatives. (Cf. Art. 452; three examples.)

fĭ t'ā pŭ k'ŏ | 他 | 可 'cannot do without him.'

464. *Wŭ* 無, which commonly means 'without,' is frequently used as a negative particle, and sometimes as a prohibitive—'do not.'

t'iĕn-shăng yiŭ, tĭ-shăng wŭ 天 上 有 地 上 | 'in heaven there is, on earth there is not.'

wŭ jŭ Sŭng-jĭn! | 若 宋 人 'do not like the man of Sung!'

wŭ ĭ ĭ yĕ | 以 異 | 'there is no difference.'

THE SYNTAX OF THE PARTICLES.   161

Phrases: *wú-jĭ* 無 日 'not for a day at a time.' *Mǎng-tsz̽.* = (*pŭ-jĭ.*)

wú-ì! | 異 'wonder not! think it not strange!'

465. *Mŏ* 莫 'do not!' when it stands alone, is prohibitive, and when joined with adjectives and *yü* 於 it enters into several expressions for the superlative degree: e. g.—

mŏ-siaú! 'do not laugh!'   *mŏ-shwŏ!* 'do not speak!'

mŏ wǎng mŏ-laí! 莫 往 莫 來 'have no intercourse with!'

mŏ shīn yü sz̽ | 甚 於 斯 'nothing could exceed this.'

mŏ tá yü t'iēn | 大 於 天 'nothing greater than heaven.'

mŏ tá chī kūng | 大 之 功 'excellent merit.'

466. *Wĭ* 未 'not yet, never yet,' supplies the place of the negative particle in many expressions: v. examples in Arts. 412 (*wĭ chī yiù yè*), 426 (*yiú wĭ weĭ pŭ-k'ŏ*), and 451 (*wú wĭ chī hô yè-ĭ-ĭ*). And sometimes *wĭ* at the close of a sentence produces an interrogation: e. g.—

shwŏ liaù yè wĭ? 說 了 也 未 'have you spoken, or not yet?'

467. *Hiú* 休, 'to cease,' and *hiú-yaú* | 要 are prohibitives, as are also *pĭ* 別, 'to separate,' and *pĭ-yaú*. And *mĭ* 靡, a synonym of *wú* 無, and *fĭ* 匪, a synonym of *fĭ* 非, are direct or absolute negatives: e. g.—

mìng mĭ chǎng-chǎng 命 靡 常 常 'destiny is not constant.'

kü tĕ mĭ chǎng 厥 德 靡 常 'his virtue is not constant.'

ngò sīn fĭ shĭ 我 心 | 石 'my heart is not stone.'

With *mŏ*, *fĭ = nisi, unless, but:* e. g.—

mŏ chĭ fĭ hú 莫 赤 匪 狐 'nothing is a purple red, if not wolves.'

mŏ hĕ fĭ wū | 黑 | 烏 'nothing is black, if not crows.'

468. *Wú* 無 very commonly has the force of the preposition 'without' (*sine*): e. g. *wú-ts'ī* 無 妻 (*sine uxore*) = 'a widower;' *wú-tsz̽* 無 子 (*sine prole*) = 'childless;' *wú-fú* | 父 (*sine patre*) = 'fatherless.' These expressions are all classical, and are to be found in the "Four books." So also *wú-jín* 無 人, which = 'nobody.'

469. Several other words are found which serve the purpose of the negative

Y

particle. Such is *wû* 无 the negative of existence, which is a synonyme of *wû* 無: e. g.—

k'î yĭ wú fâng 其益 | 方 'the increase of it has no bounds.' *Yĭ-kīng*.

470. *Wâng* 亡, 'to lose,' is also occasionally used in opposition to *yiŭ* 有, as the negative of existence, but this use of *wâng* is by no means common:

hô yiŭ, hô wâng? 何有何亡 'what had I, and what had I not?' *Shĭ-kīng*.

471. *Wâng* 罔 is more common as a negative, and it is frequently found as such in the *Shū-kīng*: e. g.—

heŭ fī mĭn, wâng shì; mĭn fī heŭ, wâng sź. *Shū-kīng*.
后非民罔使民非后罔事
'If the prince be without people, he has no service; if the people be without a prince, they have no duty to perform.'

wâng yiŭ tsź sź 罔有此事 'there is no such thing.'

chĭ jŭ wâng wǎn! 置若 | 聞 'act as if you did not hear!'

472. In the following example it is followed by a negative, and then a strong affirmative is produced: e. g.—

fân-mĭn wâng pŭ tüĭ 凡民罔不譈 'among all the people there is no one who hates him not,'=*every body hates him*.

V. Adversative particles, 而 *ŕ*, 但 *tán*, 只 *chĕ*, 尙 *sháng*, &c.

473. The adversative particles include all words which, being used as conjunctions, imply *opposition*, or the addition of something to the previous clause. The most common particle of this kind in the books is *ŕ* 而, which, however, has several other uses: (v. Art. 425.) Examples of its use as an adversative particle are very numerous. Thus in the Chrestomathy: *j'ī t'ŭ wŭ-yĭ, ŕ-yiŭ haĭ chī* (5. a. 11), 'not only is it profitless, *but* indeed it injures it.' Again, *hiaŭ-tĭ ŕ haŭ-fân-shâng-chĕ, siên-ĭ* (3. e. 17), 'those who are dutiful and kind, *and yet* are fond of rebelling against superiors, are few.' And *pǎn lĭ, ŕ taŭ sāng* (3. f. 13), 'let the first principles be established, *and then* practical principles will arise.' In the Epitaph of *Ki-tsź*,—*hwǎn ŕ wŭ-siĕ, t'üĭ ŕ pŭ-sĭ* (2. k. 20), 'in obscurity, *yet* he was not depraved; in ruin, *yet* he sighed not in despair.'

The particle *ŕ*, as such, does not appear to have been used in the ancient books, but only in those in and after Confucius' time.

shŭ ŕ pŭ tsŏ 述而不作 'to compile, *but* not to compose.'

tān ằr pŭ yên 淡而不厭 'tasteless, *but* not loathsome.'

pŭ sź ằr tĭ 不思而得 'he does not think, *and yet* he obtains it.'

pŭ-sháng ằr mín kiuén, pŭ nú ằr mín weī,
不賞而民勸不怒而民威
'He gives no reward, *and yet* the people praise him; he shows no anger, *and yet* the people fear him.'

474. *Tán* 但 'but yet, but especially,' is a common adversative particle both in the books and in the higher style of conversation. In the latter it is often joined with *shí* 是, and it frequently stands at the beginning of an independent clause, like *but* in English, as an expletive. In this sense it is joined with *chĕ* 只 'only,' and it means 'simply.' It appears to be equivalent to *doch*, 'yet,' in German, in such phrases as,—*Setzen sie doch!* e. g.—

tán tsô pŭ fāng! | 坐不妨 'but sit down! don't fear!' and
tán shwŏ pŭ fāng! 'but speak! there's no objection!'

In the Chrest. (9. b. 3), *tán chwāng ĭ-sŭ* 'but (or *only*) every thing is packed.' And again (9. c. 11), *tán-chĕ-shí* .. stands for 'but' or 'but only:'

tán chĕ wú pâng-yiŭ k'ŏ ts'ĭng 'but he had no friends *whom* he could invite.'

Tán 單 'only, single,' and *tān* 儃 are frequently used for the above *tán* 'but, only:' e. g.—

tán chĕ kwăn hú-shwŏ 單只管胡說 'but he only talks nonsense.'

475. *Chĕ* 只, 'only,' comes also into the category of adversative particles. It is often followed by *shí* 是 in the lower classes of composition, in which it is more commonly found than in the classics.

Tĭ 得, *p'á* 怕, *kwăn* 管, and *haŭ* 好 also follow *chĕ* and intensify it or add something of their own meaning to it.

Examples.

shwŏ-laĭ chĕ-p'á nĭ pŭ sìn
說來只怕你不信
'I would speak, *but* I fear that you would not believe.'

ằr-jìn mŭ-fă chĕ-tĭ kăn t'ā
二人沒法只得跟他
'The two men had no alternative *but* to follow him.'

chĕ sān-jĭ ts'iŭ laĭ | 三日就來 '*but* in three days he will come.'

yèn-k'ai yèn-k'ai, chě tsó pŭ chī,
眼 開 眼 開 ｜ 做 不 知
'His eyes were open to it, *but* he feigned not to know.' Cf. Chrest. 8. k. 10; 9. c. 11.

476. *Chě-p'à* is the common phrase for 'I suppose, perhaps,' in certain clauses, and it is often used in ironical passages: e. g.—

t'iēn-hià chě-p'à pŭ sāng tsai-tsž!
天 下 ｜ 怕 不 生 才 子
'I suppose there never was a man of genius in the world!'

chě-p'à nì kién-liaù kweī-liaù! 'perhaps you have seen a ghost!'

477. *Chĭ* 止, 'to come to a point and stop,' is often used like *chě*, or perhaps for it, though sometimes *chĭ* is the more appropriate particle: e. g.—

gai chī jû shīn, pŭ chī jû tsž,
愛 之 如 身 不 止 如 子
'He loves him as himself, and not merely as a son.'

478. *Weî* 惟 (variously written 唯 and 維) 'only, but,' and *nai* 乃 'then, but,' and *sháng* 尚 'yet,' are also used as adversative particles.

Examples.

weî kì weî kāng! 惟 幾 惟 康 '*but* be exact and firm!' (1. e. 7.)
In 2. n. 2. and 6. *weî* seems to be used in its original sense,—'to consider.'
nai ch'ŭ tá-fă 乃 出 大 法 '*then* he issued his great law.' (2. l. 20.) And *nai pì k'ŭ-k'ŭ yū shi-sŭ* . . . (9. l. 15) '*but* if one must needs scrupulously comply with the world's custom . . .'
sháng yiù yuèn-k'ě tsai tsž (10. i. 23) '*but* we have a guest here from a distance.'
niên suī laù-mai, sháng nǎng ch'i-mà,
年 雖 老 邁, 尚 能 馳 馬
'Though aged and infirm, *yet* he can ride on horseback.'

479. In addition to the above, many words are used as adversative particles in the various classes of composition, and each class often has its own peculiar words for this purpose. Examples of the uses of the following will be found in the Chrestomathy: *yīn* 因 for 'then' (8. e. 4; 10. e. 25): *tsaù* 早 'then' (8. c. 11; 8. c. 29); *pièn* 便 'then' (9. m. 18; 10. a. 21); *tsiŭ* 就 'then' (8. a. 16); *suì* 遂 'forthwith, then' (17. g. 27; 17. n. 20); *tsĭ* 則 'then' (21. d. 8; 21. d. 14): also (3. k. 23; 4. a. 29); *kiŏ* 卻 'then, in the next place, but' (8. b. 1; 17. m. 22; 14. b. 3). Cf. also *ěr-tsĭ* 而 即 'and then' (9. c. 18).

THE SYNTAX OF THE PARTICLES. 165

480. *Fāng* 方, *ts'ai* 纔, and *siuen* 旋 (in official papers especially), with *nì* 逆, *kìng* 竟, and *taú* 倒, are all found in the sense of 'then,' or 'but then,' and may be looked upon as adversative particles. The exact meanings of these words may be found in the Dictionary (Part IV); and reference be made to the following passages in the Chrestomathy: (8. h. 2.—6. e. 9.—11. k. 15.—12. o. 18.) Compare also the uses of *jing* 仍 and *jên* 然, as adversative particles.

VI. *Causative particles,* 以 *ì*, 故 *kù*, 因 *yīn*, 由 *yiû*, &c.

481. The causative particles take different positions,—being either first or last in the sentence, according as they are in construction or not with the other words of the sentence; for sometimes the original signification of the word is considered, and then it is held in construction, though the rendering in English must be by a causative conjunction: e. g. in the Chrest. 9. b. 22. *pù ì pâng-yiù weî tsing* 'for that friendship is not your feeling,' or 'since you have no friendly feeling;' *ì* commonly means 'to take, to use,' as it does in this passage.

482. The word *ì* 以 'to use, to take,—by,' is less commonly employed alone as a causative particle than as a verb to stand for the preposition 'by, with.' As a causative particle it is often joined with some other word.

It also shows the *purpose* or *intention*, the *instrument*, the *means* or *cause by which*, and *the reason why:* e. g. in the Chrest. *ì lì yü shì* (2. h. 15) 'in order to establish them in the world.' Again, *tsin sz̀ ì ping-ming* (2. i. 23) 'to proceed to death by being regardless of life.' And *weî-shin ì tsân sz̀* (2. j. 10) 'to bow down in order to preserve the ancestral rites,' and *sāng-jin ì ching* (2. l. 16) 'that the living might become upright.' In the following example from the *Lân-yû*, *ì* may be translated 'the reason why' or 'the cause wherefore;' e. g. 'our master's affability, good-nature, courtesy, moderation, and deference are the cause of his obtaining it' (*ì tì-chī*): (v. 3. m. 7—14.)

Hô-ì shì k'ì pù-ts'aì? (4. e. 1) 'by what means shall I know that they are without talent?' *Hô-ì* 何以 (4. j. 21) means 'for what cause or reason?' = 'in how far?'

Coupled with *shì* 是 (v. 4. k. 28) it signifies 'for this reason.'

Followed by *weî* 爲 (v. 4. o. 20) it means 'because.'

In *yû ì fī-lì* (19. b. 11) 'declared his intention of deposing and setting *on the throne.*' In 6. a. 7. and 8. j. 14. *ì* signifies 'in order to;' in 6. c. 2. and 17. f. 4. it means 'with.' And numerous examples will be found of its use with the above meanings in different parts of the Chrestomathy.

483. *Yiû* 由 'origin, source,' when it forms the equivalent for a causative particle, is found at the end of the clause: c. g. *chüï k'ì ching-lwân chī yiû*

'if we examine into the causes of this disordered state of the government:' (v. Chrest. litho. 11. e. 19.) But at the beginning of a clause it often means simply 'from.'

Examples.

pŭ chĭ k'i yiŭ 不知其由 'I know not the reason.'

yiŭ kìn ĭ-kí yuĕn 由近以及遠 'from the near even to the remote.'

yiŭ Yaù Shŭn chi-yŭ T'áng | 堯舜至於湯 'from Yau and Shun down to T'ang.'

ĭ-kí and *chi-yŭ* are the regular phrases for 'up to, even to' (*usque ad*).

Phrases: *yiăn-yiŭ* 緣由 or *ts'íng-yiŭ* 情 | 'the causes by which,'

yiŭ-nĭ 由你 'I permit you.'

484. *Yīn* 因 'a cause, a reason,' is variously used for 'because, therefore, when, and then:' e. g. *yīn jĭ-shān ts'aĭ-yŏ* (litho. 12. b. 7) 'in consequence of that he went to the hills to collect medicinal herbs.' *Yīn pàn-chŭ shí haŭ, ĭ shí lìng-jīn* (litho. 13. h. 20), 'as, in his native place, there was an influential military man, who, trusting in his great power, had ill-used people.' *Yīn kièn shì-chăng-taì maì kwān* (17. l. 30) 'when (or because) he saw that the ten Constant Attendants were selling the offices of state.' *Chĕ yīn laĭ tĭ tsaù* (10. m. 16) 'only as I came early.'

485. When *yīn* 因, 'because,' stands at the beginning of the *protasis, sŏ-ĭ* 所以 or *kŭ* 故, 'therefore,' is the corresponding word to begin the *apodosis:* e. g. *yīn-wei t'ā laì tĭ ch'ĭ, sŏ-ĭ mă t'ā,* 'because he came late, therefore he scolded him.' *Yīn t'ā pŭ laì, kŭ-tsž ngò pŭ-hwān-hĭ,* 'as he did not come, on account of this I was displeased.'

Phrases: *yīn hŏ yuĕn-yiŭ?* 因何緣由 'for what reason and cause?'

yīn tsž chĭ kŭ | 此之故 'for this reason.'

yīn-wei | 為 'because.' *yīn-yuĕn* | 緣 'cause or reason.'

yiŭ-yīn yiŭ-yuĕn 有因有緣 'it is providential.'

It is joined with *siŭn* 循 'to revolve, to go in a circle,' and *jīng* 仍 'as before,' in the sense of 'to continue;' thus,—*yīn-siûn* and *yīn-jīng* mean 'to act as before, to be remiss, to follow routine merely;' and are found in the Peking Gazette with these significations.

486. It will be seen by the articles just preceding that *yuĕn* 緣 also performs the part of a causative particle. It is similar in use to *yuĕn* 原 and the other causative particles, to which it is frequently united: e. g.—

yuĕn pàn tsŭi ŏ | 本罪惡 'on account of our sin and wickedness.'

yuên-tsz̀ pŭ yŭ-sīn | 此不悅心 'on this account he was unhappy.'

yuên-laî jù-tsz̀ 原來如此 'and this was its original state.'

yīn pŭ kú tsīn-tsĭ chī yuên
因不顧親戚之 |
'Because no regard was given to relatives.'

Phrase: *yuên-kú* | 故 'reason, cause,' used as a noun.

487. *Kaî* 蓋 or 葢 'for, because,' must also be placed in this category. It always begins the clause to which it belongs. It introduces something to confirm or explain a declaration, like *nam* in Latin.

kaî sháng-shî cháng-yiŭ pŭ tsáng k'ĭ tsīn chĕ
| 上世嘗有不曾其親者
'For in ancient times they never buried their relatives.'

kaî pàn láng-sāng chí pŭ wáng
| 本狼生志不忘
'For their origin, being born of a wolf, they never forgot.'

Kaî-ĭ | 以 is found as a phrase, 'for this reason.'

488. *Kĭ* 既, which is an auxiliary verb for the past tenses (cf. Arts. 194, 195), frequently marks the notion of causation, though the proper construing would be with *being* or *having;* and this may be turned into a clause beginning with *since* (*quoniam*, or *si quidem*) (cf. Chrest. 10. n. 21. and Art. 491): e. g.—

kĭ mîng tsiĕ chĕ 既明且哲 'since he is enlightened and become wise.' *Shī-kīng.*

The absolute form of the sentence often necessitates this mode of construing: thus—*chĕ-tàng* 'this rank,' *chĕ-yáng* 'this sort,' when put absolutely, or as the *protasis* of a sentence, convey either the hypothetical or the causal notion, and must be construed by 'if this is the state of things,' or 'since this is the case.' (Cf. 21. l. 1—12.)

VII. *Conditional particles,* 若 *jŏ,* 如 *jù,* 假如 *kià-jù,* &c.

489. Conditional or hypothetical particles are such as introduce a conditional or hypothetical clause; as, *jŏ* 若 'if, as,' *jù* 如 'as,' *kià-jù* | 如 'supposing:' e. g.—

jŏ-shí kŏ chĭ-ch'îng laù-shí tĭ jîn .. (14. a. 7—15) 'if he were an upright and honest man ..'

jŏ tsaî ts'ŏ wú 若再錯悞 'if he again err.'

jŏ t'ā pŭ laî, ngò tsiŭ pŭ k'ú, 'if he does not come, then I shall not go.'

490. *Shí* 是 or *jên* 然 is added to *jŏ* to strengthen it: e. g.—

jĭn jŏ-shí k'ăn-kiên tsĕ-sīng fī-kwŏ, kàn-chŏ pà k'ŭ-yaŭ-taí tà-ch'íng kì-kó sz̀ kŏ-tā, tsiú k'ŏ-ĭ kiaĭ-ch'ŭ pŭ-siáng, 'if when a man sees a shooting star (lit. 'a rebel star') flying over, he quickly, with his girdle, ties several sure (lit. 'dead') knots, he will destroy the evil omen:' (v. Wade's Cat. of *t'iĕn*, No. 130.)

491. *Kì* 旣 often has the same force as the conditional particle *jŏ*, and they are sometimes joined in one expression: e. g.—

kì yaú hìng, hô pŭ tsaù k'ŭ (10. n. 21), 'if he wanted to go, why didn't he go before?'

jŏ-kì 'it being so, if it is so,' implying that it really is so.

In the books *jŏ-chè* | 者 is employed for 'if,' when the conditional particle is placed prominently forward.

492. *Kià-jŭ* 假 如 is found most commonly in scientific works, on mathematics, &c. *Pĭ-jŭ* 譬 | and *pĭ-fāng* | 方 or *pĭ-yŭ* | 喩 more commonly occur in the language of conversation. *Kià-jŭ* generally introduces a case for comparison: e. g.—

kià-jŭ yiŭ jĭn, pŭ-sĭn lìng-hwǎn pŭ-mĭ, 'suppose a man does not believe that the soul is indestructible.'

493. *Hwŏ* 或, which is used for *either* and *or*, and implies *doubt*, may also fill the place of a conditional particle, and be construed by 'if' or 'whether;' it corresponds in some respects to the particle ἄν of the Greek: e. g.—

hwŏ yĭ - shí fūng - chŏ hiŭng..
或 一 時 逢 着 兇
'If once perchance you should meet with evil..'

494. *Keù* 苟, *shĭ* 使, *t'àng* 倘, *t'àng-jŭ* | 如, and several other conditional particles are employed in literary composition (cf. Art. 265, p. 94): e. g.—

keù pŭ hiŏ, hô wei jĭn? Sān-tsź kĭng.
苟 不 學 何 爲 人
'If he do not learn, how can he become a man?'

shĭ mŭ fī shí wŭ yŭ kiên. Siŭn-tsź.
使 目 非 是 無 欲 見
'If the eye be evil, it is useless to try to see *with it*.'

495. But the conditional notion is very often implied without any conditional particle being expressed. The absolute nature of the *protasis* of a sentence often implies a condition, the result of the carrying out of which is expressed in the *apodosis*: (cf. Wade's Cat. of *t'iĕn*, 68, 99, 183; but in 130, *jŏ-shí*, 'if,' is inserted.)

THE SYNTAX OF THE PARTICLES.

VIII. *Illative particles,* 故 kú, 就 tsiû, 乃 nai, 則 tsĭ, &c.

496. The illative particles correspond to the causative particles; the latter mark the *cause* or the *reason*, the former the *consequence* or the *inference* (cf. Arts. 484, 485): e. g.—

yīn t'ā shì pŭ tsŭng-míng, kú pŭ hiaŭ-tĕ, 'because he is wanting in intelligence, therefore he does not understand.'

yīn-wei ngò săng-píng, tsiù pŭ lai, 'because I was taken ill, therefore I did not come.' (Cf. also *tsĭ* 2. j. 5. and 2. j. 20; 3. k. 6, 10, 23.)

Some causative particles indeed are used for both purposes; as, *yīn* 因, *ĭ* 以. (Cf. *yīn* for 'then, therefore,' in Arts. 479 and 484.)

Very frequently the illative particle is not expressed in the *apodosis*, but it must be supplied in translation: e. g.—

t'ā pŭ tsŏ Hwâng-tí, ngò pŭ tsŏ Sheŭ-siāng, 'if he does not become Emperor, *then* I shall not become Prime Minister.'

497. It will be seen that the illative particles keep their illative force most clearly in those sentences in which the *protasis* may be construed as a *cause*. If the *protasis* begin with an equivalent for *when* or *if*, the illative particle is *then*, and simply marks the sequence or the result of the condition.

Examples.

heŭ ts'ŭng kién tsĕ shíng 后 從 諫 則 聖 'when the prince follows good counsels, then he will become wise and good.'

wei shíng jín tsĕ chī kī 惟 聖 人 則 知 幾 'but being a sacred sage, then he will know how to time things.'

hién-chĕ tsĕ nâng chī 賢 者 則 能 之 'when a man is wise, then he can do it.'

kí yiŭ tă, pĭ yiŭ sž 既 有 塔 必 有 寺 'as there is a pagoda, there must be a monastery.'

keŭ pŭ hiŏ, síng nai ts'iën 苟 不 學 性 乃 遷 'if one does not learn, then nature changes *for the worse*.'

IX. *Interrogative particles,* 乎 hû, 耶 yê, 何 hô, 孰 shŭ, &c.

498. The interrogative particles are very numerous. Some are *initial*, as regards position, as *hô* 何, *shŭī* 誰, *shŭ* 孰, etc.: others are *final*, as *hû* 乎, *yê* 耶, *tsai* 哉, etc. The former correspond to *what* and *who;* the latter to mere marks of interrogation which have a pronunciation (cf. Arts. 255, 256): e. g.—

k'i k'ŏ hô tsai? 其 可 | | 'how will this do?'

z

ặr chī-taú hû? 尔知道乎 'do you know it?' (尔 contr. for 爾.)

yiû jîn hû tsaī? 由人乎 | 'does this come from men?'

499. Hô 何 'what, why,' is most common in phrases and expressions for *why?* or *how?* e. g.—

tsǐ jû-chī hô? (4. b. 5; 4. c. 5) 'then how will you act?' (B.)
tsǐ hô ǐ ǐ yü ..? (4. j. 20) 'how is that different from ..?' (B.)
hô-kû tsŏ tsź t'aù (9. f. 24) 'why do you make this formal expression?'
k'án shí jû-hô? (11. h. 13) 'what do you think of it?'
nǐ jû-hô pǔ k'ǐ (11. m. 13) 'why don't you take (eat or drink) it?'

ặr hwán hô píng yê? 尔患何病邺 'with what disease are you afflicted?'

jû chíng jîn hô? 如正人 | 'how can he correct others?'

500. Some of these interrogative particles are indeed the same as interrogative pronouns (cf. Arts. 172—174), and, as such, are capable of standing for the correlative notions, which correspond to the several forms of interrogation; e. g. hô 'what?' may stand for 'any' or 'some,' so may shüǐ 'who?' or shǔ 'who?' e. g.—

shüǐ yaú shüǐ laí? 誰要誰來 'who wishes any one to come?'

shǔ yuên shǔ chí? 孰願 | 至 'who wishes any one to come?'

In reply to the question t'iēn-tsź hô-tsaí (17. n. 3) '*where* is the Emperor?' we have pû chī hô wâng (17. n. 15) 'I know not *where* he is gone.' And in the phrase wû-naí-hô '*without any* other resource,' hô is used as the correlative of hô 'what?' (Cf. 11. j. 2. and often.)

Phrases: hô-kú? | 故 'for what reason?'   weí-hô? 爲 | 'why?'
         hô-kú? | 居 'wherefore?'   yīn-hô? 因 | 'for what?'
         hô-weí? | 爲 'on what account?'   jû-hô? 如 | 'how?'
         hô-jîn? | 人 'who?' (18. h. 23.)   hô-tsaí? | 任 'where?'

501. The interrogative particles shüǐ 誰 and shǔ 孰, like hô, partake of the nature of pronouns rather than of particles, because they generally require pronouns for their equivalents in the translation; but they belong also to the class of particles, for they are often merely marks of interrogation, which is sometimes effected without them.

Examples.

shí shüǐ chī kwó yû? 是誰之過與 'whose fault is it?'

tsŏ t'íng chè shüǐ? 作亭者 | 'who made the pavilion?'

shŭ wei haŭ hiŏ? | 爲好學 'which of you love to study?'

shŭ yuén shŭ chí yĕ? | 願 | 至耶 'what does he desire which he does not obtain?'

502. The interrogative particle *tsaī* 哉 is used as a final particle, and often one of the other interrogative particles, or a word used as such, is placed at the beginning of the same clause.

Examples.

hŏ yiŭ yŭ tsz̀ tsaī? | 有於此 | 'what is this to me?'

k'ĭ yiŭ kiā yŭ tsz̀ tsaī? 豈有加於此 | 'how can any thing be added to this?'

hí k'ŏ tsaī? 奚可 | 'is it possible?' or 'how can it be?'

wŭ tsŭ taŭ tsaī? 烏足道 | 'how can we speak of it enough?'

503. The particle *hû* 乎 is joined with *tsaī* at the end of clauses: e. g—

wei jîn yiŭ kĭ ăr yiŭ jîn hû-tsaī?
爲仁由己而由人乎 |
'As for virtue, is it a matter for myself or for others?'

jîn yuèn hû-tsaī? 仁遠 | | 'is virtue so far away?'

504. The particle *hû* 乎 itself, when final, is interrogative, or a mark of exclamation or commiseration; but in other positions it generally stands for *yŭ* 於 'in, with respect to,' and 'than;' and sometimes it is a mere expletive.

Examples.

chí yŭ hû chí shè hû? 執御乎執射 | 'shall I drive the chariot or wield the spear?'

ĭ hâ fěă hâ? 宜 | 否 | 'is it right or is it not?'

heŭ-shí chī shíng chĕ, mŏ shíng hû Hán yù T'âng,
後世之盛者莫盛 | 漢與唐
'The glory of later times does not eclipse the glory of the *Han* and the *T'ang* (dynasties).'

yâng-yâng hû! 洋洋 | 'how vast!' (lit. 'ocean-like.')

505. *Yê* 耶 (sometimes written *yê* 邪) is another interrogative final particle, and, like *tsaī* and *hû*, often has an auxiliary particle at the beginning of the clause: e. g.—

k'i tai yiù píng ǎr heú t'aŭ yê?
豈 待 有 病 而 候 禱 耶
'Why wait until you are sick and then pray?'

tsz̆ k'i kìn yŭ jĭn ts'ing yê? Chwǎng-tsz̆.
此 豈 近 於 人 情 邪
'How does this accord with human feelings?'

hŏ ĭ chī k'i jên yê?
\| 以 知 其 然 耶
'How can I know that it is thus?'

506. Some of the interrogative particles imply a negation. Such are, *hŏ* 盍 'why not?' (*quare non*); *mŏ-fī* .. 莫 非 'surely, not otherwise than ..?' (*certe*); and *feŭ* 否 'or not?' (*nonne ita est*),—like a particle of doubt. *Hŏ* and *mŏ-fī* are placed at the beginning, but *feŭ* at the end of sentences.

hŏ kŏ yên ǎr chi? 盍 各 言 爾 志 'why do not you all speak your minds?'

Hŏ 害 (usu. pron. *haì* 'to injure') appears to be used for the above *hŏ*: e.g.—

hŏ pŭ weì? 害 不 違 'why do you not resist?'

feŭ yŭ mwàn niên? 否 與 滿 年 'is he indeed of full age?'

tsŭ-hià chī wù sīn yŭ feŭ yê?
足 下 知 吾 心 \| \| 也
'Do you, Sir, indeed know my intention?'

Several examples of *mŏ-fī* will be found in Art. 452, and of *feŭ* in Art. 461.

507. *K'i* 豈 'how?' is also an interrogative particle in common use in books and in some colloquial phrases: e.g. *k'ĭ-kǎn* \| 敢 'how dare I?' which is an equivalent for 'I thank you!' 'I do not deserve the honour!' *Wū* 惡, *hŏ* 曷, *hŭ* 胡, *hī* 奚, *yên* 焉, and *gān* 安, as well as *k'i*, are interrogative particles when placed at the beginning of clauses.

Examples.

k'i weì k'eŭ-fŭ yiù ki-kĕ chī haì? (Cf. ex. in Art. 501.)
豈 惟 口 腹 有 饑 渴 之 害
'Do only the mouth and the stomach suffer from hunger and thirst?'

sŭĭ tō yĭ hī ĭ-weì? 雖 多 亦 奚 以 為 'though many, yet what use are they?'

wú hû k'ŏ? 惡 | 可 'what can be done?'

wú nǎng tāng chī? 惡能當之 'how could I bear it?'

wú hû ch'ǐng míng? | | 成名 'how will he perfect his reputation?'

hŏ chī yúng? 曷之用 'what use is it?' *Yĭ-king.*

wù-tsz̀ hû pǔ lì hû? 吾子胡不立 | 'why not establish yourself?'

yên k'ǐ ts'ǔng chī? 焉其從之 'should he follow him?' (See also the first example in Art. 445.)

yên li jin yǔ ì? 焉離仁與義 'why forsake benevolence and justice?'

ān tĕ tsŭ sīn hû? 安得足心 | 'how can you be content?'

ān nǎng tŭ yĕ? 安能脫也 'how can we escape?'

508. There are various particles, or interrogative adverbs, used in the colloquial style for the question as *kĭ* 幾 'how many?' *nǎ* 那 'which?' *tsāng* 怎 'how?' (Cf. Arts. 255 and 256, and read pp. 27—30 in the Chrestomathy.)

509. The affirmative expressions *nǎn-taŭ* and *pǔ-ch'ing* (see Arts. 453 and 454), the former at the beginning, the latter at the end of the clause, also indicate a kind of question, which always expects the answer *yes* in reply to it. *Nǎn-taŭ*, lit. 'hard to say,' is in some respects similar to the German expression *viel-leicht, vielleicht* for *sehr leicht* 'probably, perhaps, doubtless;' and *pǔ-ch'ing*, lit. 'not perfect,' like *nicht wahr?* (See Schott's *Chin. Sprach.* p. 134. note.)

510. To the above *yû* 與 or *yû* 歟 must be added as an interrogative particle: e. g.—

jên tsĭ Shǎn pǔ kīn yû? 然則舜不禁 | 'if so, then why did not Shun resist?' (Cf. Chrest. 3. l. 29.)

X. *Dubitative particles,* 或 *hwŏ*, 與 *yû*, &c.

511. By dubitative particles are meant such words as give a character of *doubt* to the clause or sentence in which they occur; and according to this definition several of the conditional and interrogative particles might come under the same category. Several adverbs of *doubt* have already been given in Art. 253. It remains to give a few examples of their use here.

Examples.

hwŏ pǔ chī kiaŭ-haŭ 或不知叫號 'probably they knew not the cries *out of doors.*'

hwŏ yiù kiāng-hú 或有江湖 'perhaps you have rivers and lakes;'
hwŏ yiù wáng heú || 王侯 'perhaps you have kings and nobles;' which may be construed *either* &c. *or* &c.
hwŏ jên hwŏ pŭ-jên 或然或不然 'perhaps it is so, perhaps not.' (Cf. Art. 493.)
k'iú chī yú yĭ yú chī yú? 求之與抑|之| 'does he ask for it or do they give it him (without asking)?' (Cf. Chrest. 3. 1. 27.)

The following sentence from *Chwáng-tsź* is worth inserting here to illustrate the uses of dubitatative and interrogative particles:

Kiă yŭ Yĭ shŭ shĭ ąr shŭ fĭ hú?
甲與乙孰是而|非|
'Does Kia or Yĭ speak the truth?'

XI. *Intensitive particles*, 太 *t'ai*, 忒 *tĕ*, 絕 *tsŭ*, &c.

512. The intensitive particles are words which are used to strengthen the assertion or negation in respect of some particular quality. They are generally verbs according to their primary signification, but as intensifiers they retain only so much of the verbal notion as will serve the purpose of emphasising the word or sentence in which they occur. We shall take each separately, with one or two examples.

513. *T'ai* 太 and *tĕ* 忒 are very commonly used for *too, too much.*

Examples.

chê kĭ t'ai hièn 這計太險 'this project is too dangerous.'
t'ai làng tsáng siē 太冷靜些 'a little too cold' (of a person or a place).
hiá sheù tĕ hąn-liaù 下手|狠了 'you struck me with too much violence.'
kiŏ tĕ tsaù liaù siē 却|早了| 'but too early rather.'
nĭ yĕ tĕ tŏ sīn 你也|多心 'to take it too much to heart.'

514. *Shīn* 甚 'very,' *tsŭ* 絕 'decidedly,' *kĭ* 極 'extremely,' are all used as intensitive particles.

Examples.

wąn-lĭ pŭ-shīn t'ūng-t'eú 文理不甚通透 'his scholarship is not very profound.'
shīn shĭ k'ĭ-kwai 甚是奇怪 'it is strange indeed.'

tsŭ wú kī-hwuĭ 絕無機會 'decidedly unfortunate.'

tsŭ wú jĭn-kú 丨無人居 'utterly without inhabitants.'

ché yè-k'ŏ siaú-kĭ-liaù 這也可笑極了 'this is indeed extremely ridiculous.'

kí mŭ kiaú tí hwá 極沒竅的話 'language quite unintelligible.'

kí k'iaù tí hwá-kūng 丨巧的畫工 'a most clever artist.' (Cf. Arts. 331 and 334.)

Various other words are used as intensitive particles, such as *haù* 'good,' *shī-fān* 'the whole,' &c.

515. In literary compositions several words of intensifying power occur, which correspond to the expressions *much more, much less*, &c. Such are *yü* 愈, *yĭ* 益, *mí* 彌, and *hwāng* 況.

Examples.

tsz̀ yü kín pí yü yuèn 此愈近彼愈遠 'the nearer this approaches, the farther that recedes.'

k'ú shíng yĭ yuèn ạr yĭ pŏ 去聖益丨而益薄 'the farther we depart from the sacred wisdom, the meaner we become.'

yúng chī   ạr   mí   míng,   sŭ - chī   ạr   mí chwáng,
用 之 而 彌 明 宿 之 而 丨 壯
'Use it and the brighter it becomes, confine it and the greater it will grow.'

chīn   tĕ   pŭ   taĭ   yü   sz̀,   hwāng   yü   yên   hû!
眞 德 不 待 於 事 況 於 言 丨
'True virtue does not expect great deeds, much less does it wait on great words!'

516. *Shīn* 矧 is used in a similar way to *hwāng*, but it is far less common: e. g.—

chī   chíng   kàn   shín,   shín   tsz̀   yiù   Miaú,
至 誠 感 神 矧 茲 有 苗
'The highest integrity influences the gods, much more the *Miau* people.' (Cf. Prémare, *Not. Ling. Sin.* p. 215.)

XII. *Exclamatory particles*, 吖 *yā*, 兮 *hī*, 哉 *tsaī*, &c.

517. The particles of exclamation are very numerous in Chinese, and they vary according to the style of composition,—its antiquity and its peculiarities of literary and colloquial usage. In the books the exclamatory particles have

an important value. They serve to express in the language, with the written characters, those niceties of construction and expressions of feeling for which *sounds* and *gesticulations* are employed in oral communications.

518. Yá 吁 and á 阿 are very common. They denote *wonder* or *astonishment*: e. g.—

yá ché-sheù shī, píng pŭ-shí ngò-tsó-tĭ! 'Ah! this ode was not of my composing!'

They are sometimes joined as one exclamation: e. g.—

á-yá kīn-yè kiŏ mŭ-liaù tāng! 'Ah! to-night we are again without a lamp!'

519. Hî 兮 is a particle of exclamation, used most commonly in poetry, in the *Shī-kīng*, and in all ancient poems.

pì meí jīn hī! 彼 美 人 兮 'that beautiful person!'

520. P'ǐ 呸 and p'ǐ 啡 are used to express *contempt* or *defiance*, and are often equivalent to 'begone!' e. g.—

p'ǐ! tū-shí nì peí-heú lŭng-kweī! 'Ah! all this confusion behind one's back was all through you!'

p'ǐ! nì shí tŏ tá tĭ kwān-ḁr! 'Ah! you are indeed a very distinguished officer!'

521. In the plays of the *Yuên* dynasty, ŭ 兀 is used as an exclamation or *call* to an inferior: e. g.—

ŭ-ná fŭ-jīn pŭ-yaú tĭ-k'ŭ! 'O woman! do not cry and weep!'
wŭ-tĭ pŭ-shí ngò hiūng-tĭ? 'Ah! is it not my brother?'
wŭ-ná kí-shū-tĭ! 兀 那 寄 書 的 'Halloa! Postman!'

XIII. *Euphonic particles.*

522. Particles which may be called *euphonic* are such as serve merely to make a clause sound well. It has been the practice however to denominate *euphonic* many of the particles which we have placed under different classes. It is seldom that a particle is purely euphonic, it generally denotes some *feeling* or *desire* in the mind of the speaker. Many of the words which we call interjections come under this class. In every dialect there are sounds of this kind peculiar to the locality, and when these sounds are expressed in writing, it must be done by some well-known character, which for the time is divested of its ordinary signification, and by the addition of *keù*, 'mouth,' it becomes an interjection or a euphonic particle. This usage has given rise to the euphonic particles of the books, for they were the interjections of ancient times, and indeed some of them remain in use, as such, unto the present hour.

523. Thus *ì* 矣, *yè* 也, and *hî* 兮 are said to be euphonic, while they also denote an affirmation (cf. Arts. 447, 448): e. g.—

siàng pī-jên ĭ! 想必然矣 'I imagine it must be so!'

k'ŏ chī chī ĭ! 可知之矣 'it may be known!'

hĕ-hĭ! hiuēn-hĭ! 赫兮喧兮 'how splendid! how glorious!'

ān tsiĕ hìng hĭ! 安且幸 | 'happy and fortunate!'

sìn yiŭ yè chĕ, pŭ - k'ŏ tsŭ yè! (Cf. Arts. 415, 416, and 442.)
信友也者不可絕也
'Faithful friendship may not be dispensed with!'

t'iēn-hiá k'ŏ-kiūn yè; tsiŏ lŭ k'ŏ-ts'ź yè;
天下可均也爵祿可辭也,
'One may tranquillize the empire; one may refuse titles and office;'

pĕ jìn k'ŏ-taú yè; chūng-yŭng pŭ - k'ŏ nǎng yè!
白刃可蹈也,中庸不可能也
'One may tread on a naked sword; and not be able to keep the "golden mean!"'

524. *Tsai* 哉 and *hû* 乎 are used as euphonic or exclamatory particles, besides being used as interrogative particles: e. g—

fú tsaī yên yè! 富 | 言也 'how rich the language!'

hién tsaī Hwŭi yè! 賢 | 回也 'how worthy is Hwüi!'

kiūn-tsź tō hû tsai! 君子多乎 | 'has the great man so many (wants)!'

525. The final particle *yè* 也 also frequently occurs in the classics of the Chinese as a euphonic particle, and it then serves the purpose of a comma, by separating the characters, which precede it, from the rest of the sentence, as the following examples will show:

kīn yè tsĭ wâng 今也則亡 'the present is,—then gone for ever.'

wú sāng yè yiŭ yai ŕr chī yè wú yai
吾生也有涯而知也無涯
'My life has bounds, but knowledge, forsooth, is boundless.'

sāng kĭ yè; — sź kwei yè
生寄也, 死歸也
'Life is a trust;—at death we resign it.'

Fŭ also sometimes goes with *yĕ*, when *yĕ* is simply euphonic:

mŏ ngŏ chī yĕ fŭ! 莫 我 知 也 夫 'no one understands me!'

526. *Lī* 哩 is used in novels and in the colloquial style as a euphonic particle or as a particle of exclamation; e. g.—

mŏ shwŏ má, hwán yaū tă lī!
莫 說 罵 還 要 打 哩
'Not to speak of scolding, I shall beat him as well!'

527. Prémare gives these other particles of exclamation: *nī* 呢, *pō* 波, *nă* 那; and the student will find others in the course of his reading, but they are seldom used, therefore they need not be given here.

ché-kó nī? 這 個 | 'is it this?'

k'ŏ pŭ-shĭ pō! 可 不 是 波 'is it not thus!'

T'iēn-nă! 天 | 'O Heaven!'

528. *Ī* 噫 'Ah!' *tsiē* 嗟 'O!' in calling the attention of persons, but sometimes to incite or encourage; and in the *Shī-king*, with other particles, as an exclamation arising from pain: *hū-hū!* 'oh! alas!' *shīn-ĭ* 甚 矣 'indeed!' *pŭ-hĭng* 不 | 'unfortunately!' *gŏ* 惡 'wretch!' or 'hold!' (Lat. *nefas!*) *yū* 於 'ah!' are all found in the classics at the beginning of sentences, but they are rarely to be met with elsewhere.

529. Words formed by the imitation of natural sounds are very numerous in Chinese; e. g. *kiaū-kiaū* 'the crowing of a cock,' *siaū-siaū* 'the noise of wind and rain.' (See Dr. Morrison's Dictionary, vol. I., under the radical *k'eū* 口 'mouth,' for many expressions of a similar kind.)

530. Among the particles which the Chinese denominate *hū-tsź* are included all words which do not come under the category of nouns, or under that of verbs,—but simply denote the relations which the nouns and the verbs of the sentence bear to each other,—or the feelings which exist in the mind of the speaker at the time the sentence is uttered. Some of these occur always at the beginning, some always at the end of the sentence; others are found in both positions in different sentences. Some particles affect nouns and single words, some affect the whole clause, others bind together the whole sentence. These facts have been noted under each particle, but there still remains much to be learnt, from careful observation, by the student himself. The following *résumé* of the particles may, however, be of service.

1. *Attributive* particles are 的 (411), 之 (412), 者 (415), 所 (421), because they make the words which they affect *attributive*.

THE SYNTAX OF THE PARTICLES.

2. *Connective,* 亦 (424), 而 (425), 又 (426), 幷 (429), 並 (430), 兼 (431), 曁 (432), 且 (433), 及 (436), 連 (436), 也 (437), 夫 (438).

3. *Affirmative,* 是 (440), 然 (441), 也 (442), 焉 (445), 矣 (446), 已 (449), 莫非 and 無非 (452), 難道 (453), 不成 (454).

4. *Negative,* 不 (456), 弗 (459), 勿 (460), 否 (461), 非 (462), 無 (464), 莫 (465), 未 (466), 休, 別, 靡 (467), 无 (469), 亡 (470), 罔 (471).

5. *Adversative,* 而 (473), 但 (474), 只 (475), 止 (477), 惟, 乃, 尙 (478).

6. *Causative,* 以 (482), 由 (483), 因 (484), 故, 所以 (485), 緣, 原 (486), 蓋 (487), 旣 (488).

7. *Conditional,* 若, 如 (489), 旣 (491), 假如 (492), 或 (493), 苟, 使, 倘 (494).

8. *Illative,* 故, 就 (496), 乃, 則 (497).

9. *Interrogative,* 哉, 乎 (498 and 502—4), 何 (499), 誰, 孰 (500), 耶, 邪 (505), 盍, 否, 莫非 (506), 豈, 惡, 曷, 胡, 奚, 焉, 安 (507), 幾, 那, 怎 (508), 歟, 歟 (510).

10. *Dubitative,* 或, 與 (511).

11. *Intensive,* 太, 忒 (513), 甚, 絶, 極 (514), 愈, 益, 彌, 況 (515), 矧 (516).

12. *Exclamatory,* 呀, 阿 (518), 兮 (519), 嗟, 嗐 (520), 兀 (521).

13. *Euphonic,* 矣, 也, 兮 (523), 哉, 乎 (524), 哩 (525), 呢, 波, 那 (526), 噫, 惡 (527).

Sect. II. On sentences.

§. 1. *Preliminary remarks.*

531. The first section of this chapter relates to the various forms and modifications of words and phrases, which enter into the composition of sentences, and these simple formations have been there designated *simple constructions;* but, beyond the occasional use of the terms *sentence, subject, predicate, attribute,* and *object,* nothing has been said of the form of Chinese sentences. And, before examples are given, it will be well to explain the meaning intended by the different terms which will be employed.

532. A sentence expresses by the words which it contains not merely a number of separate notions, but a *thought,* or an *assertion,* which is ascertained by the relations which those separate notions bear to each other; e. g. 'the wind blows cold to-day' indicates a *belief* on the part of the speaker; but the words of which this sentence is composed are only the materials with which the thought is expressed; and the same words in a different construction would mean a very different thing, e. g. (1) 'the son loves the father' is one thing, (2) 'the father loves the son' is another. *Tá-fūng* is a 'great wind,' but *fūng tá* means 'the wind is high.' It is important to bear this in mind, for in the structure of sentences we have no more to do with the words themselves, whether simple or compound, but with the relations which exist between them. Relations which, in some languages indeed, are regulated by the inflections of the words themselves, but in Chinese, and in some other languages, they are shown by the relative position of the words and clauses.

533. Every sentence consists of two members only; (1) the *subject,* or that thing about which something is said or predicated, and (2) the *predicate,* or that action or attribute which is asserted of the subject. These are indeed sometimes united by a small word, called the *copula,* which is one of the substantive verbs; but more frequently this is wanting: the principal verb, which contains the predicate, being sufficient of itself to show its relation to the subject. And in Chinese very often the copula is omitted; e. g. *t'iĕn làng* 'the weather is cold;' *ngò pŭ-haù* 'I am unwell.'

534. There are, moreover, three relations which may exist in the sentence. First, the *predicative* relation,—or the relation of *subject* and *predicate* simply; secondly, the *attributive* relation,—or the relation of some qualifying expression to the *subject* or *object* of the predicate; and thirdly, the *objective* relation,—or the relation of the object (or supplemental expression) to the predicate. These terms are used to distinguish clauses in sentences. Thus a clause which contains subject and predicate simply, is a *predicative clause,* and in this the verb is the principal word. An attribute appended to a subject forms an *attributive clause,* and in this the adjective or attribute is the chief word. A clause added as an object to the predicate is an *objective clause,* and in this the object is the principal word, and if it relate *directly* to the predicate, it is the chief word in the whole sentence. The *predicative* clause conveys a definite and independent thought, and so may

stand alone; e. g. 'the rose is red.' The *attributive* clause cannot stand alone, because it does not express a complete thought, but only one of the elements of the sentence; e. g. 'the red rose,' 'the benighted traveller.' And the *objective* clause too is incomplete when standing alone,—when the object is united to the predicate of a sentence;—e. g. 'black with smoke,' 'withered this morning.' But these three elements of the sentence may be united to form a complete sentence; e. g. 'the red rose withered this morning.'

535. The *attribute* may be, (1) an *adjective*, (2) the *genitive case* of a noun, (3) a *noun in apposition*, or (4) a *noun with a preposition;* e. g. (1) 'a cold day;' (2) 'the *king's* horse;' (3) 'William, *the Conqueror;*' (4) 'a man *without bravery;*' and (5) a *relative* clause, which is explanatory, may be regarded as an attribute of its antecedent *.

536. The *object* may be (1) the *thing*, or *person*, which the principal verb of the sentence affects, or (2) it may be the *circumstances* of *time, place, manner* or *causality*, which serve to modify the action of the verb.

537. The *simple sentence* consists of only one clause, in which there is a subject and a predicate, but these may be enlarged and modified to a great extent. The subject in Chinese may consist of one word or of many; e. g. *Tî yŭ* (1. a. 11) 'the Emperor said:' *fân tá-jîn chī taú yiŭ sān* 'the principles of great men generally are three:' (cf. Art. 541.)

538. But sentences in Chinese are seldom simple, they are most frequently complex or compound. A *complex sentence* is one in which there is a *principal* clause and one or more *subordinate*. The subordinate clause stands to the principal clause in one of the following relations, either (1) as its subject, (2) as an attribute of its subject or its object, or (3) as a modification of the whole principal clause. In each case respectively it is a noun sentence, an adjective sentence, or an adverbial sentence.

539. A *noun sentence* in English begins with such words as *that, what, who, when* or *where;* and in Chinese it is recognisable by certain marks and the presence of certain particles, as *sŏ* 所 and *chě* 者 and *tî* 的: (cf. Arts. 411—422.)

540. An *adjective sentence*, which is also an attributive clause, or a relative sentence, is introduced in English by *who, which,* and words of that class, as *that, how, wherein, whither, why, wherefore;* and in Chinese it is distinguished by *tî*, but very often no particle is present.

541. *Adverbial sentences* are such as specify the conditions of *time, place, manner* or *causality*. Adverbial sentences of *time* show (1) the *point of time*, (2) the *duration of time*, or (3) the *repetition of the circumstance*, and are introduced respectively by (1) *when,* (2) *whilst,* (3) *as often as,* &c. Adverbial sentences of *place* relate to (1) *rest in,* (2) *motion to,* or (3) *motion from a*

---

* Since writing the above the author has seen an admirable little work on the "Analysis of Sentences" by Dr. Morell, one of Her Majesty's Inspectors of Schools, in which the subject is explained and applied to the English language with a clearness sought for in vain in grammatical treatises generally.

place, and in English they are introduced by (1) *where* or *wherever*, (2) *where* or *whither*, and (3) *whence*. Adverbial sentences of *manner* show (1) *similarity*, (2) *proportion*, or (3) *consequence*, and are introduced by (1) *as*, (2) the comparative degree of the adjective, or *as* after a negative in the principal clause, or by (3) *that*, or *so that*. Adverbial sentences of cause show (1) a *reason*, (2) a *condition*, (3) a *concession*, or (4) a *purpose*, and in English they are dependent upon the words (1) *because*, (2) *if* or *except*, *unless* (which=*if not*), (3) *although* or *however*, and (4) *that* or *in order that*. The infinitive mood alone is in English frequently used to express a purpose, and it then constitutes a distinct clause.

542. *Compound sentences* differ from complex sentences in that the clauses of which they consist are not mutually dependent, but are *co-ordinate*, and simply *connected*, with each other. This co-ordination may be considered as being under three relations. Thus when one clause is *supplemental* to the other, e. g. 'the ladder fell *and* the monkey ran away,' it may be called the *copulative* relation; when one clause is *opposed* to another, e. g. 'John is clever, *but* he is not profound,' it may be called the *adversative* relation; and when one clause contains the *reason* for the other, e. g. 'his army was disorganised, *hence* his despair,' it may be denominated the *causative* relation.

543. The *copulative* relation may exist in three degrees: (1) when equal stress is laid on both clauses,—each clause being distinct from the other; (2) when more stress lies on the second than on the first, as in clauses in English with *not only,—but;* (3) where the stress increases from clause to clause, as in the figure *climax*, each clause being introduced by some particle of sequence, *first, then, next, finally,* &c.

544. The *adversative* relation may exist in two forms: (1) where the second clause negatives the first (in English by *not,—but*), or (2) when the second clause limits the first; as, 'you may read it, *only* read it without stammering.'

545. The third, or *causative* relation in co-ordination, may have two divisions: (1) where the latter of two clauses expresses an effect, the former being the moral or physical cause, or (2) where the latter expresses a reason or motive, the former representing the result. This appears to be a simple inversion, which may be effected by the use of different particles of connection.

546. Compound sentences often suffer contraction by referring the same subject, the same predicate, and the same object to different co-ordinate clauses. Two or more subjects may go to one predicate; two or more predicates to one subject; two or more objects to one predicate; and several circumstances or limitations may be joined together in the same compound sentence, and may belong to the same word in that sentence.

547. Thus much has been said on the analysis of sentences, because without analysis of language in general, we can never arrive at the true analysis of the Chinese, and it is by a ready appreciation of the elementary forms and the scientific terms of grammar that clear, definite, and constant rules can be evolved from the study of Chinese. It is not the knowledge of a vast number of words which constitutes a real knowledge of any language, but it is the

right apprehension of its genius and idiomatic differences, (which is to be attained only by a careful analysis of its forms and constructions,) that will enable the student,—with a fair knowledge of words,—to read, speak, and translate correctly.

§. 2. *The forms of the simple sentence.*

548. A simple sentence may convey (1) a *command*, (2) a *wish*, (3) a *judgment*, i. e. an *assertion*, (4) a *question*, or (5) an *exclamation*. We have therefore to enquire what are the forms in Chinese for *imperative, optative, assertive, interrogative*, and *exclamatory* sentences. The imperative sentence will be dealt with first, because the simple force of the verb, without adjuncts, conveys this sense, and there is a close connexion between the imperative and the optative, at least in meaning. In the same way the root or crude form of the Latin verb expresses a *command*. (Cf. *es* 'be thou,' *ama* 'love thou,' and cf. Arts. 223 and 404.) Then after the assertion comes the question naturally, and these are often similar in form. The exclamation is often only to be distinguished from the question by the manner of its enunciation.

549. The form of the *imperative sentence* is simple and natural. The simple verb expresses the command, and the subject is generally understood; but when expressed, it stands before the verb and never, as a rule, after it, as it may in the English, 'come thou here;' e. g. *laî ché-lî*, 'come here,' or *nî laî ché-lî*, but not *laî nî ché-lî*. *Jŭ yĭ chāng yên* (1. a. 16) 'do you also throw light on the subject;' *kwʻaí kwān-mǫn, pŭ yaú tseŭ-liaù* (12. d. 20), 'quickly shut the doors, and let none go forth:' (cf. 12. i. 22.)

550. When the subject of an imperative sentence is a proper name, or the designation of a person, and not a mere pronoun, it sometimes stands after the verb; e. g. *laî, Yŭ!* (1. a. 13) 'come, Yŭ!' but the verbs *tsʻing* 請 and *jǎng* 讓 are used commonly before the subject, when that is expressed; e. g. *tsʻing-nî laî ché-lî* 'please to come here;' *jǎng tʻā kʻŭ pá* 'let him go away.'

551. The form of the *optative sentence* differs but little from that of the imperative. It is introduced by a verb which signifies to *desire* or to *wish*; e. g. *yuén nî pîng-ān* 'may you be happy!' The expressions *pā-pŭ-tĕ* and *hǫn-pŭ-tĕ* (cf. Arts. 273 and 395) should be remembered in this connexion. In the following passage in the *Sān-kwŏ* (litho. p. 13. c. 21—24) we have a noun governed by *hǫn* as a verb; thus, *hǫn lî pŭ nǫng!* 'would that my strength were adequate!' or 'would that I were able!' (lit. 'regret strength not able.')

552. Every *assertive sentence* in Chinese consists of a subject which stands first, and a predicate which follows it. Circumstances of time and place may stand before the subject, and circumstances of manner, of cause, and of effect generally stand before the predicate. The subject must be a noun or a word used as such, or it may consist of a sentence used as a noun: (cf. 7. a. 10, 11; 7. f. 15—18; 2. g. 12—16; 8. d. 13—18, which all form subjects.) The subject may be explained, parenthetically as it were, by a word or words in apposition, or by a participial phrase: (cf. 8. o. 16—19; 9. b. 22—27;

2. h. 22—24.) The subject may consist of two nouns, the former being in the genitive case, to express the *origin, cause,* or *relationship* of the latter: (cf. 2. 9. 12—16; 7. b. 29—c. 1; 2. h. 20—26.) The same remarks refer to the predicate when that is a noun.

553. The predicate generally requires one object, and sometimes two, to complete it; the first is called the *direct* object, the other the *indirect* object; e. g. *ché yǐ-kān-shú lŏ-liaù yĕ-tsz̀* 'this tree has shed its leaves;' *k'ŏ-ǐ yúng t'ā tsaí-kiā ch'ŭ-jǐ* (14. a. 16) 'I can employ him in the family to go in and out.'

554. *Interrogative sentences* have various forms in Chinese. Sometimes they are to be distinguished by the particles which are present in them, at other times the position of the clause, and of the words in it, shows the interrogative.

(1) When the particles are present, if they are final particles, the subject and predicate remain in the same position as they would in an assertive sentence; e. g. *nǐ yiù tŭng-tsiĕn* 'you have some cash;' *nǐ yiù tsiĕn mô?* 'have you any cash?' *ché yǐ-chĕ-mà shǐ kān-ts'aù* 'that horse eats hay;' *ché yǐ-chĕ-mà shǐ shimmô?* 'what does that horse eat?' (cf. Arts. 498—509.)

(2) When no interrogative particle is present, the form of the sentence may show that the sentence is interrogative. Two expressions are enunciated, one positive, the other negative, this leaves the mind in doubt, and shows that an enquiry is being made, just as *tŏ-shaù,* lit. 'many-few,' give rise to the abstract notion of *quantity,* and also to a question *how many?* e. g. *t'ā tsaí-kiā pŭ tsaí-kiā,* lit. 'he is at home,—not at home?'='is he at home?' By a reference to the articles on the interrogative particles the student will obtain many examples of interrogative sentences.

555. The forms of the *exclamatory sentence* scarcely differ at all from those of the interrogative. They are generally introduced by an interrogative particle or some word clearly of the nature of an exclamation. (See the Arts. on the exclamatory particle; and cf. 1. l. 14—17; 11. l. 9—17.)

§. 3. *The noun sentence.*

556. The noun sentence is one which occupies the place of a noun, and in Chinese may consist of a verb and its object; e. g. *haí jǐn pŭ haù* 'to injure people is bad.' The particles *chè, tǐ,* and *sŏ* generally mark the noun sentence.

557. The verb alone, or with adjuncts of time, may constitute a noun sentence, and be the subject of a sentence; e. g. *k'ŭng yǐn fǐ k'ǐ shǐ yè* (9. o. 5), lit. 'I fear, *to drink* is not this time;' *Tǐ siēn-sāng k'ŭ shǐ yaú k'ŭ kiù-liaù* (10. o. 25), lit. 'Mr. *Tǐ's going* is this, he wished to go long since.' Again, *hiŏ ǎr shǐ sǐ chǐ* (3. d. 10) is a noun sentence, and the subject to the verb *yŭ,* which follows. Also *yiù pǎng tsz̆ yuèn-fāng laí* (3. d. 19) and *jǐn pŭ chǐ ǎr pŭ-wǎn* (3. d. 29) are noun sentences: (cf. 9. b. 18—27.)

§. 4. *The adjective sentence.*

558. The adjective sentence is any set of words which explains or qualifies

THE SYNTAX OF SENTENCES. 185

a noun. A relative clause in English (and in Chinese often a clause in apposition) does this; but generally some particle, as *tĭ* 的, *sŏ* 所, or *ché* 者, throws the whole into the form of an adjective clause, the subject of which is represented by the particle; this makes the adjective sentence often to assume the character of a noun (cf. 3. e. 13. etc.); e. g. *kāng-tǎng-tĭ Tĭ kūng-tsź taú-mǎn* (8. c. 18) is an adjective sentence or relative clause, as it were in apposition to *Kwó kūng-tsź* its antecedent: it means literally, 'the one just waiting for Mr. *Tĭ* to arrive at the gate.'

§. 5. *The adverbial sentence.*

559. Adverbial sentences are such as express the circumstances of *time, place, manner,* and *cause.* They are sometimes introduced by particles in Chinese, but frequently they are without any distinctive mark of this kind; e. g. *swàn-kĭ tíng-liaù* (8. a. 6—9), *taú tsź-jĭ* (8. a. 10—12), *jĭ wí-ch'ŭ* (8. a. 13) are three adverbial sentences of *time* to the principal sentence *k'í-laí* 'he arose:' *tsiú,* 'then,' is really not wanted, but in Chinese it is idiomatic to insert it; it sums up, as it were, the three clauses just mentioned.

560. But adverbial sentences of *time* are often shown by some particle or phrase being present in the sentence; e. g. *yĭ-kién Tĭ kūng-tsź laí-paí* (8. c. 4), 'as soon as &c.,' is marked by *yĭ-kién;* and clauses beginning with *yĭ* and a verb will always mark an adverbial sentence of time. Again, *hwŭ-kién* (8. e. 28), 'on suddenly seeing,' introduces a similar expression. Phrases beginning with *yĭ,* 'as soon as,' would sometimes, when followed by *then,* mark the *repetition* which is implied in expressions beginning with *whenever* in English; e. g. *yĭ shĭ hŏ ch'á, tsiú kiàng Yīng hwá,* lit. 'one time drink tea, then speak English,' i. e. 'whenever he drinks tea he talks English:' (cf. 8. i. 2; 16. d. 2.)

561. *Duration* of time is expressed by an adverbial sentence,—by putting *shĭ,* 'time,' or *shĭ-kiēn,* 'time-interval,' in construction with the sentence; e. g. *nĭ tǎng tsai ché-lĭ tĭ shĭ-heú, ngò pŭ-yaú tŭ,* 'while you are staying here, I will not read;' *Kaū-k'iŭ k'ān-shĭ* (16. a. 11) 'while *Kaū-k'iŭ* was looking on:' (cf. Art. 337.)

562. Adverbial sentences of *place* may refer to *position in* or *motion to* or *from* a place; e. g. *suí pién taú nà-lĭ, ngò-t'ǔng nĭ k'ŭ,* 'whenever you like to proceed, I will go with you;' *ngò pŭ k'ǎng taú nĭ tĭ tí-fāng laí* 'I will not go to your place;' *ts'ûng ché-lĭ taú nà-kó tí-fāng, ngò pŭ k'ó k'ŭ,* 'I cannot go from hence to that place;' *ngò k'ŭ-tĭ tí-fāng, nĭ pŭ k'ò-ĭ laí,* 'where I go you cannot come.' The student will observe that such adverbial clauses require certain words, as *ts'ûng* 'from,' *taú* 'to,' and the word *tí-fāng,* 'place,' in construction, just as *shĭ* and *shĭ-heú* are generally necessary in adverbial sentences of time.

563. Adverbial sentences of *manner,* which relate to *likeness, proportion* or *effect,* are introduced by prepositions or appropriate particles, as *jû* 如, *siàng* 象, *sź* 似, *jĭn* 任, *chaū* 照, which mean 'as, like as, similar to,

B b

according to,' &c.; or by verbs and particles combined, as *pǐ* 比 'to compare,' *yü* 於 'than,' &c.; or causative verbs, as *lǐng* 令 'to cause,' *pǐ* 俾 'to give,' &c.: (cf. the adverbs of manner, Arts. 246—251; also Arts. 211, 213, and 144—150.)

564. Adverbial sentences which refer to *likeness* are such as the following: *t'ā, siáng fú-tsīn, tsó sǎng-ì*, 'he carries on trade, *as his father did;*' *naì pǐ k'ǔ-k'ǔ yü shǐ-sǔ jú-tsź, shīn fī-ì yè* (9. l. 15), 'but, *thus strictly to confine ourselves to the world's customs*, would certainly not be right:' (cf. 4. m. 25; 8. k. 12; 9. b. 22; 21. e. 24.)

565. Adverbial sentences which relate to *proportion, intensity, equality* are such as *yǐ-niēn shǎng-sheǔ, piēn tsīn-tsīn yiù wǐ* (10. a. 17), lit. 'one take raise hand, then relish it more and more,' which would seem to make the first clause an adverbial sentence of time (cf. Art. 560), but the sense of the passage would lean rather to the version '*as they drank* (or 'the longer they drank') they relished it the more;' *t'ā, pǔ jǔ nǐ, tǔ-shǔ-tǐ*, 'he is not so learned, *as you*,' or 'he is not such a scholar, *as you.*'

566. Adverbial sentences which relate to *effect* are such as are introduced by *pà* 把 'to take,' *ì* 以 'to use,' *lǐng* 令 'to cause,' &c.; e.g. *ché-kó jīn sié-tsź, pà nǐ pǔ k'ò tǔ*, 'this man writes, *so that you cannot read it;*' *t'ā kiàng ché-yáng tō, lǐng ngò pǔ nǎng kiàng*, 'he spoke so much, *that I could not speak at all:*' (cf. 1. j. 1—8.)

567. Adverbial sentences of *cause*, which relate to the *ground* or *reason*, *condition, concession, purpose* or *consequence*, require separate treatment, because they are generally dependent upon particles, or words used as such, as *yīn* 因 'because,' *ì* 以 'by,' *siǔī* 雖 'although,' *jǒ* 若 'if,' *tsiǔ* 就 'then,' &c.

568. Adverbial sentences which express the *ground* or *reason* are sometimes without, and are sometimes accompanied by, distinctive particles; e.g. *yīn kiēn Kwó shīn ts'ǐng* .. (9. c. 15) 'as he saw Mr. *Kwó's* deep feeling ..;' *ché-kó jīn pǔ-haù, yīn-wei t'ā má ngò*, 'that is a bad man, because he abused me;' *nǐ tsǒ-jǐ pǔ-laì, ngò tsiǔ pǔ tǔ-shǔ*, 'I did not read yesterday, because you did not come' (cf. 4. h. 2. and 18). There should be a causative particle present in the *protasis*, or an illative particle in the *apodosis*.

569. Adverbial sentences which express a *condition* are sometimes, but not always, introduced by a conditional particle (cf. Art. 265); e.g. *pǔ sǔng ngò yǐ kweǐ yáng-ts'iēn, ngò pǔ pà nǐ ch'ǔ-k'ǔ*, 'if you do not give me a dollar, I will not let you go;' *jǒ-shí t'ā pǔ-tseù, pǐ-tǐng tà t'ā*, 'if he does not go away, I must beat him;' *pǔ tsǒ haù shǔ, tsiǔ pǔ-k'ò-ǐ kiaù t'ā, tǔ-shǔ-tǐ*, 'if he had not made a good book, we could not call him a scholar:' (cf. 4. g. 24 —28. and 4. h. 9—14.)

570. Adverbial sentences which express *concession* are nearly always introduced by a particle such as *siǔī* 'although;' e.g. *siǔī-jén jǔ-kīn pǔ-k'ǔ, heù-*

THE SYNTAX OF SENTENCES. 187

laî t'ā k'ŭ tĕ tō, 'although now he does not cry, afterwards he will weep much;' *kweī-kwŏ sūī tsai chŭng-yáng ặr-wán-lī* .. (23. d. II) '*although* your honourable nation is in the vast ocean twenty thousand miles away;' *nĭ shwŏ-hū sūī-piên tō, ngò sĭn-pŭ-tĕ nĭ,* '*however* much you promise, I cannot believe you.'

571. Adverbial sentences which express a *purpose* are sometimes introduced by a particle; e. g. *tặn hiaú tĭ ì chŭng jin-lặn* (6. a. 4) 'give practical weight to filial piety and fraternal love, in order to strengthen the relative duties.' But when the purpose is contained in two or three syllables, it may be adjoined without a particle, like the English infinitive when it expresses a purpose.

572. Adverbial sentences which relate to *consequence* would seem to be similar to those under Art. 560, but these express rather the consequence which follows the principal sentence as a cause; e. g. 'he talks, *so that he is unintelligible,*' contains an adverbial sentence of *manner;* 'he runs so fast, *that he will be sure to get there in time,*' contains an adverbial sentence of *effect*. In this latter case, one clause contains the *cause,* the other the *effect;* but in the former case, the second clause simply qualifies the verb 'talks.' Examples of these distinctions in Chinese can hardly be given. So much is done by inference from the sense of a passage, that too subtle a distinction would only mislead. But a careful study of the causative and illative particles will be beneficial, and reference should be made to the exercises in Part III.

§. 6. *The complex sentence.*

573. The complex sentence differs from the compound sentence in this, that the clauses of which it is composed are mutually dependent. There is in a complex sentence one principal and one or more subordinate clauseš, which come under one of the above-mentioned classes, viz. (1) the noun sentence, (2) the adjective sentence, or (3) the adverbial sentence.

Examples.

hiŏ ặr shĭ sĭ chī 'to learn and constantly to dwell on the subject,' (noun s.) *pŭ yĭ yŭ hŭ?* 'is it not a pleasure?' (principal s.) (3. d. 10,—19,—29.)
ì Kī-tsż kweī tsŏ hŭng-fán 'by *Kī-tsz* restoring the great plan,' (noun s.) *fă sheú shĭng yĕ* 'he gave an example to the sacred sages,' (principal s.) (2. m. 13: cf. also 8. l. 12. and 9. l. 15—27.)

574. The adjective sentence is an accessory sentence, in apposition frequently to the word which it qualifies; and with the *person or thing,* for which that word is understood to stand, the adjective sentence may be said to be precisely similar to the noun sentence.

Examples.

yĭ-kiên Tĭ kŭng-tsż laî-paî 'as soon as he saw Mr. *Tĭ* coming to call,' (an adverbial s. of time.)
tsaù fī paú yŭ Kwó kŭng-tsż 'he hastened to inform Mr. *Kwo,*' (principal s.)
kāng-tặng-tĭ Tĭ kŭng-tsż taú-mặn 'who was just then waiting for Mr. *Tĭ* to arrive at the gate,' (adjective s. qualifying *Kwó.*)

§. 7. *The compound sentence.*

575. Compound sentences contain two or more co-ordinate clauses, each being independent of the other, though they are connected either actually by particles or virtually by the sense of the passage.

Examples.

t'iēn weī chĭ túng pŭ năng kiaí, shíng-jĭn chĭ yên wû-sò-yúng. (2. i. 9.)
naī ch'ŭ tá-fă, yúng weí shíng-sz̆. (2. l. 20.)
nĭ yĭ-peī ngò yĭ-chàn, piĕn pŭ fŭ tüĭ-ts'z̆. (10. a. 26.)
săn jĭn chĕ-tĕ t'ĭng-peī tsĭ-kiĕn, Kwŏ tsiŭ găn tsŏ taú. (10. c. 4.)

576. The three states or relations which may subsist in the compound sentence are, (1) the *copulative*, (2) the *adversative*, (3) the *causative*.

Examples.

(1) *tĭ-sīn yĭ yiù pŭ-găn, kīn yĭ pŭ kàn kiù liŭ.* (9. c. 26.)
    k'iŭ liŏ-t'ĭng nĭ-shĭ, shaù túng yĭ ts'àn. (9. d. 9.)
    kīn hĭng yiù yuên, yiú tĕ siăng peī. (9. i. 4.)

(2) *k'ĭ jĭ-yé chĭ sŏ sĭ* &c. (5. n. 29—o. 30.)
    siaù-tĭ yĭ pŭ jĭn yên k'ŭ, tán chwăng ī-sŭ &c. (9. a. 26.)
    Again in 9. c. 11, where an adversative clause comes in parenthetically, but may be said to be co-ordinate with the previous sentence, which is complex.

(3) *tặn hiaú-tĭ, ĭ chŭng jĭn-lặn.* (6. a. 4.)
    săng-jĭn pŭ năng yĭ-jĭ ặr wŭ yúng, tsĭ pŭ-k'ò yĭ-jĭ ặr wŭ ts'aí. (7. a. 10.)
    shĭ kŭ tsz̆ taú, ĭ lĭ yŭ shĭ. (2. h. 11.)
    wŭ yĭ wù sz̆, kŭ pŭ weí. (2. j. 1.)

577. Under the copulative relation a subdivision may be said to exist, which relates to clauses presenting an alternative, as in English clauses beginning with the particles *either* and *or*. *Hwŏ* 或 or *hwŏ-chĕ* 或者 and *hwán* 還, repeated at the beginning of each clause, mark such sentences.

Examples.

hwán shĭ tăng chīn, hwán shĭ tăng shwá?
還 是 當 眞 | 是 當 耍
'Are you in earnest, or are you joking?'

hwŏ-chĕ t'ā-laí, hwŏ-chĕ t'ā sz̆-liaù, 'either he will come, or perhaps he is dead.' (Cf. 3. l. 27, where *yĭ* is used for *or*, as a connective.)

§. 8. *Figures of speech.*

578. Under this comprehensive expression much is included, but we purpose noticing only a few of those peculiar forms which in language take this denomination: such as *ellipsis*,—the leaving out of words; *pleonasm*,—

THE SYNTAX OF SENTENCES. 189

the redundant use of words; *antithesis*,—the appropriate use of words of opposite significations; and the *repetition* of a word or phrase to give emphasis to the expression.

579. By the figure ellipsis many expressions in Chinese become intelligible, which appear, at first sight, to be in accordance with no particular rule. Such are the terms *chī-ì* (9. f. 12) 'old friends;' *paí-sheú* 'to make a visit on a person's birthday:' *paí-niên* 'to pay compliments at the new year;' *kaú-laù* 'to plead age,' *kaú-píng* 'to plead sickness' (as a reason for retirement from office).

580. It is a very common thing to leave out the personal pronouns when they are the subjects of sentences, and when no difficulty would arise in supplying them from the context or from the conversation. *Pŭ-yaú* alone might be either 'do not!' i. e. *noli*, or 'I do not want;' but *pŭ-yaú ché-kó tūng-sī* must be, 'I do not want this thing,' and *pŭ-yaù túng-sheù* must be, 'do not move!'='be quiet!' So also *sié-sié* 'thanks!' for 'I thank you;' but this expression is similar in the English, 'thank you.'

581. The obscurity which might sometimes veil the meaning of a sentence in Chinese is removed by the redundancy of repeating the same idea by negativing its opposite term: thus, *ngò yaú k'ŭ, pŭ yaú tàng*, 'I wish to go, and do not wish to stay;' *nì yaú shwŏ chīn, pŭ yaú shwŏ hwâng*, 'do you speak truly, and do not speak falsely;' *tsîn-yên k'án-kién* 'I saw it with my own eyes.'

582. The Chinese delight in forming antitheses, for which their language affords great facility, every important attribute and object having its appropriate opposite term. A list of the most common of these will be found in Appendix I. Antithesis occurs frequently in proverbs and old sayings; e. g. *yiù t'eŭ weí, mô wî chīn*, 'in front there is dignity, but behind no troops;' and *shâng yiù t'iĕn-t'âng, hiá yiù Sū Hâng*, 'above there is heaven, and below *Su-(cheu)* and *Hang-(cheu)*:' (cf. 19. i. 11.)

583. Repetition has already been referred to as being a common method of forming words and phrases and for intensifying adjectives and adverbs (cf. Arts. 99 and 136), but it is often merely for the sake of the rhythm that words and syllables are repeated. A few select expressions of this kind may be seen in Appendix I.

584. Almost all the other figures of speech which are used in European tongues are to be found in Chinese. *Climax* is especially common in this language. But it is needless to multiply examples of these figures, for they will easily be recognised by the advanced student.

§. 9. *The varieties of style.*

585. The differences of style in Chinese authors, and the marks of the period in literary works, are very great and distinct. The language of the most ancient authors is very brief and sententious, while the meaning is pregnant and expressive. There is a majesty and dignity of style, which have never been surpassed by later writers. The style of the *King* (cf. Part II. pp. 5, 6)

stands foremost in antiquity and sublimity. The *Sz̽-shū*, the *Lĭ-kĭ*, the *Taŭ-tĕ-kīng*, the *Ts'ŭ-ts'z̽*, and the *Shān-haĭ-kīng* come next in order (cf. Part II. pp. 6, 7), and to these may be added the great commentators and writers of elegant compositions, such as *Chwāng-tsz̽* and the *Shĭ-tsz̽*, or 'Ten scholars,' mentioned in Part II. pp. 7, 8. To these must be added *Măng-tsz̽*, who, though nearly equal to *K'ŭng-tsz̽* in Chinese estimation as a philosopher, has a diffuse style of composition. *Tsŏ-shĭ*, the author of the *Tsŏ-chuén* and the *Kwŏ-yŭ*, *Sz̽-mà-tsiēn* and the *Ts'aĭ-tsz̽*, or 'men of talent,' come next, with the later authors, *Hán-yŭ* (who lived in the *T'áng* dynasty), *Gaŭ-yáng Siŭ*, *Sŭ Tūng-pŏ*, *Chŭ-hī*, and many others, fragments of whose works are preserved in the *Kù-wăn yuén kién* (cf. Part II. pp. 14, 36).

586. The distinctions drawn by the eminent writer *Yáng-tsz̽* 楊子 (cf. Part II. p. 8) between the different varieties of style are as follows: *sz̽ shīng ts'z̽ tsi̽ k'áng; ts'z̽ shīng sz̽ tsi̽ fŭ; sz̽ ts'z̽ chīng tsi̽ kīng*. When the subject is greater than the power of expression, it is denominated *k'áng* 伉 'unevenly matched;' when the expression exceeds the subject, it is called *fŭ* 賦 'poetical style;' and when the subject and the expression are equally matched, it is called *kīng* 經 'classic style.'

587. *Gaŭ-yáng Siŭ* says: *Yên ĭ tsaĭ sz̽, ăr wăn ĭ shĭ yên; sz̽ sin yên wăn, tsi̽ k'ŭ kīng pŭ-yuèn*, 'let the words contain the theme or subject, and let elegant style adorn the words; let there be the subject truthfully, and the words elegantly set down, and the style will not be far from that which is called *kīng*.' In which passage the four characters 事 信 言 文 *sz̽ sin yên wăn* contain the marks of the highest style of literary composition.

588. No positive rules can be given for composition, but the length of the *kŭ*, or clauses, should be somewhat diversified. Though clauses of four characters, which form phrases, are frequent in the best authors, the style will be stiff and bald, unless occasionally a clause of five, six, or seven characters be introduced. It is usual to accumulate ideas in an opening sentence, and then to display them separately in the sequence. The admired style of Chinese compositions may be compared to the elegant style of Cicero rather than to the nervous argumentative style of Demosthenes. (Cf. Prémare's *Notitia Linguæ Sinicæ*, where examples of style will be found.)

APPENDIX I.

List of antithetical words.

商 shāng 'a wholesale merchant.' 賈 kŭ 'a retail trader.'
賞 shàng 'to reward.' 罰 fă 'to punish.'
善 shén 'good, virtuous.' 惡 ŏ 'bad, vicious.'
收 sheū 'to collect together.' 散 sán 'to scatter abroad.'
首 sheù 'the head.' 腳 kiŏ 'the foot.'
授 sheú 'to give.' 受 sheú 'to receive.'
獸 sheú 'a wild animal.' 畜 chŭ 'a tamed animal.'
始 chì 'the beginning.' 終 chūng 'the end.'
是 shí 'it is so,—true.' 非 fī 'it is not so,—false.'
是 shí 'yes.' 否 feù 'no.'
深 shīn 'deep (of water).' 淺 tsièn 'shallow.'
伸 shīn 'to extend the body.' 屈 kŭ 'to bend the body.'
身 shīn 'the body.' 神 shín 'the spirit.'
升 shīng 'to ascend.' 降 kiáng 'to descend.'
升 shīng 'to rise,' 浮 feú 'to float.' 沉 chín 'to sink.'
盛 shíng 'to flourish.' 衰 shwaī 'to decay.'
雙 shwāng 'a pair.' 隻 chĕ 'an individual.'
順 shán 'to obey.' 逆 nì 'to disobey.'
放 fáng 'to let go.' 收 sheū 'to take up.'
福 fŭ 'happiness.' 禍 hŏ 'misery.'
豐 fūng 'abundant.' 荒 hwāng 'sterile.'
富 fú 'rich.' 貧 pín 'poor.'

APPENDIX I.

愛 *gai* 'to love.'
傲 *gaú* 'proud.'
硬 *gáng* 'hard.'
寒 *hán* 'cold.'
好 *haù* 'good.'
厚 *heŭ* 'thick,—generous.'
喜 *hĭ* 'to be glad.'
賢 *hiên* 'a wise man.'
虛 *hŭ* 'empty,—vain.'
形 *hîng* 'the form,—substance.'
活 *hwŏ* 'alive.'
會 *hwuĭ* 'to meet together.'
爺 *yê* 'the father.'
筵 *yên* 'the banquet.'
友 *yiŭ* 'a friend.'
因 *yīn* 'good words and actions.'
陰 *yīn* 'the female principle in nature,—darkness,—obscure.'
熱 *jĭ* 'hot.'
吉 *kĭ* 'fortunate.'
高 *kaū* 'high.'
蓋 *kai* 'to cover.'
甘 *kān* 'sweet.'
嫁 *kiá* 'to marry (of the woman).'
教 *kiaú* 'to teach.'
結 *kĭ* 'to bind fast.'
古 *kŭ* 'ancient times.'
禽 *kîn* 'birds.'

惡 *wú* 'to hate.'
謙 *kiēn* 'humble.'
軟 *juèn* 'soft.'
暑 *shù* 'heat.'
歹 *tai* or 惡 *ŏ* 'bad.'
薄 *pŏ* 'thin,—mean.'
愁 *tsiŭ* 'to be sorrowful.'
愚 *yû* 'a foolish man.'
實 *shĭ* 'solid,—true.'
影 *yĭng* 'the shadow.'
死 *sž* 'dead.'
別 *pĭ* 'to separate from.'
娘 *niáng* 'the mother.'
席 *sĭ* 'a common feast.'
仇 *cheŭ* 'an enemy.'
果 *kò* 'the reward of them' (Budd.).
陽 *yáng* 'the male principle in nature,—light,—clear.'
冷 *làng* 'cold.'
兇 *hiūng* 'unfortunate.'
低 *tī* 'low.'
開 *k'ai* 'to open.'
酸 *swān* 'sour.'
娶 *tsüĭ* 'to marry (of the man).'
學 *hiŏ* 'to learn.'
解 *kiaĭ* 'to loosen.'
今 *kīn* 'the present time.'
獸 *sheŭ* 'beasts.'

APPENDIX I.

雄 *hiúng* 'the male (of birds).'   雌 *tsz̄* 'the female (of birds).'

禁 *kín* 'to forbid.'   許 *hiú* 'to allow.'

曲 *k'iŭ* 'crooked.' (*wān* 彎.)   直 *chí* 'straight.'

經 *kīng* 'classic text.'   傳 *chuén* 'the commentary.'

公 *kūng* 'public.'   私 *sz̄* 'private.'

功 *kūng* 'merit.'   報 *paú* 'reward.' *kwó* 過 'fault.'

空 *k'ūng* 'empty.'   滿 *mwàn* 'full.'

饑 *kī* 'hungry.' (*nüĭ* 餒.)   飽 *paù* 'satisfied.'

生 *sāng* 'raw, green.'   熟 *shŭ* 'cooked, ripe.'

遠 *yuèn* 'distant.'   近 *kín* 'near.'

去 *k'ŭ* 'to go away.'   來 *laî* 'to come near.'

君 *kiūn* 'the prince.'   臣 *chîn* 'the vassal.'

光 *kwāng* 'brightness.'   暗 *gán* 'darkness.'

理 *lì* 'the spiritual essence,—the principle which arranges.'   氣 *k'í* 'the material essence,—the matter which is arranged.'

利 *lí* 'profit or interest.'   本 *pàn* 'the original capital.'

留 *liŭ* 'to detain, to keep.'   逐 *chŭ* 'to throw away.'

流 *liŭ* 'to flow, to roam.'   止 *chì* 'to stop, to rest in.'

樂 *lŏ* 'to manifest pleasure.'   悲 *peī* 'to express sorrow.'

猛 *mạng* 'fierce.'   良 *liáng* 'gentle, good.'

門 *mạn* 'the outer door.'   戶 *hú* 'the inner door;' *mạn-hú* = 'family.'

怒 *nú* 'anger.'   忍 *jìn* 'patience.'

賓 *pīn* 'the guest.'   主 *chù* 'the host.'

僕 *pŭ* 'a man-servant.'   婢 *p'í* 'a maid-servant.'

本 *pạn* 'the beginning.'   末 *mŭ* 'the end.'

虧 *kw'eī* 'to lose.'   益 *yí* 'to gain.'

鬼 *kweì* 'ghost inferior,—the active principle of *yīn*.'   神 *shîn* 'spirit superior,—the active principle of *yáng*.'

貴 *kweí* 'noble.'   賤 *tsiên* 'mean.'

觀 *kwān* 'to look at from below, or from a distance.'   臨 *lin* 'to look at from above, or while approaching.'

燥 *saú* 'dry.'   濕 *shî* 'damp, humid.'

僧 *sāng* 'religious.'   俗 *sŭ* 'secular.'

笑 *siaú* 'to laugh.'   哭 *k'ŭ* 'to cry.'

先 *siēn* 'before.'   後 *heú* 'behind or after.'

新 *sīn* 'new.'   舊 *kiú* 'old.'

信 *sín* 'to believe.'   疑 *î* 'to doubt.'

姓 *síng* 'the name of the clan.'   氏 *shí* 'the name of the family.'

性 *síng* 'natural disposition.'   習 *sĭ* 'practice.'

送 *súng* 'to give.'   受 *sheú* 'to receive.'

送 *súng* 'to bid adieu.'   迎 *ying* 'to welcome.'

師 *sź* 'a tutor.'   徒 *tú* 'a pupil,—a disciple.'

單 *tān* 'single.'   雙 *shwāng* 'double.'

貪 *t'ān* 'covetous.'   廉 *liên* 'liberal,—not avaricious.'

淡 *tán* 'simple, moderate.'   濃 *nûng* 'strong.'

刀 *taū* 'a sword with one edge.'   劍 *k'iên* 'a two-edged sword.'

問 *wạ̀n* 'to ask.'   答 *tă* 'to reply.'

未 *wí* 'not yet.'   已 *ĭ* 'already.'

張 *chāng* 'to stretch the bow.'   弛 *shĭ* 'to relax the bow.'

章 *chāng* 'the art of counting.'   程 *ching* 'the art of weighing and measuring.'

倡 *ch'āng* 'a female musician.'   優 *yiū* 'a male performer.'

長 *ch'âng* 'long.'   短 *twàn* 'short.'

常 *ch'âng* 'constant.'   變 *piên* 'changeable.'

唱 *ch'áng* 'the leader in the song.'   和 *hô* 'the singer who replies.'

朝 *chaū* 'morning.'   暮 *mú* 'evening.'

APPENDIX I. 195

陟 *chĕ* 'to ascend.'
遲 *ch'î* 'slow.'
智 *chî* 'prudent.'
眞 *chīn* 'true.'
成 *chíng* 'to perfect.'
誠 *chíng* 'sincere.'
正 *chíng* 'straight.'
正 *chíng* 'upright.'
忠 *chūng* 'faithful and truthful.'
出 *ch'ŭ* 'to go out.'
早 *tsaŭ* 'early.'
妻 *ts'ī* 'wife.'
焦 *tsiaū* 'sad.'
借 *tsié* 'to borrow.'
疾 *tsí* 'hastily.'
積 *tsí* 'to collect.'
姐 *tsiĕ* 'elder sister.'
進 *tsín* 'to advance.'
清 *ts'īng* 'clear.'
晴 *tsíng* 'serene weather.'
左 *tsŏ* 'the left hand.'
坐 *tsŏ* 'to sit.'
從 *ts'úng* 'to follow after.'
粗 *tsū* 'coarse.'
祖 *tsù* 'ancestor.'
尊 *tsān* 'honourable.'
存 *tsṳ́n* 'to preserve.'
彼 *pì* 'that.'

降 *kiáng* 'to descend.'
快 *kw'eí* 'quick,'=速 *sŏ.*
愚 *yû* 'foolish.'
假 *kià* 'false.'
敗 *pai* 'to ruin.'
僞 *wei* 'deceitful.'
歪 *wei* 'crooked, awry.'
邪 *siê* 'depraved.'
佞 *níng* 'a flatterer.'
入 *jí* 'to enter in.'
晚 *wàn* 'late.'
妾 *tsĭ* 'concubine.'
樂 *lŏ* 'joyful.'
還 *hwán* 'to pay again.'
遲 *ch'î* 'slow,'=徐 *sú* 'leisurely.'
散 *sán* 'to scatter.'
妹 *mei* 'younger sister.'
退 *tüí* 'to retreat.'
濁 *chŭ* 'muddy.' (*hwạ̌n* 混.)
雨 *yù* 'rainy weather.'
右 *yiú* 'the right hand.'
立 *lì* 'to stand.' (*k'ĭ* 起.)
違 *wei* 'to oppose.'
細 *sì* 'fine.'
孫 *sạ̄n* 'descendant.'
卑 *pi* 'mean.'
亡 *wáng* 'to lose.'
此 *tsż̀* 'this.'

Examples of antithesis in sentences.

yiù ts'ai wi - pĭ yiù maú, yiù maú wi - pĭ yiù ts'ai,
有才未必有貌有 | 未必有 |
'There may be talent without beauty, and there may be beauty without talent.'

maú ch'ing k'i - ts'ai, ts'ai fú k'i maú,
貌稱其才 | 副其 |
'His beauty equals his ability, and his talents enhance his beauty.'

ĭ pŭ chē shīn, shĭ pŭ ch'ung k'eù,
衣不遮身,食不充口
'Not clothing to cover his body, nor food to fill his mouth.'

hô - chŭ pŭ - mĭ, shīn - chŭ pŭ - sin?
何處不覔,甚處不尋
'Where have I not looked, where have I not sought?'

yaú - k'i wŭ luĭ, yaú - yên wŭ - yŭ,
要泣無淚,要言 | 語
'He wished to weep, but he had no tears,—to speak, but he had no words.'

t'ā wei ngò sz̀, ngò pĭ wei - t'ā wáng,
他爲我死, | 必爲他亡
'As he died for me, I must sacrifice myself for him.'

sháng-t'iĕn wŭ - lŭ, jĭ - tĭ wŭ mǎn,
上天無路入地 | 門
'If he would rise to heaven there is no way, or enter earth there is no door,'
='he cannot escape.'

nĭ yĭ - yên ngò yĭ - kŭ. nĭ yĭ - chŭng ngò yĭ - chàn.
你一言我 | 句　你一鍾 | | 盞
'They are well matched at gossipping.'　'They are well matched at drinking.'

yĭ pwán - ǎr ts'z̀, yĭ pwán - ǎr k'ǒng,
一半兒辭一 | 兒肯
'He half refuses, and is half willing.'

Examples of repetition of characters.

yuèn-yuèn ts'iaú kièn 遠 | 瞧見 'to look at from a long distance.'

gai-gai t'ŭng-k'ŭ 哀 | 慟哭 'to weep bitterly.'

APPENDIX I. 197

yĭ-kŭ-kŭ tŭ t'ing-tĕ liaŭ 一 句 | 都 聽 的 了 'I heard every word.'

yĭ-pú-pú mŏ sháng-shān laí 一 步 | 摸 上 山 來 'step by step, feeling his way, he ascended the mountain.'

kīng-kīng tĭ shwŏ 輕 | 的 說 'to speak very softly.'

t'ing-t'ing tāng-tāng 停 | 當 | 'in a fixed and proper manner.'

ch'ĕ-ch'ĕ yĕ-yĕ 扯 | 拽 | 'to carry off by force.'

míng-míng pĕ-pĕ 明 | 白 | 'very clearly understood.'

twān-twān chíng-chíng 端 | 正 | 'elegant and correct.'

ts'ĭ-ts'ĭ chĭng-chĭng 齊 | 整 | 'precisely arranged.'

hwān-hwān meí-meí 昏 | 昧 | 'dull and bewildered.'

sŭ-sŭ t'aŭ-t'aŭ 絮 | 叨 | 'to reiterate vociferously.'

Phrases formed upon a similar principle.

pŭ-chī pŭ-kiŏ 不 知 | 覺 'he knows not nor perceives.'

pŭ-míng pŭ-pĕ 不 明 | 白 'quite unintelligible.'

yuén-sāng yuén-sż 願 生 | 死 'ready to live or die.'

k'ĭ-sāng k'ĭ sż 氣 生 | 死 'desperately angry.'

k'ŏ-hạ́n k'ŏ-naŭ 可 恨 | 惱 'extremely annoying.'

sż k'ĭ sż k'iaŭ 似 奇 | 巧 'apparently very clever.'

pwán k'aī pwán yèn 半 開 | 掩 'half revealed and half concealed.'

pwán jín pwán kweĭ 半 人 | 鬼 'half man and half ghost.'

lúng-shín lúng kweĭ 弄 神 | 鬼 'to play the ghost.'

lúng-laí lúng k'ú 弄 來 | 去 'to be eager at business.'

hú-yên hú-yŭ 胡 言 | 語 'to talk very foolishly.'

má-tá má-siaŭ 罵 大 | 小 'to abuse all alike.'

tá-tsiŭ tá-jŭ 大 酒 | 肉 'a great feast.'

k'iaŭ-mú k'iaŭ-yáng 喬 模 | 樣 'in a haughty manner.'

kŏ-mạ́n kŏ hŭ 各 門 | 戶 'each in his own way.'

198   APPENDIX I.

kĭ-sīn kĭ-k'ŭ 吃辛 | 若 'greatly afflicted.'
yiŭ-p'ing yiŭ-kŭ 有憑 | 據 'there is full proof of it.'
mŭ-yuên mŭ-kŭ 沒原 | 故 'there is no ground at all for it.'
mŭ-tsŭng mŭ-yĭng 沒踪 | 影 'without trace or shadow.'

Examples of synonymes used in phrases.

haŭ-kĭ gaĭ-ts'ĭng 好潔愛清 'to love cleanliness.'
t'ŭng kān kŭng k'ŭ 同甘共若 'alike happy and troubled.'
tsāṇ pīn kĭng kĕ 尊賓敬客 'to honour and respect guests.'
hwān-t'iēn hĭ-tĭ 歡天喜地 'to rejoice exceedingly.'
shĭ-t'iēn mĭng-tĭ 誓天盟地 'to swear by heaven and earth.'
shĭ-pâng tsiŭ-yiŭ 詩朋酒友 'friends of the Muse and the wine.'
paŭ ch'eŭ sŭ yuên 報讎雪怨 'to revenge an insult.'
lĭng yá lĭ ch'ĭ 伶牙俐齒 'clever at speaking.'
hŭ sź lwán siàng 糊思亂想 'to think confusedly.'
jŭ kī sź h'ŏ 如饑似渴 'like hunger and thirst.'

Select idiomatic phrases.

tsáng t'eŭ lŭ weì 藏頭露尾 'to hide the head and expose the tail.'
niên maĭ lĭ shwaĭ 年邁力衰 'years increased, strength decayed.'
shān chĭn haĭ tsŏ 山珍海錯 'sumptuous fare.'
ts'ŭ ch'á t'ăn fŭn 麤茶淡飯 'tasteless tea and rice,—poor fare.'
meĭ-laĭ yên-k'ŭ 眉來眼去 'glancing now and again.'
meĭ-hwā yên-siaŭ 眉花眼笑 'arched eyebrows and laughing eyes.'
hwaĭ-ts'aĭ paŭ-hiŏ 懷才抱學 'devoted to learning.'
ts'īng-t'iēn pĕ-jĭ 清天白日 'in open day.'
nĭ-shāng ngŏ-liâng 你商我量 'let us mutually advise.'
nĭ-tŭng ngŏ-sī 你東 | 西 'we are mutually opposed.'

pĕ-jĭ hĭ yĕ 白日黑夜 'from noon to midnight,—day and night.'
tsĭ-sz̽ pă-hwŏ 七死八活 'more dead than alive.'
tsĭ-păn pă-lĭ 七本八利 'the profit just saves the capital.'
pĕ-ling pĕ-li 百伶百俐 'very shrewd and clever.'

Elegant phrases, idiomatic and poetic.

Shĭ-yŭn 詩云 'the *Shĭ-kĭng* says,' or *Shŭ-yŭn* 書 | 'the *Shŭ-kĭng* says.'

Tsz̽ yŭ 子曰 'for *K'ŭng-tsz̽* (Confucius) says.'

jŭn-pĭ 潤筆, lit. 'to moisten the pencil,—to commit to writing.'

fŭng-fŭ 捧腹 'to laugh immoderately,' like "Se tenir les côtés de rire," or "Laughter holding both his sides." Milton.

keŭ-mĭng 鈎名, lit. 'to fish for a name,—to hunt for a reputation.'

mŭ-sŭng 目送, lit. 'with the eye to accompany,—to watch until out of sight.'

yĭn-kĭ 飲泣, lit. 'to drink tears,—to weep bitterly.'

shĭ-yên 食言, lit. 'to eat words,—to break a promise.'

Confucius denied himself in respect of four things, which are referred to in the following expressions:

wŭ-ĭ 毋意 'he did not bind himself to his own opinion.'

wŭ-pĭ | 必 'he did not hold any thing to be of necessity absolute.'

wŭ-kŭ | 固 'he was not perverse and obstinate in his views,'

wŭ-ngŏ | 我 'he held no feelings of private interest.'

T'ai-yuên 泰元, lit. 'the exalted origin of things,—heaven.'

Tŭng-kiŭn 東君, lit. 'the prince of the east,—the sun.'

T'ai-yâng 太陽 'the great light,—the sun.'—*Sol.*

Pĕ-k'ŭ 白駒, lit. 'the white colt,—the morning.'—*Aurora.*

I-hô 羲和 'the charioteer of the sun.'—*Phaethon.*

T'iēn-hăn 天狼 'a star of evil omen.'

Siēn-hô 纖呵 'the charioteer of the moon,' also called *Chāng-ngŏ.*

Ti-kūng 帝弓 'the rainbow,' also called *Ti-tŭng* 螮蝀.

Nü-i 女夷 'the Spirit presiding over flowers.'

Wāng-hwā 王化 'the royal flower,'—the *Maŭ-tān* 牡丹.

Tsāng-yiù 淨友 'the water-lily,' *Lŭng-yá* 龍牙 'the *li-chi* 荔枝.'

Li-chi-nú ｜｜奴, lit. 'slave of the *li-chi*'= the *lŭng-yè* ('fruit').

chŭī-fūng 追風 'pursuer of the wind,' or *chŭī-tién* 追電 'a pursuer of the lightning,'—a name for a fine horse.

shān-kiŭn 山君, lit. 'prince of the mountains,—the tiger.'

The 'sheep' is called *Jeú-maú* 柔毛; the 'goat,' *jèn-lâng* 髯郎; the 'swallow,' *t'iēn-nù* 天女; the 'parrot,' *yên-niaù* 言鳥; the 'tortoise,' 玄夫 *Hiuēn-fú*; the 'ant,' *hiuēn-k'ü*; the 'vine,' *Hūng-yiù* 紅友, *Hwān-pě* 歡伯, *Sāng-lâng* 桑｜ or *Lân-sāng* 蘭生. *Tsó-tsiù* 佐酒 is 'the wine for a journey.' *Chūng-tsiù* 中｜ 'half drunk.' *Chín-hiuên* 陳玄 'ink.' *Fūng-wí* 鳳味 or *lŭng-wí* 龍尾 'an inkstone.' *Li-wí* 栗｜ 'the pencil.' *Yü-pàn* 玉版 'paper.' *Shū-t'ing* 殊廷 'palace of the immortals.' *Shí-kiā* 世家 'a man of rank.' *Yü-shí* 玉食 'choice food.' *Nién-sheú* 黔首 a term for 'men.' *Yü-t'ì* 玉體 'a very fair person.' *Kaū-tsź* 高貲 'passing rich.' *Kaū-sāng* 高生 or *tāng-sāng* 登｜ 'an old man.' *Tá-tsiāng* 大匠 or *chĭ-chŏ* 執斲 'a worker in wood.' *Ts'iāng-kwei* 翔貴 'to fly after honours.' *Ts'iuên-taí* 泉臺 'a sepulchral mound,—a tomb.' *Shên-p'âng* 禪旁 'a bier.' *Wŭ-kú* 物故 'dead.' *Wâng-yáng* 亡恙 'free from disease.' *Tsiēn-lĭ k'ü* 千里駒 is 'a fine young horse.' *Shí-chūng-hú* 詩中虎 is 'a poet.' *Jin-chūng-lûng* 人中龍 is 'an illustrious man.' *Kiaí-yü-hwā* 解語花 and *hwā-kién-siū* 花見羞 and *yâng-liù-chī* 楊柳枝 mean 'a beautiful woman.' *Sź-tsź-tsó* 獅子座 'the seat of Buddha.' *Kiūng-fá* 窮髮 is 'a barren soil.' *Kwei-tīng* 貴鼎 'something very precious.' *Wŭ-tĭng-shí* 五鼎食 'the five kinds of flesh.'

APPENDIX II.

A list of Chinese family names (Pĕ-kiā sing) arranged according to the Radical characters.

(Rad. 1—44.)

1	丁 Tǐng	21	侯 Sz̄	41	包 Paū	61	唐 T'áng	81	安 Gān
2	万 Wán	22	倪 Nǐ	42	匡 Kwāng	62	喻 Yú	82	宋 Súng
3	上 Sháng	23	傅 Fú	43	卓 Chŏ	63	喬 Kiaú	83	忘 Mí
4	丘 Kiū	24	儲 Chú	44	卜 Pŭ	64	單 Chên	84	宗 Tsūng
5	乜 Mǐ	25	元 Yuên	45	卞 Piên	65	嚴 Yên	85	官 Kwān
6	于 Yǔ	26	充 Ch'ūng	46	印 Yìn	66	國 Kwŏ	86	宣 Siuēn
7	井 Tsǐng	27	党 Tăng	47	危 Weî	67	堵 Tù	87	臣 Hwán
8	人 Jìn	28	全 Tsiuên	48	厙 Shé	68	壽 Sheú	88	宫 Kūng
9	仇 Kiú	29	公 Kūng	49	厤 Lǐ	69	夏 Hiá	89	宰 Tsaì
10	令 Lîng	30	寰 Kǐ	50	叔 Chŏ	70	大 Tá	90	家 Kiā
11	仰 Yăng	31	冉 Jìn	51	古 Kŭ	71	奚 Hī	91	容 Yúng
12	仲 Chúng	32	冶 Yĕ	52	史 Sz̄	72	姚 Yaū	92	宿 Sù
13	任 Jìn	33	冷 Lăng	53	司 Sz̄	73	姜 Kiāng	93	寇 K'eú
14	伊 Í	34	凌 Lǐng	54	吉 Kǐ	74	姬 Kī	94	富 Fú
15	伍 Wù	35	刁 Tiaū	55	向 Hiáng	75	斐 Leú	95	封 Fūng
16	伏 Fú	36	别 Piĕ	56	吳 Wú	76	孔 K'ùng	96	尉 Weî
17	何 Hô	37	利 Lí	57	吕 Lù	77	孟 Mǎng	97	尚 Sháng
18	余 Yú	38	劉 Liú	58	周 Cheū	78	季 Kǐ	98	尤 Yiú
19	侯 Heú	39	勞 Laū	59	和 Hô	79	孫 Sān	99	尹 Yǐn
20	俞 Yú	40	勾 Keū	60	咸 Hiên	80	宇 Yǔ	100	居 Kū

APPENDIX II. (Rad. 44—107.)

#		#		#		#		#	
101	屈 K'ŭ	128	徒 T'ŭ	155	晁 Ch'aŭ	182	樂 Yŏ	209	滑 Hwă
102	屠 T'ŭ	129	從 Tsŭng	156	時 Shi	183	樊 Făn	210	滕 T'ăng
103	山 Shān	130	德 Tĕ	157	宴 Yén	184	權 Kiuên	211	滿 Mwăn
104	岑 Ts'în	131	惠 Hwei	158	景 King	185	欒 Lwăn	212	潘 P'ăn
105	崔 Ts'uī	132	慎 Shin	159	暴 Paŭ	186	歐 Gaŭ	213	澹 T'ăn
106	嵇 Ki	133	慕 Mŭ	160	曁 Ki	187	步 Pŭ	214	濮 Pŭ
107	巢 Ch'aŭ	134	應 Ying	161	曹 Ts'aŭ	188	武 Wŭ	215	烏 Wū
108	左 Tsŏ	135	懷 Hwaī	162	曾 Tsăng	189	歧 Ch'ĭ	216	焦 Tsiaŭ
109	巫 Wū	136	戈 Kō	163	朱 Chū	190	段 Twán	217	熊 Hiung
110	巴 Pā	137	戎 Jŭng	164	李 Lĭ	191	殷 Yin	218	燕 Yén
111	師 Sz̄	138	成 Ch'ĭng	165	杜 Tŭ	192	母 Mŭ	219	牛 Niaŭ
112	席 Sĭ	139	戚 Ts'ĭ	166	杭 Hăng	193	毛 Maŭ	220	牧 Mŭ
113	常 Ch'ăng	140	戲 Taī	167	東 Tūng	194	水 Shwuĭ	221	狄 Tĭ
114	干 Kān	141	房 Făng	168	松 Sūng	195	江 Kiāng	222	狐 Hŭ
115	平 P'ing	142	邑 Hŭ	169	林 Lin	196	池 Ch'ĭ	223	王 Wăng
116	康 K'ăng	143	扶 Fŭ	170	柏 Pĕ	197	汪 Wāng	224	班 Pān
117	庚 Yŭ	144	支 Chī	171	查 Chă	198	汲 Ki	225	璩 K'ŭ
118	廉 Liên	145	政 Ching	172	柯 Kō	199	沃 Wŭ	226	甄 Chīn
119	廖 Liaŭ	146	敖 Gaŭ	173	柳 Liŭ	200	沈 Chĭn	227	甘 Kān
120	廣 Kwăng	147	文 Wăn	174	柴 Ch'aī	201	沙 Shā	228	甫 Fŭ
121	弔 Kūng	148	方 Fāng	175	桂 Kwei	202	洪 Hŭng	229	寗 Ning
122	弘 Hŭng	149	於 Yū	176	桑 Sāng	203	浦 Pŭ	230	田 T'iên
123	張 Chăng	150	施 Shĭ	177	梔 Wăn	204	淳 Shŭn	231	申 Shin
124	強 K'iăng	151	昌 Ch'āng	178	梁 Liăng	205	溫 Wăn	232	畢 Pĭ
125	彭 P'ăng	152	明 Ming	179	梅 Mei	206	游 Yiŭ	233	白 Pĕ
126	後 Heŭ	153	易 Ĭ	180	楊 Yăng	207	湛 Chán	234	皇 Hwăng
127	徐 Sŭ	154	昝 Tsăn	181	榮 Yăng	208	湯 T'āng	235	皮 P'ĭ

(Rad. 108—163.) APPENDIX II.

#	Char	Rom	#	Char	Rom	#	Char	Rom	#	Char	Rom	#	Char	Rom
236	益	Yĭ	263	紅	Húng	290	葡	Sán	317	虞	Yû	344	越	Yuĕ
237	盛	Shíng	264	索	Sŏ	291	荊	Kīng	318	蝸	Yūng	345	趙	Chaù
238	盧	Lû	265	終	Chūng	292	莊	Chwāng	319	衛	Wei	346	路	Lú
239	相	Siāng	266	經	Kīng	293	莘	Sīn	320	衡	Hāng	347	車	Ch'ē
240	瞿	K'ú	267	繆	Miú	294	莫	Mŭ	321	袁	Yuên	348	軒	Hiēn
241	石	Shĭ	268	羅	Lô	295	華	Hwá	322	裘	K'iû	349	轅	Yuên
242	祁	K'î	269	羊	Yáng	296	萬	Wán	323	裴	P'ei	350	辛	Sīn
243	祖	Tsŭ	270	羿	I	297	葉	Yĕ	324	褚	Ch'ù	351	農	Núng
244	祝	Chŏ	271	翁	Ung	298	葛	Kŏ	325	解	Kiaì	352	通	T'ūng
245	祿	Lú	272	習	Sî	299	董	Tùng	326	計	Kì	353	逢	Fûng
246	禹	Yù	273	翟	Tí	300	蒙	Múng	327	許	Hù	354	連	Liên
247	秋	Ts'iu	274	耿	Kăng	301	蒯	Kw'ei	328	訾	Tsĕ	355	逯	Lŏ
248	秦	Ts'in	275	聞	Wăn	302	蒲	P'ú	329	詹	Chēn	356	遲	Ch'í
249	程	Ch'îng	276	聶	Niĕ	303	蒼	Ts'āng	330	談	T'án	357	邊	Piēn
250	穆	Mŭ	277	胡	Hú	304	蓋	Kaì	331	諸	Chū	358	邢	Hîng
251	空	K'ūng	278	胥	Sū	305	蓬	P'úng	332	謝	Sié	359	那	Nô
252	竇	Teú	279	能	Năng	306	蔚	Wei	333	譚	T'án	360	邰	T'ai
253	章	Chāng	280	臧	Ts'áng	307	蔡	Ts'ai	334	谷	Kŭ	361	邴	Ping
254	童	T'úng	281	臺	Tai	308	蔣	Tsiáng	335	豐	Fūng	362	邵	Shaú
255	竺	Chŭ	282	舒	Shū	309	蕭	Siaū	336	貝	Pei	363	郁	Yŏ
256	符	Fú	283	艾	Gai	310	薄	Tŏ	337	貢	Kúng	364	郗	Hī
257	管	Kwàn	284	芮	Juì	311	薊	Kì	338	費	Fei	365	郜	Kau
258	箭	Kièn	285	花	Hwā	312	薛	Sié	339	賀	Hó	366	郝	Hŏ
259	籍	Tsĭ	286	苗	Miaú	313	藍	Lán	340	賁	Pí	367	郎	Láng
260	米	Mì	287	范	Fán	314	雋	Lín	341	賈	Kià	368	鄉	Kià
261	麋	Mí	288	茅	Maú	315	夔	Kw'ei	342	賴	Lai	369	鄧	Hī
262	紀	Kì	289	茹	Jú	316	蘇	Sū	343	赫	Hĕ	370	郭	Kwŏ

APPENDIX II.   (Rad. 163—212.)

371	都 Tū	385	閔 Mĭn	399	雙 Shwāng	413	顧 Kú	427	麻 Má
372	鄂 Gŏ	386	閻 Yên	400	離 Lí, Hí	414	養 Yăng	428	黃 Hwáng
373	鄒 Tseū	387	闕 K'ŭ	401	雲 Yún	415	饒 Jaú	429	黎 Lí
374	鄔 Wú	388	關 Kwān	402	雷 Luī	416	馬 Mă	430	黑 Hĕ
375	鄧 Tăng	389	敢 Hàn	403	霍 Hŏ	417	馮 P'ing	431	黿 Tá
376	鄭 Chíng	390	阮 Yuèn	404	靳 Kín	418	駱 Lŭ	432	鼓 Kŭ
377	豐 Fūng	391	陰 Yīn	405	鞏 Kŭng	419	高 Kaū	433	齊 Ts'i
378	酈 Li	392	陳 Ch'ìn	406	鞠 Kiŏ	420	鬱 Yŏ	434	齒 Ch'ĭ
379	金 Kīn	393	陶 T'aú	407	韋 Weí	421	魏 Wei	435	騎 I
380	鈄 T'eù	394	陸 Lŭ	408	韓 Han	422	魚 Yú	436	瀧 Lúng
381	鈕 Neù	395	陽 Yâng	409	韶 Shaú	423	魯 Lù	437	龐 P'áng
382	錢 Ts'iên	396	隆 Lúng	410	項 Hiáng	424	鮑 Paú	438	龔 K'ūng
383	鍾 Chūng	397	隗 Wei	411	須 Sū	425	鳳 Fúng		
384	長 Ch'áng	398	雍 Yūng	412	顏 Yên	426	鞠 K'iŏ		

Note—64 is also called *shen*. 305 should have 'grass' above it. 314 should have 'door' with 'grass' above it. 389 should have 'a door' over it.

The following are family names of two syllables.

Ch'áng-săn (384, 79).
Chên-yú (64, 6).
Chŭ-kŏ (331, 298).
Chūng-li (383, 400).
Chúng-săn (12, 79).
Gaū-yáng (186, 395).
Hiá-heû (69, 19).
Hŏ-liên (343, 354).
Hiĕn-yuên (348, 349).
Hwáng-fú (214, 228).
Kūng-yé (29, 32).
Kūng-săn (29, 79).
Kūng-yáng (29, 269).
Líng-hú (34, 222).
Mú-yûng (133, 91).

Pú-yáng (214, 395).
Shīn-t'ú (231, 102).
Sháng-kwān (3, 85).
Shŭn-yú (204, 6).
Sz̆-k'ūng (53, 251).
Sz̆-mà (53, 416).
Sz̆-t'ú (53, 128).
Tá-chŏ (70, 50.)
T'án-t'ai (213, 281).
Tsūng-ching (84, 145).
Tūng-fāng (167, 148).
Yù-wăn (80, 147).
Wăn-jīn (275, 8).
Wăn-sz̆ (2, 21).
Wei-ch'ĭ (96, 356).

The numbers refer to the previous list.

APPENDIX III.

A list of the dynasties, the emperors, and the nién-haú.

I. *Sān-hwáng* 三 皇 'the Three emperors.'

Under this title are included the names of six persons, whose history is pure myth, but whose names ought to be known to the Chinese student.

1. *Pw'ǎn-kú* 盤古 (v. Part II. p. 104). 2. *T'iĕn-hwáng* 天 | *. 3. *Tí-hwáng* 地 | . 4. *Jin-hwáng* 人 | . 5. *Yiú-ch'aú* 有巢. 6. *Siú-jin* 燧人.

These rulers are said to have reigned myriads of years, and to have invented all the ordinary arts of life.

II. *Wŭ-tí* 五帝 'the Five emperors.' [B. C. 2852—2204.]

1. *Fŭ-hī* 伏羲 (115). 2. *Shin-núng* 神農 (140). 3. *Hwáng-tí* 黄帝 (100). 4. *Shaú-hau* 少昊 (84). 5. *Chuen-hiĕ* 顓頊 (78). 6. *Tí-kú* 帝嚳 or 佶 (78). 7. *T'áng-tí Yau* 唐 | 堯 (102). 8. *Yú-tí Shǎn* 虞 | 舜 (50).

Of this early period tradition alone renders an account. Eight sovereigns ruled, and instituted many useful methods of providing for the wants and comforts of their subjects. Ploughing, fishing, writing, keeping records of events, and the best modes of governing mankind formed the subjects of their invention. During these times *K'aī-fūng fú*, on the *Hwáng-hó* in *Hó-nán*, was the metropolis. The first cycle began in the 61st year of *Hwáng-tí*.

III. *Hiá-chaú* 夏朝 'the Hia dynasty.' [B. C. 2205—1767.]

1. *Tá Yù* 大禹 (2205—8). 2. *Tí K'ĭ* | 啟 (2197—9). 3. *T'ai*

---

* The characters *hwáng*[a], *wáng*[b], *tí*[c], *t'aí*[d], *tsŭ*[e], *tsŭng*[f], and some others will not be repeated frequently in this list. The numbers in brackets give the date of the commencement and the length of each reign.

[a] 皇 [b] 王 [c] 帝 [d] 太 [e] 祖 [f] 宗

Kǎng 太康 (2188. 29). 4. Chūng Kǎng 仲 | (2159. 13). 5. Tī siāng | 相 (2146. 28). 6. Shaù Kǎng 少 | (2118. 61). 7. Tī Chu | 杼 (2057. 17). 8. Tī Hwaí | 槐 (2040. 26). 9. Tī Máng | 芒 (2014. 18). 10. Tī Sĕ | 池 (1996. 16). 11. Tī Pŭ-kiáng 不降 (1980. 59). 12. Tī Kiūng | 扃 (1921. 21). 13. Tī Kin | 廑 (1900. 21). 14. Tī K'ùng-kiǎ | 孔甲 (1879. 31). 15. Tī Kaū | 皋 (1848. 11). 16. Tī Fā | 發 (1837. 19). 17. Kī Kweí 桀癸 (1818. 52). (Cf. Part II. p. 22, note for a notice of Yŭ.)

IV. Shāng-chaú 商朝 'the Shang dynasty.' [B. C. 1766—1122.]

1. Ch'ing-t'āng 成湯 (1766. 13). 2. T'aí-kiǎ 太甲 (1753. 33). 3. Wǔ-tīng 沃丁 (1720. 29). 4. T'aí-kǎng | 庚 (1691. 25). 5. Siaù-kiǎ 小 | (1666. 17). 6. Yūng-kì 雍己 (1649. 12). 7. T'aí-meù | 戊 (1637. 75). 8. Chūng-tīng 仲丁 (1562. 13). 9. Waí-jīn 外壬 (1549. 15). 10. Hô-tân-kiǎ 河亶 | (1534. 9). 11. Tsŭ-yĭ 祖乙 (1525. 19). 12. Tsŭ-sīn | 辛 (1506. 16). 13. Wŭ-kiǎ 沃甲 (1490. 25). 14. Tsŭ-tīng | 丁 (1465. 14). 15. Nán-kǎng 南 | (1433. 25). 16. Yáng-kiǎ 陽 | (1408. 7). 17. Pwǎn-kǎng 盤 | (1401. 28). 18. Siaù-sīn 小 | (1373). 19. Siaù-yĭ | 乙 (1352. 28). 20. Wŭ-tīng 武丁 (1324. 59). 21. Tsŭ-kǎng | 庚 (1265. 7). 22. Tsŭ-kiǎ | 甲 (1258. 33). 23. Lĭn-sīn 廩 | (1225. 6). 24. Kǎng-tīng | 丁 (1219. 21). 25. Wŭ-yĭ 武 | (1198. 4). 26. T'aí-tīng 太 丁 (1194. 3). 27. Tī-yĭ | 帝 | (1191. 37). 28. Cheù-sīn 紂 | (1154. 32).

V. Cheū-chaú 周朝 'the Cheu dynasty.' [B. C. 1122—249.]

1. Wŭ-wâng 武王 (1122. 7). 2. Ch'ing-wâng 成 | (1115. 37). 3. Kǎng-wâng 康 | (1078. 26). 4. Chaú-wâng 昭 | (1052. 51). 5. Mŭ-wâng 穆 | (1001. 55). 6. Kúng-wâng 共 | (946. 12). 7. I-wâng 懿 | (934. 7). 8. Hiaú-wâng 孝 | (909. 15). 9. Í-wâng 夷 | (894. 16). 10. Lĭ-wâng 厲 | (878. 51). 11. Siuĕn-wâng 宣 |

APPENDIX III.

(827. 46). 12. *Yiû-wâng* 幽 | (781. 11). 13. *P'ing-wâng* 平 | (770. 51). 14. *Hwân-wâng* 桓 | (719. 23). 15. *Chwāng-wâng* 莊 | (696. 15). 16. *Lí-wâng* 釐 | (681. 5). 17. *Hwŭi-wâng* 惠 | (676. 25). 18. *Sīang-wâng* 襄 | (651. 33). 19. *Kīng-wâng* 頃 | (618. 6). 20. *Kwāng-wâng* 匡 | (612. 6). 21. *Tíng-wâng* 定 | (606. 21). 22. *Kiĕn-wâng* 簡 | (585. 14). 23. *Líng-wâng* 靈 | (571. 27). 24. *Kīng-wâng* 景 | (544. 25). 25. *Kíng-wâng* 敬 | (519. 44). 26. *Yuên-wâng* 元 | (475. 7). 27. *Chīng-tíng-wâng* 貞定 | (468. 28). 28. *Kaŭ-wâng* 考 | (440. 15). 29. *Weî-li-wâng* 威烈 | (425. 24). 30. *Gān-wâng* 安 | (401. 26). 31. *Lí-wâng* 烈 | (375. 7). 32. *Hiĕn-wâng* 顯 | (368. 48). 33. *Shĭn-tsīng-wâng* 慎靚 | (320. 6). 34. *Nân-wâng* 赧 | (314. 59). 35. *Tūng-cheŭ-kiūn* 東周君 (255. 6).

During this period several great men flourished, whose names and works have come down to the present time. Such was *Wăn-wâng*, 'the prince of letters,' who at the end of the *Shang* dynasty had been imprisoned for his upright conduct. In confinement he wrote the *Yĭ-kīng* or 'Book of changes,' and was afterwards liberated through the intercession of a lady whom his son (afterwards *Wù-wâng*, the first monarch of the *Cheu* dynasty) had sent to the emperor. *Wù-wâng* and his brother *Cheŭ-kūng* were both eminent men of letters. *Laù-tsz̀*, the founder of the Tauist sect, *K'ŭng-tsz* (Confucius) (B. C. 519), and *Mặng-tsz̀* (Mencius) were all born during the *Cheu* dynasty. The doctrines taught by these worthies of antiquity were called *wâng-taú*, 'the royal doctrines,' a term which is equivalent to the term "philosophy" in Europe. The country was divided into many petty states in these times. At one time there were 125, at another they were reduced to 41. The terms *Chŏn kwŏ* 戰國 and *Lĭ-kwŏ* 列國 were the designations of these 'contending' or 'confederate' states.

VI. *Tsin-chaŭ* 秦朝 'the Tsin dynasty.' [B. C. 249—246.]

1. *Chwāng-siāng wâng* 莊襄王 (249. 3).

VII. *Heŭ T'sin chaŭ* 後 | | 'the Latter Tsin dynasty.' [B. C. 246—202.]

1. *Chĭ Hwâng-tí* 始 | | (246. 37). 2. *Ar-shĭ Hwâng-tí* (209. 7).

Ch'í Hwáng-tí was the most celebrated ruler China ever had. He built the great wall, and destroyed all existing records, as far as he could do so, and put many of the learned to death, because he feared their influence to incite the people to rebellion. He was undoubtedly a great monarch, his power extended throughout China, and he called himself the 'First emperor.'

VIII. *Hán-chaú* 漢朝 'the Han dynasty.' [B. C. 202—A. D. 25.]

1. *Kaŭ-tsŭ* 高 | (202. 8). 2. *Hwŭi-tí* 惠 | (194. 7). 3. *Lŭ-heŭ* 呂后 (187. 8). 4. *Wǎn-tí* 文 | (179. 23). 5. *Kǐng-tí* 景 | (156. 16). 6. *Wŭ-tí* 武 | (140. 54). 7. *Chaŭ-tí* 昭 | (B. C. 86. 13). 8. *Siuěn-tí* 宣 | (B. C. 73. 25). 9. *Yuěn-tí* 元 | (B. C. 48. 16). 10. *Ch'ing-tí* 成 | (B. C. 32. 26). 11. *Gaï-tí* 哀 | (B. C. 6. 6). 12. *P'ing-tí* 平 | (A. D. 1. 5). 13. *Jŭ-tsź yíng* 孺子嬰 (A. D. 6. 17). 14. *Hwaí-yáng-wáng* 淮陽 | (A. D. 23. 2).

IX. *Tŭng Hán* 東漢 'the Eastern Han dynasty.' [A. D. 25—221.]

1. *Kwāng-wŭ* 光武 (25. 33). 2. *Míng-tí* 明 | (58. 18). 3. *Chǎng-tí* 章 | (76. 13). 4. *Hô-tí* 和 | (89. 17). 5. *Shang-tí* 殤 | (106. 1). 6. *Gán-tí* 安 | (107. 19). 7. *Shǎn-tí* 順 | (126. 19). 8. *Chŭng-tí* 沖 | (145. 1). 9. *Chě-tí* 質 | (146. 1). 10. *Hwǎn-tí* 桓 | (147. 21). 11. *Líng-tí* 靈 | (168. 22). 12. *Hiěn-tí* 獻 | (190. 31).

At the end of this dynasty the empire was divided into 'Three kingdoms,' *Shŭ, Wei,* and *Wŭ.*

X. *Heŭ Hán* 後漢 'the Latter Han.' [A. D. 221—265.]

1. *Chaŭ-lĭ tí* 昭烈 | (221. 2). 2. *Heŭ-tí* 後 | (223. 42).

XI. *Tsin-chaŭ* 晉朝 'the Tsin dynasty.' [A. D. 265—317.]

1. *Wŭ-tí* 武 | (265. 26). 2. *Hwŭi-tí* 惠 | (290. 17). 3. *Hwaí-tí* 懷 | (307. 6). 4. *Mín-tí* 愍 | (313. 4).

XII. *Tŭng Tsin* 東晉 'the Eastern Tsin.' [A. D. 317—420.]

1. *Yuěn-tí* 元 | (317. 6). 2. *Míng-tí* 明 | (323. 3). 3. *Ch'ing-tí* 成 | (326. 17). 4. *Kǎng-tí* 康 | (343. 2). 5. *Mŭ-tí* 穆 | (345. 17).

6. *Gaī-tī* 哀帝 (362. 4). 7. *Tī-yĭ* 帝奕 (366. 6). 8. *Kièn-wặn* 簡文 (371. 2). 9. *Hiaú-wŭ* 孝武 (373. 24). 10. *Gān-tī* 安 | (397. 22). 11. *Kùng-tī* 恭 | (419. 1).

The literary degree of *Siŭ-ts'aĭ* was introduced A. D. 286.

XIII. *Pĕ Sŭng* 北宋 'the Northern Sung.' [A. D. 420—479.]

1. *Kaū-tsŭ* 高 | (420. 3). 2. *Shaŭ-tī* 少 | (423. 1). 3. *Wặn-tī* 文 | (424. 30). 4. *Wŭ-tī* 武 | (454. 10). 5. *Fĭ-tī* 廢 | (464. 1). 6. *Mìng-tī* 明 | (465. 8). 7. *Tsāng-wŭ-wáng* 蒼武王 (473. 4). 8. *Shặn-tī* 順 | (477. 2).

XIV. *Ts'ĭ-chaŭ* 齊朝 'the Tsi dynasty.' [A. D. 479—502.]

1. *Kaū-tī* 高 | (479. 4). 2. *Wŭ-tī* 武 | (483. 11). 3. *Mìng-tī* 明 | (494. 5). 4. *Tūng-hwạ̄n-heŭ* 東昏侯 (499. 2). 5. *Hô-tī* 和 | (501. 1).

XV. *Liáng-chaŭ* 梁朝 'the Liang dynasty.' [A. D. 502—557.]

1. *Wù-tī* 武 | (502. 48). 2. *Kièn-wặn* 簡文 (550. 2). 3. *Yuên-tī* 元 | (552. 3). 4. *Kìng-tī* 敬 | (555. 2).

About this time the people began to use chairs for seats. *Wù-tī* became a Buddhist monk, and observed the rules of the order.

XVI. *Chín-chaŭ* 陳朝 'the Chin dynasty.' [A. D. 557—589.]

1. *Kaū-tsŭ* 高 | (557. 3). 2. *Wặn-tī* 文 | (560. 7). 3. *Fĭ-tī* 廢 | (567. 2). 4. *Siuĕn-tī* 宣 | (569. 14). 5. *Hoú chù* 後主 (583. 6).

XVII. *Siŭ-chaŭ* 隋朝 'the Süy dynasty.' [A. D. 589—620.]

1. *Kaū-tsŭ* 高 | (589. 16). 2. *Yáng-tī* 煬 | (605. 13). 3. *Kùng-tī-yiŭ* 恭侑 (618. 1). 4. *Kùng-tī-t'ùng* | 侗 (619. 1).

XVIII. *T'áng-chaŭ* 唐朝 'the T'ang dynasty.' [A. D. 620—907].

1. *Kaū-tsŭ* 高 | (620. 7). 2. *T'aí-tsŭng* 太 | (627. 23). 3. *Kaū-*

tsŭng 高 | (650. 34). 4. Chŭng-tsŭng 中 | (684. 26). 5. Jŭi-tsŭng 睿 | (710. 3). 6. Hiuên-tsŭng 玄 | (713. 43). 7. Sŭ-tsŭng 肅 | (756. 7). 8. Taì-tsŭng 代 | (763. 8). 9. Tĕ-tsŭng 德 | (780. 25). 10. Shǎn-tsŭng 順 | (805. 1). 11. Hiēn-tsŭng 憲 | (806. 15). 12. Mŭ-tsŭng 穆 | (821. 4). 13. King-tsŭng 敬 | (825. 2). 14. Wǎn-tsŭng 文 | (827. 14). 15. Wŭ-tsŭng 武 | (841. 6). 16. Siuĕn-tsŭng 宣 | (847. 13). 17. I-tsŭng 懿 | (860. 14). 18. Hī-tsŭng 僖 | (874. 15). 19. Chaù-tsŭng 昭 | (889. 15). 20. Chaù-siuĕn-ti 昭宣 | (904. 3).

XIX. *Heù Liâng* 後梁 'the Latter Liang dynasty.' [A.D. 907—923.]

1. *T'aì-tsù* 太 | (907. 6). 2. *Liâng-chŭ-tien* 梁主瑱 (913. 10).

XX. *Heù T'âng* 後唐 'the Latter T'âng dynasty.' [A.D. 923—936.]

1. *Chwāng-tsŭng* 莊 | (923. 3). 2. *Mîng-tsŭng* 明 | (926. 8). 3. *Mǐn-tì* 閔 | (934). 4. *Fì-tì* 廢 | (934. 2).

XXI. *Heù Tsìn* 後晉 'the Latter Tsin dynasty.' [A.D. 936—947.]

1. *Kaù-tsù* 高 | (936. 8). 2. *Ch'ŭ-tì* 出 | (944. 3).

XXII. *Heù Hán* 後漢 'the Latter Han dynasty.' [A.D. 947—951.]

1. *Kaù-tsù* 高 | (947. 1). 2. *Yǐn-tì* 隱 | (948. 3).

XXIII. *Heù Cheū* 後周 'the Latter Cheu dynasty.' [A.D. 951—960.]

1. *T'aì-tsù* 太 | (951. 3). 2. *Shì-tsŭng* 世 | (954. 6). 3. *Kŭng-tì* 恭 | (960).

XXIV. *Sŭng-chaù* 宋朝 'the Sung dynasty.' [A.D. 960—1127.]

1. *T'aì-tsù* 太 | (960. 16). 2. *T'aì-tsŭng* 太 | (976. 22). 3. *Chīn-tsŭng* 真 | (998. 25). 4. *Jîn-tsŭng* 仁 | (1023. 41). 5. *Yīng-tsŭng* 英 | (1064. 4). 6. *Shîn-tsŭng* 神 | (1068. 18). 7. *Chĕ-tsŭng* 哲 | (1086. 15). 8. *Hwuī-tsŭng* 徽 | (1101. 25). 9. *Kīn-tsŭng* 欽 | (1126. 1).

APPENDIX III.

XXV. *Nân Sûng* 南宋 'the Southern Sung.' [A. D. 1127—1280.]

1. *Kaū-tsūng* 高 | (1127. 36). 2. *Hiaū-tsūng* 孝 | (1163. 27). 3. *Kwāng-tsūng* 光 | (1190. 5). 4. *Nīng-tsūng* | (1195. 30). 5. *Lī-tsūng* 理 | (1225. 40). 6. *Tú-tsūng* 度 | (1265. 10). 7. *Kùng-tsūng* 恭 | (1275. 1). 8. *Twān-tsūng* 端 | (1276. 2). 9. *Tī-pīng-tī* 帝昺 (1278. 2).

XXVI. *Yuên-chaū* 元朝 'the Yuên dynasty.' [A. D. 1280—1368.]

1. *Shí-tsù* 世 | (1280. 15). 2. *Ch'ing-tsūng* 成 | (1295. 13). 3. *Wù-tsūng* 武 | (1308. 4). 4. *Jín-tsūng* 仁 | (1312. 9). 5. *Yīng-tsūng* 英 | (1321. 3). 6. *T'ai-ting-ti* 泰定 | (1324. 5). 7. *Mīng-tsūng* 明 | (1329. 1). 8. *Wĕn-tsūng* 文 | (1330. 3). 9. *Shùn-tsūng* 順 | (1333. 35).

XXVII. *Mîng-chaū* 明朝 'the Mîng dynasty.' [A. D. 1368—1644.]

1. *T'ai-tsù* 太 | (1368. 30). 2. *Kién-wĕn-ti* 建文 | (1398. 5). 3. *T'ai-tsūng* 太 | (1403. 22). 4. *Jín-tsūng* 仁 | (1425. 1). 5. *Siuēn-tsūng* 宣 | (1426. 10). 6. *Yīng-tsūng* 英 | (1436. 21). 7. *Kīng-ti* 景 | (1457. 8). 8. *Hién-tsūng* 憲 | (1465. 23). 9. *Hiaū-tsūng* 孝 | (1488. 18). 10. *Wù-tsūng* 武 | (1506. 16). 11. *Shi-tsūng* 世 | (1522. 45). 12. *Mù-tsūng* 穆 | (1567. 6). 13. *Shīn-tsūng* 神 | (1573. 47). 14. *Kwāng-tsūng* 光 | (1620. 1). 15. *Hī-tsūng* 熹 | (1621. 7). 16. *Hwai-tsūng* 懷 | (1628. 16).

XXVIII. *Tá-ts'īng-chaū* 大清朝 'the Tá-ts'īng dynasty.' [A. D. 1644—1862.]

1. *Shí-tsù-chāng* 世 | 章 (1644. 18). 2. *Shíng-tsù-jin* 聖 | 仁 (1662. 61). 3. *Shí-tsūng-hién* | | 憲 (1723. 13). 4. *Kaū-tsūng-shŭn* 高 | 純 (1736. 60). 5. *Jín-tsūng-juī* 仁 | 睿 (1796. 25). 6. *Taū-kwāng* 道光 (1821. 30). 7. *Hiên-fūng* 咸豐 (1851. 9). 8. *Tūng-chì* 通治 (1860).

APPENDIX IV.

THE NIEN-HAU.

(1.) *List of the characters occurring in the niĕn-haú, arranged alphabetically.*

章 chāng 'luminous.'	淳 chặn 'pleasant.'	咸 hiên 'complete.'
昌 chāng 'splendid.'	中 chŭng 'middle' or 'second.'	顯 hiên 'illustrious.'
常 ch'áng 'constant.'	重 chŭng 'renewed.'	興 hĭng 'flourishing.'
長 ch'áng 'extensive.'	符 fú 'charm.'	訓 hiŭn 'instruction.'
昭 chaŭ 'bright.'	輔 fŭ 'assistance.'	禾 hô 'peace.'
韜 chè 'large, wide.'	福 fŭ 'happiness.'	和 hô 'harmony.'
始 chĭ 'beginning.'	豐 fūng 'affluent.'	河 hò 'the river.'
至 chí 'extreme.'	鳳 fūng 'omen of good.'	鴻 hŭng 'vast.'
治 chí 'ruling.'	封 fūng 'affluent.'	弘 hŭng 'vast.'
致 chí 'the utmost.'	安 gān 'peace.'	洪 hŭng 'vast.'
赤 chì 'carnation.'	漢 hán 'milky-way.'	化 hwá 'reforming.'
眞 chīn 'true.'	衡 hạng 'adjusting.'	黃 hwáng 'yellow.'
征 chīng 'conquering.'	亨 hạng 'success.'	皇 hwáng 'emperor.'
貞 chīng 'virtuous.'	後 heú 'second.'	徽 hwŭĭ 'excellent.'
承 chíng 'aiding.'	狩 heú 'hunting.'	會 hwŭĭ 'united.'
成 chíng 'perfect.'	喜 hĭ 'pervading.'	義 í 'justice.'
正 chíng 'upright.'	僖 hĭ 'rejoicing.'	儀 í 'correct.'
政 chíng 'regulating.'	熙 hĭ 'prosperity.'	仁 jin 'humane.'
禎 chíng 'pure.'	禧 hĭ 'bliss.'	人 jin 'man.'
垂 chŭĭ 'extending.'	孝 hiaú 'pious.'	開 k'aī 'opening.'

甘 kān 'sweet.'	露 lú 'manifest.'	瑞 shwuĭ 'good omen.'
康 k'āng 'firm.'	祿 lŭ 'happiness.'	璽 sĭ 'royal seal.'
更 kāng 'more.'	龍 lúng 'dragon.'	象 siáng 'elephant.'
紀 kĭ 'arranging.'	隆 lúng 'glorious.'	先 siēn 'first.'
啟 kĭ 'instructing.'	民 mín 'people.'	宣 siuēn 'extending.'
極 kĭ 'extreme.'	明 míng 'bright.'	朔 sŏ 'restoration.'
嘉 kiā 'increasing.'	業 niĕ 'inheritance.'	綏 suĭ 'tranquil.'
麟 kiā 'stag.'	年 niēn 'year.'	歲 suĭ 'year.'
乾 kién 'firm.'	寧 níng 'peace.'	嗣 sz̀ 'succession.'
監 kién 'controlling.'	本 pǎn 'origin.'	大 tá 'great.'
建 kién 'establishing.'	寶 paù 'precious.'	太 t'aí 'extreme.'
景 kĭng 'illumined.'	保 paù 'protecting.'	泰 t'aí 'vast.'
竟 kíng 'investigating.'	平 p'íng 'peace.'	登 tāng 'ascending.'
慶 k'ìng 'good.'	普 p'ù 'general.'	道 taú 'reason.'
君 kiūn 'princes.'	順 shǎn 'obedient.'	德 tĕ 'virtue.'
居 kū 'residing.'	紹 shaù 'continuing.'	地 tĭ 'earth.'
恭 kùng 'honouring.'	上 sháng 'superior.'	帝 tí 'ruler.'
拱 kùng 'uniting.'	攝 shĕ 'directing.'	調 t'iaú 'regulating.'
觀 kwān 'to see.'	收 sheú 'taking.'	天 t'iēn 'heaven.'
光 kwāng 'brightness.'	授 sheú 'receiving.'	鼎 tĭng 'security.'
廣 kwàng 'vast.'	壽 sheú 'aged.'	定 tìng 'fixed.'
龜 kweī 'tortoise.'	視 shĭ 'behold.'	冊 tsĕ 'plan.'
國 kwŏ 'kingdom.'	神 shín 'divine.'	載 tsaí 'containing.'
禮 lĭ 'ceremony.'	昇 shīng 'ascending.'	贊 tsán 'praising.'
曆 lĭ 'heavenly signs.'	升 shīng 'ascending.'	宅 tsĕ 'dwelling.'
麟 lín 'stag.'	聖 shìng 'sacred.'	詳 tsiáng 'felicitous.'
樂 lŏ 'joy.'	盛 shìng 'abundant.'	節 tsiĕ 'partition.'

APPENDIX IV.

爵 *tsiŏ* 'noble.'	賜 *ts'z̤* 'bestowing.'	耀 *yaù* 'glory.'
青 *tsīng* 'azure.'	通 *t'ŭng* 'thorough.'	延 *yên* 'spread.'
清 *tsīng* 'pure.'	同 *t'ŭng* 'same.'	炎 *yên* 'luminous.'
靖 *tsìng* 'quiet.'	統 *t'ŭng* 'complete.'	應 *yīng* 'replying.'
初 *tsŭ* 'beginning.'	端 *twān* 'upright.'	祐 *yiù* 'assistance.'
祚 *tsú* 'blessings.'	烏 *ū* 'a crow.'	豫 *yü* 'prepared.'
總 *tsŭng* 'general.'	萬 *wán* 'myriad.'	雲 *yŭn* 'clouds.'
宗 *tsŭng* 'ancestor.'	文 *wǫn* 'literary.'	運 *yŭn* 'revolving.'
崇 *tsŭng* 'revered.'	五 *wŭ* 'five.'	元 *yuên* 'beginning.'
總 *tsùng* 'general.'	武 *wŭ* 'military.'	雍 *yŭng* 'harmony.'
階 *tū* 'all.'	陽 *yáng* 'vast.'	永 *yǔng* 'eternal.'

Note.—All these characters are significant when they are present in the designation of a year or a reign, and the meanings here attached to them are intended to guide the student in rendering such designations into English. In some cases the translation of the character will not suit the English expression, and some words are used figuratively, or they refer to a well-known story. The expression generally runs in the usual grandiloquent phraseology of the Chinese, and intimates that "Peace and prosperity have arisen;" that "Blessings are going to be universally diffused;" or that "All things are beginning again to prosper."

The following list of the *niên-haú*, in which they are arranged according to the English alphabet, will be of immense service to the student of Chinese history. The absence of the native characters will be of little consequence, as the names of the emperors, the dynasties, and the years of the cycle are given, and one of these is generally mentioned by native authors who use the *niên-haú*.

APPENDIX IV.   215

(2.) *List of the niên-haú arranged alphabetically.*

Niên-haú.	Duration.	Emperor.	Dynasty.	Year of the cycle.	B.C.	A.D.
Chāng-hô	2	Chāng-tí	Hán	tīng-haï		87
Chāng-wŭ	2	Chaŭ-lĭ-tí	Shŭ-Hán	kāng-tsź		221
Ch'áng-sheú	2	T'iĕn-heù	T'áng	jĭn-shĭn		692
Ch'áng-gān	4	T'iĕn-heù	T'áng	sĭn-ch'eù		701
Ch'áng-kíng	4	Mŭ-tsūng	T'áng	sĭn-ch'eù		821
Ch'áng-hĭng	4	Míng-tsūng	Heú-T'áng	kāng-yĭn		930
Chê-tŭ	6	Yīng-tsūng	Hiá	tŭng-yiù		1057
Chì-yuên	6	Chaū-tí	Hán	yĭ-wí	86	
Chì-kiên-kwŏ	5	Wáng-màng	Hán	kĭ-sź	9	
Chì-kwāng	4	T'ai-wŭ-tí	Wei	kiă-tsź		424
Chí-tĕ	4	Ch'áng-chíng-kūng	Chin	kweĭ-maù		583
Chí-tĕ	2	Sŭ-tsūng	T'áng	pĭng-shĭn		756
Chí-taú	3	Chīng-tsūng	Súng	yĭ-wí		995
Chí-hô	2	Jĭn-tsūng	Súng	kiă-wŭ		1054
Chí-p'ĭng	4	Yīng-tsūng	Súng	kiă-shĭn		1064
Chí-níng	1	Chŭ-yùng-tsĭ	Kīn	kweĭ-yiù		1213
Chí-yuên	31	Shí-tsù	Yuên	kiă-tsź		1264
Chí-yuên	6	Shán-tí	Yuên	yĭ-kweī		1335
Chí-tá	4	Wŭ-tsūng	Yuên	wŭ-shĭn		1308
Chí-chí	3	Yīng-tsūng	Yuên	sĭn-yiù		1321
Chí-hô	1	T'ai-tíng-tí	Yuên	wŭ-shĭn		1328
Chí-shún	3	Wăn-tsūng	Yuên	kāng-wŭ		1330
Chí-chíng	28	Shàn-tí	Yuên	sĭn-sź		1341
Chí-ū	13	Tá-tí	Wŭ	wŭ-wŭ		238
Chĭn-yuên	3	Tí-liáng	Kīn	kweĭ-yiù		1153
Chīng-hô	4	Wŭ-tí	Hán	kĭ-ch'eù	92	
Chīng-kwān	23	T'ai-tsūng	T'áng	tīng-haī		627
Chīng-yuên	20	Tĕ-tsūng	T'áng	yĭ-ch'eù		785
Chīng-yiŭ	4	Siuên-tsūng	Kīn	kweĭ-yiù		1213
Chīng-míng	6	Chŭ-t'iĕn	Heú-Liáng	yĭ-haï		915
Chīng-kwān	13	Tsūng-tsūng	Hiá	jĭn-wŭ		1102
Chīng-shīng	3	Yuên-tí	Liáng	jĭn-shĭn		552
Chīng-míng	1	Hiaŭ-wăn-tí	Weí	pĭng-shĭn		176
Chīng-kwāng	1	Yiŭ-chŭ-liáng	Pĕ-Tsí	tīng-yiù		577
Chīng-gān	5	Chāng-tsūng	Kīn	pĭng-shĭn		1196
Chīng-hwá	23	Hiên-tsūng	Míng	yĭ-pĭng		1465
Chīng-chí	9	Chŭ-fāng	Weí	kāng-shĭn		240
Chīng-yuên	4	Chŭ-maŭ	Weí	kiă-sŭ		254
Chīng-míng	2	Ch'áng-chíng-kūng	Chin	tīng-wŭ		587
Chīng-p'ĭng	1	T'ai-wŭ-tí	Weí	sĭn-maù		451
Chīng-chí	4	Siuên-wŭ-tí	Weí	kiă-shĭn		504
Chīng-kwāng	5	Hiaŭ-míng-tí	Weí	kāng-tsź		520
Chīng-t'ùng	14	Yīng-tsūng	Míng	pĭng-shĭn		1436
Chīng-hô	7	Hwuï-tsūng	Súng	sĭn-maù		1111
Chīng-tá	8	Gaï-tsūng	Kīn	kiă-shĭn		1224

APPENDIX IV.

Niên-haú.	Duration.	Emperor.	Dynasty.	Year of the cycle.	B.C.	A.D.
Chíng-tĕ	8	Tsŭng-tsŭng	Hiá	tĭng-wî		1127
Chíng-tĕ	16	Wŭ-tsŭng	Míng	pìng-yín		1506
Chíng-lŭng	6	T'í-liáng	Kīn	yiù-tsż		1156
Chŭĭ-kùng	4	T'iēn-heù	T'ăng	yĭ-yiù		685
Chŭng-yuên	6	Kīng-tí	Hán	jĭn-shĭn	149	
Chŭng-yuên	2	Hwāng-wŭ-tí	Hán	pìng-shĭn		56
Chŭng-p'ìng	6	Lĭng-tí	Hán	kiă-tsż		184
Chŭng-hĭng	1	Hồ-tí	Tsĭ	sĭn-sź		501
Chŭng-tá-t'ŭng	6	Wŭ-tí	Liáng	kĭ-yiù		529
Chŭng-tá-t'ŭng	1	Wŭ-tí	Liáng	pìng-yín		546
Chŭng-hĭng	1	Chŭ-lăng	Wei	sĭn-haī		531
Chŭng-hồ	4	Hĭ-tsŭng	T'ăng	sĭn-ch'eù		881
Chŭng-t'ŭng	4	Shĭ-tsù	Yuên	kāng-shĭn		1260
Chŭng-hồ	1	Hwŭĭ-tsŭng	Sĭng	wŭ-sŭ		1118
Chăng-hī	24	Hīng-tsŭng	Liaŭ	jĭn-shĭn		1032
Fŭ-shíng-chíng-taú	4	Yĭng-tsŭng	Hiá	kweĭ-sź		1053
Fúng-hwáng	3	Chŭ-kaù	Wŭ	jĭn-shĭn		272
Hán-gān	2	Shăn-tí	Hán	jĭ-wù		142
Heú-yuên	7	Wặn-tí	Hán	wŭ-yín	163	
Heú-yuên	3	Kíng-tí	Hán	wŭ-sŭ	143	
Heú-yuên	2	Wŭ-tí	Hán	kweĭ-sź	88	
Hĭ-p'ĭng	6	Lĭng-tí	Hán	jĭn-tsż		172
Hī-p'ĭng	2	Hiaú-mĭng-tí	Wei	pìng-shĭn		516
Hī-nĭng	10	Shĭn-tsŭng	Súng	wŭ-shĭn		1068
Hiaú-kiĕn	3	Hiaú-wŭ-tí	Pĕ-Súng	kiă-wù		454
Hiaú-chăng	4	Hiaú-mĭng-tí	Wei	yĭ-sź		525
Hiên-fŭng	10	Tá-ts'īng		kāng-sŭ		1850
Hiên-hī	2	Yuên-tí	Wei	kiă-shĭn		264
Hiên-nĭng	5	Hwŭĭ-tí	Tsín	yĭ-wî		275
Hiên-hồ	9	Chíng-tí	Tsín	pìng-sŭ		326
Hiên-k'ăng	8	Chíng-tí	Tsín	yĭ-wî		335
Hiên-gān	2	Hiĕn-wặn-tí	Tsín	sĭn-wî		371
Hiên-hăng	4	Kaū-tsŭng	T'ăng	kāng-wù		670
Hiên-t'ŭng	14	Yí-tsŭng	T'ăng	kāng-shĭn		860
Hiên-p'ĭng	6	Chīng-tsŭng	Súng	wŭ-sŭ		998
Hiên-shặn	10	Tŭ-tsŭng	Súng	yĭ-ch'eù		1265
Hiên-yŭng	10	Taú-tsŭng	Liaŭ	yĭ-sź		1065
Hiên-tsĭng	6	Jĭn-tsŭng	Lĭ-Liaŭ	pĭng-shĭn		1136
Hiĕn-k'ĭng	5	Kaū-tsĭng	T'ăng	pĭng-shĭn		656
Hiĕn-tĕ	6	Shĭ-tsŭng	Heú-cheū	kiă-yĭn		954
Hīng-p'ĭng	2	Hiĕn-tí	Hán	kiă-sŭ		194
Hīng-nĭng	3	Gaī-tí	Tsín	kweĭ-haī		363
Hīng-gān	2	Wặn-chíng-tí	Wei	jĭn-shĭn		452
Hīng-kwăng	1	Wặn-chíng-tí	Wei	kiă-wù		454
Hīng-hồ	4	Hiaú-tsĭng-tí	Tŭng-weī	kĭ-wî		539
Hīng-yuên	1	Tĕ-tsŭng	T'ăng	kiă-tsż		784
Hīng-tĭng	5	Siuĕn-tsŭng	Kīn	tīng-ch'eù		1217
Hồ-tsĭng	3	Wŭ-chíng-tí	Pĕ-Tsĭ	jĭn-wù		562
Hồ-p'ĭng	6	Wặn-chíng-tí	Wei	kāng-tsż		460
Hồ-p'ĭng	4	Chíng-tí	Hán	kweĭ-sź	28	
Hồ-p'ĭng	1	Hwặn-tí	Hán	kāng-yín		150

APPENDIX IV.

Niên-haú.	Duration.	Emperor.	Dynasty.	Year of the cycle.	B.C.	A.D.
Húng-kiā	4	Chíng-tí	Hán	sīn-ch'eù	20	
Húng-taú	1	Kaū-tsūng	T'áng	kweî-wí		683
Húng-wù	31	T'aí-tsù	Míng	wù-shīn		1368
Húng-hī	1	Jîn-tsūng	Míng	yî-sź		1425
Húng-chí	18	Hiaū-tsūng	Míng	wù-shīn		1488
Húng-kwāng	1½	Fú-wáng	Míng	kiă-shīn		1644
Hwâng-lúng	1	Siuēn-tí	Hán	jîn-shīn	49	
Hwâng-ts'ū	7	Wǎn-tí	Wei	kǎng-tsź		220
Hwâng-wù	7	Tá-tí	Wú	jîn-yín		222
Hwâng-lúng	3	Tá-tí	Wú	kî-yiù		229
Hwâng-chī	2	Taú-wù-tí	Wei	pìng-shīn		396
Hwâng-hīng	4	Hién-wǎn-tí	Wei	tīng-wí		467
Hwâng-kién	2	Chaū-tí	Pě-Tsî	kǎng-shīn		560
Hwâng-yiú	5	Jîn-tsūng	Súng	kî-ch'eù		1049
Hwâng-kién	2	Siāng-tsūng	Hiá	kǎng-wù		1210
Hwâng-t'ùng	9	Hī-tsūng	Kīn	sīn-yiù		1141
Hwâng-k'îng	2	Jîn-tsūng	Yuên	jîn-tsź		1312
Hwùi-chāng	6	Wù-tsūng	T'áng	sīn-yiù		841
Hwùi-t'úng	10	T'aí-tsūng	Liaú	wù-sū		938
Ī-hī	14	Gān-tí	Tsín	yî-sź		405
Ī-nîng	1	Kūng-tí	Tsî	tīng-ch'eù		617
Ī-fúng	3	Kaū-tsūng	T'áng	pìng-tsź		676
Jîn-sheú	4	Wǎn-tí	Súi	sīn-yiù		601
Jîn-k'íng	5	Jîn-tsūng	Hiá	kiǎ-tsź		1144
K'aī-hwâng	20	Wǎn-tí	Súi	sīn-ch'eù		581
K'aī-yaú	1	Kaū-tsūng	T'áng	sīn-sź		681
K'aī-yuên	29	Hiuên-tsūng	T'áng	kweî-ch'eù		713
K'aī-chíng	5	Wǎn-tsūng	T'áng	pìng-shīn		836
K'aī-p'îng	4	T'aí-tsù	Heú-Liâng	tīng-maú		907
K'aī-yún	3	Tsí-wāng	Heú-Tsín	kiǎ-shīn		944
K'aī-paù	9	T'aí-tsù	Súng	wù-shīn		968
K'aī-hī	3	Ning-tsūng	Súng	yî-ch'eù		1205
K'aī-k'îng	1	Lí-tsūng	Súng	kî-wí		1259
K'aī-t'aí	9	Shíng-tsūng	Liaú	jîn-tsź		1012
Kān-lú	4	Siuēn-tí	Hán	wù-shīn	53	
Kān-lú	4	Chù-maú	Wei	pìng-tsź		256
Kǎng tíng	1	Jîn-tsūng	Súng	kǎng-shīn		1040
Kǎng-hī	61	Shíng-tsú	Tsīng	jîn-yín		1662
Kǎng-chī	2	Hwaî-yâng-wâng	Hán	kweî-wí		23
Kiǎ-p'îng	5	Chù-fǎng	Wei	kî-sź		249
Kiǎ-hǒ	6	Tá-tí	Wú	jîn-tsź		232
Kiǎ-hīng	4	Mín-tí	Tsín	kweî-yiù		313
Kiǎ-yiú	8	Jîn-tsūng	Súng	pìng-shīn		1056
Kiǎ-t'aí	4	Ning-tsūng	Súng	sīn-yiù		1201
Kiǎ-tíng	17	Ning-tsūng	Súng	wù-shīn		1208
Kiǎ-hī	4	Lí-tsūng	Súng	tīng-yiù		1237
Kiǎ-tsìng	45	Shí-tsūng	Míng	jîn-wù		1522
Kiǎ-k'îng	24		Tá-ts'īng	pìng-shīn		1796
Kiên-yuên	6	Wù-tí	Hán	sīn-ch'eù	140	
Kiên-mîng	1	Chù-yín	Pě-Tsî	kǎng-shīn		560
Kiên-fúng	2	Kaū-tsūng	T'áng	pìng-yín		666

F f

218   APPENDIX IV.

Niên-haú.	Duration.	Emperor.	Dynasty.	Year of the cycle.	B.C.	A.D.
Kiên-yuên	2	Sĭ-tsūng	T'áng	wù-sŭ		758
Kiên-fŭ	6	Hĭ-tsūng	T'áng	kiă-wù		874
Kiên-níng	4	Chaū-tsūng	T'áng	kiă-yin		894
Kiên-hwá	4	Chŭ-tiên	Heú-Liâng	kweĭ-yiù		913
Kiên-yiú	3	Yin-tí	Heú-Hán	wù-shīn		948
Kiên-tĕ	5	T'aĭ-tsʻù	Súng	kweĭ-haī		963
Kiên-hīng	1	Chīng-tsūng	Súng	jīn-sŭ		1022
Kiên-taú	9	Hiaú-tsūng	Súng	yĭ-yiù		1165
Kiên-hāng	4	Kīng-tsūng	Liaú	kĭ-maù		979
Kiên-t'ùng	10	T'iēn-tsú-tí	Liaú	sīn-sź		1101
Kiên-taú	2	Hwuĭ-tsūng	Hiá	wù-shīn		1068
Kiên-yiú	24	Jīn-tsūng	Hiá	kāng-yin		1170
Kiên-tíng	4	Hiên-tsūng	Hiá	kweĭ-woí		1223
Kiên-lûng	60	Kaū-tsūng	Tá-tsʻīng	pìng-shīn		1736
Kiên-chaú	5	Yuên-tí	Hán	kweĭ-woí	38	
Kiên-chí	4	Chīng-tí	Hán	kĭ-ch'eù	32	
Kiên-p'ìng	4	Gaĭ-tí	Hán	yĭ-maù	6	
Kiên-wù	31	Kwāng-wù-tí	Hán	yĭ-yiù		25
Kiên-tsʻù	8	Chāng-tí	Hán	pìng-tsż		76
Kiên-kwāng	1	Gān-tí	Hán	sīn-yiù		121
Kiên-k'āng	1	Shạ̄n-tí	Hán	kiă-shīn		144
Kiên-hô	3	Hwân-tí	Hán	tìng-haī		147
Kiên-níng	4	Lîng-tí	Hán	wù-shīn		168
Kiên-gān	25	Hiên-tí	Hán	pìng-tsż		196
Kiên-hīng	15	Heú-chŭ	Shŭ-Hán	kweĭ-maù		223
Kiên-hīng	2	Chŭ-liáng	Wú	jīn-shīn		252
Kiên-hạ̄ng	3	Chŭ-kaù	Wú	kĭ-ch'eù		269
Kiên-wù	1	Mĭn-tí	Tsín	tìng-ch'eù		317
Kiên-yuên	2	K'āng-tí	Tsín	kweĭ-maù		343
Kiên-yuên	4	Kaū-tí	Tsí	kĭ-woí		479
Kiên-wù	4	Mîng-tí	Tsí	kiă-sŭ		494
Kiên-mîng	1	Chŭ-yĕ	Weí	kāng-sŭ		530
Kiên-tĕ	6	Wù-tí	Cheū	kāng-yin		572
Kiên-chūng	4	Tĕ-tsūng	T'áng	kāng-shīn		780
Kiên-lûng	3	T'aĭ-tsʻù	Súng	kāng-shīn		960
Kiên-chūng tsìng-kwŏ	1	Hwuĭ-tsūng	Súng	sīn-sź		1101
Kiên-yên	4	Kaū-tsūng	Súng	tìng-woí		1127
Kiên-wạ̄n	5	Hwuĭ-tí	Mîng	kĭ-maù		1399
Kīng-tsʻù	2	Mîng-tí	Weí	tìng-sź		237
Kīng-yuên	4	Yuên-tí	Weí	kāng-shīn		260
Kīng-p'ìng	1	Yûng-yâng-wâng	Pĕ-Súng	kweĭ-haī		423
Kīng-hô	1	Fí-tí	Pĕ-Súng	yĭ-sź		465
Kīng-mîng	4	Siuēn-wù-tí	Weí	kāng-shīn		500
Kīng-lûng	3	Chūng-tsūng	T'áng	tìng-woí		707
Kīng-yûn	2	Suĭ-tsūng	T'áng	kāng-sŭ		710
Kīng-fŭ	2	Chaū-tsūng	T'áng	jīn-tsż		892
Kīng-tĕ	4	Chīng-tsūng	Súng	kiă-shīn		1004
Kīng-yiú	4	Jīn-tsūng	Súng	kiă-sŭ		1034
Kīng-tìng	5	Lĭ-tsūng	Súng	kāng-shīn		1260
Kīng-yên	2	T'wān-tsūng	Súng	pìng-sź		1276
Kīng-t'aí	7	Kīng-tsūng	Mîng	kāng-wù		1450

APPENDIX IV. 219

Niên-haú.	Duration.	Emperor.	Dynasty.	Year of the cycle.	B.C.	A.D.
Kíng-níng	1	Yuên-tí	Hán	wù-tsz̀	33	
Kíng-yaú	5	Heú-chù	Shŭ-Hán	wù-yîn		258
K'ing-lì	8	Jìn-tsūng	Súng	sīn-sź		1041
K'ing-yuên	5	Níng-tsūng	Súng	yĭ-maù		1195
Kiù-shì	1	T'iēn-heù	T'áng	kāng-tsź		700
Kŭ-shĭě	2	Shŭ-tsź-yīng	Hán	pìng-yîn		6
Kùng-tí	4	Kùng-tí	Wei	kiă-sŭ		554
Kùng-hwá	5	Yīng-tsūng	Hiá	kweĭ-maù		1063
Kwāng-hô	6	Líng-tí	Hán	wù-wù		178
Kwāng-hĭ	1	Hwŭi-tí	T'sin	pìng-yîn		306
Kwāng-tá	2	Lín-haĭ-wâng	Chîn	tīng-haĭ		567
Kwāng-tsĕ	1	T'iēn-heù	T'áng	kiă-shīn		684
Kwāng-k'ì	3	Hī-tsūng	T'áng	yĭ-sź		885
Kwāng-hwá	3	Chaū-tsūng	T'áng	wù-wù		898
Kwāng-tíng	13	Shîn-tsūng	Hiá	sīn-wí		1211
Kwàng-tĕ	2	Taí-tsūng	T'áng	kweĭ-maù		763
Kwàng-míng	1	Hī-tsūng	T'áng	kāng-tsź		880
Kwàng-shặn	3	T'aí-ts'ù	Heú-Cheŭ	sīn-haĭ		951
Kwàng-yùn	2	Kìng-tsūng	Hiá	kiă-sŭ		1034
Lîn-tĕ	2	Kaū-tsūng	T'áng	kiă-tsź		664
Lúng-hô	1	Gaī-tí	Tsin	jîn-sŭ		362
Lúng-gān	5	Gān-tí	Tsin	tīng-yiù		397
Lúng-hwá	1	Heú-chù-weí	Pĕ-Tsí	pìng-shīn		576
Lúng-sŏ	2	Kaū-tsūng	T'áng	sīn-yiù		661
Lúng-kì	1	Hī-tsūng	T'áng	kĭ-yiù		889
Lúng-tĕ	2	Chù-t'iēn	Heú-Liâng	sīn-sź		921
Lúng-hīng	2	Hiaū-tsūng	Súng	kweĭ-wí		1163
Lúng-k'ing	6	Mŭ-tsūng	Míng	tīng-maù		1567
Lúng-wù	1	T'áng-wâng	Míng	pìng-sŭ		1646
Míng-tí	2	Míng-tí	Cheŭ	tīng-ch'eù		557
Míng-taú	2	Jîn-tsūng	Súng	jîn-shīn		1032
Míng-chāng	6	Chāng-tsūng	Kīn	kāng-sŭ		1190
Níng-k'āng	3	Wŭ-tí	Tsin	kweĭ-yiù		373
Pạ̀n-chì	4	Siuēn-tí	Hán	wù-shīn	73	
Pạ̀n-ts'ŭ	1	Chì-tí	Hán	pìng-sŭ		146
Paù-tíng	5	Wŭ-tí	Cheŭ	sīn-sź		561
Paù-yīng	1	Sŭ-tsūng	T'áng	jîn-yîn		762
Paù-lì	2	Kìng-tsūng	T'áng	yĭ-sź		825
Paù-yuên	2	Jîn-tsūng	Súng	wù-yîn		1038
Paù-k'ing	3	Lì-tsūng	Súng	yĭ-yiù		1225
Paù-yiú	6	Lì-tsūng	Súng	kweĭ-ch'eù		1253
Paù-tá	5	T'iēn-tsù-tí	Liaū	sīn-ch'eù		1121
Paù-níng	10	Kìng-tsūng	Liaū	kĭ-sź		969
Paù-tíng	3	Chù-kaù	Wŭ	pìng-sŭ		266
P'ù-t'ūng	7	Wŭ-tí	Liâng	kāng-tsź		520
Shặn-chí	18	Shí-tsù	Tá-ts'īng	kiă-shīn		1644
Shặn-yiú	12	Lì-tsūng	Súng	sīn-ch'eù		1241
Shặn-hwá	5	T'aí-tsūng	Súng	kāng-yîn		990
Shặn-hī	16	Hiaú-tsūng	Súng	kiă-wù		1174
Sháng-yuên	2	Kaū-tsūng	T'áng	kiă-sŭ		674
Sháng-yuên	2	Sŭ-tsūng	T'áng	kāng-tsź		760

F f 2

APPENDIX IV.

Niên-haú.	Duration.	Emperor.	Dynasty.	Year of the cycle.	B.C.	A.D.
Shaú-t'aí	1	Kíng-tí	Liáng	yǐ-haī	555	
Shaú-shíng	4	Chě-tsūng	Súng	kiǎ-sǚ		1094
Shaú-hīng	32	Kaū-tsūng	Súng	sīn-haī		1131
Shaú-hī	5	Kwāng-tsūng	Súng	kāng-sǚ		1190
Shaú-tíng	6	Lǐ-tsūng	Súng	wù-tsz̄		1228
Shaú-hīng	12	Chíng-t'iēn t'aí-heú	Sī-Liaú	jǐn-sǚ		1142
Shaú-wù	½	Fú-wáng	Míng	pìng-sǚ		1646
Sheú-kwǒ	2	T'aí-tsù	Kīn	yǐ-wí		1115
Sheú-lǔng	6	Taú-tsūng	Liaú	yǐ-haī		1095
Shīn-tsiǒ	4	Siuēn-tí	Hán	kāng-shīn	61	
Shīn-shwùí	2	Míng-yuēn-tí	Wei	kiǎ-yín		414
Shīn-kiǎ	4	T'aí-wù-tí	Wei	wù-shīn		428
Shīn-kweī	2	Míng-tí	Wei	wù-sǚ		518
Shīn-kūng	1	T'iēn-heú	T'áng	tīng-yiù		697
Shīn-lúng	2	Chūng-tsūng	T'áng	yǐ-sź		705
Shīn-tsě	6	T'aí-tsūng	Liaú	pìng-tsz̄		916
Shīng-míng	2	Shǎn-tí	Pě-Súng	tīng-sź		477
Shīng-p'íng	5	Mǔ-tí	Tsín	tīng-sź		357
Shīng-lì	2	T'iēn-heú	T'áng	wù-sǚ		698
Siēn-t'iēn	1	Hiuēn-tsūng	T'áng	kweī-ch'eù		713
Siuēn-chíng	1	Siuēn-tí	Cheū	wù-sǚ		578
Siuēn-hô	7	Hwūī-tsūng	Súng	kì-haī		1119
Siuēn-tě	10	Siuēn-tsūng	Míng	pìng-jín		1426
Sūī-hô	2	Chíng-tí	Hán	kweī-ch'eù	8	
Sź-shíng	21	Chūng-tsūng	T'áng	kiǎ-shīn		684
Tá-míng	8	Wù-tí	Pě-Súng	tīng-yiù		457
Tá-t'ūng	2	Wù-tí	Liáng	tīng-wí		527
Tá-t'áng	11	Wù-tí	Liáng	yǐ-maù		535
Tá-paù	2	Kiěn-wǎn-tí	Liáng	kāng-wù		550
Tá-siáng	3	Tsíng-tí	Cheū	kì-haī		579
Tá-niě	12	Yáng-tí	Súī	yǐ-ch'eù		605
Tá-lì	14	Taí-tsūng	T'áng	pìng-wù		766
Tá-chūng	13	Siuēn-tsūng	T'áng	tīng-maù		847
Tá-shǎn	2	Chaū-tsūng	T'áng	kiǎ-yín		890
Tá-chūng tsiáng-fú	9	Chīng-tsūng	Súng	wù-shīn		1008
Tá-kwān	4	Hwūī-tsūng	Súng	tīng-haī		1107
Tá-k'āng	10	Taú-tsūng	Liaú	yǐ-maù		1075
Tá-gān	10	Taú-tsūng	Liaú	yǐ-ch'eù		1085
Tá-k'íng	2	Kíng-tsūng	Hiǎ	pìng-tsz̄		1036
Tá-gān	10	Hwūī-tsūng	Hiǎ	pìng-shīn		1076
Tá-tě	5	Tsūng-tsūng	Hiǎ	yǐ-maù		1135
Tá-k'íng	4	Jín-tsūng	Hiǎ	kāng-shīn		1140
Tá-tíng	29	Shí-tsūng	Kīn	sīn-sź		1161
Tá-gān	3	Chū-yùng-tsź	Kīn	kì-sź		1209
Tá-tě	11	Chíng-tsūng	Yuēn	tīng-yiù		1297
T'aí-chāng	1	Kwāng-tsūng	Míng	kāng-shīn		1620
T'aí-tíng	4	T'aí-tíng-tí	Yuēn	kiǎ-tsz̄		1324
T'aí-p'íng hīng-kwǒ	8	T'aí-tsūng	Súng	pìng-tsz̄		976
T'aí-ts'ǚ	4	Wù-tí	Hán	tīng-ch'eù	104	
T'aí-chī	4	Wù-tí	Hán	yǐ-yiù	96	
T'aí-hô	6	Míng-tí	Wei	tīng-wí		227

APPENDIX IV. 221

Niên-haú.	Duration.	Emperor.	Dynasty.	Year of the cycle.	B.C.	A.D.
T'ai-yuên	1	Tá-tí	Wŭ	sĭn-wí		251
T'ai-p'ing	2	Chŭ-liáng	Wŭ	pĭng-tsz̀		256
T'ai-shĭ	10	Wŭ-tí	Tsin	yĭ-yiŭ		265
T'ai-k'āng	10	Hwüï-tí	Tsin	kāng-tsz̀		280
T'ai-gān	2	Hwüï-tí	Tsin	jĭn-sŭ		302
T'ai-hīng	4	Mĭn-tí	Tsin	wù-yĭn		318
T'ai-hô	8	Chāng-tsūng	Kīn	sĭn-yiù		1201
T'ai-kĭ	1	Süï-tsūng	T'áng	jĭn-tsz̀		712
T'ai-ning	3	Ming-tí	Tsin	kweĭ-wí		323
T'ai-p'ing	9	Hwüï-tí	Tsin	sĭn-haĭ		291
T'ai-hô	5	Haĭ-sĭ-kūng	Tsin	pĭng-yĭn		366
T'ai-yuên	21	Wŭ-tí	Tsin	pĭng-tsz̀		376
T'ai-yuên	1	Kŭng-tí	Süí	wù-yĭn		618
T'ai-chĭ	7	Ming-tí	Pĕ-Súng			475
T'ai-yŭ	1	Ming-tí	Pĕ-Súng	jĭn-tsz̀		472
T'ai-tsīng	3	Wŭ-tí	Liáng	tĭng-maŭ		547
T'ai-hô	9	Wăn-tsūng	T'áng	tĭng-wí		827
T'ai-p'ing	1	King-tí	Liáng	pĭng-tsz̀		556
T'ai-p'ing	11	Shing-tsūng	Liaŭ	sĭn-yiù		1021
T'ai-kien	14	Siuên-tí	Chin	kĭ-ch'eù		569
T'ai-ch'áng	8	Ming-yuên-tí	Weí	pĭng-shĭn		416
T'ai-yên	5	T'ai-wù-tí	Weí	yĭ-haĭ		435
T'ai-p'ing ching-kiūn	12	T'ai-wù-tí	Weí	kāng-shĭn		440
T'ai-gān	5	Wăn-ching-tí	Weí	yĭ-wí		455
T'ai-hô	23	Wăn-tí	Weí	tīng-sz̀		477
T'ai-t'ŭng	17	Wăn-tí	Weí	yĭ-maŭ		535
T'ai-ning	1	Wŭ-ching-tí	Pĕ-Tsí	sĭn-sz̀		561
Tāng-kwŏ	10	Taŭ-wù-tí	Weí	pĭng-sŭ		386
Taú-kwāng	30		Tá-ts'īng	kāng-shĭn		1820
T'ĕ-yiŭ	1	Kŭng-tsūng	Súng	yĭ-haĭ		1275
Tí-tsiĕ	4	Siuēn-tí	Hán	jĭn-tsz̀	96	
Tí-hwáng	3	Wáng-màng	Hán	kāng-shĭn	20	
T'iaŭ-hĭ	1	Kaŭ-tsūng	T'áng	kĭ-maŭ		679
T'iēn-hán	4	Wŭ-tí	Hán	sĭn-sz̀	100	
T'iēn-fúng	6	Wáng-màng	Hán	kiă-sŭ		14
T'iēn-tsĕ	1	Chŭ-kaŭ	Wŭ	yĭ-wí		275
T'iēn-sĭ	1	Chŭ-kaŭ	Wŭ	pĭng-shĭn		276
T'iēn-kĭ	1	Chŭ-kaŭ	Wŭ	tĭng-yiù		277
T'iēn-kien	18	Wŭ-tí	Liáng	jĭn-wŭ		502
T'iēn-kiă	6	Wăn-tí	Chin	kāng-shĭn		560
T'iēn-k'āng	1	Wăn-tí	Chin	pĭng-sŭ		566
T'iēn-hing	6	Taŭ-wù-tí	Weí	wù-sŭ		398
T'iēn-sz̀	5	Taŭ-wù-tí	Weí	kiă-shĭn		404
T'iēn-gān	1	Hiēn-wăn-tí	Weí	pĭng-wŭ		466
T'iēn-p'ing	4	Tsīng-tí	Túng-Weí	kiă-yĭn		534
T'iēn-paŭ	10	Wăn-siuēn-tí	Pĕ-Tsí	kāng-wŭ		550
T'iēn-t'ŭng	5	Heŭ-chŭ-weí	Pĕ-Tsí	yĭ-yiŭ		565
T'iēn-hô	6	Wŭ-tí	Chaŭ	pĭng-sŭ		566
T'iēn-sheŭ	2	T'iēn-heù	T'áng	kāng-yĭn		690
T'iēn-tsĕ-wán-süï	1	T'iēn-heù	T'áng	yĭ-wí		695
T'iēn-paŭ	14	Hiuên-tsūng	T'áng	jĭn-wŭ		742

APPENDIX IV.

Niên-haú.	Duration.	Emperor.	Dynasty.	Year of the cycle.	B.C.	A.D.
T'iēn-fŭ	3	Chaū-tsūng	T'áng	sīn-yiú		901
T'iēn-yiú	4	Chaū-siuēn-tí	T'áng	kiă-tsź		904
T'iēn-chíng	4	Míng-tsūng	Heú-T'áng	pìng-sŭ		926
T'iēn-fŭ	8	Kaū-ts'ŭ	Heú-Tsín	pìng-shīn		936
T'iēn-fŭ	1	Kaū-ts'ŭ	Heú-Hán	tīng-wí		947
T'iēn-hī	5	Chíng-tsūng	Súng	tīng-sź		1017
T'iēn-shíng	9	Jín-tsūng	Súng	kweí-haī		1023
T'iēn-tsán	4	T'aí-tsūng	Liaú	jín-wù		922
T'iēn-hién	12	T'aí-tsūng	Liaú	pìng-sŭ		926
T'iēn-lŭ	4	Shí-tsūng	Liaú	tīng-wí		947
T'iēn-k'íng	10	T'iēn-tsú-tí	Liaú	sīn-maū		1111
T'iēn-hī	34	Chī-lŭ-kŭ	Sī-Liaú	wù-tsź		1168
T'iēn-yiú-chūi-shíng	3	Yīng-tsūng	Hiá	káng-yín		1050
T'iēn-sź-lí-shíng-kwŏ-k'íng	6	Hwuī-tsūng	Hiá	káng-sŭ		1070
T'iēn-gán-lí-tíng	1	Tsúng-tsūng	Hiá	pìng-yín		1086
T'iēn-í-chí-p'íng	4	Tsúng-tsūng	Hiá	tīng-maū		1087
T'iēn-yiú-mín-gán	8	Tsúng-tsūng	Hiá	sīn-wí		1091
T'iēn-shíng	21	Jín-tsūng	Hiá	kì-sź		1149
T'iēn-k'íng	13	Hwán-tsūng	Hiá	kiă-yín		1194
T'iēn-fŭ	7	T'aí-tsŭ	Kīn	tīng-yiú		1117
T'iēn-hwuī	15	T'aí-tsūng	Kīn	kweí-maū		1123
T'iēn-kiuén	3	Hī-tsūng	Kīn	wù-wù		1138
T'iēn-tĕ	4	Tí-liáng	Kīn	kì-sź		1149
T'iēn-hīng	3	Gaī-tsūng	Kīn	jín-shín		1232
T'iēn-lí	2	Wán-tsūng	Yuên	wù-shín		1328
T'iēn-shán	8	Yīng-tsūng	Míng	tīng-ch'eū		1457
T'iēn-k'í	7	Hī-tsūng	Míng	sīn-yiú		1621
T'iēn-ming	11	T'aí-tsŭ	Tsíng	pìng-shīn		1616
T'iēn-tsūng	9	T'aí-tsūng	Tsíng	tīng-maū		1627
Tsiáng-lūng	2	Tí-pìng	Súng	wù-yín		1278
Tsíng-lúng	4	Míng-tí	Weí	kweí-ch'eū		233
Tsíng-t'aí	3	Lú-wáng	Heú-T'áng	kiă-wù		934
Tsíng-k'áng	1	K'īn-tsūng	Súng	pìng-wù		1126
Tsíng-níng	9	Taú-tsūng	Liaú	yí-wí		1055
Ts'ŭ-yuên	5	Yuên-tí	Hán	kweí-yiú	48	
Ts'ŭ-chí	1	Shú-tsź-yíng	Hán	wù-shín		8
Ts'ŭ-p'íng	4	Hién-tí	Hán	káng-wù		190
T'súng-hiún	1	Kúng-tí	Heú-Cheū	káng-shín		960
Tsúng-níng	5	Hwuī-tsūng	Súng	jín-wù		1102
Tsúng-fŭ	14	Chíng-t'iēn-t'aí-heú	Sī-Liaú	kiă-sŭ		1154
Tsúng-k'íng	1	Chiù-yùng-tsǐ	Kīn	jín-shín		1212
Tsúng-tĕ	8	T'aí-tsūng	Tá-ts'īng	pìng-tsź		1636
Tsúng-chíng	17	Sź-tsūng	Míng	wù-shín		1628
Tsúng-cháng	2	Kaū-tsūng	T'áng	wù-yín		668
T'úng-kwáng	3	Chwáng-tsūng	Heú-T'áng	kweí-wí		924
T'úng-chí			Tá-Tsíng	sīn-yiú		1861
T'úng-hŏ	29	Shíng-tsūng	Liaú	kweí-wí		983
Twān-kúng	2	T'aí-tsūng	Súng	wù-tsź		988
Twān-p'íng	3	Lí-tsūng	Súng	kiă-wù		1234
Wán-súi t'úng-t'iēn	1	T'iēn-heú	T'áng	pìng-shīn		696
Wán-lí	47	Shín-tsūng	Míng	kweí-yiú		1573

APPENDIX IV.

Nién-haú.	Duration.	Emperor.	Dynasty.	Year of the cycle.	B.C.	A.D.
Wăn-tĕ	1	Hī-tsūng	T'ăng	wù-shīn		888
Wù-fúng	2	Chù-liáng	Wŭ	kiă-sŭ		254
Wù-tíng	8	Tsing-tí	Tŭng-Weí	kweî-haī		543
Wù-fúng	4	Siuĕn-tí	Hán	kiă-tsż	57	
Wù-p'ing	6	Heú-chù-weí	Pĕ-Tsí	kăng-yin		570
Wù-chĭng	2	Mĭng-tí	Chaū	kĭ-maù		559
Wù-tĕ	9	Kaŭ-tsŭng	T'ăng	wù-yin		618
Yăng-sŏ	4	Ching-tí	Hán	tĭng-yiù	24	
Yăng-kiā	4	Shăn-tí	Hán	jin-shīn		132
Yên-p'ing	1	Shăng-tí	Hán	ping-wù		106
Yên-kwāng	4	Gān-tí	Hán	kĭ-wí		122
Yên-hī	9	Hwăn-tí	Hán	wù-sŭ		158
Yên-hī	20	Heú-chù	Shŭ-Hán	wù-wù		238
Yên-hĭng	1	Heú-chù	Shŭ-Hán	kweî-wí		263
Yên-hŏ	3	T'aí-wù-tí	Weí	jin-shīn		432
Yên-hĭng	5	Wăn-tí	Weí	sīn-haī		471
Yên-chăng	4	Siuĕn-wù-tí	Weí	jin-shīn		512
Yên-tsaí	1	T'iēn-heù	T'ăng	kiă-wù		694
Yên-k'ing	11	Tĕ-tsūng	Sī-Liaù	yi-sż		1125
Yên-tsŭ	11	King-tsŭng	Hiá	wù-yin		1038
Yên-sź-ning-kwŏ	1	Yĭng-tsūng	Hiá	kĭ-ch'eù		1049
Yên-yiú	7	Jin-tsūng	Yuên	kiă-yin		1314
Yĭng-shăn	1	Min-tí	Heú-T'ăng	kiă-wù		934
Yĭng-lĭ	18	Mŭ-tsūng	Liaŭ	sīn-haī		951
Yĭng-t'iēn	4	Siăng-tsūng	Hiá	tĭng-maù		1207
Yuên-niên	7	King-tí	Hán	yĭ-yiù	156	
Yuên-kwāng	6	Wù-tí	Hán	tĭng-wí	134	
Yuên-sŏ	6	Wù-tí	Hán	kweî-ch'eù	128	
Yuên-heú	6	Wù-tí	Hán	jin-sŭ	122	
Yuên-tĭng	6	Wù-tí	Hán	yĭ-ch'eù	116	
Yuên-fúng	6	Wù-tí	Hán	sīn-wí	110	
Yuên-fúng	6	Chaū-tí	Hán	sīn-ch'eù	80	
Yuên-p'ing	1	Chaū-tí	Hán	tĭng-wí	74	
Yuên-k'āng	4	Siuĕn-tí	Hán	ping-shīn	65	
Yuên-yên	4	Ching-tí	Hán	kĭ-yiù	12	
Yuên-sheú	2	Gaī-tí	Hán	kĭ-wí	2	
Yuên-chì	5	P'ing-tí	Hán	sīn-yiù		1
Yuên hŏ	3	Chăng-tí	Hán	kiă-shīn		84
Yuên-hĭng	1	Hŏ-tí	Hán	yĭ-sż		105
Yuên-ts'ū	6	Gān-tí	Hán	kiă-yin		114
Yuên-kiā	2	Hwăn-tí	Hán	sīn-maù		151
Yuên-hĭng	1	Chù-kaù	Wŭ	kiă-shīn		264
Yuên-hīng	3	Gān-tí	Tsin	jin-yin		402
Yuên-hī	1	Kŭng-tí	Tsin	kĭ-wí		419
Yuên-kiā	30	Wăn-tí	Pĕ-Sŭng	kiă-tsż		424
Yuên-hwūī	4	Tsăng-yú-wăng	Pĕ-Sŭng	kweî-ch'eù		473
Yuên-tsiáng	1	Tsing-tí	Tŭng-Weí	wù-wù		538
Yuên-hŏ	15	Hiēn-tsūng	T'ăng	ping-sŭ		806
Yuên-fūng	8	Shîn-tsūng	Sŭng	wù-wù		1078
Yuên-yiú	8	Chĕ-tsūng	Sŭng	ping-yin		1086
Yuên-fŭ	3	Chĕ-tsūng	Sŭng	wù-yin		1098

APPENDIX IV.

Nién-haú.	Duration.	Emperor.	Dynasty.	Year of the cycle.	B.C.	A.D.
Yuên-tĕ	7	Tsŭng-tsūng	Hiá	kāng-tsz̀		1120
Yuên-kwāng	2	Siuên-tsūng	Kīn	jîn-wù		1222
Yuên-chīng	2	Chíng-tsūng	Yuên	yĭ-wí		1295
Yuên-tʻùng	2	Shạ̀n-tí	Yuên	kweĭ-yiù		1333
Yūng-hĭ	4	Tʻaí-tsūng	Súng	kiă-shīn		984
Yūng-níng	5	Tsŭng-tsūng	Hiá	yĭ-wí		1115
Yūng-chíng	13	Shí-tsūng	Tá-tsʻīng	kweĭ-maù		1723
Yùng-kwāng	5	Yuên-tí	Hán	wù-yîn	43	
Yùng-shĭ	4	Chíng-tí	Hán	yĭ-sź	16	
Yùng-pʻíng	18	Míng-tí	Hán	wù-wù		58
Yùng-yuên	16	Hô-tí	Hán	kĭ-chʻeù		89
Yùng-tsʻū	7	Gān-tí	Hán	tīng-wí		107
Yùng-níng	1	Gān-tí	Hán	kāng-shīn		120
Yùng-kiên	6	Shạ̀n-tí	Hán	pìng-yîn		126
Yùng-hô	6	Shạ̀n-tí	Hán	pìng-tsz̀		136
Yùng-kiă	1	Chíng-tí	Hán	yĭ-yiù		145
Yùng-hīng	2	Hwân-tí	Hán	kweĭ-sź		153
Yùng-sheú	3	Hwân-tí	Hán	yĭ-wí		155
Yùng-kʻāng	1	Hwân-tí	Hán	tīng-wí		167
Yùng-gān	7	Kíng-tí	Wú	wù-yîn		258
Yùng-hī	1	Hwüí-tí	Tsín	kāng-sŭ		290
Yùng-kʻāng	1	Hwüí-tí	Tsín	kăng-shīn		300
Yùng-níng	1	Hwüí-tí	Tsín	sīn-yiù		301
Yùng-hīng	2	Hwüí-tí	Tsín	kiă-tsz̀		304
Yùng-kiă	6	Hwaî-tí	Tsín	tīng-maù		307
Yùng-chāng	1	Mín-tí	Tsín	jîn-wù		322
Yùng-hô	12	Mŭ-tí	Tsín	yĭ-sź		345
Yùng-tʻeŭ	3	Wù-tí	Pê-Súng	kweĭ-shīn		420
Yùng-míng	11	Wù-tí	Tsí	kweĭ-haī		483
Yùng-tʻaí	1	Míng-tí	Tsí	wù-yîn		498
Yùng-yuên	2	Tūng-hwạ̄n-heŭ	Tsí	kĭ-maù		499
Yùng-tíng	3	Wù-tí	Chin	tīng-chʻeù		557
Yùng-hīng	5	Míng-yuên-tí	Weí	kĭ-pìng		409
Yùng-pʻíng	4	Siuên-wù-tí	Weí	wù-tsz̀		508
Yùng-gān	2	Chwāng-tí	Weí	wù-shīn		528
Yùng-hī	3	Wù-tí	Weí	jîn-tsz̀		532
Yùng-pʻíng	2	Fí-tí	Weí	jîn-shīn		552
Yùng-hwüí	6	Kaū-tsūng	Tʻáng	kāng-sŭ		650
Yùng-lŭng	1	Kaū-tsūng	Tʻáng	kāng-shīn		680
Yùng-shạ̀n	1	Kaū-tsūng	Tʻáng	jîn-wù		682
Yùng-chāng	1	Tʻiên-heŭ	Tʻáng	kĭ-chʻeù		689
Yùng-tʻaí	1	Taí-tsūng	Tʻáng	yĭ-sź		765
Yùng-chīng	1	Shạ̀n-tsūng	Tʻáng	yĭ-yiù		805
Yùng-gān	3	Tsūng-tsūng	Hiá	kĭ-maù		1099
Yùng-lŏ	22	Chíng-tsù	Míng	kweĭ-wí		1403
Yùng-lĭ	15	Kweí-wāng	Míng	tīng-haī		1647

APPENDIX V.

A comparison of some Chinese dialects with reference to their pronunciation.

The Chinese divide their syllables into two parts,—the *initial* and the *final*. They do not understand how to analyse the syllable into its component letters, and therefore it often happens that they are unable to distinguish slight changes in the pronunciation of certain words. Hence arises a difficulty to the student, who is frequently unable to catch the articulations of his Chinese tutor. And if the Chinese tutor is unable to discern the difference between certain letters, much less is he able to say how or why changes in various dialects have taken place, and he is also less expert at speaking various dialects of his own country than a well practised foreigner.

The want of an alphabetic system, by which articulations may be accurately expressed, is the cause of this. And the foreigner has this advantage over the untutored Chinese, who has nothing to guide his pronunciation but the ear, while the European has the sound written down for his eye, and the letters are the symbols of an analytic process. We have only to call to mind the vulgar provincialisms of our own country, and the transformation of words, produced by the unlettered rustic, to understand the value of our alphabet, in aiding us to escape the most chaotic differences of pronunciation, which would make English a Babel of dialects, were they allowed to pass from one to another by the ear alone without being written down.

Now although we cannot start a theory as to which dialect represents the original and true pronunciation of Chinese with much chance of proving it, we may for the sake of convenience assume that that which presents us with the clearest and most definite pronunciation is the nearest to that original, and to what Chinese pronunciation should be. It is an undoubted fact that changes have taken place in some syllables, but the great mass of Chinese sounds is most ancient and simple. If then we could ascertain exactly what this ancient pronunciation was, we should be in a better position to show how or why the subsequent changes have occurred.

The Chinese, as was said, do not write down the sounds of their syllables; but we do so to assist our memory, and to define clearly what those sounds are. What we value in our own language, among other things, is the orthography which shows the etymology in many words; and we obstinately refuse to entertain the new principles of the "*Fonetik Nuz;*" and we persist in keeping our ancient spelling of words, because we delight to see the remains which exist of their parentage and origin.

APPENDIX V.

China has numerous dialects with a common origin; these ought all to be represented by the Roman alphabet, and they ought to follow in a certain degree the primary and the purest pronunciation. Slight changes should be explained with the old spelling, instead of a new orthography being invented for each dialect.

Dialectic changes affect either the consonantal sounds, or the vowel sounds, or both, there is the elision of a letter, the addition of a letter to the syllable, or a change of tone. The regular changes which we find in European languages occur in Chinese. (Cf. Art. 3. Part I.) The Mandarin dialect(i. e. the *Kwān-hwá*), spoken in the central provinces, preserves the primary vowel sounds (*a, i, u*) and the simple combinations of these (*ai, au, iu, ia, ui, ua*), while the provincial dialects modify these latter considerably, and produce such sounds as those which are represented in this work by *e* (*ā*), *o* (*ŏ*), *ǫ* (*aw*), *ö* (German), *ü* (French), and the primary vowels *a, i, u* are pure, and with the Italian sounds.

It is well known that the vowel sounds affect the consonantal sounds with which they are united. In Spanish, in Italian, in Swedish, and in Polish what are called the hard vowels (*a, o, u*) and the soft vowels (*i, e, ä, ü*) affect the pronunciation of the preceding gutturals *g, k, c, ch*.

Thus in Polish *c* is generally pronounced *ts*, but before the vowel *i*, which is occasionally written above the letter (*ć*), it is like the Germ. *tsch,* but somewhat softer, as in the Italian *ci* or the Spanish *ch* in *chupa*. In this language consonants are said to have a hard or a soft pronunciation, according as they are followed by *y* or *i* respectively. The vowel *i* is the regular indication of a soft pronunciation for the preceding consonant. Thus in *śmierć* (*shmierch*) 'death,' and *siano* (*shiano*) 'hay,' *s* is pronounced like *sh* nearly, only softer. The *hs* of Mr. Wade's orthography is evidently this sound.

In Swedish *k* before *i, e, y, ä,* and *ö,* is softened in the same way; thus, *kärlek* (*chärlek*) 'love,' *kif* (*chif*) 'strife:' so also *sk* before *a, o, u* is hard, but before *i, j, e,* soft ; thus, *skjuta* (*shiuta*) 'to shoot :' *t* is hard excepting when followed by *j;* thus, *tjena* (*chena*) 'to serve,' like the Germ. *dienen;* but the spelling is not changed, or this relationship would be well-nigh lost sight of.

Thus much has been said in anticipation of the time when the Chinese dialects or languages will be written by means of the Roman alphabet alone. It will then be easy to observe the connexion between the dialects, to see the radical syllable in each word, and to learn to read, if but one system of spelling be used for all the vernacular dialects.

Dialectic differences of pronunciation relate to the changes and modifications of single letters. In Chinese the initial letter in Roman type is modified or entirely changed,—the final letter is changed (as *n* to *m* or *ng*),—or a letter is added either before the initial or after the final (as *n* before *y* or *j* in the dialects about Shanghai, and before *g* in some Canton varieties); *k, p,* or *t* is added after the syllables affected by the "entering tone" in the Canton and the Hakka dialects, and *n* is not unfrequently transformed into

APPENDIX V. 227

ng. The regular compounds (*ai, au, iu*) of the Mandarin are modified in the provincial dialects;—*ai* becoming *e* (i. e. *ä* or *ā*), *au* becoming *ō* or *ǫ* (i. e. *aw* in *law*), *iu* becoming *iau* or *iǫ*. The Mandarin keeps the pure and sharp sounds of the consonants—*k, p, t*—the flat and heavy sounds of these letters (*g, b, d*) are not found in its pure pronunciation, but in the Peking and in some local *patois* they creep out.

The letters *k, p, t* are however aspirated, and hence arise *k', p',* and *t'.* When *k* is very strongly aspirated it approximates to *ch*, and *ch* is often confounded with *ts*, especially in syllables in which an *i* follows the initial sound of *ch* or *ts*. The liquids *l, m, n* are very often interchanged in Chinese, but in southern Mandarin they are kept comparatively without alteration. In the south of China the initial *s* is used for *sh* in some vulgar dialects.

In treating of dialectic changes, the open syllables—those ending with a vowel—must be chiefly considered, for the short vowels which are produced by the closing of a syllable are very undefined, and are really very unimportant, being hardly distinguishable by a native. They may be compared to the Hebrew *sheva* and its compounds.

General changes in vowel and consonantal sounds.

1. The primary vowels—*a, i, u*—remain in open syllables in almost all the dialects of China. The Hokkien or Amoy dialect presents a few exceptions to this rule, and in some dialects the syllables made up with a consonant and one of these vowels admit another vowel between the two letters ; e. g. *ka* changes to *kia, ku* to *kiu*, and *ta* to *tǫa;* but as a rule these letters are constant. And even in many closed syllables they remain in the different dialects. This is especially the case with the vowels *i* and *u, king* in one dialect never changes to *kung* or *kang* in another, but being in a closed syllable it is shortened, and from the imperfect articulation it is difficult to determine its exact quality,—in the Hokkien dialect it would seem to be like a short *e*. So also in the Peking dialect, *ching* of southern Mandarin becomes *cheng;* the difference however is hardly perceptible to a native. If the phrase and tone be idiomatic the slight variation in the quantity of a vowel is overlooked.

2. But although these vowels (*a, i, u*) in their simple state are unchanged in the various dialects, they are generally altered when in Mandarin they are found together in the same syllable, thus *kiang* of the Mandarin becomes *keung*, and *kiung* becomes *kung* in the Canton dialect. Their regular compounds—*ai, au,* and *iu*—in open syllables are almost always changed into their proper modifications—*e, o* (*ǫ* or *ą*), and *ü*—in the dialects. The closed syllables in *ang* in Mandarin change it into *eung* in Canton, and those in *ien* change into *in*. Sometimes a nasal *ng* is added where only *n* existed, e. g. *jin,* 'man,' in Mandarin is *yąn* in Canton and *nyąng* in Shanghai. The *y* is dropped and the *n* changed to *l* in Fucheu, and it then makes *lang*. The *jin* is changed to *nyin* in Ningpo, and in Japanese the *y* is dropped and *nin* becomes the word for 'man.'

APPENDIX V.

These principal changes serve to show the uniformity which exists in Chinese dialects; the diversity being always in accordance with some well established law of euphonic change.

The following simple system of finals in Chinese may serve as the standard of comparison. They are nearly all found in Mandarin. The vowels *i* and *u* may precede any of these finals and coalesce with them, forming often the initials *y* and *w*.

(1) a, (2) i, (3) u, (4) ai, ei, e, and ạ, (5) au, eu, (6) iu,
    á   ĭ   ŭ   ĕ   ọ and ọ, ŏ   ŭ
    an   in   un (oon)   en   ạn   oi   on   ŭ
    ang   ing   ung   eng   ạng   ong   ün

Hence by prefixing *i* and *u* (*y* and *w*)—*ia, iá, ian, iang, ua, uá, uan, uang, iai, ieŭ, ien, io, iŏ*, &c. &c. are produced. Some dialects employ these vowels between the proper initial and the final, others omit them. *Sien* in Mand. becomes *sin* in Canton. The presence of such additional vowels in Mandarin may lead the student to expect considerable variation in the provincial dialects in those particular syllables.

Comparative table of changes in some finals.

Mand. D.	Cant. D.	Shang. D.	Amoy D.
a	a	o	ọa, ê
á	at, ap	á	
an	am, an, ọn, un	aⁿ, oⁿ	ọaⁿ, am
ang	eung, ong, ang	ang, ong	aⁿ, ieng, ong, uⁿ, ieng
i	ai	*i* and *yi*	ọe, e, ui, oa, i
ĭ	op, ik		it, ip, ek
in	am	ang, eng, ing	im
ing	ang, ing	ing	ieng, iⁿ, iaⁿ
u	o	ọ	iu, ŏ
ŭ	ak	ŭ	ok, ut
ung	ung	ung	iêng, eng, iong, ong
ai	oi, ai	e, i, a	ai, oe
ei	ei, i	ei	
ĕ	ak	ẹ	ap
ẹn	in, im, ün	áⁿ, öⁿ, eᵘ	am
ạn	ạn	aⁿ	ng
ạng		ạng	iⁿ
au	iu, o, u	o, ọ	ô, o, a
o		ạ	e
eu	eu	ạ	ŏ
ọ			
ŏ	ok	ŏ	ŏ, ap
iu		ạ	
ü		yü	o
ü̆	üt		ĕ
ün		ün	
üi		e	

APPENDIX V.

3. The modifications of the consonants are similar in character. Mutes change into their corresponding letters,—a *t* may change to *d*, a *p* to *b*, a *k* to *ch* or *g*, a *ch* to *ts*, and occasionally to *sh*, a *chang* may become a *tsiang* or a *shang* in different dialects.

Comparative table of changes in some initials.

Mand. D.	Cant. D.	Shang. D.	Amoy D.
h	f	h	h, k, or dropped
hw	w	w	h
s	s or sh	s or z	ch
sh	sh or s	s, z, or l	ti
shw		s	
ts	sh and ts	s	ch or k
ch	ts occ.	ts	ti or s
chw	ch	ts	chi
k	k	k	g
kw	k	k	k
j	y	ny	j
y	y or dropped	dropped	h, g, or dropped
f	f		h, p, or b
m	m		b
n	n	n or l	l or g
p	p	p or b	b
w	v, m, or ng	w	b or g
ạr (ear)	ni	nyi	hi
mŭ (eye)	muk	mŭ	bak
yĭ (one)	yat	nyĭ	chit
chŭ (bamboo)	chuk	chŭ	tiek
kwang (light)		kwoⁿg	kng
mien (face)	min	miⁿ	bien
yü (in)	ü	i	họ
shan (hill)	san	saⁿ	soaⁿ
shin (spirit, body)	sạn, shạn	zạng, sạn	sin, sieng
shang (upper)	sheung	lang or zong	tieng
nan (south)	nam	naⁿ	lam

These attempts to compare the dialects of Chinese may serve to lead the way for an extensive comparison of them, which the author hopes some one in China may undertake and carry out more completely than he has done here.

APPENDIX VI.

On the weights, monies, measures, and times.

The Chinese weigh every thing that can be weighed,—money, wood, and liquids. Their chief circulating medium is Spanish dollars, which go by weight. The *Ferdinand* dollar is at a premium of 1—1½ per cent. The *Carolus* dollar at a premium of 7—8 per cent. Those bearing the stamp *G* are only received at a discount. Mexican and U. S. A. dollars are taken *at par* by foreigners.

The highest weight in money is a *tael* (*liàng*); then come the *mace* (*ts'iên*), the *candareen* (*fān*), and the *cash* (*li*). 3 taels = 4.16 dol., but the equivalents vary; about 720 taels make 1000 dollars.

tael.	mace.	cand.	cash.	oz. troy.	gr. troy.	sterg.	dollars.
1	10	100	1000	1.208	579.84	6s. 8d.	1.389—1.398
	1	10	100		57.984	8d.	.138— .139
		1	10		5.7984	.8d.	

The common coin—the cash—of China is composed of 6 parts of copper and 4 of lead. Bullion is rated by its fineness, by dividing it into 100 parts called "touches." Sycee is cast into ingots, by the Chinese called "shoes," and these are stamped with the mark of the office that issues them, and the date of their issue. They are of different sizes, from ½ a tael to 100 taels. Gold ingots of 10 taels = cir. 22—23.

In measures for dry and liquid goods, the *pecul* (*tan*), the *catty* (*kin*), and the *tael* (*liàng*) are used.

pecul.	catty.	tael.	lbs. av.	cwt.	lbs. troy.
1	100	1600	133⅓	1.0.21¼	162.0.8.1.
	1	16	1⅓		

1 ton = 16 pec. and 80 catt. 1 cwt. = 84 catt. 1 lb. av. = ¾ catt. In long measure the *covid* (*chè*), the *punt* (*tsān*) are used. The covid varies in the measurement of clothes, distances, and vessels; by the Mathematical Board in Peking it was 13.125 Eng. inches; in the Canton trade, 14.625 Eng. in.; by engineers of public works, 12.7 Eng. in.; and for distances, 12.1 Eng. in. nearly.

The *li* or Chinese mile = 316¼ fathoms = 1897½ Eng. feet: 192½ *li* = 1 deg. of lat. or long., according to the Chinese, but the Jesuits made 250 *li* = 1 deg., each *li* being = 1826 ft. or 1/10 of a French league.

APPENDIX VI.

In land measure 1200 covids = 1 acre or *meu*, which contains 6600 sq. feet.

The Chinese measure time by dividing the 24 hours of the day and night into twelve watches, and they begin to reckon from midnight. The twelve horary characters *tsz, cheu, yin, meu,* &c. (see Part I. p. 61) are employed for the purpose of indicating their watches. *Tze* being used for the two hours from 11 p. m. to 1 a. m.; *cheu* from 1—3.

The character *ching* 正 prefixed to any horary character makes it signify the even number between the two hours; e. g. *ching-tsz* would be 12 o'clock at midnight, and *kiau* 交 being prefixed would make it mean 11 p. m.

But foreigners speak generally of *yĭ-tién-chŭng* 'one stroke on the bell,' for 'one o'clock,' *ȧr-tién-chŭng* 'two o'clock,' and the Chinese understand these expressions. *Kĕ* 刻 means 'a quarter of an hour,' and *pwán* 半 *tién-chŭng* 'half an hour.'

PART II.

A CHINESE CHRESTOMATHY.

A SHORT INTRODUCTION
TO
CHINESE LITERATURE.

The literary works of the Chinese are very extensive, and relate to very many of the subjects on which the mind of man has been engaged at all periods of his history; the higher subjects, however, of mental science, logic and philology, have met with but little attention among them. The writers of China have drawn less from the works of foreigners than the writers of almost any nation; and this has arisen from the very nature of their position, cut off as they were at an early period from the great nations of the west of Asia, surrounded by wild tribes, who were unacquainted with letters, and proud of their superior cultivation, they rejected improvements of every kind from abroad. But if the mania for foreign notions and theories was unknown among them, the imitation of ancient models of their own became so morbid as to prevent the proper development of their mental strength and the improvement of the natural growth of their minds. The power of mental production consequently became limited to their own narrow sphere of experience; and although the rules of their ancient sages inculcated no such contracted maxims, their minds narrowed by continual imitation of old models (well enough suited to the periods in which they had their origin) began to look upon these models as simple embodiments of truth. Facts, however, compel the admission that great diversities of style in the prose, and of metre in the poetry of the Chinese have characterised different periods of their history. Their works have been remarkable rather for their extent than for the originality of thought or the acuteness of judgment displayed in them.

The Chinese themselves divide their literature under four general heads; viz. I. *King* 經, II. *Sz̄* 史, III. *Tsz̄* 子, IV. *Tsĭ* 集.

I. The works placed under the first head we may call *classic*. They come under the following divisions: *a)* All sacred writings and the commentaries on them; *b)* All ritualistic writings and music; *c)* All works of a philological nature, as dictionaries and tone-books.

II. The *historical* writings of all kinds come under the head of *Sz̄*, and also *narrative* and *descriptive* works, but not works on natural history.

III. Under the head *Tsz̄* come, *a)* The writings of the ten sages of antiquity; *b)* All religious and moral works of the Tauists or Buddhists; *c)* All scientific works, and those upon the fine arts and trades; *d)* All encyclopædic works.

IV. The character *Tsĭ* signifies 'collection,' and under this head are collected works of the imagination and poems, but not novels.

This classification is that given in the Catalogue of the Imperial Library of Peking, but for the benefit of the student who will wish to be directed in his reading, the following arrangement of the different Chinese styles of composition will be found useful.

The most ancient and most concise style is that called,

I. *Kŭ-wĕn* 古文 'ancient literature,' and this includes

    1. *Kīng-shū* 經書 'ancient classics, and works composed after their model;'

    2. *Kŭ-shĭ* 古詩 'ancient poetry, and modern poetry after that model.'

II. *Shí-wĕn* 時文 'modern literature,' and this includes

    1. *Wĕn-chāng* 文章 'fine writing' or 'elegant essays;'

    2. *Shī-fŭ* 詩賦 'odes and epics;'

    3. *Yü-kī* 諭契 'edicts and official papers;'

    4. *Shū-chă* 書札 'epistles and letters of every kind;'

    5. *Chuén-chí* 傳志 'stories and romances;'

    6. *Tsă-lŭ* 雜錄 'miscellanies, plays, &c.'

The spoken language, the *Kwān-hwá* 官話 'mandarin language,' is also divided into

    1. *Pĕ kwān-hwá* 北官話 or *Kīng-hwá* 京 | 'the language of Peking' or 'the northern mandarin;'

    2. *Nân kwān-hwá* 南官 | 'the southern mandarin,' which is also called the *Chíng-yīn* 正音 'correct sound;' and the 通行的 | *T'ŭng-hīng-tĭ hwá*, i. e. 'the language of universal circulation.'

The student will find in the following extracts passages to exemplify nearly all these different styles of composition, and in the study of them with the notes he will find much that differs, and very much to admire, in the rhythm that pervades each piece.

In the *Wŭ-kīng*, 'the five classics,' are contained the most ancient monuments of Chinese poetry, history, philosophy, and jurisprudence; and portions of these are probably among the most early records of history extant. Confucius, in the sixth century before Christ, collected them from different sources, and edited them without diminishing their correctness or originality. They usually stand in the following order :

1. The *Yi-king* 易經, or *Classic of Changes*, is a work on Cosmogony, based upon a theory of the combination and transmutation of certain figures formed by straight lines, sometimes entire and sometimes broken. Beginning with two figures, a broken straight line, and an unbroken one, the author, *Fŭ-hi* 伏羲, proceeded to form a number of combinations, until he made eight diagrams. They are thus given with their names:

1	2	3	4	5	6	7	
☰	☱	☲	☳	☴	☵	☶	☷
乾	兌	離	震	巽	坎	艮	坤
k'iên	*tüi*	*li*	*chin*	*sin*	*kàn*	*kĕn*	*kw'ăn*

These are commonly called the *pă-kwá*, and represent some of the primary objects of nature, as *heaven, earth, fire, water*, &c. From these eight figures, sixty-four were constructed; and so by a regular system of combination and ever varying mutation, representative diagrams or figures have been formed for all the objects of nature *. The Chinese cannot give a very definite and clear account of the subject of this book †.

2. The *Shū-king* 書│, of which pages 1 and 2 of the Chrestomathy afford a specimen, is the *Historical Classic*, being fragments of ancient history. It contains many excellent maxims on moral philosophy and political economy; as well as lessons of practical wisdom, based upon truth and humanity ‡.

3. The *Shī-king* 詩│, or *Classic of Odes*, is a collection of ancient hymns and odes or ballads. They were collected by Confucius, and commented on by various writers §.

4. The *Li-ki* 禮記, *Book of Ceremonies*, is a compilation of laws relating to the manners and customs of life in the most ancient times, from which the Chinese of the present day derive many of their rules of conduct.

5. The *Chūn-tsiŭ* 春秋, or *Spring and Autumn* Annals, is a work by Confucius himself. It contains the history of his native country, *Lŭ-kwô* 魯國.

---

* A Latin translation of this work, "ex lat. P. Regis interpretatione," was edited by Dr. Mohl, Stuttgard, in two vols. in 1832.

† V. *Entwurf einer Beschreibung der Chinesischen Litteratur, Schott:* read in the Academy of Sciences in Berlin, 1850, and published in the "Abhandlungen" of the Academy, p. 302.

‡ The following translations of this work have appeared. In French by Gaubil *Le Chou-king*. Paris, 1770. This was revised by De Guignes. It is said to be too free, and in many respects faulty. Another translation exists in Pauthier's *Livres sacrés de l'Orient*. Paris, 1841. And a good English translation by Dr. Medhurst with the native text interspersed. Shanghai, 1846. 8º.

§ There is a Latin translation of the *Shi-king*, "ex lat. P. Lacharme interpretatione," edited by Dr. Mohl. Stuttgard, 1830. And also a German translation into verse by F. Rückert. *Chi-king, Chinesischen Liederbuch*. Altona, 1833.

These are the five classics. The style in which they are written is broken and rude, unlike the compositions of later times, and this is internal evidence of their antiquity.

Next in estimation are the following:

1. The *Sź-shû* 四 書, or *Four Books*, a collection of writings, by various persons, on moral and political subjects. The names of the separate works comprised under this title are, 1. The *Tá-hiŏ* 大 學, or *the Study for the Adult,—the Great Study*, is a short work on political science by *Tsang-tsź* 曾 子 *. 2. The *Chūng-yûng* 中 庸, or *the Due Medium*, is a work on avoiding extremes in life by means of philosophy and virtue, like the doctrines of the great Greek philosopher of old,—Aristotle. This portion was written by *Tsź-sź* 子 思, a grandson of Confucius †. 3. The *Lȗn-yü* 論 語, or *Dialogues and Discourses* of *Kūng-fū-tsź* 孔 夫 子 (Confucius), written down by two of his disciples after the philosopher's death ‡. 4. *Shâng-mạng* 上 孟 and *Hiá-mạng* 下 |. The first and second portions of the works of the philosopher *Mạng* (Mencius), who lived B. C. 350. The subject of this work is of a moral and political nature, and in the form of dialogue and exhortation §. Passages from the *Four Books* are given in the Chrestomathy, pp. 3, 4, 5 ||.

All the above works are largely annotated and commented on by native writers, and by some of them with excellent style and ability. Among the chief commentators was *Chū-fū-tsź* 朱 夫 子, who lived in the thirteenth century. His writings are held in great estimation.

In the next rank comes the *Cheū-lî* 周 禮 or *Ceremonies of the Cheu Dynasty;* then the *Hiaú-kīng* 孝 經 or *Book of Filial Piety;* *Ts'ŭ-tsź* 楚 辭 a Collection of *Poems;* and the *Shān-haî-kīng* 山 海 經 or *Book of Poetical Fictions,* a sort of mythology, from which the poets of China draw some of their allusions.

---

* An English translation of the Tá-hiŏ was appended, with the native text, to Dr. Marshman's *Clavis Sinica.* Serampore, 1814. 4°. A Latin and French translation exists by Pauthier, with the native text, Paris, 1837; and an English translation by G. B. Hillier, Hongkong, 1850.

† The Chūng-yûng was translated into Latin and French, accompanied by the native text, by Abel-Rémusat, in the *Notices et Extraits:* (vol. X.) Paris, 1817. 4°.

‡ The Lȗn-yü was translated by Dr. Marshman into English, and published with the native text, under the title of, *Works of Confucius* at Serampore, 1809. 4°.

§ The writings of Mencius were translated literally into Latin by M. Stanislaus Julien, and published with the native text at Paris, in 3 vols. 1824.

|| The Sz-shū have been frequently translated;—into Latin by *Intorcetta;* Paris, 1687: and by *Noël* also into Latin; Prague, 1711;—into English by *Collie;* Malacca, 1828. 8°.;—into German by *Schott;* 2 vols. Halle, 1828;—into French by *Pauthier;* Paris, 1841.

In addition to these there are three ancient commentaries upon the *Chŭn-tsiŭ*, which belong to the style of the *Kŭ-wān;* and the works of *Sz̤-mă-tsiēn* 司馬遷, the celebrated historian (B. C. 100), and those of several other noted writers in a similar style.

Contemporary with Confucius was *Laù-tsz̤* 老子 or *Laù-kiūn* 老君, B. C. 604.* He was the founder of a school of philosophy, and took *taú* 道 'reason,' 'λόγος,' as the foundation of his system; he discoursed about *lĭ* 理, the 'principle of order' in the universe, and was the originator of the Tauist sect. He composed a work called *Taú-tĕ-kīng* 道德 | 'Book of Reason and Virtue,' which has been translated into French, under the title of, "Le livre de la voie et de la vertu," by Professor Julien. Paris, 1842. 8º. For an account of his miraculous birth, &c., see Morrison's Dictionary, part I. vol. I. p. 707.

There were ten eminent writers of antiquity, who are associated together by the title *Shĭ-tsz̤* 十子. *Laù-tsz̤* was the first of these. The second was 莊子 *Chwāng-tsz̤*, also a Tauist, and the most celebrated disciple of *Laù-tsz̤*. He flourished about B. C. 368, in the reign of the Emperor Hien-waug. He was the author of the work *Nān-hwā-kīng*, and two satirical pieces against the Confucianists. His originality and independence of character are shown in his works and in the following anecdote: A powerful Chinese prince wished him to take office in his government, and offered him rich gifts, but *Chwāng-tsz̤* replied: "I would rather be a solitary pig and wallow in my own sty, than be a decorated sacrifice and be led by the guiding strings of the great." According to the *Sz̤-kí* 史記 of *Sz̤-mă-tsiēn* there was nothing that he had not looked into, *wŭ sŏ pŭ kw'eí* 無所不窺, though his maxim seems to have been: "Our life has limits, but knowledge is without limits."

The third philosopher was *Siūn-tsz̤* 荀子, who belonged to the *Jú-kiā* 儒家, 'the Confucian school.' He lived about B C 230, and was counted worthy of having his name associated with that of *Măng-tsz̤* 孟子 for a long period. His style is perspicuous and his knowledge correct, but he differed from *Măng-tsz̤* (Mencius) in his ethics. *Măng-tsz̤* held that the natural disposition of man is towards *virtue;* *Siūn-tsz̤*, that it is towards *vice*. His writings were of a politico-moral nature.

The fourth philosopher was *Lĭ-tsz̤* 列子, a Tauist, who was contemporary with *Laù-kiūn* (B. C. 585). His style is lucid and sublime, but he

---

* The proper name of this philosopher was *Li-pĭ-jang* 李伯陽.

prefers the lofty to the true. *Chwāng-tsź* is said to have written out a complete copy of his works.

The fifth philosopher was *Kwăn-tsź* 管子, who belonged to the *Pīng-kiā* 兵家, 'the military school.' He flourished in the third century B. C. His works are on the subjects of war and government.

The sixth philosopher was *Hān-fī-tsź* 韓非子, called *Han-tsź*, who lived about B. C. 200. He belonged to the *Fă-kiā* 法家, 'the law school.' Jurisprudence was the subject which he chiefly considered. His works commence with the aphorism: *pŭ chĭ ǎr yên, pŭ chĭ; chĭ ǎr pŭ yên, pŭ chūng,* 不知而言不智,知而不言不忠, 'not to know and yet to speak is imprudent; to know and yet not to speak is unfaithful.'

The seventh philosopher was *Hwai-năn-tsź* 淮南子, who belonged to the *Tsă-kiā* 雜家, 'writers on various subjects.' He was the grandson of 高帝 *Kaŭ-tí* of the Han dynasty, B. C. 189. He wrote upon the origin of things.

The eighth philosopher was *Yăng-tsź* 楊子, a Confucianist, who lived in the reign of *Ching-tí* 成帝, B. C. 1. He is said to have spoken little, for he had an impediment in his speech, but he was a great thinker and reader. He did not write much, but his works have received the commendation of a great authority, for *Mă-twān-lĭn*, when comparing him with *Siŭn-tsź*, says: "Siŭn-kīng had great talents, but many failings; Yăng-hiŭng was a man of limited abilities, but made few mistakes." The names of his two principal works are; *Fă-yên* 法言 'on laws,' and *T'ai-hiuĕn-kīng* 太玄經, which is devoted to an explanation of the Yĭ-kīng.

The ninth philosopher was *Wǎn-chūng-tsź* 文中子, one of the best ancient writers of the Confucian school. His proper name appears to have been *Wăng-t'ŭng* 王通.

The tenth philosopher, *Hŏ-kw'ăn-tsź* 鶡冠子, was a Tauist. He obtained this name, the *Hŏ-capped philosopher*, from the fact of his wandering about the mountains with the feathers of this bird in his cap or in his hair. His writings were first brought to light during the T'ang dynasty.

The works of these ten scholars, who are commonly called the *Shĭ-tsź*, are collected in a work called *Shĭ tsź ts'ŭng-mŭ* 十子總目 'General Index of the Ten Philosophers.' Cf. Dr. Morrison's Dictionary, part I. vol. I. pp. 707, 708.

SOME OF THE CHIEF WORKS IN CHINESE LITERATURE. 9

In addition to these general remarks on the higher class of Chinese literature we may content ourselves with a list of some of the principal works in the several departments which are likely to be more especially interesting to Europeans. The Chinese language is very rich in Buddhistic literature, as well as in works on jurisprudence, topography, history, and statistics. It possesses large encyclopædias and anthologies; researches in natural history, the healing art, and the fine arts; treatises on language and the meanings of words; on mathematics and the various applications of numbers, with works on the art of war. Poetry and the drama occupy a large place too, as do also works of fiction in the various grades of the romance and novel style. The industrial arts and trades, and the processes of manufacture extant among the Chinese are explained in detail in separate works *.

I. *Ethics, politics, and mental science* †.

1. 三字經 *Sān-tsź-kīng*, 'The three-character classic,' by Wang Pi-heu, a Confucianist of the Sung dynasty (13th cent.). Annotated by Wang Tsin-shing: "The language is simple, the principles important, the style perspicuous, the reasoning clear."

2. 千字文 *Ts'iēn-tsź-wǎn*, 'The book of 1000 characters,' by Cheu Hing-tsz, A.D. 550. This is a common school-book. The 1000 characters were collected by Wang he-che, by command of an emperor of the Liang dynasty. The emperor gave them to Cheu Hing-tsz, and asked him to form them into an ode. He did so in a single night, and his hair turned gray in consequence. Various translations of this work exist in European languages; also in Japanese, Manchu, and Corean.

3. 幼學詩 *Yiū-hiŏ-shī*, 'Odes for the young.' A translation of this by Dr. Bridgman appeared in the Chinese Repository for Oct. 1835.

4. 小學 *Siaù-hiŏ*, 'The learning for children,' was composed by 朱子 *Chū-tsź*, who is held in estimation second only to Confucius himself. The opening sentence of the work shows its subject and tendency: "In ancient times the Siaù-hiŏ taught children every thing which concerned their daily life and conduct to parents, elders, superiors, teachers, and friends; in order to a due consideration of the fundamental laws which govern the person, the family, the state, and the universe."

5. 家寶全集 *Kiā-paù-ts'uên-tsí*, 'A complete collection of family jewels.' Miscellaneous moralities, instructions, and advice, in 32 vols., by

---

* Large collections of Chinese books are deposited in the Libraries of the British Museum, the Royal Asiatic Society, the University College, London, the Bodleian Library, Oxford, the East India House, and King's College, London. The magnitude of these collections is in the order here given; from the British Museum, which contains upwards of 30,000 vols., to King's College, which possesses about 1200 vols. Almost all good works in ordinary Chinese literature will be found in one or another of these institutions.

† To these may be added several works already mentioned among the classics.

PART II.   C

T'iĕn-kî-shî 天基石, published in the time of K'ang-hi. An extract from this work was given by Thom in his Chinese Speaker, with a translation.

6. 聖諭廣訓 *Shîng-yû kwāng-hiūn*, 'Amplification of the sacred edict.' Sixteen maxims by the emperor K'ang-hi, amplified by his son, the emperor Yûng-ching, and paraphrased by a mandarin. The Rev. Dr. Milne made a translation of this work.

7. 家庭講話 *Kiā-t'îng-kiàng-hwâ*, 'Discourses for the family hall.' These are in good mandarin style, and are very suitable for practice in reading. (King's Coll.) *

8. 太上感應編 *T'ai-shàng kàn-ying-piĕn* †, 'The book of rewards and punishments.' This is a very celebrated Tauist tract. *T'ai-shàng*, 'the sublime,' is an epithet of *Laù-kiūn;* see p. 7. of this Introduction. The work consists of a number of sayings on the duties of man, with a list of the rewards and the punishments connected therewith.

9. 金剛經 *Kin-kāng-kīng*, 'The diamond classic.' A Buddhist work in 1 vol.

10. 敬信錄 *Kîng-sin-lŭ*, 'The book of the revered faith.' A collection of sayings and exhortations of the chiefs of the Tauist and Buddhist religions. The praises of *Kwān-yīn* 觀音, the merciful goddess, are given in rhyme to be sung by the faithful. Its precepts are said to act on the human mind like a clock at midnight, they awaken the devout soul, and its doctrines enlighten the darkened eye of the mind.

11. 明心寶| *Mîng-sīn-paù-kiĕn*, 'The precious mirror for enlightening the heart.' This work consists of elegant extracts from the moral writings of the Chinese. A translation appeared in Spanish by P. Navarette; Madrid, 1676. A notice of the work may be seen in the Chinese Repository.

12. 華嚴經 *Hwâ-yên-kīng*. A noted Buddhist work on the holy books or *sutras*. A copy is preserved in St. Petersburg in 81 books, which is said to have been printed in 1419. The translator was a monk from Turkistan, according to Dr. Schott: see " Entwurf, &c.," p. 333.

13. 性理大全 *Sîng-lî tá-ts'uên*, 'A complete exposition of the principles of nature.' A metaphysical work, in 20 vols. The subject of it is the Chinese philosophy respecting the dual powers, which enters into all works of this nature.

---

* When the name of a Library is noted, it is not to be inferred that the work is to be found in that collection alone.

† A translation of this work was made by Prof. Julien, and published under the title of, "Le livre des Récompenses et des Peines" par Julien, 1841.

II. *Mathematics and astronomy.*

14. 幾何原本 *Kĭ-hŏ yuên-pǎn,* 'The first principles of quantity,' is a translation of Euclid's *Elements of Geometry,* by Paul Scu, a high mandarin, and P. Ricci, the Jesuit missionary, in 4 or 6 vols. The original work is very scarce, but copies exist in manuscript, and a new edition has recently been printed by the Protestant missionaries at Shanghai. (Bodleian.) (King's Coll.)

15. 曆象考成 *Liĕ-siăng k'aù-ch'ing,* 'Mathematical tables for astronomical purposes.' (Bodleian.)

16. 數理精縕 *Sú-lĭ tsīng-yŭn.* A treatise on mathematics, containing the science of Europe in the 18th century. (Bodleian.)

17. 律歷淵源 *Lŭ-lĭ yuên-yuên,* 'The original sources of music and number,' in 100 vols. This is a work by the first Jesuits who resided in China. In it are explained the theory of music and the European system of notation; mathematics, including trigonometry, and the method of calculating eclipses, with all the necessary tables of logarithms, &c. A list of ninety-two stars is given in vol. 31, with their right ascension and declination, which are measured upon the equator. (Bodleian.)

III. *Language and the meanings of words.*

18. 說文 *Shwŏ-wǎn.* A dictionary of the ancient characters, arranged under 540 elementary characters, which was published during the *Hán* 漢 dynasty, B.C. 150. The author's name was *Hŭ-shīn* 許慎, 'official government.' (Brit. Mus.)

19. 玉篇 *Yŭ-piēn.* A dictionary of the characters, arranged according to 542 radicals, in 30 books, by Ku ye-wang. It was published in the Liang dynasty, A.D. 530. It is the basis of the Chinese-Japanese Dictionary used in Japan. The pronunciation of characters is according to the *făn-tsĭ* system.

20. 五車韻瑞 *Wŭ-kū yŭn ȯuí,* 'The tonic dictionary, called the *Wŭ-kū,*' in 32 vols., by Chin Siĕn-săng. This is one of the best dictionaries on the "tones" which exist in Chinese. Dr. Morrison made it the basis of his Syllabic Dictionary, and gives some particulars respecting it in the preface to Part II. of his dictionary, q. v.

21. 正字通 *Chíng-tsź-t'ŭng,* 'Explanation of the correct characters.' A dictionary according to the radicals. (King's Coll.)

22. 佩文韻府 *Peí-wǎn-yŭn-fù,* 'Thesaurus of literary phrases,' compiled by order of the emperor K'ăng-hī. Seventy-six of the *literati* were engaged in preparing it, and it took them seven years to complete it. It was published in 1711, in 131 vols. This Thesaurus is perhaps the

most extensive collection which exists of the words and phrases of any language. M. Callery commenced working this mine in 1842, and published the first part of an encyclopædia of the Chinese language in 1846. The work was to consist of about ten large volumes, and it was expected that sixteen years would be occupied in the execution of his project, which he was unfortunately obliged to relinquish. (Brit. Mus.)

23. 康熙字典. *K'āng-hī-tsź-tiĕn*, 'The dictionary of K'āng-hī,' the first emperor of the present dynasty. It is generally in 32 vols. The meanings are very good. The work is universally used in China, and constitutes the great national work of reference for the language. Dr. Morrison commenced his dictionary by translating K'ang-hi's lexicon.

24. 清文鑑 *Ts'ing-wăn-kiĕn*, 'Mirror of the Manchu-Tartar language,' in 26 vols. (Several works of this kind are in the Brit. Mus.)

25. 回教俗語 *Hwŭi-kiaú-sŭ-yŭ*, 'Mahommedan Proverbs (in Arabic and Chinese).'

26. 江湖尺牘分韻 *Kiāng-hŭ chĭ-tŭ făn-yŭn*, 'The rivers and lakes, papers and rhymes*.' This is the title of a popular work on letter writing &c. for travellers; and it is a sort of dictionary of phrases proper to be used in epistolary correspondence. It is in 6 vols. 12º.

27. 初集啟蒙 *Ch'ō-tsĭ kĭ-mŭng*, 'Explanations for beginners,' in 20 vols. It contains definitions of the terms employed by the student of *Wăn-chāng* ('elegant essays').

IV. *Jurisprudence.*

28. 大清律例 *Tá-ts'īng lŭ-lĭ*, 'The laws of the Tá-ts'īng dynasty,' i. e. the penal code of the present or Tartar dynasty of China, in 40 vols. A translation of this work was made by Sir George T. Staunton, Bart., F. R. S. 4º. London, 1810.

29. 科場條例 *Kō-chăng-t'iaŭ-lĭ*, 'The laws and regulations of the Examination Hall,' in 18 vols. It is published every ten years, and its contents will supply the best phrases which are employed with reference to the *literati*.

30. 大清會典 *Tá-ts'īng hwŭi-tiĕn*, 'Official details relating to the civil code and the statistics of the Tá-ts'īng dynasty,' in 260 vols. An interesting account of this work is given in Sir John Davis' work on the Chinese. See Knight's edition of 1836, vol. II. pp. 180, 181.

V. *Medicine and materia medica.*

31. 本草綱目 *Păn-tsaŭ kăng-mŭ*, 'General outline of natural his-

---

* The term 'rivers and lakes' means the 'provinces' of Kiang-si, Kiang-nan, Hu-pĭ, and Hu-nan, which are noted for beautiful scenery and commerce.

tory' with a view to medical practice. The author of this work was Lĭ-shĭ-chĭn 李時珍. It was published under the supervision of his son, and for the benefit of his family, in 1596. It contains very concise accounts of various animals, plants, and minerals; in a word, the materia medica derived from the animal, vegetable, and mineral kingdoms.

There are many other works on medicine, but their contents are uninteresting to Europeans, because they are wanting in science.

VI. History and statistics.

The affairs of each dynasty have been recorded by the imperial historiographers, and these state papers are the sources whence the various histories of China have been derived.

32. 通典 T'ŭng-tièn, 'A complete directory to history and politics,' in 200 chapters, by Tô-yiŭ 杜佑 of the T'âng 唐 dynasty. It was this work that Ma Twan-lin proposed to complete in his Wăn-hiĕn-t'ŭng-kiaŭ, which may be looked upon as a continuation of the T'ŭng-tièn.

33. 通鑑目 T'ŭng-kién-kăng-mŭ, 'The comprehensive mirror with a complete index,' in 120 vols. The history of China, edited by Chu-hi, the philosopher and annotator of the Canonical Books, who lived about the middle of the 13th century. This work is not so much an independent production as a convenient form of the T'ung-kién, which appeared above a century before, by the renowned Sz-ma-kwang. The emperor Ying-tsŭng 英宗 (A.D. 1064-67) had commanded the royal historiographer Sz-ma-kwang to compose a succinct history of China with correct chronology, making use of the historical works extant, and especially the annals. Sz-ma-kwang finished his work in 1084, and laid it at the feet of Ying-tsung's successor, Shĭn-tsŭng 神宗, who gave it the title of T'ung-kien, 'comprehensive mirror' (of events). It begins with the earliest historical period, and comes down to the beginning of the 2nd Sung dynasty, including a period of 1362 years. Facts only are related, the reader is left to form his own judgment upon them. Impressed with the worth of the T'ung-kien, and wishing to increase its usefulness, Chu-hi prefaced the accounts given in detail with a summary, but without altering the sense. These summaries, which are printed in large characters, are followed by the detailed account and a commentary; thus the work is, as it were, enclosed in a network, and on this account it obtains the name of Kang-mŭ (v. 31).

34. 二十一史 Ar-shĭ-yĭ-shĭ, 'The twenty-one historians.' A complete history of China, in 282 vols., from the highest antiquity down to the end of the Yuên 元 dynasty. This is the work of twenty-one imperial historiographers, whose duty it was to note down the events of each reign as they occurred, preparatory to publication in the succeeding reign.

35. 史記 *Shĭ-kì*, 'Records of history,' in 130 chapters, by Sz-ma-tsien, who flourished B. C. 104. This book contains the history of about 3000 years. It begins with *Hwâng-tí* 黄帝, 'The yellow emperor,' and ends in the year B. C. 122, in the Han dynasty.

36. 古文析義 *Kŭ-wăn sĭ-ì*, 'The meanings of ancient literature discriminated,' in 16 vols. 8º. This work consists of historical fragments in an elegant and much admired style, with explanatory notes.

37. 綱 | 會纂 *Kāng-kiên-hwŭi-tswăn*, 'Mirror of history,' by *Fung-cheu siên-sāng* 鳳洲 (surnamed *Wâng*), in 34 vols. (v. 2994).

38. | | 易知 *Kāng-kiên ì-chī*, 'History made easy,' is an abridgment of the *T'ûng-kiên-kāng-mŭ* (33). It was the work of three scholars of the present dynasty, and was finished in 1711, in 36 vols.

39. 歷代 | 史 *Lĭ-tai kiên-shĭ*, 'Mirror of history through successive ages.'

40. 東花錄 *Tūng-hwā-lŭ*, 'Chronicles of the flower of the east.' The official history of the Imperial house at present reigning in China. The last edition was published in 1820, in 16 vols.

VII. *Biographical notices.*

41. 歷代名臣奏議 *Lĭ-tai ming-chīn tseŭ-ì*, 'Memorials of the celebrated statesmen of successive dynasties,' in 350 chapters.

42. 古列女傳 *Kŭ lĭ-nŭ chuén*, 'An account of distinguished women of ancient times,' in 7 chapters, by Liu-hiang of the Han dynasty.

43. 唐才子傳 *T'âng tsaî-tsz̀ ch'uén*, 'An account of the men of genius of the T'ang dynasty,' by Sin Wan-fang, in 8 vols. M. Prof. Bazin says of this author, that he has a very good style of composition; that he adds to each biographical notice proper observations and criticisms; and that when he examines the qualities and the faults of the poets, he is always in the right *.

44. 學統 *Hiŏ-t'ŭng*, 'A general view of learning,' in 12 vols. It contains memoirs of the leading members of the sect of Confucius and extracts from their works, with a view to combating the errors of the Tauists and Buddhists.

45. 百家姓 †*Pĕ-kiā-sìng*, 'All the family names.' 1068 characters are

---

* V. *Siècle des Youên*, p. 58.

† Although the word *pĕ*, '100,' is used, it stands for 'all,' just as *pĕ-kwān* means 'all the officials.' This work contains 454 surnames.

contained in it, of which 510 are different. This work contains the ancient surnames of the Chinese, many of which are still in use. In some editions the origin of these names is given in notes. It is a school-book, and uninteresting to foreigners.

VIII. *Geography, topography, and statistics.*

46. 大清一統志 *Tá-ts'ing yĭ-t'úng-chĭ,* 'A complete account of the Tá-tsīng (the present) empire.' A geographical work of great importance and value. It consists of 500 chapters in 240 vols. It contains various matters connected with topography and statistics. Each province has its own descriptive work of this kind. (Brit. Mus.)

47. 海國圖誌 *Haĭ-kwŏ t'ú-chĭ,* 'Geography of the world,' in 24 vols., by the late Commissioner Lin, who caused the "Opium War" by burning all that drug then in port at Canton.

48. 瀛寰志畧 *Yĭng-hwān chĭ-liŏ,* 'A compendious description of the world,' in 6 vols. imp. 8º., by the Lieutenant-Governor of the province of Fŭ-kien. It contains very good maps of the various countries of the world, and the descriptions are tolerably correct. His Excellency was assisted by a European in making the compilation. (King's Coll.)

49. 廣輿圖記 *Kwàng-yú-t'ú-kì,* 'Geographical descriptions with maps,' by *Lŭ-yĭng-yáng* 陸應陽, in 24 *kiuen* or books. It was composed during the 明 *Míng* dynasty, when China was divided into 15 provinces, not into 18 as at present. The 25th book contains some account of the 'outside barbarians,' *waì-ĭ* 外夷, and these include Japan, Korea, Liu-kiu, Si-fan or Tangutia, Mongolia, Tonquin, Cochin-China, and Siam.

50. 佛國記 *Fŭ-kwŏ kì,* 'An account of Buddhist countries,' by 法顯 *Fă-hièn,* a Buddhist of the earlier Sung dynasty (A.D. 422). He set out from *Ch'áng-ān* 長安 in the year 405, during the *Tsìn* 晉 dynasty, and traversed thirty countries on his way to India : (v. Imperial Catalogue, large copy, kiuen 71. p. 4.)

IX. *Mythology.*

51. 神仙鑑 *Shĭn-siēn-kièn,* 'Mirror of the divine immortals.' It contains the myths relating to the Tauist deities and deified saints. The story of Shakyamuni is told in the 5th chapter, and the work contains other matter which is interesting on account of the bold independence with which the stories are related.

16   SOME OF THE CHIEF WORKS IN CHINESE LITERATURE.

X. *Poetry.*

52. 全唐詩 *Ts'uên T'áng shī,* 'The poetry of the T'ang dynasty,' in 900 chapters. (Brit. Mus.)

53. 李太白集 *Lĭ T'ai-pĭ tsĭ,* 'Lĭ-t'ai-pĭ's collection of poetry,' by Lĭ-t'ai-pĭ of the T'ang dynasty *.

54. 東坡全集 *Tŭng-pŏ ts'uên-tsĭ,* 'A complete collection of Tung-po's odes,' in 15 chapters, by Su-shĭ of the Sung dynasty *.

XI. *Painting, engraving, &c.*

55. 博古圖錄 *Pŏ-kù-t'ŭ-lŭ,* 'Investigation of antiques with plates,' in 16 vols. This work affords valuable assistance in deciphering the inscriptions upon metal and earthenware vases, some of which date from very high antiquity. The Journal of the Royal Asiatic Society contains specimens and translations taken from this work.

XII. *The drama.*

56. 元人百種 *Yuên-jīn pĕ-chúng,* 'The hundred plays of the Yuen dynasty.' A celebrated collection of dramas. The style is antiquated colloquial, but clear. Several of these have been translated by Prof. Bazin, Prof. Julien, and Sir John Davis. See *Théâtre Chinois* by Prof. Bazin.

57. 綴白裘 *Chui-pĭ-k'iŭ,* 'A collection of dramas,' in 43 vols. (Brit. Mus. and R. A. S.) (For *k'iŭ,* v. sheet, 1263.)

XIII. *Works of fiction.*

The following names of novels are worth inserting. It is by reading such works that the student will form a more lively conception of the genius of the Chinese people, their customs, manners, and principles of action. The romances are classified by the Chinese according to the quality of the composition and the nature of the story. They distinguish especially between *siaù-shwŏ* 小說, lit. 'small talk,' = *novels* of the lower order, pure fictions; and *hiēn-shū* 閒書, lit. 'leisure book,' = *romances* founded on stories from real life and history. These they classify under the ten grades of talent (*tsai* 才) exhibited in their composition. The first or *T'i-yĭ-tsai shū* is the

58. 三國志 *Sān-kwŏ-chĭ,* 'History of the three kingdoms,' a work in 20 small volumes. The style, which is terse, is very much admired for its classic elegance. The story is founded upon the history of the three

---

* *Lĭ T'ai-pĭ* and *Sū Tūng-pō* are the two great and popular poets of China. Their surnames are *Lĭ* and *Sū ; T'ai-pĭ* and *Tūng-pō* are their names.

kingdoms and the civil wars in China, which lasted nearly a century, from A. D. 168—265. The author's name was Lo Kwan-chung, who founded it upon a real history by Chin-sheu of the Tsin dynasty. See pp. 17—20, of the native text, for a specimen of this work. A translation of a portion of it has been made into French by M. Theod. Pavie, from the Tartar version.

59. 水 滸 傳 *Shwŭi-hŭ chuén*, 'History of the shores' or 'History of the robbers,' by Shi Nai-gan, in 20 vols. 12º. This appeared originally in the time of the Mongol emperors, and was reprinted in 1650. It is a romance of the comic kind, and a good specimen of the style of language used two or three centuries ago; it is therefore somewhat antiquated, and the style is very prolix, a proof probably of its being in the colloquial idiom. A specimen is to be found in the native text of the Chrestomathy, pp. 13—16.

60. 好 逑 傳 *Haú-k'iú chuén*, 'The story of the fortunate union,' in 4 vols. 12º. The style and contents of this work are admirable. A translation of it was published in England, edited by Bishop Percy in 1761, under the title of "The Pleasing History." But in the elegant translation of it by Sir John F. Davis in 1829, the English reader may find a really pleasing and instructive story, and on the accuracy of the translation he may rely: pp. 8—12, of the native text, afford a specimen of its style, which abounds in good colloquial expressions, though some of them are perhaps antiquated.

61. 紅 樓 夢 *Húng-leŭ múng*, 'Dreams of the red chamber,' in 20 vols. 12º. This is a popular work in the Peking dialect. A portion of it was published in Thom's Chinese Speaker in 1846.

62. 玉 嬌 梨 *Yŭ-kiaŭ-li*, 'The two cousins,' in 4 vols. 12º. This was translated by M. Abel-Rémusat in 1826. Like the *Haú-k'iú chuén*, it is very good reading for the beginner and the general student of Chinese.

63. 列 國 志 *Lĭ-kwŏ-chĭ*. A history of the kingdoms into which China was divided in the *Cheŭ* 周 dynasty, worked up into the form of a romance. It begins in the year B. C. 1148, under the last emperor of the *Shǎng* 商 dynasty, and ends B. C. 258, about the beginning of the *Ts'in* 秦 dynasty. It consists of 8 books. (B. M., R. A. S., Bod.)

XIV. *Agriculture and weaving.*

64. 農 政 全 書 *Núng-chíng ts'uén-shŭ*, 'A complete work on agriculture,' in 60 chapters, by Shü Kwang-hí of the *Míng* 明 dynasty. (Brit. Mus.)

65. 耕織圖詩 Kǎng-chī t'ǎ-shī, 'Plates and odes on agriculture and weaving,' by Leu-chau of the Sūng 宋 dynasty.

XV. Encyclopædias and compilations.

66. 三才圖會 Sān-tsaí tú hwüi, 'Plates and explanations on the three powers'(i.e. heaven, earth, and man), in 60 vols. An encyclopædia illustrated with woodcuts. It was composed under the Ming 明 dynasty, after the arrival of Europeans in China. The author's name was Wâng-kī 王圻. He finished the work in 1607. (Brit. Mus.)

67. 文獻通考 Wǎn-hiên t'úng-k'aù, 'Thorough examination into antiquity,' by Mǎ Twân-lîn 馬端臨, who lived A.D. 1275. It consists of 348 chapters; about 110 vols.; and includes articles upon ancient government and tenures, ancient literature and writing, and many subjects not even noticed in other works. A large amount of discrimination is displayed in the book, and it will well repay the patient student's toil*. (Brit. Mus.)

68. 淵鑑類函 Yuên-kiên-lŭi-hán, in 139 vols., compiled by order of the emperor K'ang-hi. This is an encyclopædia, and contains a very full account of subjects which come within the sphere of Chinese experience. It would afford a very large number of phrases for a good dictionary of the Chinese language. (E. I. Comp.)

69. 潛確類書 Ts'iên-kiŏ-lŭi-shū. This is an encyclopædia, like the preceding. It contains a full account of various matters connected with the antiquities of China. (E. I. Comp.)

70. 永樂大典 Yúng-lŏ tá-tiên, 'The great classic of Yûng-lŏ,' the 3rd emperor of the Ming dynasty, whose reign commenced A.D. 1403. He was the reviver of literature. It consists of 22,877 chapters, and contains many entire works, the original editions of which are lost.

71. 商賈便覽 Shāng-kŭ-piên-lǎn, 'A convenient index for merchants,' in 6 vols. This small work is calculated to prove of use to the merchant and the traveller.

72. 四庫全書總目 Sz̆-kú ts'uên-shū tsúng-mŭ, 'A general catalogue of all the books in the four departments,' published by imperial authority, in 112 vols. 12°. There is an abridgment of this in 8 vols., which was published in 1774. (Both in Brit. Mus.)

---

* M. Rémusat calls this work, in the Appendix to his Grammaire, "Le plus beau monument de la littérature chinoise, vaste collection de mémoires sur toutes sortes de sujets, trésor d'érudition et de critique, où tout ce que l'antiquité chinoise nous a laissé de matériaux sur les religions, la législation, l'économie morale et politique, le commerce, &c. &c. &c., vaut à lui seul toute une bibliothèque."

The above list will guide the student in his purchase of books and in his study of Chinese literature. It remains for us to notice the different styles of composition which will be met with, and to say a few words on the metres of Chinese verse.

The style of the *kù-wǎn* requires a separate study; there is a massive grandeur about it, which is wanting in the lower orders of prose composition. The term itself,—'ancient literature,'—is peculiarly appropriate, for the character of this style bears the stamp of antiquity.

The modern style of elegant essay writing,—*wǎn-chǎng*,—by expertness in which the government officials attain their position and their literary rank, may be characterised as the antithesis of the *kù-wǎn;* the latter being terse and expressive, pregnant in meaning and swelling with the thought, while the former is diffuse and expansive, rhythmical and smooth, but barren of fresh ideas, and elaborate only in the mode of expression. The *kù-wǎn* labours to exhibit the idea succinctly in a few words; the *wǎn-chǎng* repeats the idea, and shows it under many forms of expression; the former is the sterling gold, the latter is the same changed into the cumbrous equivalents of copper and brass; and the genuine pearl is often hidden among the spurious imitations which accompany it. Specimens of the *wǎn-chǎng*, as well as of the other styles, are given in Gonçalves' *Arte China*. Of the *kù-wǎn*, the extracts given in the Chrestomathy, from the *Shū-kīng* and the *Sź-shū*, will afford specimens.

The style of ordinary books on history, topography, &c., is a medium between the *kù-wǎn* and the *wǎn-chǎng*. Less desire for elegant composition prevails in this style; and it approaches what has been called the *business* style, which is the idiom of the government papers, edicts, and official documents. There is a simplicity, but at the same time a stiffness and precision about it. The Letter of the Commissioner Lin to the Queen of England and several other papers will be found in the text of the Chrestomathy to exemplify this style.

The literary composition in novels varies very much; some novels, such as the *Sān-kwŏ chí*, are classical. The style of this work, however, is less terse than the *kù-wǎn*, and dispenses in a great measure with the particles employed in that style, while it approaches the *kù-wǎn* in vigour of expression, although the subjects treated of are very different. The romance style thus varies from the high classical novel, down to the common story expressed in every day colloquial. The extracts from the *Sān-kwŏ chí*, the *Haǔ-k'iǔ chuén*, and the *Shwuǐ-hù chuén* will exemplify these remarks. But the language of conversation will form the first object of attention, for it is by this that the student will communicate with his learned *siēn-sāng*. This style it is which it has been our object to elucidate. The pages of mandarin dialogues and phrases display a great number of specimens of the mandarin or *kwān-hwá*, in which, with all its variations, (and it has many distinct phases,) great simplicity of style and construction will be found to prevail.

The style and metre of modern verse among the Chinese differ materially

CHINESE POETRY.

from those of ancient poetry. The common metre of the *Shī-kīng*, 'Book of Odes,' is *four* syllables, and the style is cognate with that of the *kù-wăn*. Chinese verse consists sometimes of *four*, sometimes of *five*, and sometimes of *seven* or *eight* syllables; they are regulated by the *tones*, which, when in this connection, are divided into *even* and *deflected*. If we suppose *a* to represent the *even* tone, *b* the *deflected* tone, and *c* the one or the other (common), the verse of four lines and seven or eight syllables would run thus:

c-a-c-b-b-a-a   c-b-c-a-b-b-a
c-b-c-a-a-b-b   c-a-c-b-a-a-b
c-b-c-a-b-b-a   c-a-c-b-b-a-a
c-a-c-b-b-a-a.   c-b-c-a-b-b-a.

"There are six different sorts of poetry: 1st, *Fūng* 風, which contains the principles of ancient sages for the promotion of social order. 2nd, *Fŭ* 賦, which contains a plain statement of virtues and vices. 3rd, *Pī* 比, which satirizes by allusions, when the poet is afraid to speak plainly. 4th, *Hĭng* 興, figurative allusion to encourage those who dislike flattery. 5th, *Yă* 雅, which contains correct rules and sentiments for posterity. 6th, *Sŭng* 頌, which contains direct praise of virtuous deeds *."

On the subject of the various styles of prose and metrical compositions, the student may refer to Mr. Consul Meadows' "Desultory Notes on China;" Allen, London, 1847; and "The Poetry of the Chinese" by Sir John Davis, Bart., &c. &c., which appeared in the Transactions of the Royal Asiatic Society.

The passages printed in native character may now be read by the help of the dictionary, notes, and translations.

The sounds of the characters and all the other aids have been given separate from the text, because we think that, while all needful help should be given, the *textus nudus* should be distinct, to enable the student to test his acquirements; and, as a College text-book, it is necessary that the text, without notes, should be read in class.

---

* See Dr. Morrison's Dict., Part III. p. 324.

21

The following is a list of the passages in native character in the Chrestomathy, which are also given in Roman type, with translations and notes.

Index to the native text.

1. Extract from the *Shū-kīng* (1) and (2) . . . Pages 1 and 2
2. Epitaph of *K'í-tsź* 2
3. Extract from the *Sź-shū* (1), (2), and (3) . . . . 3—5
4. Extract from the *Shīng-yü* (1) and (2) . . . . 6 and 7
5. Extract from the *Haú-k'iú chuén* (1), (2), (3), (4), and (5) . 8—12
6. Extract from the *Shwuì-hù chuén* (1), (2), (3), and (4) . 13—16
7. Extract from the *Sān-kwŏ chí* (1), (2), (3), and (4) . . 17—20
8. Selections from Æsop's Fables, translated (1) and (2) . . 21 and 22
9. Official Papers (Lin's Letter to Queen Victoria) . . 23 and 24
10. Official Papers (a Notice and a Petition) 25
11. Official Papers (Supplementary Treaty, 1844) . . . 26
12. Dialogues and Phrases in Mandarin (1), (2), (3), and (4) . 27—30
13. Extract from the *Chíng-yīn tsuí-yaú* 31
14. Epistolary Style 32
15. Poetical Extracts (Ancient and Modern) 33
16. Proverbs 34
17. Six pages lithographed come under the above heads thus:—
    pp. 9 and 10 under 13; pp. 11, 12, and 13 under 7; p. 14 under 8.

Note—The translations of the passages are in some parts free, because it was impossible to make them literal; in other parts the English may have suffered from a literal rendering. In every case the wants of the young students have been kept in view; and the author hopes that, with the aid here given and the assistance which may be derived from the dictionary, all the passages in Chinese text will be rendered clear to his intelligence.

1. Extract from the *Shū-kīng* (1), v. native text, page 1.

a. 2. *Shū-kīng. Yü-shü. Yí Tsí. Tí yŭ: "Laí Yü! jù yĭ ch'āng yên."*
a. 19. *Yü paí, yŭ: "Tū Tí! yü hŏ yên? yü sź jĭ tsź-tsź." Kaü-yaü yŭ:*
b. 5. *"Hŭ! jü-hŏ?" Yü yŭ: "Hūng-shwüĭ t'aü t'iēn haú-haú, hwaí-shān*
b. 18. *siāng-līng, hiá-mín hwān-tién, yü shīng sź-tsaí, suí-shān kàn-mŭ; kí*
c. 3. *Yí tseú shū siēn shĭ, yü kiŭ kiù-ch'uēn, k'ŭ sź-haí, siún k'iuèn kwèi k'ü*
c. 19. *ch'uēn; kí Tsí pŏ tseú shū kiēn-shí siēn shĭ, maú ts'iēn yiù wú, hwā*
d. 4. *kŭ; chīng mín naì lĭ, wán pâng tsŏ í." Kaü-yaü yŭ: "Yŭ! sź jù*
d. 19. *ch'āng yên." Yü yŭ: "Tū Tí! shin naì tsaí weí." Tí yŭ: "Yŭ!" Yü*
e. 3. *yü: "Gān jù chĭ, weí kí weí kāng, k'í pĭ chĭ; weí túng peī yíng í chí,*
e. 20. *ì chaú sheú Sháng-tí, t'iēn k'í shîn míng yúng hiù." Tí yŭ: "Hŭ!*
f. 4. *Chīn-tsaí! Lín-tsaí! Lín-tsaí! Chīn-tsaí!" Yü yŭ: "Yŭ!" Tí yŭ:*
f. 17. *"Chīn tsŏ chín kù-kwāng ạr-mŭ: yü yü tsŏ-yiú yiù mín, jù yĭ; yü*
g. 3. *yü siuēn-lĭ sź-fāng, jù weí; yü yü kwān kù-jín chī siáng, jĭ, yŭ, sīng,*
g. 20. *shîn, shān, lúng, hwá, ch'úng tsŏ hwüĭ tsūng-í, tsaù-hŏ fạn-mí fù-fŭ*

The Shu-king is the most ancient record possessed by the Chinese, and is consequently very fragmentary. It is said to have consisted originally of 100 §§., forty-two of which are lost; and some of those which remain are considered to be spurious. All the copies which could be found were burnt by the Emperor Chí of the Tsin dynasty (B. C. 220), because this work kept alive the desire to return to the ancient *régime*. But on the revival of literature under Wăn-tí of the Hàn dynasty (B. C. 178), the text was recovered from an old blind man who could repeat it from memory and understood its meaning. This imperfect restoration was afterwards improved on Kung-wang finding in the ruins of the house of K'ung-tsz (Confucius) a copy of the original, written in the ancient (tadpole) character. These are the sources of the present editions. The style is very quaint, and the meaning compressed into few words. This renders the sense obscure in many passages; the commentators are at a loss to explain it sometimes, and few of the Chinese care to understand its meaning, though the book itself is held in great veneration by them.—The first book is called "the Book of Yu," because it contains some account of the affairs of the Emperor Shun, who took the designation *Yu* on coming to the throne.

This section is called *Yí-Tsí*, because Yu mentions the names of these two men as having helped him in his great works.

Tí (a. 11) 'the Emperor,' i. e. *Shun* ª (B. C. 2200?). The commentary from which these notes are derived was written during the Sung dynasty (A. D. 1200). This passage is evidently a continuation of the last section. Kau-yau had been counselling the Emperor on the knowledge of mankind and on giving peace to the people, and then the Emperor asked Yu to speak. Yu replies: "What can I say more? I always strive to do my duty to the utmost." Kau-yau asks how he does that. *Hūng-shwüĭ* (b. 10) 'the flood.' This has led some to think the Flood of Noah was intended, but there is no evidence to prove it; great inundations have at different times devastated China. *Sz'-tsai* (b. 27) 'the four vehicles,' by which is meant *boats, carriages, sledges, and spiked-shoes*. *Siēn-shí* (c. 6) 'fresh food' or 'fish and flesh to eat.' This includes fish and fowl, and the flesh of the tortoise and of other animals. The term *kiù-ch'uēn* (c. 10), 'the nine streams,' means 'all the rivers.'

Yu exemplified the meaning of *daily exertion* by showing how he had persevered to

ª 舜

Translation of the Extract from the Shū-king (1), *v. native text,* page 1.
The Shu-king *or Classic of History* *. *The book of Yü. The section called Yi and Tsi.* The Emperor said: " Come Yu! You also throw light on the subject!" Yu bowed and said: " Good, my liege! what can I say *in addition?* but I aim daily to do the utmost." Kau-yau exclaimed: " Well, how is that?" Yu replied: " When the mighty waters rose to the skies with a swelling inundation, encompassing the mountains and overtopping the hills, and the poor people were sinking in despair, I adapted for the occasion the four methods of conveyance, and all along the mountains I cut down wood, *and,* with YI, I introduced the various kinds of fish and flesh to eat; I formed the nine streams, and led away the waters to the four seas; I deepened the ditches and brooks, and led away their waters to the streams. With Tsï I sowed seed, and brought all this into notice; as it was difficult to get food, fresh food *of animals was given* to eat. I exerted myself to promote the exchange of goods and to convert things into money. All the people then had food to eat, and all the nations were well governed." Kau-yau said: " Very good! Instructive are your excellent words!" Yu proceeded: " Yes! my liege! Cautious should those on the throne be!" The Emperor replied: " Right!" Yu continued: " Rest *in the judgment* your mind comes to; only be exact, tranquil, and firm; the ministers should be upright, then whenever any action of state arises, the result will fully answer to your expectations and schemes, and so it will be clearly shown that you are receiving God's command, and Heaven, in making known its will, will employ great blessings." The Emperor said: " Right! Ah! ministers and attendants! *How important they are!"* Yu remarked *again:* " Quite right!" The Emperor proceeded: " You ministers are my legs and arms, my ears and eyes: when I desire to assist my people, you help me; when I wish to extend my power every where, you act for me; when I wish to behold the models descended from the ancients,—the sun, the moon, the stars, the mountains, the dragon, the variegated insects, which were painted, the sacred vases (*with the monkey depicted upon them*), the water-plant, the fire, the white rice, the hatchet, the double-hook, which were all embroidered with the five colours upon the five kinds of silk to make the clothing,—you

---

carry off the waters of the deluge, and so he communicated the admonition to care and industry, as pre-requisites to success in government. *Gán jü̆ chĭ* (1. e. 4) 'rest where you arrive,' i. e. ' be satisfied with the judgment your mind naturally comes to, and let it not be affected by sinister motives afterwards.' *Jĭ, yü̆", &c.* (1. g. 17), 'sun, moon, &c.' These figures were worked in colours upon the court dresses, as symbols of the deities, and of the qualities of filial piety, cleanliness, decision, and discrimination. The first six were painted on the robe, the second six embroidered on the skirts of the dress; the mountains were the representations of the gods of the country, the dragon was employed as an emblem of change, and the 'variegated insect' or animal, which was a beautiful bird, was an example of variety in colour. The five colours were all used on each kind of silk. For pictures of these objects, the reader may refer to the Shu-king by Dr. Medhurst, p. 71.

* The words in Italics are not translations from the text.

h. 5.   chī-siŭ, ì wù ts'aì chāng shī yŭ wù sì tsŏ fŭ, jù míng; yŭ yŭ wǎn lŭ-
h. 23. liŭ, wù-shīng, pă-yīn, tsaì chí huŭ, ì ch'ŭ nă, wù yên, jù t'īng; yŭ weí,
i. 10. jù pī; jù wŭ miên ts'ăng, t'ŭi yiù heŭ-yên, kīn sź-līn! shŭ hwăn chān
i. 26. shwŏ, jŏ pŭ tsaì shī, heŭ ì mìng chī; tă ì kí chī. Shŭ yúng shì tsaì! yŭ
j. 14. píng sāng tsaì! kŭng ì nă yên, shì ặr yáng chī; kă tsì chīng chī, yúng
j. 30. chī; feŭ, tsì weí chī." Yù yŭ: "Yŭ-tsaì? Tì-kwāng t'iĕn chī hiă,
k. 14. chí yŭ haì yŭ ts'áng-sāng; wán páng lì hiên, kŭng weí Tì chīn; weí
k. 29. Tì shì kŭ, fŭ-nă ì-yên, míng-shŭ ì-kūng, kŭ-fŭ ì-yúng; shuì kān pŭ-
l. 17. jáng, kàn pŭ-kīng-yíng? Tì pŭ shì, fŭ ť'áng jì tseú kāng-kūng; wŭ
m. 2.   jŭ Tān-chŭ gaŭ, weì mǎn yiù shì haŭ, gaŭ-niŏ shì-tsŏ, kāng cheú yè
m. 18. gĕ-gĕ; kāng shwuì hīng cheŭ, páng yín yŭ kiă, yúng t'iĕn kiŭ shì; yŭ
n. 3.   chwáng jŭ-shì, tsuì yŭ T'ŭ-shān hīng jīn kwaī kiă; Kí kŭ-kŭ ặr kì, yŭ
n. 20. fŭ tsź, weí hwǎng tŏ t'ŭ kūng; pí chíng wù fŭ, chí yŭ wù ts'iĕn; cheŭ
o. 6.   shì yiù ặr sž, waì pŏ sź-haì; hǎn kiên wù chàng, kŏ tí yiù kūng;
o. 22. Miau hwăn fŭ tsì kūng, Tì k'í niên tsaí."

2.   Extract from the Shŭ-kīng (2), v. native text, page 2.

a. 1.   Tì yŭ: "Tì chīn tŭ, shì naì kūng weí sŭ; Kaŭ-yaŭ fāng k'í
a. 15. kŭ sŭ, fāng shì siáng hīng weí míng." Kw'eí yŭ: "kiă-kí míng-
a. 28. k'iŭ, tw'ǎn-fŭ k'ín-sĕ ì yúng; tsù k'aŭ laí kă, yŭ pīn tsaí weí,
b. 13. kiūn heŭ tĕ jáng; hiă kwàn ť'aŭ-kŭ, hŏ chì chŭ-yiŭ, sāng yúng ì kiên;
b. 29. niaŭ-sheŭ ts'iāng-ts'iāng; siaŭ shaŭ kiù chīng, fúng-hwǎng laí ì."

.... Ch'ŭ-nă (1. i. 2, 3) 'odes and ballads.' Ch'ŭ 'odes' from superiors; nă 'songs' from inferiors. Their respective characters were displayed in their compositions. Heŭ (1. j. 1) 'the target.' This relates to a custom mentioned in the Cheŭ-lì[b] 'the ceremonies of the Cheu dynasty.' This and the other modes of trial were probably similar in spirit to the ancient ordeal practised in other countries. The T'ŭ-shān 'the mountain Tu' was situated in Lat. 32°. 34' N. Long. 0°. 16' E. of Peking. The scene of these events was in the country now known by the name of Shǎn-túng[c], a province in the north of China.

The five tenures here mentioned are the divisions of land made in those early times; their names were Tien[d], Heu[e], Suī[f], Yaŭ[g], Hwang[h]. The people here called Miau are the Miau-tsz, a distinct tribe, supposed to be the aborigines of China. They still exist as a clan in the west-central provinces, and lead a wild life in the mountains. An account of forty-one tribes of these people is given in the Chinese Repository, vol. XIV. p. 105.

Míng-k'iŭ (2. a. 27, 28), 'the sounding stone,' means the sonorous gem which was formed of a piece of jade stone, which, being suspended in a frame, emitted a pleasant sound when struck. T'aŭ-kŭ (2. b. 19), 'the tambour,' was like a drum, but smaller; it was furnished with a handle, and, on being shook, the balls which were attached struck the instrument. Chŭ-yŭ' (2. b. 23, 24), 'the rattle,' was a tub, two cubits and four inches in diameter, and two cubits and eight inches deep. A hammer was fitted to it, by which it was struck. 'The stopper' was in form like a crouching tiger, on the back of which were twenty-seven indentations. When the music was to begin they shook the rattle, and when it was to stop they drew a style made of wood along the tiger's back.

[b]周禮 [c]山東 [d]甸 [e]候 [f]絞 [g]要 [h]荒

clearly set them *before me*. When I wish to hear the six notes, the five sounds and the eight tones of music, in what consists right government or the contrary, as concerns the odes *of the higher classes* and the ballads *of the lower classes*, each of five syllables, you listen *for me*. When I depart from the right way, you help me to return. You do not in my presence be complaisant, and on retiring have a different expression. Thoughtful should the four attendants be! All those who rudely misrepresent things, if they do not alter in time, test them by archery, in order to enlighten them; punish them with whips, so as to remind them of their duty. The Record, how useful to know it*! We wish, too, to preserve their lives! The chief musician will receive the words *appointed*, and constantly inspire these *men with them*. If they repent, recommend them and employ them; if not, overawe them." *Yu* said: "Is that right? Your majesty's glory should be *spread* through all the empire, even to the corners of the ocean, and the blue *distance* that arises, the myriads of nations, and the virtuous of your own people, would then become your subjects. But let your majesty ever raise *these men;* when they report, receive their words, and declare each according to his merits, by giving chariots and robes to render them constant. Who then would presume not to yield, and reverently to comply? If your majesty do not so, they will all be *corrupt* alike, and there will be daily reports of unworthy proceedings. Do not, as *Tan-chu*, be proud, who, while only rambling about, delighted to insult and oppress, doing evil day and night continually. Where no water was, he *wished* to sail, and he corrupted those at home; and so he caused his succession to be cut off. I was admonished by this, and having married at *Tu-shan*, only four days I remained there. When my *child Ki* fretted and wept, I did not caress him, but I considered the important duty of levelling the land. I assisted in completing the five *laws* of tenure, to the distance of five thousand lī. In every district I appointed twelve officers. Beyond these districts, even to the four seas, I established the five elders, each of whom has some merit; but the *Miau* people are stubborn and will not go to work. May your majesty bear this in mind!"

Translation of the Extract from the Shū-king (2), *native text*, page 2.

The Emperor said: "As respects walking after my virtuous rules, it is ever to your merit alone that the arrangement of it is due. *Kau-yau* then took with respect that arrangement of yours, and thereupon added the forms of punishment, being very discerning." *Kwei* said: "When they struck the sonorous stone, and swept across the harp and lyre to make their chord with the chant, then the *manes* of our ancestors and progenitors came near; the guest of *Yu* was presiding, and the multitude of nobles bravely gave homage. Below were pipes and tambours, which accompanied or ceased in accordance with the rattle and the stopper; the organ and the bell were used for the interludes. The birds and beasts were set in motion, and when they played the nine airs of *Shun* music, the *Fung* birds came and acted the rites."

* A book was kept in which the conduct of officials was noted down.

c. 11. *Kw'ei-yŭ:* "*Yŭ yŭ ki-shi fù-shi, pă-shaú sŭ wù, shŭ yŭn yŭn hiaĭ.*"
c. 27. *Tí yăng tsŏ kō, yŭ:* "*Chĕ t'iĕn chī mǐng, wei shi, wei kī;*" *naĭ kō*
d. 12. *yŭ:* "*Kù-kwāng hī tsaĭ! yuên-sheù k'ĭ tsaĭ! pĕ-kūng hī tsaĭ!*"
d. 25. *Kaŭ-yaŭ paĭ-sheù k'ĭ-sheù yăng-yên yŭ:* "*Niên tsaĭ! sŭ-tsŏ hīng sź,*
e. 10. *shín naĭ hiên! Kīn-tsaĭ! lŭ săng naĭ ching; kīn-tsaĭ!*" *Naĭ kăng tsaĭ*
e. 24. *kō yŭ:* "*Yuên-sheù mǐng tsaĭ! kù-kwāng liăng tsaĭ! shŭ sź kăng*
f. 7.   *tsaĭ!*" *Yiù kō yŭ:* "*Yuên-sheù ts'ăng-ts'ŏ tsaĭ; kù-kwāng tŏ tsaĭ!*
f. 20. *wán-sź tŏ tsaĭ!*" *Tí paĭ yŭ:* "*Yŭ! wăng kīn-tsaĭ!*"

2.   Epitaph of *Kī-tsź*, v. native text, pages 2 and 3.

g. 2.   *Kī-tsź pī. Liŭ Tsūng-yuên.—Fǎn tá-jīn chī taú yiù sān: yī yŭ,*
g. 21. *ching mŭng nán; ạr yŭ, fǎ sheù shing; sān yŭ, hwǎ kĭ mǐn. Yīn yiù*
h. 6.   *jín jín, yŭ: Kī-tsź. Shi kŭ tsź taú, ĭ lĭ yŭ shi. Kú K'ūng-tsź shŭ lŭ-kīng*
h. 25. *chī chī, yiù yīn-kīn yên. Tāng Cheú chī shí, tá taú peí-lwán, t'iĕn-weī*
i. 11. *chī túng pù-náng kiaĭ, shing jín chī yên wù-sŏ-yúng; tsin-sź ĭ píng-*
i. 27. *mǐng, chíng jín ĭ. Wù-yĭ wù-sź, kŭ pù-weĭ; weĭ-shīn ĭ tsăn-sź, ching*
j. 14. *jín ĭ. Yŭ-wăng wù-kwŏ, kŭ pù-jín; tsiĕ shi ạr taú, yiù hīng-chī-chĕ-yĕ* [a].
k. 2.   *Shi yáng paù k'ĭ mǐng-chĕ, yŭ chī fù-yàng; hwŭĭ shi mŭ-fán, jŭ yŭ*
k. 18. *ts'iŭ nŭ; hwăn ạr wŭ siĕ, t'ŭĭ ạr pŭ sĭ: kŭ tsaí Yí yŭ:* "*Kī-tsź chī*
l. 5.   *mǐng ĭ,*"—*ching mŭng nán yĕ. Kĭ t'iĕn-mǐng kī-kaĭ, săng-jín ĭ ching,*
l. 20. *naĭ ch'ŭ tá-fă, yáng weĭ shing sź. Cheú jin tĭ ĭ sŭ ĭ-lạn ạr lī tá-tiên, kŭ*
m. 10. *tsaí Shŭ yŭ:* "*ĭ Kī-tsź kweī tsŏ húng-fǎn, fǎ sheù shing yĕ;*" *kĭ fūng*
m. 26. *Chaŭ-siĕn, t'ŭĭ taú hiún-sŭ; weĭ tĭ wŭ leú, weĭ jín wŭ yuên; yúng*
n. 11. *kwăng yīn sź, pī ĭ weĭ hwǎ;—hwǎ kĭ mǐn yĕ. Sŭ shi tá-taú, tsŭ yŭ*
n. 28. *kŭ kūng; t'iĕn-t'ĭ piên-hwā, ngŏ tĭ k'ĭ chíng, k'ĭ tá-jīn yŭ!*

Kī-tsź was a relative of the tyrant *Cheú-sīn* [b] (B. C. 1112), and was obliged to save his life from the Emperor's anger, on being reproved, by feigning madness. The greatest enormities were perpetrated by this monarch and his queen *Tán-kĭ* [c], who had been taken captive by him after a victory. To please her he invented the most extravagant methods of torture, immoral songs and dances, with the worst abominations of heathen lands. *Pĭ-kăn* (2. o. 24) was the first martyr for reproving the king. *Wù-wáng* (3. a. 11), 'the martial king,' at last rid the world of this monster. He made a solemn appeal to heaven, imposed an oath on his nobles, and proceeded to battle. *Cheú* sent 700,000 men against him, but they had no will to fight; and *Cheú's* army being routed, he himself retired to the stage, which he had erected for other purposes, and burnt himself in sumptuous robes and jewels. *Tán-kĭ* was slain by *Wù-wáng*, the victorious general.

The style of this passage is very classical and elegant; for the arrangement of the words, and the antithesis to be observed in some sentences, the original text must be studied. See *Medhurst's Shoo-king*, p. 363, and *Morrison's View of China for Philological Purposes, Chronology*, p. 53.

Shing [d] (2. g. 28), which means the highest qualities of *goodness* and *wisdom*, may often be translated 'saint' or 'sacred,' and is frequently translated 'sage.' As it can apply only to those who stand apart from the rest of mankind, either on account of their virtues or their wisdom, and generally for both reasons, the rendering 'sacred sages' seems appropriate in this epitaph.

[a] 也   [b] 紂辛   [c] 妲己   [d] 聖

Kw'ei went on to say: "While I was striking and jingling the *sonorous* stones, all the beasts came forth to play, and all the officials were sincerely cordial." The Emperor composed an original ode, to wit: "that men should be careful about heaven's commands, be constant, and be exact." Then he sang, saying: "When statesmen (arms and legs) are glad to serve, the head of the state arises to action, and all public undertakings flourish." *Kau-yau* bowed with his hands and bent his head, and murmured out, saying: "Bear in mind this! *The sovereign* begins the affair, let him be careful about his regulations! Be careful, and often search into the end of affairs! Be careful!" Then he joined and completed the ode, saying: "When the head of the state is intelligent, the statesmen will be virtuous, and all affairs will be prosperous." Again he sang, saying: "If the head of the state be very stringent in his demands, the ministers will be careless, and every thing will fall into ruin." The Emperor bowed and said: "Very right! Go! and be careful!"

Translation of the Epitaph of K'i-tsz̆, v. native text, pages 2 and 3.

Ki-tsz's epitaph, by *Liu Tsung-yuen*.—Great men generally have three principles *of action;* first, they act correctly in adversity; secondly, they give an example to the sacred sages; thirdly, they reform the people. In *Yin* there was a pious man named *Ki-tsz;* he was fully furnished with these principles for an example to the world. For this reason *K'ung-tsz*, in compiling the six classics, took care diligently to *notice these points*. In the time of *Cheu*, these great principles were so utterly perverted, that the power and majesty of heaven was not sufficient to restore them to order. The words of the sacred sages were without good effect; to rush into death and to be regardless of life was *then* true piety. There being no profit in keeping the sacred rites, they kept them not; *but* to bow and reverently to preserve those rites was true piety. To give himself up to die for his country, he had not the courage; but he had two virtues;—by the preservation of his intelligence he bestowed it upon all ranks, through concealing his counsels and plans he was disgraced to imprisonment and bondage;—in obscurity he was without depravity, and when ruined he did not sigh in despair. Therefore in the *Yĭ-(king)* it is said: *Ki-tsz's* illustrious quality was contentment,—he acted correctly in adversity. The decree of heaven being changed, that the living might turn to righteousness, he issued his great law, as a model to the sacred sages. The men of *Cheu* succeeded, by arranging in order the invariable law of the human relations, in establishing the great civil code. Therefore in the *Shü-(king)* it is said: *Ki-tsz* restored the great plan, and thus he gave an example to the sacred sages. And being appointed to *Chau-sien* (Corea), he promoted virtue and taught good manners. He considered virtuous principles without reference to rank, and he regarded men without reference to distance of abode. By using widely and diligently sacrificial rites, he made the barbarians to become *civilized* Chinese;—thus he proceeded to reform the people. He followed these great laws, and united them in himself. Amid the changes and transmutations of the universe, if one succeed in upholding the right, that will be to act the great man indeed!

o. 12.   Yü hū! Tāng k'ĭ Cheŭ-shĭ wĭ chĭ, Yĭn sź wĭ t'iēn, Pĭ-kān ĭ sź,
o. 28.   Wei-tsź ĭ k'ŭ, hiáng shĭ Cheŭ ŏ wĭ jĭn ạ̈r tsź pī; Wú kāng niên lwán
a. 22.   ĭ t'ŭ tsān, kwŏ wú K'ĭ jĭn shüĭ yù hĭng-lĭ, shĭ kŭ jĭn sź chī hwŏ-jên-
b. 10.   chĕ yĕ, jên tsĭ siēn-sāng yĭn-jĭn ạ̈r wei tsź. K'ĭ yiù chĭ yŭ sź hŭ!
b. 26.   T'áng meŭ niên, meŭ yŭ, meŭ jĭ tsŏ miaŭ kĭ kiŭn süĭ shĭ chĭ sź.

3.   Extract from the *Sź-shū* (1), *Lạ̈n-yŭ*, v. native text, page 3.

d. 2.   Sź-shū. Lạ̈n-yŭ. Tsż yŭ: "Hiŏ ạ̈r shĭ sĭ chĭ, pŭ yĭ yŭ hŭ! Yiù
d. 20.   păng tsź yuèn-fāng laĭ, pŭ yĭ lŏ hŭ! Jĭn pŭ chī ạ̈r pŭ wạ̈n, pŭ yĭ
e. 7.   kiūn-tsź hŭ!" Yiù-tsź yŭ: "K'ĭ wei jĭn yĕ hiaŭ tĭ ạ̈r haŭ-fán-sháng-
e. 23.   chĕ, siēn ĭ. Pŭ-haŭ fán-sháng ạ̈r haŭ-tsŏ-lwán-chĕ, wĭ-chĭ-yiù yĕ.
f. 9.   Kiūn-tsź wú pạ̈n, pạ̈n lĭ ạ̈r taŭ sāng. Hiaŭ-tĭ-yĕ-chĕ,—k'ĭ wei jĭn chī
f. 26.   pạ̈n yŭ!" Tsż yŭ: "Kiaù yên lĭng sĭ, siēn ĭ jĭn." Tsāng-tsź yŭ:
g. 10.   "wŭ jĭ sān sāng, wŭ-shīn wei-jĭn meŭ ạ̈r pŭ-chūng hŭ? yŭ păng-yiù
g. 26.   kiaū ạ̈r pŭ-sīn hŭ? ch'uên pŭ-sĭ hŭ?" Tsż yŭ: "Taŭ ts'iên shĭng chī
h. 11.   kwŏ, kĭng sź ạ̈r sín, tsĭ yúng ạ̈r ngaĭ jĭn, shĭ-mĭn ĭ shĭ." Tsż yŭ:
h. 27.   "Tĭ tsż jĭ, tsĭ hiaŭ; ch'ŭ, tsĭ tĭ; kĭn ạ̈r sĭn, fán ngaĭ chŭng, ạ̈r tsīn jĭn:
i. 14.   hĭng yiù yŭ lĭ, tsĭ ĭ hiŏ-wạ̈n." Tsż-hiá yŭ: "Hiên hiên yĭ shĭ; sź
i. 30.   fŭ-mŭ, náng kĭ k'ĭ lĭ; sź kiūn, náng chĭ k'ĭ shīn; yŭ păng-yiù kiaū,
j. 16.   yên ạ̈r yiù sín; suĭ yŭ: 'wĭ hiŏ,' wú pĭ wei chī hiŏ ĭ."

The character *jĭn*[a] (2. h. 6), which is commonly translated 'benevolence, humanity,' &c., might be rendered 'piety' or 'virtue.' It signifies the practice of those virtues which constitute a good citizen, a kind father, a dutiful son, an affectionate husband, a loving brother and a faithful friend;—characters which are involved in the five human relations (*wŭ-lŭn*), according to the Chinese. In the first case here *jĭn* (2. i. 29) would stand for 'patriotism,' in the second (2. j. 14) for 'filial piety.'

The following notices of *Pĭ-kan, Wei-tsz*, and *Tan-ki*, which are given in Gonçalves' *Arte China*, translated by Sir John Bowring, may interest the reader: v. *Chinese Repository*, vol. XX. p. 96.   1. *Pĭ-kān*[b], 'the living one without a heart' (B.C. 1140), was the elder brother of *Cheŭ-sin*, by a concubine. He was a saint, and esteemed so by his brother, but being hated by his sister-in-law *Tán-kĭ*, on account of his admonitions, she said to *Cheŭ* it would be easy to ascertain whether he was a saint or not, for if so he would have seven holes in his heart. Moved by curiosity, *Cheŭ* ordered his heart to be extracted, and seven holes were found in it; but as the saint had secured himself against death, he went to another country. Here meeting a man who was selling onions, he asked him what vegetable it was, and the man answering that it was a vegetable without a heart, he remembered that he himself had none, and died in a swoon. 2. *Wei-tsz*'[c], 'the astronomer' (B.C. 1150), brother of *Pĭ-kan*, seeing the tyrannical acts of *Cheŭ*, fled in alarm, and carrying with him the astronomical books in which he was well versed, went to the west, to whose inhabitants he communicated his knowledge; hence it is that Europeans obtained treasures of science which China lost. 3. *Tán-kĭ*[d], 'the lovely sporter' (B.C. 1130), one of the four beautiful wives of tyrant *Cheŭ*[e]. She was fond of lighting the alarm watch-houses, to see the soldiers in movement, but when the enemy really came, and the watch-house was lighted, the soldiers did not appear; so the tyrant lost his head, and she being burned, was transformed,—some say into a guitar, which she had been before, others say into a fox.

[a]仁   [b]比干   [c]微子   [d]妲己   [e]紂

Alas! The time of the *Cheŭ* (dynasty) not yet being come, the sacrificial rites of *Yin* not yet being done away, *Pi-kan* being dead, *Wei-tsz* having departed; all tended towards the fall of *Cheŭ* (the tyrant) in death before his wickedness reached its height. While *Wu* was thinking on revolution as a means for the kingdom's preservation, had this man been absent, who would have assisted in restoring order? It was assuredly this man's work doubtless! Yea! this scholar, concealing himself patiently, worked thus; he had intended this very thing!

In the *T'ang* (dynasty) in a certain year, in a certain month, on a certain day this temple was raised to lead the city annually to perform the sacrifice.

Translation of the Extract from the Sz-shŭ (1), *Lǔn-yŭ, v. native text,* page 3.

The Master * said: "To learn, and constantly to dwell on the subject, is it not a pleasure! To have friends, come from a distance, is it not enlivening! The man *who is* misunderstood, and *who is* yet free from indignation, is he not a superior man!" *Yiŭ-tsz* said: "Those who, as men, show themselves dutiful, both as sons and as younger brothers, and yet like to resist their superiors, are few; men who dislike resisting superiors and yet like creating rebellion are not to be found! The superior man busies himself with fundamentals; the foundation being laid, then, *as a consequence, good* principles of action are produced. The duties of sons and younger brothers! these surely form the foundation of *all* reciprocal virtues." The Master said: "Crafty words and a specious exterior are seldom found with virtue!" *Tsang-tsz* said: " I daily on three points examine; viz. Have I, in acting for others, devised any thing unfaithfully? Have I, in my intercourse with friends, been insincere? Have I delivered instruction which I have not practised?" The Master said: " In ruling a country of a thousand chariots, *let there be* respect for industry and honesty; let frugality be coupled with benevolence; and, in engaging the people, let the seasons be considered." The Master said: "As for young men, while they remain at home, let them be obedient to their parents; when they go out, let them act in submission to their elders. Let them be diligent and sincere, show love to all, and make friends of the virtuous. If, after business is done, there is any surplus strength, then let them use it in the cultivation of learning." *Tsz-hiá* said: " By giving the virtuous their due, and so obtaining an equivalent for vicious desires; in serving parents, to be able to use the whole strength; in serving the prince, to be able to devote the life; in communicating with friends, to be sincere in word; although a person who does this may be deemed unlearned, I must call him learned indeed."

---

* The term 'master,' which is here adopted from Dr. Legge's translation, seems very appropriate as the translation of *tsz* ᵃ, which in this passage, and often, means 'the great teacher,'—Confucius himself. It accords with the use of the word in our translations of the Gospels for διδάσκαλος, excepting that this term *tsz*' is used by itself to mean *'the master,' par excellence,* and is never so used for any other of the philosophers.

ᴬ 子

j. 30.   Tsź yŭ: " Kiŭn-tsź pŭ chúng, tsź pŭ weî; hiŏ, tsź pŭ kŭ; chŭ chŭng
k. 15.   sîn, wú yiù pŭ jŭ ì chê; kwŏ, tsź wú tán kaī." Tsâng-tsź yŭ: " Shìn-
l. 1.   chŭng chŭī-yuên, mîn tĕ kweī heú ì." Tsź-k'în wặn yŭ Tsź-kúng yŭ:
l. 16.   " Fŭ-tsź chī yŭ shī pāng yè, pī wặn k'î ching; k'iù chī yŭ, yī yŭ chī
m. 3.   yŭ ?" Tsź-kúng yŭ: " Fŭ-tsź wặn, liâng, kūng, kiên, jâng, ì tĕ chī; fŭ-tsź
m. 19. chī k'iù chī yè, k'î chū-ì hŭ jîn chī k'iù chī yŭ!" Tsź yŭ: " Fŭ tsaì,
n. 6.   kwān k'î chī; fŭ mŭ, kwān k'î hing: sān niên wú kaī yŭ fŭ chī taú,
n. 23. k'ŏ weî hiaú ì." Yiù-tsź yŭ: " Lĭ-chī yúng hô weî kweî; siēn wâng
o. 7.   chī taú, sź weî meî: siaú tá yiú chī, yiù sŏ pŭ hing. Chī-hô ạr hô pŭ ì
o. 26. lĭ tsî chī, yī pŭ-k'ŏ hing yè."

4.   Extract from the *Sź-shŭ* (2), *Sháng-mặng*, v. native text, page 4.

a. 2.   Mặng-tsź weî Tsî Siuēn-wâng yŭ: " Wâng chī chîn yiù t'ŏ k'î ts'ī-
a. 16. tsź yŭ k'î yiù, ạr chī Ts'ŭ yiù chè; pī k'î fặn yè, tsî túng-nüī k'î ts'ī-tsź,
b. 5.   tsî jŭ chī hô ?" Wâng yŭ: " K'î chī." Yŭ: " Sź-sź pŭ nâng chī sź, tsî
b. 21. jŭ chī hô ?" Wâng yŭ: " ì chī." Yŭ: " Sź-kìng chī nüī pŭ chí, tsî jŭ
c. 7.   chī hô ?" Wâng kú tsŏ-yiú ạr yên t'ā.—Mặng-tsź yŭ: " Sŏ weî kú-
c. 26. kwŏ chè, fī weî yiù k'iaú-mŭ chī weî yè, yiù shî-chîn chī weî yè. Wâng
d. 13. wú ts'în-chîn ì; sī chè sŏ tsîn, kīn-jī pŭ chī k'î wâng yè" Wâng yŭ:
d. 30. " Wú hô ì shī k'î pŭ tsaî ạr shè chī ?" Yŭ: " Kwŏ kiūn tsîn hiên jŭ
e. 16. pŭ-tĕ-ì, tsiāng-shī pī yŭ tsūn, sú yŭ tsî, k'ŏ pŭ shìn yŭ ! Tsŏ-yiù kiaī
f. 4.   yŭ: 'hiên,' wî-k'ŏ yè; chŭ tá-fū kiaī yŭ: 'hiên,' wî-k'ŏ yè; kwŏ-jîn
f. 20. kiaī yŭ: 'hiên,' jên-heú ch'ă chī kiên: hiên yên, jên-heú yúng chī."

Sź-shŭ (3. d. 2), 'the Four Books,' may be looked upon (like the Penteteuch with the Jews), as containing the moral and political principles of the Chinese. This passage is taken from the *Lŭn-yŭ*, 'the Dialogues' or discourses of Confucius and his disciples. *Yŭ*[a] (3. d. 17) is here represented by the character *shwŏ*[b]. It expresses the internal feeling of pleasure induced by thinking over something in which the mind delights. In opposition to *lŏ*[c] (3. d. 27), which means the external manifestation of pleasure,—*cheerfulness, gladness*. *Chè*[d] might have been looked for after *chī* (e. 1) or *hwŭn* (e. 4); but the form of the sentence agrees with that of the two previous clauses, in which *chè* is omitted. Observe the change of tone in *haú* (e. 20), which here means 'to like,—to love.' *Siĕn-ì jîn*[e] (3. g. 4), 'few pious,' is an unusual construction. *Jîn* is in *apposition* here, as frequently, and this will explain the form of expression. *Siĕn-ì* is the predicate of the sentence, and *jîn* is added, as it were by apposition, and makes a relative clause like an attributive, 'who are pious.' For a critical history of the text the student may refer to Dr. Legge's *Chinese Classics*, vol. I. *Prolegomena*, p. 12. Dr. Legge translates *Lŭn-yŭ* by 'Confucian Analects.'

The subjects of the work are very various; filial piety is held to be the prime duty and the foundation of all virtue. The fragmentary nature of the work precludes any analysis of its contents. The Chinese have made two great divisions of it into *Sháng-lŭn*, 'upper or first *lŭn*,' and *Hiá-lŭn*, 'lower or second *lŭn*.' From the terseness of the style and the necessity, in translations of this kind, of giving the meaning as literally as possible, the entire sense cannot well be conveyed, it would indeed need a paraphrase to make the full idea clear to the English reader. The first passage here given, for example, would be represented in a paraphrase in some such phrase as this: 'What agreeable sensations arise in our minds when we think again on that which, by constant reiteration and practice, we have

[a] 悅   [b] 說   [c] 樂   [d] 者   [e] 鮮矣仁

The Master said: "If the superior man * be not grave, then he will not command respect; let him study and then he will not be vulgar, let him estimate in the highest degree fidelity and truth, let him be without friends excepting those like himself; when in error then let him not be afraid to change." *Tsang-tsz* said: "If care be taken about the last rites *for parents*, and they be repeated for the departed *souls*, the virtuous principle of the people will return to its *original* goodness." *Tsz-k'ïn* asked *Tsz-kŭng*, saying: "When our Master comes to this or *that* country, he needs must get information about its government;—does he ask for it, or is it given to him?" *Tsz-kung* replied: "Our Master, by affability and goodheartedness, by courtesy and moderation, coupled with a polite yielding to others, obtains it. Our Master's mode of asking it is all different from other men's *modes*." The Master said: "While the father is alive, look at the *son's* intentions; when the father is dead, look at his actions. If in three years he be without change as respects his father's principles, he may be called 'filial.'" *Yiu-tsz* said: "In acting with propriety †, to use cordiality is of importance. In the principles of the kings of days gone by, this was considered excellent. As respects following them in little things and in great, there are some which cannot be done. If any one know cordiality and do not moderate that cordiality with propriety, it should not be done."

Translation of the Extract from the Sz̆-shū (2), *Shāng-mặng, v. native text*, page 4.

Mạng-tsz, talking with *Siuen*, the king of *Tsi*, said: "Should one of your majesty's ministers, who had committed his wife and children in trust to a friend, while he made an excursion into *Tsu*, on his return find that he had starved them both outwardly and inwardly, then what should be done?" The king replied: "Cast him off." *Mạng-tsz* said: "Should the chief of the officers of justice not be able to govern his subordinates, then what should be done?" The king said: "Deprive him *of office*." *Mạng-tsz* said: "Should the interior of the four boundaries (i. e. the kingdom) not be governed *aright*, what should be done then?" The king looked left and right and spoke of another matter.—*Mạng-tsz*, at an interview with king *Siuen* of *Tsi*, said: "The reason why a country is said to be ancient, is not because it is said to have tall trees, but because it is said to have patriotic ministers. Your majesty is without the affection of your ministers. Those who formerly entered *your service*, to-day you know nothing of their loss." The king replied: "How shall I know of those without talent, and reject them?" *Mạng-tsz* answered: "When the ruler of a kingdom advances the prudent, he cannot be too cautious in employing mean men more than the honourable, or strangers more than relatives. When the attendants all say, 'he is prudent,' that is not sufficient; when the chief officers all say, 'he is prudent,' that is not sufficient; when the people of your kingdom all say, 'he is prudent,' then examine into the opinion of his prudence, if correct then employ him."

---

* Here *Kiŭn-tsz'* means rather *he who studies to be a superior man.*

† The *chi* after *li* shows that the word *li* is used as a verb, i. e. to act according to *li*, — fitness, propriety, ceremony, *etiquette.*

g. 7.   Máng-tsź kién Tsí Siuēn-wáng yŭ: "Wei kŭ shí, tsí pí shí kūng-sź
g. 23.   k'iŭ tá mŭ; kūng-sź tś tá-mŭ, tsí wáng hí, ì-wei náng shíng k'í jīn yè.
h. 10.   Tsiáng-jīn chŏ ặr siaŭ chī, tsí wáng nŭ, ì-wei pŭ shíng k'í jīn ì. Fŭ-jīn
h. 28.   yiŭ ặr hiŏ chī chwáng ặr yŭ híng chī. Wáng yŭ: 'Kŭ shè jù sò hiŏ ặr
i. 14.   ts'ŭng ngò,' tsí hŏ?" Jŭ kīn yiù p'ŏ-yŭ yŭ tsź, sŭī wán-yi, pí shí yŭ-jīn
j. 2.   tiaŭ-chŏ chī. Chī-yŭ chī kwŏ-kiă tsí yŭ: 'kŭ shè jù sò hiŏ ặr ts'ŭng ngò,'
j. 20.   tsí hŏ ì ì yŭ kiaŭ yŭ-jīn tiaŭ-chŏ yŭ tsaī!—Lŏ-chíng-tsź kién Máng-tsź
k. 10.   yŭ: "K'ŏ-kaŭ yŭ kiŭn, wei laì kién yè; pí-jīn yiù Tsáng-ts'áng chè tsŭ
k. 26.   kiŭn; kiŭn shí-ì pŭ kwŏ laì yè." Yŭ: "híng, hwŏ shí-chī; chì, hwŏ nī-
l. 12.   chī:—híng, chì, fī jīn sò náng yè. Wŭ chī pŭ yŭ Lŭ-heŭ, t'iēn yè. Tsáng-
l. 29.   shí chī tsź, yēn náng shí yŭ pŭ yŭ tsaī!"—Pí yiù sź yēn ặr wŭ chíng
m. 17.   sīn wŭ wáng, wŭ tsù cháng yè, wŭ jù Sūng jīn. Jên Sūng jīn yiù mīn
n. 3.   k'í miaŭ-chī pŭ cháng ặr yă-chī chè; máng-máng-jên kwei wei k'í jīn,
n. 19.   yŭ: "Kīn-jī píng ì, yŭ tsù miaŭ cháng ì." K'í tsź tsŭ ặr wáng shi chī
o. 6.   miaŭ tsí kaŭ ì. T'iēn-hiá chī pŭ tsù miaŭ cháng chè kwá-ì, ì-wei wŭ yí
o. 24.   ặr shè chī chè, pŭ yŭn miaŭ chè yè, tsù chī cháng chè, yă miaŭ chè yè;
a. 11.   fī t'ù wŭ yí ặr yiŭ haì chī.

5.   Extract from the Sź-shŭ (3), Hiá-máng, v. native text, page 5.

b. 2.   Máng-tsź yŭ: "Pí-ì shíng chī tsìng chè yè. I-yŭn shíng chī jīn
b. 17.   chè-yè.   Liŭ Hiá-hwŭi shíng chī hŏ chè yè. K'ūng-tsź shíng chī shí
c. 2.   chè-yè.   K'ūng-tsź chī wei tsí tá chíng, tsí tá chíng yè-chè. Kīn shíng
c. 18.   ặr yŭ chīn chī yè kīn shīng yè-chè, ch'ì t'iaŭ-lí yè; Yŭ chīn chī yè chè,
d. 6.   chūng t'iaŭ-lí yè.   Ch'ì-t'iaŭ-lí-chè, chi chī sź yè.   Chūng-t'iaŭ-lí-chè,

---

once thoroughly learnt:—the present thought associates itself with the past, and produces pleasure in the mind; but only the scholar can experience this. Again, what cheerful joy arises when a friend comes from a distance to visit us again!' The former joy is subjective, it is enkindled by our mental associations; the latter is objective, it dwells with pleasure on the external object which comes from afar.

Shin-chūng chūi-yuèn (3. k. 29). This sentence refers to the practice of reverencing the *manes* of ancestors and attending to the funeral rites of parents. Tĭ (3. l. 5), commonly translated 'virtue,' is rather the 'natural conscience.' The Chinese teachers say it is the good principle implanted in the heart of man by heaven. Heŭ (l. 7), 'thick,' is here put for 'original goodness,' and it is often used for 'generous,' in opposition to pŏ [a], 'thin,' which is used for 'meanness.' Shí (3. l. 20) is here put for 'the, this, any' (3. m. 7—16). Observe the character of Confucius here given; by doing his duty to others, he obtains from them what he wants. Gentleness, goodness (or sincerity), meekness, moderation, and courtesy were his characteristics. Chì (3. n. 8), the 'intention' or 'inclination' not yet brought into action, but only sufficiently to show a tendency:—after his parents' death, then he will act (híng, n. 13).

Máng-tsz (4. a. 2). This celebrated philosopher was born in the kingdom of Ts'ŭ [b] (now the province of Shān-tūng [c]), where he lived about B. C. 350. He was left fatherless at an early age, but his mother took great care of his education and the choice of his youthful companions. He first studied under Tsź-sź [d], one of Confucius' descendants, and finally obtained a post under the king of Tsí,—Siuēn-wáng. But as the king did not conform to Máng-tsz's doctrines, he entered the service of the king of Liáng [e],—Hwŭi-wáng.

[a] 薄   [b] 鄒   [c] 山東   [d] 子思   [e] 梁

Mąng-tsz, at an interview with king *Siuen* of *Tsi*, said: "To make a great palace, you must employ a master-builder to seek out great trees. If he find large trees, then your majesty will rejoice, because you will consider them quite fit for the purpose. But if the workman in hewing them down make them small, then your majesty will be angry, because you will consider them unfit for the purpose. Now, if a man in his youth learn manly principles, and wish in manhood to practice them, and your majesty say, 'Just abandon what you have learnt and follow me,'—how is that? Suppose now your majesty had an unpolished gem here? Although it is only twenty taels in weight, you must employ a lapidary to cut and polish it. And when, with reference to the government of a country, you say, 'Just abandon what you have learnt and follow me,'—then how does this differ from instructing a lapidary how to cut and polish precious stones?"—*Lŏ-ching-tsz*, at an interview with *Mąng-tsz*, said: "I have represented it to our prince, who was about to call upon you, *but* his favourite *Tsang-tsang* prevented him, on this account our prince is not come." *Mąng-tsz* said: "When one is promoted to office, it is some one who causes it; when one is not promoted, it is some one who prevents it. Promotion and non-promotion are not in the power of man. If I do not meet the prince of *Lu*, heaven prevents it; how could a son of the *Tsang* family prevent my meeting him*!"—You must labour at your business and not forget to regulate the heart, and do not assist growing things. Be not like the man of the *Sung* dynasty! There was a man of *Sung* who when he grieved at his grain not growing, pulled it up a little to assist its growth, and hurrying home fatigued, he said to his people: "I am unwell to-day, I have helped the corn to grow." His sons hastened to go and look at the corn, and behold it was withered away! There are few in this world who do not assist the corn to grow. Because there is little profit arising, those who abandon it, and do not weed their corn, but help it to grow by pulling it up a little, do not only no good, but positive harm.

Translation of the Extract from the Sź-shŭ (3), *Hiá-mąng, v. native text*, page 5.

Mąng-tsz said: "*Pi-i was* the pure one among the sages; *I-yün was* the trusty statesman among the sages; *Liu Hia-hwŭi was* the peaceful one among the sages, and *K'ung tsź was* the seasonable one among the sages. *K'ung-tsź* is called completely perfect. This being completely perfect, is like the sound of gold and the jingling of precious stones. The sound of gold is the commencement of harmony, the jingling of precious stones is the termination thereof. To begin harmonious arrangement is the work of wisdom,—the completion of the same is the work of sanctity. Wisdom may be likened

---

Afterwards he performed various services at the courts of the petty princes of those times. He attained the age of 94. Divine honours are paid to his memory, and twice every year sacrifices are offered at his tomb.

* This *Ping*, prince of *Lu*, had been prejudiced against *Măng-tsz* by his favourite, who said that he was a bad man because he had attended more carefully to the funeral ceremonies of his mother than to those of his father. Though the fact was, he was in affluence when he buried his mother, but at an earlier period when his father died he was in poverty.

d. 22. shíng chī sź yè. Chí pí tsï k'iaù yè; shíng pí tsï lï yè. Yiù shê yü
e. 9. pă pú chī waí yè, k'î chí ạr lï yè, k'î chūng fī ạr lï yè."
f. 2. Ts'ï-yĭn chī sīn, jĭn-kiaī yiù-chī; siŭ-ú chī sīn, jĭn-kiaī yiù-chī;
f. 18. kūng-kíng chī sīn, jĭn kiaī yiù-chī; shí-fī chī sīn, jĭn-kiaī yiù-chī.
g. 4. Ts'ï-yĭn chī sīn, jĭn yè; siŭ-ú chī sīn, ï-yè; kūng-kíng chī sīn, lï yè;
g. 22. shí-fī chī sīn, chí yè. Jĭn, ĭ, lï, chí, fī yiŭ waí lŏ ngò yè. Ngò ku
h. 10. yiù chī yè fŭ sź ạr ĭ. Kú yŭ: 'k'iŭ, tsï tĭ chī; shè, tsï shī chī.' Hwŏ
h. 28. siāng p'eì sź ạr wú swàn chè, pŭ nǎng tsín k'î tsaí chè yè. Shī yŭ:
i. 14. "T'iēn sāng chīng mín,—Yiù wŭ yiù tsï,—Mĭn-chī ĭ,—Haú shĭ ĭ-tĕ."
i. 30. K'ŭng-tsź yŭ: Weí tsź-shī chè, k'î chī taú hŭ? kú yiù wŭ pī yiù tsï
j. 17. mĭn chī pĭng ĭ yè. Kú haú shĭ ĭ-tĕ.
k. 2. Măng-tsź yŭ: "Niù shān chī mŭ cháng meì ĭ; ī k'î kiaū yŭ tá kwŏ
k. 18. yè, fŭ-kĭn fă chī, k'ŏ-ĭ weí meì hŭ? Shī k'î jī-yè chī sŏ sï, yŭ-lú chī
l. 8. sŏ jŭn, fī-wŭ míng-nĭ chī sāng yên! Niù-yáng yiú ts'ŭng ạr mŭ chī,
l. 24. shï-ĭ jŭ p'ĭ chŏ-chŏ yè. Jĭn kiên k'î chŏ-chŏ yè, ĭ-weí wí-cháng yiù
m. 12. ts'aí yên! Tsź k'î shān chī síng yè tsaī? Suī tsăn hŭ jĭn chè, k'î wú
m. 28. jĭn-ĭ chī sīn tsaī? K'î sŏ-ĭ fáng k'î liáng-sīn chè, yĭ yiù fŭ-kĭn chī
n. 16. yŭ mŭ yè: tán-tán ạr fă chī, k'ŏ-ĭ weí meì hŭ? K'î jī-yè chī sŏ sï,
o. 5. píng tán chī k'î, k'î haú-wú yŭ jĭn siāng-kĭn yè-chè, kī hī tsï k'î tán-
o. 23. cheú chī sŏ weí yiù kŭ-wáng chī."

Shĭ-chĭn (4. d. 7). The commentator Chū-hi explains this expression by lüt-shĭ hiăn-kiŭ chĭ chĭn ⁿ 'statesmen who are loyal and patriotic when affairs are in a confused state.' Ts'ĭn-chĭn (4. d. 14) 'ministers who are attached to,—have an affection for, their prince.' Măng-tsz was arguing, that if a country was to be considered ancient (that is, worthy of respect on account of its venerable and well-tried institutions) by reason of the loyalty and patriotism of its statesmen, then, where affection for the prince was wanting, such ministers could not exist long, but would depart, and consequently the kingdom would lose this mark of honour. The commentator adds: "Being without attached ministers (i. e. ts'ĭn-chĭn), much more would the state be without those patriotic men who are equal to troublous times" (i. e. shĭ-chĭn). The king's idea is, that such ministers go away because they have not ability equal to the work. His majesty assumes, that he cannot tell their capacities before he engages them, and so he may make a mistake; he therefore asks how he may guard against error in this point, and so reject them. The excellent reply of Măng-tsz needs perhaps a little explanation. He cautions the king against promoting relations and honourable men who are without prudence, and neglecting the mean man and the foreigner who may have this quality. He then proceeds to supply the case in which the man of reputed prudence may be tested in order to employment. He warns the prince against the peculiar bias of particular classes, and points to the *vox populi* as worthy of his regard, on account of its comparative freedom from party feeling and prejudice.

(4. g. 7—i. 17). In this passage Măng-tsz insinuates that the learning of the sages is great, and that the king seeks to reduce their principles to his own practice. Fán-shĭ, an eminent scholar and commentator, says on this passage: "The ancient sages ever grieved that princes could not follow their doctrines, and the princes lamented that the sages could not conform to their desires, wherefore the agreement of prince and minister was ever a matter of difficulty. K'ung-tsz and Măng-tsz seldom agreed with the princes of their times." In (4. l. 5) Măng-tsz recognises a Supreme Ruler, whom he calls *Heaven*, as the governor of human affairs. Măng-măng (4. n. 12) is explained to mean 'the appearance of stupidity;' Măng-măng signifies 'much fatigued,' according to Dr. Williams' Dictionary.

ᵃ 累 世 勳 舊 之 臣

unto ingenuity *in its practice*, and sanctity may be compared to strength. Thus, the archer, who shoots at upwards of a hundred paces, reaches *the target* merely by his strength,—should he strike the centre it will not be merely by his strength."

All men possess compassionate hearts; all men have hearts open to shame; all men have hearts inclined to reverence; all men have hearts to distinguish between truth and falsehood. A compassionate heart leads to benevolence; a heart ashamed of vice acts with justice; a reverent heart produces propriety of manners; a heart which knows truth from falsehood gives wisdom. *Now*, we are not imbued with benevolence, justice, propriety, and wisdom by things external; we assuredly possess them *innately;* they are not to be aimed at only. Therefore it is said: "Seek them and you obtain them, forsake them and you lose them." Some lose manifold, times without number, and are unable to perfect the capacity they possess. The *Shī-(king)* says: "Heaven produced all people,—they have things to do and ways to do them, —the people are ever constant in loving this beautiful virtue." *K'ŭng-tsè* has said that he who made this ode knew right principles! For if there is business to do, there must be a method of doing it, and that which the people constantly maintain is esteem for this beautiful virtue *.

Măng-tsè said: "The forest of the *Niu* mountain† was once beautiful; but since its borders verge on a great state, the axe has felled it:—can it be called beautiful *still?* Yet with the silent growth by day and night, and the genial influence of rain and dew, surely the tender sprouts will shoot again! Nay! but the oxen and the sheep have been there, and have eaten them up; so that now it is a wilderness! When people see its naked barrenness, they will think it never supported a forest. But was this the natural state of the mountain? Supposing the preservation of it in man, is there not a heart of kindness and justice there? But the means by which man loses his uprightness is like the operation of the axe on the forest. If you fell wood every morning, can it appear beautiful? By the daily and nightly growth *of virtue*, the spirit which each dawn revives, makes all men similar in their love and hate; but the deeds which each day brings to pass, wither and destroy it."

Pĭ-t (5. b. 5); *I-yün* (5. b. 12); *Liŭ Hiă-hwŭi* (5. b. 19). The virtues of these three worthies of antiquity are mentioned in order that the chief, *K'ŭng-tsè*, might be mentioned as combining the whole united in his character. *Shing* (5. b. 7) is explained by the commentator as being *tĭ chĭ sŏ tsiŭ yĕ* 'that which proceeds from the virtuous principle,' it corresponds therefore with *sanctity* among us.

(5. g. 16. 17) *k'ŭng-king*. The commentator has explained this, which is a colloquial expression, and means 'to reverence,' by saying that *k'ung* is the external expression of *king*, and *king* is the principle in the heart from which *k'ung* arises. Here we have an example of the scientific form of some Chinese words; the *objective* and the *subjective* being united to form a general term.

* This 'beautiful virtue' (*shĭ ĭ-tĭ*, 5. j. 25) is called in the *Tă-hiŏ*, *mĭng-tĕ*, 'bright virtue,' and explained in the commentary to be the virtuous principle implanted in the heart by heaven, by which man may direct both his spirit and his conduct.

† The *Niu* mountain was on the south-east frontier of the kingdom of *Tsi*, the domain of the king to whom *Măng-tsz* was speaking.

6. Extract from the *Shíng-yú* (1), v. native text, page 6.

a. 1. *Shíng-yú.* (1.) *Tṣ̌n hiaú-tí ì chǔng jîn-lṣ̌n.*
a. 11. *Nyò Shíng-tsù Jîn Hwâng-tí lín-yú lù-shí-yì niên, fǎ-tsù tsān-tsīn*
a. 27. *hiaú sź pû kweí, kin tíng Hiaú-kīng yèn-í yǐ-shǖ; yèn-shí kīng-*
b. 12. *wṣ̌n, ì-lí ts'iǔng-kwân; wú-fǐ hiaú chī t'iēn-hiá chī í. Kú Shíng-yú*
b. 28. *shí lū t'iaú sheù ì hiaú-tí k'aī k'ǐ twān.*
c. 8. *Chin peī chíng hǔng niě chüī weī wàng hiún ch'uī kwǎng li kiaú*
c. 21. *chǐ sź siēn shǐn hiaú-tí chī í, yúng shí yù ạr ping-mǐn-jîn tǎng, siuēn*
d. 8. *shí chī. Fǔ hiaú chě; t'iēn chī kīng, tí chī í, mǐn chī híng yè. Jîn*
d. 24. *pǔ chī hiaú fǔ-meù, tū pǔ sź fǔ-meù gaí-tsž chī sīn hû! Fāng k'ǐ wí*
e. 12. *lí hwaī-paù; kī pǔ nǎng tsź-pū; hǎn pǔ nǎng tsź-í. Weí fǔ-meù chě*
e. 29. *shǐn yīn-shǐng, chǎ híng-sǐ siaù, tsǐ weí chī hì; tí, tsǐ weí chī yiǔ;*
f. 15. *híng-tūng, tsǐ kweī-pǔ pǔ lí; tsě-t'úng, tsǐ ts'ǐn-shǔ k'ǖ-fí ì yàng ì kiaú*
g. 3. *chī yū ch'íng jîn fǔ weí sheú kiā-shǐ meù sāng-lí pǎ kī kīng yíng sīn*
g. 20. *li k'ǖ tsüī. Fǔ-meù chī tě shí t'ǎng haú-t'iēn-kāng-kí; jîn-tsž yù*
h. 6. *paù-tsīn gặn yū wán yǐ, tāng nüī tsin k'ǐ sīn waī kiě k'ǐ lí kīn shǐn*
h. 24. *tsǐ-yúng ì kīn fǔ laù ì lùng hiaú yàng; wú pò piên yìn tsiù; wú haú*
i. 11. *yùng teú lṣ̌n; wú haú hô-tsaī sź ts'ǐ-tsž tsúng shí ì wṣ̌n wí pí ạr*
i. 28. *chíng k'iǒ yiù yū ch'uī ạr kwǎng chī. Jǔ Tsǎng-tsž sò weí kǖ-chǖ*
j. 13. *pǔ-chwāng fí hiaú sź; kiùn pǔ chǔng fí hiaú; lí kwān pǔ kīng fí*
j. 28. *hiaú; pāng-yiù pǔ sīn fí hiaú; chēn chin wú yúng fí hiaú: kiaī*
k. 12. *hiaú tsž fặn nüī chī sź yè.*
k. 20. *Chě tí sān twǎn shí tǎn shwǒ hiaú tí taú-lí, nì-mṣ̌n t'ǐng-chǒ!*
l. 5. *Hiaú-shṣ̌n tiē-niâng, ché yǐ kiên sź shí t'iēn-tí kiēn chǎng-tsān tí taú-*
l. 21. *lí, pǎ-sǐng-mṣ̌n tsüī-tá tí tí-híng.*

The *Shíng-yu*, 'Sacred Edict,' was issued by the emperor *K'ang-hi*, the first great emperor after the Tartar invasion and conquest of China in A. D. 1644. It consisted of sixteen maxims, bearing upon social and political duties. They include admonitions to filial and fraternal duties (1); to regard for kindred and neighbours (2, 3); to husbandry and economy (4, 5); to honour learning and preserve orthodoxy (6, 7); to understand the laws and cultivate politeness (8, 9); to form a habit of determination in your calling (10); to instruct youth (11); to refrain from false accusations and from hiding deserters (12, 13); to pay up taxes (14); to form corporate bodies in order to suppress theft (15); and to settle animosities in order to avoid bloodshed (16). These maxims, each of seven characters, were written on slips of wood, and are still exposed in the public offices. They were amplified by *Yung-ching*, *K'ang-hi's* son and successor. This he ordered to be read in public on the 1st and 15th of each month, a custom which is still continued. The style is classical, and difficult for the lower classes to understand. But *Wang Yu-po*, an officer of government, paraphrased the whole in colloquial style of composition.

Laws in China were first explained to the people in the *Cheu*ᵃ dynasty (cir. B.C. 1000), on the 1st day of the month. At the present readings, the civil and military officers in uniform meet in a public hall. The *Lí-sǎng* exclaims: "Stand forth in file!" which they do according to rank: then he says; "Kneel thrice and bow nine times!" They all kneel and bow towards a platform, where a board stands with the emperor's name on it. Then he exclaims: "Rise and retire!" They then proceed to a hall where the law

ᵃ 周

Translation of the Extract from the Shing-yü (1), *v. native text*, page 6.

The Sacred Edict. (1.) Give practical weight to filial piety and fraternal love in order to strengthen the relative duties.

Our canonized ancestor, the emperor *Jin*, reigned sixty-one years, and followed the ways of his fathers in honouring his parents and in aiming unremittingly to observe the duty of filial piety. His majesty himself revised and amplified the meaning of the *Hiaŭ-king* ('Book of filial piety'). He amplified and explained the text of the work, arranging consecutively the arguments which it contained; considering filial piety alone, and nothing else, to be the means of governing the empire. For this reason the sixteen articles of the Sacred Edict start with filial and fraternal duties as their leading principles.

We, having succeeded to this vast inheritance, have investigated thoroughly his former instructions; and, having studied the object he had in view in establishing the doctrine every where, we have, in the first place, reiterated the meaning of filial piety and fraternal affection, in order that you soldiers and people all may know it. Now filial piety exists in the law of heaven, in the sentiment of the earth, and in the conduct of the people. If a man does not know how to obey his parents, he does not bear in mind their heart of affection! For before he was separated from their parental arms: when hungry, he could not feed himself; when cold, he could not clothe himself. To act as parents do, is to judge by the sound of the voice, to notice the appearance of the face; if the child laugh, then to be pleased; if he cry, then to be grieved; when he moves about to support his footsteps and not leave him; when he is in pain, through sickness, then to be regardless of sleep and food, in order to rear him and to teach him until he arrive at man's estate *.

And then they give him a home, they plan about his livelihood by a hundred schemes, they deliberate for him until their whole heart and strength are both expended. The good principles of parents are like the vastness of high heaven! The son who would fain requite his parents' kindness only in a ten-thousandth degree, must, whether at home or abroad, exercise to the utmost his whole heart and strength;—be careful about himself, be frugal, serve them with diligence, and dutifully provide for them. Let him not gamble nor drink,—neither be fond of feats of daring and trials of strength,—nor hanker after riches to expend secretly on his wife and children. Although to perform outward ceremonies he may not be prepared with means to accomplish all that he might intend, sincerity of purpose should abound, and increase it. As *Tsang-tsz* has said: Unseemly conduct is not filial; in serving the prince to be traitorous is not filial; in the office of magistrate to act in an undignified manner is not filial; with friends to be insincere is not filial; in battle to be cowardly is not filial. All these belong to the duty of an obedient son.— (Paraphrase.)—These three sections treat on the doctrine of filial piety alone. Do you listen! This one article of obedience to parents is the principle which is constantly preserved in the universe, and is the greatest act of virtuous practice amongst mankind.

---

* Cf. Xenophon's *Memorabilia* of Socrates, Bk. II. 2, 5, 6.

l. 30.	Nì-mặn ts'ŭng-pŭ-chī hiaú-shặn tiē-niàng, tsá-mŏ, pŭ-pà nā tiē
m. 15.	niàng gai-ặr-tsż tī sīn-chàng, siàng shàng yĭ siàng? Tāng nì-mặn
m. 29.	tsò hai-tsż tī shi-heú, tiē-niàng hwai-paù-chŏ; làng-liaù, pŭ hwŭï tsż-
n. 15.	kì ch'uēn-ĭ; kī-liaù, pŭ-hwŭï tsż-kì k'ĭ-fán; k'án-chŏ nì-mặn yên-sĭ,
n. 24.	nì siaú-liaù, t'à pién hì: nì tì-liaù, t'à pién ts'iŭ; nì hǐng-túng-liaù,
o. 10.	t'à tsiú kān-tǐng-liaù nì pú pŭ lĭ. Nì jŏ yiù-liaù tsē-pǐng, t'à pién
o. 27.	shŭï pŭ nằng ăn.

7.   Extract from the *Shíng-yŭ́* (2), v. native text, page 7.

a. 2.	(5.) Sháng tsĭ-kién ĭ sĭ tsai-yúng.
a. 10.	Sāng-jin pŭ-nằng yĭ jĭ ặr wú yúng, tsĭ pŭ-k'ò yĭ jĭ ặr wú tsai.
a. 27.	Jên pĭ liŭ yiù yŭ chī tsai ặr heú k'ò kŭng pŭ shĭ chī yúng. Kú tsĭ-
b. 14.	kién sháng yên! Fŭ tsai yiù shwŭï yè; tsĭ-kién yiù shwŭï chī ch'ŭ
b. 28.	yè. Shwŭï chī liŭ pŭ ch'ŭ, tsĭ yĭ-sĭ wú yŭ ặr shwŭï lĭ hŏ ĭ. Tsai
c. 15.	chī liŭ pŭ tsĭ, tsĭ yúng-chī wú tú ặr tsai lĭ kwei ĭ. Ngò Shíng-tsù,
d. 2.	Jin Hwáng-tí, kŭng lǐng tsĭ-kién, wei t'iēn-hiá siēn, hiú yàng-sāng sĭ
d. 17.	hai-nŭï. Yīn fŭ yiù kīng kīng ĭ sĭ tsai, yáng shĭ hiún kai. Tsż kù
e. 3.	min fūng kiai kwei hŭ kǐn kién. Jên kǐn ặr pŭ kién, tsĭ shĭ fŭ chī
e. 19.	lĭ pŭ-tsŭ kŭng yĭ fŭ chī yúng. Tsĭ sŭï sò ts'áng pŭ-tsŭ kŭng yĭ jĭ
f. 6.	chī sŭ. K'ĭ hai nai kằng shīn yè.—Chê t'eŭ yĭ twán shĭ shwŏ.
f. 21.	Shíng-tsù, Jin Hwáng-tí, yīn-yīn chŭï-hiún tī yuên-yiù. Tá fàn jin
g. 6.	sāng shĭ-sháng pŭ nặng yĭ-jĭ mŭ-yiù fĭ, tsiú pŭ k'ò yĭ-jĭ mŭ-yiù yên-
g. 24.	ts'iên. Jên pĭ tǐng tsĭ-ch'ŭ-hiá siē yên-ts'iên, taú nà hwŭ-jên shĭ t'à
h. 10.	tī shĭ-heú, ts'ai tī tsĭ-kì; sò-ĭ shwŏ tsĭ-kién yĭ-chŏ. Shí-kŏ tsŭ-miaú-
h. 28.	tĭ fă-tsż! Tsiè chê yên-ts'iên, tsiú jŭ shwŭï yĭ-pān; jin tsĭ-kién t'à,
i. 14.	tsiú siàng tsŭ-shwŭï-tĭ yĭ-pān. Liŭ tĭ shwŭï pŭ tsŭ-chŭ siē yiù tō-
i. 30.	shaù liŭ tō-shaù, tsiú yaú kān-hŏ-liaù. Yúng tsai jŭ liŭ shwŭï jŏ pŭ
j. 16.	tsaï-sĭ-chŏ-siē, jin ts'ŭng tō-shaù yên-ts'iên chuên yên yè-tsiú k'ǐng-
k. 1.	liaù.—Fŭ pīng-tǐng ts'iên-liàng yiù yĭ tǐng chī sŭ, nai pŭ-chī tsặn

---

is usually read. Here the people are assembled to listen. The *Lĭ-sāng* then calls out: "Respectfully begin!" The *Sz-kiàng-sāng*, or orator, kneels before an altar of incense, takes a board with a maxim, and ascends a pulpit or platform. An old man then presents the board to the people, calls for silence with a rattle, and, kneeling, reads the maxim. The *Lĭ-sāng* next demands the explanation from the *Sz-kiàng-sāng*, who stands up and gives the meaning. See Dr. Milne's *Preface* to his *Translation of the Sacred Edict*.

The original preface by *Yung-ching* is in elegant classical style, and worthy of careful perusal. We will give a version of a portion, which may be of assistance to the young student. "The *Shu-(king)* says: 'Every year, in the 1st month of spring, a herald with a bell went round on the roads.' The *Lĭ-(kĭ)* says: 'The *Sz-tu* prepared the six ceremonies to chasten the dispositions of the people; and illustrated the seven doctrines in order to exalt their virtue!' All these, by giving proper weight to first principles, and reverence for realities, became the means of enlightening the people and awakening the age. A plan the very best! An idea the most noble! Our canonized father, the emperor *Jin*, for a long time taught the doctrine of complete renovation. His virtue was wide as the ocean, and his favour extended every where. His benevolence nourished every thing, and his justice regulated all people. For sixty years, morning

If you do not at all understand obedience to your parents, how can you, unless you consider your parents' heart of affection towards their child, give it a thought? At that time when you were a little fellow, and in your parents' embrace,—being cold, you knew not how to clothe yourself; being hungry, you could not feed yourself*. They beheld the colour of your countenance. When you smiled, they were pleased; when you wept, they were sorrowful. When you moved about, they, at your heels, supported your steps and remained with you. If you were sickly, they could not sleep in peace.

Translation of the Extract from the Shíng-yü (2), *v. native text,* page 7.

(5.) Attend carefully to frugality so as to spare the waste of your means.

Mortals cannot exist for a day without expending something, and consequently they may not exist for a day without the means of doing so. Well then, they must lay up their superfluous money, so that bye and bye they may apply it to future necessities. For this reason let frugality be exercised! Now money is like water, and frugality is like the accumulation of water. If the flowing away of water be not stopped, then the water will leak out and be completely exhausted. And if the flowing forth of money be not limited, then the expenditure of it will be lavish and your means will fail. Our canonized ancestor, the emperor *Jin*, himself practised a frugal economy, for a leading example to the empire; while he aimed at making provision for the people and giving prosperity to the state †. In times of abundance he was so careful to spare the wealth of the country, that he used to issue proclamations to instruct the people to lay up store. From olden time all the feelings of the people were in favour of industry and frugality. But *if we suppose* industry without frugality, then ten men's labour would not suffice to supply one man's wants. The store which comes of a year's hoarding is insufficient for one day's need. The harm which arises is greater still *than the loss.*—(Paraphrase.)—This first section tells the reason why our canonized ancestor, the emperor *Jin,* gave us such careful instructions. All men in general born into the world are unable to live for a day without expense. Therefore they cannot exist for a day without money, so they must determine to store up and accumulate a little money, to meet sudden emergencies. Then they will be able to relieve the embarrassed; on this account he speaks of frugality. It is an uncommonly good plan of his! Now as for money, it is just like water; and if people take care of their money, it is just as if one collected a quantity of water together. Now, if flowing water be not confined and stopped, a good deal will escape, and then all will be dried up. Using money is like letting water flow, if you do not employ a little care as to the quantity, then your money will by little and little be exhausted.—Now the amount of the soldier's pay is fixed, but he does not know how to be frugal. As to his

---

* It will be observed that several characters, which are wanting in the native text, have been supplied in the Roman character.

† This passage is rather obscure, but the translation given above appears to convey the meaning intended. The expressions 'within the seas' and 'below the skies' are translated by 'the state' and 'the empire.'

k. 17. *tsĭ; i haú sièn-lí, shĭ k'iŭ kān-meì. Yi yŭ fĭ, sú yŭ chī liáng shīn,*
l. 4.   *chí chūng t'aì, ĭ súi k'ĭ yŭ. Tsz̀-mù siāng kiuén; jĭ fù yi jĭ, chai*
l. 20. *shīn lüī-chúng, kĭ hǎn pŭ mièn.—Ché tĭ-ạ̀r-twán shi shwŏ pīng pŭ-chī*
m. 7. *tsĭ-kién-tĭ; nĭ-mḁ̀n pīng-tīng tĭ ts'iên-liáng, yuên yiù yi-tīng chī sú-*
m. 23. *mŭ, jŏ-shĭ pŭ chĭ-taú tsḁ̀n-tsĭ; ĭ-fú yaú hwâ-lí, fān-shĭ yaú meĭ-k'eù,*
n. 11. *kwó yi-kó yŭ jĭ-tsź, taú hwâ fĭ kī-kó yŭ ts'iên-liáng, ché ts'iên-liáng*
n. 28. *tsāng-tĭ keú fĭ. Shīn-tsiè yiú pŭ gān-sāng-tĭ. Hwán yaú kiĕ siē*
o. 13. *chai jĭn i hwüī-shà, chĕ kú yi-shĭ kw'aī-hwŏ.*

8. Extract from the *Haú-k'iŭ chuén* (1), v. native text, page 8.

a. 2.   *Haú-k'iŭ chuén. Swàn-ki tíng-liaù, taú tsź-jĭ, jĭ wí-ch'ŭ, tsiú k'ĭ*
a. 18. *laí, kiaū Siaù-tān sheū-shĭ hing-lĭ, tà-tièn k'ĭ-shīn; tsź-kiŏ chuên-yáng*
b. 4.   *tièn-sháng yi-kó-siaù-sź, nâ-liaù tĭ-tsz̀ laí, hwüī-paì Kwó kūng-tsz̀.*
b. 20. *Pŭ-k'ĭ Kwó kūng-tsz̀ ĭ-fú hiá-jĭn tsaí hiá-chú tà-t'íng; yi-kiên T'ĭ*
c. 7.   *kūng-tsz̀ laí-paì, tsaù fĭ paú-yù Kwó kūng-tsz̀ kāng-tàng-tĭ T'ĭ kūng-*
c. 23. *tsz̀ taú mḁ̀n. Kwó kūng-tsz̀ tsaù ĭ-kwān tsĭ-ts'ù siaù-hâ-hâ tĭ yíng-*
d. 9.   *tsiāng-ch'ŭ-laí taú: "Siaù-tĭ tsŏ-jĭ tsin-yĕ, pŭ-kwó liaú-piaù-yàng-*
d. 24. *mú chĭ chíng; T'ĭ kàn laú taí-hiūng tsź-kú;" yīn liên-liên tà-kūng-*
e. 9.   *kùng ts'íng tsin-k'ŭ. T'ĭ kūng-tsz̀ yuên tà-cháng, chĕ taú mḁ̀n t'eù yi-*
e. 24. *míng-tĭ, piên tseù. Hwŭ-kién Kwó kūng-tsz̀ chí ch'ŭ-mḁ̀n yíng-tsĭ,*
f. 8.   *shĭ-fān yīn-kín, yi-tw'ạ̀n-hŏ-k'í, piên-fáng pŭ-hiá làng-lién laí, chĕ-tĕ*
f. 25. *t'eù liaù míng-tĭ, liáng-siāng-yi-jáng taú t'íng. T'ĭ kūng-tsz̀ tsiú yaú*
g. 10. *shī-lĭ. Kwó kūng-tsz̀ chĭ-chú taú: "Tsź-kiên pŭ-piên ts'íng kiaú."*
g. 24. *Súi tsiāng T'ĭ chĭ-yaú taú heú-t'íng; fāng-ts'aí shĭ-lĭ sú-tsó. Yi-mién*
h. 10. *hién-sháng-ch'â-laí, Kwó kūng-tsz̀ yīn shwŏ-taú: "Kiù wḁ̀n taí-hiūng,*
h. 24. *yíng-hiūng chĭ míng, kĭ-sź yi-hwüí; ts'iên múng-jŭ lín pĭ-yi shĭ, tsĭ*
i. 10. *meù tsín-yĕ ạ̀r yiú ts'úng-ts'úng fā-kiá, paù-hḁ̀n chí-kīn; kīn-hīng*
i. 25. *tsaí-lín, yiú chíng chüī-kú, chíng yiú kw'aī-sź! Kàn pàn-tsŏ píng-*
j. 9.   *yuên shĭ-jĭ chī yìn, ĭ weí kĭ-kĕ chī hwaí?" T'ĭ-kūng-tsz̀ ch'â pá, tsiú*
j. 26. *lĭ-k'ĭ-shīn-laí, taú: "Chíng chàng-hiūng heú-gaí, pḁ̀n tàng lĭng-kiaú;*

and evening, even while eating and dressing, his only concern was to excite all, both within and without the empire, to exalt humanity, to speak with deference to each other; to put away meanness and keep faith with one another perfectly; that by cultivating the spirit of kindness and humility, they might for ever enjoy a reign of universal peace. Therefore with this intention he gave these superior instructions, consisting of sixteen articles, to acquaint the Bannermen (i. e. the Tartars), together with all descriptions of men and soldiers throughout the provinces, of the bounds of their common and uncommon duties, of the culture of the ground and of the mulberry tree, of working and resting, principles and results, of fine and coarse, public and private, great and small, and whatsoever else the circumstances of the people called on them to practice,—these are the things which his sublime intelligence aimed at. He affectionately treated you, his subjects just as his own children; he issued his sacred instructions, clearly aiming at your certain protection, every age should observe them, they cannot be changed."

Shing (6. a. 12) here means 'canonized' or 'sacred.' It is the custom in China to place the names of great men in the temple of ancestors, they thus become canonized and receive the prefix *shing*. The temple of Confucius is called the *Shing-miaú*. (Cf. note on page 26, Part II.)

clothes, he likes to have them fine; as to his food, he seeks for what is nice and good. One month's expenditure amounts to several months' pay, until he borrows to follow out his wishes. The child and the mother become of equal size. Every day adds to the burden of debt, and hunger and starvation become inevitable.—(Paraphrase.)—This second section speaks about the soldier's ignorance of frugal economy. The pay of you soldiers is a regularly fixed amount. If you don't know how to be economical, but as far as your clothes are concerned you wish for finery, and as respects your food you have a dainty mouth; when a month is passed, you find that you have spent several months' wages; how can your pay be sufficient? Moreover you cannot live happily, but you must run into debt, in order to carry out your habits of dissipation, and you regard only the pleasures of the moment.

Translation of the Extract from the Haŭ-k'iŭ chuén (1), *v. native text*, page 8.

The Story of the Fortunate Union.

His plans being determined on; the next day, before the sun was up, he arose and called *Siau-tan* to collect the luggage, and to prepare himself *for departure: while* he himself, on the other hand, having solicited *the services* of a boy from the inn, took his card to return the visit of Mr. *Kwo*. Without intimation Mr. *Kwo* had set a menial to play the spy in the lower room. Directly *this man* saw Mr. *T'ĭ* going to visit, he hastened to give information to Mr. *Kwo, who was* just waiting for Mr. *T'ĭ* to arrive at the gate. Mr. *Kwo*, ready dressed, came out to receive *him*, smiling, and with a respectful but cordial 'Ha! ha!' he said: "*I*, your humble servant, in waiting upon you yesterday, intended merely to show a slight mark of the sincerity of my respect. *You* Mr. *T'ĭ*, I fear, have troubled yourself, Sir, to take notice of it." Then repeatedly he bowed respectfully and invited him to enter in. Mr. *T'ĭ* at first intended only to go to the door and present a card, and then to walk away. *But* on seeing all at once Mr. *Kwo* straightway coming out to receive him, very urgent and full of cordiality, (then) he did not lay aside his reserve, but merely presented his card, and the two *gentlemen* kept bowing to each other until they reached the reception room. Mr. *T'ĭ* was then about to perform the salutations, but Mr. *Kwo* stopped him, saying: "This place is inconvenient to invite your commands;" and forthwith he invited *T'ĭ* into the inner hall, where they saluted each other, and sat down in due form. Tea having been served up, Mr. *Kwo* then said: "*I* have long heard of you, Sir, you have a hero's name, ardently have I looked forward to an interview. When, on a former occasion, you condescended to come to our poor place, I then planned to wait upon you, and in a hurried manner to pay my compliments; *but you were absent*, and I have felt the annoyance up to the present time. Now that happily you are again come, and have once more condescended to regard us, it is assuredly a significant circumstance; may I presume to engage you in a ten days' entertainment to make even my original plan, and to gratify our feelings of hunger and thirst?" Mr. *T'ĭ*, however, having finished his tea, then arose and said: "In return, Sir,

k. 10. *chĕ-shí 'kweī-sīn-sz̀-tsién,' kīn-jĭ lĭ-kĕ tsiú-yaú hîng-liaù, pà pĭ chī*
k. 27. *hwān, liŭ-taí í-jĭ, k'ŏ-yĕ!" Wâng-waí tsiú tseù. Kwó lân-chŭ taú:*
l. 12. " *Siāng-fûng pŭ-yĭn, chīn lîng 'fûng-yŭ siaú-jĭn.' Jîn shí hîng-kĭ, yĕ*
l. 27. *yaú kŭ-liŭ sān-jĭ." T'ĭ taú: " Siaù-tí shí-shí yaú-hîng, pŭ-shí kŭ-ts'z̀,*
m. 14. *kĭ châng-hiûng siāng-liâng." Shwŏ-pá, yiú wàng waí tseù. Kwó yĭ*
m. 27. *sheù chĭ-chŭ, taú: " Siaù-tí süī pŭ-ts'aí, yĕ t'iĕn weí hwán-kiā tsz̀-tí;*
n. 13. *t'aī-hiûng pŭ-yaú k'án-tĕ shĭ-fān k'īng-liaù jŏ kò k'án-k'īng, tsiú pŭ-*
n. 29. *kaī laí tsz̀-kŭ-liaù; ki-mûng tsź-kú, pién yaú swàn tsŏ pīn-chŭ; siaù-*
o. 15. *tí k'ù-k'ù siāng-liŭ, pŭ-kwó yŭ shaù tsín pīn-chŭ chī ĭ ạr, fĭ*

9. Extract from the *Haú-k'iú chuén* (2), v. native text, page 9.

a. 1.   *yiù sŏ k'iú yĕ; pŭ-shí taī-hiûng hô kién k'ŭ-chī shín yĕ." T'ĭ k'ûng-*
a. 17. *tsz̀ taú: " Mûng châng-hiûng yĭn-yĭn yŏ-ngaí, siaù-tí yĭ pŭ jĭn yên*
b. 2.   *k'ŭ; tán chwāng-ì-sŭ; hîng-sĭ kūng-ts'ûng, shí pŭ yûng hwán ạr."*
b. 16. *Kwó taú: " Kī-shí, t'aī-hiûng, pŭ ì pâng-yiù weí ts'îng, kw'aí-í yaú-*
c. 1.   *hîng; siaù-tí k'iâng-liŭ, yĕ tsz̀-kiŏ hwâng-kweí; tán chĕ-shí ts'îng-*
c. 15. *shín ngŏ-fŭ ạr laí, yiú lîng ngŏ-fŭ ạr k'ŭ, tĭ-sīn shí yiù pŭ-gān:*
d. 2.   *kīn yĭ pŭ kàn kiù liŭ, chĕ k'iú liŏ-t'îng-nĭ shí, shaù túng yĭ-ts'àn, ạr*
d. 19. *tsĭ t'îng k'ŭ-chĕ tsiú taú, shŭ-kĭ jĭn-ts'îng liâng tsín. Nân-taú t'aī-*
e. 4.   *hiûng hwán pŭ-k'ạng fù-ts'âng!" T'ĭ pạn pŭ-yŭ liŭ, yĭn kién Kwó*
e. 18. *shīn-ts'îng heú-maú, k'ạn-k'ạn kw'àn-liŭ, chi-tĕ-chŭ-hiá taú: " Taú-*
f. 2.   *ts'aí tsín-paí tsạng-pién haù siāng-jaù!" Kwó taú: "Chī-ì siāng-fûng,*
f. 16. *tāng wáng pŭ-ngŏ; t'aī-hiûng kw'aí-sź, hô-kŭ tsŏ tsz̀ t'aú-yên?" Chîng*
g. 1.   *shwŏ pŭ-liaù, chĕ-kién Shwüī-yŭn hwŭ tseù-liaù tsín-laí. K'án-kién*
g. 15. *T'ĭ, mâng-shī-kwó-lĭ, mwán-liên t'üī siaú, taú: " Tsŏ-jĭ shé-chĭ-nŭ*
g. 30. *kàn T'ĭ siēn-sāng yuĕn laí kaŭ-í, tĕ tŏ ngŏ-hiŏ-sāng kŭ-kièn, fûng-kŭ*
h. 17. *shaù-piaù wĭ shīn, pŭ shí T'ĭ siēn-sāng hô-kú kién waí k'ù-k'ù ts'z̀-liaù.*
i. 4.   *Kīn hîng yiù yuĕn, yiú tĕ siāng-peī." T'ĭ taú: " Ngŏ-hiŏ-sāng laí*

The *Hiaú-kīng* (6. b. 3) 'the Classic of Filial Piety,' is a collection, in sixteen chapters, of sentences by Confucius and his disciple *Tsang-tsz̀*, upon duty to parents and superiors. The author's name is unknown. A translation by Dr. Bridgman appeared in the *Chinese Repository*, vol. V.

Wŭ-fī . . . . . . ĭ (6. b. 17—25). Here are two negatives to intensify an assertion. The whole may be construed: 'By nothing else but filial piety he considered that the empire could be governed.' (See Art. 450 of Part I.) *Chĭ t'iĕn-hiá chĭ* ĭ = 'the idea (or thought, or purpose) for governing the empire,' i. e. 'he *considered* that the empire could be governed,' *wŭ-fī hiaú*, 'only by filial piety *being inculcated*.'

Fŭ hiaú-chŏ . . . . . . yĕ (6. d. 10—22) is an elegant passage, which cannot be literally translated; it contains an allusion to the three great powers of the universe, *sān-ts'aí*ᵃ as the Chinese call heaven, earth, and man. It is intended to convey the idea that filial piety is that duty which contains the germ of all good principles and virtuous conduct, and the fulfilment of which produces harmony in the universe.

Chĕ tí-sān-tw'àn (6. k. 20). This annotation might have referred to an earlier portion, but here begins the subject of filial piety, and the author having but a limited space, he deemed it right to omit the first two sections of notes.

ᵃ 才

for your generosity and kindness, I ought to receive your commands, but the fact is this,—'My heart returns like arrow fleet,'—to-day, and at once, I am about to proceed on my journey; as regards the enjoyment of your hospitality I will remain to receive it another day, that will do." Going towards the outer *door* he was about to depart, *when* Mr. *Kwo* stopped him, saying: "*For* good friends to meet without drinking, would truly cause the wind and the moon to smile (at men)! Admitting that you are in haste to travel, still you ought to yield, and remain three days." *Tĭ* said: "I am really about to travel, it is not a mere refusal, I beg of you, Sir, to excuse me." Having spoken, he again turned to the door; but *Kwo* with one hand took hold of him and said: "*I*, although I, your humble servant, am without talent, yet you should consider that I am the son of an official family, you, Sir, should not look upon me very lightly, if indeed you do despise me, then you ought not to have come to take notice of *me*. Having obliged me with your kind regard, then you should look upon me as your host; and I, in thus urging you to remain, only wish in a slight degree to fulfil a host's friendliness and nothing more.

Translation of the Extract from the Haú-k'iŭ chuén (2), *v. native text*, page 9.

I have nothing else to ask. I do not know what you can see to oppose so much." Mr. *Tĭ* said: "Being under obligation, Sir, for your extreme kindness, I, for my part, can hardly allow myself to speak of going; but as every thing is packed, and my face is set (homewards) like a running stream in haste, the circumstances will not permit me to delay at all." *Kwo* said: "It being so, Sir, that you take not friendly feeling as your disposition, *but* are in a hurry to depart; if I were to urge your stay, I should be ashamed of myself. But the fact is just this, early in the morning you come fasting, and if I were to allow you to depart without breakfast, my mind would be truly ill at ease. As it is I would not presume to detain you for long, only a very little time, to take a slight meal, and then we may hear of your departure, and it may be said that all those human feelings of ours are mutually satisfied. You cannot, Sir, still be unwilling to remain." *Tĭ*, who as far as he was concerned did not wish to stay, when he saw the deep feeling and generous behaviour (of his host) entreating him to wait, abode where he was, and said, "In a mere visit why should I trouble you so much?" *Kwo* said: "When good friends meet, then they forget personal feelings; you, Sir, are a shrewd man of learning, why do you make use of this formal expression?" Just as he was speaking and before he had finished, who should they see but *Shwŭi-yŭn* walking up and coming in. On seeing *Tĭ*, he rapidly went through the salutations, and with his face all smiling he adressed him and said: "Yesterday my little niece being moved by your coming so far Mr. *Tĭ* to honour us with your compliments, deputed me to present a card, and to offer an invitation, as a slight indication of our cordial feelings. We could not understand what reason you had Mr. *Tĭ* for objecting and so decidedly refusing. Now happily we have had the good fortune to meet again to-day." *Tĭ* said: "I came in great haste,

i. 18.	*shŭ tsaŭ-tsaŭ, k'ŭ fŭ ts'ūng-ts'ŭng; yŭ lĭ yuên-wú ch'eŭ-tsŏ, kŭ kíng tŏ*
j. 4.	*shí-chĕ ts'z̆-sié; tsĭ kin-jí chĭ laĭ, yĭ pŭ-kwó yuên yĭ shĭ-kīng, yè ợr*
j. 22.	*múng Kwó-hiŭng, tsĭ chạn-chạn t'eŭ-hiá; yŭ-liŭ, k'ŭng fĭ lĭ; yŭ k'ŭ,*
k. 2.	*yiŭ k'ŭng fĭ ts'íng; chíng tsaĭ-tsz̆ fĭ ch'eŭ-ch'ŭ, híng laŭ-ūng yiŭ ĭ kiaŭ-*
k. 18.	*chĭ." Shwŭĭ-yŭn taŭ: "Kù-chĭ haŭ pâng-yiŭ, k'íng kaĭ jŭ kú; Tĭ siĕn-*
l. 3.	*sāng yŭ Kwó shé-ts'ĭn, nân-taŭ tsiŭ pŭ-jŭ kŭ jin! naĭ pĭ k'ŭ-k'ŭ yŭ*
l. 20.	*shí-sŭ jŭ-tsz̆, shīn fĭ-ĭ yè !" Kwó siaŭ taŭ: "Hwân-shĭ laŭ-tà-jīn*
m. 6.	*shwŏ-tĕ t'ūng-kw'aĭ!" Tĭ kiên ợr jīn hŭ-siāng kw'àn-liŭ, kìng pŭ kĭ*
m. 21.	*ts'iên tsīng, chĕ jĭn-tsó haŭ-ĭ, piên siaŭ-yĭ-siaŭ tsŏ-hiá, pŭ fŭ yên k'ŭ.*
n. 8.	*Pŭ-tō-shĭ peĭ-shâng tsiŭ laĭ. Kwó tsiŭ súng tsŏ. Tĭ taŭ: "Yuên*
n. 22.	*múng liên chaŭ-kĭ ợr sheŭ ts'àn, weĭ-hô yiŭ laŭ tsz̆-tsiŭ ? k'ŭng yìn fĭ*
o. 8.	*k'ĭ shĭ yè !" Kwó siaŭ taŭ: "Mán-mán yìn k'ŭ, shaŭ-pŭ-tĕ yŭ-chŏ*
o. 23.	*yìn-shĭ." Sān-jĭn kŭ-kŏ tá-siaŭ tsiŭ tsŏ ợr yìn.*

10. Extract from the *Haŭ-k'iŭ chuên* (3), v. native text, page 10.

a. 5.	*Yuên-laĭ sān-jĭn yŭ kiŭ-pĭ-sāng, k'ŭ shĭ haŭ-yiŭ; yĭ-niên shâng*
a. 20.	*sheŭ, piên tsīn-tsīn yiŭ wĭ;—'nĭ yĭ-peĭ, ngŏ yĭ-chàn,' piên pŭ fŭ tūĭ-tsz̆.*
b. 7.	*Yĭn-liaŭ pwán-shàng, Tĭ chíng-yiŭ kó chŭ-sheŭ chĭ ĭ, hwŭ-jên tsŏ-yiŭ*
b. 22.	*paŭ Wâng, Pĭng-pú tĭ, sān kŭng-tsz̆ laĭ-liaŭ. Sān jĭn chĕ-tĭ t'íng-peĭ*
c. 8.	*tsĭ-kiên. Kwó tsiŭ gān-tsó taŭ: "Wâng-hiŭng laĭ tĭ shīn-miaŭ!"*
c. 21.	*Yĭn yâng sheŭ chĭ-chŏ Tĭ taŭ: "Tsz̆ weĭ Tĭ-hiŭng, haŭ-kĭ sz̆ yè !*
d. 6.	*Pŭ-k'ŏ pŭ-hwŭĭ !" Wâng taŭ: "Mŏ-fĭ tsiŭ-shĭ tà-jĭ Tá-gān-heŭ yàng-*
d. 22.	*hiên-tâng tĭ Tĭ T'ĭng-sāng mó ?" Shwŭĭ-yŭn mâng tá-taŭ: "Chíng-*
e. 5.	*shĭ ! chíng-shĭ !" Wâng yĭn chŭng-fŭ kŭ sheŭ-tsŭ kùng-taŭ: "Kiŭ-*
e. 18.	*yàng ! kiŭ-yàng ! Shĭ-kìng ! shĭ-kìng !" Yĭn mwàn Chīn yĭ-kŭ-shâng,*
f. 1.	*súng-yŭ Tĭ taŭ: "Tsiĕ Kwó-hiŭng chĭ tsiŭ, liaŭ-piaŭ siaŭ-tĭ yàng-*
f. 15.	*mŭ chĭ sz̆." Tĭ tsĭ-liaŭ yè chīn yĭ-shâng hwŭĭ-kíng taŭ: "Siaŭ-tĭ*
f. 30.	*ts'ŭ haŭ, hô-tsŭ taŭ taĭ-hiŭng, jŭ kīn, jŭ jŭ." Fāng-tĭ wạn-p'ĭn chĭ*
g. 16.	*chíng, pĭ-tsz̆ kiaŭ-tsán. Yĭ-liên tsiŭ-shĭ sān-kŭ-shâng; Tĭ chíng*
g. 30.	*yaŭ kaŭ chĭ, hwŭ tsŏ-yiŭ yiŭ paŭ Lĭ, Hán-lín tĭ ợr kŭng-tsz̆ laĭ-liaŭ.*

The maxim on page 7 is the 5th of the sixteen original maxims.

The pages 8—12 of the Chrestomathy contain a passage from the *Haŭ-k'iŭ chuên*, a notice of which will be found on page 17 of Part II. In this work, a perusal of the whole of which we would recommend to the student of Chinese, we see, as Sir John Davis aptly says, "portrayed by a native hand this most singular people in almost every variety and condition of human life.

"Quicquid agunt homines—votum, timor, ira, voluptas,
    Gaudia, discursus—nostri est farrago libelli."

See the Preface to his admirable translation, "The Fortunate Union."

The student will observe that the absolute clause, which may be translated by a clause beginning with *having* or *being*, is of very frequent occurrence in Chinese composition. The first thing to do is to unite the characters and syllables which form phrases or grammatical words,—nouns, verbs, or attributive expressions. Such are *swàn-kĭ* (8. a. 6, 7), which, though verbs generally, are here united to form a noun,—'plans.' Then *tíng-liaŭ* is a verb, 'being fixed;' *tsz̆-jĭ* (a. 11, 12) is a phrase, 'the next day,' just as in English, 'he came next day' for 'he came on the next day,' the word *on* being omitted in Chinese, as in

and I am going again without delay;—with respect to greetings, for my own part, I have no politeness, therefore respectfully relying upon you Sir, the messenger, I must decline with thanks; for my coming to-day was only to acknowledge a visit and to render my obligations to Mr. *Kwo*, who most assiduously invited me to stay. Should I wish to stay, I fear it would be improper; should I wish to go, I also fear lest it might not be kind: just at this troublesome juncture of my embarrassment, fortunately you, respected Sir, are come to direct me." *Shwüi-yŭn* said: " Good friends of the olden time were inclined to conceal such reasons; you Mr. *T'ĭ* and my relation Mr. *Kwo* are forsooth as good as the ancients!—but to confine yourselves strictly to the world's customs in this manner, would certainly not be right." *Kwo* laughed and said: " Of a surety my old friend speaks with an acute shrewdness." *T'ĭ* seeing that they both were alike wishing to detain him as a guest, now forgot his earlier dispositions, and feeling well disposed in mind, (then) he smiled, sat down, and spoke no more of going. Soon after this, wine was served up; Mr. *Kwo* then showed him a seat. But Mr. *T'ĭ* said: " I am much obliged indeed for your consideration of my morning fast, and for giving me refreshment, *but* why do you also trouble yourself to bestow wine *on me;* I suspect this is not a time to drink." *Kwo*, laughing, said: " Go on drinking a little, and presently we shall find it is drinking time." All three laughed outright, and sat down to their cups.

Translation of the Extract from the Haŭ-k'iŭ chuên (3), *v. native text,* page 10.

Now the three happened to be good friends with the wine, and directly they raised their hands *to drink,* (then) they felt an increasing relish for it; and when they had once *pledged* each other, (then) they did not again decline drinking. After drinking three horns, and just as Mr. *T'ĭ* thought of stopping, all at once the attendants announced that the third son of *Wang*, of the Board of War, had arrived. The three gentlemen had merely put down their glasses to receive him, when *Kwo* proceeded to seat him comfortably, saying: "Mr. *Wang* it is a good thing that you are come." Then with his hand he pointed to *T'ĭ*, saying: "This gentleman, Mr. *T'ĭ*, is a hero and a scholar, you ought to make his acquaintance." *Wang* replied: "Surely it is no other than that *T'ĭ t'ing-sang*, who forcibly entered the Pleasure palace of *Tá-gān-heŭ?*" *Shwüi-yŭn*, hastily replying, said: "Quite so! quite so!" *Wang* then renewing his salutations with respect said: "I have looked forward to this pleasure! I was ignorant of the honour!" Then, filling a large wine-cup, he presented it to *T'ĭ*, saying: "I borrow Mr. *Kwo's* wine to show in a small degree my private feelings of respect." *T'ĭ* received it, and having poured out a cup in return, politely said: "I am a common person, what have I worthy of mention; *but* your qualities, Sir, may be compared to gold and jewels." Then after reciprocal praises on degree of scholarship and rank had been passed between them, and three cups had been drunk in succession, just as *T'ĭ* was about to say he must stop, on a sudden the attendants again made an announcement that the second son of

46   SHI-WAN.—SIAU-SHWO.—HAU-K'IU CHUEN.   [10. h. 17.—11. j. 28.]

h. 17.   Sz̽-jin ching yaú k'ĭ shīn siāng-yíng; nà Lì kūng-tsz̽ ĭ-tseù taú si-
i. 3.   ts'iên chi-chú taú : " Siāng-shŭ hiūng-tí, pŭ siaū túng-shīn, siaù-tí
i. 17.   kīng tsiú tsŏ pá !" Kwó taú : " Sháng yiù yuèn-k'ĕ tsaí-tsz̽." Tí t'íng
j. 1.   shwŏ, yiú tĭ lĭ sĭ yaú tsŏ lĭ. Nà Lì tsiĕ pŭ tsŏ yĕ, siēn k'án-chŏ Tí
j. 19.   wa̧n taú : " Haù yīng tsiún jin-wŭ !" Tsiĕ tsìng-kiaú chàng-hiūng-tí
k. 2.   sīng taí-haú ? Tí taú : " Sîaù-tí naĭ tá-ming, Tí Chúng-yŭ." Lì taú
k. 17.   chĕ-ta̧ng shwŏ shí, Tí Tū-hiên tĭ chàng kiūn-tsz̽; liên-liên tsŏ-yĭ taú:
l. 3.   " Kiù-wa̧n tá-ming, kīn-jĭ yiù yuên-híng hwüï !" Kwó-tsiú yaú jĭ-tsó.
l. 18.   Tí tsz̽-shí tsiù-ĭ-pwán-hān, yiú siàng yaú-híng; yīn ts'z̽ shwŏ-taú:
m. 4.   " Lì hiūng ts'aĭ laĭ, siaù-tí pa̧n-pŭ-kaĭ tsiú yaú k'ŭ, chĕ yīn laĭ tĭ tsaù,
m. 21.   t'aū yin kwó tō, hwáng hîng sĭ kūng-tsūng, pŭ na̧ng kiù-chú; chĕ-tĭ
n. 6.   yaú siēn pĭ-liaù." Lì yīn tsŏ-sĭ taú: " T'ĭ-hiūng yĕ t'aí-k'ĭ jin ! kī-
n. 22.   yaú-híng, hŏ pŭ tsaù k'ŭ ? Weí-hŏ siaù-tí kūng taú, tsiú yĭ-k'ĕ yĕ pŭ
o. 9.   na̧ng liŭ ? chĕ-shĭ mîng k'ĭ siaù-tí ! Pŭ tsŭ yù yìn-liaù !" Shwüï-yūn
o. 24.   taú: " Tí siēn-sāng k'ŭ, shí yaú k'ŭ-kiù-liaù !"

11.   Extract from the *Haú-k'iú chuén* (4), v. native text, page 11.

a. 5.   Tí wŭ-naí chĕ-tí yiú fŭ tsó-hiá, yŭ Lì tüí yìn-liaù sān-kŭ-shāng.
a. 22.   Yīn-ts'aí-wán, hwŭ tsŏ-yiú yiú paù-taú Cháng ka̧ng-k'iŏ tĭ tá kūng-tsz̽
b. 8.   laí-liaù. Chúng-jīn hwán wĭ kĭ tá-yíng, chĕ-kiên ná Cháng kūng-tsz̽
b. 23.   waí-taí-chŏ yĭ-tĭng fāng-kīn yĕ siĕ-chŏ liàng-chĕ sĭ-yèn, tsaú-paù-chŏ
c. 10.   yĭ-kŏ mà-liên, tsaù k'ĭ-tí tsüí hiūn-hiūn, yĭ-lú kiaú tsiāng-tsìn-laí taú:
c. 27.   " Nà yĭ-weí shí Tí hiūng, kí yaú taú ngò lí ch'ing-hiên laí, tsó haù-kĭ,
d. 14.   tsāng pŭ-hwüï ngò yĭ-hwüï ?" Tí ching lĭ-k'ĭ shīn laí tà-cháng yù t'ā
d. 30.   shĭ lĭ, kiên t'ā yên-yŭ pŭ-sa̧n, piên lĭ-chú tá-yíng taú: " Siaù-tí piên-
e. 17.   shí T'ĭ t'ing-sāng, pŭ-chĭ chàng-hiūng yaú hwüï siaù-tí, yiù hŏ tsz̽-
f. 2.   kiaú ?" Cháng yĕ pŭ-weí lĭ, ch'ing-chŏ yèn k'ān Tí, k'ān-liaù yiú-k'ān,
f. 17.   hwŭ tá-siaú shwŏ-taú: " Ngò chĕ-taú T'ĭ-hiūng shí tsĭ-kó t'eŭ pă-kó
g. 3.   tàn tĭ haù Hán-tsz̽ !—K'iŏ yuên-laí ts'ing-ts'ing meí-mŭ, pĕ-pĕ mién-
g. 18.   k'ùng !—wŭ-í yŭ nŭ-tsz̽ !—siāng-shí Tsīn-heú ! heú tsŏ-liaù sz̽ yŭ, tsiĕ
h. 4.   mán-kiàng; tsiĕ siēn kiaú-yĭ-kiaú tsiù-liáng, k'ān shí jŭ-hŏ ?" Chúng-
h. 18.   jīn t'ing-liaù, k'ŭ tsán-meĭ taú : " Cháng-hiūng miaú-la̧n tá-tĭ yíng-
i. 2.   hiūng pa̧n-sĭ !" Tsiĕ ts'ing yĭ-shāng yĭ-yìn a̧r ʟuu tsz̽ kān-liaù, süï
i. 17.   lù k'ùng-shāng yaú chaú-kān. Tí kiên t'ā kān-tí shwa̧ng-kw'aí, wŭ-
j. 1.   naí-hŏ yĕ chĕ-tí miên-k'iáng k'ĭ-kān-liaù. Cháng-taú : " Ts'aí siàng
j. 15.   kó páng-yiù yĭ-miên !" Yiú kiaú tsò-yiú chīn-k'ĭ liàng-shāng. Tí

English. Observe that words expressing 'then' as a mark of sequence are often used in Chinese, where in English we should omit them : e. g. tsiú (8. n. 16), tsaù (8. c. 14), fāng-tsat (8. h. 1, 2), and often. Several expressions occur in this extract, which are set phrases for particular occasions, and partake of the nature of proverbs or common sayings, and, as such, cannot be explained by the ordinary rules of grammar : e. g.—

kweí-sīn sz̽-tsiên (8. k. 12) 'returning heart as arrow (fleet).'
fūng-yū siaù-jīn (8. l. 18) 'the winds and moon would smile at man.'
hîng-sĭ kūng-ts'ūng (9. b. 7) 'my face is set like running stream to go.'

Li, Fellow of the Imperial Acadamy, had come. Just as the four gentlemen were rising to receive him, this Mr. *Li* had walked into the festive scene, and stopping, said: "Old friends like us will not take up time in moving, I am already seated." *Kwo* said: "But there is a guest here from a distance!" When *Tĭ* heard this said, he left the table, and sought to make the salutations. The aforesaid Mr. *Li* did not make any bow, but he first looked at *Tĭ* and said: "A fine superior sort of man! Be so good, Sir, to tell me your surname and name (eminent designation)." *Tĭ* replied: "My proper name is *Tĭ Chūng-yŭ*." *Li* said as follows: "It is *Tĭ*, the Censor's eldest son." Repeatedly bowing, he went on to say: "I have long ago heard of your great name, to-day by some good providence we have happily met." *Kwo* then invited him to be seated. *Tĭ* at this time being half-overcome with wine, and besides that thinking of taking his departure, (then) declined with these words: "Since Mr. *Li* is just come, I properly ought not to go, but I came early, and I feel ashamed of having drunk so much, and much more for this reason that I am in great haste to travel, and cannot remain long, indeed I wished before to go." *Li* then changed countenance and said: "Mr. *Tĭ* is very insulting, if he wished to go, why did he not go sooner? Why just when I came, then all on a sudden he could not stay? this is clearly an insult to me; I am not good enough to drink with!" *Shwŭi-yün* said: "Mr. *Tĭ* wished to leave a good while ago."

Translation of the Extract from the Haú-k'iŭ chuén (4), *v. native text,* page 11.

Tĭ had no other alternative but to sit down again, and with *Li* to drink three large cups. When they had finished drinking, suddenly the attendants announced that the eldest son of *Chang*, a person of distinction, had arrived. Before any one had time to reply, they see Mr. *Chang*, with his dress all awry, with his eyes askant, and with a rakish air, having made himself drunk betimes, come rolling in, crying: "Which is Mr. *Tĭ*, who is come to our ancient city and place to play the hero? how is it he did not favour me with a visit?" *Tĭ* was just then standing up, preparing to salute him, *but* when he saw that his expressions were uncivil, he drew himself up and replied: "Your humble servant's name is *Tĭ t'ing-sang*, I was ignorant that you, Sir, wished to meet me; pray what are your commands?" *Chang* still made no bow, *but*, looking straight at *Tĭ*, he stared and stared again; then, bursting into a loud laugh, he said: "Why I expected to find Mr. *Tĭ* a seven-headed and eight-hearted Chinaman, and behold he has fine blue eyes and a pale countenance, just like a girl. I believe he is a mere effeminate, and bye and bye we will say more about it, but first let us try his capacity for wine and see what it is." They all heard and praised the plan highly, saying: "Mr. *Chang* speaks well, with the real spirit of a great hero!" Then they proposed a bumper to be drained, and when it was drained they raised the empty cup to show that it was dry. *Tĭ*, seeing that they drained theirs without being the worse for it, had no alternative but, perforce, to drink off his own. *Chang* said: "Come now, that's friendly!" and called the attendants to refill the cups. But *Tĭ*

48   SHI-WAN.—SIAU-SHWO.—HAU-K'IU CHUEN.   [11. j. 29.—12. l. 9.]

j. 29. *taú:* "*Siaù-tĭ tsŏ-kiù tĭ yiú p'eĭ Wáng-hiŭng săn-shăng, Lĭ-hiŭng*
k. 13. *săn-shăng, fáng ts'aĭ yiú k'ŭ p'eĭ cháng-hiŭng yĭ-shăng. Tsiên-liàng*
k. 26. *yiù hien.*" *Cháng-taú:* "*Kĭ Wáng, Lĭ, ạr-hiŭng k'ŭ liên săn-shăng,*
l. 9. *hŏ tŭ siaù-tĭ yaú yĭ shăng ạr chĭ?—shĭ k'ĭ siaù-tĭ liaù! ts'ŭng-pŭ*
l. 25. *sheú jĭn chĭ k'ĭ!*" *Chăng piên mwàn-liên t'ạn-nú taú:* "*Kiàng-*
m. 7. *mĭng tŭi-yĭn ngò k'ĭ-liaù, nĭ jŭ-hŏ pŭ-k'ĭ? mŏ-fĭ nĭ ì k'iàng k'ĭ ngò*
m. 25. *mŏ?*" *Tĭ yĭ-shĭ tsŭi-tĭ shĭn tŭ yuèn-liaù, kaú-chŏ ĭ-tsź, chĕ yaŭ-t'eŭ*
n. 12. *taú:* "*K'ĭ-tĭ-piēn, k'ĭ; k'ĭ-pŭ-tĭ-piēn, pŭ-k'ĭ; yiù shĭn-mŏ k'iàng?*"
n. 27. *Cháng-taú:* "*Chĕ peī-tsiù, nĭ kàn pŭ k'ĭ mŏ?*" *Tĭ taú:* "*Pŭ-k'ĭ!*"
o. 11. *Chăng tá-nú taú:* "*Nĭ tsăng kàn taú ngò Shān-tŭng laĭ chwăng-*
o. 24. *k'iàng. Nĭ pŭ-k'ĭ ngò chĭ-peī-tsiù ngò piēn yaú nĭ k'ĭ liaù k'ŭ!*"

12.   Extract from the *Haú-k'iŭ chuên* (5), v. native text, page 12.

a. 9. *Yīn ná-k'ĭ ná peī tsiù laĭ chaú chŏ Tĭ kiă-t'eŭ kiă-liên, chĕ yĭ-kiaŭ.*
a. 26. *Tĭ, sŭī-jên tsŭi-liaù, sĭn-shăng kiŏ-wán mĭng-pă. Yĭ-kĭ kĭ-tĭ hŏ-sĭng*
b. 13. *lwán-pĭng; yĭn tsiăng-tsiù tŭ kĭ-sĭng-liaù; wáng-t'iaú k'ĭ-shĭn laĭ,*
b. 27. *tsiăng Chăng yĭ pà chaú chŭ jaù liaù liàng jaù taú:* "*Tsăng kàn taú*
c. 11. *hù-t'eŭ shăng laĭ, sĭng sź!*" *Chăng tá kiaŭ taú:* "*Nĭ kàn tà ngò mŏ?*"
c. 26. *Tĭ piên yĭ-chùng taú:* "*Tà nĭ piên tsăng-mŏ?*" *Kwŏ ts'aĭ hwá-taú:*
d. 10. "*Haù-ĭ liŭ yĭn, naĭ kàn ĭ-tsiù să yè! kw'aĭ kwăn mạn pŭ-yaú tseŭ-*
d. 26. *liaù! tsiè tà t'ā kŏ tsiù-sĭng!*" *Tsaù liàng siăng tseù-ch'ŭ ts'ĭ-pă-kŏ*
e. 11. *tá-hán. Tĭ siaú-yĭ-siaú taú:* "*Yĭ-k'iŭn fŭng keù! tsăng-kàn laĭ k'ĭ*
e. 26. *jĭn!*" *Yīn yĭ-sheú chŭ-chŭ Chăng pŭ-fáng, yĭ-sheú tsiăng taĭ-tsź yĭ-*
f. 11. *hiên nà siē hiaú-chán wàn-chàn, tà-fān yĭ-tĭ. Shwŭi-yŭn kăng tseù-taú*
f. 27. *shĭn-piên, p'ĭ Tĭ chĕ yĭ-t'ŭī taú:* "*K'án Shwŭi siaù-tsiē fān-shăng,*
g. 11. *jaú nĭ; tà tsaù t'ŭī-tĭ-k'ŭ, yiù cháng yuèn-kĭn tĭ-taú tĭ shăng; pă*
g. 28. *pŭ-k'ĭ-laĭ. Tĭ tsiăng Chăng t'ĭ tsiăng k'ĭ-laĭ chĕ yĭ-sheù saú-tĭ chŭng-*
h. 15. *jĭn tŭng-taú-sĭ-waĭ. Chăng yuèn-shĭ kŏ sĭ-lĭ, niŭ hwā tsiù hiŭng hŭ*
i. 1. *tĭ mwàn-k'eù kiaú-taú:* "*Tá-kiă pŭ-yaú tŭng-sheù! yiù hwá haù-*
i. 15. *kiàng!*" *Tĭ taú:* "*Mŭ shĭn hwá kiàng; chĕ haù-haù sŭng ngò ch'ŭ*
i. 28. *k'ŭ, piên wán sź tsiuên hiŭ. Jŏ yaú kiuên-liŭ, kiaú nĭ jĭn-jĭn tŭ sź.*"
j. 14. *Chăng liên-liên yĭng-chĭng taú:* "*Ngò súng nĭ! Ngò súng nĭ!*" *Fáng*
j. 27. *Tĭ tsiăng Chăng fáng-pĭng, shán wạn-liaù yĭ-sheù t'ĭ-chŏ tsź-pŭ-liaù*
k. 12. *ch'ŭ-laĭ, chúng-jĭn yèn tsăng-tsăng k'án, chŏ-k'ĭ tĭ-pĕ-t'ĭng, yiù pŭ kàn*
k. 28. *shăng-ts'iên, chĕ-haù tsaĭ-p'áng shwŏ-ngáng-hwá, taú:* "*Kàn tsăng*

Kiŭ-pĭ-săng (10. a. 10) is a cake used in the fermentation of wine. *Pĭ-săng* refers probably to the sprouting of the grain from which the liquor is made; and this whole expression seems to be used here, by *metonomy*, for the wine itself, just as *John Barleycorn* is employed in our own language for ale or beer.

Nĭ yĭ-peī, ngò yĭ-chàn (10. a. 26) is a graphic form of expression, perhaps the proper form for inviting another to take wine, in pledging one another. *Pwán-shàng* (10. b. 9), lit. 'half the forenoon,' consequently 'three hours.' Observe that *chíng*, when used for 'just as,' takes the second place when the subject of the sentence is mentioned (cf. 10. b. 12).
The polite expression in 10. e. 17—24. is hard to translate into English, but the version we have given conveys very nearly the signification intended in the original.

exclaimed: "Your humble servant has been sitting a long time, and has just now taken three cups with Mr. *Wang,* three cups with Mr. *Li,* and now one cup with you, Sir; my shallow capacity has a limit." *Chang* replied: "Having taken three cups with each of our brethren, *Wang* and *Li,* why with me, only one cup and then stop? This is to insult me! I have never yet been insulted by any body!" He then swelled with suppressed rage, and said: "Apologise by drinking in reply to me! Why don't you drink? Surely you intend to insult me excessively, don't you?" *Tĭ* now being nearly overcome with what he had drunk, leaned back in his chair and, shaking his head, exclaimed: "When it is convenient to drink, then I drink; when it is not convenient to drink, I won't drink; where is the excessive insult?" *Chang* said: "This cup of wine will you dare not to drink it?" *Tĭ* said: "I won't drink it!" *Chang,* in a great rage, cried: "Why do you dare to come to our *Shan-tung* to show these airs; if you will not drink this cup of wine of mine, I will make you drink it."

Translation of the Extract from the Haŭ-k'iŭ chuên (5), *v. native text,* page 12.

He then took up the cup of wine and dashed it completely over the head and face of *Tĭ,* who, although in a state of intoxication, yet had his wits about him. Suddenly his ardent temper was roused, and all confusion of mind was dissipated; and, as far as the wine went, he was sobered. He jumped up in an instant and, having seized *Chang* with a firm grasp, he swung him round twice, saying: "How dare you venture to come, seeking death, with a tiger?" *Chang,* with a loud voice, cried: "Do you dare to strike me?" *Tĭ,* then giving him a slap, replied: "If I strike you, what then?" *Kwo* then put in a word: "A fine idea to stay drinking, and then, relying on the wine, to make a disturbance!—quickly shut the door and let no one go out! Then beat him until he is sober!" At once from two adjacent rooms came forth seven or eight strong fellows. But *Tĭ,* with a smile, said: "You pack of mad dogs, how dare you come to insult a man!" Then with one hand he gripped tightly hold of *Chang* and with the other he lifted the whole table of refreshments and scattered them on the ground. *Shŭĭ-yŭn* just then having approached him, was pushed by *Tĭ* with the words: "Having a regard for your niece I spare you a little:" as he hurled him several feet away, where he fell sprawling on the ground unable to rise. *Tĭ* then took *Chang,* and with one hand sweeping him round, he scattered them all in every direction. Now *Chang,* who was a man of vicious habits and was enervated with wine and debauchery, cried out with all his might: "Every one be still!—we will hold a parley!" *Tĭ* replied: "There is no need of that; only show me out, and then a host of troubles will be avoided; but if you should force me to remain, I will be the death of every one of you!" *Chang* then repeatedly answered: "I'll show you out!— I'll show you out!" Then *Tĭ* took *Chang* and set him up, and having placed him firmly upon his legs, with one hand he held him and marched out, while the rest fiercely looked on and angrily stood forward, but not daring to advance, they merely uttered aside their boasts, saying: "How dare he thus

l. 10. *jŭ-tsz̀ hŭ weî, tsiè jaŭ t'ā k'ŭ, shaù-pŭ-tĭ yaŭ kien kô kaŭ hiä !" T'ĭ*
l. 27. *chĕ tsŏ-pŭ-t'ing-kién, t'ĭ-chŏ Chāng chĭ t'ŭng tseù-ch'ŭ tá-mẹ̆n chī waî,*
m. 13. *fāng tsiāng-sheù fáng k'aī taŭ: "Fān Chāng-hiŭng ch'uên yŭ chŭ-*
ın. 25. *hiŭng; ngŏ, Tī Chāng-yŭ, jŏ yiù tsặn tĭ tsaí sheù, tsiēn-kiŭn wán-mà*
n. 10. *chŭng, yè pŭ-k'ŏ ch'ŭ-jîn, hŏ hwāng sān-wù kô tsiù-sĭ chī t'ŭ, shĭ sú*
n. 27. *kô Hán chī-wáng-yaŭ liŭ màng hù chī pín ! Hô k'ĭ yŭ yè !" T'siāng-*
o. 12. *sheù yī-kù taŭ : " Tsìng-liaù !" K̄ing tá-tă pŭ-hwŭĭ liá-chŭ laĭ.*

13.   Extract from the *Shwŭĭ-hù chuén* (1), v. native text, page 13.

a. 1. *Shwŭĭ-hù chuén. Hwá-shwŏ kù Súng Chĕ-tsūng Hwáng-tĭ tsaî-*
a. 14. *shĭ. K'ĭ-shĭ Súng Jîn-tsūng T'iēn-tsz̀ ĭ yuèn, Tūng-k̄ing, K'aī-fūng*
a. 28. *fŭ Piēn-liáng, siuēn-wù-kiŭn piēn yiù yī-kô feŭ-lâng p'ŏ-lŏ-hŭ tsz̀-tí,*
b. 15. *sîng, Kaŭ; p'aī-hâng, tì-ạr; tsz̀-siaŭ pŭ-ch'îng kiä-nĭ; chĕ haù ts'z̀-*
b. 30. *ts'iâng shĭ-p'àng, tsŭĭ-shĭ t'ĭ-tĕ-haŭ kiŏ-k'ĭ-k'iŭ. K̄ing-sz̀ jîn k'eù-shặn*
c. 16. *pŭ-kiaŭ Kaŭ-ạr, kiŏ tū kiaŭ t'ā tsŏ, Kaŭ-k'iŭ. Heŭ-laĭ fŭ-tsî piên*
d. 2. *tsiāng k'ĭ-k'iŭ nù-tsz̀ k'ŭ-liaù maŭ p'àng t'iēn tsŏ-lĭ jîn piên-kaî-tsŏ*
d. 18. *sîng, Kaŭ; mîng, K'iŭ. Chĕ jîn ch'uī, t'ân, kō, wù, ts'z̀-ts'iâng, shī-*
e. 1. *p'àng, siāng-pŏ, wân-shwà; yĭ hŭ-lwán hiŏ shī-shŭ ts'z̀-fŭ; jŏ lặn jîn-*
e. 17. *ĭ-lĭ-chĭ-sîn-hîng-chūng-liâng, kiŏ-shĭ pŭ hwŭĭ; chĕ tsaí Tūng-k̄ing,*
f. 2. *ch'îng-lĭ ch'îng-waí pāng-hién. Yîn pāng-liaù yī-kŏ sâng, Tĭ-wâng*
f. 16. *yuên-waí ạr-tsz̀, shĭ-ts'ién. Meī-jĭ sān-wà liàng-shê, fūng-hwá-sŭ-*
g. 1. *yŭ; p'ĭ t'ā fŭ-tsīn K'aī-fūng fŭ-lĭ kaŭ-liaù yī-chí wặn-chwáng fŭ-yŭn*
g. 18. *pù Kaŭ-k'iŭ twán-liaù ạr-shī kiuén chấng shĭ p'eī ch'ŭ-kiaī fā-fâng*
h. 3. *Tūng-k̄ing, ch'îng-lĭ jîn-mîn pŭ hŭ-yŭng t'ā tsaí kiä sŭ-shĭ. Kaŭ-k'iŭ*
h. 19. *wŭ-t'aù naī-hô, chĕ-tĕ laĭ Hwaî-sī Lîn-hwaí cheŭ t'eŭ-pặn yī-kô k'aī*
i. 6. *tù-fâng tĭ hién Hán Liŭ Tá-lâng, mîng-hwán Liŭ Shí-kiuén. T"ā*
i. 20. *pîng-sāng chuén haù sī k'ĕ yàng hién-jîn chaŭ nă sz̀-fāng yŭ kă laŭ*
j. 6. *Hán-tsz̀. Kaŭ-k'iŭ t'eŭ-tŏ-tĕ Liŭ Tá-lâng kiä yī-chŭ sān-niên.*

Liaŭ-piaù (10. f. 10) and *yàng-mŭ* (10. f. 14), 'a slight mark of respect,' seem to be the formal expressions for these notions. They are united in one expression in 8. d. 21—26, and are in both places thrown into the position of an attribute; and, though the form of the sentence cannot be preserved, the force of it will be easily seen in each case.

Haù yîng tsiún jîn-wŭ ! (10. j. 21) is a combination of irony and contempt. *Chŏ* in the description of Mr. *Cháng* (11. b. 25; c. 2; and c. 9) is the proper auxiliary verb (cf. Art. 197 of Part I) to form the past tense or past participle; it is, however, frequently used where, in some languages, no past tense would be employed, but only the 'historical' present. The above passages may be translated by *having*, or *being* so and so, as in an absolute clause.

Shwŭĭ-hù chuén (13. a. 1—3). The student may refer to page 17 of the Introduction to the Chrestomathy for a few notes on this work. The title of it does not clearly indicate the nature of its contents, which are of a very varied character; but it conveys an allusion to a story in the *Shi-king*, where a certain ancient prince is said to have escaped with some of his loyal followers from a horde of Tartars. The events narrated in this novel are so far similar to his adventures, that they treat of the troubles which arose out of the wars which happened in China at the end of the *Sung* dynasty (A. D. 1281). (Cf. *Bazin, Le Siècle des Youên*, p. 111.) The style of this work is peculiar, and cannot be deemed a good specimen for imitation. The construction of the sentences however, and the use of appropriate par-to act violently? but let him go, we shall soon see his loftiness brought down!" *Tī* only made as though he heard them not, but keeping fast hold of *Chang* he walked with him out at the front door; then, having loosed his grasp of him, he said: "I will trouble you, Mr. *Chang*, to return and tell your friends, that, with an inch of steel in my hand, I, *Tī Chung-yŭ*, even though amidst troops of cavalry, would not permit any one to stop my exit,—how much less likely is it that three or four drunken and profligate rascals, with the help of a dozen fellows, should beard the tiger in his fury! What a piece of folly!" So saying, he raised his hands, ceremoniously bowed, and then strode homewards.

Translation of the Extract from the Shwuǐ-hù chuén (1), v. *native text*, page 13.

History of the River's banks, or Stories of Banditti.

It said that in the time of the Emperor *Chĕ-tsung* of the ancient *Sung* dynasty, at a period remote from the days of his celestial majesty *Jin-tsung*, there lived in the eastern capital, *Kai-fung fu* in the *Pien-liang* garrison, a dissipated youth belonging to a decayed family, of the name of *Kau*. He was the second son, and *consequently* he had not for himself any of the family fortune, but he was clever in the use of the spear and the cudgel, and very expert at kicking the foot-ball. The men of the metropolis did not call him *Kau-ur* (*his proper name*), but, with freedom of speech, they all called him *Kau-k'iu* ('foot-ball'), hence we see the cause of this character *kiu* ('ball') being attached to this man's name; so that it was changed thus: surname *Kau*, name *K'iu*. This man could play on wind instruments and stringed instruments; he could sing and dance, fence and cudgel, and was fond of trifling amusements; he had * also studied in a desultory manner the *Shi-king*, the *Shu-king*, and both prose and poetry; but as for deeds of kindness, justice, propriety, prudence, and fidelity, he knew just nothing *about them*. He merely spent his time within and without the city, aiding idlers in their pursuits; and he formed a connection in this way with the son of an officer of superior rank, named *Wang*, and helped him to spend his money. Every day brought with it a round of dissipation. But *Wang's* father wrote an accusation against him to the chief magistrate of the capital, and *Kau-k'iu* was sentenced to twenty strokes on the back, and, besides that, to go into exile. All the inhabitants of the metropolis were forbidden to receive him into their houses to board or to lodge. *Kau-k'iu* having no other resource, just proceeded to *Hwai-si;* and having come to *Lin-hwai cheu*, he repaired at once to a certain vagabond Chinaman, *Liu Ta-lang*, who had opened a gambling-house, and went by the name of *Liu Shi-kiuen*. He took pleasure in receiving and feeding all idle loungers; and had also invited, from all sides, the Chinamen *engaged* in the dykes and drains. *Kau-k'iu* found a home in *Liu Ta-lang's* family, where he remained three years.

---

* Cf. Prémare's *Notitia Linguæ Sinicæ*, p. 140.

j. 21.   Heú-laî Chĕ-tsūng T'iēn-tsż, yīn paí Nán-kiaū kàn-tĕ fūng t'iaù
k. 5.   yù shḍn fáng kwān yīn tá shé t'iēn-hiá; nà Kaū-k'iù tsaí Lín-hwaī
k. 20.   Cheū, yīn tĕ-liaù shé-yiú tsüī-fàn, sż-liáng yaú hwüī Tūng-kīng. Ché
l. 5.   Liù Shí-kiuên kiŏ hŏ Tūng-kīng ch'ing-lì Kīn-liáng k'iaù-hiá k'aī-
l. 20.   yŏ-pú-ti, Tùng Tsiāng-sż shí tsīn-sì siè-liaù yī-fūng-shŭ-chă sheú-shì
m. 7.   siè jīn-sż pu'àn-ch'ēn tsī fă Kaū-k'iù hwüī Tūng-kīng t'eù-pḍn Tùng
m. 22. Tsiāng-sż kiā kwŏ-hwŏ. Tāng-shì Kaū-k'iù ts'ż-liaù Liù Tá-láng peī
n. 7.   sháng paū lì, lì-liaù Lín-hwaī cheū ì-lī hwüī-taú Tūng-kīng kíng-laì
n. 23. Kīn-liáng k'iaù-hiá Tùng-sāng yŏ-kiā, hiá-liaù ché-fūng-shŭ. Tùng
o. 7.   Tsiāng-sż yī-kièn Kaū-k'iù k'án-liaù Liù Shí-kiuên laī-shŭ, tsż-t'ù-lì
o. 23. sìn-sż taú: " Ché Kaū-k'iù ngò kiā jù-hô gān-chŏ-tĕ t'ā?

14.   Extract from the Shwüī-hù chuén (2), v. native text, page 14.

a. 7.   Jŏ-shi kô chí-ch'ing laù-shì tĭ jîn, k'ò-ì yúng t'ā tsaí kiā ch'ŭ-jî, yè
a. 25. kiaú haî-ạr-mḍn hiŏ siē haù; t'ā kiŏ-shì kô pāng-hiên tĭ p'ó-lŏ-hú, mŭ
b. 13. sìn-hîng tĭ jîn; yī-tsiè tāng-ts'ù yiù kwó-fàn-laì, pí-twán-p'eî tĭ jîn,
b. 30. kiú-sìng pí-pŭ-k'ạng kaī. Jŏ liù chú tsaí kiā-chūng, taú-yè-tĕ haî-ạr-
c. 17. mḍn pú-hiŏ haù-liaù, taí pú-sheŭ liù t'ā yiù p'ī-pú-kwó Liù Tá-láng
d. 4.   miên-p'î." Tāng-shì chĕ-tĕ k'iuên tsiè hwán-t'iēn-hì-tì siāng-liù tsaí kiā
d. 20. sŭ-hì; meī-jī tsiù-shì, kwàn taí chú-liaù shì sŭ jĭ, T'ùng Tsiāng-sż sż-
e. 7.   liáng-ch'ŭ yī-kó-lú sŭ-tsiāng ch'ŭ yī-t'aú ì-fù, siè-liaù yī-fūng shŭ-
e. 24. kièn, tüī Kaū-k'iù shwŏ-taú: " Siaù-jîn kiā-hiá, 'yíng-hŏ chī kwāng,
f. 8.   chaú jîn pŭ liáng,' k'ùng heú wŭ-liaù tsŭ-hiá ngò chuên tsiên tsŭ-hiá
f. 23. yù Siaù-sū Hiŏ-sż, chŭ; kiù-heú yĕ tĕ-kó ch'ŭ-shīn. Tsŭ-hiá ĭ-nüî
g. 10. jù-hô?" Kaū-k'iù tá-hì, sié-liaù Tūng Tsiāng-sż. Tùng Tsiāng-sż
g. 24. shí kó-jîn tsiāng-chŏ shŭ-kièn yìn-līng Kaū-k'iù kíng-taú Hiŏ-sż fŭ-
h. 10. nüî. Mḍn-lì chuên paù Siaù-sū Hiŏ-sż. Ch'ŭ-laù kièn-liaù Kaū-k'iù
h. 25. k'án-liaù shŭ, chī-taú Kaū-k'iù yuên-laí shí pāng-hiên feù-láng tĭ jîn,
i. 11. sìn-hiá siāng-taú: "Ngò ché-lì jù-hô gān chŏ-tĕ t'ā?—pŭ-jù tsó kó jîn-
i. 29. ts'ing,—tsièn t'ā kŭ fù-mà Wáng Tsîn-liù fù-lì, tsó kó-tsīn süī-jîn;
j. 15. tŭ hwān t'ā tsó Siaù-wáng Tŭ T'aí-weí t'ā piên hì-hwān ché-yáng-tĭ
k. 1.   jîn." Tāng-shì hwüī-liaù Tùng Tsiāng-sż shŭ-chă liù Kaū-k'iù tsaí

---

ticles, as marks of the sequence of clauses, are good and worthy of the student's observation: (cf. p. 14. a. and b.) He should also notice the frequent union of two syllables, of like signification, to make one word, even among the particles: (cf. 13. c. 27; 14. b. 17; 14. l. 17; and often.)

Piên-liáng (13. a. 29) was the ancient name of *Kaī-fúng fù.*

Jîn-ì-lì-chì-sìn (13. e. 16—20), 'kindness, justice, propriety, prudence, and fidelity,' are the cardinal virtues among the Chinese.

Yuên-waī (13. f. 16) is the title of an officer of the fifth rank.

The advanced student will observe that many phrases in the *Shwüī-hù* differ from those in use at present: (cf. *shì-ts'iên* 13. f. 20.) The use of *peī* or *pī* (13. g. 2) to make a passive form of the verb is not unfrequent: (cf. 14. b. 25.)

The expression *sān-wā liàng-shé* (13. f. 24) cannot be literally translated so as to convey the sense, which is a sort of euphemism for a dissolute way of life. The following phrase *fūng hwā-süh-yüh* (13. f. 28) has also a similar signification, for the words 'wind, flowers,

After a time his celestial majesty, *Chĕ-tsung*, when he worshipped in *Nan-kiau*, being moved with gratitude for the propitious winds and the genial rain, then extended his favour, and sent a general pardon throughout the empire. Our *Kau-k'iu*, in *Lin-hwai cheu*, took advantage of the amnesty, and contemplated returning to the capital. Now this *Liu Shi-kiuen* had, in the metropolitan city of *Tung-king*, at the foot of the *Kin-liang* ('Golden-beam') bridge, keeping an apothecary's shop, a relative named *Tung Tsiang-sz*. So, having written a letter of introduction, he collected a few things, with some money for the journey, and presented them to *Kau-k'iu*, bidding him on his return to *Tung-king* to seek a home in the family of *Tung Tsiang-sz*. Then *Kau-k'iu*, having taken leave of *Liu Ta-lang* and shouldered his bundle, departed from *Lin-hwai cheu*, and by easy stages returned to *Tung-king*. He drew near to the foot of the *Kin-liang* bridge, and when he had arrived at the apothecary's shop belonging to *Tung*, he presented his letter of introduction to *Tung Tsiang-sz*. Directly *Tung* saw *Kau-k'iu* and had glanced over *Liu Shi-kiuen's* letter, he thought within himself, saying: "How can I receive this *Kau-k'iu* into my family?

Translation of the Extract from the Shwiŭ-hŭ chuén (2), *v. native text*, page 14.

If indeed he were an honest man and sincere in purpose, he might be useful in going in and out of the house, and also in teaching the children some good things; but the fact is, he has been an associate of idlers, he is of a bankrupt house, and a man of no principle;—and besides, those who have been offenders, and have been cut off from society, certainly will not change their former dispositions. If he remain in my family, he will subvert the good principles of my children, and teach them nothing good; and if I do not treat him civilly and keep him, it will be about equal to brushing the skin off my friend *Liu Ta-lang's* face." Then he just considered within himself, and, by way of pleasing both parties, he received *Kau-k'iu* into his family to take up his abode, daily gave him wine and food, and treated him well for a fortnight. At last *Tung Tsiang-sz* meditated a way out of this awkward business; he took out a new suit of clothes; and, having written a letter, he addressed himself to *Kau-k'iu*, saying: "My poor family, like the light of the glow-worm's fire, cannot make any body illustrious; and I am afraid that bye and bye it will be injurious to you, Sir. But I will recommend you, Sir, to Dr. *Siau-su*, and after a time you will obtain promotion. What do you think of this, Sir?" *Kau-k'iu* was much pleased, and thanked *Tung Tsiang-sz*. The latter then sent a messenger to take the letter and to direct *Kau-k'iu* to the Doctor's mansion. The porter announced his arrival to Dr. *Siau-su*, who came forth to see him. But when he had read the letter, and knew that *Kau-k'iu* was originally an idle vagabond, he communed with himself, thus: "How shall I manage in treating this man?—but it will be best to appear friendly, and I can recommend him to go to the palace of the Emperor's son-in-law *Wang Tsin-liu*, to be a private attendant on the Governor *Siau-wang;*—he is fond of such men." He then replied to *Tung Tsiang-sz's* letter, and kept

k. 15. fù-lì chú-liaù yĭ-yé. Ts'z̄-jì siè-liaù yĭ-fŭng shŭ ch'ing, shĭ kién kān
l. 2. jìn, súng Kaŭ-k'iŭ k'ŭ nà Siaù-wáng Tŭ T'aí-wei chŭ. Ché T'aí-wei
l. 17. naĭ-shí, Chĕ-tsūng Hwáng-tí mĭ-fŭ, Shìn-tsūng Hwáng-tí tĭ fù-mà.
m. 2. T'ă hĭ-gaĭ fŭng-liŭ jìn-wù, chíng yúng ché-yáng tĭ jìn; yĭ-kién Siaù-
m. 18. sŭ Hiŏ-sź chaī-jìn ch'ĭ shŭ, súng ché Kaŭ-k'iŭ laĭ, paĭ kién-liaù, piĕn-
n. 4. hĭ, sūi tsĭ siè hwūi-shŭ, sheŭ-liŭ Kaŭ-k'iŭ tsaī fù-nūi tsŏ kŏ tsīn-sūi.
n. 21. Tsź-tsź Kaŭ-k'iŭ tsaŭ-tsí tsaī Wáng Tŭ-wei fù-chūng ch'ŭ-jì jŭ t'ŭng
o. 7. kiă-jìn yĭ-pān; Tsź-kù taŭ jĭ yuèn jĭ sŭ jĭ ts'īn jĭ kìn. Hwŭ yĭ-jĭ
o. 25. Siaù-wáng, Tŭ T'aí-wei, k'ing-

15. Extract from the *Shwŭĭ-hù chuén* (3), v. native text, page 15.

a. 1.   tán sáng-shīn fặn-fŭ fù-chūng ăn-p'aĭ yèn-yén chuén tsīng siaù-kiù
a. 16. Twān-wáng. Ché Twān-wáng naĭ-shí Shìn-tsūng T"iēn-tsź tĭ shĭ-yĭ
a. 30. tsź, Chĕ-tsūng Hwáng-tí yŭ tí, kién cháng tūng kiá, p'aĭ haŭ kiù tá-
b. 15. wáng; shĭ kŏ tsūng-míng tsiún-siaù jìn-wù, feŭ-láng tsź-tí mặn fŭng-
b. 30. pāng-hiĕn chĭ sź, wŭ yĭ-pān pŭ-hiaŭ, wŭ yĭ-pān pŭ-hwūi, kặng wŭ yĭ-
c. 17. pān pŭ-gaĭ, jŭ kīn-kīn shŭ-hwá wŭ-sò-pŭ-t'ăng; tĭ-k'iŭ, tă-tán, pīn-
d. 4. chŭ t'iaŭ-sź; ch'iŭ, tán, kō wù, tsź pŭ-pĭ-shwŏ. Táng-jĭ Wáng Tŭ-wei
d. 21. fù-chūng, hwaĭ pĭ yèn-yén, shwūĭ lŭ kŭ-pĭ tsīng Twān-wáng kŭ-chūng
e. 6. tsŏ-tíng, T'aí-wei lūi-sź siáng-p'eĭ; tsiù tsīn sŭ-peĭ, shī-kūng liáng
e. 21. t'aŭ, nà Twān-wáng k'ĭ-shīn tsīng-sheŭ, gaŭ-laĭ shŭ-yuên-lĭ; shaŭ-kĭ
f. 6. mảng-kién shŭ-kiă-sháng yĭ tūĭ ặr-yáng chĭ yŭ nièn ch'ing. Chín-chĭ
f. 22. sz̄-tsź kĭ-shí tsŏ-tĭ haŭ sí-k'iaŭ líng-lăng. Twān-wáng nà-k'ĭ sź-tsź
g. 9. pŭ-lŏ sheŭ, k'aŭ-liaŭ yĭ-hwūi, taŭ haŭ. Wáng Tŭ-wei, kién Twān-
g. 23. wáng sīn-gaĭ, piĕn shwŏ-taŭ: "Tsaī yiù yĭ-kŏ yŭ-lŭng pĭ-kiă, yè-shĭ
h. 9. ché-kŏ tsiáng-jìn yĭ-sheŭ tsŏ-tĭ, kiŏ pŭ tsaī sheŭ-t'eŭ; míng-jĭ ts'ŭ haĭ
h. 26. yĭ-píng siáng-súng." Twān-wáng tá-hĭ taŭ sín siè heŭ-i siáng, nà pĭ-
i. 12. kă pĭ-shí kặng-miaŭ. Wáng Tŭ-wei taŭ: "Míng-jĭ ts'ŭ-ch'ŭ-laĭ,
i. 26. súng chĭ kūng-chūng, piĕn kién Twān-wáng yiú siè-liaù liáng-kó, ī-
j. 10. k'iŭ jĭ sĭ yĭn-yén chĭ mŭ tsìn tsūi fāng sān.—Twān-wáng siáng-pĭ,
j. 26. hwūĭ kūng k'ŭ-liaù. Ts'z̄-jĭ Siaù wáng, Tŭ T'aí-wei ts'ŭ-ch'ŭ yŭ-lŭng
k. 11. pĭ-kiă hŏ liáng-kó chín-chĭ yŭ sz̄-tsź, chŏ yĭ-kŏ siaù-kīn hŏ-tsź chíng-
k. 29. liaù, yúng hwáng-lô paŭ-fŭ paŭ-liaŭ, siè-liaù yĭ-fŭng shŭ ch'ing, kiń
l. 14. shĭ Kaŭ k'iŭ sảng-k'ŭ. Kaŭ-k'iŭ líng-liaŭ Wáng Tŭ-wei kiūn-chĭ
l. 28. tsiáng-chŏ liáng-pān yŭ wán k'ĭ hwaĭ-chūng, ch'ūi-chŏ shŭ-ch'ing, kíng-
m. 12. t'eŭ Twān-wáng kūng-chūng, laĭ; pà mặn-hwān-lĭ chuén-paŭ yŭ

---

snow, moon,' frequently imply 'an unrestrained and gay career of pleasure:' (cf. 14. m. 5. and *feŭ-láng* 13. b. 8.)

The word *Hán*[a] is frequently used to designate 'natives of China,' especially such as are brave and manly, like the word *Briton* in English: (v. 13. j. 6; also 12. e. 12.)

Fù-mà (14. j. 3), 'son-in-law of the Emperor,' appears to be used as a title (cf. 15. n. 24), and *tsiè-fū* (16. g. 28), 'brother-in-law,' is used in speaking of another in the third person, for *mĭ-fŭ* (14. l. 23).

[a] 漢

Kau-k'iu in his mansion for the night. The next day he wrote a letter of recommendation, and sent it by a business-like man, who was to guide *Kau-k'iu* to the mansion of the Governor *Siau-wang*. Now this Governor was a brother-in-law of the Emperor *Chĕ-tsung*, and a son-in-law of the Emperor *Shin-tsung*. He was very fond of elegant and rare men and things, and especially of such men as our hero. As soon as he saw Dr. *Siau-su's* messenger bearing a letter and introducing *Kau-k'iu*, he bowed and was pleased; and, having at once written a reply, he received *Kau-k'iu* into his house as a private attendant. From this time forward *Kau-k'iu* was treated in Governor *Wang's* mansion just as one of the family, and thus on all occasions. Now it happened one day that the Governor,

Translation of the Extract from the Shwŭĭ-hŭ chuên (3), *v. native text*, page 15.

Siau-wang, on the occasion of the celebration of his birthday, ordered a banquet to be held in his palace, to which he invited his brother-in-law Prince *Twan*. Now this Prince *Twan* was the eleventh son of the Emperor *Shin-tsung*, and the younger brother of the Emperor *Chĕ-tsung*. He had the supervision of the chariots and the standards of war, and he had the title of viceroy. He was a man of intelligence and beauty, and was acquainted with all the gay and frivolous people of the age; for gallantry and knowledge of the world there was not his equal. Music, literature, and painting he had thoroughly investigated, and it would be superfluous to speak of his powers in kicking foot-ball, playing on the guitar, carving, netting, and the other accomplishments of singing and dancing. On the appointed day, the Prince came to the Governor's mansion, where the feast was prepared. Having invited Prince *Twan* to be seated at the head of the table, the Governor took the opposite end. After the wine had gone round several times, and ten courses had been despatched, Prince *Twan*, on rising to wash his hands, accidently entered the library, where, on a book-shelf, suddenly his eye fell on a pair of beautifully wrought ornaments representing two lions in jade-stone. They were ornamental paper-weights, very finely carved and curiously figured with dragons. Prince *Twan* took up the lions and held them in his hands, while he kept admiring them, and saying that they were beautiful. *Siau-wang*, seeing that Prince *Twan* liked them, (then) said: "I have besides these a pencil-stand in jade wrought with dragons, made by the same artist, but just now it is not at hand; tomorrow I will find it and send it to the palace." Then Prince *Twan* having thanked him again and again, they returned to the saloon, where, after further carousal, they separated.—*Twan-wang* having departed, returned to his palace, and on the following day *Siau-wang*, the Governor, took out the ornamented pencil-stand of jade and, with the two paper-weights,—the lions of the same material,—he placed it in a little silver casket; and, having wrapped the whole in a handkerchief of yellow gauze, he wrote a letter, which he sent *Kau-k'iu* to deliver. *Kau-k'iu*, having received Governor *Wang's* orders, took the two precious articles, and with the letter in his pocket, he proceeded to Prince *Twan's* palace. The keeper of the gate announced him to the steward, who

m. 30. *yuên-kŭng. Mŭ tō-shì yuên-kŭng ch'ŭ laí, wǫ̆n:* "*Nì-shì nà-kó fù-*
n. 10. *lì laí-tì jìn?*" *Kaū-k'iŭ, shī-lì-pá, tă-taú:* "*Siaù-jìn shì Wāng fù-mà*
n. 27. *fù-chŭng, tĕ-sŭng yŭ-wán-k'ì laí-tsìn tá-wáng.*" *Yuên-kŭng taú:*
o. 11. "*Tiēn-hiá tsaí t'ìng-sān-lì hô siaù hwáng-mǫ̆n tì-k'ì-k'iŭ, nì tsź kwó-*
o. 27. *k'ŭ.*" *Kaū-k'iŭ taú:*

16. Extract from the *Shwŭì-hù chuên* (4), v. native text, page 16.

a. 1. "*Siāng-fǎn yìn-tsìn.*" *Yuên-kŭng yìn-taú t'ìng-mǫ̆n. Kaū-k'iŭ*
a. 13. *k'án-shì kiēn Twān-wáng t'eŭ taí juēn-shá T'áng-kīn, shīn ch'uēn*
a. 26. *tsź-siŭ-lŭng p'aŭ-yaū hì wǫ̆n-wù chwáng sŭi t'iaŭ pà siŭ-lŭng p'aŭ*
b. 11. *ts'iēn k'īn ì chă k'ì ch'ŭì tsaí tiaŭ-ặr piēn, tsŭ ch'uēn yĭ-chwáng kàn-*
b. 26. *kīn-siēn fī-fŭng hiŭ, sān-wù kó siaù hwáng-mǫ̆n siāng-pwán chŏ-*
c. 10. *ts'ŭ k'ì-k'iŭ. Kaū-k'iŭ pŭ-kàn kwó k'ŭ ch'ŭng-chwáng, lì tsaí*
c. 24. *ts'ŭng-jìn peí-heú sź-heú yè. Sź Kaū-k'iŭ hŏ-tāng fǎ-tsź shì yŭn taú*
d. 11. *laí nà-kó k'ì-k'iŭ t'áng t'ì k'ì-laí, Twān-wáng tsì-kó pŭ-chŏ hiáng-jīn*
d. 28. *ts'ŭng lì chì kwàn taú Kaū-k'iŭ shīn-piēn. Nà Kaū-k'iŭ kiēn k'ì-*
e. 12. *k'iŭ laí, yĕ-shì yĭ-shì tì tàn liáng shì-kó yuēn-yáng kwaì tì hwán*
e. 28. *Twān-wáng. Twān-wáng kiēn-liaù tá-hì, piēn wǫ̆n taú:* "*Nì shì*
f. 11. *shīn jìn?*" *Kaū-k'iŭ hiáng-ts'iēn kweí-hiá taú:* "*Siaù-tì shì Wáng*
f. 24. *Tū-weí tsīn-sŭì, sheú tŭng-jīn shì lìng tsź sŭng liáng pān yŭ-wán-k'ì*
g. 10. *laí tsìn-hiēn Tá-wáng, yiù shŭ-ch'ìng tsaí-tsź paí-sháng.*" *Twān-*
g. 23. *wáng t'ìng-pá, siaù taú:* "*Tsiè-fū chīn jŭ-tsź kwá-sīn.*" *Kaū-k'iŭ*
h. 7. *ts'ŭ ch'ŭ shŭ-ch'ìng tsìn-sháng. Twān-wáng k'aī hŏ-tsź k'án-liaù*
h. 20. *wán-k'ì tū tì yù t'áng heú kwān sheŭ-liaù k'ŭ. Nà Twān-wáng tsiè*
i. 5. *pŭ-lì yŭ-k'ì hiá-lŏ; kiŏ sīn-wǫ̆n Kaū-k'iŭ taú:* "*Nì chè-laí hwŭì-tì*
i. 22. *k'ì-k'iŭ, nì hwán tsŏ shīn-mŏ?*" *Kaū-k'iŭ yiŭ sheŭ kweí-feú taú:*
j. 6. "*Siaù-tì kiaū-tsŏ Kaū-k'iŭ, hŭ lwán tì tĕ kì paì.*" *Twān-wáng taú:*
j. 21. "*Haù! nì piēn hiá ch'áng laí tì yĭ-hiáng shwà.*" *Kaū-k'iŭ paì taú:*
k. 5. "*Siaù-tì shì hô tāng-yáng jìn, kàn yŭ gān Wáng hiá kiă!*" *Twān-*
k. 19. *wáng taú:* "*Chè-shì ts'ì-yŭn shè mìng weí t'iēn-hiá yuēn, tán t'ì hô*
l. 4. *shāng?*" *Kaū-k'iŭ tsaí paì taú:* "*Tsǎng kàn!*" *Sān-hwŭì wù-tsʼź kaū-*
l. 17. *tsʼź. Twān-wáng tìng-yaú t'ă t'ì. Kaū-k'iŭ chĕ-tĕ k'eŭ-t'eŭ siè-tsŭì,*
m. 2. *kiaì-sì-hiá, tsʼaí t'ì kì-kiă. Twān-wáng hŏ tsʼaì; Kaū-k'iŭ chĕ-tĕ pà*
m. 19. *pìng-sāng pàn-sź tū shì ch'ŭ-laí fŭng-fŭng. Twān-wáng nà shīn-fǎn*
n. 4. *mŭ-yáng, chē k'ì-k'iŭ yĭ-sź p'iaŭ-kiaū niēn tsaí shīn-sháng tì Twān-*
n. 19. *wáng tá-hì nà-lì k'ǎng fáng Kaū-k'iŭ hwŭì fù k'ŭ, tsiŭ liŭ tsaí kŭng-*
o. 5. *chŭng kwó yì-yè. Tsʼź-jì p'aì kó yēn-hwŭì chuēn tsʼìng Wáng Tū-weí*
o. 20. *kŭng-chŭng fŭ yēn.*

The use of *tǎng*ᵃ, for 'that,' is frequent, especially in the phrases *tǎng-jì* 'on that day' and *tǎng-shì* 'at that time:' (cf. 13. m. 27; 14. k. 2; 15. d. 16.)

The accumulation of attributes and epithets for nouns is a characteristic of the style of the *Shwŭì-hù*; e. g. *feŭ-lǎng p'ŏ-lŏ-hŭ tsz-tì* (13. b. 8—14): (cf. 13. l. 23—27; 13. l. 14—21; and *chì-ch'ìng laù-shì tì jīn* 14. a. 10—15.)

ᵃ 當

soon came out and asked, "From whose mansion do you come?" *Kau-k'iu*, having paid his respects, replied: "I am from Son-in-law *Wang's* house, and am come to present some precious articles of *vertu* to His Highness." The steward said: "He is down in the court of the palace, kicking foot-ball with other members of the imperial family;—go over there." *Kau-k'iu* said:

Translation of the Extract from the Shwŭĭ-hŭ chuén (4), *v. native text*, page 16.

"I will trouble you, Sir, to show me the way." Then the steward showed him to the door of the court. While *Kau-k'iu* was looking on, he saw Prince *Twan*, having a turban of the *T'ang* dynasty, made of soft gauze, upon his head; he wore a nankeen vest embroidered with dragons, and adorned with streamers of fine muslin, with embroidered lappets turned down in front, but loosely adjusted on the side of his dress. On his feet were boots elegantly adorned with gold thread and the flying phœnix. Three or four members of the imperial family were assisting him to play at foot-ball, and therefore *Kau-k'iu* dared not to cross over to him, but he stood waiting behind the attendants. Now it happened that *Kau-k'iu* had some experience at foot-ball, and when the ball arose from the ground and Prince *Twan* failed to receive it well, it fell towards the crowd at the side of *Kau-k'iu*. As he saw the ball coming, in a moment he boldly gave it a magnificent kick and sent it back again to Prince *Twan*. When Prince *Twan* saw it, he was greatly pleased, and at once asked, saying: "Who are you?" *Kau-k'iu* came forward and, kneeling, said: "Your humble servant is Governor *Wang's* private attendant, I have received some precious articles to present to Your Highness, and I have a letter also with reference to these things." When Prince *Twan* heard this, he smiled and said: "My brother-in-law has truly great consideration for me!" *Kau-k'iu* then took out the letter and presented it, and Prince *Twan* having opened the casket and looked at the precious articles it contained, committed them unto an attendant; but before they were gone from his hand, he asked *Kau-k'iu*, saying: "You know how to kick foot-ball, what is your name?" *Kau-k'iu* again made obeisance and said: "Your humble servant is called *Kau-k'iu*, and has had some inconsiderable experience in kicking foot-ball." Prince *Twan* replied· "Very good! Come down to the ground and have a game." *Kau-k'iu* bowed and said: "Your humble servant is a person of no rank, how can he presume to engage with Your Serene Highness?" Prince *Twan* replied: "That is, by classifying the clouds and associating great names, to make the world harmonise, but what objection is there to your kicking?" *Kau-k'iu* again bowed and said: "How can I presume?" and after declining several times, Prince *Twan* insisted on his playing. So *Kau-k'iu* just bowed his head and asked pardon, and then, rising from his knees, he went down to the playing ground and took a few kicks. Prince *Twan* called to the people to stand back. *Kau-k'iu* only used his ordinary skill, but he displayed a refined and elegant deportment. Prince *Twan* was pleased with his manner, and requested him to stay at his palace. The next day he prepared a great feast, to which he invited Governor *Siau-wang*.

17. Extract from the Sān-kwŏ chí (1), v. native text, page 17.

a. 2. Sān-kwŏ chí. Tsiè-shwŏ Chāng-jáng Twán-kweī kiĕ-yùng shaù-tí,
a. 16. kĭ Chín-liù Wáng, maú-yēn-tʻŭ-hò, liên-yé pǎn-tseù Pī-máng shān.
b. 1. Yŏ sán kāng shí-fān, heú-mién hán shīng tá kù jìn-mà, kàn chí tāng-
b. 17. tsʻiên Hò-nán Chūng-pú chʻuên-lí Mín-kúng, tá hū: "Yĭ-tsĕ hiŭ
c. 1. tseù!" Chāng-jáng kiēn sź kĭ, siŭí tʻeú hò ạr sź. Tí yù Chín-liù
c. 16. Wáng, wí chī hū-shí, pŭ kàn kaù-shīng, fŭ yŭ hò piēn, lwán-tsʻaù chī
d. 2. nüí. Kiūn-mà sź sán kʻú kàn, pŭ-chī Tí chī sò-tsaí. Tí yù Wáng
d. 18. fŭ-chí sź-kāng, lú-shwüí yiú hiá, fŭ chūng kī nüí, siáng-paù ạr kʻŭ, yiú
e. 5. pʻá jìn chī-kiŏ, tʻān-shīng tsʻaù-máng chī chūng; Chín-liù Wáng yŭ:
e. 19. "Tsż kiēn pŭ-kʻò kịù-lwán, sŭ-pĭ sìn hwŏ-lú. Yŭ-shí ạr jìn ì ì siáng-
f. 7. kĭ, pʻá sháng gán piēn, mwán-tí kīng-kĭ, hĕ-gán chī chūng, pŭ-kiēn
f. 22. hīng-lú; chíng wŭ-naí-hò, hwŭ yiù liù-yíng tsʻiēn-pĕ chʻing-kʻiŭn,
g. 6. kwáng máng chaú yaú, chĕ tsaí Tí-tsʻiên fī-chuên Chín-liù Wáng
g. 19. yŭ: "Sź tʻiēn tsù ngò liūng-tí yè, siŭí siŭí yíng-hò ạr hīng tsiēn-tsiēn
h. 5. kiēn-lú, hīng chí wù kāng, tsŭ tʻúng pŭ-náng híng, shān kāng piēn
h. 19. kiēn yĭ-tüī. Tí yù Wáng ngó yŭ tsʻaù-tüī chī chūng. Tsʻaù-tüī
i. 4. tsʻiên-mién shí yĭ-sò chwāng-yuên, chwāng-chù shí yè múng liàng
i. 17. hùng jí, chüí yŭ chwāng heú. Kʻing-kiŏ pʻĭ-ì chʻù-hú, sź hiá kwān
j. 2. wáng-kiēn chwāng-heú tsʻaù-tüī-sháng húng-kwáng chʻúng tʻiēn.
j. 13. Hwáng-máng wàng shí, kiŏ-shí ạr-jìn ngó yŭ tsʻaù-tüī-pwán. Chwáng-
j. 27. chù wặn yŭ: "Ặr shaù-niên shüí-kiā chī tsż?" Tí pŭ-kàn yìng;
k. 11. Chín-liù Wáng chī Tí yŭ: "Tsż shí tāng-kīn Hwáng-tí; tsaù Shĭ-
k. 25. chǎng-shí chī lwán, tʻaù-nán taú tsż; Wù naí Wáng tí, Chín-liù Wáng
l. 10. yè." Chwáng-chù tá kʻing tsaí paí yŭ: "Chĭn siēn-chaù Sź-tʻú, Tsʻüí-
l. 24. lí chī tí, Tsʻüí-ī yè. Yīn kiēn Shĭ-cháng-shí maí-kwān tsź-liên, kú yìn
m. 11. yŭ-tsż." Süí fù Tí jī chwāng, kweī tsín tsiù-shí.—Kiŏ-shwŏ Mín-

The appositional form of construction is more frequent in the Shwüí-hù than in the Haú-kʻiû. By the appositional form we mean to denote the aggregation of clauses, beginning with verbs which have no apparent subject, but they proceed (without any connective particle being used) to explain something in the preceding clause, and on this account we have designated them *appositional*.

The Sān-kwŏ chí, or 'History of the Three Kingdoms,' has been referred to in p. 16. of Part II. Sir John Davis speaks of the same work, in his book on the Chinese, as being "the only readable Chinese Chronicle;" and he considers that it contains matter as likely to be genuine as the stories detailed in Livy. The style of this work is remarkable for its classic terseness, but it is without the adornment of particles to any great extent. A few are used; but the sequence of clauses, which are generally of four or five characters, suffice to show the connection and the mutual dependence of ideas. Absolute clauses are of frequent occurrence, and there is a general absence of pronouns and particles. Nouns and verbs form the staple material, by the different position of which the grammatical relations are expressed.

Tsiè-shwŏ (17. a. 6) is the regular phrase for the beginning of a new chapter, and *kiŏ-shwŏ* (17. m. 22) for the resumption of a subject which was previously mentioned. *Shaù* (17. a. 14), 'few,' here means 'young,' the word *niên*, 'year,' being understood, or rather the *shaù* being put for the full phrase *shaù-niên* (17. k. 1); a part being used for the whole, which is a common rule in Chinese phraseology. This fact should be born in mind,

Translation of the Extract from the Sān-kwŏ chí (1), *v. native text*, page 17.

The History of the Three Kingdoms.

The story goes on to say, that *Chang-jang* and *Twan-kwei*, having with violence laid hands upon the young Emperor and the Prince *Chin-liu*, rushed blindly through the smoke and fire; and, under cover of the night, fled to the *Pi-mang* mountain. About the third watch, voices were heard behind them, and a great multitude of horsemen pursued them. In the fore-front was *Min-kung*, an official of the second class, from *Ho-nan;* with a loud voice he cried: "Ye obstinate rebels cease to run!" *Chang-jang*, seeing that the crisis had arrived, immediately plunged into the river and died. The Emperor with the Prince *Chin-liu*, unconscious of the real state of things, and not daring to speak aloud, hid themselves among the tangled grass on the river's bank. The cavalry dispersed in all directions in the pursuit, without becoming acquainted with the Emperor's whereabouts. *But* the Emperor and the Prince concealed themselves until the fourth watch, *when*, as the dew was falling, and they felt the cravings of hunger, they embraced each other and cried; but fearing lest any one should find them out, they stifled their voices in the jungle; *then* Prince *Chin-liu* said: " In this place we cannot long beguile the time, we must seek for a means of saving our lives." Thereupon, having girded up their clothes, they crawled up the side of the bank. The ground was all thick with prickly brambles, and, in the darkness, they could not see to walk on the road. Just when they had no other resource, all at once there appeared an innumerable swarm of fireflies streaming past; the light shone splendidly, and they wheeled in their flight only before the Emperor. Prince *Chin-liu* exclaimed: *"*This is indeed Heaven assisting us, my brother!" and forthwith they followed the fireflies' light and proceeded until shortly after they saw the road, and travelled upon it until the fifth watch. *Then* being footsore and not able to proceed, and seeing on a mountain side a heap of grass, the Emperor and the Prince lay down in the midst of it. *Now* in the front of the heap was a farm, and the farmer was dreaming in the night that two red suns had fallen at the back of his farm. Awaking in a fright he threw on his clothes, and, issuing from the house and scanning every side of it, he saw at the back of the farm, on the heap of grass, a red light shoot upwards to the sky. In a state of trepidation he went to look, and behold, there were the two *little* fellows on the side of the grass heap. The farmer asked, saying: "You two youngsters, whose sons are you?" The Emperor not daring to reply, Prince *Chin-liu*, pointing to the Emperor, said: "This is the present Emperor, who, when the revolution of the ten *Chang-shi* broke out, fled, and with difficulty reached this place. I am the Prince junior, Prince *Chin-liu.*" The farmer, in alarm, bowed twice and said: " I am *Tsüi-i*, the younger brother of *Tsüi-li*, the Minister of Instruction during the late reign. Because I saw the ten *Chang-shi* selling office and envying good men, therefore I withdrew in private to this place." He then supported the Emperor to enter the farm, and on his knees presented wine and food.—But to return to the story:—*Min-kung*

m. 25. *kúng kàn-shǎng Twán-kweī, nǎ-chǔ wǎn:* " *T'iēn-tsz̀ hô-tsaí?*" *Kweī*
n. 8. *yên ì tsaí pwán-lǔ siāng-shì, pǔ-chī hô wàng, kúng sùi shǎ Twán-*
n. 23. *kweī, hiên t'eǔ yǔ mà hiáng-hiá, fǎn píng sz̀ sǎn sīn-mǐ. Tsz̀ kì kiǒ*
o. 9. *tǔ shǐng yí-mà sùi lǔ chiǔ-sǐn. Ngeù chī Ts'ǔi-í chwāng; kiên sheù-*
o. 25. *kǐ, wǎn chī. Kúng shwǒ tsiáng-sī.*

18. Extract from the *Sān-kwǒ chi* (2), v. native text, page 18.

a. 2. *Ts'ǔi-í yìn Kúng kiên Tí. Kiūn-chīn t'úng-k'ǔ. Kúng yǔ:*
a. 14. "*Kwǒ pǔ-k'ǒ yi-jī wǔ kiūn, ts'ǐng Pí-hiá hwán Tū.*" *Ts'ǔi-í chwāng-*
a. 29. *shǎng chí-yiù seǔ-mà yí-pǐ; pí yǔ Tí shǐng. Kúng yǔ Chín-liǔ Wáng,*
b. 15. *kúng-shǐng yí-mà, lì chwāng ǎr hǐng. Pǔ-taú sān-lǐ, Sz̀-t'ǔ Wáng-*
b. 30. *yùn, T'aì-weǐ Yáng-più, Tsò-kiūn Kiaú-weǐ,—Shǎn Yǔ-k'iúng:*
c. 12. *Yiú-kiūn Kiaú-weǐ,—Chaú-míng; Heǔ-kiūn Kiaú-weǐ,—Paǔ-sín;*
c. 24. *Chūng-kiūn Kiaú-weǐ,—Yuên-shaú; yí-hǐng jīn chúng, sǔ-pě jīn-mà;*
d. 8. *tsǐ-chǒ kǔ-kiá, kiūn-chīn kiaì-k'ǔ. Siēn shǐ jīn tsiáng Twán-kweī sheù-*
d. 23. *kǐ, wàng kīng-sz̀ haú-líng líng-hwán haù-mà yǔ Tí kì Chín-liǔ Wáng*
e. 9. *k'ǐ-tsǒ. Tsǔ-tí hwán kīng, siēn shǐ Lǒ-yáng siaù-ǎr yaù, yǔ:* "*Tí*
e. 24. *fī Tí, Wáng fī Wáng; Ts'iēn shǐng wán-k'ǐ tseǔ Pě-máng,*" *chí-tsz̀*
f. 8. *kò yǐng k'ǐ ts'ín. Kǔ-kiá hǐng pǔ taú sǔ-lǐ, hwǔ-kiên tsīng-k'ǐ pí-jī*
f. 25. *ch'ǐn-tǔ chē-t'iēn, yǐ-chī jīn-mà taú-laí. Pě-kwǎn shǐ-sǐ, Tí yǐ tá-*
g. 12. *kīng. Yuên-shaú tseǔ-mà ch'ǔ wǎn:* "*Hô-jīn?*" *Siǔ-k'ǐ-yǐng-lǐ, yí-*
g. 26. *tsiáng fī-ch'ǔ, lǐ-shīng wǎn:* "*T'iēn-tsz̀ hô-tsaí?*" *Tí chên-lǐ pǔ-nǎng*
h. 11. *yên. Chín-liǔ Wáng lě-mà, hiáng-ts'iēn ch'ǐ yǔ:* "*Laí-chè hô-jīn?*"
h. 25. *Chǒ yǔ:* "*Sī-liáng Ts'z̀-lǐ, T'úng-chǒ yè.*" *Chín-liǔ Wáng yǔ:* "*Jǔ*
i. 8. *laí paù-kiá yè? Jǔ laí kiě-kiá yè?*" *Chǒ yǐng yǔ:* "*Tí-laí paù-kiá.*"
i. 24. *Chín-liǔ yǔ:* "*Kí-laí paù-kiá, T'iēn-tsz̀ tsaí-tsz̀, hô-pǔ hiá-mà?*" *Chǒ*
j. 10. *tá kīng hwǎng-máng hiá-mà, paì yǔ taú-tsǒ. Chín-liǔ Wáng ì yên*
j. 25. *fǔ-weí Túng-chǒ. Tsz̀-ts'ǔ-chi-chūng, píng-wǔ shǐ-yǔ; Chǒ gán kí-*
k. 10. *chī, ì-hwaì fī-lǐ chī ì. Shǐ jī hwán kúng, kiên hô t'aì-heǔ, kǔ-kǒ*
k. 27. *t'úng-k'ǔ kiên-tiēn kúng chūng pǔ kiên liaù ch'uên-kwǒ-yǔ-sǐ. T'úng-chǒ*

because by this rule only can many expressions be understood which defy a literal rendering.

Liên-yè (17. n. 24), lit. 'connecting night,' i. e. 'joining night to day,' becomes equivalent to our adverbial expression, *day and night*. The translations of titles of officers mentioned in this work cannot, in all cases, be considered satisfactory. The changes which have taken place in the Chinese political world at different periods, and the whimsical alterations in the names of offices, present great difficulties to an English translator.

The use of *yü*[a] (17. c. 26; 17. m. 11) or *yü*[b] (17. e. 30. and h. 27) for *tsaí*[c], 'in,' and *chī*[d] (17. d. 1. and e. 13) for *tī*[e] the genitive particle, with *ǎr*[f] as the mark of *result*, are peculiarities of this style, and in which it approaches that of the ancient classics.

Hǐng-lǔ (17. f. 22), 'to walk on the road,' is an expression which would mean literally 'to walk the road,' but it must be explained either as we have translated it, 'to walk on the road,' or be understood to make a phrase, or, as it were, one word, meaning 'to travel, to proceed *on their way*.'

[a] 於   [b] 于   [c] 在   [d] 之   [e] 的   [f] 而

overtook *Twan-kwei*, seized him, and demanded where the Emperor was; *Kwei* said that he had missed him when half-way on the road, and that he did not know where he was gone. *Kung* forthwith killed *Twan-kwei*, and hung his head from *his* horse's neck. Having divided his soldiers to scour the country in every direction; he himself mounted a horse, and, following the road, went alone in quest *of the fugitives*. By chance he arrived at *Tsüi-i's* farm. *I*, seeing the head, asked about it. *Kung* having explained minutely,

Translation of the Extract from the Sān-kwŏ chí (2), *v. native text*, page 18.

Tsüi-i led *Kung* to see the Emperor. The Sovereign and his minister both wept bitterly, and *Kung* said: "The state cannot exist for a day without a prince, I beseech Your Majesty to return to the Capital." *Now* at *Tsüi-i's* farm there happened to be a lean steed, which they prepared for the Emperor to mount, *while Kung* and Prince *Chin-liu* rode together upon one horse, and so left the farm and proceeded on their way. Before they had gone three short miles, the Minister of Instruction—*Wang-yün*, the Governor *Yang-piau*, the Governor of the Army of the left—*Chun Yü-kiung*, the Governor of the Army of the right—*Chau-mang*, the Governor of the Army of the rear—*Pau-sin*, and the Governor of the Army of the centre—*Yuen-shau*, with a crowd of people and several hundreds of horsemen, met them. The Prince and ministers all wept aloud; and, as a first measure, they sent a man with *Twan-kwei's* head to the city, with the command to expose it, and to bring back some suitable horses for the Emperor and the Prince to ride. These being obtained, they proceeded towards the city; and thus was fulfilled the former saying of the children in *Lŏ-yang:* "The Emperor is not an emperor, the Prince is not a prince; a thousand chariots and a myriad of riders come in from *Pi-mang*." Before the cavalcade had moved many furlongs, what should they see but a host of people coming to meet them, with banners and flags darkening the sky and marching amid clouds of dust. The officers changed colour, and the Emperor also was exceedingly afraid; but *Yuen-shau*, putting spurs to his horse, rode forward and demanded who they were. From behind an embroidered flag, a general burst forth and, with a stern voice, asked: "Where is the Emperor?" The Emperor himself, in a state of fear, dared not to speak; but *Chin-liu* urged his horse forward and shouted · "Who is this coming?" *Chŏ* replied: "The overseer of *Si-liang*,—*Tung-chŏ*." *Chin-liu* said: "Do you come to protect His Majesty, or do you come to seize His Majesty?" *Chŏ* replied: "I am come on purpose to protect him." *Chin-liu* then said: "As you are come for that purpose, why do you not descend from your horse?" *Chŏ*, in a state of fear and confusion, at once dismounted, and made the salute on the left side of the road. Prince *Chin-liu* then spoke to him and calmed his troubled mind. *Tung-chŏ* from first to last carefully observed his expressions, and secretly cherished the desire of making him Emperor. On the same day they returned to the palace and saw the dowager Empress, and they all wept together; but on searching in the palace they were unable to find the imperial seal. *Tung-chŏ* had stationed

l. 11. tŭn-pīng ch'ĭng-waí; meī-jĭ taí tĭ-kiŭ mà-kiūn, jĭ-chĭng hwặng hĭng
l. 26. kiaī-shĭ; pĕ-sĭng hwâng-hwâng pŭ-gān. Chŏ ch'ŭ-jĭ kūng-tĭng liŏ wŭ
m. 11. kí-tán; Heŭ-kiūn Kiaŭ-weí, Paŭ-sín, laí kiên Yuên-shaú yên: "Tûng-
m. 25. chŏ pí-yiŭ ĭ-sīn sŭ ch'ŭ chĭ." Shaú yŭ: "Chaŭ-t'ĭng sĭn-tĭng, wī-k'ŏ
n. 11. kĭng-túng." Paŭ-sín kiên Wâng-yŭn, yĭ yên k'í-sź. Yŭn yŭ: "Tsiè
n. 25. yûng shâng-ĭ." Sĭn-tsź yĭn pạ̀n-pú kiŭn-pīng t'eú Taí shān k'ŭ-liaŭ.
o. 10. Tûng-chŏ ch'aŭ-yiŭ Hô-tsín hiŭng-tí pŭ-hiá chĭ pīng, tsín kweī châng-
o. 25. ú; sź weí Lī-jŭ yŭ:

19.   Extract from the Sān-kwŏ chí (3), v. native text, page 19.

a. 1.   "Wŭ yŭ fĭ Tí, lĭ Chĭn-liŭ Wâng hô-jŭ?" Lī-jŭ yŭ: "Kīn-chaŭ-t'ĭng
a. 17.   wŭ chŭ, pŭ-tsiŭ tsź-shĭ hĭng-sź, chī tsī yiŭ piên ĭ. Laí-jĭ yŭ Wặn-mĭng
b. 5.   yuên-chŭng, chaŭ-tsī pĕ-kwān, yŭ ĭ f ī-lĭ; yiŭ pŭ ts'ŭng chè, chàn-chī;
b. 21.   tsī weí-k'iŭen chī hĭng, chĭng tsaí kīn-jĭ." Chŏ lĭ; tsź-jĭ tá p'aí yên-
c. 7.   hwŭi p'iên, tsĭng kūng-hiâng. Kūng-hiâng kiaī kŭ T'ûng-chŏ, shŭī
c. 19.   kàn pŭ-taŭ. Chŏ taí pĕ-kwān taŭ-liaŭ, jên-heŭ sŭ-sŭ taŭ yuên-mặn hiá-
d. 6.   mà, taí-kiên jĭ sĭ; tsiŭ hĭng sú siŭn, Chŏ kiaŭ t'ĭng tsiŭ chī yŏ; naí
d. 22.   lĭ-shĭng yŭ: "Wŭ yiŭ yĭ yên, chúng kwān tsĭng-t'ĭng." Chúng-kwān
e. 5.   tsĕ ặr. Chŏ yŭ: "T'iēn-tsź weí wân-mĭn chī chŭ, wŭ weī-ĭ, pŭ k'ŏ-ĭ
e. 22.   fûng tsūng-miaŭ shĭ-tsī; kīn Shâng nŏ-yŏ, pŭ-jŭ Chĭn-liŭ Wâng,
f. 6.   ts'ūng-mĭng haŭ-hiŏ, k'ŏ chĭng tá-weí, wŭ yŭ fī Tí lĭ Chĭn-liŭ Wâng;
f. 22.   chū tá-chĭn ĭ-weí hô-jŭ?" Chū kwān t'ĭng pá, pŭ kàn ch'ŭ shĭng.
g. 7.   Tsŏ-shâng yĭ jĭn t'uī gán, chĭ ch'ŏ lĭ yŭ yên-ts'iên, tá hū: "Pŭ k'ŏ!
g. 21.   pŭ k'ŏ! Jŭ-shĭ hô-jĭn? kàn fā tá-yŭ? T'iēn-tsź naī siēn-Tí tĕ tsź,
h. 10.   ts'ŭ wŭ kwŏ-shĭ; hô tĕ wâng-ĭ f ī-lĭ; jŭ yŭ weí tswàn-nĭ yê?" Chŏ shĭ
h. 28.   chĭ, naī Kīng-cheŭ Ts'ź-lĭ, Tĭng-yuên yè. Chŏ nú ch'ĭ-yŭ: "Shặn-
i. 12.   ngò-chè, sāng! nĭ-ngò-chè, sź!" Sŭí chĭ peī-kiên yŭ chàn T'ĭng-yuên.
i. 27.   Shĭ Lī-jŭ kiên Tĭng-yuên peí-heú yĭ-jĭn sāng-tĕ k'í-yŭ hiēn-gáng,

Very few connective particles are employed in the Sān-kwŏ chí for 'and' or 'with:' yŭ [a] is found (17. h. 24); but kiŭn-chĭn (18. a. 8. and d. 12), 'prince and ministers,' is without any connective: (cf. Part I. Art. 288. 1.)

Pŭ-k'ŏ yĭ-jĭ wŭ (18. a. 15), 'cannot be a day without,' seems to be a usual form for the expression 'cannot dispense with.' Compare Chrest. 7. a. 10. et seq. and pŭ-k'ŏ pŭ-hwŭi 'you could not dispense with meeting him.' (10. d. 6.)

Observe that chĭ [b] (18. a. 30) is used for, and is similar in meaning to, chĕ [c] 'only.' Yŭ [d] (18. b. 7) is used appropriately for the datival sign 'for,' as it means 'to give;' but a little farther on it is used for the conjunction 'and' (= to cum 'with'), and it is followed by kúng [e] (18. b. 15).

Kí [f] (18. e. 5) is here used for 'and,' because perhaps yŭ had been just employed for the mark of the dative; and its original meaning suits better the idea of union than does that of yŭ ('to give').

Lŏ-yâng (18. e. 17) was an ancient city in Ho-nan, the capital of the ancient monarch Fŭ-hi.

[a] 與   [b] 止   [c] 只   [d] 與   [e] 共   [f] 及

his troops outside the city, and every day he marched them, heavily armed, through the streets and markets, causing terror and uneasiness to the people. Moreover, he went in and out of the palace without the least concern. This being the state of things, Governor *Pau-sin*, of the Army of the rear, paid a visit to *Yuen-shau*, and said: "*Tung-chŏ* certainly has some sinister intention which he will carry out if he is not removed." *Shau* replied: "The government is but recently become settled, we must not lightly make any move." *Pau-sin* went to see *Wang-yün*, and repeated his thoughts on the state of affairs. *Yün* replied: "It will be well to hold a consultation about it." *Sin* himself thereupon led away the troops under his command to the *Tai* mountain, where they encamped. *Tung-chŏ* induced also the soldiers under the command of *Ho-tsin* and his brother to give him their support, and he then privately consulted *Li-ju* and said:

Translation of the Extract from the Sān-kwŏ chí (3), *v. native text*, page 19.

" I wish to depose the Emperor and to set up *Chin-liu,* the Prince. What think you?" *Li-ju* said: " The present government is without a head, surely this is the time to execute the business, if you delay there will be some change of course. To-morrow, in the *Wăn-ming* garden, summon all the high officials, and proclaim your intention of causing an abdication; those who do not follow you, kill; for the present is just the time to impress them with your power." *Chŏ* was gratified, and the next day he had a great feast, and an assembly, and invited the nobles and gentry. Now the nobles and gentry all feared *Tung-chŏ;* who then might dare to stay away? *Chŏ* waited for all the officials to arrive, and afterwards leisurely riding up to the gate, he dismounted, and came in to dinner, wearing his sword. When the wine had gone round several times, *Chŏ* bade them to cease drinking, and to stop the music, and then in a stern tone he said: "I have a word to say, let all the officers present quietly listen." Then they all inclined the ear, while *Chŏ* said: "The Emperor is the lord of all people, if he has not a dignified appearance he cannot perform the rites in the temple of ancestors and to the gods of the land. *Now* his present majesty is timid and weakly, not like the Prince *Chin-liu,* who is intelligent and fond of learning, and may well succeed to the great throne. I wish therefore to depose the Emperor and to set up *Chin-liu,* the Prince, what do you think of it, my lords?" All the ministers, when they had heard it, were afraid to utter a word. *But* among those who were seated was a man who arose, pushed away the table, and standing erect before the assembly, with a loud voice said: " It cannot be! It cannot be! Who are you that you should dare to utter such great words? The Emperor is the son of the late Emperor's lawful queen. From the first he has been without fault or error, why take traitorous measures to dethrone *him?* Do you wish to become a usurper and a rebel?" *Chŏ* beheld him, and *saw* that it was the *Ts'z-li* of *King-cheu*, —*Ting-yuen* by name. *Chŏ* in a rage shouted out: "Those that obey me, live! those that are adverse, die!" Forthwith grasping the sword at his girdle he wanted to destroy *Ting-yuen,* when *Li-ju,* on seeing behind *Ting-yuen's*

j. 13. *weï-fŭng pīn-pīn, sheù chī fāng-t'iēn hwă kĭ, nŭ mŭ ǫ̊r shí. Lĭ-jŭ kĭ*
j. 30. *tsĭn yŭ:* "*Kīn jĭ yìn yèn chī chŭ, pŭ k'ŏ t'ăn kwŏ-chíng, laì-jĭ hiáng*
k. 16. *Tŭ-t'ăng kŭng-lǎn.*" *Wĭ chī chúng-jĭn kiaī kiuén Tīng-yuên sháng-*
k. 29. *mà ǫ̊r k'ŭ. Chŏ wǎn pĕ-kwān yŭ:* "*Wŭ sò-yên hŏ kŭng-taŭ feù?*"
l. 14. *Lŭ-chī yŭ:* "*Míng kūng chā ĭ; sĭ T'aĭ-kiă pŭ míng, I-yŭn fáng*
l. 29. *chī yŭ T'ăng-kwān; Ch'áng-yĭ wáng tăng weí, fāng ǫ̊r shī tsī jĭ, tsaú*
m. 14. *ŏ săn shī yŭ t'iaŭ; kŭ Hŏ-kwāng kaŭ T'aĭ-miaŭ ǫ̊r fī chī. Kīn-sháng*
m. 30. *suī yiŭ, tsŭng-míng jĭn-chī, píng-wŭ fǎn haù kwŏ-shī; kūng naì waì*
n. 15. *kiŭn Ts'ź-lĭ, sŭ wĭ ts'ăn yŭ kwŏ chíng yiŭ wŭ I-Hŏ chī tá tsaĭ. Hŏ*
o. 2. *k'ŏ kiāng chù fī-lĭ chī sź?* *Shíng-jĭn yŭn yiù I-yŭn chī chĭ, tsĕ k'ŏ*
o. 19. *wŭ I-yŭn chī chĭ tsĕ tswàn yè.*" *Chŏ tá nŭ pă* *

20. Extract from the *Sān-kwŏ chí* (4), v. native text, page 20.

a. 1. *kiên hiáng-ts'iēn yŭ shă chī; I-lâng, P'áng-pĭ kiên yŭ:* "*Lŭ*
a. 14. *Sháng-shū haĭ nüĭ jĭn wáng, kīn siēn haĭ chī k'ùng t'iēn-hiá chĭn-pŭ.*"
a. 29. *Chŏ naì chī; Sź-t'ŭ Wáng-yŭn yŭ:* "*Tĭ-lĭ chī sź pŭ k'ŏ tsiù-heŭ*
b. 16. *siāng-sháng, lĭng-jĭ tsaĭ-ĭ.*" *Yŭ-shí pĕ-kwān kiaĭ sán. Chŏ gān-kiên*
c. 1. *lĭ yŭ yuên-mǎn. Hwŭ-kiên yĭ jĭn yŏ mà ch'ī kĭ, yŭ yuên-mǎn waì*
c. 17. *wàng-laĭ. Chŏ wǎn Lĭ-jŭ:* "*Tsź hô jĭn yè?*" *Jŭ yŭ:* "*Tsź Tĭng-*
d. 1. *yuên ĭ-ǫ̊r, síng, Lù; míng, pŭ, tsź, Tŭng-siēn chè yè. Chù-kūng tsiè-*
d. 16. *sŭ pĭ chī.*" *Chŏ naì jĭ yuên ts'iên-pĭ. Ts'ź jĭ jĭ paŭ Tĭng-yuên yĭn-*
e. 2. *kiŭn chíng-waĭ nĭ-chén. Chŏ nŭ yìn-kiŭn t'ùng Lĭ-jŭ ch'ŭ-yíng;*
e. 16. *liàng-chĭn tuĭ yuên, chĕ kiên Lù-pŭ, tìng sŭ-fă kīn-kwān, p'ī pĕ-hwā*
f. 2. *chên-p'aŭ hwán t'ăng-maŭ k'aĭ-kiă, kĭ sź-lwán paŭ-taĭ, tsŭng mà tĭ kĭ,*
f. 18. *suī Tĭng Kiên-yáng, ch'ŭ taŭ chĭn tsiēn. Kiên-yáng chĭ Chŏ má yŭ:*
g. 2. "*Kwŏ-kiă pŭ hīng, yēn-hwàn lûng-kiuên, ĭ-chĭ wán-mín t'ŭ-t'ăn.*
g. 16. *Ǎr wŭ chĭ-tsǎn chī kūng; yên kàn wáng-yên fī-lĭ, yŭ lwán chaŭ-*

Paŭ-kiá (18. i. 22) 'to protect His Majesty.' Here *kiá*, 'an imperial carriage,' is employed, by metonomy, for royalty itself: (cf. Part I. Art. 182.)

Híng kiaĭ-shì (18. l. 25), 'to walk the streets and markets,' is a use of the verb *híng*, already referred to in the case of *híng-lŭ* 'to proceed on the way,—to travel:' (cf. 18. f. 22.)

Kiên (18. m. 20) 'to see,' in the sense of 'have an interview with,' is very classical: (cf. Chrest. 4. g. 8. and often in the *Sź-shŭ*.) *Yên* (18. m. 23) with the signification 'to speak, to deliberate,' is a mark of classic style, and is different from *weĭ* (18. o. 27), which means simply 'to tell:' *t-sīn* (18. m. 28), lit. 'another heart,' or a 'different mind' from that which he manifested, here means, 'sinister design.' *Wĭ-k'ŏ* (18. n. 9), 'cannot as yet,' is a very elegant expression: indeed the whole reply of *Shaŭ* is worthy of careful notice.

The rapid transition from the narrative of *Pau-sin's* interviews with *Yuen-shau* and *Wang-yŭn* to his placing himself at the head of his troops is a characteristic of the style of the *Sān-kwŏ*.

Tsiŭ (19. a. 20) is used here in an uncommon sense, with the negative *pŭ* before it; it assimilates in meaning to *jŭ* 'as.' The whole expression in this passage means, 'There is no time like the present for action.'

* *Chŏ tá nŭ pă* ª ' *Chŏ* in a great rage drew his sword.' These characters were inadvertently omitted in the native text.

卓 大 怒 拔

back a man of great ability, of a bold and upright figure and a dignified deportment, holding in his hand a long ornamented spear, and looking round with earnest eyes, came forward and said: "To-day this is the place of feasting, we cannot parley about the affairs of state; to-morrow in the Imperial Hall we may publicly discuss." Soon afterwards all present exhorted *Ting-yuen* to mount his horse and go. But *Chŏ* asked the officers, saying: "Is that which I have said in accordance with justice or not?" *Lu-chi* replied: "Your Excellency is in error; in ancient times the Emperor *T'ai-kiă* was of weak mind, and *I-yün* dismissed him to *Tang-kung;* and when the Prince *Chang-yĭ* ascended the throne, and in twenty-seven days did more than thirty acts of wickedness, *Hŏ-kwang* accused him in the Great Temple and deposed him. *But* although the present Emperor is young, he is intelligent, humane, and prudent, and he is without the least fault of any kind; and *you*, my lord, are the *Ts'z-li* of a foreign state, and have hitherto had no concern in this government, moreover you have not the great talents of *I* and *Hŏ;* how then can you take on yourself the business of deposing and raising *to the throne?* A sacred sage *once* said: 'Those who have the mind of *I-yün* may *act as he did;* those who have not his mind will act like rebels.'"

Translation of the Extract from the Sān-kwŏ chí (4), *v. native text,* page 20.

Chŏ was enraged, and, grasping his sword, he sprang forward wishing to kill *Chi;* but the councillor *P'ang-pĭ* restrained him, and said: "President *Lü* is looked up to by all the people, and if you should begin by injuring him, it is to be feared that there will be a commotion in the empire." *Chŏ* then stopped, and the Minister of Instruction, *Wang-yün,* said: "It is not convenient to discuss public affairs after wine, another day we will talk about it." Upon this all the ministers departed. Now as *Chŏ* was leaning on his sword, standing at the entrance to the garden, he chanced to see a mounted horseman prancing up and down in front of the place and flourishing his lance. *Chŏ* asked *Li-ju* who the man was. *Ju* replied: "He is *Ting-yuen's* illegitimate son, his surname is *Lü,* his name is *Pu,* and his title is *Fung-sien,* your lordship should avoid him." *Chŏ* then re-entered the garden, and so got out of the way. The next day it was reported that *Ting-yuen* was at the head of troops outside the city and challenging to battle. *Chŏ* in a rage went forth, accompanied by *Li-ju,* leading troops to meet him. The two lines in semi-circles stood opposite to each other, and there was *Lü-pu,* having a golden band round his hair, and having on a military cloak beautifully embroidered, armour also of the *T'ang* period, and a girdle wrought with lions and gems. He spurred his horse, raised his lance, and following *Ting Kien-yang,* came out to the front of the line. *Kien-yang* pointed to *Chŏ,* and upbraided him, saying: "The government is in misfortune, and the eunuchs are managing affairs to the ruin and desolation of the people and the country. While you, who have not an atom of merit, are desirous of creating rebellion. How dare you traitorously attempt to cause an abdication?" *Chŏ* had not time to reply

h. 1.	t'*íng*." *Tŭng-chŏ wĭ-kĭ hwŭï-yèn, Lù-pū fĭ-mà shă-kwŏ-laĭ. Tŭng-*
h. 16.	*chŏ hwăng-tseù. Kién-yáng sŭ kiūn yèn shă. Chŏ píng tă-paĭ, tŭï*
h. 30.	*săn-shĭ yŭ lĭ hiá-chaĭ. Tsŭ chúng shăng-ĭ. Chŏ yŭ: " Wŭ kwăn Lù-*
i. 15.	*pŭ fĭ ch'áng-jīn yè. Wŭ, jŏ tĕ tsz-jīn, hŏ lŭ t'iĕn-hiá tsaĭ ?" Ch'áng*
j. 1.	*ts'iĕn yĭ-jīn ch'ŭ yŭ: " Chù-kūng wŭ yiù, meŭ yŭ Lù-pū t'ŭng hiáng,*
j. 16.	*chĭ k'ĭ-yŭng ạr wŭ-meŭ, kiĕn-lì wáng-ĭ; meŭ p'íng săn-tsăn pŭ-lăn-*
k. 2.	*chĭ-shĭ shwŏ, Lù-pū kŭng-sheù laĭ kiáng: k'ŏ hŭ ?" Chŏ tă-lĭ, kwăn*
k. 17.	*k'ĭ jīn naĭ Hù-fạn Chūng-lăng tsiāng, Lĭ-sŭ yè. Chŏ yŭ: " Jŭ tsiāng*
l. 2.	*hŏ-ĭ shwŏ chī ?" Sŭ yŭ: " Meŭ wặn Chù-kūng yiù míng-mà yĭ-pĭ, haŭ*
l. 18.	*yŭ: "Chĭ-t'ŭ,"jĭ-híng ts'iĕn lĭ ; sŭ tĕ tsz-mà, tsaĭ yúng kīn-chŭ, ĭ-lĭ kĭ k'ĭ*
m. 7.	*sīn; meŭ kăng tsin shwŏ-tsz, Lù-pū pĭ fặn Tíng-yuēn, laĭ t'eŭ Chù-*
m. 22.	*kūng ĭ." Chŏ wặn Lĭ-jŭ yŭ: " Tsz-yĕn k'ŏ hŭ ?" Jŭ yŭ: " Chù-kūng*
n. 7.	*yŭ-ts'ù t'iĕn-hiá, hŏ-sĭ yĭ-mà ?" Chŏ hiĕn-jĕn yŭ-chĭ, kặng yŭ hwăng-*
n. 23.	*kīn yĭ-ts'iĕn-liàng, míng-chū sŭ shĭ-kŏ, yŭ-taĭ yĭ-t'iaŭ. Lĭ-sŭ ts'ĭ-liaù*
o. 10.	*lĭ-wŭ, t'eŭ Lù-pū chaĭ laĭ fŭ-lŭ, kiūn-jīn weĭ-chŭ. Sŭ yŭ: " K'ŏ sŭ-*
o. 27.	*paŭ Lù Tsiāng-kiūn."*

21. Selections from Æsop's Fables, translated (1), v. native text, page 21.

a. 2.	*Sŭ-mŭ kìng-yŭ.*
a. 7.	*Sĭ yiù weĭ fŭ-chĕ, ngŏ-píng tsaĭ ch'wáng tsiāng-tsŭ, chúng-tsz hwăn*
a. 21.	*t'íng fặn-fŭ, k'ĭ-fŭ yŭ: " Wŭ yiù yĭ-wŭ, jŭ-tặng shí chī ; siŭ chī mŭ-*
b. 8.	*t'iaŭ yĭ-sŭ, líng k'ĭ-tsz chĕ chī, shí năng-twán feŭ ?" Chúng-tsz jŭ-míng*
b. 24.	*chĭ-chĭ, pŭ năng-twán. Fŭ hwŭï chī yŭ: "Jŭ tsiĕ chŭ-t'iaŭ ch'eŭ-ch'ŭ,*
c. 9.	*ts'z-tĭ fạn-chĕ, shí nặng-twán feŭ ?" Yŭ-shí mŏ-pŭ sŭï-sheù ạr twán.*
c. 25.	*Fŭ yŭ: " Ngŏ sz chī heŭ, jŭ-tặng pŭ-ĭ fạn-lĭ ; hŏ, tsĭ pŭ sheŭ jīn-k'ĭ,*
d. 13.	*fặn, tsĭ ĭ yŭ chĕ-twán. Tsz-mŭ tsŭ ĭ-weĭ chíng ĭ." Sŭ-yŭ yŭn: " Shặn*
d. 30.	*ch'ĭ siāng-ĭ ;—liĕn, tsĭ wán wŭ yĭ-shĭ ; jŏ fặn-chī, shặn wáng, tsĭ chī*
e. 16.	*hặn, wŭ-yiù pŭ-shĭ yè." Shín chī! Jŭ ĭ yĭ-kwŏ ạr lạn ; kŏ-kŭ yĭ-fāng-*
f. 4.	*chĕ, siēn yiù pŭ-paĭ, fặn pŭ-jŭ hŏ-lĭ siāng-liĕn chī weĭ meĭ yè.*

g. 2.	*Paŭ gặn shŭ.*
g. 6.	*Sz-tsz shŭ-shwŭï yŭ kiaŭ-waĭ, siaŭ-shŭ tsaĭ-pàng wăn-t'iaŭ, kīng-*

Kiaŭ (19. d. 16), commonly 'to teach,' is here used, like *kiaŭ*[a] 'to call,' for 'to command, to bid ;' and the next words, *t'ing-tsiù chī-yŏ*, which are the object of this *kiaŭ*, are exactly in accordance with the use of the figure metonomy in the construction of phrases ; e. g. *tsiù*, 'wine,' is here put for 'drinking the wine.' The whole phrase must be taken as the object of *kiaŭ*, in one expression. (Cf. Part I. Art. 211.)

Observe the use of the qualifying expression *lĭ-shíng* (19. d. 22), 'stern voice,' before the verb *yŭ* 'to say,' meaning 'in a stern tone he said,' or 'he said sternly.' A language like the Chinese, which is wanting in marks for the different cases, admits of great variety in translation without inaccuracy, but good judgment is requisite to an idiomatic version from or into this language. The words of *Tung-chŏ* (19. d. 25) exemplify the remarkable terseness of the style of the *San-kwŏ ;* here we have literally, 'I have one word, all officers quietly listen,'—'all officers incline ear.' (See the translation on page 63.)

[a] 叫

before *Lü-pu*, at a flying speed, darted across. *Chŏ* at once withdrew in a state of trepidation, but *Kien-yang* followed him with his troops also in pursuit, and *Chŏ's* soldiers were completely routed. After retreating for about thirty furlongs, they threw up a stockade, and a council of war was held. *Chŏ* said: "I perceive that *Lü-pu* is no ordinary man; if I could obtain him, what need should I have to be anxious about the empire?" A man then came out and said: "My lord, be not concerned, I am a fellow-townsman of *Lü-pu*,— I know that he is brave, *but* without much sense, he looks at gain and forgets right principles; I can, with a very small amount of fine talking, cause *Lü-pu* to come and pay his respects to you. Will you allow it?" *Chŏ* was much pleased, and observed that the man was the veteran adjutant-general *Li-seu*. *Chŏ* said: "But how will you speak to him?" *Seu* replied: "I have heard that your lordship has a celebrated horse, named the 'Purple-hare,' which can go a thousand furlongs a day, I must have this horse, and with gold and pearls obtain possession of his heart; and I will so manage to address him that he shall turn against *Ting-yuen* and come over to your lordship." *Chŏ* asked *Li-ju*, saying: "Will this do?" *Ju* replied: "Your lordship wishes to take the empire, why should you have any concern for a horse?" *Chŏ* then gladly gave it up, together with gold, a thousand ounces, several tens of bright pearls, and a jewelled girdle. *Li-seu* took the presents to give to *Lü-pu* in the entrenched camp. While hiding himself in the road, the soldiers surrounded him, but *Seu* said: "I have a message to general *Lü-pu*."

Translation of the Selections from Æsop's Fables (1), *v. native text*, page 21.

The comparison of the bundle of wood.

Once upon a time there was a father laid in sickness upon a bed, and, being about to die, all his sons stood around to hear his *dying* commands. The father said: "I have something which I wish you to attempt," and forthwith he threw down a bundle of sticks, bidding his sons to break them, and to try whether they could snap them in two or not? All his sons did as they were bidden, but they were unable to break them in two. The father *then* instructed them, and said: "Do you now pull out each stick! and snapping them one after the other, try if you can break each in two or not?" Upon doing this, there was not one which remained unbroken. The father said: "After my death you should not separate! If you are united, you will not be insulted by others; if you divide, then it will be easy to break and disperse you, just as this bundle of sticks shows. The proverb says: 'When the lips and teeth are alike united, not one in ten thousand will be lost; but separate them, and then the lips are dead and the teeth grow cold, and every thing is lost.' Pay attention to this! Like as in a kingdom where each man considers his own house alone; there are few who are not destroyed; but there is nothing so desirable as united strength!"

The rat that returned a kindness.

While a lion was soundly sleeping in a wild region, a little rat came playing near him. The lion having awoke in a fright began to play with him.

g. 20. sīng ặr hí-chī. Sz̀ süt ì chaŭ feŭ-chī, shŭ pŭ-nâng tŭ, gaí-mīng chaŭ-
h. 7. hiá. Sz̀ nién siaù shŭ kŭ-kŭ chī tʻì, shá chī wŭ-yí, pŭ-jŭ shè-chī. Shŭ
h. 25. tĕ-mièn, heŭ yŭ sz̀-tsz̀ wŭ-tʻeŭ lǐ-chè chī wàng, shí pŭ-nâng tŭ. Shŭ
i. 12. nién chaŭ-hiá chī gặn, süt tsiāng wàng yaŭ-pʻó, sz̀-tsz̀ chī tĕ-tŭ-shīn.
i. 28. Jŭ shí sò-wet: "Shí-ặr tʻiaŭ liâng, pŭ-chī hô tʻiaŭ tĕ-lt!" Yiŭ yŭn:
j. 14. "Tĕ fâng-sheŭ-shí, sŭ fâng-sheù; tĕ jaŭ-jīn-chŭ, tsiè jaŭ-jīn; tsı̆ wŭ
j. 30. kīng-shí jīn siaù. Chʻing kʻùng kin-jī chī siaù-jīn, shí tsiāng-laı̆ chī
k. 15. gặn-jīn, yı̆ wĭ-kʻò tíng yè?"

l. 2. Chē-fŭ kʻiŭ Fŭ.
l. 7. Yı̆-jī chē-fŭ tsiāng chē-lặn hién yŭ siaù-kʻāng, pŭ-nâng kʻì. Chē-fŭ
l. 23. kʻiŭ kiŭ yŭ A-mi-to Fŭ. Fŭ kò kiâng-līn wặn yŭ: "Nı̆ yiù hô-sz̆
m. 10. siāng-kʻiŭ?" Fŭ yŭ: "Ngò chē lŏ-kʻāng kʻiŭ Fŭ-lı̆ pă-kiú." Fŭ yŭ:
m. 25. "Jù tāng kièn kāng kʻt chē, ặr pièn kʻt mà; tsz̀-jèn tāng-chʻŭ tsz̀ kʻāng,
n. 11. jŏ-jù chüt sheù ặr taí, ngò yı̆ wŭ-nâng wet ì." Jŭ shí-jīn, kı̆-shí kʻiŭ
n. 29. Fŭ, yı̆ tāng-sièn tsīn kʻi-lı̆, naı̆ kʻò. Jín ặr súng Fŭ wặn-shīng, pŭ-jŭ
o. 16. tsz̀-hīng mièn-lı̆.

22. Selections from Æsop's Fables, translated (2), v. native text, page 22.
a. 2. Lâng tuán yâng-gán.
a. 7. Kù yiù hiŭng-kiuèn, kŭ-pīn yŭ lâng, wet yâng fŭ-ì, kŭ-liâng sŭ-hŏ,
a. 23. tsūng pŭ-kʻặng hwặn, kʻiŭ lâng tsŏ-chŭ. Lâng tst chʻŭ-chʻaı̆, tsiāng
b. 6. yâng nả-hwŏ, sín yŭ: "Ặr kʻién meù-kiuèn kŭ-liâng; jı̆-kiù pŭ-
b. 20. hwặn, shí hô taŭ-lı̆?" Yâng yŭ: "Pʻíng-wŭ tsz̀-sz̆, naı̆ kwʻāng-kiuèn
c. 4. wŭ-kaú yè." Lâng wặn kiuèn yŭ: "Yâng pŭ-kʻặng chaŭ, ặr yiù
c. 17. pʻíng-kŭ feù?" Kiuèn yŭ: "Yīng, kiŭ, kiaı̆ kʻò tsŏ-chíng." Lâng tst
c. 30. chüèn-laı̆ yīng, kiŭ, mièn-mién siāng-chī. Yīng, kiŭ, chʻíng chīn-sz̆!
d. 13. yâng kʻién kiuèn liâng, ngò-tặng mŭ-kı̆; pʻíng-fī wŭ-kaú, kı̆ gặn tsiāng
d. 28. yâng, gán-liŭ chī tsüt." Lâng tüt yâng yŭ: "Hién yiù tı̆-chíng, ặr
e. 12. shâng laı̆ hŭ?" süt shă-chī. Yŭ-shí kaú-chī-kiuèn, yiù shīn-sz̆-chī

Shì-tst (19. e. 25) should be *shè-tst* 'the gods of the land and the grain,' which are worshipped by the Emperor and his suite, in person, on particular occasions. *Tsŭng-miaù* (19. e. 23) is the 'Temple of Ancestors,' which also receives a periodical visit from the Emperor.

Shâng (19. e. 28) 'upper' for 'superior,' and is here put for the Emperor, as the highest individual of all the superior classes.

Tsūng-mīng (19. f. 6), 'intelligent-bright,' is here put as an attribute to *Chīn-liá*, but *after* instead of *before* it, and where we should use a relative clause. It may be looked upon as an apposition to the previous word, and its position is worthy of attention.

Tʻing-pá (19. g. 1) 'having heard,' in which *pá*, 'to cease,' gives the force of the perfect tense in European tongues: (cf. Part I. Art. 197.) *Tsŏ-shâng* (19. g. 7) 'among those sitting;' *shâng* 'upon, upper,' stands for several ideas in different constructions. Compare *tién-shâng* (8. b. 4) 'at the inn,' as we say, "on 'Change" for "*at the Exchange*."

Tĕ-tsz̀ (19. h. 8) means the legitimate son of the Emperor, the son of the principal wife,— the Queen, who is called *Chíng-shı̆* [a].

[a] 正室

The lion with his paw covered him, so that the rat, being unable to escape, cried piteously from beneath the claws. The lion bethought himself that the rat had a very small body, and that if he killed him no profit would accrue, so he deemed it best to let him go. The rat was therefore let off, but on another occasion he met with the lion caught by mistake in the hunter's net, and with all his strength he could not get out. The rat remembered the favour while under the claws, and at once set about gnawing the net through with his teeth, and at last he gave the lion his liberty. Just as in the world we say: "Of twelve beams of wood, we know not which is the strongest." And again they say: "When you can deliver any one, you should do so; when you can spare any one, you should spare, and on no account look upon others as insignificant. Lest indeed the mean man of to-day should be our benefactor to-morrow,—who knows?"

The coachman praying to *Fŭ* (*Buddha* for *Hercules*).

One day a coachman got his carriage wheel sunk into a little pit and was unable to raise it out, so he begged for assistance from *Amida Buddha*, who really descended and enquired, saying: "What do you want?" The man said: "My carriage has fallen into this pit, and I pray for the power of *Buddha* to pull it out." *Buddha* replied: "You ought with your shoulder to raise the vehicle, and lash your horses, *then* assuredly it will arise from this pit; *but* if you let your hands hang down and wait, even I shall be powerless to help you." Thus it is in the world; when affairs are urgent, men pray to *Fŭ;* but they ought first to exhaust all their energy, and then they would be able to manage them. *For* if you call on *Fŭ* ten thousand times, it will not be so good as using your own exertions.

Translation of the Selections from Æsop's Fables (2), v. native text, page 22.

The sentence of the wolf in the suit about the sheep.

In former times there was a savage dog, who petitioned a wolf, saying that a sheep owed him several measures of corn, and that he would on no account pay, and he begged the wolf to act as arbiter. The wolf sent out a bailiff to seize the sheep, and having caught him, he examined him, saying: "You have owed a certain dog some corn for a good while, and have not paid, what sort of principle is that?" The sheep replied: "It is no such thing, but that mad dog has accused falsely." The wolf asked the dog, saying: "The sheep is unwilling to confess, have you any proof against him?" The dog replied: "The eagle and the kite can both bear witness." The wolf then summoned the eagle and the kite to appear before his face and to testify. They declared that it was all true; that the sheep owed the dog the provision, "We have seen it," *said they*, "and he is not falsely accused, we beg you graciously to take the sheep and deal with him as the law directs to cure him of this crime." The wolf *then* took the sheep and said: "Now we have strong proof, do you still persist?" and forthwith killed him. Thereupon the dog which had at first accused him, with the wolf which had adjudged the affair, together

e. 28. láng-kwān, pìng kān-chíng-chī yīng-kiŭ, (shê-hiĕ yi-wō,) kúng fān k'ĭ
f. 13. yáng.   Jŭ shí-jìn, jŏ yiù tsz̄-ts'aí, meí chaú hwáng-hó! yiú; yŭ t'ān
f. 28. láng chī kwān, yuên-kaú jŭ kiuèn, kān-chíng jŭ yīng-kiŭ; tsĭ pŭ-pí
g. 13. wáng k'ĭ pìng-kūng twán-sz̆ ĭ! Yén yŭn: "Siáng yiù ch'ĭ, fán k'ĭ
g. 27. shīn." K'ĭ pŭ hŭ?
h. 2.   Tŭ-shê yaù ts'ó.
h. 7. Sĭ yiù tŭ-shê, yuên-jí tí-p'ŭ; yŭ wŭ, tsĭ yaù; shĭ yiù lĭ-ts'ó tsaí-ts'iên;
h. 25. shê tsĭ ch'ên ár yaù-chī. K'eŭ chŭ ts'ó ch'ĭ, hŭ-tĭ k'ò-kién, ĭ-weí yaù
i. 12. shāng tsz̄-ts'ó, fŭ tsaí yaù-chī. Ts'ó yŭ: "Jŭ sìn kiuèn-tŭ, pŭ-náng
i. 27. haí jìn, fán haí tsz̆-kì." Jŭ shĭ yiù láng-sīn-chê, cháng tsaí gán-lĭ, ĭ
j. 14. yên-yŭ hwüi-jìn, ár pŭ-chī shĭ tsz̆ hwüï. Shín chī!

k. 2.   Fù-t'eŭ k'iŭ píng.
k. 7. Sĭ yiù fù-t'eŭ, süï jüï ár wŭ-yúng, tsz̆-sz̆ pĭ-tĕ yĭ-píng, fāng k'ò
k. 24. kién-yúng yŭ-shĭ; naì k'ĭ k'ĭ shŭ yŭ: "Siēn-sāng, tsz̆ ngò yĭ-mŭ, pŭ-
l. 10. kwó kìn-weí yĭ-píng tsŭ ĭ; t'ā-jí tsz̆-táng t'ŭ-paí." K'ĭ shŭ tsz̆-kú chī-kō
l. 29. fán-shíng; "Hô-sĭ yĭ-píng?" K'aí-jên yŭ-chī. Fù tĕ k'ĭ píng; sò-yiù
m. 15. shŭ-lìn, tsìn p'ĭ fŭ-k'ŭ! Hô k'ĭ shŭ-chī yŭ tsaī! Jŭ shí-jìn sò weí:
n. 2. "Tsù hù t'iēn yĭ." Yiú yŭn: "Tí-taŭ, ki-míng;" shĭ yĕ! Fān-jìn
n. 16. pĭ-sŭ kŏ sheŭ k'ĭ fān tsĭ, wŭ chī-ts'án yiù jìn, ch'íng-k'ùng (yiù jŭ fŭ
o. 3. píng), tsĭ hwaí chī wàn ĭ.

23. Official Papers (Lin's Letter to Queen Victoria (1)), v. native text, page 23.

a. b. 1. Kīn-ch'aī, Tá-chin, Pīng-pú Sháng-shŭ, Liàng-Hŭ Tsūng-tŭ, Lín,
a. 17. Pīng-pú Sháng-shŭ, Liàng-Kwāng Tsūng-tŭ, Tang,
b. 17. Pīng-pú Shí-láng Kwāng-tūng Siùn-fŭ, I,
c. 1. hwüï-t'úng chaú-hwüï Yīng-ki-lí kwŏ wáng, weí líng-kín ā-piên
c. 15. yēn-sz̆; chaú-tĕ t'iēn-taú wŭ-sz̄ pŭ-yúng haí-jìn, ĭ lĭ kì; jìn-ts'ìng

---

Kwó-shī (19. h. 12) is a union of two verbs, 'to pass over' and 'to fail,' put for 'transgression' or 'fault.' (Cf. Part 1. Art. 101.)

Hiáng (19. k. 15), 'towards,' is used here for 'at:' (cf. Part I. Art. 407. 4.) *Kūng* (19. k. 18) here means 'public,' as often; e. g. *kūng-wŭn* (14. d. 15) 'public despatch,' but in *kūng-hiáng* (19. c. 10) it means 'nobles,' and *kūng-taŭ* (19. l. 11) means 'just,' because justice is founded on the *common* rights of mankind. Again, *kūng* (19. n. 12) is 'you, my lord:' (cf. 20. d. 13, 14.) *Tsiù-heŭ* (20. b. 14) 'after wine.' Here *tsiŭ*, 'wine,' is put for 'drinking wine.'

Observe the ellipsis of the substantive verb in *tsz hŏ jìn yĕ* (20. c. 23—26).

The description given of the dress of great men and heroes in Chinese romances is generally elaborate, as is that of *Lü-pū* (20. e. 24—f. 13), who played an important part in this story of the *San-kwŏ*.

Fī-mă (20. h. 10), lit. 'flying-horse,' is an example of the use of the verb to qualify the noun; but in such cases the qualifying verb or participle has often to be translated by an adverbial expression; and here we must construe, 'his horse going at full speed,' *Shă* (20. h. 12), 'to kill,' is here used to intensify the expression, to imply that he darted across the intermediate space. The use of *hiá* (20. i. 4) 'down,' or 'lower,' for 'throwing up' a stockade, or 'entrenching themselves,' is very idiomatic. In fact *shăng* and *hiá*, as will

with the false witnesses,—the eagle and the kite (a nest of birds of the same feather),—divided the sheep among themselves. Thus it is in the world, if a man possess wealth, it will daily bring crosses and woes upon him, and should he cross the path of a magistrate who is greedy like the wolf, and an accuser like the dog, and false witnesses like the eagle and the kite, then he must not expect to have it decided according to any justice in the case. So the proverb says: "The elephant has tusks *of ivory*, and we burn his body *for them*, is it not so?"

The venomous snake bites the file.

Once upon a time a venomous snake wound itself into a blacksmith's shop, and every thing which fell in its way it gnawed. Now it happened that a sharp file came in its way, so the snake coiled itself round it and began to gnaw it, but his mouth suddenly coming in contact with the sharp teeth of the file, drops of blood were to be seen; he thereupon thought that these were from the wounds inflicted on the file, so he went on gnawing it. But the file said: "Your heart is very venomous, you are not able to hurt others, but, on the contrary, you may injure yourself."

Just so in this world, those who have the hearts of wolves are constantly in secret slandering others, but they unwittingly defame themselves. Beware of such!

The axe-head begs for a handle.

There was once an axe-head, which, although sharp, was useless, so he thought within himself that he must obtain a handle, and be useful in the world. Then he besought a tree, saying: "Sir, give me a piece of wood, only sufficient to make a handle, and some other day I will, as in duty bound, reward you." The tree on seeing his branches so abundant, thought, 'Why should I grudge a handle?' And so generously gave him one. The axe now having obtained a handle, cut down completely all the trees which were in the forest. What stupidity it was in this tree! So the men of the world have the saying: "Help the tiger by adding wings." Also they say: "Present a knife and beg your life;" and so it is. Let every one keep his own share and on no account give to others, lest truly (as in the case of the axe handle) he may repent of it too late!

Translation of Official Papers (Lin's Letter to Queen Victoria (1)), v. native text, page 23.

Imperial Commissioner *Lin*, a Minister of State, a President of the Board of War, Governor-General of the Two *Hu* (*Hu-nan* and *Hu-pĕ* provinces),

President *Tang*, of the Board of War, Governor-General of the Two *Kwang* (*Kwang-tung* and *Kwang-si* provinces), and

Vice-President *I*, of the Board of War, and Lieutenant-Governor of *Kwang-tung*,

unite in making a communication to the Ruler of the English nation, in order to cause the prohibition of the opium traffic; showing that Providence does not allow any private arrangements soever to be injurious, so that they

d. 2.   pŭ-yuèn. Shŭ fī wú-shă ặr haú-sāng ? Kweí-kwŏ, süï tsaí chŭng-yăng
d. 17: ặr-wán lī waí ; ặr tʻŭng tsž tʻiēn-taú, tʻăng tsž jīn-tsʻing, wí-yiù pŭ-
e. 3.   mìng, yŭ sāng-sž lī-haí chè yè.   Ngò tʻiēn-chaū sž-haì weí kiă ; tă
e. 19. Hwăng-tì, jŭ tʻiēn chī jīn, wú-sò-pŭ-feú, ặr hiă-hwăng tsŭ-yì, yì tsaí píng-
f. 7.   sāng, pìng-yŭ chī chŭng. Kwăng-tŭng, tsž kʻaī haì-kin ì-laì, liŭ-tʻŭng
f. 22. meú-yì ; făn Nüï-tì min-jīn, yŭ waí-laí făn-chʻuên siāng-ān, yŭ lŏ-lì chè,
g. 10. yiù sú-shǐ niên yŭ-tsž ì.   Tʻsiè yŭ tă-hwăng, chʻă-yě, hŭ-sž, tặng-lüï,
g. 27. kiaī. Chŭng-kwŏ paù-kweí chī chʻăn ; waí-kwŏ jŏ pŭ-tě tsž, tsï wŭ ì-weí
h. 14. ming ; ặr tʻiēn-chaū yì-shí tʻŭng jīn, hŭ kʻî făn-maí chʻŭ-yăng, tsŭ pŭ
h. 30. kin-sï, wú-fī tʻüï-sž waí fŭ ì tʻiēn-tì chī sīn weí sīn yè.   Naì yiù yì
i. 19. chŭng kān ì chī weí ā-piēn kiă-taí făn-maí, yiù-hwŏ yŭ-mîn, ì haí kʻî
j. 7.   shīn, ặr meú kʻî lì, tsʻiēn hĭ-shǐ chè.   Sháng shaŭ kĭn tsï hú-siāng
j. 22. chʻuên jèn liŭ-tŭ jǐ-shīn tsaí chŭng yuên, fŭ shŭ făn chʻăng, süï tsaī-
k. 7.   tsž-tặng yŭ-mîn tʻān-kʻeŭ-fŭ, ặr tsʻiăng kʻî sāng, yì shŭ nì yiù-tsž tsʻù
k. 24. hô-pí weí gaí-sǐ yè jên ì.   Tă-tsʻîng yì-tʻŭng chī tʻiēn-hiă, wú tsaí
l. 11. twăn fŭng-sŭ ì chíng jĭn-sīn, kʻì-kʻặng shì haì-nüï sāng-ling kān-sīn
l. 27. chín-tŭ, shí-ì hiên tsiāng Nüï-tì făn-maí ā-piēn, pìng hĭ-shǐ chī jīn, yĭ-
m. 15. tʻî yên-hing chī tsüï yŭng kín liŭ chʻuên ; weí-sž tsž-tặng tŭ-wŭ hí
n. 1.   kweí-kwŏ sò-shŭ, kŏ-pŭ hiă-nüï kweí-yì kān-jīn sž-hing tsaú-tsŏ ; tsž-fī
n. 19. kweí-kwŏ wăng, lìng kʻî chī-tsaú tsž-wŭ pìng-fī chŭ-kwŏ kiaī jên-yiŭ
o. 5.   wặn kweí-kwŏ yì-pŭ chặn mîn-jīn hǐ-shǐ făn-chè, pǐ chʻing : tsž hĭ chī
o. 22. kʻî haí-jīn, kú tï-weí chī lǐ-kín.

---

have been seen, enter into many pure Chinese idioms. *Wŭ* (20. j. 8) 'not, do not,' being employed for *pŭ-yaú*ᵃ, is one of the characteristics of the terse style of this work. *Tŭng-hiang* (20. j. 14), 'of the same village,' is another example of the predicate being of pregnant meaning, and like the attribute only being placed after the noun which it qualifies. This form is common in the *San-kwŏ*. We have *chŏ tă-hĭ* (20. k. 13).

Mark *hô-ì* (20. l. 2) 'by what means?' and compare this use of *ì* with *ì-weí hô-jŭ?* (19. f. 25) 'how do you consider this?' or 'what do you think of it?' (cf. 4. j. 20. and 4. e. 1.) *ì* often has the force of the final particle 'that, to the end that,' or 'for the purpose of:' (cf. 19. e. 21 ; 23. l. 14 ; and Part I. Art. 482.)

Fŭ-lŭ (20. o. 17) 'to hide on the road.' In this expression the noun *lŭ* follows the verb 'to hide' directly, without any particle to show the relation ; but the sense of the passage compels the above rendering, just as in *hing-lŭ* above (17. f. 22). This form is frequent. We have a case in the next page; *ngò-pǐng* (21. a. 12) 'lying in sickness.'

Pages 21 and 22 of the native text contain extracts from a work entitled: "Esop's Fables written in Chinese by the learned *Mun Mooy Seen-shang*, and compiled in their present form (with a free and literal translation) by his pupil, Sloth," an allusion to which will be found in the Preface to this work, page viii. The style is quaint, easy, and well adapted for the expression of fable. It cannot be considered, however, as a very good model for composition, though it may serve as a stepping-stone to something better, and to familiarise the student with the expression of native modes of thought. But these fables abound in good colloquial phrases, to which the student will be directed by the hyphen in many cases. And here it may be observed, that the hyphen in this work is often placed between syllables which are merely grammatically united, and not absolutely, as is the case in compound words ; e. g. the negatives *pŭ* 'not,' *wú* 'without ;' some verbs, as *süï* 'to follow,'

ᵃ 不要

may serve the interests of individuals; and that the feelings of all men are similar, (*for* who is there that does not hate death and love life?) And although your honourable nation is two myriads of *li* across the vast ocean, yet you acknowledge the same Providence and the same human feelings, and there is not one of you ignorant respecting life and death,—profit and loss. Now the Celestial dynasty looks upon all within the four seas * as one family, and the benevolence of our great Emperor (like that of heaven) comprehends all; even desert places and disconnected regions alike receive their life and nurture from thence. There has existed at Canton, from the time of the removal of the restrictions on maritime communication up to the present, regular commercial dealing, and the people of China, generally, have held a peaceful and profitable intercourse with those who came from abroad in foreign ships during a period of several tens of years until now. Moreover, with reference to rhubarb, teas, and the silks of the Lake *provinces* and such other commodities, which are the valuable and rich productions of China; were foreign nations unable to procure them, they would be without the means of *enjoying* their lives; but the Celestial court, looking with benevolence towards all alike, has permitted trade to be carried on with foreigners, without the least stint or grudge, and has in this course undoubtedly had no other aim in view than to imitate the beneficent principles which unite heaven and earth. But there is a class of unprincipled Barbarians, who manufacture opium, and bring it here for sale. And thus, in order to contrive profit for themselves, they tempt the common people of our land to the injury of their bodies. Formerly the consumers were only a few, *but* latterly the habit has spread its contagion, *while* it extends more deeply every day towards the centre of the land,—with its rich, fruitful, and flourishing population. But although, among the common people, there are many who gratify their appetites at the expense of their lives, and as this is the origin of the evils resulting from the habit, their case does not call for pity. Yet, when we consider the empire as a whole, under the rule of the *T'á-tsing* ('Great Pure') dynasty, it is a matter of importance that the minds of men should be directed in the formation of correct customs. How then can we be willing to cause the inhabitants of the world to take with pleasure this deadly poison? Therefore from henceforth both those in the Inner land (China) who deal in opium, and also those who eat it, shall alike be liable to the severest punishment; and a perpetual prohibition against it shall be enacted and be made known every where. We have considered that this poisonous article is the secret production of artful and designing people within the boundaries of your honourable nation's tributary kingdoms, and that neither the sovereign of your honourable nation has caused it to be made, nor that even all these kingdoms manufacture it;—yea, we have heard that your honourable nation does not allow your own people to consume it, and that offenders will surely be reproved. It is certainly from knowing its evil effects that these severe prohibitions have been made.

---

* The expression 'four seas' sometimes means 'China,' at other times 'the world.'

24. Official Papers (Lin's Letter to Queen Victoria (2)), v. native text,
page 24.

a. 1.   *Jên kín k'í kí-shĭ,—hô-jú kín k'í fán-maí, píng kín k'í chí-tsaú?—*
a. 17. *naĭ weí ts'ĭng-yuên chĭ taú. Jŏ tsź pŭ-shĭ, ǫr-jíng kàn chĭ-tsaú fán-maí*
b. 4.   *yìn-yiù Nüí-tí yŭ-mín; tsĭ-shĭ yŭ-kĭ chĭ sāng, ǫr liên-jín chĭ sź; yŭ-kĭ*
b. 23. *chĭ lĭ, ǫr ĭ-jín ĭ haĭ. Tsź-kiaĭ jín-ts'ĭng chĭ sŏ t'ûng-hǫ̆n, t'iēn-taú chĭ sŏ*
c. 12. *pŭ-yûng. Ĭ ĭ T'iēn-chaū lĭ-chín Hwâ-Ĭt; hô-nǎn lĭ-chĭ k'í míng? ǫr yàng-*
c. 29. *t'í shíng-míng kwān-tá, tsź ĭ kaú-kiaĭ yŭ siēn; tsiè ts'ûng-ts'iên wí yûng-*
d. 15. *kūng-wǫ̆n, î-hwüĭ kweí-kwŏ Wâng; yĭ-tān kín-yên, tsĭ yiŭ tĕ-yiŭ weí*
e. 2.   *pŭ-chĭ. Kín yŭ kweí-kwŏ Wâng yŏ tsiāng tsź haĭ-jín chĭ ā-piĕn,*
e. 18. *yûng-yuèn twán-tsŭ; ngò Nüí-tí kín-jín kĭ-shĭ, yĭ shŭ-kwŏ kín-jín*
f. 4.   *chí-tsaú; k'í ts'ûng-ts'iên ĭ-kíng tsaú-tsŏ-chè, kweí-kwŏ lĭ-tsĭ pān-líng*
f. 20. *hĭng seù tsîn-t'eŭ chĭ haĭ-lí; twán pŭ-hŭ t'iēn-tí kiēn kāng-yiù tŭ-wŭ.*
g. 7.   *Fī-tŭ Nüí-tí mín-jín pŭ-sheú k'í haĭ, tsĭ kweí-kwŏ mín-jín (kĭ-yiù*
g. 24. *tsaú-tsŏ, ān chĭ k'í pŭ kĭ-shĭ) kwŏ píng tsaú-tsŏ shǎng kín chĭ, tsĕ kaĭ-*
h. 11. *kwŏ yĭ pŭ-sheú k'í haĭ. K'í pŭ-kŏ hiàng t'aĭ-píng chĭ fŭ! Yĭ-chaú*
h. 27. *kweí-kwŏ kūng-shǫ̆n chĭ chín, jú-tsź tsĕ míng yŭ t'iēn-lí, ǫr Shāng-t'iēn*
i. 14. *pŭ-chĭ kiáng tsaĭ. Hĭ hŭ jín-ts'ĭng ǫr shíng-jín. Yĭ-pĭ chĭ hŭ, hwáng*
i. 29. *Nüí-tí kí-kíng yên-kín, wŭ-shí kĭ-shĭ, tsĭ-shí kaĭ-kwŏ chí-tsaú, tsūng-*
j. 16. *yĭ wŭ-chŭ k'ò-maĭ, wŭ-lĭ k'ò-t'ŭ. Yù k'í kw'eĭ-pǫ̆n t'û-laú, hô-pŭ kaĭ*
k. 4.   *t'ŭ pĭ-niĕ? Hwàng Nüí-tí seù-ch'ŭ ā-piēn tsín-hĭng fŭ-hò yiŭ shaŭ-*
k. 20. *weĭ, tsaĭ yiù Ĭ-ch'uên kiă-taĭ ā-piēn, ts'iên-laĭ pŭ-nǎng-pŭ yĭ-t'í shaŭ-*
l. 7.   *weĭ. K'ùng (ch'uên nüĭ sŏ tsaĭ t'â hô) nǎn miên yŭ-shĭ, k'ŭ fǫ̆n. Shĭ lĭ-*
l. 23. *pŭ-tĕ ǫr haĭ ĭ-hĭng, yŭ haĭ-jín ǫr siēn haĭ-kĭ yè. T'iēn-chaū chĭ sŏ-ĭ*

ĭ 'to use,' which are employed as prepositions (then meaning 'with' or 'by'); and auxiliary verbs, as *nǎng* 'to be able,' *k'ò* 'can, may;' and demonstratives, as *tsz* 'this,' and *k't* 'his;' and the reflexive particles *tsz* 'self,' *siáng* 'mutual,' are generally united by the hyphen to the words which they affect. Very much might be done in this way to make Chinese, even the terse, classical style, intelligible in Roman letter; and it is devoutly to be wished that the various dialects may, before long, be represented by the Latin alphabet, and be freed from the cumbrous characters, which, for the masses, clog the path to knowledge.

Sŭĭ-ĭ (21. g. 25), lit. 'follow,—use,' forms a redundant expression for 'with.' We have *sŭĭ* alone in *sŭĭ-sheŭ* (21. c. 21) 'with the hand.'

There is a great mixture of classical and colloquial terms in the style of these fables; o. g. (in 21. a. 10) we have *fŭ-chĕ* instead of *fŭ-tsín*, which is the colloquial term. Again, "the lion was sleeping *in* (*yŭ*—21. g. 10) a wild region;" "the mouse was playing *in* (*tsaĭ*—21. g. 15) (or *at*) his side." Here different words are employed for 'in,' perhaps to avoid tautology, but *yŭ* is not often used in colloquial style. *Fǎn-fŭ* (21. a. 22) 'command, bidding,' is the common expression for commanding an inferior.

The expression *pŭ-jú* (21. h. 20) has occurred several times. It signifies literally, 'not as' or 'not like,' and must be explained to mean 'there is nothing like' or 'the best thing to do is:' (cf. 14. i. 24. and 21. o. 14.)

*Tsiáng*ᵃ (21. i. 18) in the sense of 'to take' is not very common; it corresponds in use to *pa*ᵇ 'to take,' meaning 'referring to, touching, concerning,' it refers to the object mentioned, and helps to form an expression, like the "accusative of closer specification"

ᵃ 將   ᵇ 把

Translation of Official Papers (Lin's Letter to Queen Victoria (2)), *v. native text, page* 24.

But though you forbid the eating of it,—what is that compared with the prohibition of its sale and the restriction on its manufacture?—this latter would be the rational means of cleansing the source. If you do not eat it yourselves, yet by continuing presumptuously the manufacture and the sale of it, you tempt the lower orders of the Inner land (China),—you truly desire to live yourselves and to overwhelm others in death,—you seek your own profit, and bring loss upon other men. All these things are what the common feelings of humanity hold in abhorrence, and what Divine Providence will not tolerate. And since the power of the Celestial dynasty moves both Chinese and Barbarians, what difficulty would there be in establishing regulations respecting their fate? But having regard to propriety, sacred honour, and magnanimity, it is certainly proper, in the first place, to issue commands; and, as heretofore no public despatch has been sent to the Sovereign of your honourable kingdom, if the matter be the subject of rigid prohibition on a sudden, then some may be tempted to plead ignorance as an excuse. *But* as the case stands, we would with the Sovereign of your honourable nation, covenant to abolish for ever this hurtful opium drug, we should forbid the consumption of it in the Inner land (China), and the tributary kingdoms also should forbid the manufacture of it. As for that which has already been made, your honourable government should issue commands for its collection from every quarter, and for its complete destruction in the bottom of the sea, nor let any more of the poisonous article exist any longer in the world. *Then* not only will the people of the Inner land (China) not be injured by it, but also the said people of your honourable nation (who being the makers of it certainly know how to eat it), when the manufacture is forbidden, will of necessity be also uninjured by it. Will not each party then enjoy the happiness of peace? And in addition to this, by your honourable nation's respectful and sincere obedience, you will show a clear apprehension of divine principles, and Heaven will not bring down calamities *upon us.* This will be in harmony with the feelings of humanity and with those of the sacred sages. Also let it be remembered besides, that the people of the Inner land (China), being under severe prohibitions against the eating of it, if the aforesaid nations still manufacture it, there will assuredly be no market for it, and no device will cause profit to arise therefrom. Thus, with the prospect of losing the capital and labouring in vain, will it not be better to change your plans for another employment?

Furthermore, all the opium which can be found in the Inner land (China) has been delivered over to be consumed by fire, and if in future there happen to be any Barbarian ships conveying opium hither, the whole must be destroyed by fire. But we fear (as there will be other goods in the same ships) it will be difficult to distinguish the jewel from the stone, and all must be burnt alike. Thus, not obtaining any profit, and injury taking a substantial form, in wishing to hurt others, you will hurt yourselves first. The Celestial dynasty's

m. 12. chîn fŭ wán-kwŏ chè, chíng yiù pŭ-tsʻè chŭ shîn, weï wŭ weï, yên chŭ
m. 28. pŭ-tsaù yè. Kweï-kwŏ Wáng tsï-taú tsz̀-wǎn, tsï tsiāng kŏ haï-kʻeù
n. 13. twán-tsŭ, yuên-yiù sŭ-hîng î feú hîng. Wŭ-hwáng shï chŭ tʻîng
n. 27. chʻŭ tsï.
o. 3.   Taú-kwāng shï-kiù niên ḁr yŭ ——— jï, î-hwŭï Yīng-kwŏ chŭ
o. 21. chaŭ.

25. Official Papers (From the 'Supplementary Treaty of 1844'), v. native text, page 25.

a. 1.   I. Yï sò-yiù Kīn-chʻaī, Kūng-shï, Tá-chîn hwá-yá kʻiên-yín, tsín
a. 15. chʻŭ-kʻeù hó-wŭ shwŭï-hiàng, tsï-lí fú-niēn chŭ tsĕ, sź-heú Kwǎng-cheū,
b. 1.   Fŭ-cheū, Hiá-mǎn, Nîng-pō, Shǎng-haï, wù kiàng-kʻeù, kiūn fúng î-
b. 15. weï shï.
b. 18. II. Yï sò-yiù Kīn-chʻaī, Kūng-shï, Tá-chîn ‾hwá-yá kʻiên-yín sīn-
c. 2.   tíng meú-yï chāng-chʻíng fú-niēn chŭ kién, sź-heú wù kiàng-kʻeù, kiūn-
c. 17. fúng î-weï shï.
c. 22. III. Yï sīn-tíng meú-yï chāng-chʻíng tí-sān tʻiaŭ, hó-chʻuên tsín
d. 5.   kʻeù paú kwān yï-kwʻàn, nŭï sò yên fǎ yín jŏ kān yuên, kŭ hó-wŭ chʻá
d. 22. chʻaū jï kwān tǎng yŭ, tsz̀ yín liên hó yíng-kweï Chūng-hwá kwŏ nú,
c. 8.   ï chʻūng kūng-hiáng.
e. 13. IV. Yï Kwǎng-cheū, Fŭ-cheū, Hiá-mǎn, Nîng-pō, Shǎng-haï, wù
e. 25. kiàng-kʻeù, kʻaī kwān chŭ heú, kʻï Yīng-shāng meú-yï chú-sò, chĕ chǎn
f. 10. wù kiàng-kʻeù. Pŭ-chǎn fú tʻā-chú kiàng-kʻeù, yï pŭ-hŭ Hwá-mín tsaí
f. 26. tʻā-chú kiàng-kʻeù, chʻuén tʻūng sz̄ siāng meú-yï, tsiāng-laï Yīng-kwŏ
g. 10. Kūng-shí yiù yú-shï míng, pŭ-hŭ tʻā-wàng, ḁr Yīng-shāng jú hwŏ peï
g. 26. yŏ, pŭ-fŭ kìn-líng, kï tsiāng Kūng-shí kaú-shï chí jŏ wàng wǎn, shén
h. 12. wàng tʻā-chú kiàng-kʻeù, yiù piên fán-maï jïn pʻíng Chūng-kwŏ yuên-
h. 26. piên, liên-chʻuên liên-hó yï-píng chʻaū tsŭ jï kwān, Yīng-kwān pŭ-tĕ
i. 11. tsǎng-lǎn, tʻǎng Hwá-mín tsaí tʻā-chú kiàng-kʻeù, yù Yīng-shāng sz̄
i. 25. chʻuén meú-yï, tsï Kwŏ fǎ kŭ tsaí, yíng-chaŭ lí pán-lï.
j. 11. V. Yï tsiên tsaí Kiāng-nán niĕ-kīng ï-tíng, î-heú shāng kʻiên, twán
j. 25. pŭ-kʻò kwān weï paù kiaŭ, yiù sīn tíng meú-yï chāng-chʻíng tí-sá tʻiaŭ,
k. 11. Yīng-shāng yŭ Hwá-shāng kiaú-yï yï-kwʻàn, nŭï-fú tsiāng pŭ-náng
k. 25. chŭ yáng-háng taï pʻeï-chï kiú lï, chʻíng chú chŏ pʻeï. Tsï shï shīng
l. 10. míng tsaí gán. Sź-heú pŭ-kʻŭ Hwá-shāng kʻiên Yīng-shāng, kï Yīng-

---

in Greek: (cf. Part I. Art. 407. 6.) There is another example of this use of tsiāng in 21. l. 11.

A-mi-to Fŭ (21. l. 26). This is the common name of Buddha in China. The name which serves for all the various forms of calling upon the deity, whether in oaths or in prayers.

Observe the use of siāng[b] in siāng-kʻiù (21. m. 10), in which expression it corresponds to the use of the middle voice in Greek. It implies two parties: (cf. Part I. Art. 215.)

[a] 盟 約 'a treaty' (between two nations).   [b] 相

means of holding the myriads of nations in subjection is unfathomable and divine, and produces reverence beyond the power of words to tell! Let it not be said that early warning was not given! When Your Majesty receives this despatch, then take measures for seizing all the opium at every sea-port, and send us a speedy reply. Do not, by false embellishments, evade or delay! Earnestly reflect on these things, and earnestly observe them!

In the nineteenth year of *Tau-kwang*, in the second month, on the —— day. A communication addressed to England.

Translation of Official Papers (From the 'Supplementary Treaty of 1844'), *v. native text,* page 25. *

Art. I. † The tariff of export and import duties which is hereunto attached, under the seals and signatures of the respective plenipotentiary and commissioners, shall henceforward be enforced at the five ports of Canton, Fu-chau fu, Amoy, Ningpo, and Shanghai.

Art. II. The general regulations of trade which are hereunto attached under the seals and signatures of the respective plenipotentiary and commissioners shall henceforward be in force at the five afore-named ports.

Art. III. All penalties enforced, or confiscations made, under the third clause of the said general regulations of trade, shall belong, and be appropriated to, the public service of the government of China.

Art. IV. After the five ports of Canton, Fu-chau, Amoy, Ningpo, and Shanghai shall be thrown open, English merchants shall be allowed to trade only at those five ports. Neither shall they repair to any other ports or places, nor will the Chinese people, at any other ports or places, be permitted to trade with them. If English merchant vessels shall, in contravention of this agreement, and of a proclamation to the same purport, to be issued by the British plenipotentiary, repair to any other ports or places, the Chinese government officers shall be at liberty to seize and confiscate both vessels and cargoes; and should Chinese people be discovered clandestinely dealing with English merchants at any other ports or places, they shall be punished by the Chinese government in such a manner as the law may direct.

Art. V. Formerly in *Kiang-nan* it was agreed that the government could not be responsible for the debts of merchants, and according to the 4th clause of the newly established regulations concerning 'commercial dealings between English and Chinese merchants,' it is no longer allowable to ask for the repayment of debts by appealing to the old laws, which required the Hong merchants to pay the debts of each. This is truly and clearly declared in the records. Henceforth, whether a Chinese merchant owe any thing to an English merchant, or an English merchant owe to a Chinese merchant, if the

---

* Page 25 of the native text was erroneously headed 'a notice and a petition,' which should have been the heading for page 26.

† The version here given is that published as the English treaty, which was in fact the original, and of which the Chinese text in the Chrestomathy is the translation.

l. 24. shāng k'iĕn Hwá-shāng chī chaí, jú kò cháng-kú k'iŏ-tsŏ, jìn tsai ch'ān
m. 9.   ts'ăn, kiūn yíng yiù Hwá Yíng kaī kwàn-sź-kwān, yĭ-t'ĭ ts'ăng kūng-
m. 23. chú kí, ì-chaú píng-yún. Jìng-chaú yuén-yŏ p'í-tsź taí-weí chŏ-chuī,
n. 9.   kiūn pú taí-weí paù-ch'ăng.
n. 16. VI. Yí K'wàng-cheū tăng wù kiàng-k'eù, Yíng-shāng, hwŏ cháng
n. 27. ch'uén kú-chú, hwŏ pú-shí wàng-laí, kiūn pú-k'ŏ wáng taú hiáng-kiĕn,
o. 12. jìn-í yiú-hìng, yiú kăng pú-k'ŏ yuén-jí nüí-tí meú-yí.

26.   Official Papers (a notice and a petition), v. native text, page 26.
a. 2.   Kín yé-hìng yŏ.
a. 7.   Lí kín yŏ jìn meū-meū tăng, weí yén kín yé-hìng, ì tsíng tí-fāng
a. 23. sź. Kwŏ-kiă chúng-măn kí-sí, yú-taí hú paú-kĕ, hiáng-mín t'í-lìng haú-
b. 10. păng, kīn fāng k'í taú-tsĕ. Kiaī yiù míng kín. Shuī kàn weí făn. Kín
b. 15. kiĕn tí-fāng făn-lwăn, taú-tsĕ ch'āng-kw'āng, tsūng yiù yé-hìng pú-kìn.
c. 10. Hí piĕn k'í-chă? Shí ì shìng-kí gán taú, shìn chí míng-hŏ ki'āng-kiĕ,
c. 26. ts'ìn pú-găn chìn, kiă pú-liaù sāng. Haí mŏ tsí ì! Hŏ shŭ tá yên! Weí-
d. 13. tsź shĕ tsiù hwuī chúng, yén shĕ kín-yŏ. Yí yú hwāng hwăn, tsí kín
d. 28. jìn hìng, chí chí wù-kăng sān-tiĕn, fāng k'ŏ-jìn k'í laí-wăng. Meī-jí
e. 14. lăn-liú siún lŏ, jú yiù făn-kín-chĕ, míng-lŏ weí haú, kŏ-kŏ sheù-chí
f. 1.   ts'iang, taú, nù, ch'úng, shă-sź wŭ-lăn, t'ăng míng-lŏ shí, ch'ă tièn yí
f. 16. míng pú-taú, laí-jí ts'íng-shìn, hwuī-chúng kúng-fă, kiù pú k'íng taí.
g. 1.   Tí sié lí sú chí, shă chú chāng-kwá, shú p'í sìng taí yú chī jìn, chī sŏ
g. 19. kiaī: ăr kī-míng keù-taú chī jìn tĕ ch'íng ì.   Kín-yŏ.

The pronoun k'í[b] 'he, his,' in the expressions k'í-chĕ (21. m. 29), k'í-mă (21. n. 3), is used like our definite article 'the,' for the second person jú (21. m. 25) has just been used, therefore k'í could not be construed as 'his' in this place.

Yŭ[c] frequently means 'with reference to;' so in to beg something of somebody, it signifies 'of' or 'from,' as in 22. a. 13.

Tsŏ-chú (22. a. 29), lit. 'to be the master,' is 'to act as judge:' (cf. Part I. Arts. 221, 361. 5, and 371.) Tsŏ is again used for the verb to be in 22. c. 26. Taú-lí (22. b. 23) 'law of reason, rule of right,' is the general term for 'good principles' of justice, taste, feeling, or judgment. It is to a Chinese that indefinable standard of right and wrong, which suits his own peculiar habits, tastes, or feelings: (cf. Mr. Commissioner Yeh's dialogues with his interpreter, Mr. C. Alabaster, given in the Times during the war of 1856.)

Mŭ-kí (22. d. 19), lit. 'eyes struck at,' must here mean 'happened to see.'

Tí-chíng (22. e. 9), lit. 'iron evidence,' means 'strong testimony.'

Lín, the author of the paper addressed to the Queen of England, which is to be found on pages 23 and 24, was, like Yeh of recent notoriety, a good representative of the exclusive policy of the Chinese. He was an able writer, and a sincere upholder of the government which he served. He was the tool of the then dominant party in Peking, whose plan was to suppress the opium trade and to humble foreigners. His great literary work, the Hai-kwŏ t'ú-chí, has been noticed on page 15 of Part II. Many errors exist in those parts of it which relate to foreign nations, but a good deal of information is to be found in it upon other subjects, which relate to China and the neighbouring countries.

[a] 告白 'a notice.'   [b] 其   [c] 於

accounts and vouchers be well authenticated, the persons present and the property still existing shall be dealt with by the Chinese and English authorities, according to the principles of justice, so as to manifest impartiality. And, according to the original stipulations, both these authorities shall prosecute in behalf of creditors, but in no case shall they be made responsible for them *.

Art. VI. It is agreed that English merchants and others, residing at or resorting to the five ports to be opened, shall not go into the surrounding country beyond certain short distances, to be named by the local authorities in concert with the British consul, and on no pretence for purposes of traffic.

Translation of Official Papers (a notice and a petition), v. native text, page 26.

A prohibition against walking out after nightfall.

It has been agreed upon to forbid strictly any person walking out after nightfall, in order that the state of the neighbourhood may be peaceful.

When the city gates of the kingdom have been shut, the night watches shall be rung with the bell, to warn off persons of bad character; the country people shall sound little bells and strike the watchman's bamboo, diligently to keep in check thieves and robbers. These all are definite prohibitions. Who will dare to oppose and transgress? Of late the land has been in much confusion, thieves and robbers have been ungovernable, generally going out by night without restraint. *Such being the case,* how can they conveniently be taken up for examination? Thus, availing themselves of the darkness, they contrive to go on plundering until the morning dawns, while the people cannot sleep at peace on their pillows, and the lives of the household are in danger. Evils, how immeasurable! calamities, how great! This is the reason why, having called a meeting of the whole body, it has been determined to issue this strict prohibition. As soon as the dusk of evening comes on, it is forbidden for persons to walk abroad, until three quarters after the fifth watch, when they may go to and fro as they list. Every day, by turns, persons shall go the rounds, and, if they find any one transgressing this prohibition, they shall strike the gong as a signal, and whoever is found with a spear, a sword, a cross-bow, or a musket, shall certainly be punished, whoever he be. If, at the striking of the gong, any person does not come to seek out the matter, on the next day, in the morning, he shall be punished before all, and he shall not lightly be pardoned. Let, then, several copies of this notice be written out and posted up every where, that all passers by may know of this prohibition, and that those thieves, who crow like cocks (to get the gates opened) and who steal like dogs, may not presume too much on their powers. Respect this agreement.

---

* The 5th clause is not given in full in the English copy, we have therefore consulted the student's benefit by taking another version, which follows the Chinese text more closely. (Cf. a version of this treaty given in the Chinese Repository, vol. XIII. p. 143.)

h. 5.	*Ts'ǐng chǐ-ch'ǔ pìn.*
h. 11.	*Shīn-k'īn Meǔ-meǔ kìn-pìn.*
i. 1.	*Pìn weí shī-taú liên-p'ǎng, kàn ts'ǐng chǐ-ch'ǔ, ǐ shīn hǒ-tsaī-sź.*
i. 16.	*Chaú-tĕ hǒ-yāng yǐ-sź, siūi yǔ: "T'iēn-míng," k'ǐ-fī jìn-sź! Tǎng-*
j. 1.	*chǔ pǔ-shīn, tsū-jēn hǒ-k'ǐ siaú-ts'iǎng; lǔ-tsaú sū yǔ, siūi àr yāng kǐ*
j. 18.	*ch'ǐ yǔ. Jǒ pǔ-yǔ weí fāng yǔ, k'ǐ haí tsiāng yiù pǔ-k'ǒ shíng yēn.*
k. 4.	*P'ǐ shǐ-taú-shāng, liàng pàng liēn-p'ǎng haí-mǐ, t'àng yiù hǒ-chǔ,*
k. 18.	*tsüí yǐ yè-chǒ, tsiĕ p'ǎng hǐ yìn-hǒ chī wǔ, hìng-taú-chī jìn, yēn-hǒ*
l. 5.	*wǔ kǐ, tsǐ hìng fàn liaù. Hwàng kìn lǔng-tūng chī tsì, wán-wǔ*
l. 19.	*tsiaú-kán, siūi shān-ts'aù yǐ weí chī chǒ-hǒ, àr shīn p'ǎng chī sú i weí*
m. 6.	*lǐ hǔ? T'àng pǔ ch'ī k'ú, shīn weí pǔ-piēn, lǐ-hǒ pìn ts'ǐng. Lǐ-kiaī.*
m. 23.	*Chǐ-ch'aí chǒ líng hwüī ch'ǐ, miēn weí hǒ tsaī. Tsź k'ǐ tǔ meū-tàng sheǔ*
n. 9.	*k'ǐ yǐ, shǎ p'ǐ tsź k'ǔ-tĕ siāng ān àr. Weí-tsź pìn k'aú-fǔ weí chüī*
n. 26.	*kiēn, chēn gān tsǐ fǔ laù-yê taī ts'iên shē hìng.*

27. Dialogues and Phrases in the Mandarin Dialect (1), v. native text, page 27.

a. 1.	*Ngǒ yiù yǐ-kiēn-sź-ts'ǐng k'iú nǐ. Shímmǒ sź-ts'ǐng? Fāng-sīn shwǒ*
a. 16.	*pá! K'iǔ-nǐ kǐ-ngǒ yǐ-pá-taú-tsź. Kǐ-ngǒ tsǒ chĕ-kó. Kàn-kiǔ Tá-*
b. 4.	*yê chĕ-kó gān-tiēn. Hàn tsīng-yuēn Tō-siĕ. Haù-shwǒ! Sheú-liaù*
b. 18.	*nǐ-tǐ gān wǎng-pǔ-liaù. Nǐ hạn chǐ-lǐ. Ngǒ kiēn-weí nǐ. Yuēn-i*
c. 4.	*shímmǒ? Pǔ-pǐ tō-lǐ. Ngǒ hwān-hǐ nǐ. Pǔ kaī-tāng. Lǐ-tāng.*
c. 19.	*Nǐ nǎng-keú ī-kaú ngǒ. Kiaū ngǒ tsǒ shímmǒ? Nǐ yǐ-shwǒ, ngǒ tsiú*
d. 5.	*tsǒ. Nǐ yaú shímmǒ, ngǒ tsiú tsǒ shímmǒ. Pǔ-kàn. Kiǔ-nǐ tī-ngǒ*
d. 21.	*wǎn Chǎng siēn-sāng haù*. Shǐ ngǒ tī haù pǎng-yiù. Liú-hiá chĕ-*
e. 5.	*mǒ-siĕ-kó lǐ-maú. Kiaū ngǒ shī-lǐ mǒ? Pǔ-yaú. Chĕ-yáng haù.*
e. 20.	*Ngǒ yaú shwǒ yǐ-kǔ-hwá, k'ùng-p'á tǐ-tsüí nǐ. Suī-piēn shwǒ. Nǐ*
f. 5.	*ts'ǐng-fàn tá.—Shǐ pǔ-shǐ? Shǐ-tsaī shǐ. Ngǒ shwǒ laù-shǐ hwá.*
f. 20.	*Kwǒ-jēn shǐ chĕ-yáng. Shüī ǐ-hwǒ? Ngǒ siàng shǐ. Ngǒ shwǒ pǔ-shǐ.*
g. 5.	*Tá-tǔ pa. Nǐ tǔ-shāng tō-shaù? Yǐ liàng yìn-tsź. Shwǒ-chīn.*
g. 19.	*Shwǒ-hwǎng. Kiǎ-hwá. Shwǒ hú-hwá. Ngǒ fá-shǐ. Yǐ-tíng tǐ hwá.*
h. 3.	*Yǐ-kǒ-jīn shwǒ-liaù yǐ-tsź hwáng, heú-laī siūi-jēn shwǒ shǐ-hwá, mǔ-*
h. 19.	*yiù jìn sìn. Fàn-jìn sá-hwáng, tsiú tiū-liaù liēn.—Pǔ-yaú siūi-k'où*
i. 5.	*tá-ying. Chĕ-kó hwǎn-ylǔ jìn-sìn mǒ? Chĕ-kó shǐ wǎng-hwǎng yēn.*

Tsūng-tǔ (23. a. b. 12), lit. 'general-leader' or 'guide of all,' is the title given to the supreme governor of one or two provinces, and is nearly equivalent to our term *viceroy*.

Siùn-fù (23. b. 23) is the title of the deputy governor of a province; the word itself would seem to imply that his duty was to see that peace was preserved,—*siùn* means 'to go round' and *fù* 'to tranquillize.'

The Two *Hu* provinces are *Hu-pĕ* (north) and *Hu-nán* (south), and the Two *Kwang* provinces are *Kwang-tung* (east) and *Kwang-sī* (west).

Hwüī-t'ǎng (23. c. 1), 'to unite together,' is also expressed by *hwüī-hǒ*ᵃ.

Chaú-hwüī (23. e. 3) 'communicate.' In the treaty which was negotiated by Lord Elgin, an article is inserted to render the use of this term obligatory when communications

* This character should be *heú* 侯 : (cf. p. 32. native text.)   ᵃ 合

A petition asking for the removal [of old houses].

M. M——, Gentleman, respectfully petitions.

He makes a representation respecting the mat-sheds in the market-place, and earnestly begs that they may be removed, in order to guard against the calamity of a conflagration. Although the misfortune of fire is indeed said to be "a judgment from heaven," still it is assuredly the work of man. If lamps and candles be not taken care of, on a sudden misery arises among the wretched screens; and if the cooking stoves be not looked after, presently misfortune comes, even the fish in the ponds (will not escape). If we do not prepare and guard against (fire), the evils arising therefrom will be beyond the power of words to tell.

The mat-sheds on both sides of the market-place are covered thickly together, and if they should take fire, there would be disastrous consequences. The matting is, moreover, a material easy of combustion, and passers by who were smoking would endanger it, and might set the whole on fire. Besides, now on the approach of the winter quarter, every thing is in a dry state, and the mountain grass, with which the sheds are thatched, might take fire, to which the latter have always been liable. And if they are not taken away, it will be very inconvenient indeed. This is the reason why I petition, and beg of your worship to order the officers to pull them down, in order to avoid the calamity of fire. This will assuredly not only benefit individuals, but it will truly avail in preserving the peace. Therefore this petition has been presented; and should you deign to consider it, a great favour will be conferred. We hasten to present this to your worship for approval and execution.

Translation of Dialogues and Phrases in the Mandarin Dialect (1),
v. native text, page 27.

I have something to ask of you. What is it? Speak freely! I want you to give me a knife. Do this for me. I beseech you, Sir, to do me this favour. Gladly! Many thanks! Very well! If I receive your favour I shall never forget it. You are very polite! I am troubling you. What do you want? Do not use so much formality. I like you! Nonsense! It is not! You may depend upon me. What do you want me to do? Directly you speak I will act. Whatever you want I will do it. I could not think of it. I beg of you to give my compliments to Mr. *Chang*. He is a good friend of mine. Lay aside so much of this etiquette. Do you wish me to forget my manners? No, indeed! This is a good way. I want to speak a word, *but* I fear that it may offend you. Say what you like! You are very kind.—Is it so or not? It is indeed so! I speak honestly. Certainly it is so. Who doubts it? I think so. I say it is not so. Let us bet. How much will you bet? A dollar (lit. 'an ounce'). To speak the truth. To speak falsely. Untruth. To speak nonsense. I swear. It is positively asserted. If a man speak once falsely, afterwards, although he speak the truth, nobody will believe him. Every man who tells a lie, throws away his reputation. Do not answer without thinking. Are there any who still

i. 20. *Ngò wân-ặr. Ngò pŭ-kwó shwŏ siè-hwá. Shí-tĭ. Kaĭ-tāng tsŏ*
j. 4. *shimmô? Yiù shímmô k'ò tsŏ tĭ? Jŭ-kīn ngò-mặn tsŏ shímmô haù?*
j. 20. *Nĭ kĭ-ngò shímmô chŭ-í? Ché-kó tsặng-mô-yáng pán-fă-ặr. Tặng-*
k. 6. *yĭ-tặng, ngò ché-yáng tsŏ pă. Nĭ siàng ché-yĭ-kiên-sź-tsîng tsặng-*
k. 21. *mô-yáng? Tū-shĭ yĭ-kó-yáng.—Nĭ ts'ŭng nà-lĭ laĭ? Wàng nà-lĭ k'ŭ́.*
l. 10. *Ngò k'ŭ́ Pĕ-kīng. Ts'ŭng chaŭ-lĭ laĭ. Ts'îng tsín-laĭ. Kín ngò laĭ.*
l. 24. *Lĭ-k'aĭ! Tseù-pá! K'ŭ́-pá! Wàng-heú t'ŭĭ yĭ-tièn-ặr. Laĭ ché-lĭ.*
m. 9. *Tặng yĭ-hwuĭ-ặr. Tặng ngò laĭ. T'ā-mặn yĭ-tsĭ k'ŭ́-liaù. Pŭ-yaú*
m. 24. *ché-mô k'waĭ tseù. Nĭ tseù-tĭ t'aĭ-k'waĭ. Pŭ-yaú tŭng-sheù. Tsaĭ*
n. 8. *ché-lĭ tsó. Mặn kwān-liaù. K'aĭ-mặn. Ts'ŭng ché-lĭ kwó. Kwó-*
n. 21. *pŭ-k'ŭ́. Nĭ tiŭ-liaù shímmô? Ngò mŭ tiŭ shímmô. Weĭ-shímmô?*
o. 6. *Yīn-weĭ ngò shĭ-liaù yĭ-kiên-tŭng-sī.—Kaŭ-shīng shwŏ. Tĭ-shīng*
o. 21. *shwŏ. Nĭ shwŏ-tĭ t'aĭ-k'waĭ, pŭ-nâng tŭng-tĭ.*

28. Dialogues and Phrases in the Mandarin Dialect (2), v. native text, page 28.

a. 1. *Nĭ hwŭĭ-shwŏ Chūng-kwŏ hwá mô? Nĭ shwŏ-liaù mô? Tsūng mŭ-*
a. 15. *yiù t'îng-kiên ché-kó. Meú-jîn kaú-sŭ-liaù ngò. Heú-laĭ ngò kaú-*
a. 30. *sŭ t'ā. Nĭ shwŏ-liaù ché-kó mŭ-yiù? Mŭ-yiù. Ts'îng-wặn ché-kó*
b. 15. *shĭ shimmô? Chī-taú ché-kó mô? Shwŏ-tĕ. Shwŏ-pŭ-tĕ. Weĭ-*
b. 29. *shimmô nĭ pŭ tă-yîng?—Nĭ t'îng-kiên ngò shwŏ mô? Ngò t'îng-pŭ-*
c. 15. *kiên. Shwŏ ts'īng-ts'ú yĭ-tièn-ặr. Laĭ ché-lĭ t'îng. Ngò lĭ ná-kó-jîn*
d. 1. *yuèn, t'îng-pŭ-kiên t'ā-tĭ-hwá. Chīn-lŭng-liaù ngò-tĭ ặr-tò.—Nĭ tŭng-*
d. 18. *tĕ ts'îng t'ā-tĭ-hwá mô? Nĭ tŭng-tĕ, t'ā shwŏ-kwó-tĭ? Ngò shwŏ-tĭ,*
e. 4. *nĭ tŭ tŭng-tĕ mô? Nĭ shwŏ-tĭ, ngò ts'iuèn tŭng-tĕ. Tŭ tŭng-tĕ. Tŭ*
e. 20. *pŭ-tŭng-tĕ. Míng-pĕ-liaù mŭ-yiù? Ché-kó shín-mô í-sź; Tsặng-mô-*
f. 6. *yáng kiaĭ-shwŏ. Ngò tsaĭ-nĭ-t'eŭ-lĭ chī-taú. Pĭ-fāng pŭ chī-taú, yiù*
f. 22. *shimmô kwán-hī? Ché-kó ngò pŭ-kwó siàng shĭ ché-yáng.—Jīn-tĕ t'ā*
g. 9. *mô? Kiên-kwó t'ā kĭ-tsź nĭ? Pŭ kĭ-tĕ tsź-sú. Wàng-liaù ngò mô?*
g. 25. *Ngò kí pŭ ts'īng-ts'ú. Kĭ-tĕ hặn-ts'īng. Siàng-pŭ-k'ĭ-laĭ: Siàng-k'ĭ-*
h. 10. *laĭ-liaù. Nĭ kĭ süĭ? Siên-sāng kweĭ-kāng? Tō-tá niên-kĭ? Yiù ặr-*
h. 25. *shĭ süĭ. Nĭ pĭ-ngò tá. Nĭ tá-kaĭ lŭ-shĭ tō süĭ. Ts'ŭ́-liaù-tsīn mŭ*
i. 12. *yiù? Nĭ fú-mŭ tŭ tsaĭ mô? Siên-fú sź-liaù yiù liàng-niên. Mŭ-tsīn*
i. 28. *tsaĭ-kiā-liaù yiù sān-kó-yŭ. Yiù kĭ-kó ặr-tsź? Yiù kĭ-weĭ lîng-lâng?*
j. 15. *Yiù kĭ-weĭ kweĭ-nŭ? Sān-kó kŭ-niâng. Hiūng-tĭ kĭ-kó? Tsaĭ-tĭ tān*
k. 1. *ngò yĭ-kó, pĭ-tĭ tŭ sź-liaù. Nĭ shwŏ ché yĭ-kŭ-hwá, ngò k'ĭ-liaù yĭ-kó-*
k. 20. *niên-t'eŭ. Siàng-k'ĭ-liaù shimmô? Miên-pŭ-liaù sź.—T'iên-k'ĭ hặn-*
l. 4. *haù; ngò-mặn ch'ŭ-k'ŭ́, kwáng-yĭ-kwáng pá. Ngò-mặn k'ŭ́ liàng-kw'aĭ*
l. 17. *liàng-kw'aĭ. Ngò-mặn sháng-ch'īng pá! Lú pŭ-piên;—pŭ fāng-*
l. 29. *piên;—pŭ piên-í. Yaú tsó-ché mô? Ngò shīn-sháng juèn-jŏ, mŭ-yiù lĭ-*
m. 15. *liàng tseù. Ngò tseù-pŭ-tŭng. Yaú hīng kān-lú, yaú hīng shwuĭ-lú*
m. 29. *nĭ? Yaú sháng-ch'uên mô? Yaú kĭ-ts'iàng-tĭ ch'uên? Hŏ-kĭ! nĭ taĭ*

are held between superior officers of each nation. *Chaŭ-tĕ* (23. e. 17) means 'whereas, according as,' and is a common phrase in official papers. *T'iên-taú* (23. c. 29), lit. 'the way of heaven,' means 'Divine Providence.' *T'ŭng* (23. d. 22), 'together with,' appears here to signify 'with reference to' or 'as for.'

believe in this? This is a falsehood. I was playing. I was only joking. Truly! What ought I to do? What can I do? If we should do this well, what opinion should you have of us? How shall we manage this? Wait a while, let us do it in this way. How do you think this thing is? It is quite the same.—Where do you come from? Where are you going? I am going to Peking. I am come from Court. Please to come in. Come near to me. Stand further off. You may go. Go away! Go behind; fall back a little. Come here! Wait a little while. Wait until I come. They went all together. Do not walk so fast. You walk too fast. Be quiet! Sit down here. The door is fastened. Open the door. Come over here. I cannot come over. What have you thrown away? I have not thrown any thing away. Why? Because I have picked up something.—Speak loud! Speak low! You speak too quickly, I cannot understand.

Translation of Dialogues and Phrases in the Mandarin Dialect (2),
v. native text, page 28.

Do you know how to speak the Chinese language? Have you spoken? I have not indeed heard that. A certain man told me. Afterwards I told him. Did you say this or not? If you please, what is this? or, Allow me to ask what this is. Do you know this? I can say; I cannot say. What! do not you reply?—Do you hear what I say? I cannot hear. Speak a little more distinctly. Come here and listen. At a distance from that man, I cannot hear what he says. It has deafened my ears.—Do you understand clearly what he says? Do you understand what he said? What I said, did you quite understand? What you said I perfectly understood. I quite understood. I did not understand at all. Were you clear about it or not? What is the meaning of this? How do you explain it? I knew before you. Suppose I do not understand, what would be the consequence? I only think this is so.—Do you know him? How many times have you seen him? I do not remember the number of times. Have you forgotten me? I cannot recollect distinctly. I remember very well. I cannot think *or* recollect. I have just remembered. How old are you? What is your honourable age, Sir? How great is your age? *or,* How many are your years? I am twenty years (old). You are older than I am. You are (I should say) above sixty years (old). Are you married or not? Are your parents alive? My late father died two years ago. My mother married again three months ago. How many children have you? How many young gentlemen? How many young ladies? Three daughters (lit. 'misses'). Brothers, how many? I am by myself alone, the others are dead. When you uttered that expression, a thought arose in my mind. What did you think of? One cannot avoid death.—The weather is very fine, let us go out to take a walk. Let us go to take the air. Let us go into the city. The road is bad, (lit. ' not convenient,')—not in a good state,—not good for walking. Do you wish to ride? I am weak, I have not strength to walk. I cannot walk. Do you wish to go by land or by water? Will you go in a boat? What sized boat would you like? (lit. ' how many oared-boat?')

n. 14.	ngò kwó hô pá?| Kān-sīn! Ché-yī-chĕ-ch'uên mŭ-yiù weî mô? Yaú-
n. 29.	ts'iáng-tseù, yiù nĭ-fūng, yiù tìng-t'eú-fūng. Yaú tsaí nà-lĭ sháng-
o. 13.	gān? Tsaí tá-mà-t'eú ná-lĭ. Lin-kīn-liaù hô-piēn, hiá-maú. Ché-lĭ
o. 29.	haù yā!

29. Dialogues and Phrases in the Mandarin Dialect (3), v. native text,
page 29.

a. 1.	Aĭ-yā! ché-kó-tĭ-fāng hặn-haù-k'án;—wặn-hô-tĭ, liáng-shwáng-tĭ?
a. 16.	K'ān shŭ́ tŭ k'aĭ-liaù hwá-ạr. Ché-yī-kān lŏ-liaù yĕ-tsż. Mĕ-tsż shŭ́-
b. 4.	liaù. Nĭ fă-liaù mô? Shĭ-tsaí kwặn-kiuên-liaù. Tsaí-ché-kó ts'īng-
b. 18.	tsaù-sháng t'ĭ-chŏ, haù. T'sīn nà-kó shŭ́-lin. Tsaí ché-siē shŭ́-tĭ-hiá
c. 4.	hặn-haù-tĭ yīn-liáng. Kīn-niên kwò-tsż tō. Shŭ́ tō kĭ-liaù kwò-tsż.
c. 20.	Kīn-niên, niên-fūng. Kiú-niên shĭ hwáng-niên. Ché-lĭ yiù hặn-
d. 3.	haù-tĭ p'in-kwò, shā-lĭ, lĭ-tsż, yīng-t'aú. Ngò nîng-yaú hĕ-t'aú, hwó-
d. 19.	shĭ lĭ-tsż. Ngò hặn siáng-k'ĭ t'aú-ạr, kŭ-tsż, kān-tsż, tsáng-tsż. Ché-
e. 7.	siē meî-tsż kāng haù. Yiù pŭ-t'aú maí mô? Chĭ tō-shaù ts'iên yĭ-kīn?
e. 23.	Maĭ-tĕ sź-shĭ-kó tá-ts'iên yĭ kīn. Maí shĭ-kī kīn pá!—T'iēn wán-liaù.
f. 10.	Jĭ-t'eú yaú lŏ-shān. Tạ̀ng-yĭ-hwüĭ t'iēn tsiú hĕ liaù. Kw'aí tseù pá;
f. 25.	nĭ-fă-liaù. K'ĭ wán-fán. T'iēn-k'ĭ tsạ̀ng-mô-yáng-haù? T'iēn-k'ĭ
g. 9.	làng. T'iēn yīn-liaù. Ché-kó wán-sháng haù t'iēn-k'ĭ. Yiù ch'aú-
g. 22.	k'ĭ. Yiù yŭn-tsaĭ, k'án-pŭ-kién sīng-sŭ. Lwán-k'ĭ-fūng laî-liaù.
h. 6.	Shĭ yĭ-kó paú-fūng. T'iēn-k'ĭ ch'áng-piên. Haù hiá-yŭ. Hiá
h. 19.	pŏ-tsż. Hiá-sŭ̆. Sŭ̆-hwā k'aĭ liaù. Tà-lüĭ. Lüĭ-hiáng. Tà-shén.
i. 3.	Lüĭ tà-sź-liaù yĭ-kó-jīn. Fūng-chuī. Fūng-tá. Paú-fūng kwó-k'ú́-
i. 18.	liaù, k'án-tĕ-kién t'iēn-hâng. Shĭ kó haù t'iēn-k'ĭ tĭ p'ing-k'ú́. Yiù-
j. 3.	wú́. Jĭ ch'ŭ mán-mán-tĭ, tsiú sán-liaù. Hiá-lú́. Hiá-shwáng.—
j. 17.	Shimmô shĭ-heú? Kĭ-hiá-chūng? Pŭ-wán. Hwüĭ-kiā k'ú́ pá!
j. 30.	Hwán yiù-shĭ-heú, tsaí sháng-wù. Chā-pŭ-tō yĭ-hiá-chūng. Tà-
k. 14.	liaù yĭ-hiá sān-kạ. Hwán mŭ-yiù tà sān-hiá ạr-kạ. Nĭ tsạ̀ng-mô
k. 30.	chĭ-taú? T'īng-kién chūng tà-liaù. Ngò siáng pŭ-shĭ ché-yáng ch'ĭ.
l. 14.	K'án nĭ-tĭ piaù. Ngò-tĭ piaù tseù-tĭ-k'waí pŭ-tüĭ. Piaù mán kĭ-
l. 29.	fặn. Sháng-k'án jĭ-kweí. Shā-tsż-piaù tsaí nà-lĭ?—Nĭ hwán-hĭ
m. 14.	nà-kó shĭ-heú? Chặn-t'iēn shĭ tsüĭ-haù-tĭ. Ché-kó t'iēn-k'ĭ wặn-
m. 29.	hô-tĭ, yĕ pŭ-jĭ, yĕ pŭ-lâng. Ché pŭ-swàn chặn-t'ien, swàn shĭ tūng-
n. 15.	t'iēn. Shŭ́ tŭ mŭ-yiù fă-yă. Ché hiá-t'iēn jĭ-tẹ-hặn. Ngò ch'ŭ-liaù
o. 1.	hán, yaú jĭ-sź. Tsūng mŭ-kiŏ-tĕ ché-yáng jĭ. Kaī-tāng hú́-tō tĭ
o. 17.	mŭ-sŭ̆-tsaù. Yaú sheú chwáng-kiā; kŏ-wán-liaù chwáng-kiā. Tsiú-
o. 30.	t'iēn.

30. Dialogues and Phrases in the Mandarin Dialect (4), v. native text,
page 30.

a. 2.	Sháng-hiŏ.—Nĭ ché-yáng kw'aí wàng nà-lĭ paù. Ngò shàng-hiŏ.
a. 15.	Ngò yĕ wàng nà-lĭ k'ú́. Tạ̀ng yĭ-chên-yên. Pŭ-yaú maĭ-taĭ. Tsaí
a. 30.	ngò-mặn t'eú-lĭ tseù-tĭ nà-yĭ-kó shĭ shüĭ? Shĭ ngò-mặn t'ŭng-hiŏ-tĭ.
b. 17.	Tsà-mặn tŭ yĭ-kweī-ạr tseù pá!—Nĭ weî-shimmô laî-tĭ ché-mô ch'ĭ.

Friend! Take us over the river! Gladly! Has this boat no masts? We must row; there is a contrary wind,—the wind is right a-head. Where do you want to go ashore? At that great jetty there! When you have approached the shore let go the anchor. Here is a good place!

Translation of Dialogues and Phrases in the Mandarin Dialect (3), *v. native text*, page 29.

Ah! this country is very pretty! pleasant and cool! See the trees have all blossomed. This one has shed its leaves. The corn is ripe. Are you spent? I am indeed tired. To fling ourselves down on this green grass will be pleasant. Enter that forest. Under the trees it is very shady. This year there is plenty of fruit. Many trees have borne fruit. This year was an abundant year. Last year was a year of scarcity. Here there are very good apples, pears, plums, and cherries. I prefer walnuts or chestnuts. I am very fond of eating peaches, small oranges, or large thin-skinned oranges or coolie oranges. Those plums are better. Have you any grapes to sell? They cost how much a pound? I can sell them at forty large cash a pound. Buy a few pounds!—The day is very fine. The sun is going to set. Wait a while, it will soon be dark. If you walk fast, you will be wearied. Eat your evening meal. How is the weather? The weather is cold. The sky is overcast. This evening it is fine weather. It is damp. It is cloudy; I cannot see the stars. The wind has risen in gusts. It is a gale. The weather is ever changing. It rains hard. It hails. It snows. It is snowing in flakes. It thunders. The thunder roars. It lightens. The thunder (bolt) has killed a man. The wind blows. The wind is high. The storm is past, we can see the rainbow. It is a sign of fair weather. It is misty. The sun will come out by-and-by, then it will be dispersed. The dew is falling. The hoarfrost is falling.—What time is it? What o'clock is it? Not late. Let us go home! There is time (enough) yet, it is still forenoon. It is nearly one o'clock. It has struck one and three quarters. It has not yet struck three and two quarters. How do you know? I heard the clock strike. I do not think it is so late. Look at your watch. My watch goes fast, it will not agree. Your watch is slow, how many minutes? Go and look at the sun-dial. Where is the sand-glass? Do you like this season? Spring is the best. This weather is pleasant; it is neither hot nor cold. This is not like spring; it is like winter. The trees have not yet budded. This summer it is very hot. I am perspiring, I shall die of heat. I never experienced such heat. We ought to have a large crop of millet. You should reap. I have reaped. Autumn.

Translation of Dialogues and Phrases in the Mandarin Dialect (4), *v. native text*, page 30.

On going to school.—Where are you running so fast? I am going to school. I am going there too. Wait a minute. Don't loiter. Who is that walking in front of us? It is our school-fellow. Let us all walk together!—Why do you come so late? I was up late last night, and could not rise early. At what

c. 5. *Ngò tsŏ-jî ngaú-liaù yè, pŭ-nǎng tsaù k'ĭ-laî. Nĭ shî kĭ-hiá-chŭng*
c. 21. *k'ĭ-laî-tĭ ? Nĭ haù-lǎn-tó. Weî-shîmmŏ tsʻiên-jî pŭ laî? Nà yî-jî-sź-*
d. 9. *tsʻing hǒn-mǎng, pŭ-tĕ kʻŭng-ḏr laî. Liaú-lĭ shí-sŭ tĭ sź-tsʻing*
d. 24. *shǎng-t'eŭ yiù-tĭ weî-hiên pŭ-shaù. Jŏ pĭ-jĭn míng-nĭ pá-liaù, taú-*
e. 10. *tĭ nĭ-tĭ sź-fŭ míng-nĭ, pŭ-tʻing, chê-kŏ liaù pŭ-tĕ; hwáng-tsiè nĭ tǎn-*
e. 28. *kŏ-liaù nĭ-tĭ sź-tsʻing yiù tá kwǎn-hî. Sŭî-piên tʻā tà, pŭ-wú yaú*
f. 15. *liaù nĭ-tĭ pǫn-fǎn. Chê-sǎn-tʻiên nĭ pŭ niên-shŭ, pŭ-haù. Tsaî pŭ-*
g. 1. *yaú chê-yáng. Tsʻiên yî-tsź nĭ laî chê-lĭ, ngò fǎn-fŭ-liaù nĭ shîmmŏ ?*
g. 18. *Kʻú nĭ-tĭ fǎng tsŏ. Taî nĭ-tĭ maú-tsź. Kʻán-nĭ-tĭ shŭ. Yŭ-pí nĭ*
h. 5. *yaú peî-tĭ-shŭ. Tʻing-míng! Niên-wǎn-liaù mŭ-yiù ? Hwǎn mŭ-*
h. 18. *yiù. Nĭ pĭ-mĕ-yén tŭ yiù-liaù mŏ ? Chê-kŏ maî tsź shîmmŏ shīng-*
i. 4. *yîn? Yîn maî. Tsǫng-mŏ kiaî-shwŏ ? Yiù tsáng tĭ î-sź. Tsūng*
i. 17. *mŭ-yiù kʻán-kiên chê-yáng-tĭ yî-kó-tsź. Chê-yî-pǫn-shŭ nǎn-tǔng.*
j. 3. *Ngò mŭ-yiù hŭ-tō tĭ kūng-fŭ. Yīn-weî ngò kaī-tǎng kàn-kʻú maî*
j. 19. *tūng-sī; líng-waî hwǎn yiù pĭ-tĭ sź-tsʻing kaī-tǎng pán. Nĭ siaù-sīn*
k. 5. *meî-jĭ niên-tĭ-shŭ; līng-waî yî-kó-yŭ hwǎn yaú-tsŏ liàng-piên wǫn-*
k. 21. *chǎng.—Nĭ haù yā? Hǫn-haù. Nĭ yáng-liaù fán mŏ ? Kʻĭ-liaù.*
l. 5. *Líng-tsān haù ? Kiā-fŭ haù. Nĭ tĭ kʻiù-kʻiù tsǫng-mŏ-yáng ? Tʻā jŭ-*
l. 20. *kīn pì tʻeŭ-lĭ haù-tĕ-tō. Míng-jĭ tsaî-kiên! Ngò kaī-tǎng súng-hīng.—*
m. 7. *Tʻiên tsiǎng-hĕ. Taú-liaù shŭî-kiŏ tĭ shî-heú. Hò-kî, nĭ tʻǎng ngò laî.*
m. 23. *Pʻá-kweî mŏ ? Pŭ-pʻá. Fǎng-hiá wǫn-chʻǎng. Liŭ-hiá tǎng. Mí-*
n. 6. *tǎng. Míng-tʻiên tsaù-siē kʻĭ-laî, kiaù-ngò. Ngò kaī-tǎng tsʻing-tsaù*
n. 20. *kʻĭ-laî. Yĭ-tíng kĭ-tĕ mŏ ? Yĭ-tíng kĭ-tĕ. Tà-hò. Tiên-tǎng. Mŭ-*
o. 6. *yiù hò-shî. Hò-meî-ḏr.—Shŭî tà-mǫn? Shî shuî ? Ngò hwǎn mŭ-*
o. 21. *yiù kʻĭ-laî. Tsaù sīng-liaù. Tʻiên tá-liáng-liaù.*

31. Extract from the *Chíng-yīn tsŭî-yaú*, v. native text, page 31.

a. 1. *Yĭ-kó-jĭn hiŏ Kwǎn-hwá laî, tsŏ shîmmŏ tĭ nî ? Tʻeŭ-yî-kiên yŭ-pé*
a. 18. *tsź-kĭ tsiǎng-laî chʻŭ-shīn tsŏ-kwǎn, sź-heú shǎng-sź, lĭn-lĭ shŭ-yuên,*
b. 4. *yaú tsŏ yî-kó yiù-pǫn-sź-tĭ Kwǎn yā! Kʻĭ-tsʻź, tsiŭ tsŏ tá-kʻĕ-shǎng,*
b. 21. *hwŏ kʻaī hǎng-tiên, hwŏ wàng waî-sǎng tseù shwŭî, yaú-tsŏ yĭ-kó mà-*
c. 6. *lĭ-tĭ kʻĕ-shǎng. Tsaî kʻĭ-tsʻź, tsiŭ-shî kŭ-kiă pá-tsĕ,—nĭ shî kó yiù-*
c. 23. *ĭ-shĭ-tĭ jĭn, yiù-tʻĭ-miên-tĭ jĭn, tsaî hiáng-tsŭ-chŭng, niên-chʻǎng yŭ-*
d. 9. *chʻǎng, hiǎng-tsʻing tsŭ-sź, shaù-pŭ-liaù; yè yĭlŭ kiên pà sź-ḏr, yaú tʻĕ*
d. 25. *jĭn-kiă liaú-lĭ liaú-lĭ; yè tĕ kiên-kiên tĭ-fǎng, pà sź-ḏr shwŏ kó tĭ-sĭ*
e. 14. *tsʻing-tsŭ, yî-tsĕ weî-kú hiǎng-tsŭ, ḏr-tsĕ paù-hú mǫn-meî ; yuên-shî weî*
f. 1. *chê sǎn-mǫn kʻĭ-kiên, pîng pŭ shî shwŏ kĭ-kŭ Kwǎn-hwá, tsaî tá-kiaī*
f. 17. *shǎng, naú-wǎn í-ḏr, siaú-hwá jĭn-kiă, hĕ-húng jĭn-kiă, hwǫn-hiūn*
g. 2. *jĭn-kiă, tsiŭ swǎn-liaù sź-lŏ. Sò-ĭ nĭ-mǫn tsūng-yaú pà tá-fǎng tĭ*

Jín (23. e. 14) 'benevolence, kindness;' see note on p. 28 of Part II.
Wŭ sŏ-pŭ-feŭ (23. e. 26) ' it overshadows every thing;' cf. Art. 422 of Part I.
The repetition of *píng* (23. f. 6. and 8) means ' both'—' and,' or ' at once'—' and.' In classical compositions, the Chinese are fond of using *chŭng* 'centre' (23. f. 11) and *sīn* ' heart' (23. i. 12) for the *origin* or the *moving principle* of that with which it is joined.

Tsz——î-*laî* (23. f. 14), ' from —— to the present time,' is a good example of this form of construction.

o'clock did you rise? You are very lazy. Why did you not come the day before? On that day I had to do some very urgent business and I could not find time. To managing affairs in the world there are obstacles not a few. If any one else command you, you are content; but if your tutor bid you do any thing, you do not obey. This will not do. Besides, if you shirk your work, great consequences will result. No matter whether he beats you or not, you do not hasten to your duty. You have not learnt any thing for these three days;—this is bad. Don't do it again. Once, on a former occasion, when you came here, what did I order you to do? Go to your room and sit down! Take your cap! Look at your book! Prepare your lesson to repeat. Obey! Have you learnt your lesson or not? Not yet. Have you your pencil, ink, and inkstone? What is the sound and tone of this (*mai*) character? The sound is *mai*. What is its meaning? It has the meaning of *burying*. I have never seen such a character as this. This book is difficult to understand. I have not much time, because I have to fetch many things; and besides, I have other things to do. You take care and learn your book every day; besides every month write two chapters of elegant composition.—Are you well? Very well! Have you dined? I have. Is your good father well? My father is well. How is your uncle? He is much better than he was formerly. I shall see you again to-morrow. I will see you out!——It is getting dark. Bed-time has arrived. Friend! Come with me! Are you afraid of ghosts? No! Put down the mosquito curtains. Set down the lamp. Put out the lamp. Get up rather early in the morning and call me. I must get up early. Will you be sure to remember? I will certainly remember. Strike a light. Light the lamp. I have no flint. Coal.—Who is knocking at the door? Who is it? I am not up yet. Awake quickly, it is broad day-light.

Translation of the Extract from the Chíng-yīn tsüí-yaú, v. native text, page 31.

When a man learns the Mandarin dialect, what is it for? In the first place, it is to prepare himself for future advancement as a Mandarin, so as to be able to attend on his superiors and to superintend his subordinates, and to be an officer of ability. In the next place, if he would be a mercantile man of the first class, whether he open an establishment (at home), or travel abroad in the provinces by land and water, he ought to be a shrewd and clever merchant. And again, even if a man must stay at home and do nothing much, being a man of independence and respectability, still among his country relatives, in the course of months and years, their affairs will not be a few, and each of these he will have to consider for them. And, if he see clearly his ground, he may take each matter and speak of it in detail and with much acuteness, then he will at once have a regard for his kinsmen's interests, and, at the same time, protect his own door. Now it is for these reasons, and lest also you be not able to speak a few sentences of Mandarin on the great thoroughfares, of a noisy, joking character, to make fun of people, or to deceive and make fools of them, that you must make it your business *to learn Mandarin.* Therefore you should take language of a liberal character, language suitable for receiving and waiting

g. 19. *hwá-ạr, tsĭ-tai chàng-sháng tĭ hwá-ạr, yíng-cheŭ pâng-yiù tĭ hwá-ạr,*
h. 5. *kiaŭ-taú wàn-pei tĭ hwá-ạr, shī hwān tĭ-hiá-jin tĭ hwá-ạr, taŭ-liaù*
h. 22. *waĭ-t'eŭ, yiù kiaŭ-kwān tsĭ-fú tĭ hwá-ạr, tüí chŏ maì-maĭ jin tĭ hwá-*
i. 9. *ạr, yáng-yáng tū-yiù kó kw'àn-shì. Yaú tsai ché sháng-t'eŭ liŭ-sīn-*
i. 24. *ts'aĭ-shì ching-king tĭ yā! T'sai pŭ-wàng-liaù hiŏ Kwān-hwá tĭ ché*
j. 9. *yĭ-fān kūng-fū yā!*
k. 2. *Nĭ tsŏ hiŏ-sāng tĭ jin, sháng shŭ-fâng nien-shŭ, shimmŏ-tū-yaú*
k. 17. *yiù kó kweĭ-kiù; ts'ing-tsaù k'ĭ-laĭ, sĭ-liaù liên, hŏ-liaù ch'à, pin-kaú*
l. 3. *tiĕ-tiĕ mā-mā, haĭ-ạr wàng shŭ-fâng k'ŭ-liaù, shwŏ-kwó chī heú, paŭ*
l. 19. *k'ĭ shŭ-pạn, ch'ŭ tá-mạn-k'eŭ, twàn-twàn ching-ching, chīn-chīn chŭng-*
m. 3. *chŭng tĭ k'ŭ, liàng-chĕ-kiä pŭ yaú hwạn-ti'aŭ, liàng chĕ yên-ts'ing pŭ-*
m. 18. *yaú hwạn-ts'iaŭ tūng-sī, yĭ-chĭ tseù taù shŭ-fâng lĭ-t'eŭ, pà shŭ pạn*
n. 4. *fâng-hiá, wáng Shíng-jin shâng-t'eŭ, tsŏ kó yĕ, yiú t'ĭ siēn-sāng tsŏ*
n. 19. *kó yĕ, jên-heú tsó-chŏ nien-shŭ, pà shŭ peĭ-tĕ shŭ-shŭ ạr tĭ, ts'aĭ súng*
o. 7. *taú siēn-sāng chŏ-sháng; peĭ-shŭ shĭ-heú, yiú yaú yĭ-kū-kū līng-yá lí-*
o. 24. *ch'ĭ, pŭ-yaú hān hû tsó-leŭ!*

32.   The Epistolary Style, v. native text, page 32.

a. 2.   *Wạn-heú.*
a. 5. *Kiù ts'ĭ chēn Hān, wĭ hú jŭ yuên; kín wạn ĭ tsīng Kiāng yiú, tĕ*
a. 21. *hwá jĭ sīn, yīn-siên chī sz̄, kāng shīn wú-meĭ. Hạn pŭ-nâng ch'à-ch'ĭ*
b. 6. *ạr fī-ts'iàng tsò-yiú, kwān shíng hwá ạr ling tĕ yên yè! K'īn yuên*
b. 21. *lúng-piên, tĭ tsiê yĭ-hàng, ĭ shīn tsĭ-kw'ān. Kiēn ts'ing kīn gān; Jŭ*
c. 6.   *weĭ kién nien.*
d. 2.   *Tà.*
d. 4.   *Shíng míng kwán ạr, fĭ yĭ-jĭ ĭ. Hwaĭ ĭ jin ạr pŭ-kién, ching*
d. 19. *ts'ing ts'ĭ yū kién-kiä, naĭ hwà hán hiá pān, yuên-jŭ tĭ mién. Tạn kiaĭ*
e. 5. *sāng-píng chī kĭ-kĕ. Hô híng jŭ chī! Weĭ shĭ siēn shĭ chī yà, chuēn shŭ*
e. 22. *jin jin, wĭ miên p'ĭ-yè ts'àn-fŭ, tsź-tsāng nüĭ-kw'eĭ ạr. T'àng yiù*
f. 7. *liàng-yuên, tĕ yaŭ hwüĭ kú, tsĭ ts'àn tsiù lạn wạn. K'ò pŭ-líng kù-jin*
f. 23. *shên meĭ yū ts'iên ĭ. Shĭ wáng! Shĭ t'aù! Kíng tsž ts'aĭ fŭ.*

The English are variously characterized in this composition either as *fán* (23. g. 2) 'foreign,' (a word used originally for the inhabitants of the southern frontier of China,— the southern barbarians,) or as *í* (24. c. 20. and 24. k. 23) 'the western barbarians,' a tribe on the western frontier of China. Foreign nations are generally called *waì-kwŏ* (23. h. 4) 'outside kingdoms,' and *sĭ-yâng-kwŏ* 'western ocean kingdoms.'

The Supplementary Treaty, a part of which is given on p. 25 of the Chrestomathy, was published at Hongkong, in July 1844, by Sir John F. Davis, who was then Governor of Hongkong. It contains the very important provisions that the five ports of Canton, Amoy, Fu-cheu, Ningpo, and Shanghai should be opened to British trade, and for the resort and residence of British merchants; by it the close system of the Hong merchants at Canton was broken up, and free-trade allowed with any native merchants. This treaty was supplementary to the treaty of Nanking, which is indeed referred to in it: (cf. *kiâng-nán* &c. 25. j. 11.)

Hān (32. a. 8) or *Hān Kíng-cheŭ* was an eminent statesman, whose friendship reflected his own bright fame on those who enjoyed it. Intercourse with him ennobled the recipient

upon seniors and superiors, phrases for polite intercourse with friends, the expressions appropriate for instructing young people, and language for calling upon inferiors. And when you go out of doors you will require expressions to use to mandarins, and others to address to merchants. There are models for all these (kinds of expression). You should pay attention to what has been said above: then it will be all right! Then you will not have wasted your time in studying the Mandarin dialect.

If you are a young student, you go up to school to study; now every thing has a rule. Rise early; and having washed your face and drunk your tea, announce to your parents that their son is going to school. Having said that, wrap up your book, go out at the front door, and proceed (to school) in a becoming manner. Your feet should not be skipping disorderly, nor your eyes be listlessly gazing at every thing. But proceed straight into the schoolhouse, take your book and lay it down, reverently look up to the sage above and make a bow, then make a bow to the tutor, and afterwards sit down to study. Having learnt off your lesson perfectly, then present it to your tutor and lay it on his desk. When you say your lesson, you should repeat every sentence distinctly and fluently, you should not mumble or leave out any words.

Translation of the Passages in the Epistolary Style, v. native text, page 32.

A letter of greeting.

For a long time I have looked reverently to *Han, but* have as yet not attained my desire. Recently I heard that you had removed your banner to the River's right, and that your virtue increases, and is renewed daily; my private feelings of joy become deeper, whether awake or asleep. Would that I were able to put on wings and fly to hover on your right and left! To behold your abounding progress, and to listen with delight to your gracious words! At present I am fortunately able to despatch a letter, and I just employ one line, in order to manifest my accumulated feelings of respect, and to wish you wealth and happiness. Humbly I bow, considering that you know my thoughts.

Reply.

Your flourishing reputation is ever sounding in mine ears, and that daily. I cherish kind regards for him whom I do not see. My feelings are just like those towards a distant relative, and in the favours conferred by his flowery pencil, I seem to see him face to face. I respectfully salute you with gratification on the fulfilment of my longings for peace. What fortune like this! But the praises which you have lavished upon me are simply such as belong to a really good man, and not to an insignificant and rude countryman; and they only increase my confusion. If a convenient opportunity should arise, pray accept my invitation, and favour me with your regard, that we may decant our wine and chat about literature. Let not our past differences stand in the way of our former esteem. This is my hope! This is my prayer! Respectfully I offer this in reply.

h. 3.   *Kw'eí-wŭ.*
i. 1.   *Liáng-páng kiù-kw'ŭ, yīn maŭ ts'iuên-wŭ, kiāng-haì chī tsù jīn t'aì*
i. 15.   *shīn.   K'ĭ tĕ yŭn yuèn tsaì yĭ-fāng hŭ?   Weī shí tsź sīn wáng hing,*
i. 30.   *tāng pŭ fŭ ts'ạn sŭ-hwŭì wŭ tsź chī tsiĕ, chí kwaì hán yàng.   Hwáng-*
j. 15.   *heŭ hwŭì yiù k'ĭ, pŭ-tsaí yŭ shí, yuén tsaí yŭ t'iēn; k'ĭ k'ĭ kŏ-tsź nù*
k. 2.   *lĭ k'ŏ ạr.   Tsź yuên húng-piên, fŭ-sháng sheù-kīn yĭ-fāng, siaù-taŭ*
k. 17.   *liáng-pà; siĕ wĭ hiù-wŭ, pạn pŭ-tsŭ tāng mŭ lĭ chī t'eŭ, ạr ts'iēn lĭ*
l. 4.   *ngŏ-maŭ.   Wŭ-līng ts'ing cháng, liáng pĭ tù-tsź ạr yĭ-liên yŭ-lŭ chī*
l. 20.   *lŭ-jīn ĭ.   Chŭ weī chí-chĕ, mĕ t'aŭ nŭì, wŭ k'ĭ p'iên k'ĕ lŭ-shīn.*
m. 7.   *K'ĭn tsź yuèn-tá, shạn-ts'ing fŭ-gān, píng heŭ kín chì, píng heŭ*
m. 20.   *kāng níng.   Sháng*
                    Meŭ-meŭ Hiŭng-t'aì Tá-jīn wạn-kì,
                         Yŭ-tĭ Meŭ-meŭ tsź tạn.

33. Poetical Extracts (Ancient and Modern), v. native text, page 33.

a. 2.   *Kŭ-shī.   1. Tá-fūng kō.*
a. 5.   *Tá-fūng k'ĭ hĭ!—Yŭn fĭ yáng!*
a. 16.   *Weī kiă haì-nŭì hĭ!—Kweī kŭ hiāng!*
a. 24.   *Gān tĕ màng sź hĭ!—Sheù sź fāng!*

b. 5.   *2. Chạn-kūng kiŭ.*
b. 9.   *Tsŏ-yĕ fūng-k'aī lú tsìng-t'aŭ,   Wĭ-yāng ts'iên tiên yŭ lạn kaŭ,*
b. 23.   *Píng-yáng kō-wŭ sīn chīng ch'ùng,   Liên-waì chạn-hán tsź miên-p'aŭ.*

c. 9.   *Wŭ-yên.   3. Yiŭ-kŭ.*
c. 15.   *Kweí-tsiên sŭì ĭ-tạng,   Ch'ŭ mạn kiaī yiù yíng;*
c. 25.   *Tŭ wŭ waí-wŭ kiĕn,   Sŭì tsź yiŭ-kŭ ts'ing!*
d. 5.   *Wĭ yŭ yĕ laī-kwŏ,   Pŭ-chī chạn ts'aŭ sāng!*
d. 15.   *Ts'īng-shān hwŭ ĭ-shŭ,   Niaù-tsiŏ jaù shĕ míng.*
d. 25.   *Shí yŭ taŭ-jīn ngaù,   Hwŏ sŭì ts'iaŭ-chĕ híng.*

---

of his favours, and his approbation was held to be a great recommendation for honourable employment: (cf. Gonçalves' *Arte China*, Historical Extracts, No. 130.) This name is used therefore, by way of praise, and in honour of the person's reputation, to whom the letter is addressed. Such allusions in letters sometimes make the epistolary style difficult to be understood, and they always defy a literal rendering.

It-tsíng (32. a. 15), 'remove-banner,' here means to 'change your residence.'

Kiāng-yiŭ (32. a. 17), ' the River's right,' is put for the city of Nan-king, which is situated on the right bank of the Great River, the *Yáng-tsz* ('son of the ocean').

The student will observe the peculiar terseness and formality of the phraseology in the epistolary style, which abounds also in allusions of various kinds. This does not imply, however, any great degree of learning in the writer, for the phrases suitable for fashionable letter-writing are set down in a book, which is known to all educated persons: (cf. Part II. p. 12. 26. *Kiáng-hŭ chī-tŭ fán-yŭn.*)

Yĭn-siĕn or *hĭn-siĕn* (32. a. 23) 'joyful expectations.'

Ch'ă-ch'ĭ (32. b. 4), 'to insert wings,' is a phrase peculiar to this style.

A letter sent with a present.

My good friend, you have been long absent, not the slightest sound of you has reached us. The navigation of the river has been much interrupted. How can it be said that we are living in the same country? But I think myself that we should forget the present aspect *of our affairs*, and not be again careful about stemming the torrent with vain regrets about those who have forgotten us. How much more when *we know that* a meeting time will arrive, not indeed in this world, but, we hope, in heaven. Let us each console ourselves thus, and use our best endeavours to this end, and it will be well. By this opportunity I beg to send you, by the bearer, a pocket-handkerchief and two small knives, things valueless in themselves: they are not worthy to be sent as presents, but they are foreign curiosities, and though insignificant things, they show my good feelings. I can well suppose that in viewing them you will pity the poor stupid little travellers. After due reverence to your lord, I hope you will remember me, and in your prayers bear me for a moment in mind. Respectfully at this distance I communicate, wishing you tranquillity and happiness, as well as present good fortune and perfect peace.

To be placed upon the desk of my honourable and worthy elder brother M. M.,

With the salutations of his humble servant M. M.

Translation of the Poetical Extracts (*Ancient and Modern*), v. native text, page 33.

Ancient poetry. 1. The song about the high wind.
A high wind arises!—The clouds come flying along!
Majestic heaves the ocean!—We return to the old abode!
Peace we possess, and heroes!—to keep us on every side!

2. The ballad about the Spring-palace, by *Wang Chang-ling*.
Last night the peach tree by the well bloomed forth
In the temple before *Wi-yang*, when the moon was at her full,
Ping-yang danced and sang with ever-increasing grace,
Or without the porch-screen in cool of spring she wore a quilted robe.

Verses of five syllables. 3. The hermit, by *Wei Ying-wŭ*.
The noble and the mean, although they differ in rank,
Alike proceed from home, and have their plans for gain.
Here by myself no outward things disturb me.
Freely am I come to dwell in this retirement.
The small rain by night falls all around,
The grass buds forth in spring I know not how,
The blue mountain, anon, gleams with the rising sun,
The little birds keep singing as they fly about my cot,
Oft-times I join the traveller on his way,
Oft follow, perhaps, the woodman in his rounds;

e. 5.	*T'sz̽ tāng ān kièn-liŭ,*	*Shŭı̀ weı̆ pŏ shı̆-yŭng ?*
e. 17.	4. *Kwŏ tsiù kiă.*	
e. 21.	*Tsz̽-jı̆ chăng hwặn yı̄n,*	*Fı̄ kwān yàng sı̆ng lı̆ng !*
f. 1.	*Yèn k'ān jı̆n tsı̄n tsŭı̆,*	*Hò jı̆n tŭ weı̆ sı̆ng ?*
g. 2.	*Liŭ-shı̄.—Wŭ-yèn liŭ.*	5. *Yiŭ-cheŭ yĕ yı̄n.*
g. 14.	*Liăng-fŭng ch'ŭı̆ yĕ-yŭ,*	*Siaŭ-sĕ tŭng hăn-lı̂n,*
g. 24.	*Chı̆ng yiù kaŭ-tăng yèn,*	*Năng wăng ch'ı̆ mŭ sı̄n,*
h. 4.	*Kiŭn-chūng ı̆ kièn wŭ,*	*Sĕ-shặng chŭng kiă-yı̄n:*
h. 14.	*Pŭ-tsŏ piēn ch'ı̆ng-tsiăng,*	*Shŭı̀ chı̄ gặn yŭ shı̄n.*
i. 2.	6. *Sŭng Hăn-lı̂n Chāng Sz̽-mă Năn-haı̀ lĕ-pı̄.*	
i. 13.	*Kwăn-mièn t'ūng năn-kı̆,*	*Wặn-chāng lŏ shăng-t'aı̀,*
i. 23.	*Chaŭ ts'ăng sān tièn k'ŭ,*	*Pı̄ taŭ pĕ măn k'aı̄.*
j. 3.	*Yè-kwăn nŭng hwā-fă,*	*Chặn-făn sı̆ yŭ laı̀.*
j. 13.	*Pŭ-chı̄ ts'āng haı̀-shăng,*	*T'iēn-k'ièn kı̀-shı̆ hwŭı̀.*
k. 5.	*Tsı̆ yên liŭ.*	7. *Yiŭ-cheŭ sı̄n-sŭı̆ tsŏ.*
k. 15.	*K'ŭ-sŭı̆ Kı̄ng-năn meı̆ sz̽ sŭ,*	*Kı̄n-nièn Kı̆-pĕ sŭ jŭ meı̆.*
k. 29.	*Kŭng chı̄ jı̆n-sz̽ hŏ ch'ăng-tı̆ng,*	*Tsiĕ hı̀ nièn-hwă k'ŭ fŭ-laı̀.*
l. 13.	*Piēn-chı̄n-shŭ kō liēn-jı̆ tŭng,*	*Kı̄ng-ch'ı̆ng liaŭ-hò ch'ĕ mı̆ng k'aı̄*
l. 27.	*Yaŭ-yaŭ sı̆ hiăng Chàng-ān jı̆,*	*Yuĕn shăng năn-shān sheŭ yı̆ peı̄.*
m. 12.	*Wŭ yên p'aı̆ liŭ.*	8. *Pĕ-tı̄ hwaı̆ kŭ.*
n. 1.	*Jı̆-lŏ ts'āng-kiăng wăn,*	*T'ı̆ng-jaŭ wặn t'ŭ-fŭng.*
n. 11.	*Ch'ı̆ng lı̂n Pā-tsz̽ kwŏ,*	*T'aı̆ mŭ Hăn-wăng kūng.*
n. 21.	*Hwăng fŭ jı̆ng Cheŭ tièn,*	*Shı̄n shān shăng Yŭ kŭng.*

Tsŏ-yiŭ (32. b. 9) must here mean literally 'on the right and left,' not 'attendants' or 'officers' as the phrase commonly signifies.

Hŭng-piĕn (32. b. 21) is the regular phrase, in letters, for 'sending a letter.' *Hŭng* means literally 'a swan or wild goose,' and is applied figuratively to a 'letter-carrier.' *Piĕn* commonly signifies 'convenience, opportunity.'

Fŭ weı̆ kièn-niĕn (32, c. 5) 'I how and consider that you know my thoughts.' *Kièn* 'to mirror back, to reflect.'

Kı̄-kĕ (32. e. 8), lit. 'hunger and thirst,' expresses 'intense longing,' and here stands as a noun. It is qualified by *săng-pı̆ng* (32. e. 5) 'the growth of peace;' then the whole expression forms the object of the verb *kiaı̆* 'to dissipate, to dissolve.'

Ts'ān-tsiŭ lăn-wăn (32. f. 14), lit. 'bottle-wine discourse-letters,' which has been translated, 'decant our wine and chat about literature,' might have been, 'take a glass of wine together and discuss the subject of letters.'

Ts'iēn-lı̆ ngŏ-maŭ (32. l. 2), lit. 'thousand miles goose feathers,' appear to be put for 'foreign curiosities.'

The specimens of ancient and modern poetry, which are given on page 33, present in some parts even greater difficulties than the epistolary phraseology. The ancient poetry of the Chinese was irregular; each verse consisted of an equal number of syllables, and assimilated in rhyme and ending. But this was not always according to strict rule, or at equal distances. The metre of modern verse consists commonly of five (*wŭ-yên shı̆,*—33.

I am happy in my fortuneless and humble lot,
Yet who can say that I mock at the world's glory?

4. The man too fond of wine, by *Wang Tsi*.

This day till evening let us drink,
Nor care for our reasoning souls!
Our eyes see that all love wine,
Why then should we alone abstain?

Stanzas of eight verses.—Verses of five syllables.

5. The nocturnal banquet at *Yiŭ-cheŭ*, by *Chăng Shwŏ*.

The cold blast blows, the night rain comes down,
A desolate moaning shakes the wintry woods,
But here in the high hall there is feasting,
It makes me forget that my evening of life draws on.
Among those soldiers it is meet to flourish the spear.
In that gay crowd they repeat the flageolet's note:
He who has not been the governor of a state
Can never know the depth of favour given.

6. To the Academician *Chăng Sź-mà* going to *Nan-haì* to erect an epitaph.

Chaplets and wreaths extend to the southern pole,
Fair words are scattered on the elevated cross,
Commands by three high officers are sent,
An epitaph for the southern barbarians is revealed.
On the hostleries of the wild thick flowers shoot forth,
On the white sails in spring-tide the small rain falls.
We know not when, from the vast ocean,
The messengers of the throne may return.   By *Tu Fu*.

Verses of seven syllables.   7. Made in *Yiŭ-cheŭ* at the new year.

Last year the plum-tree *blossoms* in *King* of the south were like snow,
This year the snow in *Kī* of the north was like the plum blossom.
Thus may we perceive the inconstancy of human affairs.
And we rejoice though the varying year goes and returns.
The officers in the garrisons sing the live-long day.
In the capital there are illuminations until the morning dawns.
The distant west longs for the sun of *Chang-an*.
Let us drink to the long life of the southern mountain.

Verses of five syllables.   8. The antiquity of *Pĕ-tí*, by *Chin Tsz-gang*.

The sun sinks into the vast river;—it is night;
The oars rest; and the dialogue turns on the customs of the land.
The city (*Pĕ-tí*) looks down upon the kingdom of *Pa-tsz*.
Its high towers eclipse the palaces of the *Han* kings,
Its barren wastes were brought under culture by *Cheu*.
Its great mountains do honour to the merits of *Yu*.

o. 1.   *Gán-hiuên ts'ĭng-pĭ twán,*   *Tí hièn pĭ liú t'ŭng,*
o. 11. *Kù mù sāng yŭn tsí,*   *Kweĭ-fân ch'ŭ wú-chŭng.*
o. 21. *Chuên t'ŭ k'ŭ wû hièn,*   *K'ĕ sź tsó hô-k'iûng.*

34.   *Sŭ-yŭ̂*, Proverbs, v. native text, page 34.

a. 4.   1. *Yĭ-kŭ liàng-tĕ.*   2. *Sāng-t'iaû ts'ŭng siaù-jeù.*   3. *Shán-fŭng pù-*
a. 16. *k'ĭ làng.*   4. *Tsaí-kiā kíng fú-mù, hô-pĭ yuèn shaŭ-hiáng?*   5. *Suĭ-*
a. 29. *fūng taú t'ô, shán-shwüĭ t'üĭ ch'uên.*   6. *Hŏ-sháng t'iēn-yiû.*   7. *Kŏ-*
b. 11. *jìn tsź-saú mán-ts'iên sŭ̆; mŏ-kwàn t'ā-jîn wà-sháng shwāng.*   8. *Tĕ*
b. 25. *miaú-wán wú-shĭ.*   9. *Jîn piên: jŭ-tsź! jŭ-tsź! T'iēn lĭ: wí-jên! wí-*
c. 12. *jên!*   10. *Shú kaū ts'iēn cháng, yĕ lŏ kweī kān.*   11. *Kiŭn-tsź yĭ-yên,*
c. 25. *kw'aí-mà yĭ-piên.*   12. *Kwāng-yîn sź tsièn, jĭ-yŭ jù sō.*   13. *Kùng-*
d. 10. *kíng pù-jù ts'ŭng-míng.*   14. *Pŭ-tāng shǎn, pù-chī t'iēn chī kaū; pù-*
d. 25. *lìn k'ĭ, pù-chī tí chī heú; pù-wán siēn-wáng chī weĭ yên, pù-chī*
e. 11. *hiŏ-wán chī tá.*   15. *Kíng míng, tsĕ ch'ĭn-gaī pù-jèn, chí-míng, tsĕ*
e. 25. *siĕ-ŏ pù-sāng.*   16. *Shwüĭ tī yù, t'iēn piēn yīng-kaū k'ò; shé, tĭ k'ò-*
f. 12. *tiaú; weī yiù jìn-sīn pù-k'ò liaú. T'iēn k'ò-tú, tĭ k'ò-liáng, weī yiù*
f. 28. *jìn-sīn pù-k'ò fáng. Hwá-hù hwá-p'í, nán hwá-kiù; chī jîn miên*
g. 14. *pŭ-chī sīn, tüĭ miên yù yú, sīn kă ts'iēn shān.*   17. *Kwá-yên tsĕ-*
g. 28. *kiaū, k'ò-ĭ wú hwüĭ-lín, k'ò-ĭ wú yiù-jù.*   18. *Yŭ kwá, tsīng-shin*
h. 13. *shwáng; sź tō, hŭ-k'í shwaī.*   19. *Ts'iú-chī múng shé, k'ò-chī múng*
h. 26. *tsiāng.*   20. *Tsiù pù tsüĭ jîn, jîn tsź-tsüĭ.*   21. *Húng-yên pŏ míng.*
i. 8.   22. *Yĭ k'ĕ pù-fân ár chù.*   23. *Tsó yĭ-jĭ hô-sháng, chwáng yĭ-jĭ chúng.*
i. 23. 24. *Yŭ mĭ tsi, ár tseù sŭ chúng.*   25. *Shú taù wú yìn.*   26. *Kiŭn-tsź*
j. 7.   *pŭ-niên kiú ŏ.*   27. *Tān-sź pù-ch'ìng siên.*   28. *Yaú chī sīn-fŭ sź, tán*

---

c. 9) or seven syllables (*tsĭ-yên shĭ*,—33. k. 5), but there are verses of three, four, six, and nine syllables. These syllables are regulated by the *tones* of the words, which are formed into two classes, viz. the *píng* [a] 'even' and the *tsè* [b] 'deflected.' The *píng* tones are the *upper* and *lower even* tones (*shàng-píng* and *hiá-píng*); the *tsĕ* tones are the *rising*, the *departing*, and the *entering* tones (*shàng*, *k'ù*, and *jĭ*). In verses of five syllables, the first and the third are subject to no rule, the second and fourth must vary between the *píng* and the *tsè* tones; and in the second and third verses these two (2nd and 4th syllables) must be the converse of the first, and the fourth verse must be like the first in this respect. In verses of seven syllables, the first, third, and fifth are subject to no rule, the tones of the second and the fourth must vary, and that of the sixth must be like that of the second. In verses of five or seven syllables, three of the four final syllables must have the same class of termination and accent. As a general rule the final syllable of the third verse does not rhyme, and in the other verses rhyme is often dispensed with. The student can make out for himself a table of the metres by using an open circle (○) to represent the *píng* tones, and a black circle (●) for the *tsĕ* tones. In some verses the third syllable in five-syllable verses and the fifth in seven-syllable verses are called the *eye* of the verse, which corresponds to the *cæsura* or the *ictus* in the poetry of European languages, and this 'eye' must always be a *noun* or a *verb*,—i. e. a word of full meaning (*shĭ-tsz* [c]), not a particle,—and it must either rhyme or alternate with the following verse. Above forty different

[a] 平   [b] 仄   [c] 實字

But the ancient green walls are cut down.
The dangerous places are made accessible.
The ancient trees grow to the limits of the clouds.
The returning sail shoots out from the midst of the mist.
The trace of that stream goes on without a limit.
The traveller sits gazing on the scene without being wearied.

Translation of Proverbs (Sŭ-yŭ), v. native text, page 34.

1. At one lift to obtain two. "To kill two birds with one stone." 2. The mulberry branch follows the (direction of the) small bend. "As the twig is bent the tree's inclined." 3. A fair wind raises no waves. 4. If at home you respect your parents, there will be no need of humbling yourself abroad (lit. ' going to a distance to burn incense'). 5. To sail with wind and tide. 6. To pour oil in the fire. "To add fuel to the flame." 7. Let every man sweep the snow from his own door-way, and not concern himself with the frost on other men's roofs. "Let every man mind his own business." 8. Virtue requires no colouring. 9. Man's convenience (says): thus and thus! Heaven's order (replies): not yet! not yet! "Man plans; but heaven disposes." 10. Though a tree be a thousand *chang* high, its leaves fall and return to the root. 11. One word to the superior man and one lash to the good horse (are enough). "A word to the wise is sufficient." 12. Time flies like an arrow: days and months like a weaver's shuttle. 13. To feel reverence is not so good as to give obedience. "Obedience is better than sacrifice." 14. If you do not ascend the mountain, you cannot know the height of heaven; if you descend not to the stream of the valley, you cannot know the depth of the earth. If you do not listen to the *wise* words bequeathed by the ancient kings, you cannot know the greatness of *true* learning. 15. If the mirror be bright, then the dust will not defile it; if the intelligence be clean, then licentiousness will not grow up. 16. The fishes at the bottom of the stream, and the birds in the sides of heaven, may both be reached with the arrow and the hook; but man's heart is beyond conjecture. Heaven may be measured, and earth may be surveyed, but man's heart is without bounds. In drawing the tiger, you may paint his skin, but it is hard to depict his bones. In acquaintance with a man, you may know his face, but you cannot know his heart. Though you converse *tête-à-tête*, his heart is separated from you as by a thousand mountains. 17. If your words be few and your acquaintance select, there will be no need for repentance, sorrow, and shame. 18. If desires be few, good spirits will abound; if aims be many, cheerfulness will languish. 19. The prisoner dreams of pardon; the thirsty of a cordial. 20. The wine does not intoxicate the man; the man makes himself drunk. 21. A fair countenance is a poor inheritance. 22. A single guest does not require two lodgings. 23. To be one day a priest and the next a bell-ringer. 24. He wishes to hide his track, and yet he walks on the snow. 25. When the tree falls there is no shadow. 26. The superior man thinks not on old evil deeds. 27. A single thread is not enough to make a rope. 28. If you wish to know the thoughts which

j. 22. t'íng k'eù-chúng yên. 29. Jŏ yaú twán tsiù-fă, sīng-yèn k'ān tsiŭ jĭn.
k. 6. 30. Tsz̀ yŭ: "Jĭn wŭ yuèn lŭ́, pĭ yiŭ kín yiŭ." 31. Yŭ chī k'ĭ kiūn,
k. 20. siēn-shí k'ĭ chín; yŭ shí k'ĭ-jĭn, siēn-shí k'ĭ-yiù; yŭ chī k'ĭ-fŭ́, siēn
l. 7. shí k'ĭ-tsz̀. 32. P'ing-fūng siŭ̀ p'ó, kwŭ-kĕ yiŭ tsắn; kiūn-tsz̀ siŭ p'ín,
l. 22. lĭ-ĭ chăng tsaí. 33. Pŏ-yŭ ĭ yŭ wŭ-ni, pŭ-náng chīn-shĕ k'ĭ-sĕ; kiūn-
m. 9. tsz̀ chŭ́ yŭ chŭ́-tí, pŭ-náng jèn-lwán k'ĭ-sīn; sŭng-pĕ k'ŏ-ĭ naí sŭ́-
m. 26. shwāng, míng-chí k'ŏ-ĭ shĕ kiēn-weí. 34. Jĭ-yŭ siŭ̀ míng, pŭ-chaú fŭ-
n. 12. pw'ăn chī hiá: taŭ-kiēn siŭ̀ kw'aí, pŭ-chàn wŭ-tsiŭ chī jĭn; fī tsaí
n. 27. húng hó, pŭ jĭ shīn-kiā chī mắn. 35. Jĭn-sāng, chí wí sāng; chí-sāng,
o. 14. jĭn ĭ laù; sīn chí yĭ-tsĭ sāng, pŭ-kiŏ wŭ-chăng taú.

9. Extracts from the *Chíng-yĭn tsŭi-yaú*, v. native text (lithographed), page 9.

a. 2.   *Tí-yĭ twán. Jĭ-chăng.*
a. 8. Ts'ĭng-tsaù k'ĭ-laí, kiaù haí-tsz̀-mắn, saú-saú tí, kiaù-kiaù hwā, gaú
a. 23. shwŭĭ sì liên, p'aú wàn haù ch'ă k'ĭ-k'ĭ. Mŭ́-yiù sź̀ tĭ shí-heú, k'ān-
b. 14. k'ān shŭ́, siĕ-siĕ tsz̄, sān-liăng-kó sź̀-wắn păng-yiù tsŏ-kó shī, hiá kó
c. 6. weí-k'ī, kiaì-kiaì mắn-ḑr, tsiú k'ŏ-ĭ kwó-tī jĭ-tsz̀ liaù. Taú-liaù hiá-
c. 23. wù, lā kì păng-kūng, shĕ kì t'iaú tsiên, pá chĕ-shīn kīn-kwŭ, hwŏ-túng
d. 14. hwŏ-túng. Jĭn yiŭ yiù tsīng-shīn, yiù chàng-kíng; chĕ-tū shí haù
e. 3. sź. Pŭ-yaú wàng waí-t'eŭ t'ān-wán, pŭ-yaú teú-k'í, pŭ-yaú tă-kiā
e. 18. piên-tsiŭ, pŭ-yaú tŏ-sź̀, pŭ-yaú naú-tsiù, pŭ-yaú kwó-kiā. Wŭ shwŏ
f. 9. tĭ hwā yĭ-tiēn ḑr tsŏ-tí tŭ mŭ́-yiù ā! Nì yaú t'íng-chŏ, pŭ-yaú wàng-
g. 2. kí liaù ā!—Tiên kó tăng-ḑr laí ā; hĕ-kù yĭng-tsz̀, tsăng-mŏ ts'iaú tĭ
g. 20. kiên nī?

h. 2.   *Tí-ḑr twán. Tsĕ-kiaù.*
h. 8. Yí-kó-jĭn ch'ŭ́-laí, siāng-yŭ̀ păng-yiù, tsŭng-yaú taí shwāng yèn-
h. 22. ts'ĭng, kiên-liaù nà-siĕ chíng-kīng jĭn, kiàng lĭ-ĭ-tĭ, kiēn-hŏ-tí, laù-shí-
i. 14. tĭ, túng-tí kweí-kŭ-tí yiù liăng-sīn-tĭ, kiên-kwó shí-miēn-tí, yiù tsaí-
j. 6. ts'ĭng-tí, yiù pḑ̀n-sź-tĭ, k'ŏ-ĭ kaú-tĕ-chŭ́-tí, nì ts'aí haù t'ĭ-t'ā siāng-
j. 24. yŭ̀, kăn-chŏ t'ā tseù, kùng-kíng t'ā, pŭ-haù t'aĭ-mắn t'ā; yiù-shên
k. 14. siāng-kiuên, yiù-sź̀ siāng-pāng; piên tá-kiā yiù yĭ liaù. Jŏ ts'iaù-

---

kinds of poems are enumerated, but many of these are inconsiderable in extent and importance. The best specimens are full of metaphorical and allegorical expressions, ancient and obsolete words, allusions to history and fable, with references to customs and opinions, known only to the learned. This renders Chinese poetry very difficult for foreigners to understand.

The specimens given on page 33 are, with the exception of the first, to be found in the *Kŭ T'áng-shī hŏ-kiaì*, 'the poetry of the ancient *T'ang* (dynasty) explained,' a work in 5 vols. 12º.

Wí-yáng (33. b. 16) was the name of a royal palace in *Ch'áng-ān*ᴬ, during the *Hán* dynasty, which ended A. D. 260.

ᴬ 長安

occupy a man's heart, just listen to the words of his mouth. 29. If you want to break through drunken habits, look at a drunken man when you are sober. 30. Confucius said: "If a man will not care for the future, he certainly will have present sorrow." 31. If you wish to know the character of a prince, first look at his ministers; if you would understand a man, first look at his friends; if you would know a father, first look at his son. 32. Though the screen be broken, its frame is still preserved; though the superior man be poor, propriety and rectitude still remain. 33. Though the white gem be cast into the dirt, its purity cannot be sullied: though the good man live in a vile place, it cannot taint and disorder his heart. The fir and the cypress can endure snow and frost; and bright wisdom can walk through difficulty and danger. 34. Though the sun and moon are bright, they cannot shine beneath an up-turned bowl: though the sword (of justice) be swift, it cannot decapitate the innocent, nor can unlooked-for calamity, with its evil genius, enter the dwelling of the prudent. 35. Man is born, but knowledge is not born (with him); when knowledge is acquired, man soon grows old; when his mind has obtained a fulness of knowledge, before he is aware, the great change comes over him.

Translation of the Extracts from the Ching-yin tsüi-yaú, v. native text (lithographed), page 9.

First section. On every-day affairs.

Rise early and call the servant-boys to sweep the floor, to water the flowers, to warm water for washing the face, and to make a cup of good tea to drink. When you have nothing to do, look at a book, or write some characters, or with two or three literary friends make a verse (or two), or play a game at chess (lit. 'conquest' or 'siege'), to dissipate sadness, thus you will be able to pass the day. When noon is come, pull a few twangs of the bow, and shoot a few arrows; as for that body of muscle and bone of yours, exercise it well. Thus a man will get good spirits, and will grow strong: all these are good things to do. But don't go abroad hankering after amusement, don't create disturbances, don't fight and brawl, don't be a busy-body, don't be noisy over your wine, don't wander from house to house. What I have said is perfectly correct, there is no mistake in it. Do you listen and don't forget it.

Light the lamp and bring it here, it is as dark as midnight, how can I see?

The second section. On selecting acquaintances.

When a man goes out to hold intercourse with friends, he should carry a pair of eyes in his head; and when you see those who are men of rectitude, or those who speak with propriety and justice, the cordial and honest men, and those who understand customs, those who have a conscience, and those who have seen the world, those who have natural talent and good sense, on whom you may rely,—do you then seek their acquaintance, and walk in their footsteps, respect them and do not slight them; if you have any good project in hand, consult with them, and in matters of business mutually assist one another, thus both

l. 3.   kién-liaù nà-siē pŭ-haù jîn, yĭ tièn-ą̊r pą̊n-sź, tŭ mŭ-yiù; yĭ pá
l. 20. kwāng-kw'ą̊n tsüí, húng-p'ièn jĭn-kiā,

10. Extracts from the *Chíng-yĭn tsüí-yaú*, v. native text (lithographed),
page 10.

a. 2.   yiŭ pŭ-haù pī-k'ĭ, ts'iuên-kàn siē hwą̊n-cháng tĭ sź, yiŭ pŭ-
a. 16. tŭng yèn, yiù pŭ-kú liên, yiŭ t'aù jĭn hiên.   Jĭn-kiā mà t'ā, t'ā yè
b. 7.   pŭ-haí saù; chê-yáng tĭ jîn, ngò ts'iaŭ-kiên-liaù, tsiú naù-liaù t'ā, nì
b. 23. ts'iēn-wán pŭ-yaú t'ĭ-t'ā tseù-lùng, t'ā tsiú kw'aĭ-p'ièn nĭ-tĭ yĭn-tsź
c. 21. ts'ièn: hwán pŭ tà-kìn, t'ā hwán yaú wú nĭ-tĭ sź, sāng-ch'ŭ hŭ-tŏ sź
d. 13. laí.   Yiù shímmŏ pién-ĭ nĭ ?   Ts'úng-kĭn-ĭ-heú nì yaú tà chŭ-ĭ, ts'aĭ
e. 5.   haù yā!

f. 2.   Tĭ-sān twán.   Tsă-hwá.

f. 8.   Jĭn tsüí yaú-kìn shĭ shwŏ-hwá.   Nĭ ts'iaú nà-siē yiù mĭng-sĕ tĭ jîn,
f. 24. fą̊n-waí pŭ-t'úng, t'ā shwŏ-ch'ŭ tĭ hwá, tsūng-shĭ ch'ŭ-kūng jĭ-tièn, yiù
g. 15. wą̊n-yà, tsź pŭ-yúng shwŏ lŏ.   T'ā tsiú süí-k'eù shwŏ kŭ pá ts'ín-ch'áng
h. 7.   tĭ hwá-ą̊r, yè kiŏ-tĕ tá-fāng, yiù t'ĭ-kiù,—pŭ-kiaŭ-ngaú, pŭ-hiá-tsŏ.
h. 24. Jĭn-kiā t'ĭng-liaù, tsź-jên kw'ā-t'ā hwüí-shwŏ hwá liaù.   Jên ą̊r
i. 13. chíng-kĭng hwá, kú-jên yaú-t'íng, tsiú-shĭ shí-tsīng-sháng, nà-siē hiên-
j. 3.   tsź jîn-tą̊ng tĭ hwá, yè yaú fáng ch'áng-ą̊r-tò t'íng-t'íng.   Süí-jên pŭ-
j. 19. pĭ hiŏ t'ā, yè yaú chū-taú, kŏ-chú fūng-sŭ; tsăng-mò shĭ tsą̊n-hwá,
k. 10. ts'ŭ-hwá, yà-hwá, niŏ-pŏ hwá, fúng-chíng jĭn tĭ hwá, siaú má jĭn tĭ
l. 1.   hwá; jĭn-kiā shwŏ-ch'ŭ-laĭ, nì pŭ-tŭng tĭ, tsiú ch'íng-liaù kó tsŭ-
l. 16. t'iaú-tsź liaù.

11. Extract from the *Sān-kwŏ chí*, chap. I, v. native text (lithographed),
page 11.

a. 2.   Tĭ-yĭ hwüí.

a. 7.   Yèn t'aú-yuên haú-kĭ sān kĭ ĭ.
b. 7.   Chàn Hwáng-kĭn yĭng-hiúng sheù lĭ kŭng.
c. 1.   Hwá-shwŏ t'iēn-hiá tá-shĭ; 'fą̊n-kiù pĭ-hŏ, hŏ-kiù pĭ-fą̊n.'   Cheŭ
c. 16. mŭ tsĭ-kwŏ fą̊n-tsāng, píng jĭ yŭ Ts'ín; kĭ Ts'ín mĭ chĭ heú Ts'ŭ Hán
d. 7.   fą̊n-tsāng, yiŭ píng jĭ yŭ Hán.   Hán chaŭ, tsź Kaŭ-tsŭ chàn pĕ-shê
d. 22. ą̊r k'ĭ ĭ, yĭ-t'úng t'iēn-hiá.   Heú laí Kwāng-wŭ chūng-hĭng, ch'uên
e. 11. chí Hiên-tí, süí fą̊n-weí Sān-kwŏ.   Ch'üí k'ĭ chí lwán chĭ yiŭ, t'aĭ-ch'ĭ

Kweí-tsién (33. c. 15), 'the noble and the mean,' both have their plans of aggrandisement; the former at court, the latter in the market. The poet wishes to show that the noble man and the mean man are alike different from the ascetic, who alone can retire from the world and its projects for getting gain. He alone can enjoy the outward things,—the soft rain, the bright grass, the blue mountain, and the singing birds,—which arise without his arrangement and yield him pleasure.

parties will be profited. But you will see those bad men, who have not the slightest particle of good sense, a set of sharpers, who deceive people,

Translation of the Extracts from the Ching-yīn tsüi-yaú, v. native text (lithographed), page 10.

who are of a quarrelsome disposition, entirely taken up with questionable affairs,—men who will not take hints, and who have no regard for appearances, who draw down upon themselves the displeasure of others; and when they are scolded, they do not feel ashamed. When I see such men, I directly give them a scolding. You should on no account whatever have any thing to do with them. If you associate with them, they will swindle you out of your money: but that would be of little consequence, if they did not prejudice your affairs and produce a great deal of trouble. Then what benefit will there be in that? From the very first do you be decided, and then all will be well!

The third section. On miscellaneous phrases.

The most important thing for a man is to speak *well*. Now when you see men of note, different from the common herd, you will find that their language has a classic elegance about it, and an air of refinement, of which it is needless to speak. Even when they utter the first expression which comes to their lips in ordinary parlance, you may perceive a liberality of sentiment and a regularity about it,—it is neither haughty nor mean. When people hear them, they, of course, praise them highly, as being able to speak properly and classically. Assuredly you should listen to them. Then there is the language of the market-place and the well, and the talk of loungers and of various classes of men; you must stretch your ears to catch these; *for* although you need not learn them, you should know them, as well as the customs of every place; what is village talk, coarse language, elegant language, cruel, insulting language, the language of flattery, ridicule, abuse, &c., for when men utter such, and you do not understand, you will seem exactly like a country clown.

Translation of the Extract from the Sān-kwŏ chí, chap. I, v. native text (lithographed), page 11.

Chapter the first.

At the banquet in the peach-garden three brave men form a righteous league. By exterminating the Yellow-turbans the heroes raise their reputation.

It is a common saying with respect to the state of nations, that 'the long-divided must unite, the long-united must divide.' At the end of the *Cheu* dynasty the empire was divided into seven kingdoms; these contended together and were finally united in the *Tsin* dynasty; and after the extinction of the *Tsin* family, the houses of *Ts'u* and *Han* strove together and were at last merged in the *Han* dynasty. The universal dominion of the *Han* commenced with the Emperor *Kau-tsu*, who destroyed the white serpent and raised a body of patriot soldiers. Afterwards *Kwang-wu* arose as his successor, and he in turn transmitted the throne to *Hien-tí*. The power of the state was then divided, and became Three Kingdoms. If we proceed to investigate

SAN-KWOH CHI.   [Lith. 11. f. 2.—12. i. 3.]

f. 2.   yŭ Hwán-Líng, ǎr tí. Hwán-tí kín-kú shén-lùi, tsǔng-sín hwán-kwān,
f. 17. kǐ Hwán-tí p'áng. Líng-tí tsǐ weí; Tá-tsiāng-kiūn, Teú-wù; T'aí-fú,
g. 7.   Chīn-fān, kúng-siāng fú-tsŏ. Shí yiù hwán-kwān Ts'aú-tsǐ tàng líng-
g. 21. k'iuên; Teú-wù Chīn-fān meú chŭ chī; kī-sź pǔ-mǐ, fàn weí sò haí;
h. 12. Chūng-kiuēn tsź tsź yǔ hùng. Kiēn-níng ǎr-niên, sź-yŭ, wáng-jǐ, Tí
i. 2.   yŭ Wǎn-tě tiên, fāng shǐng tsó; tiên-kŏ kw'āng-fūng tseú-k'ǐ, chě-kiên
i. 17. yǐ-t'iaú ts'īng-shê, ts'áng liàng-sháng fǐ tsiāng-hiá-laí, fān yŭ í-sháng.
j. 8.   Tí kīng taù, tsŏ-yiù kǐ kiú jǐ-kūng, pě-kwān k'ǔ pǎn pǐ, sū-seù shê pŭ-
k. 1.   kiên-liaù. Hwǔ-jên tá-lùi tá yǔ, kiā ǐ pīng-pŏ, lŏ taú pwán-yě, fāng-
k. 18. chù; hwaí k'iŏ fǎng-ú wú-sú. Kiēn-níng sź-niên ǎr-yù, Lŏ-yáng tí
l. 8.   chín, yiú haì-shwùǐ fán-yǐ, yuên-haì kŭ-mín, tsín p'ǐ tá láng kiuèn jǐ
l. 24. haì chūng.

12. Extract from the *Sān-kwŏ chí*, v. native text (lithographed), page 12.

a. 1.   Shí Kŭ-lŭ kiuēn yiù hiūng-tí sān-jǐn; yǐ míng, Chāng-kiŏ; yǐ míng,
a. 17. Chāng-paù; yǐ míng, Chāng-liáng.   Nà Chāng-kiŏ pǎn-shí kó pǔ-tí
b. 5.   Siú-ts'aí, yīn jí-shān ts'aí-yŏ; yǔ yǐ laù-jǐn, pí-yên túng-yên, sheù
b. 22. chí lí-cháng, hwán Kiŏ chí yǐ túng chūng, ǐ t'iēn-shŭ sān kiuèn sheú
c. 11. chí, yŭ: "Tsź míng, 'T'aí-píng yaú-shŭ,' jù tě chí, tāng taí T'iēn
c. 25. siuēn hwá p'ù kiú shí-jín, jŏ míng í-sīn, pǐ hú gŏ paù."   Kiŏ paí,
d. 16. wǎn sǐng míng. Laù-jín yǔ: "Wǔ naì Nán-hwá laù-siēn yě." Yēn-
e. 5.   kǐ hwá chín-ts'īng-fūng ǎr k'ǔ.   *   *   *   *
e. 13. Tsíng yǔ: "Tsě-píng chúng, ngò-pīng kwá, míng-kūng ǐ tsŏ sǔ
f. 1.   chaū-kiūn yíng-tí." Liŭ-yên jên k'ǐ shwŏ, suì tsǐ ch'ǔ pàng, chaū-mú
f. 16. í-píng. Pàng-wǎn hǐng taú Chŏ-hiên yìn ch'ǔ Chŏ-hiên chūng yǐ-kó
g. 6.   yíng-hiúng. Nà jǐn pǔ shǐn haú tŭ-shŭ, sìng kwān-hŏ, kwá yên yŭ,
g. 21. hǐ-nú pǔ hǐng yŭ sě, sú yiù tá chí, chuēn haú kǐ-kiaŭ t'iēn-hiá haú-kǐ,
h. 14. sāng-tě shǐn-chàng pǎ-chě, liàng-ǎr chùǐ-kiên, shwāng-sheù kwŏ yŭ sǐ,

---

Kǐ-pě (33. k. 24) here means *Yiŭ-cheū* itself, which was the name of *Shíng-kīng*[a], (Moukden, the capital of Manchuria,) under the *Hán* dynasty.

The city of *Pŭ-tí* (33. m. 17) was in *Kweí-cheū fú*.

The lithographed pages (9—14) which follow here, were printed in London from the author's handwriting, but they are not so satisfactory as the 34 pages of letter-press which were done in Hongkong. This accounts for the absence of pages 1—8, page 9 having been printed first to suit the convenience of pupils who did not need the earlier pages, which were extracts from the Ancient Classics &c., and which were subsequently printed in Hongkong. The extracts from the *Chíng-yīn tsůǐ-yaú* are likely to prove very serviceable to the student, they present him with a good many expressions in the Peking dialect, though not of the extreme kind, and they would easily pass current in the southern provinces. Among the general characteristics of the Peking dialect is the frequent use of the perfect particle *liaù*[b] and the formative particle *ǎr*[c]. There is a redundancy of expression, and, in pronunciation, an uncommon sharpness of utterance in the case of all letters which admit it (*kí, tsí, chí, sí, hí*).

[a] 成京　　[b] 了　　[c] 兒

the cause of this revolution, we shall find that it began with the two Emperors *Hwan* and *Ling*. When the Emperor *Hwan* died, *Ling* came to the throne. The marshal *Teu-wu* and the guardian *Chin-fan* became coadjutors in the government. Now it happened that when the eunuch *Ts'au-tsĭ* and his party were intriguing for power, *Teu-wu* and *Chin-fan* formed a counter-plot to exterminate them; but the scheme was discovered, and turned out injurious to themselves; and the eunuchs from this time increased in audacity.

On the 15th day of the 4th month of the 2nd year, *Kien-ning* ('tranquillity established') the Emperor proceeded to the Hall of Audience, and just as he was ascending the throne, a violent wind suddenly rushed from a corner of the Hall, and what should they see but a great green snake, seeming to fly down from the beam above, which coiled itself up upon the imperial seat. The Emperor fell down in terror, but the attendants quickly rescued him and carried him into the palace. The mandarins, one and all, hastened away; and, in a moment, the serpent itself vanished. On a sudden it began to thunder loud and to rain heavily, accompanied with hail stones. This continued until midnight, and laid in ruins an immense number of dwellings.

In the 2nd month of the 4th year of this same Emperor, an earthquake was felt in *Lŏ-yang*, the sea inundated the lands, and the inhabitants of the coasts were washed away.

Translation of the Extract from the Sān-kwŏ chí, v. native text (lithographed), page 12.

At this time there lived in the district of *Kü-lŭ* three brothers, named *Chang-kiŏ, Chang-pau,* and *Chang-liang*. Now this *Chang-kiŏ* did not take the degree of *Siu-tsai* (B. A.), *but* proceeded to the hills to gather medicinal herbs. There he met one day an aged man with a fair and youthful countenance, who held in his hand a staff of cane. He called *Kiŏ* into a cave, and gave him three sacred volumes, saying: "These are called, 'The Arts necessary for producing Peace.' Take them, and in the name of Heaven proclaim the doctrine of reform, that the world may be saved. And should contrary thoughts arise in your mind, you will suffer the reward of the wicked." *Kiŏ* bowed and enquired his name and surname. The old man said: "I am the aged genius of *Nan-hwa*;" and having uttered these words he vanished into thin air and was gone. * * * *

Tsing said: "The rebel soldiers are many, our soldiers are few; your Excellency should at once raise an army to oppose the enemy." *Liu-yen* acquiesced in this advice, and immediately issued a placard, calling upon patriots to enlist. This document reached the town of *Chŏ*, and a brave man of the place responded to the call. He was not much of a scholar, but his disposition was magnanimous and kind, and his words were few; the feelings of anger and pleasure were rarely visible in his countenance, and he was a man of a strong will. He loved to form friendships with the brave men of the empire. His height was eight *chĕ* (near seven feet); his two ears hung down on his shoulders; his hands reached down to his knees; he was able to

i. 4.   mŭ náng tsź kŭ k'í ạr; mién jŭ kwán-yŭ, shạn jŭ t'ŭ chī; Chŭng-
i. 19. shān Tsíng wáng Liŭ shíng chī heú, Hán Kīng-tí Kiŏ-hiá hiuên sạn;
j. 8.   síng Liŭ, míng Peí, tsź Hiuên-tĕ.
j. 17. Tāng-jí kién-liaù páng-wạn, k'aí-jén ch'áng-t'án, suí-heú yí-jīn lí-
k. 7.   shīng yên yŭ: "Tá-cháng-fū pŭ-yŭ kwŏ-kiă ch'ŭ-lí, hô-kŭ ch'áng-
k. 22. t'án?" Hiuên-tĕ hwuí shí k'í jīn, shīn pă-chĕ, shīng jŭ kŭ-liŭ, shí jŭ
l. 13. pạn-mà. Hiuên-tĕ kién t'ā hîng-maú í-cháng, wạn k'í síng-míng.

13. Extract from the Sān-kwŏ chí continued, v. native text (lithographed),
page 13.

a. 1.   K'í-jīn yŭ: "Meŭ Síng Chāng, míng Fī, tsź Yí-tí. Shí kŭ Chŏ-
a. 15. kiŭn, p'ŏ yiù chwāng-t'ién, maí-tsiù t'ŭ-chū, chuēn haú kí-kiaŭ t'ién-
b. 5.   hiá haú-kí; kiă-ts'aí kién kūng k'án páng ạr t'án, kŭ-tsź siāng-wạn."
b. 20. Hiuên-tĕ yŭ: "Ngò pạn Hán-shí tsūng-tsīn, síng Liŭ, míng Peí;
c. 8.   kīn wạn Hwáng-kīn ch'áng-lwán, yiù chí yŭ p'ó-tsĕ gān-mín. Hạn lí
c. 23. pŭ-náng! Kŭ ch'áng-t'án ạr." Fī yŭ: "Ngò p'ŏ yiù tsź-ts'aí, tāng
d. 12. chaŭ-mú hiāng-yûng, yŭ kūng t'ûng kiŭ tá-sź. Jŭ-hô?" Hiuên-tĕ
e. 1.   shīn-hí, suí yŭ t'ûng jí ts'ạn-tién chùng yín-tsiù. Chíng yín kién,
e. 15. kién yí tá Hán, tuī-chŏ yí liáng chĕ-tsź, taú tién mạn-sheù hiĕ-liaù.
f. 6.   Jí tién tsó-hiá pién hwán tsiù-paù: "Kw'aí chīn-tsiù-laí k'í, ngò taí-
f. 21. kàn jí-ch'íng-k'ŭ t'eŭ-kiŭn."
g. 2.   Hiuên-tĕ k'án k'í jīn, siāng-maú t'áng-t'áng, weí-fūng pín-pín,
g. 15. tsiù yaŭ t'ā t'ûng tsó, t'aú k'í síng míng. K'í jīn yŭ: "Wù síng
h. 4.   Kwān, míng Yù, tsź Sheú-ch'áng, heú kaí Yŭn-ch'áng, Hô-tūng Kiaí
h. 17. liáng jīn yĕ. Yīn pạn-chù shí-haú, í-shí líng jīn, peí wù shă-liaù,
i. 8.   t'aŭ nán Kiāng-Hŭ wù-lŭ nién ì. Kīn wạn tsź chŭ, chaŭ-kiŭn p'ó-
i. 23. tsĕ, tí-laí yíng-mú." Hiuên-tĕ suí ì kí chí kaú-chí. Yŭn-ch'áng tá-hí,
j. 15. t'ûng taú Chāng-fī chwāng sháng, kúng-ì tá-sź. Fī yŭ: "Ngò
k. 4.   chwāng heú yiù t'aú-yuên, hwá-k'aí chíng shíng, míng-jí tāng yŭ
k. 16. yuên chūng tsĕ kaú t'ién-tí; ngò sān-jīn kí-weí hiūng-tí, hiĕ lí t'ûng-
l. 7.   sīn, jên-heú k'ò t'ŭ tá-sź." Hiuên-tĕ, yŭn-ch'áng tsí-shīng yíng yŭ:
l. 22. "Jŭ-tsź shín haù."

The passages given on pages 11—13 are from the Sān-kwŏ, with which the student is
already acquainted (v. Chrest. pp. 17—20). The 'Yellow-turbans' (Hwáng-kīn, 11. b. 8)
were rebels under the leadership of Chāng-kiŏ (12. a. 13), who, besides being a general,
pretended to perform cures by charms and exorcism. He raised an immense army, which
he organized and allotted to subordinate generals. At the close of the Hán dynasty
(A. D. 226), after the reign of the last Emperor Hien-tí (11. e. 12), the division of the
country into three kingdoms took place. The two Emperors Hwán and Líng (11. f. 3, 4)
were weak and lax in their government, and this brought on a rebellion, which assumed
larger proportions under Tūng-chŏ, a man of great strength and military ability. His
career of cruelty, during which he slaughtered vast numbers of his enemies, was brought to
an early close, for Lŭ-pu (v. 20. d. 5, 7) destroyed him and all his family. The Imperialist
cause was upheld by the generals Lŭ-pí (13. c. 5, 7) a mat-seller, Kwan-yŭ (13. h. 4, 6) a
seller of sour-curds, and Chāng-fī (13. j. 17) a pork-butcher. These were the three brave

see his own ears; his face was like the jewel on a crown; and his lips were ruddy *like rubies*. He was a descendant of the ninth generation from *King-ti* of the *Han* dynasty; his clan name was *Liu*, his surname *Pei*, and his title was *Hiuen-tĕ*.

When he saw the above-mentioned placard, he heaved a deep sigh, and immediately behind him a man exclaimed with a loud voice: "When a fine fellow does not exert his strength for his country, why does he sigh so deeply?" *Hiuen-tĕ* turned round and beheld a man about seven feet high, having a voice like thunder, and a *physique* like that of a vigorous charger. When *Hiuen-tĕ* saw this extraordinary figure, he enquired his name and surname.

Translation of the Extract from the Sān-kwŏ chí continued, v. native text (lithographed), page 13.

The man replied: "My name is *Chang*, my surname *Fī*, and my title *Yĭ-tĕ*. For generations we have dwelt in this district of *Chŏ*, and we have a small landed property here. I deal in wine and slaughter pigs. I am fond of forming the acquaintance of the brave men of the empire. When I saw you just now looking at the placard and sighing, I could not help speaking to you." *Hiuen-tĕ* said: "I am descended from the house of *Han*, my name is *Liu* and my surname *Pei*. When I lately heard that the Yellow-turbans were in rebellion, the wish arose in my mind to break their power and to give peace to the people. Would that my strength were adequate to it! It was for this reason that I sighed." *Fī* replied: "I have some small means, let us call out our brave countrymen, and with you, Sir, begin to put the great affair into execution, what do you think of that?" *Hiuen-tĕ* was much pleased, and they forthwith entered the village inn to take some wine. Just as they were drinking, they saw a fine son of *Han* (a Chinaman), pushing along a hand-cart, who, coming up, stopped at the door of the inn. Having entered the inn, he sat down and called to the waiter: "Pour out quickly some wine for me to drink, I am in haste to reach the city to join the army." *Hiuen-tĕ*, seeing that the man had a noble aspect and a dignified bearing, invited him to join them, and then enquired his name and surname. The man replied. "My name is *Kwan*, my surname *Yu*, and my title *Sheu-ch'ang*, which has been altered to *Yün-ch'ang*. I am a native of *Kiai-liang* in *Ho-tung*. When a man of influence in my native place, relying on his power, had insulted and oppressed the people, I killed him; and, having escaped with difficulty, for five or six years I have been in the River and Lake provinces. Having recently heard in this place that an army is being raised to subdue the rebels, I am going (to the city) on purpose to enlist." *Hiuen-tĕ* at once told him of his own project. *Yün-ch'ang* was much pleased, and they went together to *Chang-fī's* farm to consult about the matter. *Fī* said: "At the back of my farm there is a peach garden, the flowers are just in full bloom. Let us to-morrow in that garden sacrifice to Heaven and Earth, and we three men will unite as brethren, with all our hearts, and then we may plan about this great matter." *Hiuen-tĕ* and *Yün-ch'ang* with one voice exclaimed: "That is very good."

14. From Æsop's Fables, by Robert Thom, Esq., v. native text (lithographed), page 14.

a. 2. *Ch'ai p'āng yáng.*
a. 6. *Pw'ăn-kù ts'ŭ, niaù-sheŭ kiaī năng yên. Yī-jī ch'aî yŭ yáng, t'úng*
a. 20. *kiēn yìn-shwŭì; ch'aî yŭ p'āng k'ì yáng; tsź-niên wŭ ì tsiè ts'ź, naì*
b. 10. *kiāng tsĕ chī yŭ: "Jŭ hwặn-chŭ tsż shwŭì, shī laù-fŭ pŭ-năng yìn,*
b. 25. *kaī shá. Yáng tŭí yŭ: "Tá-wáng tsaí sháng liŭ, yáng tsaí hiá liŭ;*
c. 14. *sŭí chŭ wŭ gaī." Ch'aî fŭ tsí yŭ: "Jŭ k'ú-niên meū-jī ch'ŭ-yên tĕ-*
d. 5. *tsŭí yŭ ngò, yī kaī shá." Yáng yŭ: "Tá wáng wŭ ì; k'ŭ niên meū-*
d. 20. *jī yáng wí ch'ŭ-shī, gān-năng tĕ-tsŭí tá-wáng?" Ch'aî tsí piên-siŭ weí*
e. 11. *nŭ, tsí chī yŭ: "Jŭ chī fú-mŭ tĕ-tsŭí yŭ ngò, yī jŭ chī tsŭí yè." Sŭí*
f. 4. *p'āng chī. Yên yŭn: "Yŭ kiă chī tsŭí, hô hwán wŭ ts'ź ?" Tsí tsż*
f. 18. *chī weí yè.*

g. 2. *Ăr shŭ.*
g. 5. *Ts'ān-lô chŭng yiù ặr shŭ, pặn-shŭ tsīn-ī, yī tsaí kīng-sz̄ kwŏ-hwŏ.*
g. 21. *Hwŭ yī-jī laí ts'ān t'án-kiá, ts'ān-shŭ liŭ ặr kw'ăn chī. Sò ch'ŭ chī*
h. 12. *shì ts'ŭ-cheŭ pŭ-k'ăn. Kīng-shŭ yŭ: "Jŭ kŭ wŭ hwá, ŭ-shī wŭ meí-*
i. 3. *wí, hô-pŭ sŭí ngò taŭ kīng, yī-kiēn shí-miên?" Ts'ān-shŭ hīn-jên,*
i. 18. *t'úng wáng kī taŭ kīng, kwò-jên shí-yíng kiaī ì yī-jī ặr shŭ t'úng*
j. 9. *chŏ mĕ! Laí yī-hiŭng kiuèn, kì tsiāng ts'ān-shŭ hwŏ k'ŭ! Ts'ān-shŭ*
j. 23. *tá hiaí, wặn yŭ: "Tsź chŭ ch'áng yiù tsż haī hŭ?" Yŭ: "Jên."*
k. 11. *Ts'ān-shŭ ts'ź, yŭ: "Fī ngò chī fŭ yĕ, yŭ k'ì páng-hwáng ặr kān-chī;*
l. 2. *shŭ jŏ gān-tsíng ặr tsaŭ-k'áng?" Sŭ yŭn: "Nìng shì k'aī meî-chŭ,*
l. 16. *mŏ-shì ts'iŭ meî-fân!" Tsí tsż chī weí yè!*

---

men who are mentioned in the opening stanza (*Haŭ-kĭ săn*, 11. a. 10). They united with a solemn oath to retrieve the fortunes of the *Hán* family. They associated with themselves *Lŭ-pŭ*, *Kŭng-mìng*, and *Yuèn-shaŭ*, and finally established the kingdom of *Shŭ* [a]. Another famous general, *Tsaŭ-tsaŭ*, succeeded in forming the kingdom of *Weí* [b], and *Sān-kiuĕn* raised for himself the kingdom of *Wú* [c]: these were the *Sān-kwŏ*, 'the Three Kingdoms,' which form the subject of this, the best historical romance of the Chinese.

Pw'ăn-kù (14. a. 6) is a mythical personage, who is described in Chinese books as the first man, who, though not the creator of the world, had the Herculean task allotted to him of bringing the chaos into a cosmos, of making order and beauty out of confusion. The Rationalists of China, commonly called *Tauists*, have proceeded to particularise the acts of this individual; they describe his work of splitting the heavens and chiselling the rocks. His efforts, they say, were continued eighteen thousand years. On his death his head became a mountain, his breath the winds, and his voice thunder, with other ridiculous stories, similar however to the Scandinavian myths on this subject. For a long account of this myth see Dr. Williams' *Middle Kingdom*, vol. VI. p. 196, where a curious picture is given of *Pw'ăn-kù* at work.

[a] 蜀 [b] 魏 [c] 吳

Translation of Æsop's Fables, by Robert Thom, Esq., v. native text (lithographed), page 14.

The wolf devours the sheep.

In the primitive times of *Pwan-ku*, when all the birds and beasts could speak, one day a wolf and a sheep were drinking at the same stream. The wolf wished to devour the sheep, but, thinking within himself that he had no excuse, he reproached him sternly and said: "You are making this water muddy, so that I, your superior, cannot drink, I must kill you." The sheep replied: "Your Honour is at the upper part of the stream, and I am at the lower; though the water is muddy it is no obstacle *to your drinking*." The wolf again reproached him and said: "Last year on a particular day you said something offensive against me; I ought to kill you." The sheep said: "Your Honour is under a mistake, *for* last year on that particular day I was not born. How could I offend against Your Honour?" The wolf then, instead of being ashamed, became angry, and, reproving him, said: "Your parents offended against me, and it is your fault too," and forthwith devoured him. The proverb says: "If you want to impute a crime to any one, why distress yourself at the want of an excuse?" This is what is meant.

The two mice.

In a retired village were two mice, who were both relatives and friends. One of them went to live in the city, and one day unexpectedly she came to the village to visit her old friend. The country mouse begged to be allowed to entertain her. But the provisions which she brought out were coarse and foul, and were not good enough for the city mouse, who said: "Your abode is not very beautiful, and your household food is neither fine nor savoury, why not come with me to the city and take a look at the world?" The village mouse gladly went with her, and on arriving at the city *she found* certainly that the food was very different. But one day, as the two mice were together drinking, a fierce dog suddenly made his appearance, and was nearly seizing upon the country mouse and carrying her off. The country mouse, in great alarm, enquired, saying: "Are these evils always here?" *Her friend* replied: "Yes." Then the country mouse begged to be excused, and said: "This is no happiness to me, with all this terror and good victuals. There is nothing like peace and coarse husks." The common saying is: "It is better to drink rice-water with pleasant feelings, than to eat the rice that produces sorrow*." This is just what it means.

---

* Lit. 'opening eye-brow rice-water' than 'sorrowing eye-brow rice.'

第一段日常清早起來叫孫子們掃掃地澆澆花熬水洗臉泡碗好茶吃吃沒有事的時候看看書寫寫字三兩個斯文朋友作個詩下個圍棋解解悶兒就可以過得日子了到了下午拉幾骹弓射幾條箭把這身筋骨活動活動人又有精神又長勁這都是好事不要往外頭貪甜一點兒錯的都沒有阿你要聽着不要開酒不要過家我說的話一點兒錯的都沒有阿你要聽着不要忘記了阿點个灯兒來阿黑鼓影子怎麼瞧得見呢
第二段擇交一個人出來相與朋友總要帶雙眼睛見了那些正經人講禮義的謙和的老實的董得規矩的有良心的見過世面的有才情的有本事的可以靠得住的你繞好替他相與跟着他走恭敬他不好急慢他有善相勸有事相幫便大家有益了若瞧見了那些不好人一點兒本事都沒有一把光棍嘴哄騙人

家又不好脾氣全幹些混賬的事又不董眼又不顧臉又討人嫌人家罵他他也不害臊這樣的人我瞧見了就惱了他你千萬不要替他走攏阿你若替他走攏他就拐騙你的銀子錢還不打緊他還要慫恿你的事生出許多事來有甚麼便宜呢從今以後你要打主意纔好阿。

第三段雜話

人最要緊是說話你瞧那些有名色的人分外不同他說出的話總是出經入典有文雅氣自不用說咯他就隨口說句把尋常的話兒也覺得大方有體局不驕傲不下作人家聽了自然誇他會說話了然而正經話固然要聽就是市井上那些閒雜人等的話也要放長耳聚聽聽雖然不必學他也要知道各處風俗怎麼是村話粗話雅話虐薄話奉承人的話笑罵人的話人家說出來你不董得就成了個耷條子了。

第一回

宴桃園豪傑三結義
斬黃巾英雄首立功

話說天下大勢分久必合合久必分周末七國分爭并入于秦及秦滅之後楚漢分爭又并入于漢漢朝自高祖斬白蛇而起義一統天下後來光武中興傳至獻帝遂分爲三國推其致亂之由殆始於桓靈二帝桓帝禁錮善類崇信宦官及桓帝崩靈帝即位大將軍竇武太傳陳蕃共相輔佐時有宦官曹節等弄權竇武陳蕃謀誅之機事不密反爲所害中涓自此愈橫建寧二年四月望日帝御溫德殿方陞座殿角狂風驟起只見一條大青蛇從梁上飛將下來蟠于椅上帝驚倒左右急救入宮百官俱奔避須臾蛇不見了忽然大雷大雨加以冰雹落到半夜方止壞却房屋無數建四年二月洛陽地震又海水泛溢沿海居民盡被大浪捲入海中

時鉅鹿郡有兄弟三人。一名張角。一名張寶。一名張梁。那張角本是箇不第秀才。因入山採藥。遇一老人。碧眼童顏。手執藜杖。喚角至一洞中。以天書三卷授之曰。此名太平要術。汝得之。當代天宣化普救世人。若萌異心。必獲惡報。角拜問姓名。老人曰。吾乃南華老仙也。言訖。化陣清風而去。○靖曰。賊兵衆我兵寡。明公宜作速化縣中一箇英雄。那人不甚好讀書。性寬和寡言語。喜怒不形於色素有大志。專好結交天下豪傑。生得身長八尺兩耳垂肩雙手過於膝。目能自顧其耳。面如冠玉。唇若塗脂。中山靖王劉勝之後招軍應敵。劉焉然其說。隨卽出榜。招募義兵。榜文行到涿縣引出漢景帝閣下玄孫。姓劉名備字玄德。○○當日見了榜文。慨然長嘆。隨後一人厲聲言曰。大犬夫不與國家出力。何故長嘆。玄德回視其人身八尺聲若巨雷勢如奔馬。玄德見他形貌異常。問其姓

名其人曰、某姓張、名飛字翼德、世居涿郡頗有莊田賣酒屠猪專好結交天下豪傑、恰縫見公看榜而嘆、故此相問、玄德曰、我本漢室宗親姓劉名備、今聞黃巾倡亂、有志欲破賊安民、恨力不能故長嘆耳、飛曰、吾頗有資財當召募鄉勇與公同舉大事如何、玄德甚喜、遂與同入村店中飲酒、間見一大漢推著一輛車子到店門首歇了、入店坐下、便喚酒保快斟酒來吃、我待趕入城去投軍、玄德看其人相貌堂堂威風凛凛、就邀他同坐、叩其姓名、其人曰、吾姓關名羽字壽長、後改雲長、河東解良人也、因本處勢豪凌人、被吾殺了、逃難江湖五六年矣、今聞此處招軍破賊特來應募、玄德遂以已志告之、雲長大喜、同到張飛莊上、共議大事、飛曰、我莊後有桃園花開正盛、明日當於園中祭告天地、我三人結為兄弟協力同心、然後可圖大事、玄德雲長齊聲應曰、如此甚好、

豺烹羊

盤古初鳥獸皆能言。一日豺與羊同澗飲水、豺欲烹其羊、自念無以措辭、乃強責之曰、汝混濁此水、使老夫不能飲、該殺羊對曰、大王在上流、羊在下流、雖濁無礙、豺復責曰、汝去年某日出言得罪於我、亦該殺羊曰、大王悞矣、去年某日、某未出世、安能得罪、豺則變羞為怒、責之曰、汝之父母得罪於我、汝亦汝之罪也、遂烹之、諺云、欲加之罪、何患無辭、即此之謂也。

二鼠

村落中有二鼠、本屬親誼、一在京師過活、忽一日來村探舊、村鼠留而欵之、所出之食、粗臭不堪、京鼠曰、汝居無華屋、食無美味、何不隨我到京一見世面、村鼠欣然同往、及到京、果然食用皆異、一日二鼠同酌、蓦來一雄犬、幾將村鼠櫻去、村鼠大駭問曰、此處常有此害乎、曰、此執若安靜而糟糠俗云、寧食開眉粥、莫食愁眉飯、即此之謂也。

俗語○一舉兩得桑條從小揉順風不起浪在家敬父母何必遠燒香隨風到
舵順水推船火上添油各人自掃門前雪莫管他人瓦上霜德妙文無色
人便如此如天理未然未如從命○不登山不知天之高不臨谿不知地之
光陰似箭日月如梭恭敬不如從命○不登山不知天之高不臨谿不知
水底魚天邊鷹高可射低可釣人之有人心對面則明塵埃不染智明則邪惡不生
厚不聞先王之遺言不知學問之大鏡明則塵埃不染智明則邪惡不生
可防盡畫皮難畫骨知人知面不知心惟有人心隔千山寡言擇交可以
無悔吝可以無憂辱慾寬精神爽思多血氣衰因之夢魘酒不醉人
人自醉奢可以無命一客不煩二主做一日和尚撞一日鐘口中言若要斷酒法
樹倒無陰君子不念舊惡單絲不成線要知心腹事但聽口中言若要斷酒法
醒眼看醉人先視其父屏風雖破骨格猶存君子雖貧禮義常在白玉可以
友欲知其父先視其子
泥不能沾淫其色君子處於濁地之下刀劍雖快不斬無罪之人非災橫禍不入
涉艱危○日月雖明不照覆盤之下刀劍雖快不斬無罪之人非災橫禍不
慎家之門○人生智未生智生人易老心智一切生不覺無常到

古詩
大風歌。
大風起兮雲飛揚威加海內兮歸故鄉安得猛士兮守四方。○
春宮曲。
昨夜風開露井桃未央前殿月輪高平陽歌舞新承寵簾外春寒賜錦袍。○
五言
幽居貴賤雖異等出門皆有營獨無外物牽遂此幽居情微雨夜來過不知春草生青山忽已曙鳥雀繞舍鳴時與道人偶或隨樵者行自當安寒劣誰謂薄世榮。○
過酒家。此日長昏飲非關養性靈眼看人盡醉何忍獨為醒
律詩·五言律
幽州夜飲。涼風吹夜雨蕭瑟動寒林正有高堂宴能忘遲暮心軍中宜劍舞塞上重笳音不作邊城將誰知恩遇深○
送翰林張司馬南海勒碑。冠冕通南極文章落上台詔從三殿去碑到百
登閶野館濃花發春帆細雨來不知滄海上去歲荊南梅似雪今年薊北雪如梅共知
人事何嘗定且喜年華去復來○邊鎮戍歌連日動京城燎火徹明開遙遙
長安日願上南山壽一杯○五言排律 白帝懷古 荒服仍周甸深山尚禹功
日落滄江晚停橈間土風城臨巴子國臺沒漢王宮
嚴懸青壁斷地險碧流通古木生雲際歸帆出霧中川途去無限客思坐何窮。

問候。久切瞻韓未獲如願近聞移旌江右德化日新欣羨之私更深寤寐。
恨不能插翅而飛翔左右觀盛化而聆德言也今緣鴻便特借一行以申積悃
兼請金安伏惟鑒念○
答盛名貫耳非一日矣懷伊人而不見。正情切于蒹葭乃華翰下頒宛如
覿面頓解生平之飢渴何幸如之惟是先施之雅專屬仁人未免鄙野村夫自
增內愧耳倘有良緣得邀惠顧則樽酒論文可不令古人擅美于前矣是望是
禱敬此裁覆○
艮朋久闊音耗全無江海之阻人殆豈得云宛在一方乎惟是自信忘形當
努力可耳茲緣鴻便附上手巾一方小刀兩把些微朽物本不足當木李之投
不復可溯洞無自之嗟致乖涵養況後會有期不在于世願在于天祇期各自
而千里鵝毛物輕情重諒必覯此而益憐愚魯之旅人矣主威心尺默禱內
期片刻留神謹此遠達頓請福安并候康寧。
某某兄台大人文几
　　　愚弟某某字頓

一個人學官話來做甚麼的呢一件預備自己將來出身做官伺候上司臨
涖屬員要做一個有本事的官阿其次就做大客商或開行店或往外省走水
要做一個廝俐的客商再其次就是居家則你是個有衣食的人有體面的
人在鄉族中年長月長鄉情族事少不了也有件兒要替人家料理料
也得見見地方把事兒說幾個官話細情節一則衛顧鄉族二則保護門楣原是為
這三門人家就箕了事略所以你們總要把大方的話兒接待長上的話兒有交官接府的話
薰人家教道晚輩的話兒使喚下人的話兒到外頭留心幾是正經的阿
友的話兒對着買賣人的話樣樣都有個欵式要在這上頭留心幾
兒對着學官話的這一翻工夫阿○
不枉了學官話的
你做學生的人上書房念書甚麼都要有個規矩清早起來洗了臉喝了茶
禀告爹爹媽媽孩兒往書房去了說過之後包起書本出大門口端端正正珍
珍重重的去兩隻脚不要混跳兩隻眼睛不要混瞧東西一直走到書房裡頭把書背得
把書本放下望聖人上頭作個揖又替先生作個揖然後坐着念書把書
熟熟兒的幾送到先生卓上背書時候又要一句句伶牙俐齒不要含糊錯漏

DIALOGUES & PHRASES IN THE MANDARIN DIALECT. (1) 30

○上學你這樣快往那裡跑我們上學我也往那裡去等一展眼們頭裡走的那一個是誰我們同學的咱們都一塊兒走罷你好懶惰為什麼來的這麼遲我昨日熬了夜不能早起來你是幾下鐘起來的你好有的危險了你不前日不來那一日事情狠忙不得空兒來料理世俗的事情上頭有的就擱了你不少若別人命你罷了到底你的師傳命你不聽這個了不得況且你念書不好再的這事情有大關係隨便他打盼不要快了你什麼的本分這三天你不念書不要這樣預備你要背的書聽說念完了沒有還沒有你筆墨硯都帶有的帽子看你不書預備前一次的書念我盼咐了你快了你去你的房坐三天你的帽子這個埋字的什麼聲音你要買怎麼解說命有葬的意思我該當趕去買東西另外還有一個字難懂我沒有許多的工夫因為我該當一個月還要做兩篇文章○你好呀狠好辦麼你小心每日念的書另外的舅舅怎麼樣他如今比頭裡好的多明日再見飯吃了令尊好家父好你的舅舅的時候怎麼計你同我來怕鬼麼不怕放下蚊我該當送行○明天將黑些到了睡覺的時我該當清早起來一定記得麼一定記得帳留下燈減燈明天早打火點燈沒有火石火煤兒○誰叫打門是誰我還沒有起來早醒了天大亮了

噯呀這個地方狠好看溫和的涼爽的看樹都開了花兒這一根落了葉子
麥子熟了你乏了麼實在困倦了在這個青草上踢着好進那個樹林在這些
樹底下狠好的蘋菓沙梨李子櫻桃多麼好那多結菓子了今年是荒年這裡
有狠好的柑子橙子這些梅子頭要落山等一會天氣有潮氣雲彩看不見星宿
斤買十幾斤罷天氣晚了這晚上好天氣下雨下雹子下雪花開了打雷雷响
子怎麼樣好天冷天陰了這個晚上好天氣有潮氣走罷你乏了吃晚飯一
天氣怎麼來了一個暴風風大暴風過去了看得見天虹是個好天氣的懲還
亂起雷打死了慢慢的就散了露下霜○什麼時候下鐘不晚回家去罷
打閃雷打出午差不多一下鐘打了一下三刻還沒有打三下二刻你怎麼知
據有時候繞日出慢的○你歡喜那個時候春天是最好的這個天氣溫和的
道聽見鐘打了我想不是這樣遲看你的表我的表是走的快不對表慢幾分
有時候暑沙子表在那裡你歡喜那個時候春天這
看日暑沙子表在那裡這不冷這不算春天算是冬天樹都沒有發芽這夏天熱的狠我
也不熱也不冷這不算春天算是冬天樹都沒有發芽這夏天熱的狠我
汗要熱死總沒覺得這樣熱該當許多的苜蓿草要收莊稼割完了莊稼秋天

有耍便天我有你得想麼我遠他你
逆上易氣一三大狠意說聽不你會
風船狠要個個概是思的不你說說
有麼要坐別月六想這的你答說中
頂　好車的十起樣懂都應了國
頭幾麼我們多來認得得他這話
風槳我出死個娶得得他的個麼
耍的我身去了兒了說解他話沒你
在船夥上一子你親麼說震有說
那　計曠你說有沒見我聾沒了
裡　你軟曠這幾有過在了有什
上　帶弱我一位你你你的請麼
岸　我沒們句令幾幾頭我問總
在　過有涼話郎父次裡的這沒
大　河力涼我有母先知耳個有
馬　罷量快起幾都生道朶是聽
頭　甘走涼了位在不比不什見
那　心我快一閨閒貴方見麼這
裡　這走我個先庚多不說知個
　　一不們念父多大數知清道某
臨　隻動上頭死大年忘道楚這人
近　船要城想了年紀了有一個告
了　沒行罷起有紀有我什點麼訴
河　有旱　了兩　麼麼兒來了
邊　槳路不什母　　關來說我
下　麼不便麼親　記係說得後
錨　搖便　幾再　這了得說來
這　槳水　個嫁　個沒他不我
裡　　路　方了　我有說得告
好　　呢　不大　不這過離訴
阿　　　　便　　清個的那
　　　　　不　　楚甚人
　　　　　死　　不
　　　　　單　　過

我有一件事情求你什麽事情郭情放心說罷求你給我一把刀子給我作這個

懇求大爺這個恩典狠情願多謝你不好說當了你的恩勾忘不了你狠知禮我作什麽懇為

你願意什麽不必多禮我歡喜你不該當理你能勾倚靠我叫我作什麽朋

友一說下這麽個禮貌叫我失禮不要求你這樣好替我問張先生好是我得好朋

我隨便說一說你情分大是不是寶在是我說老實寶話果然說這樣一句話誰疑惑我想罪你

的話隨口答應這個說了一次賭上多少兩銀子說話真說謊假是說虛樣話誰疑惑我想罪你

不要說不是打賭罷一次後來雖然說沒有人信凡人撒謊就丟了脸一定

該當作隨什麼說這個還有多少來信麽這個是妄話說好我給我麽主意這個怎麽

樣辦法兒等一等我這樣作的如今想這們一件事情怎麽樣都是一個樣

你從那裡來往那裡去我作罷你今想這們作什麽好請進來近我來離開走罷你去罷的

後退一點兒來在這裡等一會兒等我從朝他們一齊過去不去你要這麽快走我沒走

太快不要動手在這裡坐門關了開門從這裡過不去你丟了什麽

什麽為什麽因為我拾了一件東西高聲說低聲說你說的太快不能懂得

OFFICIAL PAPERS (SUPPLEMENTARY TREATY 1844).

待禁夜行約立禁約人某某等為嚴禁夜行以靖地方事國家重門擊柝預
賊猖狂總由夜行不謹奚便稽察是以乘機暗盜甚至明火強刼見地方紛亂盜
不乎暴客鄉民提鈴敲梆緊防其盜賊皆有明禁誰敢違犯近見地方不安枕家盜
至五更三點方可任其來往每日輪流巡邏如有犯禁者一遇黃昏即禁人行直
鎗刀弩銃殺死勿論倘鳴鑼時查點一名不到來日清晨會眾共罰決不輕貸
特寫立數紙寶處張掛庶紳衿某某謹禀之人知所戒而雞鳴狗盜之人無得逞矣
謹約飭請飭除禀
禀為市道連逢懇請飭除以愼火災事竊禀
燭不慎猝然禍起蕭牆爐竈疎密倘有火燭最易惹着且逢係引火之物行道
可勝言彼市道上兩傍連逢蓋倘爾映及池魚一事雖曰天命豈非人事燈
之人素易烟火悞及即行焚燎况今隆冬之際萬物焦乾雖山草亦為之着火而剡
逢之此豈獨某力乎倘不拆去深為不便理合禀請台階飭差着令毀拆免為
火災
老爺臺前施行等受其益寶彼此俱得相安耳為此禀叩伏為垂鑒沾恩切赴

欽差大臣兵部尙書兩湖總督林．

兵部尙書兩廣總督鄧．
兵部侍郎廣東巡撫怡．

會同照會英吉利國王爲令禁鴉片烟事照得天道無私不容害人以利已人情不遠孰非惡殺而好生貴國雖在重洋二萬里外而同此天道同此人情未有不明於生死利害者也我天朝四海爲家大皇帝如天之仁無所不覆而退
荒絶域亦在並生並育之中廣東自開海禁以來流通貿易凡內地民人與外來番船相安於樂利者有數十年於茲矣且於大黃茶葉湖絲等類皆中國寶
貴之產外國若不得此即無以爲命而天朝一視同仁許其販賣出洋絕不靳
惜無非推思外服以天地之心爲心也乃有一種奸夷製爲鴉片夾帶販賣誘
惑愚民以害其身以害其生殘其心豈肯使海內生靈甘心受愛惜也然
富庶蕃昌雖在此等務在端風俗以正人心豈肯使海內生靈甘心受愛惜也然
以大淸一統之天下務在此等愚民食口腹而戕其生亦屬由自取何必爲愛惜也然
現將內地販賣鴉片並吸食之人一體嚴行治罪永禁流傳惟思此等毒物非
貴國所屬各部轄內鬼蜮奸人私行造作自非貴國王令其製造此物並非諸
國皆然又聞貴國亦不准民人吸食犯者必懲自係知其害人故特爲之厲禁

o n m l k j i h g f e d c b a

○狼斷羊案○古有兒犬具稟於狼謂羊負伊穀糧數斛總不肯還求狼作主狼則出差將羊拏獲訊曰爾欠穀糧日久不還是何道理羊曰爾不肯招爾有憑據否犬曰鷹鶻皆可作證狼卽傳羊按律來鷹犬誣告面面相質鷹鶻稱眞事羊欠犬糧我等目擊並非誣告將羊按律乃往犬誣告也狼問犬曰鷹鶻間真事羊欠犬糧我等目擊並非誣告將羊按律治罪狼對羊曰現有鐵證爾尚賴乎遂殺之於是原告之犬與審事之狼官並干證如犬干證如鷹鶻則不必望其如世人若有貲財每招橫禍又遇貪狼之官豈不寃乎。
○原告如犬干證如鷹鶻則不必望其秉公斷事矣諺云象有齒焚其身蛇則纏而咬之官干證狼蠍一窩共分其羊如世人若有貲財每招橫禍又遇貪狼之官豈不寃乎
○毒蛇如鷹鶻則不必望其秉公斷事矣諺云象有齒焚其身蛇則纏而咬之
○口觸鉎齒血滴○昔有毒蛇沿入鐵舖遇物卽咬適有利鉎復再咬之鉎曰汝心太毒不能害人反害
○自已如世有狠心者常在暗裡以言語譛人而不知實自譛也。○
○斧頭求柄○昔有斧頭雖銳而無用自思必得一柄方可見用於世乃乞其
○樹曰先生賜我一木不過僅爲一柄足矣他日自當圖報其樹自顧枝柯繁盛
何惜柄慨然與之斧得其柄所有樹林盡被伐去何其樹之愚哉如世人所
謂助虎添翼又遞刀乞命是也。凡人必須各守其分切勿尺寸與人誠恐有
如斧柄則悔之晚矣。○

相依連則萬無一失若分之唇亡齒寒無有不失也愼之如以一國而論各據一方者鮮有不敗反不如合力相連之爲美也

○報恩鼠　獅子熟睡於郊外小鼠在旁玩耍驚醒而戲之獅隨以爪覆之鼠不能脫哀鳴　爪下獅念小鼠區區之體殺之無益不如捨之鼠得免後遇獅子始得脫身如世所謂人小誠恐不知何係得力之小人是將來之恩人亦未可定也　一日獅將網嚙破獅子得饒人處且饒人切勿輕

視人小誠恐不知何係得力之小人是將來之恩人亦未可定也

○車夫求佛　一日車夫將車輪陷於小坑不能起車夫求救於阿彌陀佛佛謂車夫曰我車落坑求佛力拔救佛曰汝當肩扛其車而鞭其馬自然騰出此坑若汝垂手而待我亦無能爲矣如世人急時求佛當先盡其力乃可任爾誦佛萬聲不如自行勉力

劍向前欲殺植議郎彭伯諫曰盧尙書海內人望今先害之恐天下震怖卓乃止司徒王允曰廢立之事不可酒後相商另日再議于是百官皆散卓按劍立于園門忽見一人躍馬持戟于園門外往來卓問李儒此何人也儒曰此丁原義兒姓呂名布字奉先者也主公且須避之卓乃入園潛避次日入報丁原引軍城外搦戰卓怒引軍同李儒出迎兩陣對圓只見呂布頂束髮金冠披百花戰袍環唐猊鎧甲繋獅蠻寳帶縱馬提戟隨丁建陽出到陣前建陽指卓罵曰國家不幸閹宦弄權以至萬民塗炭爾無尺寸之功焉敢妄言廢立欲亂朝廷卓未及回言呂布飛馬殺過來董卓慌走建陽率軍掩殺卓兵大敗退三十餘里下寨聚衆商議卓曰吾觀呂布非常人也吾若得此人何慮天下哉帳前一人出曰主公勿憂某與呂布同鄕知其人乃虎賁中郎將李肅也卓曰汝將何以說之肅曰某聞主公有名馬一匹號曰赤兎日行千里須得此馬再用金珠以利結其心某更進說詞呂布必反丁原來投主公矣卓問李儒曰此言可乎儒曰主公欲取天下何惜一馬卓欣然與之更與黃金一千兩明珠數十顆玉帶一條李肅齊了禮物投呂布寨來伏路軍人圍住肅曰可速報呂將軍

吾欲廢帝立陳留王何如李儒曰今朝廷無主不就此時行事遲則有變矣來
日于溫明園中召集百官諭以廢立有不從者斬之則威權之行正在今日卓
喜次日大排筵會遍請公卿公卿皆懼董卓誰敢不到卓待百官到了然後徐
徐到園門下馬帶劍入席酒行數巡卓教停酒止樂乃厲聲曰吾有一言眾官
靜聽眾官側耳而聽卓曰天子為萬民之主無威儀不可以奉宗廟社稷今上
不若陳留王聰明好學可承大位吾欲廢帝立陳留王諸大臣以為何如諸官
聽罷不敢出聲坐上一人推案直出立于筵前大呼不可不可汝是何人敢發
大語丁原也卓怒叱曰順我者生逆我者死遂掣佩劍欲斬丁原時李儒見丁
州剌史丁原背後一人生得器宇軒昂威風凜凜手執方天畫戟怒目而視李
儒急進曰今日飲宴之處不可談國政來日向都堂公論未遲眾人皆勸丁原
上馬而去卓問百官曰吾所言合公道否盧植曰明公差矣昔太甲不明伊尹
放之于桐官昌邑王登位二十七日造惡三十餘條故霍光告太廟而廢之今
上雖幼聰明仁智並無分毫過失公乃外郡剌史素未參與國政又無伊霍之
大才何可強主廢立聖人云有伊尹之志則可無伊尹之志則篡也

崔毅引貢見帝。君臣痛哭貢曰國不可一日無君請陛下還都崔毅莊上止
有瘦馬一匹備與帝乘貢與陳留王共乘一馬離莊而行不到三里司徒王允
太尉楊彪左軍校尉淳于瓊右軍校尉趙萌中軍校尉鮑信另換一
行人眾數百人馬接着車駕君臣皆哭先使人將段珪首級往京師號令
好騎馬到來百官應其識車駕行不到數里洛陽帝非王千乘換一
萬騎走來百官失色帝亦大驚袁紹勒馬出問何人繡旗蔽日塵土遮天一枝
人馬到來帝失色帝亦大驚袁紹勒馬向前此日來者何人卓日西涼刺史
問天子何在帝日汝來保駕耶陳留日既來保駕自初
董卓也。陳留日汝來保駕耶陳留日汝來何太后俱各痛哭董卓檢點
天子在此何不下馬卓大驚慌忙下馬拜于道左陳留王以言撫慰董卓自初
至終並無失語卓暗奇之已懷廢立之意是日還宮見何太后俱各痛哭檢點
宮中不見了傳國璽董卓屯兵城外每日帶鐵甲馬軍入城橫行街市百姓惶
惶不安卓出入宮庭無忌憚後軍校尉鮑信來見袁紹言董卓必有異心速
除之紹曰朝庭新定未可輕動鮑信見王允亦言其事允曰且容商議信自引
本部軍兵投泰山去了董卓招誘何進兄弟部下之兵盡歸掌握私謂李儒曰

EXTRACT FROM THE SAN-KWŌ-CHI. (1)

三國誌。且說張讓段珪劫擁少帝及陳留王冒烟突火連夜奔走北邙山約三更時分後面喊聲大舉人馬趕至當前河南中部掾吏閔貢大呼逆賊休走讓見事急遂投河而死帝與陳留王未知虛寶不敢高聲伏於河邊亂草內張讓軍馬四散去趕不知帝之所在帝與王伏至四更露水又下腹中飢餒相抱而哭又怕人知覺吞聲草莽之中陳留王曰此間不可久戀須別尋活路于是二人以衣相結爬上岸邊滿地荊棘黑暗之中不見行路正無奈何忽有流螢千百成羣光芒照耀只在帝前飛轉陳留王曰此天助我兄弟也遂隨螢火而行漸漸見路行至五更足痛不能行山崗邊見一草堆帝與王臥于草堆之後螢火草堆前面是一所庄院庄主是夜夢兩紅日墜於庄後驚覺披衣出戶四下觀望見庄前後草堆上紅光冲天慌忙往視却是二人臥于草堆之間曰二少年誰家之子草堆不敢應陳留王指帝曰此是當今皇帝遭十常侍之亂逃難到此庄主大驚再拜曰臣先朝司徒崔烈之弟崔毅也因見十常侍賣官嫉賢故隱於此遂扶帝入庄跪進酒食却說閔貢趕上段珪擒下問天子何在珪言在半路相失不知何往貢遂殺段珪懸首級問兵四散尋覓自己却獨乘一馬隨路追尋偶至崔毅庄毅見首級問之貢說詳分

相煩引進。院公引到庭門。高俅看時見端王頭戴軟紗唐巾身穿紫繡龍袍腰繫文武雙縧條把繡龍袍前襟拽札起揣在縧兒邊，足穿一雙嵌金線飛鳳靴三五個小黃門相伴着蹴氣毬。高俅不敢過去衝撞立在從人背後伺候也是高俅合當發跡時運到來那個氣毬騰地起來端王接個不着向人叢裏直滾到高俅身邊。那高俅見氣毬來也是一時的膽量使個鴛鴦拐踢還端王。端王見了大喜便問道。你是甚人。高俅向前跪下道小的是王都尉親隨。受東人使令齊送兩般玉玩器來進獻大王。有書呈在此拜上。端王聽罷笑道。姐夫眞如此掛心。高俅取出書呈進上。端王開盒子看了玩器都遞與堂候官收了去那端王且不理玉器下落却先問高俅道你這來會踢氣毬你喚做甚麼。高俅叉手跪覆道小的叫做高俅胡亂踢得幾腳。端王道好你便下塲來踢一向。要高俅拜道。小的是何等樣人。敢與恩王下腳。端王道這是齊雲社名爲天下圓。但踢何傷。高俅再拜道。怎敢。三回五次告辭。端王定要他踢。高俅只得叩頭謝罪。解膝下塲纔踢幾腳端王喝采。高俅只得把平生本事都使出來奉承端王那身分模樣。這氣毬一似鰾膠粘在身上的端王大喜那里肯放高俅回府去。就留在宮中過一夜。次日排個筵會專請王都尉宮中赴宴○

誕生辰分付府中安排筵宴專請小舅端王這端王乃是神宗天子第十一子哲宗皇帝御弟見掌東駕排號九大王是個聰明俊俏人物浮浪子弟門風幫閒之事無一般不曉無一般不會更無一般不愛如琴書畫無所不通踢毬打彈品竹調絲吹彈歌舞自不必說酒進數杯食供兩套那端王起身淨手偶來請端王居中坐定太尉對席相陪書院裏少歇猛見書架上一對兒羊脂玉鎮紙獅子極是做得好細巧玲瓏端王拿起獅子不落手一同道好王都尉見端王心愛便說道再一併相送端王大喜道深謝厚意想那筆架必是更妙王都尉道明日取來送一個玉龍筆架也是這個匠人一手做的却不在手頭明日取出來回宮去了次日王都尉取出玉龍筆架和兩個鎮紙玉獅子着一個小金盒子盛着用黃羅包複包了寫了一封書呈却便着高俅送去高俅領了王都尉鈞旨將着兩般玉玩器懷中揣着書呈投端王宮中來把門官吏轉報與院公沒多時院公出來問你是那個府裏來的人高俅施禮罷答道小人是王駙馬府中特送玉玩器來進大王院公道殿下在庭心裏和小黃門踢氣毬你自過去高俅道

如何安着得他。若是個志誠老實的人。可以用他在家出入。也教孩兒們學些好。他却是個孽閒的破落戶。沒信行的人。亦且當初有過犯來被斷配的人。舊性必不肯改。若留在家中。倒惹得孩兒們。不學好。待不收留他又撇不過舊面皮。當時只得權且歡天喜地相留。在家宿歇。每日酒食管待。住了十數日。董將仕思量出一個路數。將出一套衣服。寫了一封書簡。對高俅說道。小蘇學士出來見。我轉薦足下。與小蘇學士處。久後也得仕進。發跡有分。高俅大喜。謝了董將仕。董將仕使個人。將着書。引領高俅逕到學士府內。門人轉報。小蘇學士出來。見了高俅。看了來書知道。來歷原是幫閒浮浪的人。心下相道。我這裏如何安着得他。不如做個人情。薦他去駙馬王晉卿府裏做個親隨。人都喚住了他。小王太尉好。人當時回了董將仕書札。留高俅在府裏住了一夜。次日寫了一封書呈。使個幹人送高俅。去那小王都太尉處。這太尉乃是哲宗皇帝妹夫。神宗皇帝的駙馬。這高俅。馬他便喜愛風流人物。正用這樣的人。一見小蘇學士差人持書送這高俅。來拜見了便喜。隨即寫回書。收留高俅在府內做個親隨。自此高俅遭際在王都尉府中出入。如同家人一般。自古道。日遠日疎。日親日近。忽一日小王都太尉慶

水滸傳〇話說故宋哲宗皇帝在時其時宋仁宗天子已遠東京開封府汴梁宣武軍便有一個浮浪破落戶子弟姓高排行第二自小不成家業只好刺鎗使棒便將氣毬踢得好脚氣毬傍添作立人口順不叫高二却叫他做高毬後來發跡便棒相撲頑耍亦胡亂學詩書詞賦仁義禮智信行忠良却是不會只在東京城裏城外弄閙因擊了一個生鐵王員外兒子使錢斷了二十脊杖迭配出界月被他父親告了一紙文狀府尹把高俅無奈何只得來淮西臨准州發放東京城裏閙開坊的閑漢柳大郎名喚柳世權他平生專好惜客養閑人招納納四方迯于隔涳漠大郎的托得柳大郎家宿食高俅無討奈何只得來淮西臨准州投逩董將仕家過活當時高俅感得風調雨順浚放寛恩大赦天下那高俅在臨准州因得了赦宥罪犯思量要一封東京調柳世權却和東京城裏金梁橋下開生藥舖的董將仕家過活當時高俅辭了柳大郎背上包裹離了臨准州迤邐囘到東京投奔董將仕家金梁橋下董生樂家下了這封書董將仕一見高俅看了柳世權來書自肚裏尋思道這高俅我家

酒我偏要你吃了去因拿起那杯酒來焌着鐵夾頭夾臉只一澆鐵雖然醉了心上却還明白一急急得火星亂迸因將酒都急醒了亡跳起身來將一掌抓住揉了兩揉道怎敢到虎頭上來尋死將張大叫道你敢打我麼鐵便一把打你便怎麼過纔話道好意留飲乃敢倚酒撒野關門不要走鐵道且打他個酒醒早兩廂走出七八個大漢鐵笑一笑道一羣風狗怎敢來欺人因一手捉住張不放 提將水小姐分一手掀那些餚饌碗盞打翻一地水運剛走到身邊被鐵只一推道看起來只一饒你打早推跌去西至張原是個色厲內扎不起來的滿口叫道大家不要動手有話好講鐵道沒甚話講只好好送你出去將事全休若一手提着圈留叫你人人都死張連連應承道我送你白挺下鐵又不敢上前只平站穩了硬話道敢如此胡為且饒他去少不得要見個高下鐵只作不聽若好在傍說一話道怎如此走出大門之外方將手放開道煩張兄傳語鴿兄我鐵中玉若見提鐵張直同走出大門之外不可出人何况三五個酒色之徒十數個漢指望有寸鐵在手千軍萬馬中也不可出人何其思也將手一舉道請了要將猛虎之鬚何其思也將手一舉道請了竟大踏步囘下處來

去久了。鐵無奈只得又復坐下與李對飲了三巨觴飲纔完忽左右又報道張更却的大公子來了。衆人還未及答應只見那張公子歪戴着一頂方巾也斜着兩雙色眼糟包着一個麻臉早吃得醉醺醺一路叫將進來道那一位是鐵兄既要到我歷城縣來做豪傑怎不會我一會鐵正立起身來打帳與他施禮見他言語不遜便立住答應道小弟不知長兄要會小弟有何賜教。張也不爲禮瞪着眼看鐵看了又便忽大笑說道我只道鐵兄是晉後七個頭。鐵見他言語不遜禮見他言語不爲禮瞪着眼看鐵看了又便忽大笑說道我只道鐵兄是晉後七個頭。
八個膽的好漢子却原來青青眉目白白面孔無異於女子想是晉後坐了頭。
事餘本色。且慢講且先較一觴較酒量看是如何。衆人聽了俱贊美道張兄妙論大得了。
奈何也只得勉強吃乾了。張道纔像個朋友遂舉空觴又叫一觴賊量有限張道小
英雄本色。且請一觴較乾而飲酒量自乾了衆人見他兩觴的爽快無小
弟坐久又陪王兄三觴李兄要一觴而止莫非你倚强欺人之欺張道醉的
王李二兄俱連三觴何獨小弟如何不吃不得便不吃有甚麼强鐵一咋醉的
滿臉怒道講明對飲我吃了。你如何不吃吃不得便不吃有甚麼强張道這
身都軟了靠着椅子只搖頭道吃不吃不得便不吃有甚麼强張道這
酒你敢不吃麼鐵道不吃張大怒道你怎敢到我山東來裝腔你不吃我這
杯杯杯杯杯杯杯

就坐而飲。原來三人與曲蘗生俱是好友一拈上手便津津有味你一杯我一盞便不復推辭飲了半晌鐵正有個住手之意忽左右報王兵部的三公子鐵來了三人只得停杯接兒鐵正有道王兄來得甚妙因用手指着鐵挺生道這位鐵兄豪傑士也不可不會王道莫非就是打入大安侯養閒堂的鐵挺生麼水運兄答道正是王因重復舉手足恭道久仰久仰失敬失敬因敬道小弟粗送與鐵道借過兄之酒聊表小弟仰慕之私鐵接了一觴就是三巨觴回敬道小弟豪何足道台兄如金如玉方得文品之正四公子已走告止忽左右又報如翰林的二公子小弟竟就坐罷過道尚有遠客在此請教長兄到席前止住道相熟那兄弟不消動身先看着鐵問道好英俊人物且連作說又得離席要作禮那李且不作揖李道這等說是鐵都憙的長君子連連作弟姓台號鐵道小弟乃大名中玉李道過酒已半酣又想着要行揖道久聞大名今日有緣幸會就要邀入坐鐵來得早叨飲過多況行色倥偬不因弟能久住只得總來別了李因作色道鐵兄也太欺人旣要行何不早去為何辭說道李兄小弟本不該就去只弟剛到就一刻也不能留這是明欺小弟不足與飲了水運道鐵先生去是要

有所求也。不識台兄何見拒之甚也。鐵公子道蒙長兄殷殷雅愛，小弟亦不忍
言去。但裝己束。行色淒匆。勢不容緩耳。過道既是台兄不以朋友爲情。快意不要
行。小弟強留也。自覺惶愧。但只是清辰一餐而來。又令愕腹而去。幾人情實兩道盡不
安今台兄亦不敢久留。只求從鐵暑停尼時。少動見一過深。情厚貌懇懇欵留，庶得住。一道寶
難道今台兄繞進只見高誼特走了進來。具束鐵忙施禮。滿臉怒笑道昨日舍姪女感
說不了。只見水運忽相擾。從過知已看相逢。當見忘不我台兄推笑士。何故止作此舍姪女苦
鐵先生了。今幸有緣。又得相托我學生。奉屈少表微草草而去。不識鐵先生於禮何故見外酬
苦辭了。今幸辭有緣。又得相陪。亦不過以敎之。水運道古之好朋友。即譚譚傾蓋如轄欲
故敬托使者正在此今日之來。亦不過有以敎之拘拘於世俗古之好朋友。即譚譚傾蓋如轄故。
去又恐非情。正在此費躊躇。不如古人乃必拘拘於世俗古如此甚非宜也。過笑笑笑一道
鐵先生與過親道就見二人互相欵留。竟不記前情。只認做好意。便笑
還是下老大人說得痛快鐵備見上酒來。過就送坐鐵道原蒙憐朝飢而授餐爲何
笑坐不復言去不多時也。過笑道慢慢飲去少不得遇着飲時三人俱各大
又勞賜酒。恐飲非其時也。過笑道慢慢飲去少不得遇着飲時

好逑傳算計定了。到次日日未出。就起來叫小丹收拾行李打點起身自
處打聽上一個小厮拿了帖子來拜過公子不期過公子已伏下人在下
冠齊楚笑哈哈的迎將出來道小弟昨日晋謁不過聊表仰慕之誠敢勞台
兄賜顧因連連打恭拱請進去鐵公子原打帳只得投名帖便走忽見過兩相
公子直出門迎接十分殷勤一圑和氣便放不下冷臉來。只得投一名帖兩相
揖讓到廳施禮序坐。一面獻禮過公子止住道此間不便請敎遂將鐵投名帖直邀到
應方纔敢作平原只是謀晉謁而又匆匆發駕抱恨至今。今幸再臨又承垂顧一
會又蒙厚辱本當領敎上茶來過公子因說道久聞台兄英雄之名急思一
誠又快事敢板邪。十日之飲以慰飢渴之懷。鐵公子茶罷就立起身來道
承長兄厚受。過欄住道相逢不飲眞令立風月笑人任是行急也要扯住道
日可也往外就走。過欄住道相逢不長兄相諒說罷又往外走過一手扯住不該來
日鐵道小才實實要行不是故辭乞長兄相諒說罷又往外走過一手扯住不該來
小弟雖不才也忝爲官家子弟。台兄苦苦相留不過欲少盡賓主之誼耳非
賜顧了既蒙賜顧便要筭做賓主小弟苦苦相留不過欲少盡賓主之誼耳非

○尚節儉以惜財用。○生人不能一日而無用卽不可一日而無財。然必留有餘之財而後可供不時之用故節儉尚焉夫財則水也節儉猶水之蓄也我聖祖不靄則一洩無餘而水立涸矣財不節則用之無度而財立罄矣我聖祖仁皇帝躬行節儉爲天下先休養生息海內殷富猶兢兢以惜財用積歲所藏盡自古民風皆貴乎勤儉然而不儉則十夫之力不足供一夫之用訓示訓藏不足供一日之需其害乃更甚也。○這頭一段是說聖祖仁皇帝那般般垂訓的緣由大凡人生世上不能一日沒有費就不可一日沒有銀錢必定積蓄下的不足大凡人生世上不能一日沒有費就不可一日沒有銀錢必定積蓄下的些銀錢到那忽然一用財如流水若不仔細着些一般從多少銀錢轉眼也就馨且這銀錢就如水了。一般人節儉他就得濟急所以說節儉一着是個絕妙的法子。流多少就要乾涸了。○夫兵丁錢糧之數乃不知撙節衣好鮮麗食求甘美不免○這第二段了。○夫兵丁錢糧之數乃不知撙節衣好鮮麗食求甘美不免○這第二段之糧甚至稱貸以遂其欲子母相權日復一日債深累重饑寒不知撙節是說兵丁不知節儉的你們兵丁的錢糧原有一定之數若是不知道撙節衣服是要華麗飯食要美口過一個月日子到花費幾個月錢糧這錢糧怎的够費甚且有不安生的。還要揭些債任意揮霍只顧一時快活。

聖諭敦孝弟以重人倫我聖祖仁皇帝臨御六十一年法祖尊親孝思不匱欽定孝經衍義一書衍釋經文義理詳貫無非孝治天下之意故聖諭十六條首以孝弟開其端朕丕承鴻業追維往訓推廣立教之思先申孝弟之義用是條與爾兵民人等宣示之夫孝者天之經地之義民之行也人不知孝弟之義獨不思父母愛子之心乎其未離懷抱饑不能自哺寒不能自衣為父母者審聲察形色笑則為之喜啼則為之憂行動則趨步不離疾痛則寢食俱廢以養以教至於成人復授家室謀生理百計營心力俱瘁父母之德寶同昊天罔極而養毋膚髮奚報親恩於萬一自當內盡其心外竭其力謹身節用以勤服勞以誠以孝餘隆推孝養毋博奕飲酒毋好鬬狠毋好貨財私妻子縱使儀文未備而誠慤有不信非孝而勇陳無勇非孝皆孝子分內之事也〇這第三段是單說孝的道理百姓們最大的孝德行孝的道理你們聽着孝順爹娘這一件事是天地間常存的道理你們縱不知孝順爹娘怎麼不把那爹娘愛兒子的心腸想一想當你們做孩子的時候爹娘懷抱着冷了不會自己穿衣饑了不不信非孝而勇陳無勇非孝皆孝子分內之事也啼了他便愁你行動了他就跟定了你步不離你若有了疾病他便睡不能安

者也助之長者揠苗者也非徒無益而又害之〇
〇孟子曰伯夷聖之淸者也伊尹聖之任者也柳下惠聖之和者也孔子聖之
時者也孔子之謂集大成集大成也者金聲而玉振之也金聲也者始條理也
玉振之也者終條理者智之事也終條理者聖之事也智譬則巧也
聖譬則力也由射於百步之外也其至爾力也其中非爾力也〇
〇惻隱之心人皆有之羞惡之心人皆有之恭敬之心人皆有之是非之心人皆有之惻隱之心仁也羞惡之心義也恭敬之心禮也是非之心智也仁義禮智非由外鑠我也我固有之也弗思耳矣故曰求則得之舍則失之或相倍蓰而無筭者不能盡其才者也詩曰天生蒸民有物有則民之秉夷好是懿德孔
子曰爲此詩者其知道乎故有物必有則民之秉夷也故好是懿德〇
〇孟子曰牛山之木嘗美矣以其郊於大國也斧斤伐之可以爲美乎是其日
夜之所息雨露之所潤非無萌蘖之生焉牛羊又從而牧之是以若彼濯濯也
人見其濯濯也以爲未嘗有材焉此豈山之性也哉雖存乎人者豈無仁義之
心哉其所以放其良心者亦猶斧斤之於木也旦旦而伐之可以爲美乎其日
夜之所息平旦之氣其好惡與人相近也者幾希則其旦晝之所爲有梏亡之

EXTRACT FROM THE SZ-SHU. (2) SHANG-MANG. 4

孟子謂齊宣王曰王之臣有託其妻子於其友而之楚遊者比其反也則凍
餒其妻子則如之何王曰棄之曰士師不能治士則如之何王曰已之曰四境
之內不治則如之何王顧左右而言他孟子見齊宣王曰所謂故國者非謂有
喬木之謂也王無親臣矣昔者所進今日不知其亡也王曰吾
何以識其不才而舍之曰國君進賢如不得已將使卑踰尊疏踰戚可不慎與
左右皆曰賢未可也諸大夫皆曰賢未可也國人皆曰賢然後察之見賢焉然
後用之○○孟子曰為巨室則必使工師求大木工師得大木則
喜以為能勝其任也匠人斲而小之則王怒以為不勝其任矣夫人幼而學之
壯而欲行之王曰姑舍女所學而從我則何如今有璞玉於此雖萬鎰必使玉
人彫琢之至於治國家則曰姑舍女所學而從我則何以異於教玉人彫琢玉
哉○○樂正子見孟子曰克告於君君為來見也嬖人有臧倉者沮君君是以不
果來也曰行或使之止或尼之行止非人所能也吾之不遇魯侯天也臧氏之子
子為能使子不遇哉○必有事焉而勿正心勿忘勿助長也無若宋人然宋人
有閔其苗之不長而揠之者芒芒然歸謂其人曰今日病矣予助苗長矣其子
趨而往視之苗則槁矣天下之不助苗長者寡矣以為無益而舍之者不耘苗

去向使紂惡未稔而自斃武庚念亂以圖存其人誰與與理是固人事之
或然者也然則先生隱忍而為此其有志于斯乎唐某年其月某日作廟汲郡
歲時致祀。○論語。
四書。
子曰學而時習之不亦說乎有朋自遠方來不亦樂乎人不
知而不慍不亦君子乎有子曰其為人也孝弟而好犯上者鮮矣不好犯上而
好作亂者未之有也君子務本本立而道生孝弟也者其為仁之本與子曰巧
言令色鮮矣仁。曾子曰吾日三省吾身為人謀而不忠乎與朋友交而不信乎
傳不習乎子曰道千乘之國敬事而信節用而愛人使民以時子曰弟子入則
孝出則弟謹而信汎愛眾而親仁行有餘力則以學文子夏曰賢賢易色事父
母能竭其力事君能致其身與朋友交言而有信雖曰未學吾必謂之學矣子
曰君子不重則不威學則不固主忠信無友不如己者過則勿憚改。曾子曰慎
終追遠民德歸厚矣子禽問於子貢曰夫子至於是邦也必聞其政求之與抑
與之與子貢曰夫子溫良恭儉讓以得之夫子之求之也其諸異乎人之求之
與子曰父在觀其志父沒觀其行三年無改於父之道可謂孝矣有子曰禮之
用和為貴先王之道斯為美小大由之有所不行知和而和不以禮節之不可

THE EPITAPH OF KI-TSZ.

帝曰迪朕德時乃功惟叙皇陶方祗厥叙方施象刑惟明蘷曰戞擊鳴球搏拊
琴瑟以詠祖考來格虞賓在位羣后德讓下管鼗鼓合止柷敔笙鏞以間鳥獸
蹌蹌簫韶九成鳳凰來儀夔曰於予擊石拊石百獸率舞庶尹允諧帝庸作歌
曰勑天之命惟時惟幾乃歌曰股肱喜哉元首起哉百工熙哉皐陶拜手稽首
颺言曰念哉率作興事愼乃憲欽哉屢省乃成欽哉乃賡載歌曰元首明哉股
肱良哉庶事康哉又歌曰元首叢脞哉股肱惰哉萬事墮哉帝拜曰俞往欽哉

箕子碑 柳宗元
凡大人之道有三一曰正蒙難二曰法授聖三曰化及民殷有仁人曰箕子實具
當紂之時大道悖亂天威之動不能戒聖人之言無所用進死以併命誠仁矣與
無益吾祀故不為也委身以存祀誠仁矣與亡吾國故不忍且是二道有行之者
矣是用保其明哲與之俯仰晦是謨範辱於囚奴昏而無邪隤而不息故在易
曰箕子之明夷正蒙難也及天命旣改生人以正乃出大法用為聖師周人得
以序彝倫而立大典故在書曰以箕子歸作洪範法授聖也及封朝鮮推道訓
俗惟德無陋惟人無遠用廣殷祀俾夷為華化及民也率是大道叢於厥躬天
地變化我得其正其大人歟於虖當其周時未至殷祀未殄比干已死微子已

書經虞書益稷帝曰來禹汝亦昌言禹拜曰都帝予何言予思日孜孜皐陶曰吁如何禹曰洪水滔天浩浩懷山襄陵下民昏墊予乘四載隨山刊木暨益奏庶鮮食予決九川距四海濬畎澮距川暨稷播奏庶艱食鮮食懋遷有無化居烝民乃粒萬邦作乂皐陶曰俞師汝昌言禹曰都帝慎乃在位帝曰俞禹曰安汝止惟幾惟康其弼直惟動丕應徯志以昭受上帝天其申命用休帝曰吁臣哉鄰哉鄰哉臣哉禹曰俞帝曰臣作朕股肱耳目予欲左右有民汝翼予欲宣力四方汝為予欲觀古人之象日月星辰山龍華蟲作會宗彝藻火粉米黼黻絺繡以五采彰施于五色作服汝明予欲聞六律五聲八音在治忽以出納五言汝聽予違汝弼汝無面從退有後言欽四鄰庶頑讒說若不在時侯以明之撻以記之書用識哉欲並生哉工以納言時而颺之格則承之庸之否則威之禹曰俞哉帝光天之下至于海隅蒼生萬邦黎獻共惟帝臣惟帝時舉敷納以言明庶以功車服以庸誰敢不讓敢不敬應帝不時敷同日奏罔功無若丹朱傲惟慢遊是好傲虐是作罔晝夜頟頟罔水行舟朋淫于家用殄厥世子創若時娶于塗山辛壬癸甲啟呱呱而泣予弗子惟荒度土功弼成五服至于五千州十有二師外薄四海咸建五長各迪有功苗頑弗即工帝其念哉

www.ingramcontent.com/pod-product-compliance
Lightning Source LLC
Chambersburg PA
CBHW022108290426
44112CB00008B/599